GALLERY OF
OF
Best
RESUMES

for People Without a Four-Year Degree

THIRD EDITION

DAVID F. NOBLE

jist Works

America's Career Publisher

Gallery of Best Resumes for People Without a Four-Year Degree, Third Edition

A Special Collection of Quality Resumes by Professional Resume Writers
Originally published as *Gallery of Best Resumes for Two-Year-Degree Graduates*

© 1990, 2000, 2005 by David F. Noble

Published by JIST Works, an imprint of JIST Publishing, Inc.
8902 Otis Avenue
Indianapolis, IN 46216-1033
Phone: 800-648-JIST   Fax: 800-JIST-FAX   E-mail: info@jist.com

Visit our Web site at **www.jist.com** for information on JIST, free job search tips, book chapters, and ordering instructions for our many products. For free information on 14,000 job titles, visit **www.careeroink.com**.

Other books by David F. Noble:
Gallery of Best Cover Letters
Gallery of Best Resumes
Professional Resumes for Accounting, Tax, Finance, and Law
Professional Resumes for Executives, Managers, and Other Administrators

Quantity discounts are available for JIST books. Have future editions of JIST books automatically delivered to you on publication through our convenient standing order program. Please call our Sales Department at 1-800-648-5478 for a free catalog and more information.

Acquisitions Editor: Lori Cates Hand
Project Editor: Gayle Johnson
Proofreader: Paula Lowell
Interior Designer: Debbie Berman
Cover Designer: DesignLab, Seattle
Page Layout: Trudy Coler
Indexer: Virginia Noble

Printed in the United States of America

10 09 08 07 06   9 8 7 6 5 4 3 2

Library of Congress Cataloging-in-Publication Data

Noble, David F. (David Franklin), 1935-
  Gallery of best resumes for people without a four-year degree : a
  collection of quality resumes by professional resume writers / by David
  F. Noble.-- 3rd ed.
      p. cm.
  Includes index.
  ISBN 1-59357-068-6
  1. Résumés (Employment) I. Noble, David F. (David Franklin), 1935-
  Gallery of best resumes for two-year degree graduates. II. Title.
  HF5383.N622 2004
  650.14'2--dc22
                    2004015333

We have been careful to provide accurate information throughout this book, but it is possible that errors and omissions have been introduced. Please consider this in making any career plans or other important decisions. Trust your own judgment above all else and in all things.

Trademarks: All brand names and product names used in this book are trade names, service marks, trademarks, or registered trademarks of their respective owners.

ISBN-13: 978-1-59357-068-2
ISBN-10: 1-59357-068-6

In memory of my brother,
Maynard A. Noble (1929–1995),
and to Peggy, Ron, Chris, and Wendy,
who made him rich with their loving care

Acknowledgments

To all those who helped make possible this updated Gallery for people without a four-year degree, I would like to acknowledge my appreciation. I am most indebted to all the professional resume writers who sent me examples of their latest work for inclusion in this book. These writers took the time on short notice to supply more than 350 new documents. The result is that all the resume and cover letter examples selected for this book are new. No example in the Second Edition is repeated in this Third Edition. Because the Third Edition of this book is not just a tweak of the Second Edition, the Second Edition is worth keeping, and the Third Edition is worth acquiring. Together, the two provide an expanded collection of more than 400 professionally written resume examples for those without a four-year degree.

I want to express again my gratitude to Bob Grilliot, who suggested that the Second Edition of this book should include resumes for people without a four-year degree. I am altogether indebted to my wife, Ginny, for the many tasks she performed online, on-screen, and on hard copy so that this new edition could be completed on time.

Contents

Introduction...1

    Why a Gallery for People Without a Four-Year Degree? 2

    How This Book Is Organized 3

    Who This Book Is For 4

    What This Book Can Do for You....................................5

Part 1: Best Resume Tips 7

Best Resume Tips at a Glance 8

Best Resume Writing Tips..9

    Best Resume Writing Strategies...................................10

    Best Resume Design and Layout Tips.........................11

    Best Resume Writing Style Tips 16

Part 2: The Gallery of Professional Resumes 21

The Gallery at a Glance 22

How to Use the Gallery..23

      Accounting...25

      Administrative Support..37

      Communications...61

      Construction 67

      Customer Service...75

      Design...93

      Education 105

      Events Planning...109

      Finance 115

Firefighting...129
Health and Safety 135
Healthcare 145
Hospitality..167
Human Resources...199
Information Systems/Information Technology 205
Law/Law Enforcement 233
Maintenance 241
Management 253
Manufacturing 289
Purchasing..301
Real Estate 307
Recruiting...313
Sales and Marketing 319
Technology...353
Transportation...367

Part 3: Best Cover Letter Tips 373

Best Cover Letter Tips at a Glance 374

Best Cover Letter Writing Tips.............................375

Myths About Cover Letters 375

Tips for Polishing Cover Letters 376
Using Good Strategies for Letters...376
Using Pronouns Correctly...377
Using Verb Forms Correctly..378
Using Punctuation Correctly 379
Using Words Correctly 383

Exhibit of Cover Letters 385

Appendix: List of Contributors 399

Occupation Index 415

Features Index 419

Introduction

Like the *Gallery of Best Resumes*, the *Gallery of Best Resumes for People Without a Four-Year Degree* is a collection of quality resumes from professional resume writers, each with individual views about resumes and resume writing. Unlike many resume books whose selections look the same, this book contains resumes that look different because they are representations of *real* resumes prepared by different professionals for actual job searchers throughout the country. (Certain information in the resumes has been fictionalized by the writers to protect the clients' privacy.) Even when several resumes from the same writer appear in the book, most of these resumes are different because the writer has customized each resume according to the background information and career goals of the client for whom the resume was prepared.

During the past several years, the resume writing industry has matured because of the following factors:

- The increase in the number of professional organizations for resume writers.

- The ready sharing of ideas at these organizations' national conventions.

- Easy access to e-mail and the World Wide Web.

- The greater availability of higher-resolution, lower-cost printers (black-and-white and color) for personal computers.

- The increase in the number of books like this Gallery that display collections of quality resumes and cover letters by professional writers. Often these books serve as idea books that emerging writers use as they develop their own expertise.

Instead of assuming that one resume style fits all, the writers featured here believe that a client's past experiences and next job target should determine the resume's type, design, and content. The use of Best in this book's title reflects this approach to resume making. The resumes are not "best" because they are ideal types for you to copy, but because the resume writers interacted with their clients to fashion resumes that seemed best for each client's situation at the time.

This book features resumes from writers who share several important qualities: good listening skills, a sense of what details are appropriate for a particular resume, and flexibility in selecting and arranging the resume's sections. By "hearing between" a client's statements, the perceptive resume writer can detect what kind of job the client really wants. The writer then chooses the information that best represents the client for the job being sought. Finally, the writer decides on the best arrangement of the information for that job, from most important to least important. With the help of this book, you can create this kind of resume yourself.

Most of the writers of the resumes in this Gallery are members of the Career Masters Institute (CMI), the National Résumé Writers Association (NRWA), the Professional

Association of Résumé Writers & Career Coaches (PARW/CC), or the Professional Résumé Writing and Research Association (PRWRA). Many of the writers belong to more than one of these organizations. Each organization has programs for earned certification. For example, writers who have the CPRW certification, for Certified Professional Résumé Writer, received this designation from the PARW/CC after they studied specific course materials and demonstrated proficiency in an examination. Those who have the NCRW certification, for National Certified Résumé Writer, received this designation from the NRWA after a different course of study and a different examination. For contact information for the CMI, NRWA, PARW/CC, and PRWRA, see their listings at the end of the appendix (the List of Contributors).

Why a Gallery for People Without a Four-Year Degree?

First of all, it should be made clear that people without a four-year degree are not people without education or who go to college for a couple of years, grow tired of studying, drop out, and get a job. This stereotypical misconception is refuted by almost every resume in this Gallery. People without a four-year degree include diverse kinds of individuals:

- Those who took courses of a particular curriculum to work in a specialized field, such as paralegals

- Those who got a two-year degree as a step toward getting a bachelor's degree

- Those who are job changers—people in transition—who acquired a two-year degree and possibly additional certification(s) to move to a new field of opportunity

- Those who had to interrupt their education for various reasons

- Those who had to work for economic reasons rather than study

- Those who took different paths (military training, technical education, and so on) to their current occupation

People without a four-year degree have special resume needs. Compared to traditional four-year students, who may have more campus activities and less full-time work experience to report on a resume, people without a four-year degree may have more full-time work experience to report. This means that Skills and Achievements tend to be emphasized more than Education.

People without a four-year degree also need resumes that help them compete successfully for jobs of employers who traditionally prefer workers with four-year and higher degrees. This Gallery showcases resumes that have helped people without a four-year degree compete successfully for better jobs in today's job market.

How This Book Is Organized

Like the first and second editions, this edition has three parts.

Part 1, "Best Resume Tips," presents resume writing tips, design and layout tips, and resume writing style tips for making resumes visually impressive. Some of these tips were suggested by the resume writers who contributed resumes to *Gallery of Best Resumes* (Indianapolis: JIST Works, 1994).

Part 2 is the Gallery itself. It contains 195 resumes from 84 professional resume writers throughout the United States, Australia, and Canada.

Resume writers commonly distinguish between chronological resumes and functional (or skills) resumes. A *chronological resume* is a photo—a snapshot history of what you did and when you did it. A *functional resume* is a painting—an interpretive sketch of what you can do for a future employer. A third kind of resume, known as a *combination resume,* is a mix of recalled history and self-assessment. Besides recollecting "the facts," a combination resume contains self-interpretation and therefore is more like dramatic history than news coverage. A chronological resume and a functional resume are not always that different; often, all that is needed for a functional resume to qualify as a combination resume is the inclusion of some dates, such as those for positions held. Almost all the resumes in this edition are combination resumes.

The resumes in the Gallery are presented in the following occupational categories:

Accounting
Administrative Support
Communications
Construction
Customer Service
Design
Education
Events Planning
Finance
Firefighting
Health and Safety
Healthcare
Hospitality
Human Resources
Information Systems/Information Technology
Law/Law Enforcement
Maintenance
Management
Manufacturing
Purchasing
Real Estate
Recruiting
Sales and Marketing
Technology
Transportation

Within each category, the resumes are generally arranged from the simple to the complex. Many of the resumes are one page, but a number of them are two pages. A few are more than two pages.

The Gallery offers a wide range of resumes with features you can use to create and improve your own resumes. Notice the plural. An important premise of an active job search is that you will not have just one "perfect" resume for all potential employers, but different versions of your resume for different interviews. The Gallery, therefore, is not a showroom where you say, "I'll take that one," alter it with your information, and then duplicate your version 200 times. It is a valuable resource for design ideas, expressions,

and organizational patterns that can help make your own resume a "best resume" for your next interview.

Creating multiple versions of a resume may seem difficult, but it is easy to do if you have (or have access to) a personal computer and a laser printer or some other kind of printer that can produce quality output. You also need word processing, desktop publishing, or resume software. If you don't have a computer or don't know someone who does, most professional resume writers have the hardware and software, and they can make your resume look like those in the Gallery. See the List of Contributors in the appendix for the names, addresses, phone numbers, e-mail addresses, and Web sites (if any) of the professional writers whose works are featured in this book. A local fast-print shop can make your resume look good, but you will probably not get there the kind of advice and service the professional resume writer provides.

Many employers now encourage the electronic submission of resumes or cover letters because of timeliness and expediency in processing. Any of the resumes in this book can be prepared for electronic transfer. If you intend to apply online for positions, be sure you follow the submission guidelines posted by the employer. If they are not clearly explained, phone or e-mail the company to inquire. You don't want to be disqualified for a job that suits you well because you did not follow the steps for successful submission.

Part 3, "Best Cover Letter Tips," discusses some myths about cover letters and offers tips for polishing cover letters. Much of the advice offered here also applies to writing resumes. Included in this part is an exhibit of 12 cover letters. Most of these letters accompanied resumes that appear in the Gallery.

The List of Contributors in the appendix is arranged alphabetically by country, state or province, and city. Although most of these resume writers work with local clients, many of them work nationally or internationally with clients by phone or e-mail.

You can use the Occupation Index to look up resumes by the current or most recent job title. This index, however, should not replace careful examination of all the resumes. Many of the resumes for some other occupation may have features that you can adapt to your own occupation. Limiting your search to the Occupation Index may cause you to miss some valuable examples. You can use the Features Index to find resumes that contain representative resume sections that may be important to you and your resume needs.

Who This Book Is For

Anyone who wants ideas for creating or improving a resume can benefit from this book. It is especially useful for active job seekers—those who understand the difference between active and passive job searching. A *passive* job seeker waits until jobs are advertised and then mails copies of the same resume, along with a standard cover letter, in response to a number of help-wanted ads. An *active* job seeker believes that a resume should be modified for a specific job target *after* he or she talks in person or by phone to a prospective interviewer *before* a job is announced. To schedule such an interview is to penetrate the "hidden job market." Active job seekers can find in the Gallery's focused resumes a wealth of strategies for targeting a resume for a particular interview. The section "How to Use the Gallery" at the beginning of Part 2 mentions how to do this.

Besides the active job seeker, any unemployed person who wants to create a more competitive resume or update an old one should find this book helpful. It shows the kinds of resumes professional resume writers are writing, and it showcases resumes for job seekers with particular needs.

What This Book Can Do for You

Besides providing you with a treasury of quality resumes whose features you can use in your own resumes, this book can help transform your thinking about resumes. There is no one "best" way to create a resume. This book helps you learn how to shape a resume that is best for you as you try to get an interview with a particular person for a specific job.

You might have been told that resumes should be only one page long; however, this is not necessarily true. The examples of multiple-page resumes in the Gallery help you see how to distribute information effectively across two or more pages. If you believe that the way to update a resume is to add your latest work experiences to your last resume, this book shows you how to rearrange your resume so that you can highlight the most important information about your experience and skills.

After you have studied "Best Resume Writing Tips" in Part 1, examined the professionally written resumes in Part 2, and reviewed "Tips for Polishing Cover Letters" in Part 3, you should be able to create your own resumes and cover letters worthy of inclusion in any gallery of best resumes.

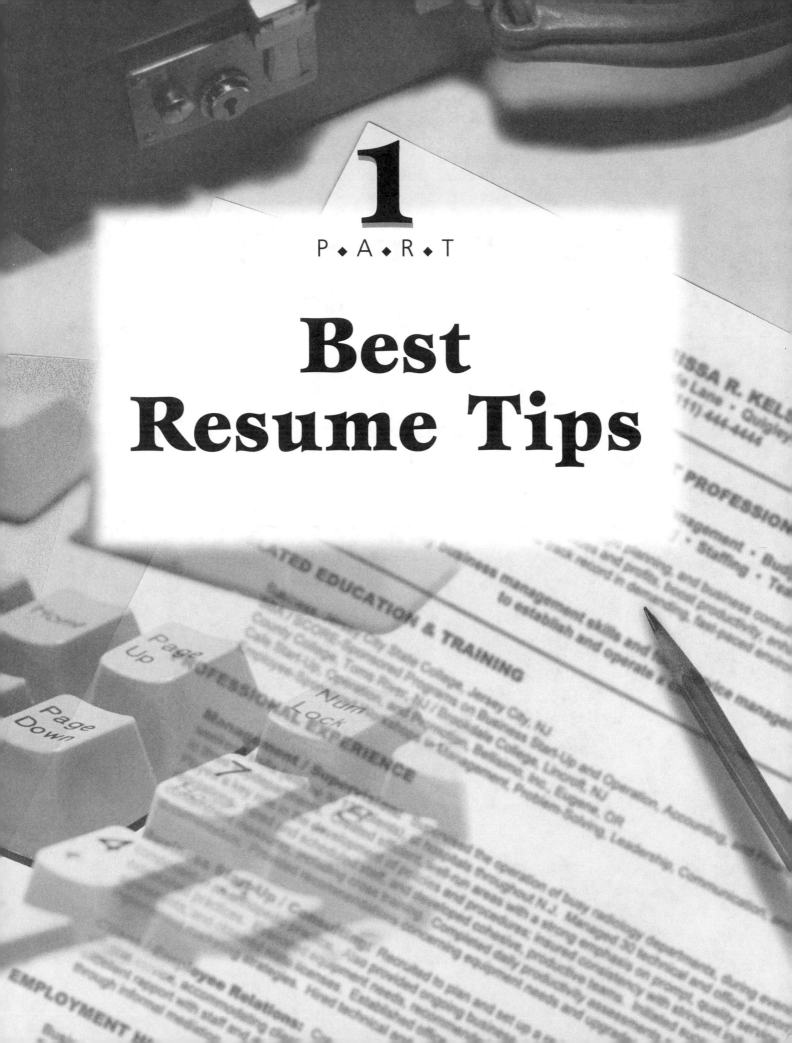

Best Resume Tips

1
P•A•R•T

Best Resume Tips at a Glance

Best Resume Writing Tips 9

   Best Resume Writing Strategies. 10

   Best Resume Design and Layout Tips 11

   Best Resume Writing Style Tips 16

Best Resume Writing Tips

In a passive job search, you rely on your resume to do most of the work for you. An eye-catching resume that stands out above all the others may be your best shot at getting noticed by a prospective employer. If your resume is only average and looks like most of the others in the pile, chances are you won't be noticed and called for an interview. If you want to be singled out because of your resume, it should be somewhere between spectacular and award-winning.

In an active job search, however, your resume complements your efforts at being known to a prospective employer *before* that person receives it. For this reason, you can rely less on your resume to get someone's attention. Nevertheless, your resume plays an important role in an active job search, which may include the following activities:

- Talking to relatives, friends, and other acquaintances about helping you meet people who can hire you before a job is available

- Contacting employers directly, using the yellow pages to identify types of organizations that could use a person with your skills

- Creating phone scripts to speak with the person who is most likely to hire someone with your background and skills

- Walking into a business in person to talk directly to the person who is most likely to hire someone like you

- Using a schedule to keep track of your appointments and callbacks

- Working at least 25 hours a week to search for a job

When you are this active in searching for a job, the quality of your resume confirms the quality of your efforts to get to know the person who might hire you, as well as your worth to the company whose workforce you want to join. An eye-catching resume makes it easier for you to sell yourself directly to a prospective employer. If your resume is mediocre or conspicuously flawed, it will work against you and may undo all your good efforts in searching for a job.

The following list offers ideas for making your resume visually impressive. Many of the ideas are for making your resume pleasing to the eye, but a number of the ideas are strategies to use for special cases. Other ideas are for eliminating common writing mistakes and stylistic weaknesses.

As you work on your resume, be sure to check out the writing advice in Part 3. You can apply many tips for writing cover letters to the writing of your resume, especially its text portions.

Best Resume Writing Strategies

1. **Although many resume books say you should spell out the name of the state in your address at the top of your resume, consider using the state's postal abbreviation instead.** The reason is simple: It's an address. Anyone wanting to contact you by mail will probably refer to your name and address on the resume. If they appear there as they should on an envelope, the writer or typist can simply copy the information you supply. If you spell out the name of your state in full, the writer will have to "translate" the name of the state to its postal abbreviation. Not everyone knows all the postal abbreviations, and some abbreviations are easily confused. For example, those for Alabama (AL), Alaska (AK), American Samoa (AS), Arizona (AZ), and Arkansas (AR) are easy to mix up. You can prevent confusion and delay simply by using the correct postal abbreviation.

   If you decide to use postal abbreviations in addresses, make certain that you do not add a period after the abbreviations, even before ZIP codes. Be sure to use the postal abbreviations in the addresses of references if you provide them.

   Do not, however, use the state postal abbreviation when you are indicating only the city and state (not the mailing address) of a school you attended or a business where you worked. In these cases, it makes sense to write out the name of the state in full.

2. **Adopt a sensible form for phone numbers, and then use it consistently.** Do this in your resume and in all the documents you use in your job search. Some forms of phone numbers make more sense than others. Compare the following:

123-4567	This form is best for a resume circulated locally, within a region where all the phone numbers have the same area code.
(222) 123-4567	This form is best for a resume circulated in areas with different area codes.
222-123-4567	This form suggests that the area code should be dialed in all cases. But that isn't necessary for prospective employers whose area code is 222. Avoid this form.
222/123-4567	This form is illogical and also should be avoided. The slash can mean "or" in an alternate option such as ON/OFF (ON or OFF). In a phone number, this meaning of a slash as "or" makes no sense.
1 (222) 123-4567	This form is long, and the first 1 is unnecessary. Almost everyone will know that 1 should be used before the area code to dial a long-distance number.
222.123.4567	This form, which resembles a Web address, is becoming more popular, particularly with people in computer and design fields.

Note: For resumes directed to prospective employers *outside* the United States, be sure to include the correct international prefixes in all phone numbers so that you and your references can be reached easily by phone.

---

3.   **If you include a Goal or an Objective statement, indicate what you hope to do for the company, rather than what the company can do for you.** See Resumes 118 and 163. Resume 45 begins with a bulleted list showing what the applicant can do for the company.

4.   **Near the top of the first page, consider including a focused Profile section.** If your Profile fails to grab the reader's attention, he or she might discard your resume without reading further. A Profile can be your first opportunity to sell yourself. For examples of Profiles, see Resumes 6, 26, 44, 54, 79, 83, 85, 101, 113, 168, and 183. Resumes 74, 77, 165, and 173, along with many others, include a profile without a heading for it.

5.   **In the Experience section, state achievements or accomplishments, not just duties or responsibilities.** The reader often already knows the duties and responsibilities for a given position. Achievements, however, can be interesting. See, for example, Resumes 93, 107, 136, 142, 169, and 172. Resume 175 presents achievements as Benchmarks and Milestones.

6.   **Consider quantifying your achievements (using dollar amounts, percentages, and so on) to make their value more visible.** See, for example, Resumes 16, 37, 38, 55, 91, 110, 116, 152, 155, 156, 158, 161, 171, 173, and 177. Resumes 133 and 174 use charts to quantify achievements.

7.   **When skills and abilities are varied, group them according to categories for easier comprehension.** See, for example, Resumes 56, 96, 106, 166, and 181.

8.   **Create a prominent Expertise section that draws together skills and abilities you have gained in previous or current work experience.** See, for example, Resumes 22, 63, 85, 89, 104, 123, and 149.

9.   **Consider including a Highlights section to draw attention to special accomplishments or achievements.** See, for example, Resumes 4, 64, 121, and 161.

10.   **If you have a noticeable gap in your employment, consider omitting dates and indicating instead the number of years in each position.** See Resume 183.

11.   **Summarize your qualifications and work experiences to avoid having to repeat yourself in the job descriptions.** See, for example, Resumes 2, 22, 127, 134, 137, and 139.

12.   **Instead of just listing your achievements, present them as challenges or problems solved, indicating what you did when something went wrong or needed fixing.** See, for example, Resumes 138 and 159. Resumes 21 and 124 present achievements as Results, and Resumes 45 and 135 indicate Payoffs. Resume 78 presents Outcomes.

Best Resume Design and Layout Tips

13.   **Use quality paper correctly.** If you use quality watermarked paper for your resume, be sure to use the right side of the paper. To know which side is the right side, hold a blank sheet of paper up to a light source. If you can see a watermark and read it, the right side of the paper is facing you. This is the surface for typing or printing. If the watermark is unreadable or if any characters

look backward, you are looking at the "underside" of the paper—the side that should be left blank if you use only one side of the sheet.

14. **Use adequate white space.** A sheet of paper with no words on it is impossible to read. Likewise, a sheet of paper with words all over it is impossible to read. The goal is to have a comfortable mix of white space and words. If your resume has too many words and not enough white space, it looks cluttered and unfriendly. If it has too much white space and too few words, it looks skimpy and unimportant. Make certain that adequate white space exists between the main sections. For examples that display good use of white space, see Resumes 4, 20, 30, 54, 68, 69, 71, 83, 85, 88, 176, 184, 187, 192, and many others.

15. **Make the margins uniform in width and preferably no less than an inch.** Margins are part of a resume's white space. If the margins shrink below an inch, the page begins to have a "too much to read" look. An enemy of margins is the one-page rule. If you try to fit more than one page of information on a page, the first temptation is to shrink the margins to make room for the extra material. It is better to shrink the material by paring it down than to reduce the size of the left, right, top, and bottom margins. Decreasing the type's point size is another way to save the margins. Try reducing the point size of text in your resume to 10 points. Then see how your information looks with the font(s) you are using. Different fonts produce different results. In your effort to save the margins, be certain that you don't make the type too small to be readable.

16. **Be consistent in your use of line spacing.** How you handle line spacing can tell the reader how good you are at details and how consistent you are in your use of them. If, near the beginning of your resume, you insert two line spaces (two hard returns in a word processing program) between two main sections, be sure to put two line spaces between the main sections throughout your resume.

17. **Be consistent in your use of character spacing.** If you usually put two spaces after a period at the end of a sentence, make certain that you use two spaces consistently. The same is true for colons. If you put two spaces after colons, do so consistently.

   Note that an em dash—a dash the width of the letter *m*—does not require spaces before or after it. Similarly, an en dash—a dash the width of the letter *n*—should not have a space before and after it. An en dash is commonly used between a range of numbers, such as 2002–2004. If you use "to" instead of an en dash in a range of numbers, be sure to use "to" consistently in other ranges.

   No space should go between the *P* and *O* of P.O. Box. Only one space is needed between a state's postal abbreviation and the ZIP code. You should insert a space between the first and second initials of a person's name, as in I. M. Jobseeker (not I.M. Jobseeker). These conventions have become widely adopted in English and business communications. If, however, you use other conventions, be sure to be consistent. In resumes, as in grammar, consistency is more important than conformity.

18. **Make certain that characters, lines, and images contrast well with the paper.** The printed quality depends on the device used to print your resume. If you use an inkjet or laser printer, check that the characters are sharp and clean, without smudges or traces of extra toner.

19. **Use vertical alignment in tabbed or indented text.** Misalignment can ruin the appearance of a well-written resume. Try to set tabs or indents consistently throughout the text instead of having a mix of tab stops or indents in different sections.

20. **Try left- or right-aligning dates.** This technique is especially useful in chronological resumes and combination resumes. For examples of left-aligned dates, see Resumes 32 and 140. For right-aligned dates, look at Resumes 3, 40, and 71.

21. **Use as many pages as you need to portray your qualifications adequately to a specific interviewer for a particular job.** Try to limit your resume to one page, but set the upper limit at four pages. No rule about the number of pages makes sense in all cases. The determining factors are your qualifications and experiences, the requirements of the job, and the interviewer's interests and pet peeves. If you know that an interviewer refuses to look at a resume longer than a page, that says it all: You need to deliver a one-page resume if you want to get past the first gate. For examples of two-page resumes, see Resumes 9, 75, 94, 108, 110, 111, 136, 156, 169, and 189. For three-page resumes, look at Resumes 62, 66, 100, and 120.

22. **Make each page a full page.** More important than the number of pages is whether each page you have is a full page. A partial page suggests deficiency, as if the reason for it is simply that information on page 1 has spilled over onto page 2. In that situation, try to compress all your information onto the first page. If you have a resume that is almost two pages, make it two full pages.

23. **When you have letters of recommendation, use quotations from them as testimonials in your resume.** Devoting a whole column to the positive opinions of "external authorities" helps make a resume convincing as well as impressive. See, for example, Resumes 6, 23, 47, 75, 80, 90, 94, and 167.

24. **Unless you enlist the services of a professional printer or skilled desktop publisher, resist the temptation to use full justification for text (to make each line go all the way to the right margin).** The price you pay for a straight right margin is uneven word spacing. Words may appear too close together on some lines and too spread out on others. Although the resume might look like typeset text, you lose readability. See also Tip 4 in the section "Using Good Strategies for Letters" in Part 3.

25. **If you can choose a typeface for your resume, use a serif font for greater readability.** *Serif* fonts have little lines extending from the tops, bottoms, and ends of the characters. These fonts tend to be easier to read than *sans serif* (without serif) fonts, especially in low-light conditions. Compare the following font examples:

Serif	Sans Serif
Century Schoolbook	Gill Sans
Courier	Futura
Times New Roman	Helvetica

Words such as *skills* and *abilities,* which have several consecutive thin letters, are more readable in a serif font than in a sans serif font.

26. **If possible, avoid using monospaced fonts, such as Courier.** A font is monospaced if each character takes up the same amount of space. For example, in a monospaced font, the letter *i* is as wide as the letter *m*. Therefore, in Courier type, iiiii is as wide as mmmmm. Courier was a standard of business communications during the 1960s and 1970s because it was the font supplied with IBM Selectric typewriters. Because of its widespread use, it is now considered "common." It also takes up a lot of space, so you can't pack as much information on a page with Courier type as you can with a proportionally spaced type such as Times New Roman.

27. **Think twice before using all uppercase letters in parts of your resume.** A common misconception is that uppercase letters are easier to read than lowercase letters. Actually, the ascenders and descenders of lowercase letters make them more distinguishable from each other and therefore more recognizable than uppercase letters. For a test, look at a string of uppercase letters and throw them gradually out of focus by squinting. Uppercase letters become a blur sooner than lowercase letters do.

28. **Think twice about underlining some words in your resume.** Underlining defeats the purpose of serifs at the bottom of characters by blending with the serifs. In trying to emphasize words, you lose some visual clarity. This is especially true if you use underlining with uppercase letters in centered or side headings.

29. **Use italic carefully.** Whenever possible, use italic instead of underlining when you need to call attention to a word or phrase. You might consider using italic for duties or achievements, as in Resumes 5 and 36. Resumes 93 and 95 use italic to describe the companies where the applicant worked. Think twice about using italic often, however, because italic characters are less readable than normal characters.

30. **To make your resume stand out, consider using unconventional display type for headings.** See, for example, Resumes 49, 50, 58, and 169.

31. **If you have access to many fonts through word processing or desktop publishing, beware of becoming "font happy" and turning your resume into a font circus.** Frequent font changes *can* distract **the reader**, ΛND SO CΛN GΛUDY DISPLΛY TYPE.

32. **Be aware of the value differences of black type.** Some typefaces are light; others are dark. Notice the following lines:

    A quick brown fox jumps over the lazy dog.

    A quick brown fox jumps over the lazy dog.

    Most typefaces fall somewhere between these two. With the variables of height, width, thickness, serifs, angles, curves, spacing, ink color, ink density, and boldfacing, you can see that type offers an infinite range of values from light to dark. Try to make your resume more visually interesting by offering stronger contrasts between light and dark type. See, for example, Resumes 21, 49, 50, 58, 73, 155, and 171.

33. **Use boldfacing to make different job experiences more evident.** See, for example, Resumes 4, 5, 12, 59, 66, 71, 74, 110, and many others.

34. **If you use word processing or desktop publishing and you have a suitable printer, use special characters to enhance the look of your resume.** For example, use curly quotation marks (" ") instead of their straight, "typewriter" equivalents (" "). For a dash, use an em dash (—). Don't use two hyphens (--) or a hyphen with a space on either side (-). To separate dates, try using an en dash (a dash the width of the letter *n:* –) instead of a hyphen, as in 2001–2004.

35. **To call attention to an item in a list, use a bullet (•) or a box (▫)instead of a hyphen (-).** Browse through the Gallery and notice how bullets are used effectively as attention getters.

36. **For variety, try using bullets of a different style, such as diamond (♦) bullets, rather than the usual round or square bullets.** Examples with diamonds are Resumes 2, 6, 39, 62, and 182. For other kinds of bullets, see Resumes 9, 12, 16, 20, 25, 27, 36, 45, 47, 48, 56, 58, 72, 87, 95, 151, 161, and 178.

37. **Make a bullet a little smaller than the lowercase letters that appear after it.** Disregard any ascenders or descenders on the letters. Compare the following bullet sizes:

    • Too small   ● Too large   • Better   • Just right

38. **When you use bullets, make certain that the bulleted items go beyond the superficial and contain information that employers really want to know.** Many short bulleted statements that say nothing special can affect the reader negatively. Brevity is not always the best strategy with bullets. For examples of substantial bulleted items, see Resumes 96 and 100.

39. **When the amount of information justifies a longer resume, repeat a particular graphic to unify the entire resume.** Resume 50, for example, displays a series of small black boxes, each containing a large letter. Resume 98 uses arrow tips repeatedly.

40. **If possible, visually coordinate the resume and its companion cover letter with the same font treatment or graphic to catch the reader's attention.** See, for example, Resumes 63, 102, and 123 and Cover Letters 2, 7, and 8, respectively.

41. **Try to make graphics match your field.** See, for example, Resumes 11, 40, 44, 46, 48, 72, 74, 80, 82, 84, 90, 95, 150, and 180. Resume 37 includes company logos. Some of the information presented in Resume 82 is in the shape of a cake!

42. **Use a horizontal line or lines to separate your name or contact information from the rest of the resume.** If you browse through the Gallery, you can see many resumes that use horizontal lines this way. See, for example, Resumes 13, 20, 34, 75, 118, 125, 127, 154, 160, 182, 188, and 194. Resume 148 contains a snazzy green line as a separator.

43. **Use horizontal lines to separate the different sections of the resume.** See, for example, Resumes 43, 61, and 67. See also Resumes 4, 8, 37, 57, 80, 114, and 162, whose lines are interrupted by the section headings.

44. **To call attention to a resume section or certain information, use horizontal lines to enclose it.** See, for example, Resumes 19, 65, 99, and 107. See

also Resumes 68, 109, and 153, in which two or more sections are enclosed by horizontal lines.

45. **Change the thickness of part of a horizontal line to call attention to a section heading below the line.** See, for example, Resumes 101 and 185. Use short horizontal lines to call attention to headings, as in Resumes 64 and 106.

46. **Enclose your resume within a page border for visual interest.** See, for example, Resumes 9, 35, 47, 52, 63, 123, 157, 160, 166, 170, and 173. Place a box around information you want to stand out, as shown in Resumes 27, 28, 122, and 193.

47. **Use a vertical line or lines to spice up your resume.** See, for example, Resumes 1, 23, 49, and 169. See also Resumes 44 and 86, in which both vertical and horizontal lines are used.

48. **Use shaded boxes to make a page visually more interesting.** See, for example, Resumes 37, 94, 163, and 167. Compare these boxes with the shadow boxes in Resumes 49 and 85. Note the shaded bars used for headings in Resumes 27 and 77. See also the vertical black bars for headings in Resume 42, and look at the vertical black bar for displaying contact information in Resume 108.

Best Resume Writing Style Tips

49. **Avoid using the archaic word "upon" in the References section.** The common statement "References available upon request" needs to be simplified, updated, or even deleted in resume writing. The word "upon" is one of the finest words of the 13th century, but it's a stuffy word at the beginning of the 21st century. Usually, "on" will do in place of "upon." Other possibilities are "References available by request" and "References available." Because most readers of resumes know that applicants can usually provide several reference letters, this statement is probably unnecessary. A reader who is seriously interested in you will ask about reference letters.

50. **Check that words or phrases in lists are parallel.** For example, notice the bulleted items in the Employment Summary section of Resume 34 and in the Accomplishments section of Resume 35. All the verbs are in the past tense.

51. **Use capital letters correctly.** Resumes usually contain many of the following:

    - Names of people, companies, organizations, government agencies, awards, and prizes

    - Titles of job positions and publications

    - References to academic fields (such as chemistry, English, and mathematics)

    - Geographic regions (such as the Midwest, the East, the state of California, and Oregon State)

    Because of such words, resumes are minefields for the misuse of uppercase letters. When you don't know whether a word should have an initial capital letter, don't guess. Consult a dictionary, a handbook on style, or some other

authoritative source, such as a reputable Web site. Often a reference librarian can provide the information you need. If so, you are only a phone call away from an accurate answer.

Use headline style in headings with upper- and lowercase letters. In other words, capitalize the first letter of the first word, the last word, and each main word in the heading, but not articles (*a, an,* and *the*), conjunctions (*and, but, or, nor, for, yet,* and *so*), and short prepositions (such as *at, by, in,* and *on*) *within* the heading. Capitalize prepositions of five or more letters.

To create a heading with small caps, first create a heading with upper- and lowercase letters. Then select the heading and assign small caps to it through the Format, Font, Small caps command. The original uppercase letters will be taller than the original lowercase letters, which will now appear as small capital letters.

52. **Check that you have used capital letters and hyphens correctly in computer terms.** If you want to show in a Computer Experience section that you have used certain hardware and software, you may give the opposite impression if you don't use uppercase letters and hyphens correctly. Note the correct use of capitals and hyphens in the following names of hardware, software, and computer companies:

AutoCAD	Microsoft Word	Photoshop
dBASE	MS-DOS	PostScript
Hewlett-Packard	NetWare	QuarkXPress
LaserJet III	PageMaker	Windows
Microsoft	PC DOS	WordPerfect

The reason that many computer product names have an internal uppercase letter is for the sake of a trademark. A word with unusual spelling or capitalization can be trademarked. When you use the correct forms of these words, you are honoring trademarks and registered trademarks and showing that you are in the know.

53. **Use all uppercase letters for most acronyms.** An *acronym* is a pronounceable word usually formed from the initial letters of the words in a compound term, or sometimes from multiple letters in those words. Note the following examples:

BASIC	Beginner's All-purpose Symbolic Instruction Code
COBOL	COmmon Business-Oriented Language
DOS	Disk Operating System
FORTRAN	FORmula TRANslator

An acronym such as *radar* (*r*adio *d*etecting *a*nd *r*anging) has become so common that it is no longer all uppercase.

54. **Be aware of the difference between an acronym and an abbreviation.** Remember, an acronym is a combination of letters making a word that you can pronounce as a word. An abbreviation, however, may consist of uppercase letters (without periods) that you can pronounce only as letters and never as a word. Examples are CBS, NFL, YWCA, and AFL-CIO.

55. **Be sure to spell every word correctly.** A resume with just one misspelling is not impressive and may undermine all the hours you spent putting it together. Worse than that, one misspelling may be what the reader is looking for to screen you out, particularly if you are applying for a position that requires accuracy with words.

    Your computer's spelling checker will catch many misspellings. It will not, however, detect when you have inadvertently used a wrong word (*to* for *too*, for example). Also be wary of letting someone else check your resume. If the other person is not a good speller, you may not get any real help. The best authority is a good dictionary.

56. **For words that have more than one correct spelling, use the preferred form.** This form is the one that appears first in a dictionary. For example, if you see the entry **trav·el·ing** *or* **trav·el·ling**, the first form (with one *l*) is the preferred spelling. If you make it a practice to use the preferred spelling, you will build consistency in your resumes and cover letters.

57. **Avoid British spellings.** These slip into American usage through books and online articles published in Great Britain. Note the following words:

British Spelling	American Spelling
acknowledgement	acknowledgment
centre	center
judgement	judgment
towards	toward

58. **Avoid hyphenating words with such prefixes as *co-*, *micro-*, *mid-*, *mini-*, *multi-*, *non-*, *pre-*, *re-*, and *sub-*.** Many people think that words with these prefixes should have a hyphen after the prefix, but most of these words should not. The following words are spelled correctly:

coauthor	midway	nonfunctional
coworker	minicomputer	prearrange
cowriter	multicultural	prequalify
microcomputer	multilevel	reenter
midpoint	nondisclosure	subdirectory

    Note: If you look in the dictionary for a word with a prefix and you can't find the word, look for just the prefix. You might find a small-print listing of a number of words that begin with that prefix.

59. **Be aware that compounds (combinations of words) present special problems for hyphenation.** Writers' handbooks and books on style do not always agree on how compounds should be hyphenated. Many compounds are evolving from *open* compounds (two different words) to *hyphenated* compounds (two words joined by a hyphen) to *closed* compounds (one word). In different dictionaries, you can therefore find the words *copy editor, copy-editor,* and *copyeditor.* No wonder the issue is confusing! Most style books do agree, however, that when some compounds appear as an adjective before a noun, the compound should be hyphenated. When the same compound appears after a noun, hyphenation is unnecessary. Compare the following two sentences:

    I scheduled well-attended conferences.

    The conferences I scheduled were well attended.

For detailed information about hyphenation, see a recent edition of *The Chicago Manual of Style* (the 15th Edition is the latest). You should be able to find a copy at your local library.

60. **Hyphenate so-called *permanent* hyphenated compounds.** Usually, you can find these by looking them up in the dictionary. You can spot them easily because they have a long hyphen (–) for visibility in the dictionary. Hyphenate these words (with a standard hyphen) wherever they appear, before or after a noun. Here are some examples:

all-important	self-employed
day-to-day	step-by-step
full-blown	time-consuming

Note that *The Chicago Manual of Style,* 15th Edition, recommends that permanent hyphenated compounds should no longer be considered permanent but may be used without a hyphen (or hyphens) when they appear after a noun or are used adverbially. (See Tip 58.)

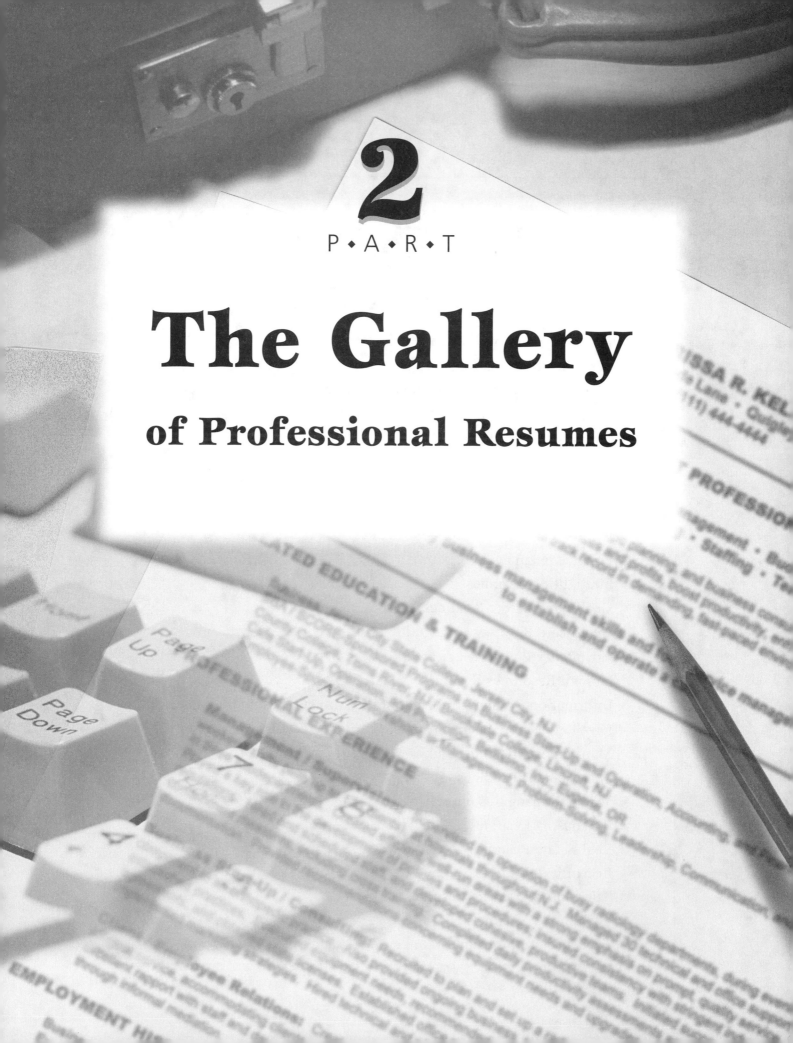

The Gallery

of Professional Resumes

The Gallery
at a Glance

How to Use the Gallery. 23
■ Accounting Resumes 25
■ Administrative Support Resumes 37
■ Communications Resumes. 61
■ Construction Resumes. 67
■ Customer Service Resumes 75
■ Design Resumes. 93
■ Education Resumes 105
■ Events Planning Resumes 109
■ Finance Resumes 115
■ Firefighting Resumes 129
■ Health and Safety Resumes 135
■ Healthcare Resumes. 145
■ Hospitality Resumes 167
■ Human Resources Resumes. 199
■ Information Systems/Information Technology Resumes 205
■ Law/Law Enforcement Resumes. 233
■ Maintenance Resumes. 241
■ Management Resumes. 253
■ Manufacturing Resumes 289
■ Purchasing Resumes 301
■ Real Estate Resumes 307
■ Recruiting Resumes 313
■ Sales and Marketing Resumes 319
■ Technology Resumes 353
■ Transportation Resumes 367

How to Use the Gallery

You can learn much from the Gallery just by browsing through it. To make the best use of this resource, however, read the following suggestions before you begin.

Look at the resumes in the category containing your field, related fields, or your target occupation. Notice what kinds of resumes other people have used to find similar jobs. Always remember, though, that your resume should not be "canned." It should not look just like someone else's resume but should reflect your own background, unique experiences, and goals.

Use the Gallery primarily as an "idea book." Even if you don't find a resume for your specific occupation or job, be sure to look at all the resumes for ideas you can borrow or adapt. You may be able to modify some of the sections or statements with information that applies to your own situation or job target.

Study the ways in which professional resume writers have formatted the applicants' names, addresses, and phone numbers. In most instances, this information appears at the top of the resume's first page. Look at typestyles, size of type, and use of boldface. See whether the personal information is centered on lines, spread across a line, or located near the margin on one side of a page. Look for the use of horizontal lines to separate this information from the rest of the resume, to separate the address and phone number from the person's name, or to enclose information for greater visibility.

Look at each resume to see what section appears first after the personal information. Then compare those same sections across the Gallery. For example, look just at the resumes that have a Profile as the first section. Compare the Profiles for length, clarity, and use of words. Do the Profiles contain complete sentences or just one or more partial lines of thought? Are some Profiles better than others in your opinion? Do you see one or more Profiles that come close to matching a Profile for you? After you have compared Profiles, try writing *in your own words* a Profile for yourself.

Repeat this "horizontal comparison" for each of the sections across the Gallery. Compare all the Education sections, all the Qualifications sections, and so on. As you make these comparisons, continue to note differences in length, the kinds of words and phrases used, and the effectiveness of the content. Jot down any ideas that might be useful for your own resume.

As you compare sections across the Gallery, pay special attention to the Profile, Summary, Areas of Expertise, Career Highlights, Qualifications, and Experience sections. (Most resumes don't have all of these sections.) Notice how skills and accomplishments are worked into these sections. Skills and accomplishments are *variables* you can select to put a certain "spin" on your resume as you pitch it to a particular interviewer or job. Your observations here should be especially valuable for your own resume versions.

After you have examined the resumes "horizontally" (section by section), compare them "vertically" (design by design). To do this, you need to determine which resumes have the same sections in the same order, and then compare just those resumes. For example, look for resumes that have personal information at the top, a Profile, an Experience section, and an Education section. (Notice that the section heads may differ slightly. Instead of the word *Experience,* you might find *Work Experience, Employment,* or *Career Highlights.*) When you examine the resumes in this way, you are looking at their *structural design,* which means the order in which the various sections appear. The same order can appear in resumes of different fields or jobs, so it is important to explore the whole Gallery and not limit your investigation to resumes in your field or related fields.

Developing a sense of resume structure is extremely important because it enables you to emphasize the most important information about yourself. A resume is a little like a newspaper article—read quickly and usually discarded before the reader finishes. That is why the information in newspaper articles often dwindles in significance toward the end. For the same reason, the most important, attention-getting information about you should be at or near the top of your resume. What follows should appear in order of descending significance.

If you know that the reader will be more interested in your work experience than your education because you don't have a four-year degree, put your Experience section before your Education. If you know that the reader will be interested in your skills regardless of your education and work experience, put your Skills section at or near the beginning of your resume. In this way, you can help ensure that anyone who reads only *part* of your resume will read the "best" about you. Your hope is that this information will encourage the reader to read on to the end of the resume and, above all, take an interest in you.

Compare the resumes according to visual design features, such as the use of horizontal and vertical lines, borders, boxes, bullets, white space, graphics, and inverse type (light characters on a dark background). Use the Features Index for help here. Notice which resumes have more visual impact at first glance and which ones make no initial impression. Do some of the resumes seem more inviting to read than others? Which ones are less appealing because they have too much information, or too little? Which ones seem to have the right balance of information and white space?

After comparing the visual design features, choose the design ideas that might improve your own resume. You will want to be selective here and not try to work every design possibility into your resume. As in writing, "less is more" in resume making, especially when you integrate design features with content.

Accounting

Resumes at a Glance

RESUME NUMBER	LAST OR CURRENT OCCUPATION	GOAL	PAGE
1	Accounting Clerk/Technology Specialist	Not specified	27
2	Office/Billing Clerk	Payroll Clerk	28
3	Accounts-Payable Clerk	Not specified	29
4	Office Manager	Office Manager	30
5	Office Manager	Bookkeeper	32
6	Senior Bookkeeper	Not Specified	34
7	Full Charge Bookkeeper	Full Charge Bookkeeper	36

C. NICHOLAS DONATO, MCP, A+
8899 FORTIN ROAD
NAPLES, FLORIDA 34134

donatoc@earthlink.net

(239) 777-9999

OBJECTIVE	Position offering growth opportunity in a computer-networking environment.
SUMMARY	▶ Broad knowledge of current computer industry, including networking. ▶ Experienced retail store manager of national footwear chain. ▶ Highly motivated and resourceful; formal and self-taught in developing professional business acumen and technical skills. ▶ Proven abilities in sales, merchandising, and customer service in computer industry and retail business.
EXPERIENCE	**Accounting Offices of Fritsch, Botts, Leonard, CPAs,** Naples, FL *Accounting Clerk/Technology Specialist*, 2001–present • Prepare worksheets, taxes, accounts payable and receivable. • Set up and care for computer hardware and other office equipment. • Install and effectively maintain general business and accounting software. **Cordell Business Technologies,** Fort Meyers, FL *Executive Teleservices Account Analyst*, 2000–2001 • Called commercial entities for copier and network integration divisions. • Generated leads, set appointments after discovering needs and interests. • Made customer calls, servicing existing accounts in database. • Successfully prospected for new accounts and their development. **CompUSA,** Cape Coral, FL *Account Executive*, 1998–2000 • Sold computer merchandise from busy nationally recognized retail outlet. • Managed account deck of 50 private and government clients. • Actively participated in lucrative state and local client bidding. • Earned Top Seller of the Month award six times; highest commissions 1999. **Thom Mcan Shoes, Inc.,** Raleigh, NC *Manager and Assistant Manager*, 1994–1998 • Managed until corporate downsizing called for store closing. • Hired and trained sales staff in proper company merchandising techniques.
EDUCATION	**Southwest Florida Community College,** Fort Meyers, FL *A.S. Degree in Business Administration, Accounting,* May 2000 *Accounting certificate,* July 2001 **Stephens University,** Raleigh, NC *Microsoft Certified Professional,* 1999 *CompTIA's A+ Certified,* 1998 **Sanders-Michaelson College,** Raleigh, NC Attended two semesters, 1992–1993

1

Edward Turilli, Newport, Rhode Island

Boxes enclose the contact information, the section headings, and the body of information. Bullets point to Summary items and to duties and achievements in the Experience section.

KATRINA LARSON

7889 Forest Avenue • Huntington Beach, CA 55555 • (555) 555–5555

OBJECTIVE: Payroll Clerk

SUMMARY OF QUALIFICATIONS

- Well-organized and detail-oriented with experience in payroll, office support, data entry and billing. Computer skills include MS Word and Excel and various proprietary software programs.

- Self-motivated employee who performs diligently to accomplish business goals. Ability to learn new skills quickly and effectively.

- Adept in customer relations with the ability to handle and resolve issues. Team-oriented; thrive in fast-paced environments. Record of dependability.

EXPERIENCE

Payroll / Billing

- ◆ Maintaining up-to-date payroll data and records, including entering changes in exemptions, insurance coverage, savings deductions, job title and department transfers.
- ◆ Compiling summaries of earnings, taxes, deductions, leave, disability and nontaxable wages for report preparation.
- ◆ Calculating employee federal and state income and Social Security taxes and employer's Social Security, unemployment and workers' compensation payments.
- ◆ Researching and resolving payroll discrepancies in a timely manner.
- ◆ Maintaining accurate customer billing information and preparing invoices in an efficient, timely manner.

Reception / Customer Service

- ◆ Greeting visitors; answering busy multiline telephone systems; screening and transferring calls while handling general inquiries.
- ◆ Addressing customer concerns, researching and resolving problems to ensure service satisfaction; extensive interface with all levels of internal personnel.

Administrative Support

- ◆ Performing diverse administrative duties such as word processing correspondence, creating presentations and maintaining confidential files/records.
- ◆ Scheduling and coordinating meetings and appointments; ordering department supplies.

EMPLOYMENT HISTORY

SULLIVAN CORP., Huntington Beach, CA
Office/Billing Clerk (1996 to present)

JENSEN INC., Huntington Beach, CA
Payroll Clerk (1994 to 1996)

FINLANDIA INC., Huntington Beach, CA
Payroll Clerk (1992 to 1994)

WARNER PACKAGING, Huntington Beach, CA
Receptionist/Accounting Clerk (1989 to 1992)

EDUCATION

Fullerton Community College, Huntington Beach, CA
Accounting courses

Louise Garver, Enfield, Connecticut

Horizontal lines under the main section headings help separate the sections visually before you read any of their content. Thickening of the line under the person's name helps call attention to it.

Melissa Simon

99 Norman Road • Wellesley, MA 02481
781-555-1234 • msimon@xyz.com

Summary

Experienced and detail-oriented accounting professional, with a proven ability to perform a broad range of functions quickly and accurately in a fast-paced environment. Skilled at multitasking. Recognized for dedication, work ethic, and going the extra mile to get the job done. Excellent interpersonal skills. Expertise includes

- Accounts payable
- Bank statement reconciliations
- Expense reports
- Payroll

- Collections
- Bank deposits
- Spreadsheets
- Problem resolution

Selected Achievements

- Resolved price discrepancies and past-due balances with up to 700 vendors, including subcontractors.
- Oversaw accounts-payable functions for 10 divisions nationwide; set up and maintained new accounts for multiple divisions.
- Uncovered and reported fraudulent activities, enabling company to recover $10,000.
- Streamlined procedures to ensure timely production of all accounting reports.
- Managed twice-weekly check run of 400 checks per week and verified them manually for accuracy.

Experience

Accounts-Payable Clerk—First Data, Watertown, MA   1997–2004
Oversaw the day-to-day A/P operations for a 450-person company with 10 divisions throughout the U.S. Processed codes and supervised check runs and mailings. Input expense reports. Assisted auditors at year-end. Communicated with vendors to expedite processing of checks. Performed collection calls regarding outstanding accounts. Assisted with bank reconciliations.

Assistant to Controller—Boston Lighting Company, Brighton, MA   1991–1997
Supervised daily A/P functions for light fixture company. Detected fraudulent activities that enabled company to recover $10,000. Maintained daily cash and deposits. Performed daily audit from all payroll activity, credit cards, and accounts receivable. Issued invoices for accounts receivable. Monitored petty cash and bank deposits.

Accounting Clerk—Town of Westwood, Westwood, MA   1988–1991
Processed payments of property taxes and water/sewer bills.

Computer Skills

Deltek, Peachtree, proprietary accounting software, MS Word, MS Excel

Wendy Gelberg, Needham, Massachusetts

The Summary consists of a profile statement and a two-column list of areas of expertise. The Selected Achievements section contains five bulleted accomplishments—most of them quantified.

WENDY A. CARUTHERS

965 Old Bridge Lane
Lansdale, PA 00000

(555) 555-5555
wcaruthers@dotresume.com

OFFICE MANAGER

Bookkeeping
Human Resources Administration
General Operations

HIGHLIGHTS

Areas of Expertise

Bookkeeping: AP/AR, bank reconciliations, financial reports, payroll
HR Administration: 401(k) and medical benefits, employee manuals, training
General Operations: Office procedures, moves, startups, closings

Key Strengths

♦ Adept at handling multiple tasks in an organized manner.

♦ Proven ability to train and supervise staff.

♦ Experience working with vendors and building operations personnel.

♦ Sensitive to confidentiality of employee records and financial data.

♦ Excellent written and verbal communication skills.

♦ Proficient in Intuit QuickBooks Pro and MS Excel and Word; working knowledge of Microsoft Outlook, Windows 95/98/NT, and Internet Explorer.

EXPERIENCE

Office Manager
E-PRAXIS, INC., Blue Bell, PA (2000–2004)

Set up office procedures and bookkeeping system that accommodated growth of Internet startup from 10 to 40 employees. Developed orientation program and accompanying manual to quickly integrate new hires. Prepared monthly and annual financial reports for top management. Hired, trained, and supervised two administrative assistants.

Selected Accomplishments

♦ Managed two office moves with minimal inconvenience and downtime.

♦ Selected to assist with office closing—employee layoffs, contract terminations, and final audit.

Jan Holliday, Harleysville, Pennsylvania

This resume has two kinds of horizontal lines: a full line under the individual's name on each page, and partial lines on each side of the centered section headings. These lines with the section headings make it easy to see at a glance the resume's overall design because you can quickly view

WENDY A. CARUTHERS

page 2

EXPERIENCE
continued

Office Manager
EASTERN OFFICE SUPPLY, INC., Montgomeryville, PA (1997–1999)

Performed full-charge bookkeeping services and human resources administration for an independent office equipment dealership. Using QuickBooks Pro, prepared invoices, accounts payable, accounts receivable, bank reconciliations, financial statements, and payroll. Maintained confidential employee files and administered medical benefits and 401(k) program.

> *Selected Accomplishments*
> ♦ Increased efficiency by training staff in standard office procedures.
> ♦ Consistently received top ratings on performance evaluations.

Family Care and Home Management
(1994–1997)

Cared for two small children. Handled day-to-day household operations and acted as general contractor for building a home addition. Managed family finances in Quicken—established budget, paid bills, and balanced bank accounts. Prepared tax returns for three households using TurboTax.

Bookkeeper
CONCORDIA FABRICATIONS, INC., Telford, PA (1991–1994)

Prepared accounts payable/accounts receivable for manufacturing company with 50 employees. Maintained employee payroll and processed expense reports. Implemented conversion from manual to computerized bookkeeping system without disrupting normal operations.

Administrative Assistant
NEWMAN MEDICAL SUPPLY COMPANY, Quakertown, PA (1990–1991)

Assisted with broad range of bookkeeping functions, including bank reconciliations, accounts payable, accounts receivable, and payroll processing. Served as primary point of contact with vendors and building maintenance personnel.

EDUCATION

Courses in Word and Excel, Franklin Area Adult School, Morrisville, PA (1996–1997)

A.S., Accounting, Gateway Business College, Somerfield, PA (1990)

---

the relative length of each section. In the Experience section the paragraph under each job position indicates responsibilities. Bullets point to achievements. Boldfacing makes the positions evident.

LISA A. WELLER

(555) 555-5555

7030 Birmingham Road   mynameis@aol.com   Grand Rapids, MI 49000-9476

BOOKKEEPER

More than 18 years of experience in accounting and executive support.
Detail orientation and perfectionism support high accuracy and zero audit issues.
Proven ability to multitask, driven by self-motivation and high ethical standards.
History of timely financial report preparation for small to midsized businesses.

Grand Rapids, MI	**Rock Solid Piping Company**	2002–2004
	Office Manager	

Assistant to Chief Financial Officer; audited, entered, and processed all accounts receivable and payable, including a conversion to automated cost accounting; served as only backup to weekly payroll consisting of three different union groups and one nonunion group of employees.

- Trained project managers and support staff; simplified retrieval of job costing info
- Automated complex handwritten system for sales and use tax computations
- Customized downloads from integrated business software to generate quarterly MESC reports, departmental profit-and-loss statements, and customer mailing data

Grand Rapids, MI	**Cracker Company**	1994–2002
	Transportation Assistant	
	(1997–2000)	

Prepared contracts for 40+ frozen-food carriers; managed off-site pallet-tracking program for four manufacturing locations; solely maintained rate and route database information used to ensure most cost-effective transportation method; audited transportation invoices.

- Performed data entry with 99% accuracy
- Calculated customer freight allowances
- Provided detailed specifications to develop new database software

Administrative Secretary
(1995–1997 and 2000–2002)

Managed time to support Vice President, two Directors, and five Managers simultaneously; trained secretarial staff of 15 in spreadsheet, presentation, and word processing applications; provided expedient turnaround on typing, transcription, and filing projects; quickly overcame learning curves to maintain use of cutting-edge software.

- Assigned as backup secretary for Executive Vice President of Marketing
- Compiled weekly market analysis reports
- Promoted from staff secretary after one year of service, 1994–1995

5

Tammy J. Smith, Olivet, Michigan

Center-justifying the company names and job positions in boldface makes it easy to see these items at a glance if you look down the middle of each page. On the second page, you view the information about the individual's education and software expertise. In the untitled

LISA A. WELLER

(555) 555-5555

mynameis@aol.com

Grand Rapids, MI **Stevenson Marketing Company** 1993–1994
Office Manager

Reconstructed accounting activity for 1993, including an extensive audit of the G/L cash account; recommended procedural changes to classify subcontractors as employees, as well as changes to sales allocation policies; processed accounts payable and accounts receivable.

- Developed standardized procedures for accounts payable and receivable
- Calculated payroll
- Prepared all related tax payments and documentation

Grand Rapids, MI **Packaging Converting, Inc.** 1990–1993
Office Manager / Assistant to Plant Manager

Processed accounts payable and receivable; prepared trend analysis, balance sheet, and profit-and-loss statements; generated job-by-job profitability analysis; completed Department of Labor and Workman's Compensation reports.

- Calculated machine-hour costs and production standards
- Determined operational efficiencies by analyzing production versus payroll hours
- Managed office staff of three, including hiring, evaluating, and training

Accounting Certificate, GPA 4.0
Grand Rapids Community College, MI
Phi Theta Kappa National Honor Society

Administrative Assistant, GPA 3.72
Bright Future Business College, Grand Rapids, MI
formerly Alabaster Business College

Covey Leadership Seminars
Seven Habits of Highly Effective People
Time Management

Software Expertise

○ Intuit QuickBooks	○ Intuit Quicken	○ Peachtree III	○ Dac Easy Accounting
○ Microsoft Excel	○ Lotus 1-2-3	○ Microsoft PowerPoint	○ Freelance Graphics
○ Microsoft Word	○ WordPerfect	○ Professional Write	○ IBM System 6/450
○ Netscape Navigator	○ Calendar Creator	○ Corporate Time	○ TimeSlips

experience section, statements in italic mention responsibilities for each position held. Bullets point to achievements and duties. Bullets as shadowed circles stand out at the end. See Cover Letter 1.

Angela Goodman

20 Main Street ♦ Nyack, NY 00000 ♦ Home: (555) 555-5555 ♦ Email: agood2@yahoo.com

Bookkeeping / Supervision / Training / Data Management

Profile

Highly accomplished professional with more than 15 years of experience and demonstrated success in all aspects of bookkeeping, accounting, and financial supervision. A versatile, dynamic, and strategic-thinking specialist skilled in creating spreadsheets and databases designed to increase efficiency. Demonstrated ability to acquire new skills, thoroughly research projects, apply theoretical knowledge, and work individually or in a team environment. Received numerous commendations.

"I would like to commend Angela for her work on the Client Database project. Her ability to work independently and to collaborate, which involved many last-minute changes to the requirements, make her an outstanding team person." — Fred Smith, President/CEO, County Health Association of New York

Summary of Abilities, Skills, and Attributes:

♦ Accounts Payable ♦ Accounts Receivable ♦ Cash Receipts and Deposits ♦ Payroll
♦ Bank Reconciliations ♦ Cash Disbursements ♦ Month-End Close ♦ Billing / Invoicing
♦ Employee Training ♦ Computer Skills (Excel, ADP Payroll, QuickBooks, Data Ease, Internet)

Professional Experience

County Health Association of New York, Nyack, NY   1988–2004
(A medium-size not-for-profit agency specializing in the care and education of the mentally ill and their families)

Senior Bookkeeper (1996–2004)
Assistant Manager (1993–1996)
Full Charge Bookkeeper (1989–1993)
Accounts Payable Administrator (1988–1989)

BOOKKEEPING

- Performed a full range of bookkeeping duties, including A/R, A/P, cash receipts and deposits, bank reconciliations, and month-end closings.
- Reviewed contracts and prepared vouchers for various funding sources in the county, state, and federal governments.
- Prepared and posted journal entries to the general ledger for the month-end close.
- Processed and submitted the payroll for up to 225 employees to ADP.
- Maintained time and accruals for eligible employees.
- Prepared Excel worksheets containing benefits data and posted information to the general ledger.
- Assisted with the preparation of financial reports.

"I am aware that this office has been short-staffed and that you worked overtime to ensure that all bookkeeping functions and other important fiscal matters were attended to in a timely manner. Your cooperative attitude and good humor have been a great support to me. I am appreciative of your hard work."

— Mary Frank, Vice President, County Health Association of New York

Joseph Imperato, Thiells, New York

This resume was for a person who had attended college many years ago, did not complete her degree, and had worked for only one company. The writer presented her accomplishments as bulleted items under her three functional areas of expertise. The distinctive feature of this resume is

Angela Goodman

SUPERVISION / TRAINING

- Supervised the daily activities of four full-time employees.
- Wrote and delivered annual evaluations.
- Scheduled staff vacations and time off while ensuring that all necessary functions continued to be performed without interruption.
- Provided accounting expertise on an ongoing basis and ensured that the staff understood and correctly implemented their duties in accordance with accepted accounting principles.
- Trained employees in the use of various software applications such as Data Ease, Payroll, and Medicaid billing.

"I would like to express my appreciation to you for your tremendous support. You willingly took over many tasks and completed everything on time. My thanks again for doing an excellent job. It made my transition to a new position much easier."
— Yolanda Rodriguez, Administrative Bookkeeper, County Health Association of New York

DATA MANAGEMENT

- Researched automated bookkeeping systems for the Association and was instrumental in the selection and purchase of the Data Ease software.
- Designed and implemented a personnel database giving management access to detailed information instantaneously.
- Developed a system to track employees and expenses by program, decreasing processing time by three days.
- Created a series of client databases based on the specific needs of each program, resulting in the automation of manual intensive processes, increased efficiency, and accuracy.
- Devised a database to track membership, contributions, events attended, and special mailings.
- Decreased processing time from one week to two days by computerizing the billing and client information for Alcohol and Substance Abuse programs.
- Created a time and accrual system, using Excel, to track employee time used and remaining time available.
- Performed updates to the Data Ease system: set up new programs, revised existing records, coded expenses, entered Medicaid billing information, and generated reports.
- Set up numerous Excel spreadsheets to track costs relating to payroll and other expenses and automated the posting of items to the general ledger.

"I want to thank you for all of your help with the specialized Billing Software. We have come quite a way with the computerization of our billing, and this would not have been possible without your assistance."
— Jack T. Peters, Program Manager, County Health Association of New York

Education

Accounting: New York City University, Bronx, NY

◆ ◆ ◆

the use of testimonials at the end of a section or subsection to back up the individual's accomplishments. Testimonials are powerful devices that promote respect and offset gaps or limitations.

CATHERINE HARRISON

CatHarrison@email.com

5555 Swanson Avenue ● Granada Hills, California 55555
(818) 555-5555 ● Mobile (919) 555-0000

FULL CHARGE BOOKKEEPER

Experienced in Full Range of General Bookkeeping and Accounting Procedures
AR/AP ● GL ● Balance Sheet ● P&L ● Journal Entries ● Payroll / Payroll Taxes ● Reconciliations

- A hardworking professional with a strong work ethic, excellent organizational abilities and attention to detail.

- Superior record of low absenteeism and punctuality.

- Experienced in both manual and computerized systems, including conversion from manual to automated system.

- Computer skills: MS Word, Excel; Intuit Quicken, QuickBooks; Peachtree

Notary Public

PROFESSIONAL EXPERIENCE

Full Charge Bookkeeper ● 1996 to Present
A. B. CHAMBERS, INC., Sherman Oaks, CA
Initially hired as receptionist for full-service insurance agency servicing broad range of commercial clients. Achieved promotions to bookkeeping positions of increasing responsibility as company grew from 6 staff members to 16.

- Perform all bookkeeping and accounting functions, including accounts receivable, accounts payable, collections, general ledger, payroll, bank reconciliations, trial balance.
- Generate financial statements and other financial reports.
- Handle licensing documentation for customer service representatives, agents and 40 nonresident insurance licenses.
- Prepare all quarterly and year-end payroll tax reports.
- Administer group health insurance and pension plan.
- Audit customer and general ledger accounts to resolve disputes and identify exceptions.
- Maintain office and computer supplies inventories; purchase as required.

EDUCATION

LOS ANGELES VALLEY COLLEGE, Van Nuys, CA; 2002
A.A. Degree; Extensive Course Work in Accounting
Graduated with Honors; Completed Studies While Working Full-Time

—Member, National Notary Association—

Vivian VanLier, Los Angeles, California

This candidate earned an A.A. degree concurrently with full-time employment. Her record of progressive promotions from an entry-level position is indicated in italic after her job title.

Administrative Support

Resumes at a Glance

RESUME NUMBER	LAST OR CURRENT OCCUPATION	GOAL	PAGE
8	Receptionist	Receptionist	39
9	Receptionist	Executive Personal Assistant/ Receptionist	40
10	Secretary	Administrative Assistant/Office Manager	42
11	Secretary	Technical Assistant	43
12	Secretary	Secretary	44
13	Administrative Assistant	Administrative Assistant	45
14	Administrative Assistant	Administrative Assistant/ Project Secretary	46
15	Administrative Assistant	Administrative Support Professional	48
16	Executive Assistant	Administrative/Executive Assistant	50
17	Executive Assistant	Fundraising/Event Planning Position	51
18	Executive Administrative Assistant	Office Management/ Administrative Support Position	52
19	Executive Administrative Assistant	Executive Administrative Officer	54
20	Office Manager/Executive Assistant	Not specified	56
21	Credit Portfolio Specialist/ Executive Assistant	Executive Assistant/Projects Manager	58
22	Leisure Travel Consultant	Office Professional	60

PATRICIA THOMAS

85 Barclay Road ~ East Brunswick, New Jersey 08816
Phone: 732.678.1691

RECEPTIONIST ~ OFFICE ADMINISTRATION

Well-organized and versed in many areas of production, sales, customer service, telephone communications and overnight shipping. Computer-literate with Internet experience. Possess excellent telephone and communications skills.

• Self-disciplined	• Motivated
• Problem solver/Troubleshooter	• Telephone techniques
• Excel under pressure	• Superb memory
• Professional	• Quick learner

HIGHLIGHTS

- Detail-oriented employee with pleasant speaking voice.
- Serve as a liaison to match customers with the right staff professional.
- Perform computer data processing in Word, daily office operations and filing.

PROFESSIONAL EXPERIENCE

AMERICAN BOUQUET COMPANY, *Edison, NJ*   1987–Present
Receptionist

- Answer telephone and greet visitors.
- Schedule conference room for various meetings.
- Type letters and perform general secretarial work.
- Assist with payroll.
- Make hotel and flight reservations, finding least-expensive plans through the Internet.
- Serve as liaison between sales and manufacturing.
- Proof all product orders to ensure accuracy.

HOWARD GRAPHICS, *New Brunswick, NJ*   1977–1987
Secretarial, proofreading, receptionist, quality control

~ Excellent References Upon Request ~

8

Beverly and Mitch Baskin, Marlboro, New Jersey

A page border, three strong horizontal lines, and relatively large font sizes are the dominant visual elements. Bulleted lists throughout make the resume a quick read. Keywords are near the bottom.

Leah Brooks

28 Flip Road • Ringwood, Vic., 3333 Australia • (613) 9888 8888 (A/H)

EXECUTIVE PERSONAL ASSISTANT / RECEPTIONIST

Professional Representation ♦ Outstanding Communication ♦ Customer Service Excellence

Commercial Construction / Financial & Investment / Health & Medical Field

QUALIFICATIONS PROFILE

Highly motivated, solutions-focused professional with extensive experience and an impressive record of achievements within all facets of reception, administrative and customer-service management across diverse industries. Combine sound time- and resource-management skills to implement strategic administrative and operational initiatives to enhance productivity, quality, client service and overall bottom-line performance.

➢ Exceptional interpersonal and communication skills with proficiency to promote confidence and build and maintain strategic business/client relationships while interfacing positively with people of diverse backgrounds.
➢ Ability to manage multiple tasks without compromise to quality or productivity.
➢ Sound organizational skills achieving results beyond company goals and objectives.

CORE COMPETENCIES

- Client Relationship Management
- Switchboard / Telephone Answering
- Process & Productivity Improvement
- Functions Planning & Management
- Vendor & Supplier Negotiations
- Correspondence Authoring
- Diary Management & Scheduling
- Senior Executive Support

PROFESSIONAL EXPERIENCE

ADCO CONSTRUCTIONS   2001–Present

Receptionist

Fully accountable for professional representation as first point of contact for this commercial construction company, implementing initiatives to ensure the smooth functioning of a busy reception area and efficient operation of an extremely demanding switchboard, proficiently handling 300–400 calls per day. Type and distribute documentation, correspondence and relevant reports, including site-meeting minutes. Perform diverse administrative and clerical procedures, including preparing subcontractor agreements, cover letters and associated photocopying/dissection into relevant procedures; ordering and maintaining stock of Adco procedural manuals for site foreman, including site instruction, site diary and request for information; and multiple photocopying as required. Coordinate mail-outs and special notices; compile and prepare priority invoices using sophisticated database and write accompanying letter. Oversee and coordinate incoming/outgoing correspondence, ensuring procedures are maintained and deadlines are achieved. Monitor and procure inventory, office stationery and kitchen consumables.

♦ Outstanding ability to liaise with difficult clients, utilizing exceptional communication skills to handle complex situations professionally to ensure that successful outcomes are achieved.
♦ Effective collaborator, demonstrating sound interpersonal skills striving toward the achievement of common goals and objectives.
♦ Track record in operating independently, prioritizing commitments to meet deadlines.

Continued…

Annemarie Cross, Hallum, Victoria, Australia

A drop cap in the individual's name is the first distinctive design element. Page borders and horizontal lines both in the contact information and under the section headings tie the two pages together visually. Bullets change within the Qualifications Profile but persist as diamonds

LEAH BROOKS

PERPETUAL   1995–2001

Receptionist / Telephonist

Distinguished track record within all facets of receptionist/telephonist procedures when interfacing with clients to meet/greet and respond to their needs; maintained Perpetual's overall corporate image through professionalism and outstanding customer service. Managed diaries and scheduled appointments for Financial Consultants; directed client introductions for Senior Consultants involving research and reporting of client's relevant data; and collaborated with Client Relationship Managers and Senior Financial Consultants. Supported Executive Personal Assistant with word processing, inbound/outbound mail, reconciliation of accounts, and preparation of invoices. Coordinated conference rooms and car bookings; maintained tearooms; monitored and procured supplies; and ensured reception area was well presented at all times.

♦ Spearheaded development and implementation of benchmarking customer liaison techniques, which secured ongoing accolades from senior executives and clients.

♦ Placated irate and concerned customers using diplomacy and tact, ensuring that clients' needs were addressed appropriately and professionally.

♦ Empowered relief staff through training, supervision and support in company procedures.

♦ Skillfully operated a 20-line Meridian 2000 switchboard, implementing outstanding communication skills/telephone techniques; requested to record corporate business message on answering machine and mobiles across the entire company.

♦ Coplanned and coordinated special corporate functions involving sourcing, qualifying and organizing caterers and facilitating the entire function to ensure successful completion.

HOSPITAL MANAGEMENT ASSOCIATION   1990–1994

Corporate / Customer Service Officer (1993–1994)

Steady promotion demonstrating expertise and professionalism through increasingly responsible positions, becoming fully accountable for the research, planning and implementation of innovative product marketing and promotional initiatives to a diverse corporate client base. Responded to technical inquiries; supported and advised companies providing Payroll Deduction Schemes to HMA clientele on a global level; provided onsite support to businesses; and assisted with general telephone inquiries.

♦ Enhanced corporate image of the company through continually representing HMA as a professional and committed organization, maintaining key alliances with a diverse client base of corporate customers.

♦ Provided strategic customer relationship management techniques to maintain client satisfaction, retention and ongoing business.

Front Desk Receptionist (1990–1993)

Maintained highest level of professionalism when greeting and assisting clients and guests; handled internal/external telephone inquiries; and coordinated internal/external deliveries. Prepared correspondence and reports using MS Word; maintained HMA's library, including distribution of daily papers, periodicals and associated literature.

EDUCATION & PROFESSIONAL DEVELOPMENT

PERPETUAL IN-HOUSE TRAINING
Professional Letter Construction / Concise Writing ♦ **First Impression**
Customer Service ♦ **Telephone Techniques** ♦ **Time Management**

Office & Secretarial Studies Certificate—BOX HILL COLLEGE OF TAFE

Word for Windows—POLLAK PARTNERS

TECHNOLOGIES

MS Word ♦ MS Excel ♦ MS Outlook

in the Professional Experience section as it extends from page 1 to page 2. The resume contains much paragraph text, but many blank lines provide white space and prevent a crowded appearance.

JACKIE D. GUENTHER

605 Bellevue Drive, Springboro, OH 44444

Residence: (000) 000-0000   Office: (555) 555-5555

PROFILE

Highly motivated and cooperative **Administrative Assistant/Office Manager** with many years in the clerical field. Interface with all levels of management. Strong secretarial ability, initiative, confidentiality and diversified administrative/secretarial duties.

EXPERIENCE PROFILE

CH2M HILL MOUND, INC., MIAMISBURG, OH   1988–2004
Environmental restoration of the former nuclear weapons site.

Secretary/Environmental Restoration and Site Transition (1999–2004)
Support Project Manager and 4 managers in office operations.
- Maintain records of correspondence
- Track training for individual training plans
- Work effectively with a wide variety of people
- Skilled in WordPerfect 6.1 and Microsoft Word, PowerPoint and Excel
- Order supplies for the department; reconcile credit card statement for payment
- Assemble, type, and disseminate correspondence to the customer and regulators

Secretary/Environmental Safeguards & Compliance (1994–1999)
Supported manager and 5 supervisors in office operations.
- Entered SAR Library into database
- Maintained record of correspondence
- Assembled and typed various correspondence
- Reviewed Daily Time Check Report for plant site
- Entered department's correspondence into database
- Ordered office and lab supplies; reconciled statement for payment

Clerk/Operations Department (1993–1994)
Supported two supervisors in general office work—letter writing, reports and presentations.
- Maintained time card records
- Acted as courier for classified documents
- Prepared tables of technical information for management
- Maintained and controlled salary administration of groups
- Answered telephone/fax and directed to proper personnel
- Assisted in preparing travel schedules and developing expense reports
- Skilled in many software programs, such as WordPerfect, Microsoft Word, Freelance 2.1 and Lotus 1-2-3

Data Control Clerk/Performance Assurance (1992–1993)
Program Support to aid management in prioritizing workload.
- Coordinated company presentations for local schools
- Managed the classified files and maintained classified log
- Provided information to management, aiding their decision-making and creating a more efficient management structure

Secretary (1988–1992)
Office Management of all secretarial duties and prepared for audit teams.
- Supported Manager of Material Analysis; coordinated and disseminated information to supervisors
- Managed the classified files and responsible for classified log and classified workstation

10

Diana Ramirez, Seatac, Washington

A thin box around the name of the chief workplace makes it evident immediately. Boldface and underlining make the different positions stand out. Bullets pull the reader's eyes down the page.

Jane Mullen

433 Roemer Avenue
Hermitage, PA 16148

724-555-5511
jmullen@yahoo.com

TECHNICAL ASSISTANT   MECHANICAL DESIGN
CAD

Project Management • Productivity Improvements • Document Management

➢ More than 12 years of experience in using CAD programs for industrial, mechanical and electrical design projects. Prepare and maintain technical drawings for use throughout organization. Understand workflow process. Drive organizational change and improvement.

➢ Direct and coordinate multiple projects and services. Strong work ethic and sense of responsibility. Keep team members motivated to achieve goals. Commitment to quality. Prepare reports and studies as needed.

➢ Use document management and AutoCAD tools. Deliver efficient data access for safety, regulatory, environmental, maintenance and grounds drawing information. Help ensure data integrity. Adept at recognizing/launching steps needed to attain objectives.

➢ Readily develop rapport with people from diverse cultures and all professional levels. Exceptional oral and written communication skills. Speak fluent Portuguese.

➢ Computer proficiency includes MS Word, MS Excel, MS Publisher, QuickBooks, Quest, 3D-Architect, CAD/AutoCAD, Design Jet, Internet communication and research.

_____ **PROFESSIONAL EXPERIENCE** _____

SECRETARY, Conrad Construction Inc.—West Middlesex, Pennsylvania   *2002–Present*
• Perform clerical duties to maintain drawing and work records, equipment and supplies. Track job status and relay information to job supervisor. Commended for exceptional organizational, administrative and computer skills. Trained owner in use of computerized estimating program.

YOUTH COORDINATOR, St. Joseph's School—Mercer, Pennsylvania   *2001–2002*
• Organized educational and recreational programs for middle school and high school students. Created a youth group for teens. Commended by parents and youth for initiating fun, inspiring activities.

TECHNICAL ASSISTANT, McFly Engineering—Warren, Ohio   *1989–2000; 2001*
• Organized engineering director's office for optimum productivity. Commended by supervisor for applying computer programs to advance production. Created Excel files to track sales, profits, accounts payable and accounts receivable. Implemented customer tracking system, which was adopted by parent company.

• Produced 2-D mechanical designs and drafting documents using AutoCAD (various versions from 2.6 through Auto LT2000i).

ENGINEER, Wheatland Industries—Wheatland, Pennsylvania   *2000–2001*
• Produced mechanical designs on CAD R13 for fabrication. Generated design details of mechanical parts; structured Bills of Materials (BOMs). Collaborated with vendors to optimize detail parts design. Checked drawings per company standards.

• Selected as technical advisor liaison regarding fabrication, sales and clients. Created "user-friendly" system for sales department through use of Excel files for all drawings.

• Assembled technical manuals for customers. Produced engineering documentation.

_____ **EDUCATION / CONTINUING EDUCATION** _____

Material Science Engineering Course Work, Youngstown State University—Youngstown, Ohio
Pre-Engineering Course Work, Kent State University–Trumbul—Warren, Ohio
Certificate, Computer-Aided Drafter and Designer, 1989, East Ohio Machinery—Alliance, Ohio

11

Jane Roqueplot, Sharon, Pennsylvania

The drafting-table graphic makes this resume unique and invites interest. Good touches are the slanted name on the drawing board, a font with drafting characters, and a good use of boldfacing.

Melissa Sky
987 Sky Way Lane, Mount Batten, New York 00000
Residence: (555) 555-5555 • E-mail: sky@aol.com

OBJECTIVE
Secretarial/Administrative

SUMMARY
More than 15 years of secretarial/administrative experience in busy and intensely demanding environments.
Such positions included:
- *Unit Secretary in a hospital intensive care unit*
- *Head Secretary for a hospital program director*
- *Secretary for a hospital outpatient clinic*
- *Victim's Advocate for the Rape Crisis Center*
- *Parent Advocate for a committee on special education*

SKILLS
*• **Typing** • **Phone work** • **Dictation** • **Scheduling** • **Customer Service** • **Filing***
*• **Computer** (Windows 98 platform) • **Research** (library and Internet)*

❖ **Organization.** *Demonstrated skill in managing simultaneous tasks, coordinating departmental activities, and meeting deadlines under strict time constraints and stressful work situations.*
- *Coordinated multiple tasks in hospital ICU. Heavy phone work. Patient, family, nurse, and doctor contact. Transcribed orders from nurses into patient charts.*
- *Headed up office of hospital residency program. Coordinated activities of Director, Assistant Director, and up to 12 residents. Screened and catalogued over 100 residency program applications a year. Scheduled residents' presentations and secured necessary slides and equipment.*
- *Organized presentations made by pharmaceutical sales representatives and other medical sales professionals. Determined the formats for their presentations.*
- *Coordinated extensive patient contact with heavy phone work and scheduling for six clinics as secretary of an outpatient clinic.*
- *Scheduled appointments for five social workers and scheduled patient tests as secretary of hospital social work department.*

❖ **Communication.** *Extensive direct contact with a variety of individuals and groups, including professional and administrative hospital staff, patients, families, sales representatives, students, teachers, and the general public. Poised under pressure. Personable and approachable.*
- *Adept at fielding a lot of questions, both in person and on the phone. Able to keep the communication process going under the stressful and multiple demands of job situations.*

EXPERIENCE
*Rape Crisis Center, **Victim's Advocate** (part-time volunteer), Wheaton, NY, 2000 to 2001*
*Committee on Special Education (Island Elementary School), **Parent Advocate** (part-time volunteer), Sandler, NY, 1996 to 2001*
Sandler (NY) School District (volunteer half-day once a week in special-ed class), 1996 to 2001
Ronald McDonald House (volunteer), Fulmont, NY, 1993-1994
*Community General Hospital, **Secretary** (Social Work Department), Athens, NY, 1989 to 1990*
*Community General Hospital, **Unit Secretary** (part-time, twice a week, 3-11:30 p.m.), Athens, NY, 1987 to 1989*
*St. Margaret's Hospital, **Head Secretary** (Residency Program), **Promoted,** Athens, NY, 1985 to 1987*
*St. Margaret's Hospital, **Secretary** (Outpatient Clinic), Athens, NY, 1984 to 1985*
*Community General Hospital, **Mail Clerk,** Athens, NY, 1982 to 1984*
*Athens Newspapers, **Clerical** (Classified Ad Department), Athens, NY, 1982*

EDUCATION
*Adirondack Community College, Mount Batten, NY, **A.A. degree in Humanities,** December 2002*
South Madison High School, North Adams, NY, 1982

12

Bruce Baxter, Liverpool, New York

With a recent degree, this applicant had been out of the workforce for a number of years to raise a family. The writer combined the individual's volunteer and job experience into one Experience section.

Mary Labunski

306 Parker Road
Schenectady, New York 12306

Residence: (518) 353-2367
Office: (518) 458-1342, Ext. 7001
xxx@aol.com

OBJECTIVE

To obtain a challenging position as an Administrative Assistant

SUMMARY OF QUALIFICATIONS

- Ability to execute multiple tasks and projects simultaneously.
- Skilled in administrative and office procedures.
- Competent with computers and numerous software applications.
- Strong analytical and negotiating skills; ability to find cost-effective solutions.
- Excellent organization and communication skills.
- Skilled in acting as liaison between senior executives, staff/outsiders.
- Dependable, loyal, discreet, trustworthy, innovative team player who can work independently.

EXPERIENCE

TRANS WORLD ENTERTAINMENT, Schenectady, NY
With more than 1,000 stores nationwide and annual sales of more than $1 billion, Trans World Entertainment is one of the nation's largest and most successful music and movie retailers.

Administrative Assistant   1992–Present
As Administrative Assistant of MIS, report directly to Vice President/Chief Technology Officer, Director of Operations, and Director of Development. Perform a variety of high-priority, time-critical, confidential activities for company. Oversee department budget and vendor accounts and manage office.
Selected contributions:

- Saved $5,000 annually by selecting new phone vendor for internal phone system.
- Negotiated with phone vendors to save more than $8,000 in annual maintenance.
- Reduced long-distance phone service by $10,000 per month by selecting new carrier.
- Improve customer service for in-store and online shopping as member of E-Works Committee.
- Cut MIS spending by creating tracking report using Excel spreadsheets to track all purchases by account.
- Assisted in coordinating national meeting to introduce a Point of Sale register system to more than 800 stores.
- Participated in selection of new cabling vendor for voice and data communication upgrades.
- Participated in Y2K testing.
- Handle travel arrangements and convention planning.

Data Entry Supervisor   1987–1992
Supervised staff of 5 data entry clerks in MIS Department. Monitored accuracy and quality of all data entries. Performed data entry, typing, and filing and diverted incoming calls. Wrote and oversaw accuracy of purchase orders, new-store orders, and receiving orders. Posted catalog items in computer system.

Data Entry Clerk   1984–1987
Entered and verified data into computer system in MIS Department. Filled purchase orders, receiving orders, and catalog orders. Conducted daily billing, physical inventories, and canceled A/P checks. Handled store returns, new-release information, inventory and back-order adjustments, promo LP and cassette catalogs, gift certificates, and other miscellaneous projects.

Payroll Clerk   1982–1984
Served as Payroll Clerk in the Payroll Department, preparing weekly payroll for 150 employees. Recorded and verified hours worked by employees. Prepared quarterly, monthly, and annual taxes. Responsible for new-hire paperwork, insurance forms, and all other Payroll Department paperwork.

COMPUTER SKILLS

Thoroughly familiar with all components of Microsoft Office (Word, Excel, PowerPoint, Access), WordPerfect, and Nortel Phone System.

Highly skilled and experienced at setting up templates and organizational systems for company records and procedures.

13

John Femia, Altamont, New York

Like a resume for an experienced executive, this one-page resume contains much information through the use of a relatively small font size. Blank lines ensure adequate white space.

SUSAN L. MILLER
9999 Saturn Court
Alpharetta, Georgia 33333
(777) 888-0000

ADMINISTRATIVE ASSISTANT / PROJECT SECRETARY

Dynamic professional with 15 years of various administrative responsibilities. An energetic self-starter with a strong sense of dedication to a job well done. Areas of expertise include:

- Organizational Skills
- Accounts Payable
- Business Correspondence
- Receptionist Duties
- Microsoft Office Applications

- Interpersonal Communication Skills
- Customer Service
- Attention to Detail
- Team Environment Contribution
- Problem Resolution

PROFESSIONAL EXPERIENCE:

Administrative Assistant / Brokerage Department, Alpharetta, Georgia   2001–2004
JONES PROPERTIES, INC.
(Commercial real estate corporation)

Prepared, assembled, and distributed sales packages for potential investors, outside brokers, and bankers. Responsible for refining and arranging business documents including leases, agreements, and other real estate contracts for tenants and owners. Ordered and negotiated pricing for all office supplies. Also, light receptionist duties that included sorting and delivering mail and providing assistance with telephone duty as needed.

Notable:
- Organized company's supply unit to make items more accessible and easy to obtain, which created higher employee productivity and efficiency.

Project Secretary, Doraville, Georgia   1999–2001
CRESTPOINT CONTRACT MANAGEMENT
(Construction management corporation)

Complete autonomy over field office's operations. Heavily involved in the accounting process. Managed project accounting systems, including petty cash account, accounts payable, and Crestpoint's field office billing while maintaining the monthly cost reports. Updated project-specific certified payroll logs, compiled monthly progress reports, and created and maintained project files. Responsibility for preparing all bid documents and packages for distribution to general contractors and subcontractors. Handled business correspondence to residents, school districts, and outside construction companies. Also organized and delivered mail, maintained office schedules, and handled telephone duties.

Notable:
- Developed strong relationships with general contractors and subcontractors from daily communication.

14

Heather Eagar, Glen Carbon, Illinois

The duties of this Administrative Assistant were task-oriented, so it was difficult for the writer to identify true achievements. The applicant, however, did have one notable achievement for each position, so the writer drew attention to each accomplishment by highlighting it with the

SUSAN L. MILLER
–Page Two–

Administrative Assistant II, Atlanta, Georgia 1998
BADGE BEHAVIORAL CARE CORPORATION
(Behavioral management corporation)

Managed diverse workloads for both Vice President and Director. Composed business correspondence, typed dictation, and organized and maintained company files. Scheduled interviews, meetings, and appointments.

Notable:
- Complete responsibility for successful company-wide, three-day training seminar for 75–100 people. Duties included preparing training material, flight and hotel reservations, meeting room accommodations, individuals' meals, and audiovisual equipment.

Administrative Assistant, Atlanta, Georgia 1993–1997
POST ENGINEERED METAL PROCESSES, INC.
(Metal and aluminum manufacturer)

Verified, distributed, audited, and archived all accounts payable. Composed and distributed both internal and external business correspondence. Arranged travel itineraries and coordinated every departmental seminar and meeting.

Notable:
- Reorganized entire accounts-payable archival system, which increased departmental documentation retrieval efficiency.

Team Support Specialist, Business and Financial Services, Marietta, Georgia 1991–1993
WIRELESS CORPORATION
(Global Information Solutions Division)

Accounts-payable responsibility, including invoicing and payroll, for the entire five-state Midwest region. Issued and processed purchase orders for components. Prepared proposals, sales presentations, and business correspondence. Organized company-wide recycling program.

Notable:
- Developed automated vendor database to be used as a quick reference in accounts payable.

Customer Support Specialist, Finance and Administration 1989–1991

Provided accounts-payable support. Managed all incoming calls on AT&T System 75 Call Director with 6 lines and 400 extensions. Coordinated meetings and arranged travel itineraries for associates.

Notable:
- Created an automated internal telephone directory for all AT&T divisional associates.

COMPUTER SKILLS & PROFESSIONAL TRAINING:

Microsoft Windows, Office, and Outlook; Macintosh; Print Shop; RF Flowcharting software.
Fred Pryor Enrichment Seminars: The Exceptional Assistant, Interpersonal Communication Skills.
Corporate educational programs covering Process Management, Diversity/Common Bonds, Opportunity, Vision, and Values.

repeated subheading "*Notable*" and a bullet. The recurrence of the subheading and bullet makes each job position seem important. The overall effect is that of strength for each position held.

CARA WAVERLY

58 Chelsea Way • Bridgeport, CT 22222 • (333) 333-3333 • cara@aol.com

Executive-level administrative support professional whose accomplishments reflect excellent administrative skills and a demonstrated commitment to providing exemplary service

SUMMARY OF QUALIFICATIONS

- Capable executive assistant with extensive experience in administrative roles.
- Organized and detail-oriented with demonstrated project coordination skills. Practiced in prioritizing and managing tasks. Effective at balancing the competing demands of multiple projects.
- Excellent interpersonal skills. Able to develop easy rapport with others while building trust.
- Versatile and resourceful team player who is willing to do whatever is necessary to complete goals and meet deadlines. Polished and professional, yet warm and accommodating.
- Recognized "go-to" person for a broad range of issues and concerns.
- Committed to providing the highest levels of customer service.

PROFESSIONAL EXPERIENCE

PETPHARMA CORP., Bridgeport, Connecticut   2001 to present
Administrative Assistant

As lead administrative assistant, provide effective support to VP of Global Marketing, VP of International Operations, and three other managers. Handle administrative details such as maintaining calendars, making travel arrangements, scheduling meetings, and coordinating conferences.

Administrative Leadership

- Established strong record in developing best practices for administrative support. Proactively provide support, looking beyond immediate need to maximize effectiveness.
- Hired as first administrative assistant in newly relocated group; developed and documented group processes and procedures. Trained and mentored new administrative assistants.
- Developed administrative checklist for new hires, ensuring smooth transition for more than 20 new employees.
- Implemented filing system for all product-related literature, creating easy-to-use resource for customer inquiries. Also developed individual product binders for each sales rep.
- Effectively support group training efforts by developing manuals and presentations, and scheduling and facilitating training sessions.
- Consistently explore lower-cost options in keeping with company's "Smart Initiatives."

Project Coordination

- Successfully arranged numerous domestic and international conferences, effectively planning and coordinating events for groups of more than 100 people.
- Oversaw all administrative details to ensure flawless events. Booked all facilities, negotiating favorable pricing. Made travel arrangements and scheduled ground transportation for all attendees. Generated handouts and purchased gifts and awards. Shipped materials to site, meeting all project timetables.
- Implemented effective follow-up system to ensure all projects and tasks remain on schedule.
- Effectively supported Transition Team, collecting and collating staff résumés for timely presentation to management.

15

Carol A. Altomare, Three Bridges, New Jersey

This applicant wanted an executive-level administrative position but did not hold that title at the time even though she supported executives and was functioning as an Executive Assistant. To show that the applicant had executive-level experience, the writer organized accomplishments

CARA WAVERLY   PAGE 2

PETPHARMA CORP., Westport, Connecticut   1998 to 2001
Administrative Assistant

Provided effective administrative support for Customer Development, Sales Training, and Sales Operations groups following relocation. Maintained all personnel and customer files.

- Developed guidelines and procedures for administrative assistants. Documented procedures for new hires.
- Established and managed system to track broker payments.
- Developed process for customer scorecarding, following up with clients to determine satisfaction with products, delivery times, and customer service. Developed spreadsheet to record and track response.
- Maintained divisional "dashboard"—a prominent display that tracked key performance measures and staff awards.
- Successfully planned and coordinated large-scale conferences and sales meetings.

BOYD, INC., Mullica Hill, New Jersey   1992 to 1998
Executive Secretary

Assisted president and controller in managing International Division. Prepared all correspondence and assisted in preparing all confidential salary reviews, business plans, budgets, and presentations.

- Organized office, setting up effective filing systems and archiving old files.
- Developed and implemented more efficient procedures for office operations.
- Effectively organized numerous conferences and sales meetings.
- Served as Board Member for Boyd's Federal Credit Union in addition to regular duties.

Corporate Flight Coordinator

Assisted Manager of Flight Operations and scheduled flights for corporate executives.

- As first full-time coordinator, set up effective scheduling system to accommodate increasing demand for flight services.

UNITED CHEMICALS, Clifton, New Jersey   1985 to 1992
Administrative Assistant

Assisted Region Administrative Manager, providing support in the area of marketing, administration, office services, information systems, and annual planning activities.

- Gathered background information for reports and special projects.
- Coordinated and scheduled system usage, enforcing region guidelines. Mobilized system specialists to handle problems and requests.
- Provided instruction for all software packages.

COMPUTER SKILLS

Word ◆ Excel ◆ PowerPoint ◆ Outlook ◆ Internet ◆ E-mail
DCIS (database for sales reporting)

References Available Upon Request

in the most recent job under the headings Administrative Leadership and Project Coordination. This approach pleased the applicant and proved to be a strong way to feature her relevant experience.

JUANITA SANCHEZ

jsanchez@email.com

5555 West 5th Street
Los Angeles, California 55555

Residence (323) 555-5555
Mobile (323) 555-0000

ADMINISTRATIVE/EXECUTIVE ASSISTANT
Special Expertise in Fashion Industry/Private Label

➢ Motivated self-starter who consistently goes beyond the requirements of the job to meet organizational objectives.

➢ Proven ability to multitask with attention to detail and accuracy in a fast-paced environment.

➢ Solid reputation for a strong work ethic and managing trusting relationships with public, clients and coworkers at all levels.

➢ Excellent computer skills, including Microsoft Word, Excel, PowerPoint, Access and Outlook.

—Core Competencies—

Multitasking • Account/Client Relations • Time & Task Management
Oral & Written Communications • Travel & Event Coordination • Problem Solving • Troubleshooting

PROFESSIONAL EXPERIENCE

SOUTHERN CALIFORNIA BEACHWEAR, Los Angeles, CA • 1998 to Present
Achieved fast-track promotions through positions of increasing challenge and responsibility for leading swimwear designer/manufacturer that generates $25 million in annual revenues with 300 employees.

Executive Assistant/Corporate Sales Support (2001–Present)
Pattern Maker (1999–2001); **Designer** (1998–1999)

Report concurrently to company President, Vice President/Sales Director and Vice President/Private Label Sales. Provide broad range of support, including client relations, report preparations, correspondence, overseeing shipping and inventory for private-label accounts, coordinating trade show participation and special events.

- Oversee inventories, supplies ordering and report preparation for private-label business that comprises more than 25% of annual profit.
- Manage excellent working relationships with 12 national key accounts, promoting positive company image.
- Coordinate all trade show participation, including working closely with agencies on casting calls for trade show models.
- Download routing and vendor guides for 90% of major accounts.
- *Accomplishments:*
  - o Accurately tracked and ensured compliance with shipping and EDI process for major account, avoiding thousands of dollars in charge-backs.
  - o Upgraded order entry processes, ensuring that appropriate inventory levels are maintained.
  - o Arranged all travel and accommodations for 30+ people attending annual sales meetings in Florida.

LAGUNA LEISUREWARE, Los Angeles, CA • 1996 to 1998
Design Assistant

Provided direct assistance to swimwear designer, including developing screens, monitoring and reporting on fashion/consumer trends and interfacing with contractors and screeners.

EDUCATION

FASHION INSTITUTE, Los Angeles, CA • **AA Degree in Fashion Design,** 1996
Honors: Awarded 1st place in design category

—Bilingual English/Spanish—

16

Vivian VanLier, Los Angeles, California

This candidate had an A.A. degree in Fashion Design and moved from being a designer to becoming an Administrative/Executive Assistant. Her goal was to become a manager in the fashion industry.

PATRICE PACKARD

45 Chestnut Street, Cold Spring Harbor, New York 55555 • (555) 555-5555 • ppackard@mail.com

---

~ Seeking a Position in a Not-for-Profit Organization ~
Emphasis on Fundraising and Event Planning

➢ Strong skills in initiating and pulling together all aspects of projects.
➢ Meticulous with details. Capable of autonomously handling a diverse array of responsibilities.
➢ Strength in anticipating problems before they arise.
➢ Excellent computer proficiency: Windows, Word, Excel, Access, PowerPoint, Outlook, and Internet.

~NOT-FOR-PROFIT EXPERIENCE~

Executive Assistant, 2003. Alzheimer's Association, Long Island Chapter, Smithtown, NY

Assistant to the Executive Director, 2001–2003. Child Care Council, Commack, NY

Public Relations / Writing / Promotions

▪ Wrote press releases for television and print promotion. Designed and produced flyers for special events.
▪ Assisted with the preparation of grant proposals and quarterly reports delineating accomplishments relative to goals set.
▪ Edited/proofread materials for Web site and for voice scripts used in public service announcements.
▪ Initiated and composed correspondence to acknowledge donors.
▪ Cultivated and maintained excellent relationships with professionals from related organizations.

Correspondence / Mailings / Information Management

▪ Handled mass mailings for fundraising initiatives. Coordinated projects and delegated activities to volunteers and interns.
▪ On a monthly basis, updated a mailing list of 12,000 names. Electronically transferred information to an outside printing vendor for widespread dissemination.
▪ Prepared budgets and verified calculations for accuracy.
▪ Maintained several databases to track contact information.

Executive Administrative Support

▪ Supported an executive director, a managing director, board members, and other professional staff. Handled virtually every type of administrative support function.

    -Managed office supply and repair needs. Dealt with vendors and repair technicians.
    -Processed and batched credit card and check donations. Handled bank deposits.
    -Troubleshot a variety of challenging and unique office problems.

Special Events

▪ Assisted in the planning, promotion, and execution of numerous special events. Attended events to actively promote organizational missions.

    -Conducted community outreach to secure donations and ensure solid levels of event participation.
    -Researched, evaluated, and made recommendations regarding event activities.
    -Assessed, priced, and hired caterers in accordance with budgetary guidelines.

~EDUCATION~

Bachelor of Arts Program, Sociology. 96 credits completed. Adelphi University, Garden City, NY

Excellent References on Request

17

MJ Feld, Huntington, New York

A few years out of college without a bachelor's degree, this applicant wanted to work for a not-for-profit organization. Because she had little relevant experience, the writer played up prior activities.

KYLA WALTERS

7558 South Fremont Way • Butte, MT 55555
Home: 777.777.7777 • kyla@aol.com • Mobile: 777.777.7777

Office Management/Administrative Support

Accomplished Administrative Manager with more than 15 years of experience in instituting organizational strategies and measures for continuous improvements and efficient business operations. Self-starter who meets project deadlines and requirements while performing multiple tasks within fast-paced environments. Respond rapidly and appropriately to changing circumstances; evaluate problems, make astute decisions to effect positive change and refocus on new priorities. Thrive as team player and coordinator for special events and programs. Outstanding interpersonal communication skills; quickly establish rapport with patients, physicians and staff members. Key strengths include

- Project Control & Management
- Human Resources Functions
- Law & Regulation Compliance
- Problem Identification & Resolution
- Team Building & Leadership

- Administrative Support
- Office Management
- Scheduling & Event Coordination
- Budgeting & Financial Affairs
- Interpersonal Communications

◆◆◆

"Kyla proved to be one of the most conscientious and hard-working associates that I have worked with in many years. Her attention to detail, dedication to her job, and positive attitude helped to make her a leader and an example for her peers and a tremendous asset to our department."

— Fred Knight, Risk Operations Manager, Rhapsody, Inc.

Professional Experience

MOUNTAIN HOSPITAL, Butte, MT   2000–Present
Executive Administrative Assistant
Provide administrative support to CEO and up to 12 management team and hospital staff members. Scope of responsibility is diverse and includes patient communications, special-event coordination, operations management, executive administration, human resources and regulatory compliance.

- Designed and implemented administrative programs to reduce redundancy, streamline processes and improve daily operations.
- Led internal office training to ensure compliance with all local, state and federal regulatory agencies; extensive knowledge of HIPAA, JCAHO and HCFA laws and regulations.
- Performed and assisted with human resources functions; interviewed, recruited and conducted new general employee orientations. Built work teams that consistently exceeded goals for productivity, efficiency and quality.
- Implemented Employee Incentive Award programs designed to promote outstanding work performance, which delivered measurable improvements in employee morale and satisfaction.
- Planned and facilitated a broad range of administrative functions, including travel arrangements, calendar management, business correspondence and outlining agendas for various functions and meetings.
- Designed and instituted a new database system for marketing, enabling the department to track areas of expertise and work history of specific licensed employees. Ultimately streamlined the process of submitting documentation to become certified or provider within network.
- Trained more than 12 staff members in equipment operations and various processes; developed team members committed to optimal productivity.
- Organized all charitable functions, special events and ongoing employee activities such as Christmas parties and picnics. Managed yearly budget of $6000 and events for 240 employees and 25 physicians; consistently stayed under budget and saved $1000–$2000 annually.
- Served as backup HR Director, frequently sought out by employees to handle issues and defuse problem situations.

18

Denette Jones, Boise, Idaho

This two-page resume offers much information through smaller type, wider lines from narrower left and right margins, and a variety of sections with shorter lines in the last half of the second page. The strong testimonial at the end of the opening section near the top of the

KYLA WALTERS – Page 2

Professional Experience continued…

RHAPSODY, INC., Butte, MT   1999–2000
Administrative Assistant/CRS Representative
Provided assistance to customers regarding various issues with accounts; established operational policies and procedures necessary for smooth business operations; developed recognition awards and motivational incentives for employees, which enhanced office environment.

MEDICAL SERVICES, Butte, MT   1999
Administrative Assistant
Directly reported to President and Vice President; oversaw projects and progression; prepared job costing, reports and materials; updated files; implemented new forms providing better efficiency and accuracy, clearing 2-month backlog within 3 weeks; accountable for new software installation, setup and maintenance of user profiles on NT environment; developed key database program for critical $1 million project, streamlining materials process, enhancing efficiency and ultimately saving costs.

BUTTE MEDICAL CONSULTING, Butte, MT   1995–1999
Administrative Assistant
Participated in assigning risk assessment to products inventoried, data entry, report updates and analysis, formal and informal research and manufacturer and vendor correspondence; collaborated with Project Manager during meetings to generate new ideas that would facilitate Y2K project.

BEAL TRANSPORTATION, Fontana, CA   1987–1995
OS & D Clerk/Supervisor
Developed and implemented new procedures that reduced claims by 12%; honored with award for completing Excellence Training Program within top 2%.

Education & Professional Development

A.A.S., Business Technology Administration (with honors), ITT Technical Institute, Butte, MT, 1999

Continuing in-service training courses sponsored by Mountain Hospital included

- Access Advanced Techniques
- Speak with Confidence & Clarity
- How to Discipline Employees
- Recruiting for Vacant Positions
- Workmen's Compensation Verification
- Knowledge of FLSA, FMLA & EEOC

- Management Skills for Administrative Assistants
- Coaching & Teambuilding Skills for Managers
- Basic Functions of HR
- Conducting Employee Orientations & Meetings
- JCAHO, HCFA, State & Federal Regulatory Agencies
- Computer/Business Software Applications

Technical Proficiencies

Access · Word · PowerPoint · Publisher · Excel · Windows XP · Outlook · Lotus Organizer · Transcription

Professional Associations

Member, Executive Women in Sales
Member, Business Professionals of America

Community Activities

Speaker/Volunteer, Suicide Awareness Program
Volunteer, Hope House
Volunteer, United Way

first page speaks louder than the impressive bulleted lists before it. Such a testimonial can help offset a gap in employment, questions about unrelated jobs, or doubts about a candidate's worth.

BELLA DORNO

| 25481 Crocker Avenue | Downey, California 90242 | 323 798-1418 |

EXECUTIVE ADMINISTRATIVE OFFICER
PERSONAL EXECUTIVE ADMINISTRATIVE ASSISTANT
Driving Organizational Change, Quality, and Continuous Improvement

Meticulous, detailed, multitasking professional with experience planning and directing executive-level administrative affairs and support to Boards of Directors and Senior Management. Combines strong planning, organizational, and communications skills with the ability to independently plan and direct high-level business affairs.

Background encompasses managing cross-functional business affairs for small and large service organizations, providing hands-on leadership, direction, and focus with positive results and outcomes. Proactive in analyzing existing operations and implementing strategies, processes, and technologies to improve organizational performance. Possess unique sense of innovation and resourcefulness with proven expertise in devising original solutions to complex problems. Effective troubleshooter whose strengths include the following:

- ◆ Administrative Policies and Procedures
- ◆ Board of Directors Meetings
- ◆ Facilities Management
- ◆ Budgeting and General Accounting
- ◆ Purchasing and Vendor Negotiations
- ◆ Regulatory Reporting and Communications
- ◆ Executive Office Management
- ◆ Confidential Correspondence and Data
- ◆ Special Project Management
- ◆ Customer Communications and Liaison Affairs

Professional and articulate; work well with all levels of management in a professional, diplomatic, and tactful manner. Delivered improvements in productivity and operating efficiency, cost reduction, and earnings. Sharp presentation, negotiation, and team-building qualifications. Outstanding interpersonal skills. Energetic and decisive business leader able to merge disparate technologies and personnel into a cohesive team-centered unit. Hardworking, dependable, trustworthy. Dedicated with a strong work ethic.

Proficient in the use of Word 2000, Excel 2000, and Access 2000. Experienced with shorthand and machine transcription.

PROFESSIONAL EXPERIENCE

EXECUTIVE ADMINISTRATIVE ASSISTANT 2001–Present
Downey Bank & Trust, Downey, CA

High-profile, executive-level administrative position supporting the Executive Vice President / Chief Lending Officer and other top management personnel throughout the organization. Scope of responsibility is diverse and includes Board affairs, customer communications, special events, regulatory reporting, and executive administration (assemble loan packages, collect reports, set appointments, keep calendar, screen calls).

- Executive liaison between Chairman, Senior Management, and employees to plan, schedule, and facilitate a broad range of corporate initiatives, company operations, and large-scale business functions. Communication is of the utmost importance in order to function independently and be self-starting in implementation.
- Built rapport with all departments and all branches. Recognized as principal Consultant.
- Handle confidential operating and financial information; maintain corporate records and minutes.
- Maintain / update files for regulatory review, oversight, and approval.

19

Myriam-Rose Kohn, Valencia, California

Two horizontal lines work together to call attention to the information between them. In this resume the two lines at the top of the first page appear together as a banner announcing the applicant's job goals and drive. The information below the banner provides a profile of the

BELLA DORNO   Page 2

- Organize all bank community involvements:
  - American Cancer Society: Heart Walk, Relay for Life: selected as coteam captain, recruit people to participate, coordinate fund raising.
  - Fourth of July Parade: assist with float decoration, participate in annual parade.
  - Office holiday party: serve on the committee to organize and facilitate all activities, handle invitations.
- **Several commendations** from President and Board of Directors.

College Assistant, Communications Department   2001
Mission College, Mission, CA

Obtained significant experience in primary research; very resourceful at finding data and developing primary and secondary sources for Department Chair / Professor. Aided with brochure creation for the Communications Department. Provided general office support. Tabulated and recorded grades.

Administrator   1993–2001
Various community activities in Downey, CA

- Participated in reading programs at elementary and junior high schools.
- Acted as Recording Secretary at Franklin Roosevelt Elementary School Site Council Meetings.
- Planned and organized social events for high school sports team.
- Designed flexible administrative systems and processes for dissemination of reports to parents of confirmation students at Christ Lutheran Church. Transitioned from manual operations to complete automation.

Executive Assistant / Administrative Assistant   1990–1993
Sumitomo Bank of California, Business Development Offices, Los Angeles, CA

Executed complex administrative duties for Executive Vice President. Assisted in budget planning and monitored / analyzed monthly operating statement. Compiled reports using various research sources. Widely recognized as information source on executive policies and procedures as well as general personnel policies. Administered all personnel functions for office staff.

Executive Assistant   1979–1990
Crocker National Bank, Los Angeles, CA

Managed confidential correspondence, appointments, meetings, and schedules. Personally planned and coordinated bank and intercompany meetings. Performed executive administrative duties as outlined under current position.

EDUCATION

Currently pursuing **Associate of Arts, Business Information Management**
California State University, Los Angeles, CA

Diploma, Executive Secretarial Program
Patricia Stevens Career College and Finishing School, Milwaukee, WI

Numerous AIB Courses, Fred Pryor Seminars, and Internal Training Classes

applicant, indicates her background and strengths, and mentions some of her worker traits and job skills. Boldfacing makes conspicuous the applicant's former positions as you glance through the Professional Experience section.

Rachel Osborne

Floral Gardens, Apartment 5-C
Idaho Falls, ID 00000

000-000-0000
luckyladybug@woohoo.com

SKILLED IN
- ☐ **Office Management**
- ☐ **Executive Assistance**
- ☐ **Sales and Business Support**

PROFESSIONAL QUALIFICATIONS
- ☐ More than 20 years of experience as a loyal, dedicated and trusted assistant to high-level corporate executives
- ☐ Recognized by management as a perceptive and assertive problem solver who thrives in a multitasking environment and can adapt quickly to new challenges
- ☐ Extremely well organized with strong project orientation and major strength in coordinating the details of business affairs with minimal direction
- ☐ Willingness and initiative to handle the numerous clerical responsibilities that keep an office functioning smoothly
- ☐ Proficient in building solid relationships, enabling people to work together as a team
- ☐ Continually contribute new ideas to increase efficiency and add value to the organization

BUSINESS PROFICIENCIES
- ☐ Computer knowledge: Windows NT, Word, Excel, PowerPoint, Quicken, ACT customer database, Macola accounting program, PC Anywhere, Delrina Winfax and Omnipage OCR program used with HP scanner
- ☐ Keyboarding of daily correspondence, customer quotes and statistical reports
- ☐ Fast longhand note taking
- ☐ Mail routing/letter composition for routine responses
- ☐ Transcription from taped dictation
- ☐ Setup and maintenance of complex filing systems
- ☐ Safeguarding of confidential matters
- ☐ Courteous and knowledgeable telephone and interpersonal communications

ADMINISTRATIVE MANAGEMENT
- ☐ Total responsibility for office services: facility maintenance, cleaning, equipment repair, telephones and building security system
- ☐ Implementation/enforcement of policies and procedures for increased efficiency
- ☐ Purchasing/inventory control of stationery supplies, printed forms and lunchroom items
- ☐ Minor troubleshooting of various office equipment, including computers and network server
- ☐ Bookkeeping assistance: invoicing, cash receipts, expense report reconciliation and commissioned payroll
- ☐ Training of clerical assistants to assume advanced responsibilities
- ☐ Control over company credit cards, leased vehicles, telecommunications pass codes and keyholder access

PROJECT COORDINATION
- ☐ Sales staff liaison for up-to-date product information, price quotes, delivery scheduling and credit terms
- ☐ Travel and meeting arrangements, domestic and international
- ☐ Company luncheons and social events
- ☐ Office moves to larger quarters
- ☐ Comparative analysis/recommendation for new capital equipment acquisitions
- ☐ Follow through on others' assignments to ensure timely completion

(Continued)

20

Melanie Noonan, West Paterson, New Jersey

An uncluttered, hanging-indent layout provides pleasing white space and makes it easy to view this resume's chief headings and subsections. A single vertical path of square, shadowed bullets directs the reader's eyes down both pages. The first page displays the breadth of the

Rachel Osborne
Page 2

CAREER HIGHLIGHTS

U.S. PACKAGING SYSTEMS, INC., POCATELLO, ID   1992 TO PRESENT
Office Manager/Executive Assistant, reporting directly to CEO of $10 million manufacturer of customized packaging machinery

❒ Hired permanently following temporary assignment with the company, having established a positive rapport with a difficult manager in a position where prior turnover was exceptionally high.

❒ Took charge of all office services, previously unassigned and often neglected in the past.

❒ Interfaced with CFO and Controller for preparation of confidential financial reports.

❒ Given joint check-signing authority for up to $10,000 and was empowered to carry out corporate directives.

❒ Supervised a receptionist, ensuring phone coverage at all times and timely completion of clerical work.

❒ Organized all historical data, specifications, drawings, contracts, invoices and general correspondence related to hundreds of machine projects into orderly binders. As a result, facilitated the quotation process, provided immediate information on the progressive stages of each project and saved countless hours in responding to customer requests.

❒ Worked closely with consultants to implement new accounting and order entry systems, eliminating redundant steps. Trained clerical staff in the use of these systems.

❒ Coordinated all aspects of 2 office moves to accommodate company's growing needs, from 15 employees initially to 47 currently. Conducted both moves smoothly with no disruption to normal business routines.

BEACON POLLUTION CONTROL CORPORATION, SHELLEY, ID   1984 TO 1992
Administrative Secretary to the Senior Vice President of Finance

❒ In addition to normal secretarial duties, assumed responsibilities of office service manager and personnel assistant, each for a period of several months during incumbents' respective absences.

❒ Successfully handled a large renovation project that involved securing and working with various building tradespeople as well as arranging for movement of large machinery.

❒ Reorganized departmental files from a paper system to electronic access of data.

❒ Cross-trained clerical employees to perform accounting and human resources functions.

❒ Designed formats that streamlined ongoing financial reporting and contributed to more efficient monthly closings.

CONTINUING EDUCATION

Groupwise IV: *Scheduling and Project Management Program*
Computer Applications Learning Center: *Microsoft Professional Office Suite*
Dun & Bradstreet: *Effective Writing Techniques*
Fred Pryor Seminar: *Management Skills for Executive Secretaries*

applicant's experience, skills, responsibilities, and activities. The bulleted items on the second page include some of her achievements at the two companies where she has worked since 1984.

Nadine L. Larson

9530 East 33rd Street ◆ West Palm Beach, FL 45612
913-490-8562 ◆ nlarson33@juno.net

EXECUTIVE ASSISTANT / PROJECTS MANAGER
Administration... Budget Management... Office Management

PROFESSIONAL PROFILE

Analytical, intelligent, organized, and resourceful professional who is a recognized **"go-to person," consummate team player,** and **innovative problem solver.** A **quick study** who seeks and **enjoys new challenges** and excels at exceeding established objectives. **Highly flexible** and masterful in reacting quickly and effectively to **corporate changes.** Extensive experience planning and implementing **administrative solutions** and directing **special projects.** Especially adept at **developing strong, positive relationships** with executive management, colleagues, clients, and vendors. Areas of expertise include

- ◆ Executive Office Management
- ◆ Special Events & Projects Management
- ◆ Confidential Correspondence & Data
- ◆ Problem Analysis & Resolution
- ◆ Budget Analysis & Administration
- ◆ Staff Training & Development
- ◆ Independent Research
- ◆ Travel Arrangements

Greatest asset is the ability to perform independently or within a team environment to achieve corporate goals that bring increased efficiency, effectiveness, revenues, and profits.

SELECTED ACCOMPLISHMENTS

- ◆ In response to a nationwide corporate directive for each facility to establish a disaster plan, charged with developing a local program based on collaborations with building, bank properties, information technology, and voice systems managers. **RESULT:** Produced a suitable report format for use as a template for other facilities across the U.S., met corporate deadline, and received accolades from the National Manager.

- ◆ Coordinated with several in-house departments the shipping of hundreds of boxes of retention files for storage. **RESULT:** After in-depth research and discussion with various carriers, selected an option that reduced department's costs from $2,000 to $200 per shipment and realized an equitable cost distribution among other participating departments.

- ◆ Revamped a credit filing system handling approximately 100 customers with multiple loans. Established a paper trail for loan underwriting, due diligence, approvals, financial records, correspondence, and documentation. **RESULT:** Received an excellent rating from a corporate auditing team.

- ◆ Planned and implemented numerous special events, both independently and as a team member, for managers hosting bank clients. **RESULT:** As part of a team, reduced expenses for a golf tournament by $10,000 from the previous year while receiving high praise from participants for the quality; consistently maintained budget parameters on all other functions.

21

Kay Bourne, Tucson, Arizona

A distinctive feature is the use of boldfacing to (1) call attention to key phrases in the Professional Profile section, (2) highlight the results of selected accomplishments, and (3) make conspicuous key responsibilities in the Skills and Abilities section. A partial dual-horizontal line appears in the

Nadine L. Larson

PROFESSIONAL EXPERIENCE

BANK ONE, Tucson, AZ   1983–2004
Credit Portfolio Specialist, Loan Analyst, Executive Assistant
Maintained position as major contributor and executive assistant for Senior Vice Presidents, Vice Presidents, and Assistant Vice Presidents in the commercial real estate lending departments staffed by up to 20 employees. Client portfolios averaged $250M, and each loan value amounted to a minimum of $1M.

Skills & Abilities

- **Provided direct support** and assistance with management calendars, meeting arrangements, general and confidential communications, corporate-culture initiatives, and travel arrangements.
- **Oversaw departmental budget** of $100K that covered operational expenses, special projects, and charitable contributions. Processed all Accounts Payable invoices and interacted with vendors regarding invoice issues.
- **Generated statistical reports** on loan sales, closings, payoffs, fee income, profitability, and financial and operating statements for each real estate project.
- **Reviewed** all loan documentation, which was between 30 and 80 pages. Ensured consistency with underwriters' reports, examined compliance issues, and established a monitoring system for financial and performance requirements.
- **Established computer** aptitudes that ensure quick adaptability to newly developed proprietary software and ongoing updates.
- **Acted as liaison** between management and clients, vendors, staff, and other local and national corporate departments.
- **Ensured compliance** with corporate Human Resources, purchasing, and expense policies. Generated memos to entire department on changes and updates.
- **Trained** new and established employees on company-specific databases, corporate policies, and equipment.
- **Maintained personnel files,** including performance reviews, annual bonus statistics, time and leave records, and benefits issues for 20 department employees.

COMPUTER SKILLS

MS Word 2000 & 2002 ◆ MS Excel, PowerPoint, Access ◆ MS Outlook ◆ WordPerfect ◆ Lotus Notes

CERTIFICATION & EDUCATION

Microsoft Office User Specialist (MOUS), expected completion August 2004
General Studies, University of Illinois, Champaign/Urbana, IL

PROFESSIONAL DEVELOPMENT

Courses in Accounting and Banking Law
Franklin Covey Project Management

contact information on page 1 and the header on page 2. Full dual lines enclose the targeted positions and the Professional Profile. Full single lines separate the three sections at the end of the resume.

Jennifer M. Jilleman

1234 N.E. Register   Gresham, Oregon 12345   555-555-5555

Office Professional

Professional Profile

Dynamic, enthusiastic, and conscientious **Office Professional** with extensive experience in a variety of office environments and proven ability to work well with others in fast-paced working conditions. Extensive expertise in the travel industry. Learn and adapt quickly to new situations. Possess excellent communication skills, both verbal and written. Thoroughly enjoy working with the customer—a definite "people person." Outstanding troubleshooting skills with efficient and successful solutions. Highly motivated, dependable, goal-oriented, and flexible. Committed to a job well done and professional excellence.

Expertise Includes:

- Administrative Skills
- Alpha/Numeric Filing
- Customer Service
- Data Entry
- Effective Coordinator
- Flexibility
- Leadership & Motivation
- Management Abilities
- Multiline Phones
- Organizational Skills
- Project Management
- Sales Techniques
- Strong Follow-Through
- Supervisor
- Team Leader
- Thoroughness

Professional Experience

Administrative Support

Experienced in a variety of environments with expertise in administrative assistance, organization, and attention to detail. Well-developed communication skills and experience in handling multiline phones along with balancing the demands of coordinating office responsibilities. Efficient, reliable, and thorough.

Customer Service

Excellent talent in "reading" the customer, gleaning information, and providing appropriate solutions. Professional appearance with proficiency in greeting customers/clients and making them feel comfortable. Strong problem-solving skills. Performance-driven.

Teamwork/Supervision

Work well in a team atmosphere or independently. Experienced in accepting a variety of projects and working them to completion with effective follow-through. Capable of accepting challenges and providing solutions. Not afraid of digging in and working with a project, as well as successfully delegating various responsibilities. Outstanding listening and assessment skills with positive results-oriented solutions.

Career Progression

Leisure Travel Consultant • Imperial Tour and Travel • Portland, Oregon • *2001–2004*
Senior Travel Consultant • Fairview Travel Service • Portland, Oregon • *2000–2001*
Owner/Manager • Jen's Travel • Portland, Oregon • *1998–2000*
General Travel Agent • Walker Travel • Gresham, Oregon • *1996–1998*
Owner/Manager/Agent/Instructor • The Cruise Shoppe • Portland, Oregon • *1991–1996*
Owner/Manager/Bookkeeper • Uniglobe Atlas Travel • Bend, Oregon
Agent • Cascade Travel • Bend, Oregon
Executive Secretary • Sunriver Lodge and Resort • Sunriver, Oregon
Agent • Tour-Time Travel • Bend, Oregon
Agent/Assistant Manager/Cruise Director • C P Travel Systems • Portland, Oregon
Substitute Teacher • SST Travel Schools • Portland, Oregon
Owner/Manager • First Class Tour and Travel, later known as Ted Boyd's Travel • Portland, Oregon

Certifications, Licenses, & Affiliations

Certified Travel Counselor • Institute of Certified Travel Agents
Accredited Cruise Counselor • Cruise Lines International Association
Member & Past President • Columbia Business Association

22

Rosie Bixel, Portland, Oregon

Note how the use of italic ties together the centered and side headings and subheadings, including the individual's name in the contact information. Boldfacing makes key information stand out.

Communications

Resumes at a Glance

RESUME NUMBER	LAST OR CURRENT OCCUPATION	GOAL	PAGE
23	Senior Editor	Not specified	63
24	Media Services Intern	Public Relations Internship	64
25	Database Marketing Coordinator	Sales and Marketing Support Position	66

Rebekka Johnson

1234 Baker Road ▼ Albany, Ohio 45710 ▼ 740.698.0000 ▼ bekka0000@yahoo.com

Excerpts from Letters of Recommendation...

"...demonstrated leadership qualities and is looked up to by the other individuals in our classes...very sincere regard for relationships...will be a wonderful success at whatever career path she chooses...Rebekka is a winner!"

—Teresa South
Youth Group Leader

▼ ▼ ▼

"...a pleasure to be around...a role model for her peers...acted responsibly, with integrity and maturity beyond her years— definitely standing out among her peers...without reservation we recommend Rebekka for any employment opportunities you may have available."

—David Kasler
Alexander Local School Board

▼ ▼ ▼

"...proven to be very dependable, responsible, and trustworthy... completed several college courses in an attempt to enter college a step ahead...her efforts are an indication of her personality because she always wants to accomplish more than what is expected...would be a great asset to any employer."

—Katie Chaney
Teacher

SUMMARY OF QUALIFICATIONS

Outgoing and enthusiastic individual with a strong work ethic and career goals focused on the field of journalism. Highly self-motivated, as evidenced by successful college studies during high school years, including achieving Dean's List status. Innate talent for writing and experience as Senior Editor of school newspaper. Good listening skills and a sense of humor—elements of success in my chosen field!

EDUCATION

OHIO UNIVERSITY, *College of Communication,* Athens, Ohio (start Fall 2004)
Media Studies Sequence—International Communication Major

ALEXANDER HIGH SCHOOL, Albany, Ohio (May 2004)
Diploma

HOCKING COLLEGE, Nelsonville, Ohio (2003–2004)
General Studies for transfer credit while still completing high school education
  ▼ Received Dean's List Certificate of Merit for Outstanding Academic Achievement
  ▼ Phi Theta Kappa International Honor Society of the Two-Year College

OHIO UNIVERSITY, Athens, Ohio (2001–2002)
General Studies for transfer credit while still completing high school education

RELATED EXPERIENCE

Senior Editor—SPARTAN TIMES NEWSPAPER, Alexander High School, Albany, Ohio (2003–2004)
  Gained valuable experience in layout and design while assisting with production of school newspaper. Assigned articles to appropriate staff members. Performed copy editing and proofreading. Coordinated sales and distribution of newspaper. Learned to work efficiently under deadline pressure.

COMMUNITY INVOLVEMENT

  ▼ Volunteer work with Toys for Tots, Ohio Educational Support Group, and the Athens County Sheriff's Department DARE program. Received a Certificate of Achievement for Outstanding Citizenship and Volunteer Work.
  ▼ Member of Athens Church of Christ. Active in Youth Group activities and volunteer with Community Meals Program.

EXTRACURRICULAR INVOLVEMENT

  ▼ Member of Dance Team, Marching Band, Flag Corps, Spanish Club, and Cheerleading Squad at Alexander High School
  ▼ Member of NASA STARS—Competitive Cheerleading Squad

23

Melissa L. Kasler, Athens, Ohio

This candidate was looking for a summer position before starting her college career in communication. The testimonials are from recommendation letters used with scholarship applications.

Erica C. Herman

School Address
4444 Alder Avenue
Eugene, OR 97401
(555) 444-4444

ericaherman@aol.com

Permanent Address
8888 N.W. 15th Place
Beaverton, OR 97229
(333) 555-5555

GOAL

A Public Relations Internship

RELEVANT QUALIFICATIONS

- Fully capable of handling assignments that require research, creativity and decision-making skills. Deadline-oriented...can produce under pressure.
- Exceptional language skills...good interviewer...creative writer...able to express thoughts clearly and effectively both verbally and in writing.
- Extensive knowledge of and experience with PageMaker, Photoshop, Microsoft Office applications and Internet communication.
- Achiever with an outgoing, enthusiastic personality; comfortable with individuals of all ages and professional levels.
- Bilingual: fluent in Spanish.
- Editor, high school newspaper.

EDUCATION

University of Oregon, Eugene, OR
Major: Journalism/Concentration: Public Relations
Minor: Spanish

Fall 2003–Present
Cumulative GPA: 3.5

Activities
- Chi Omega Sorority—Marketing/Public Relations Director
- Vice President, National Honor Society
- Public Relations Student Society of America
- Order of Omega

University of Georgia, Athens, GA
Major: Pre-Public Relations
Minor: Spanish

Fall 2002–Spring 2003
Dean's List honors
Cumulative GPA: 3.5

RELATED EXPERIENCE

Media Services Intern
University of Oregon Athletic Media Services, Eugene, OR

Jan. 2004–Present

Research and develop press releases covering various collegiate athletic events. Regularly update the media with information on all UO home athletic events. Write copy for team media guides; manipulate photos for media and public use. Post releases and team results on *www.goducks.com*.

Public Relations Intern
Portland Art Museum, Portland, OR

June 2003–Aug. 2003

As key media contact, coordinated media interviews for staff, curators and directors; fielded inquiries regarding current exhibitions; and assisted in coordinating and staffing special events to gain the public's interest and participation. Researched and produced press releases, public service announcements and copy for the PAM newsletter. Created exhibition press kits.

Continued....

24

Karen L. Conway, Media, Pennsylvania

The applicant hoped for an internship that would turn into a full-time position. She was successful in landing the internship for a Fortune 500 communications firm, with the promise of receiving a full-time position after she graduated. (She took a term off from school to gain this

ERICA C. HERMAN   Page 2

RELATED EXPERIENCE
Continued

<u>Oregon Public Affairs Intern</u>   Dec. 2001–Aug. 2002
XYZ Corporation, Hillsboro, OR
Participated in coordinating community and media relations events. Wrote for worldwide PA newsletter on an Internet website; monitored correspondence between the corporation and Oregon legislators. Assisted with the Strategic Investment Program.

HONORS & AWARDS

National Society of Collegiate Scholars
Ancient Order of Druids Honor Society
Outstanding Freshman in PRSSA (2001–2002)
PRSA Codispoti Technology Section Grant (2003)
Erik Elder Memorial Journalism Scholarship (2002)
Outstanding Junior: service and performance in journalism (2004)

COMMUNITY SERVICE

American Cancer Society administrative volunteer
Oregon Humane Society foster family member
Oregon Public Broadcasting telethon volunteer
Spanish tutor for mentally handicapped student
Make-A-Wish Foundation contributor

valuable experience.) Main section headings are centered with all capital letters. Underlining makes the side headings stand out. Many blank lines ensure white space. The last two sections make a strong ending.

188-17 Greenway, Salt Lake City, UT 00000
000-000-0000
jacqueline@alois.net

Jacqueline Alois

Marketing Communications ❖E-mail Template Design ❖Database Management

Profile

Sales and Marketing Support Professional with more than 14 years of experience in time-sensitive, fast-paced environments. Highly developed skills in oral and written communications, multitasking, attention to detail, and perseverance to completion. Keen insight into clients' perspectives, goals, and target audiences. Proficient with various software programs, including Word, Excel, Access, and Goldmine.

Key strengths include:

- ❖ Promotional copywriting
- ❖ Market research
- ❖ Sales lead qualification
- ❖ Proactive problem solving
- ❖ Database administration

- ❖ Internal/external customer service
- ❖ Computer and procedural training
- ❖ Project coordination
- ❖ Relationship building
- ❖ New-account development

Professional Employment History

GRAYROCK COMMUNICATIONS, INC., BEAR CREEK, UT   1999–PRESENT
Database Marketing Coordinator for trade show design firm

- ❖ Assist the President, Creative Director, and sales force of 7 in developing targeted messages to promote company's services (trade show display design and client training seminars). Contribute ideas in brainstorming sessions and translate concepts into persuasive written materials (brochures, web pages, and e-mail templates).
- ❖ Generate leads through extensive phone contact, which has facilitated the closing of numerous sales by determining clients' interests and addressing their specific needs or concerns.
- ❖ Enter and update all pertinent information for up to 500 clients and prospects on Goldmine system; create profiles and periodically send electronically distributed promotional pieces to keep company in the forefront for future business.
- ❖ Initially train new sales consultants on data mining to their best advantage as well as empower them for success in prospecting and cold calling. Organize sales assignments to avoid duplication of efforts.
- ❖ Coordinate all pre- and post-sale details with various departments.
- ❖ Demonstrated versatility and talent in several areas; was retained on staff despite 2 company downsizings.

QUIGLEY & VANCE, CARRINGTON, UT   1997–1999
Inside Sales Representative for graphic arts supply company

- ❖ Performed duties of sales liaison, assistant purchasing agent, and customer service representative.
- ❖ Streamlined department by automating the quote process and systematizing sales literature.

Education

Westview County College, Randolph, UT—A.A.S., Marketing Communications, 1997

Shelton Institute, Shelton, UT—Applied Writing and Database Administration courses, 1998

25

Melanie Noonan, West Paterson, New Jersey

Note how the fonts are enhanced. Look for boldfacing, bold italic, italic, and small caps. Note also the use of a different font (Albertus Medium) for the person's name, expertise areas, and headings.

Construction

Resumes at a Glance

RESUME NUMBER	LAST OR CURRENT OCCUPATION	GOAL	PAGE
26	Inventory/Receiving/Laborer	Laborer	69
27	General Foreman	General Foreman	70
28	Manager	Building Materials Professional	72
29	Owner/Operator of Excavating Company	Construction	74

Mark A. Benton

520 E. Ogden Avenue • Naperville, Illinois 06060 • 000–983–8882

PROFILE

Focus: Laborer position in the construction industry

Excel in troubleshooting and problem solving, readily understand instructions of a complicated nature, and respond to challenges with a "get the job done" attitude. Grasp client's requirements and management's needs quickly and apply appropriate actions to complete tasks in a timely manner. Constantly seeking new and more effective methods for performing professional duties. Working knowledge of Microsoft Windows and Word. Focused on personal and professional growth.

EXPERIENCE SUMMARY

- **Tradesman/Warehouseman/Laborer:** Light carpentry, painting, window preparations, frame building, shipping and receiving, loading of building supplies, use of various power tools and forklift operator.
- **Housekeeping Technician:** General housekeeping for one of the largest hotels in Chicago. Responsible for servicing up to 20 floors.
- **Building Services Technician:** General office cleaning, horizontal and vertical dusting, stripping/buffing of floors and restroom maintenance. Provided office security.
- **Security:** Ensured safe, clean and proper order of facility.
- **Administrative Support Technician:** Setup and maintenance of administrative files; answering and routing of phone calls; typing file labels, memos and letters using Microsoft Word. Copying and faxing documents, sorting incoming mail and preparing outgoing mail.

RELATED SKILLS

- Forklift Operator—Certified
- Computer Training and Enhancement
- Building Maintenance Services
- Equipment Maintenance Training

EMPLOYMENT HISTORY

Inventory/Receiving/Laborer, M&P Construction, Chicago, IL (02/01–Present)
Quality Control Coordinator, Teracotta Data Systems, Inc., Chicago, IL (04/99–02/01)
Laborer, Western and Block Construction, Chicago, IL (04/92–04/99)
Laborer, Buillion Construction/Cook County Hospital, Chicago, IL (01/89–04/92)
Housekeeper, Holiday Inn, Chicago, IL (03/86–01/89)
Warehouseman/Mover/Loader/Driver, We Move You, Chicago, IL (05/83–03/86)
Security, Your Answering Service, Bedford Park, IL (08/80–05/83)

EDUCATION

New Cycle Ministries, Inc., Chicago, Illinois. **Computer Training & Enhancement. 2004 Graduate**
Chicago High School, Chicago, Illinois. **1980 Graduate**

26

Patricia Chapman, Naperville, Illinois

This resume was for a Laborer with a variety of job experience and no degree. Boldfacing draws attention to the contact information, the centered headings, and the various positions.

Shawn Burleson

153 Asbury Lane McAllen, TX 78501 915-552-1562 915-582-4635

GENERAL FOREMAN
CONSTRUCTION / PIPE FITTER

30 years of comprehensive piping experience,
primarily in chemical plants, refineries, and oil fields on both short- and long-term projects throughout the United States. Proven track record of success with an excellent reputation for
- *quality*
- *troubleshooting*
- *safety compliance*

Knowledgeable in all facets of the construction field. Effective in supervising 20- to 100-man crews.

CORE STRENGTHS

Competent, reliable, and committed professional repeatedly earning promotions throughout career history. Sound and aggressive decision maker utilizing resources and organized processes to achieve success.
- Manage safety regulations according to OSHA and EPA regulations.
- Oversee complex projects and successfully complete them on deadline while exceeding quality standards and staying within budget guidelines.

Willing to travel

Additional core competencies include:

Detail-Oriented	Multitask-Oriented	Analytical
Proficient in OSHA / EPA Regulations	Safety Compliance	Budget Management
Excellent Presentation Skills	Supervision	Quality-Focused
Excellent Communication Skills	Keen Problem-Solving Ability	Assertive Troubleshooting Ability

---

PROFESSIONAL EXPERIENCE

Most recent history:

General Foreman and Pipe Foreman

10 years as a general foreman in multiple locations throughout the United States.

ACHIEVEMENTS:
- Refurbished and remanufactured a disassembled plant that had been out of service for 10 years. It was eventually shipped to Trinidad.—*CORP ENGINEERING.*
- Supervision:
  - Crew of 45 fabricating and erecting piping on 3 new HRSG boilers—*TRU-COR.*
  - Pipe Support and Hanger crew—*BFM CONTRACTORS.*
  - Installation crew for steam piping in paper mill expansion—*BJ COLE CONTRACTORS.*
  - Crew of 40 fabricating and erecting piping in 865 MW power plant—*HOLCOMB INDUSTRIAL.*
  - Crew of 25 responsible for installing a cold box and associated piping—*SOL-CHEM.*
  - Crew of 34 in fabrication, erection, and weld out of all vendor-furnished piping on 5 new heaters—*J.C.C. JENKING.*
  - Crew of 85 personnel in all activities of Pipe Department—*JACKSON REINOLD.*
  - Crew of 30 in fabrication and erection of process piping, punch out, and hydro test for gas plant expansion in Amarillo, Texas—*CORP ENGINEERING.*

27

MeLisa Rogers, Victoria, Texas

This candidate had a 30-year background in the construction/pipe fitting field. Within 11 years he had worked for 16 different companies but was not a "job hopper." To avoid giving this impression, the writer presented all expertise, achievements, and core strengths that the individual could

Shawn Burleson   Page 2
Professional Experience – Continued

Pipe Fitter and Pipe Superintendent

3 years of pipe fitting background includes experience in multiple United States–based plants, primarily in power and gas settings.

ACHIEVEMENTS:
- Erected steam piping in 1100 MW generating facility—*CRAIG CONSTRUCTION.*
- Fabricated and erected small-bore piping on STG—*REON INDUSTRIAL.*
- Fabricated and erected piping in new paper machine addition—*R.P. STANLEY.*
- Fabricated piping for shutdown—*KARL-ZACHRY.*
- Pepsi plant expansion—*BILMER MECHANICAL.*
- Building of computer chip plant—*JESTER REYNOLD.*

EMPLOYMENT HISTORY

General Foreman	TRU-COR—San Antonio, Texas	Mar 2003–Jun 2003
Pipe Fitter	CRAIG CONSTRUCTION—Phoenix, Arizona	Nov 2002–Feb 2003
Pipe Foreman	BFM CONTRACTORS—Boise, Idaho	Feb 2002–Oct 2002
Pipe Fitter	REON INDUSTRIAL—Tucson, Arizona	Nov 2001–Jan 2002
Pipe Foreman	BJ COLE CONTRACTORS—Austin, Oregon	Jun 2001–Oct 2001
Pipe Fitter	R.P. STANLEY—Wharton, Texas	Sep 2000–May 2001
Pipe General Foreman	HOLCOMB INDUSTRIAL—Houston, Texas	Aug 1999–Jul 2000
Pipe Fabricator	KARL-ZACHRY—Shreveport, Louisiana	Feb 1999–Jun 1999
Pipe Fitter	BILMER MECHANICAL—Tyler, Texas	Oct 1998–Dec 1998
General Foreman	SOL-CHEM—Abilene, Texas	May 1998–Aug 1998
Pipe Fitter	JESTER REYNOLD—Wichita, Kansas	Oct 1997–Jan 1998
Pipe General Foreman	J.C.C. JENKING—Ardmore, Oklahoma	Feb 1997–Jul 1997
Pipe Superintendent	JACKSON REINOLD—Tulsa, Oklahoma	Jun 1995–Aug 1996
Foreman	CORP ENGINEERING—Amarillo, Texas	Oct 1994–Apr 1995
General Foreman / Foreman	CORP ENGINEERING—Lubbock, Texas	May 1993–Sep 1994
General Foreman	CORP ENGINEERING—Amarillo, Texas	May 1992–Jul 1993

SPECIALIZED TRAINING & CERTIFICATIONS

Interaction Management Program

Sol-Chem's STOP Program—certificate of completion

OSHA's Construction Safety Course—10 Hours—certificate of completion

Certified Pipe Fitting and Welding Teacher

bring to the table. The first page focuses on all these categories instead of referring to the numerous places where he had worked. These are mentioned all at once in the Employment History on page 2.

Dennis Rogers

12 Van Buren Drive ▪ Dix Hills, NY 55555 ▪ (555) 555-5555 ▪ dennisrogers@mail.com

BUILDING MATERIALS PROFESSIONAL

Strong Knowledge Base and Network of Contacts in the Building Materials Industry

SUMMARY OF QUALIFICATIONS

- More than 17 years of industry experience. Skilled in sales, purchasing, and operations management.
- Track record of building loyal, profitable customer relationships through excellent service delivery.
- High level of accountability, professional ethics, and dedication to profitability and organizational improvements.

SPECIFIC SKILL AREAS:

• Sales & Marketing	• Quality Assurance Standards	• Problem Resolution
• Inventory Management	• Cost Reduction & Avoidance	• Vendor Negotiations
• New-Product Evaluation	• Warehouse Management	• Delivery Coordination
• Strategic Business Planning	• Staff Training & Mentoring	• Customer Relationships

BUILDING MATERIALS EXPERTISE:

> **Gypsum, steel structural products, ceiling systems, insulation, sheet goods, plywood, lumber, roofing materials, hardware, moldings, paint, screws, and fasteners**

PROFESSIONAL EXPERIENCE

Manager	KLEET LUMBER, Syosset, NY	2000–2004
Manager	BUILDERS' SUPPLY COMPANY, Queens, NY	1992–2000
Owner	ROGERS CONSTRUCTION SUPPLY, Queens, NY	1985–1992

Maintained consistent performance and progressive growth in business development/management operations through full-career experience in wholesale/retail distribution of building materials. Diverse scope of responsibility spanned customer and vendor relationship management, sales and marketing, purchasing, shipping and receiving, warehouse and inventory coordination, and financial management functions. Kept abreast of national and global issues affecting the industry. Fostered extremely loyal customer relationships.

SELECTED SKILL AREAS AND ACCOMPLISHMENTS:

<u>**SALES & MARKETING**</u>

- Produced 75% of sales for Kleet and 90% of Builders' Supply sales as sole salesperson within each organization. Managed inside sales activities at both companies and outside sales activities, including local travel, for Kleet.
- Recaptured three large Kleet accounts by addressing prior problems in service delivery and restoring customer confidence.
- Managed complex negotiations with customers for commodity-based supplies with fluctuating price structures. Ensured profitability by buying low and selling high.
- Created marketing materials that informed customers of in-stock items. Led effort to bring in new product (lumber) for Builders' Supply that resulted in an additional, profitable revenue stream.

Continued...

28

MJ Feld, Huntington, New York

This resume has many different areas and formats. The Summary of Qualifications itself has three different areas of interest: three bulleted items, followed by Specific Skill Areas, which are followed by Building Materials Expertise items as keywords. Under Professional Experience the three

Dennis Rogers

SALES & MARKETING *(continued)*

- Explored and opened new accounts on Long Island through cold calling and lead generation strategies (Kleet).
- Overcame premium-pricing objections through the strength of customer relationships.

PURCHASING

- Worked closely with approximately 30 companies for the procurement of various building materials. Secured better pricing through negotiation of volume discounts.
- Achieved best prices for customers by keeping abreast of fluctuating markets/prices and conducting favorable negotiations with material suppliers.
- Analyzed supply versus demand and balanced existing inventory with purchasing to ensure profitability.

INVENTORY/WAREHOUSE COORDINATION

- Played key role in reorganizing warehouses at Kleet (20,000 sq. ft.) and Builders' Supply. Employed space-saving strategies at Builders' Supply warehouse to accommodate all materials and fulfill workspace needs.
- Coordinated delivery schedules, verified accuracy of orders against load, and fixed delivery problems to uphold high standards for warehouse operational performance.
- Maintained high quality standards to avoid inventory losses.
- Maximized warehouse utilization through the routine clearing of "dead" inventory, some of which I was able to sell.

MANAGEMENT

- Addressed and resolved occasional customer issues regarding damage and quality of purchased materials.
- Hired and retained skilled workforce members, conducted employee evaluations, and held team members accountable for individual performance.
- Cross-trained administrative and yard personnel to cover instances of employee absence. Improved individual capabilities of team members.
- Managed accounts-receivable and accounts-payable functions.

EDUCATION

Business Administration, 64 credits
STATE UNIVERSITY OF NEW YORK AT STONY BROOK, Stony Brook, NY

COMPUTER SKILLS

Word, Excel, Internet

Excellent References Provided on Request

positions are mentioned together to avoid repetition that would appear in detailed, separate descriptions. Presenting Selected Skill Areas and Accomplishments by categories makes them easily understood.

Jerry Issacs

322 E. Jackknife Lane • Eagle Creek, Oregon 99999
555-555-5555

Construction • Underground Site Preparation

Professional Profile

Highly motivated, meticulous and hardworking **Construction** professional with more than 10 years of experience working on a variety of projects, including supplying strong **Supervisory** skills. Work well with all types of personalities; effective independently or as a team member. Extremely loyal and conscientious, with an eagerness to provide top-quality work and strong public relations for company.

Skills Summary

Pipe Laying	Layout	Equipment
3034	Catch basin	Backhoe
C-900	Complete sewer	Crane
Cast-iron ductile	systems	Dump truck
pipe	Concrete vaults	Flatbed
HDPE	Manholes	Forklift
Sewer	Tank setting	Front-end loader
Storm sewer	Sand filters	Low boy
Water		Scraper
		Track hoe
		Water truck

Projects
• Ball fields • Parking lots • Roads • RV parks • Subgrades for track and field

◆

History of Employment
Owner/Operator • JKI Enterprises • Eagle Creek, Oregon • *2002–present*
  Excavating and trucking. Pipe laying, including water, sewer, storm and electrical conduit. Set grade.
Partner • TLFTT Construction • Troutdale, Oregon • *2001–present*
Operator • Brandt Construction • Vancouver, Washington • *2002–2003*
  Track hoes and loaders.
Construction • Paul Brothers • Boring, Oregon • *1996–2001*
Eastside Recycling *Curbside Recycling* • Portland, Oregon • *1991–1996*
Owner/Operator • Mt. Hood Hydraulics • Sandy, Oregon • *1990–1991*
  Provided all facets of hydraulic repair.
Furnace Operator • Eagle Foundry • Eagle Creek, Oregon • *1979–1982; 1986–1991*

Military
U.S. Air Force • E-4—Crew Chief • *Honorable Discharge* • *1986*

Licenses and Certifications
• EMT Intermediate—State-Certified   • Oregon Class A CDL *(Driver's License)*

Community
Volunteer • Boring, Oregon Fire Department • *9 years*

Education
Mt. Hood Community College • Gresham, Oregon • *2000*
Clackamas Community College • Oregon City, Oregon • *1992*

29

Rosie Bixel, Portland, Oregon

A three-column Skills Summary highlights specific skills for this Construction Professional. The History of Employment section lists all his positions together without repetitious commentary.

Customer Service

Resumes at a Glance

RESUME NUMBER	LAST OR CURRENT OCCUPATION	GOAL	PAGE
30	Customer Service Representative	Customer Service Representative	77
31	Customer Service Representative	Banking Customer Service Representative	78
32	Customer Service Supervisor	Not specified	80
33	Customer Service Coordinator	Computer Systems Manager	82
34	Customer Service Trainer	Not specified	84
35	Senior Account Executive	Not specified	86
36	Supervisor	Customer Service Manager	88
37	Senior Site Manager	Senior Site Manager	90
38	Director of Customer Relations	Customer Service Manager	92

Samantha Rodriguez

475 Red Bridge Road
Melville, NY 11747
sam@email.com
(631) 382-2425

Customer Service Representative

Experienced in providing direct customer support by answering inbound calls and providing in-person customer service. Solid customer satisfaction and account-management skills that result in increased revenue and longstanding customer relationships.

Qualifications include the following:

- Timely assessment and understanding of customer expectations. Take a hands-on approach in clarifying customer expectations and resolve issues efficiently.
- Answer and follow up on customer inquiries, generate sales, and handle complex discrepancies related to transaction processing.
- Maintain existing client accounts and process inbound paperwork after receipt, including system update and customer notification.
- Have been described as courteous, patient, and respectful of client concerns.
- Portray a professional image and properly handle confidential information.
- Strong verbal, written, and interpersonal communication and data entry skills. Focus on detail and accuracy.
- Solid computer skills, including MS Word, Excel, Access, and Outlook.

PROFESSIONAL EXPERIENCE

CUSTOMER SERVICE REPRESENTATIVE, Advantage Banking Services, 1998–2001, Dix Hills, New York

Serviced customers, including processing and disbursing loans; opening, closing, and reconciling accounts; processing payroll deductions and direct-deposit requests; processing modifications to existing accounts; and marketing additional banking services and products to customers.

CUSTOMER SERVICE ASSOCIATE, Bank of Long Island, 1996–1998, Huntington, New York

Provided information to customers on issues such as account balances, CD rates, and loan rates. Recommended services such as stop-payment orders, check cards, and fund transfers and processed online applications. Verified deposits and answered questions regarding products and services.

SUPPORT SERVICE REPRESENTATIVE, Mortgage Homes and Loans, 1994–1996, Huntington, New York

Input member information in main system for easy, up-to-date access of data. Maintained files and documentation regarding member accounts. Carried out various clerical duties, including answering phones, distributing mail, and filing. Offered support to other members of Service Center team.

EDUCATION

Liberal Arts, Suffolk County Community College, Brentwood, New York, 1995

30

Linda Matias, Smithtown, New York

The applicant took three years off to raise her first child. The writer made three years of unemployment less evident by playing up qualifications and embedding dates in the Professional Experience section.

JULIE PETERSON

555 Park Lane, Lewiston, NY 14092	(716) 555-8837	peterj@adelphia.net

BANKING CUSTOMER SERVICE REPRESENTATIVE

Dependable, outgoing and conscientious professional seeks position as a bank teller/service representative. Experience in ensuring customer satisfaction and handling complaints and problems. Excellent organization and planning skills. Previous bank teller experience in a busy branch.

Administration	★ Chosen to settle and restock the ATMs daily
	★ Reorganized office filing system, updated accounts receivable and processed collections
Customer satisfaction	★ Worked as customer service representative taking custom orders and ensuring delivery on a tight timetable
Dependable	★ Worked overtime and unscheduled hours to make sure all holiday orders were filled in time
Managing the public, resolving unpleasant situations	★ Ran the drive-through window as a bank teller and resolved issues
	★ Coordinated many public fund-raisers and committees
Organization, planning & multitasking skills	★ As President of an organization, ran a 33-board-member group with multiple projects
Computer skills	★ Proficient in Microsoft Word and bank teller systems

PROFESSIONAL EXPERIENCE

The Village Bakeshop, Lewiston, New York, 2001–2002
CUSTOMER SERVICE REPRESENTATIVE
Answered phones, answered questions, resolved problems and wrote orders for custom baskets generated from this bakery's advertising and website. Developed and communicated priorities with the shipping/local delivery department and filled orders to meet customer needs. Worked overtime assisting owner with organizational challenges of running a small business.

Dentist's Office, Lowell, Massachusetts, 1985–1986
RECEPTIONIST/OFFICE MANAGER
Started as dental assistant, and then began completing insurance forms and directly billing insurance companies. Set up and confirmed appointments. Reorganized and improved office filing system. Dramatically improved dentist's financial situation by getting caught up on insurance payments for services already completed, as well as identifying accounts receivable and ensuring collection of balances due.

31

Gail Frank, Tampa, Florida

This candidate had been a military wife and mom for years. With her youngest child in school, she wanted to go back to work. She had been a Bank Teller long ago and wanted to be in banking again. The writer therefore highlighted experience, worker traits, and skills related to a Teller.

JULIE PETERSON

PAGE 2

Arlington Trust Bank, Lowell, Massachusetts, 1984–1985
BANK TELLER/CUSTOMER SERVICE REPRESENTATIVE

Cashed checks, managed the drive-through, created cashiers checks and money orders. Selected for additional responsibility to monitor, balance, settle and restock the ATM with supplies and cash. Verified customers' identities for transactions.

Officers' Spouses Club (OSC), Del Rio, Texas, and Grand Forks, N. Dakota, 1994–2000
PRESIDENT
1ST VICE PRESIDENT
2ND VICE PRESIDENT
CHAIRPERSON OSC WAYS AND MEANS COMMITTEE/FUND-RAISING
CHAIRPERSON OSC PROGRAMS

The Officers' Spouses Club is a nonprofit charitable/social organization composed of U.S. Air Force officer spouses. Elected President due to leadership skills, strong work ethic, ability to listen and enjoying the challenge of making more money for charitable projects.

As President, led OSC to largest amount of charitable funds collected in 3 years. Presented charitable funds to Girl and Boy Scouts troops, Red Cross, public schools and individual scholarships. Fund-raisers included a live auction, an art auction, booths at air shows, craft shows that necessitated coordination of vendors from the entire state and a murder mystery play.

Set agenda and ran monthly 33-person board meeting, ran social dinner/meetings and wrote monthly newsletter for the 200 members. Conducted biannual budget meeting to establish budget. Maintained and evaluated budget throughout year. Learned accounting/checking system and tax code requirements. Attended base hospital quarterly health care meetings and communicated changes in programs and services to OSC members.

86 Flying Training Squadron Spouses Organization, Del Rio, Texas, 1998–1999
DIRECTOR/COORDINATOR
Planned and coordinated monthly meetings to assist spouses with information and support.

PTA Grand Forks Elementary School, Del Rio, Texas, 1994–1998
SECRETARY AND FIRST GRADE VOLUNTEER

Compiled and published monthly meeting notes and assisted with fund-raisers. Volunteered in first grade classroom twice a week. Entrusted with reading groups of 4–5 children.

EDUCATION

Degree, Lowell High School, Lowell, Massachusetts, 1984. Awarded scholarship as a senior.

Bold sans serif type on both pages suggests confidence and reliability. Five-pointed stars as bullets are a different touch on page 1. Under Professional Experience, paragraphs indicate responsibilities and achievements.

BENJAMIN THOMAS MUELLER

177 Squantum Avenue
Midtown, Rhode Island 02888
(401) 000-9999

SUMMARY

➢ Highly qualified professional with extensive experience in customer service, sales, and management.
➢ Consistently maintain a high degree of effectiveness in balancing daily responsibilities with concurrent participation on special committees.
➢ High-energy, client-focused, and goal-oriented manager and team player.
➢ Proven capable and reliable in handling multiple tasks while maintaining an orderly efficiency of operations.

EXPERIENCE

1997–present   **Edgewood Sensors, Inc.,** Pawtucket, RI
Customer Service Supervisor

- Discuss, advise, and assist in selection and sale of appropriate products to satisfy customer requirements, providing formal quotes, tracking orders, and solving problems.
- Address and resolve customer issues, expedite orders, and increase business.
- Upgrade and streamline online data system, providing training in manufacturing systems, sales, and incentive programs.
- Coordinate and administer major account activities, resulting in 60% net growth and customer satisfaction.

1994–1997   **AT&T Communications,** Providence, RI
Customer Service Representative

- Responded to 70 customer calls per day, managing resolution of billing inquiries to full customer satisfaction.
- Calmed and counseled irate and difficult customers, clarifying their needs and recommending appropriate actions, thus enhancing customer loyalty, company reputation, and overall increase in annual sales.
- Contributed generously to team's success in meeting aggressive sales objectives.

1989–1994   **Victor Auto Group,** Midtown, RI
1991–1994   *General Sales Manager*

- Managed operation of auto dealership with $7M gross sales, including staffing, sales, service, and general office.
- Increased unit sales volumes by 120% and gross sales averages by 22% through rebuilding of sales staff and improved marketing procedures.
- Automated finance and insurance function utilizing PC system and TRW reporting, resulting in increased efficiency, information capture, and sales closures.
- Standardized advertising strategy and format, thus improving customer recognition and increasing sales per advertising dollar.

32

Edward Turilli, Newport, Rhode Island

Although prospective employers like to read about an applicant's most recent experience first, you can view an individual's career development by starting at the end of the resume and reading to the beginning. Here you can trace the person's growth after he got out of the Air Force:

BENJAMIN THOMAS MUELLER   Page Two

1989–1991   ***Sales Manager and F&I Manager***

- Directed auto sales and finance and insurance departments for busy dealership.
- Established profitable finance and insurance department, representing 30% of gross sales profits.
- Implemented tracking system to provide a central standardized profile of customers and customer traffic, resulting in better utilization of sales strategies and increased sales.

1988–1989   **Rally's Auto Sales,** Dartmouth, MA
Finance and Insurance Manager

- Negotiated financing between customers and lending institutions, leading to acceptable terms during a soft sales market.
- Coordinated auto delivery operations, including all necessary paperwork.

1986–1988   **Oldsmobile, Cadillac, GMC Auto Sales,** Midtown, RI, and Fall River, MA
Sales

- Sold autos and trucks to individual and commercial customers, averaging 15 sales per month, or $225,000 in monthly gross sales.
- Coordinated dealer swaps and special orders for auto and truck sales, ensuring accurate, efficient sales and deliveries.

1984–1986   **The Foxboro Company,** Foxboro, MA
Several positions held over four-year employment:

- Manager of Operations Support Services, Supervisor of Software Support Services, Associate Programmer, Software Technical Writer, and Lead Software Technician.
- Supervised and managed staffs up to 20 employees.

EDUCATION / TRAINING

- Took several courses in Business Management and Computer Science at Montana State University and Northwestern University.
- Throughout career completed numerous management programs and courses, particularly in computer technical operations, programming, and software.

MILITARY

United States Air Force, 1980–1984 (Honorably Discharged)

- Rank of Computer Specialist, First Class

– Excellent references and letters of recommendation furnished upon request –

from a Support Services Manager, to a Car Salesperson, to a Finance Manager, to a Sales Manager, and so on, until he became a Customer Service Supervisor at his present company. The Summary now makes sense.

MARK JOHNSON

1234 Oak Street ▪ Irving, CA 96051
Home: (555) 555-5555 ▪ Cell: (555) 555-5555
Email: mark@isp.com

COMPUTER SYSTEMS MANAGER
Project Management • Strategic Planning & Analysis • Staff Training

- 19 years of experience in information technology, including network/voice communications
- Extensive experience in implementing Internet access across a LAN
- Articulate in explaining complex data processing/communication concepts/processes to non-technical clients, resolving problems while providing supplemental training
- Able to provide effective support and training to Windows 95/98/XP users in person and via telephone
- Experienced in the evaluation and acquisition of hardware/software systems
- More than 14 years of direct experience in installation, troubleshooting, and maintenance of communications equipment and working with equipment/software vendors
- Utilization of information technology/communications delivery systems to ensure customer satisfaction

PROFESSIONAL EXPERIENCE

Technology Company, Some City, California

CUSTOMER SERVICES COORDINATOR   1990 to Present

Manage Customer Support Group, providing telecommunications and system applications support and training to clients. Facilitate systems corrections and enhancements. Supervise accounting, payroll, and telecommunications systems support staff. Establish procedures, goals, and objectives. Evaluate computer and telecommunications hardware and software systems.
- Develop and implement in-service training for central office and remote clients
- Interpret policies, procedures, and guidelines in the course of providing client services
- Analyze complex Information Technology systems, including local- and wide-area networks; identify system problems and develop logical conclusions/solutions

DATA COMMUNICATIONS TECHNICIAN   1988 to 1990

Built and maintained a data communications network connecting remote offices to a data processing center, providing time-share access to an online financial accounting and payroll system. Diagnosed and resolved data communications problems.
- Trained clients on proper use of microcomputers, terminals, and printers connected to network
- Installed microcomputers, terminals, and printers per client requests at multiple locations
- Determined source of network failures and took steps to remedy them through logical analysis and by obtaining services from appropriate vendors
- Analyzed data communications needs and formulated cost-effective solutions
- Built custom data communications cables per client requests

33

Carla Barrett, Redding, California

This applicant went to college but did not complete work for his degree. He had worked for the same company for all of his career. His original resume was lengthy, so the writer pared it down to two pages without sacrificing important information. Although this resume could have been

MARK JOHNSON – Page 2

DATA PROCESSING TECHNICIAN   1983 to 1988

Initiated and monitored processing of student scheduling and grade reporting. Worked closely with clients on report changes and ensured that output was clear and accurate. Identified and resolved production problems or communicated failure to appropriate manager. Followed up on requests to ensure high quality of service to clients.

- Provided instruction and assistance to online application clients
- Resolved problems with online applications, documenting as necessary for programming modifications
- Generated special reports per client requests and expedited delivery of all production reports
- Trained clients in proper use of computer terminals, printers, and data communications equipment
- Wrote and maintained system application documentation distributed to clients

MAJOR PROJECTS

- Responsible for installation of one T-1 and 22 56K Frame Relay wide-area network circuits for WAN implementation and disconnection of previous network
- Implemented a Lucent ProLogix phone system, which included 200 phone stations with integrated Audix voice mail, 17 fax stations, and 79 modems
- Coordinated feature selection and Lucent phone system training assignments for work groups; completed project on time with minimal staff disruption
- Responsible for the installation of two ISDN PRI T-1 telephones
- Coordinated with vendor the installation of a countywide communications network
- Built and installed custom serial communications network cabling at 22 separate client district office locations
- Documented entire interface of Student System, composed of 25 online programs

TECHNICAL SKILLS

- WAN and LAN Technologies
- Client/Server Architectures
- Remote Systems Access
- Security and Data Recovery

- Network Engineering
- Infrastructure Design
- System & Multiuser Interface
- Document Retrieval & Management

EDUCATION AND PROFESSIONAL DEVELOPMENT

Wave Technologies (Cisco CCNA)	2000
General Automation, Anaheim, California	1989
College of San Jose, California	1979 to 1983

placed in the group of Information Systems/Information Technology resumes, it is presented here to display a technically oriented customer service resume. Look for achievements under Major Projects.

KARRIE SYKES
2222 WEST SANFORD TERRACE
KANSAS CITY, MO 66210

888.888.8888   **ksykes14@kcmo.com**

PROFILE

Customer service professional who thrives on multitasking and providing service to internal and external customers. Expert in service methods that focus on customer retention, customer satisfaction, staff productivity, and team effectiveness. Literate in PC applications and mainframe inventory and ordering systems. Basic proficiency in Word, Excel, and Internet functions.

- Call Center Trainer
- Customer Service Trainer
- Field Operations Support
- Relationship Management

EMPLOYMENT SUMMARY

Architectural Doors   **Mar 1999–Mar 2004**
Kansas City, MO

Customer Service Trainer

Recruited from Check Documents Corporation to develop a training department serving all Architectural Doors locations throughout the South and Midwest. Addressed training needs in customer service, collections, operations, sales, and administration in this national firm providing architectural doors and services to the construction industry. Position eliminated during corporate downsizing.

- Trained customer service representatives to arrange service, provide follow-up to orders, and sell add-ons to residential and commercial customers.

- Provided oversight of quality performance in the call centers of the Kansas City, St. Louis, and Atlanta divisions.

- Delivered weekly training in Kansas City; installed weekly training in St. Louis and Atlanta divisions.

- Developed annual training objectives to support Architectural Doors's corporate mission.

34

Evelyn E. Maddox, Kansas City, Missouri

The applicant had been out of work for two years, and she was finding it difficult to get a job that would use her trainer abilities. Traditional trainer jobs require a four-year degree, but she had less than one semester of college. Most of her experience was centered in customer-service

Check Documents Corporation   **Sep 1982–Mar 1999**
Kansas City, MO

Customer Support Expert (1998–1999)
Division Trainer/Environmental, Health, and Safety Coordinator (1990–1998)
Customer Service Representative/Trainer (1982–1990)

Successively promoted from new-account kit coordinator to Customer Service Representative, Trainer, and Customer Support Expert by this national designer and printer of forms for the financial industry. Coordinated customer service for national accounts such as Worldwide Brokerage and Credit Cards Express. As Customer Support Expert, was responsible for coordinating support of a multimillion-dollar account conversion project from MegaBank to America's Bank, from ramp-up through final conversion.

- Quoted prices, shipment terms, and delivery date to sales staff and customers. Resolved purchase order issues involving customers and production. Regularly coordinated new-product implementation, product changes, customer updates, billing integrity, and customer support between customers and any/all internal departments affected.

- Developed, coordinated, and conducted training for customer service and internal sales representatives regarding product use knowledge, product sales techniques, sales fulfillment, and phone skills.

- Provided skills training to employees of the sales, customer service, information services, and manufacturing groups—letter shop, Xerox press, inserter, folding, bindery, call center.

- Trained manufacturing operators in production of customized products—coupons and letter checks—from order, design, and printing to customer's specifications.

- Conducted OSHA compliance training for lockout-tagout, bloodborne pathogens, hazardous-materials communication, spill response, back safety, MSDS documentation, and accident prevention.

PROFESSIONAL DEVELOPMENT

Certified Instructor, Learning Corporation
Certified Team Facilitator, Johnson County Community College
Certificate of Completion, Computer Learning Center

training, so the writer designed the resume to make the applicant competitive for any job in customer service. With this resume the applicant was being considered for a customer service job in a marketing firm.

Christina Christen

222 2nd Street
Tampa, FL 22222
222.222.2222
xxxxx@xxxxx.xxx

CUSTOMER SERVICE PROFESSIONAL
Problem Resolution
Marketing Research
Results-Oriented
Strong Client Contact

Extensive diversified business and marketing experience with focus on client service and account management. **Ignited stagnant sales operation, showing 28% gain after four prior years of flat sales.** Elected by peers as department representative for new technology task force. Excellent written and oral communication ability. Comfortable multitasking. Able to provide products/services to meet client needs. Interface effectively with diverse populations of clients and all levels of company personnel.

COMPUTER SKILLS

Word, Windows, Excel, ACT, Outlook, PowerPoint, mainframe and network experience.

ACCOMPLISHMENTS

TROUBLESHOOTING
- ❖ Tackled and completed difficult projects abandoned by former incumbents.
- ❖ Installed hardware and software to interface with customers using various systems, coordinating needs with technical contacts.
- ❖ Identified products to meet clients' concerns and needs.

CUSTOMER SERVICE
- ❖ Linked customers with informational resources as value-added service.
- ❖ Nurtured relationships with key accounts, increasing frequency of call cycle from 6 to 3 weeks.
- ❖ Convinced customers to shift loyalties from competitors through unparalleled customer service and creative promotions.
- ❖ Leveraged position with new customers, offering impressive record of service and reliability.

PUBLIC SPEAKING
- ❖ Brought creative new vision to position by composing multimedia presentations for collateral marketing materials.
- ❖ Addressed groups of 20–30, on a volunteer basis, to promote company's commitment to the community.

(Continued on next page)

35

Ellen Mulqueen, Hartford, Connecticut

A unique design in the upper-left corner of each page makes this resume stand out from others. A thin-line box on each page encloses the main information with right-aligned side headings. Boldfacing draws attention to a notable achievement in the opening paragraph.

Christina Christen, Page 2

MARKETING
- ❖ Outdistanced competitors by securing new business in the electronic commerce sector.
- ❖ Strengthened reputation of marketing department by providing timely, accurate responses and follow-up while simultaneously promoting new products.
- ❖ Nurtured long-term business relationships with clients, offering impressive record of service and reliability.
- ❖ Made inroads and headway with previously inaccessible clients.
- ❖ Won service contract with long-sought institutional account.

PROFESSIONAL EXPERIENCE

Credit Data, Tampa, FL
Senior Account Executive — 2001–2004

Ace Company, Tampa, FL
Client Services Representative — 1998–2001

Tampa Company, Tampa, FL
Customer Service Representative — 1995–1998

Greenbriar Services, Atlanta, GA
Customer Service Representative — 1994–1995

Radley's, Atlanta, GA
Sales Associate — 1992–1994

EDUCATION

Atlanta Community College, Atlanta, GA
AS, Computer Science

Accomplishments are grouped according to four left-aligned categories and are highlighted with compound diamond bullets. Repetition is avoided by only listing the five workplaces under Professional Experience.

Debra Lockstedt

752 Lakewood Drive   Lubbock, Texas 79411-5838   (806) 897-5583

CUSTOMER SERVICE MANAGEMENT PROFESSIONAL

with 16 years of multifaceted experience offers effective and decisive leadership in a fast-paced, results-oriented environment with an emphasis on client development and customer satisfaction.
Background includes 5 years of staff supervision and 11 years in technology.

Career Highlight
"Supervisor of the Quarter –Fourth Quarter 2002"
Presented by the Vice President of Operations of Titan Communications, Inc., in recognition of the attainment of the highest achievement of outstanding quality in customer service among a corporate supervisor team of 60 personnel.

PROFESSIONAL ACHIEVEMENTS

➢ ***Achieved an A+ rating*** on the research, creation, and delivery of a PowerPoint presentation titled "T.E.A.M.—Together Everyone Achieves More." This presentation was graded by an audience of site management personnel and peers as part of a communication module in our operation's supervisor development training series.

➢ ***Recognized as a leader in quality*** by maintaining the highest team quality average of 96% for both quality and retail operations teams. These teams consist of approximately 15–18 agents each.

➢ ***Managed a client dial-up project for 45 days,*** resulting in client satisfaction. Implemented the following strategies: daily statistical analyses of call volume; tracked number of calls per variety of card; produced analytical reports of calls and consumer data.

➢ ***Exceeded client customer service goals*** through troubleshooting customer service quality issues during 6–7 client calibration conference calls per week. Quality enhancement plans are implemented as a result of these calls, and the success of these changes is measured through the daily monitoring and scoring of agent customer service skills and is reported to the client.

PROFESSIONAL TRAINING

Supervisory Skills and Certifications
- Time Management
- Sexual Harassment Recognition and Prevention
- Fundamental Skills of Managing / Communicating
- Performance Counseling I & II
- People-Trak Human Resource Information Management Systems

Technical Skills

Hardware	Software
PCs (IBM, Dell, Compaq)	UNIX
Liebert Datawave Battery Backup	HBO Clinical
Laser, line, dot-matrix, and barcode printers	Keane Financial
DG Hardware – MV10, 000 and MV20, 000	HBO STAR Navigator (GUI)
Clarion/Avion 8500	Rhino X Medical Communication
Interfaces	Watch Child
Modems	Physician Access
Networks (basic)	Versys
	HBO Laboratory

36

MeLisa Rogers, Victoria, Texas

The applicant had a diverse background in computer technology and customer-service management. She wanted to become an Office Manager. The writer presented all professional achievements on the first page before indicating in the Professional Experience section where the

Debra Lockstedt   page 2

PROFESSIONAL EXPERIENCE

TITAN COMMUNICATIONS, INC.
Supervisor (Customer Care and Retail Teams)   *June 2000–Present*
- Coach and develop agents through agent evaluations, reviews, and attendance records
- Process and manage payroll hours and QRP (quality reward program) monthly incentives
- Implement new products as they are introduced into the call center
- Create a productive working environment for agents through positive communication and leadership

HIGHLAND MEDICAL CENTER
Information Services Operations Supervisor   *February 1999–June 2000*
- Supervised the operations staff and assigned work duties
- Scheduled, trained, and monitored software calls/resolutions of employees
- Maintained all computer systems, backups, and networks
- Managed upgrades to computer systems
- Created Ad-Hoc reports as required (Keane Cyberquery, UNIX, SQL, and basic Crystal Reports); set up Interface Management systems—created menus and forms and wrote procedure manuals
- Worked closely with LAN/WAN administrator, PC technicians, and internal departments; managed communication with outside vendors

Acting Information Services Operations Supervisor   *August 1998–February 1999*
- Upgraded computer system
- Managed inventory of all equipment, computer system backups, and report maintenance and delivery; monitored help desk, troubleshooting all computer problems
- Supervised operations Staff: assigned work duties and scheduled and trained employees
- Created Ad-Hoc reports as needed

PC Technician   *April 1998–August 1998*
- Installed and configured PCs and performed troubleshooting on PC-related problems
- Loaded software and managed delivery and setup of PCs to medical personnel
- Managed inventory of equipment and tested/ordered supplies from vendors

Computer Operator   *April 1987–April 1998*
- Provided maintenance of the HBO Clinical and Keane Financial systems, which involved system backups; table maintenance; report creation, generation, and distribution; optical disk backups; data entry; and creation of Ad-Hoc reports
- Processed payroll and managed employee security schedules and training
- Managed the troubleshooting of hardware/software and assisted with upgrades, system decision making, and help desk support

EDUCATION AND PROFESSIONAL CERTIFICATIONS

Lakeridge High School—Graduate, Lubbock, Texas
Lubbock Christian University—One Semester September 1998
Highland Medical Center—Courses and certifications: Local-Area Network, SynOptics Communication Termserver, Ethernet connectivity DG UNIX Basic, Medical Communications software Keane Cyberquery Reporting, SQL, Crystal Reports (basic), GUI Interface Management, and Forms and Menus

person worked before. Career highlights near the top of the first page focus on her management ability in her current position as a supervisor. Technical skills are listed at the bottom of page 1.

> ### Proven Winner
> **of the organization's most prestigious awards presented to the top 10% of performers achieving excellence in both performance and profit objectives.**
>
> | CIRCLE OF EXCELLENCE | PERFORMANCE FORUM | AWARD OF EXCELLENCE |
> |:---:|:---:|:---:|
> | 2000, 2001, 2003 | 2000, 2001, 2002 | 2000 |

REBECCA JOHNSON

1258 Birsch Rd.
Billings, Montana 59102
rebecca.johnson@billings.rr.com

Cell: (406) 649-3378
Home: (406) 210-8532
Work: (406) 839-4432

SENIOR SITE MANAGER

Leveraging 30 years of Call Center and Customer Service experience to achieve successes in the management and execution of

Management of multimillion-dollar revenues.
Ramp-up and stabilization of a 1,000-agent, dual-client call center.
Operations, quality support, product training and workforce management.

SELECTED PROFESSIONAL ACHIEVEMENTS

- Generated quick and positive resolutions to *9.1M annual calls and mail concerns.*
- *Increased* Call Center *service level by 14%* and *agent performance by 10%.*
- *Provided call center operational expertise* to the design and "startup" of a *$2M project* for a major expansion of *18,000 square feet* to a new location, minimizing service disruption.
- Participated in the development and implementation of the corporation's **Quality Reward Program,** recognized as a "Best Practice" in the organization's employee incentives.

Professional Experience

CUSTOMER SERVICE / CLIENT MANAGEMENT
→ Directed call center and correspondence staff consisting of up to 900 personnel.
→ Managed direct reports in technology, training, quality assurance and human resources.
→ Implemented an atmosphere of positive communication and relationships with client executives.
→ Created and maintained executive reporting procedures documenting bottom-line achievements.
→ Initiated statistical reports to monitor and evaluate department and agent progress.
→ Organized training and development activities for existing staff and new-hire training classes.

CALL CENTER
→ Successfully managed an inbound/outbound call center with focus on customer service and sales.
→ Handled a call volume of 7.7M calls per year.
→ Minimized service disruption during the multistate consolidation of two client call centers.
→ Implemented sales performance measurements based on conversion rates and revenue per call.
→ Maximized the utilization of IEX and TCS software to forecast and schedule staff.
→ Mastered a working knowledge of ACD, call routing, forecasting and scheduling.

BUDGETING
→ Developed and oversaw a $22.6M annual operating budget.
→ Increased annual profit projections by 20% over forecast.
→ Administered operations routinely under budget.
→ Developed incentive budget for call center recognition program.

Professional Employment Background

SPHERION WORKFORCE ARCHITECTS
www.spherion.com
1997–Present

Forbes Magazine recognizes Spherion as one of "America's Leading Companies." *Call Center Magazine* has recognized Spherion as the "Best Call Center" and "Call Center of the Year." Spherion's headquarters are in Ft. Lauderdale, Florida, and it has more than 310,000 employees worldwide. The Customer Contact Center Solutions business unit has 2,000 employees in seven locations throughout the United States and abroad, serving major clients such as AT&T, Sprint and Cisco.

37

MeLisa Rogers, Victoria, Texas

This individual had an extensive 30-year background, which had to be communicated as precisely as possible in a two-page resume. She had been laid off and therefore needed to be positioned as competitively as possible in the call center industry. Because the applicant had won multiple

REBECCA JOHNSON
– Page Two –

Senior Site Manager, Customer Contact Center—Great Falls/Helena/Billings, Montana **2000–Present**
- Increased client satisfaction scores by 22% in less than one year.
- Center was recognized by organization for top quality agents in consecutive periods.
- Maintained the highest percentage of staff promoted within the organization.
- Used several temporary agencies to meet fluctuating business demands.
- Controlled all sensitive correspondence for the business referred to Better Business Bureau, Attorney General, media or private law firms.
- Created ongoing programs to recognize achievements and participation for employees.
- Organized celebration festivities for the prestigious "Call Center of the Year Award."

Manager, Services Integrity—Fairbanks, Alaska **1999–2000**
- Identified, communicated, and implemented "best practices" in Spherion call centers.
- Assisted with start-up operations, acquiring operations transition knowledge and experience.

Manager, Consumer Relations—Fairbanks, Alaska **1997–1998**
- Responsible for all consumer relations processing for Spherion products.

BERTELSMANN MUSIC GROUP
www.bmg.com
Fairbanks, Alaska 1981–1997

BMG's company headquarters are located in New York, New York. Primary areas of business include record labels, music publishing and music distribution. BMG has offices worldwide with a total of 4,500 employees and annual revenues of $2.7 billion.

Manager, Doubleday Member Services **1994–1997**
- Coached analysts utilizing proprietary software package, M/Text, for written communications.
- Co-chaired and implemented company-wide incentive program.
- Managed six direct reports, two support staff and 150+ employees.

Manager, Customer Support Services **1981–1994**
- Oversaw the auditing process of customer transactions for scanned, data entry and CSR input.
- Managed customer correspondence generated from the site for CSR and communication inserts.
- Executed 100% of all sensitive correspondence, such as escalated concerns, BBB, Attorney General, law office and special enforcement agencies.
- Coordinated all insertion and manual club mailings.
- Supervised two correspondence analysts, eight supervisors and three support staff with 200+ employees.

RCA RECORD CLUB *(Name changed to Bertelsmann)*—Fairbanks, Alaska **1976–1981**

Supervisor, Music Service

- Processed enrollment applications for mail order music.
- Verified post office information and edited documents to set up accounts in the database.
- Mailed out and processed return correspondence from members.
- Conducted two-week new-hire training classes four times a year to meet the direct marketing spring, summer, fall and winter enrollment campaigns.
- Supervised call center activities and processed online transactions relating to customer accounts.

Education

Business and General Studies
   Fairbanks Community College—Fairbanks, Alaska

Committees and Memberships
   Board of Directors, Boys and Girls Club—Billings, Montana
   Board Member of Montana Workforce Innovative Networking—Great Falls, Montana
   Board Member of Montana Workforce Commission—Helena, Montana
   International Association of Reservation Executives

awards, the writer headed up the resume with "Proven Winner" to generate interest and to intrigue the reader. The first time the applicant used this new resume, she got called for an interview.

Bobbi Jean Reyna

(111) 111-1111   *8089 3rd Avenue*   **San Pedro, CA 99999**   *bjreyna2@tcb.com*

Manager ▪ Customer Service Specialist

PROFILE

Diligent, diplomatic **Customer Service & Management Professional** and decisive team leader, recognized as fair and effective, with a hands-on style and outstanding motivational skills.

QUALIFICATIONS SUMMARY

Well-Disciplined. Strong organizational skills and tenacity to execute major projects and realize goals.
Deadline-Oriented & Conscientious. Consistently strive to surpass set standards for project completion dates and turnaround times without sacrificing quality. Adaptable and versatile; proficient in multitasking.
Perceptive & Persuasive. Skilled at recognizing and averting potential problems, determining the root of conflicts and negotiating to reach equitable solutions.
Personable & Communicative. Excellent written and oral communications skills. Interact well with all corporate levels, colleagues and customers of diverse cultures. Proficient in relationship building.
Computer Skills: Microsoft Office Professional / Lotus Notes

EXPERIENCE

OPTICAL ALLUSIONS, Juneau, CA—Wholesaler / distributor of designer eyewear. Annual sales $50M.
Director of Customer Relations   **1999–Present**
Customer Service Manager   **1996–1999**

- Supervise team of 28 customer service representatives to manage 14,000 accounts, handle daily average of 1200 incoming calls and assist and interact with 55 sales reps operating nationwide.
- Hire, train, develop and motivate employees; monitor and evaluate performance; coordinate staff activity for optimal allocation of abilities and resources.
- Manage department budget, inventory and product pricing; analyze sales data to create reports.
- Oversee credit/returns department; evaluate products to identify defects or other causes for returns.

  Achievements & Contributions

  ✓ Grew department staff from 10 to 32 to accommodate company's evolution.
  ✓ Achieved substantial savings in costs and man-hours by devising and executing policy that resulted in **28% reduction in returned items.**
  ✓ Improved customer relations and boosted efficiency by developing and implementing system that **decreased average wait and on-hold time by 66%** (from 90 seconds down to 30 seconds).
  ✓ Skillfully negotiated equitable resolutions to difficult problems, often **preventing account loss.**
  ✓ Engendered congenial, productive atmosphere. Employee satisfaction and excellence evidenced by **department's earning the most "Employee of the Month" awards** during a 2-year period.

DELANEY OPTICAL, ORANGEWOOD, CA—Wholesale distributor of eyewear. Annual sales $16M.
General Manager   **1991–1996**
- Managed Customer Service, Shipping, Receiving and Inventory until company closed.

CONTINUING PROFESSIONAL DEVELOPMENT

Courses & Workshops: Budgeting / Critical Thinking / Managing Managers / Inventory Management / Assertiveness Training for Managers

38

Gail Taylor, Torrance, California

The writer needed to highlight the applicant's best skills. The Continuing Professional Development section shows the candidate's enthusiasm for learning and her attempts to increase her value as a worker.

Design

Resumes at a Glance

RESUME NUMBER	LAST OR CURRENT OCCUPATION	GOAL	PAGE
39	Graphic Designer	Graphic Designer	95
40	Vice President	Designer	96
41	Vice President	Designer	97
42	Mac Operator	Graphic Designer	98
43	Senior CAD Designer	CAD Designer	99
44	Instructor's Assistant/ Laboratory Technician	CAD Drafter/Designer	100
45	Manager, Design and Drafting	Facilities Manager	102
46	Aviation Flight Line Hostess	Interior Decorator	104

jason blue

433 darby drive, huntington, new york 11743 ♦ bluemagic@mail.net ♦ 555.555.5555

award-winning graphic designer

top-notch creative skills ... project management & production ... graphics business management

full advertising campaigns ♦ corporate identity/communication packages
business-to-business & business-to-consumer project design and management

brochures ♦ logos ♦ sales kits ♦ newsletters ♦ direct mail ♦ posters ♦ press kits ♦ sell sheets ♦ signage

professional experience

graphic designer, The Design Team, Northport, NY (2001–Present)

- ♦ Assess clients' needs and develop successful designs for promotional, marketing, and collateral materials across a wide variety of industries. Utilize an intuitive knack for appreciating clients' business goals as well as distinguishing clients' campaign from the competitive field.
- ♦ Establish rapport with clients, communicating vision of project with ease and passion. Through confident interpersonal interactions, secure sales and ensure clients' ultimate satisfaction with finished product.
- ♦ Meet client deadlines through judicious project management, orchestrating and coordinating milestones against timetables.
- ♦ Ensure profitability and competitiveness on projects through astute pricing of jobs.
- ♦ Evaluate and choose vendors for select outsourcing and materials purchasing. Credited with negotiating favorable prices, saving clients thousands of dollars.
- ♦ Brought in on several client projects requiring expert-level guidance. Provided consultation on conceptual and technical approaches, which ultimately allowed the client's in-house design staff to proceed with minimal supervision.

senior designer/art director, The Regional Letter, Melville, NY (1985–2001)

- ♦ Hired and supervised designers, interns, photographers, and freelance illustrators for Newsday's promotion & marketing department.
- ♦ Developed content-driven marketing programs that generated millions in new revenue for Newsday. Successes of these programs were noticed and subsequently rolled out as a model for all Tribune Media companies.
- ♦ Oversaw production scheduling and traffic management, ensuring that the tight weekly deadlines of the newspaper business were always met.
- ♦ Managed the department's budget for projects (allocation between departments, printing, studio rentals, and outside vendors).
- ♦ Designed special-events sections for the paper's city editions. Directed photo shoots and created illustrations to complement written material.
- ♦ Implemented new software/hardware and brought in products that enhanced the efficiency of the creative team. Trained staff on new technologies.

awards

Numerous Best of Long Island (BOLI) Ad Club Awards ♦ Art Directors' Club of New York Award ♦ Society of Illustrators Award ♦ NMA/Editor & Publisher Award ♦ 57th AGC Graphic Arts Award ♦ General Excellence Award, Newspaper Association of America

software proficiencies

Quark — Illustrator 10 — Photoshop — Acrobat — Flatbed scanning technology
Word for PCs and Macs

39

M J Feld, Huntington, New York

The original version of this resume lacked visual appeal. The writer replaced many initial caps with lowercase letters, and the resume became a hit—one of the nicest formats seen.

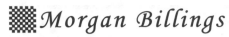

Morgan Billings

332 West 57th Street
New York, New York 00000
212.000.0000
xxxxxxx@xxx.xxx

Designer

Creative designer with experience in upscale women's fashions and accessories and home furnishings. Won distinguished awards at the Fashion Institute of Technology, including the Lentzel Cowan Memorial Award for the person with the highest potential in accessory design; Departmental Honors in Accessory Design for the student with the highest GPA; Accessory Design President; and Student Director of the Accessories Fashion Show. Knowledge of sewing techniques, pattern making, illustration, fabric dyeing, and hand embroidery. Strong computer skills.

Experience

Creative Embroidery, Los Angeles, California
Vice President   2001–Present
- **Increased sales by more than 50% FY 2002, by 73% 2003.**
- Design original embroideries.
- Manage all contracts.
- Liaise with overseas clients, including travel to Europe and India.
- Source new materials.

Zanzibar, Inc., New York, New York
Production Manager/Assistant Designer   1999–2001
- Introduced successful upscale line for European market.
- Calculated all fabric and trim orders for production.
- Oversaw all aspects of production through liaisons at factories and with private contractors.
- Assisted in design of bed linens, tabletops, lingerie, towels.
- Illustrated and created line sheets and all promotional press materials.

Superior Designs, New York, New York
Public Relations Coordinator   1998–1999
- Researched and prepared dossiers for prospective clients.
- Conceptualized press packets and promotional mailers.
- Maintained designer sales database.

Anastasia, New York, New York
Assistant to the Designer   1997–1998
- Sourced fabrics, leathers, findings.
- Developed, formatted, and maintained extensive fabric library.
- Designed and produced first samples for market evaluation.

Education

Fashion Institute of Technology, State University of New York
- AAS, Fashion Design, **Summa Cum Laude**
- AAS, Accessory Design, **Summa Cum Laude**

40

Ellen Mulqueen, Hartford, Connecticut

The writer used a weave graphic and a distinctive font (Monotype Corsiva) in the name and section headings to give the resume an artistic look. Boldfacing calls attention to Summa Cum Laude.

```
Morgan Billings
332 West 57th Street
New York, New York 00000
212.000.0000
xxxxxxx@xxx.xxx
~~~~~~~~~~~~~~~~~~~~~~~~~~~~~~~~~~~~~~~~~~~~~~~~~~~~~~~~
DESIGNER
Creative designer with experience in upscale women's
fashions and accessories and home furnishings. Won
distinguished awards at the Fashion Institute of Technology,
including the Lentzel Cowan Memorial Award for the person
with the highest potential in accessory design; Departmental
Honors in Accessory Design for the student with the highest
GPA; Accessory Design President; and Student Director of the
Accessories Fashion Show. Knowledge of sewing techniques,
pattern making, illustration, fabric dyeing, and hand
embroidery. Strong computer skills.
~~~~~~~~~~~~~~~~~~~~~~~~~~~~~~~~~~~~~~~~~~~~~~~~~~~~~~~~
EXPERIENCE
Creative Embroidery, Los Angeles, California
Vice President, 2001-Present
* Increased sales by more than 50% FY 2002, by 73% 2003.
* Design original embroideries.
* Manage all contracts.
* Liaise with overseas clients, including travel to Europe
and India.
* Source new materials.

Zanzibar, Inc., New York, New York
Production Manager/Assistant Designer, 1999-2001
* Introduced successful upscale line for European market.
* Calculated all fabric and trim orders for production.
* Oversaw all aspects of production through liaisons at
factories and with private contractors.
* Assisted in design of bed linens, tabletops, lingerie,
towels.
* Illustrated and created line sheets and all promotional
press materials.

Superior Designs, New York, New York
Public Relations Coordinator, 1998-1999
* Researched and prepared dossiers for prospective clients.
* Conceptualized press packets and promotional mailers.
* Maintained designer sales database.

Anastasia, New York, New York
Assistant to the Designer, 1997-1998
* Sourced fabrics, leathers, findings.
* Developed, formatted, and maintained extensive fabric
library.
* Designed and produced first samples for market evaluation.

EDUCATION
Fashion Institute of Technology, State University of New
York
* AAS, Fashion Design, Summa Cum Laude
* AAS, Accessory Design, Summa Cum Laude
```

41

Ellen Mulqueen, Hartford, Connecticut

This resume is a text (.txt) file version of the preceding resume for online distribution and posting. The graphic, the special font, font enhancement (boldfacing), and square bullets have been removed.

SHERRY TANG

1818 Newridge Drive • Augusta, Ontario A1A 1A1
(555) 999-4444 • tang@email.com

GRAPHIC DESIGNER
Packaging Design • Prepress Production

 **Profile**

- Talented graphic designer balancing imagination and creative design sense with solid technical skills and printing expertise
- Proficient in trapping, image setting, fixed-type flow correction, film proofing, and dyluxs; additional experience in working with scanners (flatbed and drum) and Misomex sample-cutting tables
- Hands-on experience and training in packaging design and prepress for major corporate clients
- Extremely self-motivated and organized; able to work both independently and as part of a team and to multitask effectively in high-pressure, deadline-driven environments
- Proficient with the following design and graphics programs:

Mac: QuarkXPress; Adobe Illustrator, Photoshop; INposition
PC: CorelDRAW, AutoCAD Designer Workbench, Artios, Spaceman Merchandiser

Professional Experience

Mac Operator   2002–Present
Graphco Imaging, Augusta, ON
Provided a variety of end-to-end prepress functions on major advertising projects for high-profile corporate accounts.
- Receive files from corporate clients and design houses, check all image and document formats, and complete all client changes as required.
- Complete trapping, set or replace images, fix type-flow errors, establish printing parameters, prepare film proofs and dyluxs, and output film to image setter.
- Set up scans for drum scanner (reflective and transparency).
- Major clients include **Bank of Augusta**, **Ford Motors**, **Kodak**, and **LogiTech**.

Structural Designer   Summers 2001, 2002
Norapex Lithotech, Augusta, ON
Worked exclusively on merchandising display and packaging projects for **Augusta Pharmacy**, **Wal-Mart**, and **Business Depot**.
- Based on basic product design, created a wide variety of eye-catching flip trays, end caps trays, and floor standing displays for use in national merchandising campaigns.
- Designed plan-o-grams using Spaceman Merchandiser, designed and created fillers using Designer Workbench, and operated Misomex sample cutting table to create end product.
- Consistently received positive feedback from clients and superiors for creativity, technical proficiency, work ethic, and consistent commitment to ensuring a quality product.

Other experience:
Sales Clerk—Sal's Work Warehouse, Augusta, ON   (P/T) 1999–2000
Waitress—Cheryl's Desserts, Augusta, ON   (P/T) 1998–1999

Education

Formal Education:
Package & Graphic Design—Diploma   Augusta College, 2003

Packaging Training:
AutoCAD Artios Certification (1 week)   Norapex Lithotech, 2002
Retail Spaceman   ABC Wilson, 2002

Portfolio available upon request.

42

Ross Macpherson, Whitby, Ontario, Canada

Adding a little flair for a Graphic Designer with little experience, this resume shows creativity, illustrates her technical skills, and highlights some big-name client projects she has worked on.

Maxwell E. Robinson

2982 Virginia Pearly Road, Dayton, Ohio 44444
Home: (000) 000-0000

PROFILE

Highly qualified **CAD Designer** with over 20 years of industry experience in preparing complex designs and drawings

PROFESSIONAL EXPERIENCE

MOUND APPLIED TECHNOLOGIES, MIAMISBURG, OHIO   **1981–2004**
DOE government contractor involved in environmental remediation activity.

Senior CAD Designer—BWXTO / CH2MHILL (1994–2004)
● Prepared complex designs/drawings in the following discipline areas:

● Architectural	● Surveying	● HVAC
● Electrical	● Mechanical	● Piping
● Geographic Information System (GIS)	● Global Positioning System (GPS)	● Construction/Demolition

CAD Designer II—EG&G (1990–1994)
● Prepared and developed complex detailed design projects utilizing Computer-Aided Design systems.
● Performed field verifications against industry standards to compile final design information. Also coordinated efforts with several personnel, including engineers and other design personnel.
● Advanced to Intergraph CAD system.

CAD Layout Draftsman IV—Monsanto / EG&G (1983–1990)
● Developed drawings with Applicon 895 CAD system and advanced to Applicon BRAVO/VAX CAD system.
● Aided in the development of CAD system standards.
● Trained drafters and designers on the use of CAD systems.
● Created drawings and packages for office, lab, shop and site renovations.
● Assimilated information both in field work and contact with peers, engineers and project personnel to complete detail work and design revisions pertaining to each job package.

Detail Draftsman—Monsanto (1981–1983)
● Created Mylar drawings from architectural, mechanical, electrical, HVAC and piping specifications.
● Created drawings of schematics and flow charts.
● Worked closely with lead designers and management.

EDUCATION

● **AAS,** Architectural Engineering Technology, September 1981
ITT Technical Institute, Dayton, Ohio

TRAINING

● INTERGRAPH—MGE Foundations–Windows NT
● INTERGRAPH—IFM Property Portfolio and CAD Integrator
● INTERGRAPH—Project Layout (Interactive Graphic System)
● INTERGRAPH—MicroStation PC Graphics
● ELLERBUSCH—Survey Equipment Training

43

Diana Ramirez, Seatac, Washington

When this resume with centered headings is printed on a color printer, the horizontal lines print in color (aqua over gold). The bulleted discipline areas appear in a three-row, three-column table.

1000 ALBERTA DRIVE
AUGUSTA, MI 49009
269.555.5551
rcox@yahoo.com

REBECCA COX

FOCUS

CAD drafter/designer seeking an opportunity to utilize demonstrated strength in computer-assisted mechanical drawing in an industrial setting.

PROFILE

Exhibit advanced knowledge and skills in the completion of computer-assisted technical drawings that reflect current industry standards. Will excel in fast-paced industrial environments where demonstrated organizational and time-management skills are the keys to success. Successfully plan, execute, and manage special projects to meet tight deadlines. Recognized by instructors and peers as a focused individual who is goal- and success-driven. Demonstrate expert teambuilding and communication skills. Effectively build and manage relationships with coworkers and supervisors. Acknowledged for high degree of self-confidence and a strong commitment to excellence. Education and experience have provided excellent working knowledge in the following key areas:

AREAS OF
EXPERTISE

♦ *Technical Drafting*　♦ *Mold Design*　♦ *Machine Design*　♦ *Tool Design*

Specialized Talents

♦ Team Building & Leadership ♦ Project Planning & Coordination ♦ Training & Development
♦ Confidence Building & Coaching ♦ Efficiency Improvement ♦ Time Management

Computer Skills: Proficient in **Pro/E 2001, Pro/E 2000i, AutoCAD, CADKEY,** and **Microsoft Office Suite**

EDUCATION

Associate of Applied Science, DRAFTING / CAD DESIGN, May **2004**
Associate of Applied Science, DRAFTING / CAD DRAFTER, December **2003**
LAKE MICHIGAN COMMUNITY COLLEGE, Benton Harbor, Michigan

Achievements

- ♦ Dean's List
- ♦ GPA 3.5 all four semesters
- ♦ Sole instructor's assistant/tutor/laboratory technician for entire drafting department

PROFESSIONAL
EXPERIENCE

LAKE MICHIGAN COMMUNITY COLLEGE, Benton Harbor, Michigan　　**2001–Present**
(A comprehensive, public, two-year college with a student enrollment between 10,000 and 11,000 each semester. The college offers associate of applied science degrees in 25 areas. The Drafting/CAD Design program is certified by the American Design Drafting Association.)

Instructor's Assistant/Laboratory Technician

As a result of demonstrated aptitude in CAD drafting and design and proven ability to build positive rapport with other students, hired as primary tutor/laboratory technician for LMCC's drafting department. Effectively gear individual instruction to accommodate different academic levels and learning styles.

Notable Achievements

- ♦ Assist students in developing basic drafting skills needed for industrial-level geometric construction, multiview projection, and auxiliary views and dimensioning.

- ♦ Instruct students in the operation and application of CAD systems used to create, modify, store, and plot technical drawings.

44

Richard T. Porter, Portage, Michigan

This applicant was a student graduating with an Associate of Applied Science degree in CAD Drafting and Design. As a top-flight student who was recognized for her skills, she was hired by the drafting department of the community college to tutor other CAD students—the only

PROFESSIONAL EXPERIENCE (**CONTINUED**)	**PRINTING PLUS PRINTING COMPANY**, Augusta, Michigan **1998–2000**

(Midsized commercial printing company specializing in layouts, typesetting, high-resolution scanning, and single- and multiple-color offset printing.)

Assistant Manager

Responsible for helping manage the day-to-day business activities of the print shop. Scheduled projects and used printing software to design brochures, business cards, letterhead, newsletters, and other business-related projects. Effectively worked with customers to fulfill orders. Used creative and critical-thinking skills to approach and resolve problems.

Notable Achievements

- ◆ Constantly monitored quality control/customer satisfaction issues, seeking new ways to improve customer service.

- ◆ Effectively assumed responsibilities as office manager, meeting with customers, selling products and services, and performing day-to-day general office management duties, including bookkeeping and ordering supplies.

COMMUNITY OUTREACH

Secretary, Judson Middle School PTA, 2003–Present

Volunteer, Kalamazoo County United Way, 2000–Present

Volunteer tutor, English as a Second Language, Community Outreach Center, 2001–2004

Nursery school teacher for family church, 1999–Present

Assistant coach for AYSO girls soccer association, 1999–2000

Assistant Cub Scout den leader, 2001–Present

— Outstanding References and CAD Drafting Samples Available on Request —

◆ ◆ ◆

student in the department considered for this position. Although she does not have field experience in her search for an industrial position, her teaching experience attests to her aptitude and abilities.

CONFIDENTIAL   *Will consider relocation*

Howard J. Charles

4412 Millhaven Road, Conner City, Alabama 35000
☎ 256.555.5555 ✉ hjchjc@lakeone.net

WHAT I CAN OFFER **YOUR ORGANIZATION** AS YOUR NEWEST **FACILITIES MANAGER**

❑ Capable leader with a proven track record of **maximizing ROI** and ROE (return on energy) by matching your facilities to employees' and customers' needs

❑ Skilled facilities professional who helps people tie their personal success to your **corporate growth**

❑ Thoughtful workplace planner who can turn your vision into **rising productivity** and profits

❑ Effective communicator whose written and spoken words get **results**

RECENT WORK HISTORY WITH EXAMPLES OF PROBLEMS SOLVED

❑ Draftsman *promoted over four competitors, some with six years more experience, to be* **Manager of Design and Drafting** (CAD Department Supervisor), Conner Corporation, Conner City, Alabama   86–Present

Conner is an international manufacturer of sportswear and textiles.

Sought out by senior management to get a stalled office space reorganization plan moving again. Folded in the views of 10 department managers. Then wrote and briefed every detail. *Payoffs:* Work done **five months early** and **50 percent below budget.**

Found a better way to install a critical material-handling system. My ideas were approved by the manufacturer and our leadership team. The vendor's plan: $75K in materials and lots of labor. *Payoffs:* My modular approach **saved $45K** in material and **cut labor** needs in half. My system is now our corporate standard—and the worldwide vendor's as well.

Tapped by CFO and COO to play a key role in designing and building three new plants in Mexico—without ever leaving my office and with no ability to speak Spanish. Worked everything from bidding to construction. *Payoffs:* Dropped design time **from two months to two weeks.** Not a single change order. Our work was the **most cost-effective ever.**

Helped keep us competitive when transition to new technology nearly crippled our ability to reply to RFPs. Wrote new foolproof procedures that let unskilled temps do the work accurately. Transformed skeptics into strong supporters. *Payoffs:* Converted more than 1,100 drawings a month. **Vendors wanted $300K;** I did it for only **$20K.**

45

Don Orlando, Montgomery, Alabama

This individual was being downsized in two ways: his field of drafting was being displaced, and his company was letting him go. He learned through career coaching that Facilities Manager would be an ideal position for him. The writer focused on the benefits the applicant could offer

CONFIDENTIAL

| Howard J. Charles | **Facilities Manager** | 256.555.5555 |

Chosen by our CEO over four more-senior people to help a community college produce a drafting curriculum from scratch. Wrote the lesson plans and exams and then taught the classes. ***Payoffs:*** Everything was **ready in six weeks.** Eighty percent of students passed this challenging course.

EDUCATION

❑ Associate of Applied Technology, Patterson State Technical College, Montgomery, Alabama 86

Paid my own way to earn this degree by working full time and carrying a full academic load at night.

❑ Course work in Industrial Design, Auburn University, Auburn, Alabama 82–83

❑ Course work, Chattachoogee Valley Community College, Phenix City, Alabama 80–81

❑ Course work in Building Science, Auburn University, Auburn, Alabama 78–79

COMPUTER SKILLS

❑ Expert in AutoCAD, Photoshop, Word, Excel, Windows XP, Internet search protocols

❑ Proficient in PowerPoint; Adobe Acrobat; MS Project; Windows 3*x*, 9*x*, 2000, XP, NT; UNIX

❑ Working knowledge of Means Data Estimating Software, Adobe Illustrator, Access, **Aperture CAFM software**

PROFESSIONAL AFFILIATIONS

❑ Member and former Secretary (92–94), Alabama Design & Drafting Association 86–Present

❑ Member, National Association of Photoshop Users 98–Present

❑ Chairman, Committee for the Drafting and Design Technology Department, Trenholm State Technical College, Montgomery, Alabama 00–03

an employer, because competing applicants might focus instead on narrow task-based experience alone. For the benefits, look for "Payoffs" and boldfacing in the resume in connection with each problem solved.

Julia Lynn Patton

900 Mountainview ♦ Mineola, TX 75701
903-777-0000 (Home) ♦ 903-555-9999 (Cellular)

Professional Interior Decorator
*Unique eye for color, texture, and coordination of fabric & furnishings
Highly creative, innovative, & insightful ~ Identify client desires & achieve their goals
Superb client relations & customer service talents ~ Cultivate professional alliances with clients*

Education, Honors, & Academic Achievements

Honors Graduate, MINEOLA SCHOOL – Mineola, TX (2003)
Interior Decorating ♦ Fashion Design ♦ Marketing & Advertising ♦ Visual Media
Structures, Textures, & Colors ♦ Photography ♦ Public Speaking ♦ Art ♦ Theater
♦ ♦ ♦
Member, NATIONAL HONOR SOCIETY
Profiled in WHO'S WHO AMONG AMERICAN HIGH SCHOOL STUDENTS
Won 1st Alternate in **State Competition** and **Qualified for Nationals** at DECA Marketing/Advertising State Competition
Voted by Senior Class peers as "Best Dressed"
♦ ♦ ♦
Graduate, BARBIZON MODELING SCHOOL
Won **"Most Outstanding Female Model" Award** ~ Selected to attend **Modeling Seminar in New York City**

Relevant Experience & Selected Projects

Independent Interior Design
Redesigned and decorated living quarters. Selected colors, textures, and fabrics for interesting contrast and eye appeal. Assisted friends and family members with interior decorating, including making pillows, flower arrangements, and fountains.

Sample Boards
Fabricated sample boards of entire house for school project, coordinating color scheme, fabric, and textures of carpet, tile, wallpaper, paint, design, décor, and arrangement of furnishings. **Received grade of 100.**

Floor Plan
Designed floor plan of "Dream House" for class project. House consisted of four bedrooms, three baths, great room, dining room, kitchen, utility room, and garage. Encompassed intricate measurement, drawing furniture to scale, and arranging furniture and accessories for entire house. **Received grade of 100.**

Work History

Aviation Flight Line Hostess, GALLIANT AIRWAYS—Tyler, TX (2004–Present)
♦ Make reservations (hotel and car rental) and do catering for VIPs/business professionals on chartered flights. Enter flight times, fuel costs, and plane rentals into computer. Foster business alliances with clients and ensure needs are met.

Customer Service Associate / Cashier, THOMPSON'S—Tyler, TX (2003–2004)
♦ Created "Four-Ways" (selected/coordinated end-cap displays). Assisted customers with clothing, accessories, and furnishings. Processed cash and credit card transactions. Reconciled cash drawer at closing.

Sales Associate, T & M MEN'S WEAR—Tyler, TX (2002)
♦ Orchestrated visual merchandising and window displays. Created enticing displays, which increased sales. Assisted customers with selections and color coordination. Spearheaded manual to computerized system conversion; set up and configured entire computer system, which greatly improved efficiency.

46

Ann Klint, Tyler, Texas

Two graphics (in color on a color printout) enhance this resume. Horizontal lines enclose and thereby direct attention to the applicant's profile. Boldfacing makes important information easy to spot.

Education

Resumes at a Glance

RESUME NUMBER	LAST OR CURRENT OCCUPATION	GOAL	PAGE
47	Preschool Teacher	Not specified	107
48	Basketball Coach	Basketball Coach	108

Heather Hammond

52 Lancaster Avenue
Newbold, AR 00000
(000) 000-0000
heatherhammond@email.com

QUALIFICATIONS

*More than 7 years of experience working in private preschool settings
with exposure to all childhood development stages*

Early Childhood Education Certificate, 1997
Willis County College

Certified in CPR and First Aid

TESTIMONIALS

"Heather has a natural talent for building immediate rapport with children. Her patience, confidence, and commitment make her a valuable member of our day care staff."
—Liz Kaufman, Director

"It is such a pleasure to work with Heather. She always stays calm, even in stressful moments with the children."
—Maryann Bradley, Teacher's Aide

"Kelsey loves you, and we can certainly tell she means the world to you. What we didn't realize was that you would bring out the musician in her."
—Linda and Greg Mills

"The following two words are simple but truly express our feelings for the fine job you did in helping Justin enjoy his first experience with academics. Thank you!!!"
—Sean and Deanna McFarland

"We came to you last year with our precious rosebud and have watched her bloom. We alerted you of her thorns, but you overcame most of them with your tender pruning and weeding."
—Annette and Frank DeMartino

"Thank you so much for all of your love and nurturing. Jolie loves coming to school every day, and I know you play the greatest role in her happiness."
—Janet Tremain

"Because of your gentle, kind and patient love for Rico, he has become more interested in learning. Thank you for keeping cool in the face of such great challenges."
—Consuelo and Pedro Cortez

"Thank you so very much for looking after our precious angel Adrianna. As a working mother, words can never express how thankful I am for your patience and guidance."
—Karen Fortner

"We, the parents of Kirit, wish to thank you from the bottom of our hearts for nurturing our child and expanding his horizons, opening his mind and heart in a caring and affectionate way."
—Pradeep and Naila Ashrani

PROFESSIONAL EXPERIENCE

SESAME STREET CHILDREN'S ACADEMY
Newbold, AR   1997–2004

Preschool Teacher
Promoted from Teacher's Aide after 1 year

✱ Taught 3 classes of 12 children each, ages 3–4, and supervised 2 teacher's aides.

✱ Used a variety of hands-on activities to instill an early love of learning in culturally diverse children.

✱ Created a safe, relaxed environment, which allowed the development of social and physical skills as well as creativity.

✱ Encouraged reading and writing through innovative alphabet games. By end of each school year, all children were able to print their names and orally spell them.

✱ Helped to build self-esteem by designating helpers and pairing shy children with assertive ones in play activities such as "Caterpillars and Butterflies."

✱ Contributed to a friendly, family-type work environment, sharing ideas with other teachers.

HOUSEHOLD OF MITCH AND DELIA BASCOMB
Newbold, AR   1994–1997

Nanny

✱ Assisted with educational and after-school activities for 3 children.
✱ Recommended by Mr. Bascomb for employment at Sesame Street Children's Academy.

47

Melanie Noonan, West Paterson, New Jersey

This resume shows the value of testimonials. If you read just the Professional Experience column, you read typical information. If you then read the Testimonials, you're ready to hire the person.

JAY B. GABRIEL

5451 SR 338   740.247.0000 (H)
RACINE, OHIO 45771   740.248.0000 (W)

 OBJECTIVE

Alexander Varsity Boys Basketball Coach
Talented basketball coach offering a lifetime of involvement in and broad knowledge of the game of basketball

 SUMMARY OF QUALIFICATIONS

- Alexander graduate and district resident with 17 years of successful coaching experience ranging from Biddy League through junior varsity level at Alexander
- Demonstrated talent for motivating players and building cohesive teams focused on a common goal
- Excellent communication skills—proven ability to work effectively with all parties, including players, parents, community, and administration
- Effective fundraising skills—organize various fundraisers, including recruiting numerous volunteers; oversee all expenditures
- 22 years of experience as a basketball referee

 COACHING HISTORY AND ACCOMPLISHMENTS

- Achieved first-ever undefeated season in the history of Alexander Basketball
- 12 years of coaching experience with a combined 135–80 record
    - 3 years of coaching at the junior varsity level—undefeated season
    - 3 years of coaching at the freshman level—won 2 freshman tournaments
    - 6 years of coaching at the 8th grade level—won the 8th grade tournament

 COACHING PHILOSOPHY

Coaching philosophy is based on fundamentals. Promote fast-paced, exciting game of getting the ball up and down the court quickly with a mixture of offensive and defensive strategies. Firm believer in teaching fundamentals while motivating players to perform at peak levels. Continuously promote sportsmanship and mutual respect in all aspects of program.

48

Melissa L. Kasler, Athens, Ohio

Because the resume was more of a formality, the writer decided to have some fun with the design. Using basketballs as the focus, the writer integrated the graphics with the layout.

Events Planning

Resumes at a Glance

RESUME NUMBER	LAST OR CURRENT OCCUPATION	GOAL	PAGE
49	National Program Coordinator	Event Planner and Promotions Specialist	111
50	Assistant Stylist Coordinator	Fashion Events Planner	112
51	Conference Coordinator (Intern)	Political Analyst	114

Benjamin Hall

86 Sunny Knoll Drive ✦ Poughkeepsie, NY 12601 ✦ 845.454.9900

Experienced Event Planner & Promotions Specialist

Energetic and progressive-minded individual with financial aptitude and a special strength in cause-related marketing. Consistently successful in generating philanthropic support through superior communication skills, excellent writing abilities and a service-oriented philosophy. Vast experience in planning, marketing and executing local and national events involving VIP relations, high-profile galas and corporate functions.

Special Skills

Promotions

Press Releases
Media Relations

Event Planning
Fund Development
Media Participation
Industry Partnerships
Event Coordination

Financials

Operational Budgets
Activity Analysis
Forecasting

Public Relations

Celebrity Support
Corporate Sponsors

Management

Staff Development
Employee Supervision
Scheduling/Training

Honors

Award of Distinction
Corporate Leadership
Honored by WEPR
Social Responsibility
Beauty Industry Hero
American Salon
Magazine, 2001

Summary of Qualifications

✦ Able to perform in highly visible roles, capitalize on opportunities and deliver strong results
✦ Skilled at concepting events, enhancing promotional efforts and designing ad and collateral materials
✦ Consistently successful in blending creative and administrative abilities to deliver seamless events
✦ Function well in a multidimensional role and can perform under a great deal of pressure
✦ Proven ability to assemble cohesive staffs and build consensus among groups with conflicting interests

Selected Highlights

▸ Recruited by the Beautiful Foundation with the challenge to strengthen its annual event and advance its overall philanthropic efforts. Initiated a shift in the Foundation's focus that tripled corporate **Expense** sponsorships, doubled event revenues and secured celebrity involvement for its annual gala.

▸ Provided strategic direction, administrative guidance and financial oversight for Clairol's "Color Can Make a Difference." Coordinated a national media tour as well as several cause-related fundraising and marketing campaigns. Increased campaign participation while simultaneously reducing the budget by 10%.

▸ Coproduced Beautiful's annual gala fundraiser, which generated $80,000. Successfully raised $375,000 for "Color Can Make a Difference" and obtained $100,000 in corporate donations.

▸ Directed media relations and helped complete fundraising events for the Hudson Valley Film Festival. Executed a large media campaign, enlisted celebrity cochairs and coordinated a fundraising gala ($67,000).

▸ Established b•cause, a professional beauty industry foundation that supports specific causes including Count-Me-In (online lender dedicated to helping women-owned businesses) and Locks of Love (organization that provides wigs and hairpieces to children with long-term illnesses).

Employment History

b•cause Foundation, *Poughkeepsie, NY*	National Program Coordinator	**2000 to Present**
Les Cheveaux Group, *White Plains, NY*	Salon Manager	**2001 to 2002**
Beautiful Foundation, *New York, NY*	Director of Special Events	**1999 to 2000**
Peter Coppola, *New York, NY*	Front Desk Manager	**1998 to 2001**
Hudson Valley Film Festival	Director of Media Relations	**1996 to 1997**
Clairol Professional, *New York, NY*	National Program Director	**1992 to 1995**
Heidi's Salons, Inc., *New York, NY*	Assistant Manager / Salon Promotions	**1990 to 1992**

Professional Development

Member of the Association of Fundraising Professionals   NYS Licensed Hairdresser & Cosmetologist

49

Kristin M. Coleman, Poughkeepsie, New York

This two-column resume has a shadowed page border and a vertical line separating the columns. The vertical positioning of the text lines in the left column matches that in the right column.

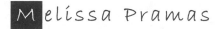

Melissa Pramas

240 Augusta Gate ▪ Pinehurst, Ontario A1A 1A1
Home: (555) 999-2222 ▪ Cell: (555) 777-9999

FASHION INDUSTRY PROFESSIONAL
Stylist / Stylist Coordinator / Fashion Events Planning

Diesel ▪ Guess ▪ Nike ▪ Parasuco ▪ Indian Motorcycle

Talented, detail-oriented professional balancing exceptional fashion sense, a strong eye for visual style, and sound fashion event-planning and project-management skills. Outgoing and personable with strong communication, negotiation, and problem-resolution skills. Strongly motivated to "get the job done" and exceed expectations.

- **Styling Expertise**—Experienced and skilled in working with a wide range of fashion styles, from urban casual (Diesel, Guess, Indian Motorcycle) to sportswear (Nike). Exceptional skills in coordinating clothes, accessories, hair, and makeup.

- **Fashion Event Planning & Vision**—Able to stage both simple and elaborate shows for any size audience, fit the show and all details to available space, and develop all details to fit theme and tone. Experienced in both public and corporate fashion events.

- **Creativity & Vision**—Creative outlook for styling the most eclectic apparel, staging innovative shows, and envisioning dynamic event themes to showcase products and generate audience excitement.

- **Communication & Leadership**—Skilled in communicating with all models, staff, catering, security, and volunteers to ensure all members of the event team are on track and fully engaged.

- **Media & Event Details**—Experienced in coordinating media, food, music, floral, lighting, props, and other special needs to create a cohesive look and feel to all visuals. Extensive industry contacts.

- **Industry Knowledge**—Additional expertise includes talent scouting, modeling, sales, and model training. Extensive industry contacts.

RELATED EXPERIENCE

Assistant Stylist Coordinator
Fashion Entertainment, Toronto, Ontario ▪ January '03–Present

Play key roles in the planning, styling, and staging of major events for a fashion consultancy coordinating fashion shows and special events throughout the Greater Toronto Area. Coordinate critical process and logistics details for major public and corporate events attended by 400–600 people. Major clients include **Nike, Diesel, Guess, Indian Motorcycle,** and **Parasuco Jeans.**

- Coordinate all clothes and accessories with available models to present products in the best possible light, taking into consideration the show theme and tone as well as the label's branding strategy.

- Coordinate upfront logistics to ensure that all event details and processes are in place. Communicate theme and details to models, dressers, makeup, and hair specialists.

- Oversee lighting, props, camera placement, and audience seating. Ensure open sightlines and present an attractive and professional presentation.

- Control backstage by coordinating sequencing and timing between models and themes.

*Additional industry experience includes positions in model scouting and sales,
modeling, and model training (John Casablanca)*

50

Ross Macpherson, Whitby, Ontario, Canada

This applicant wanted to transition to the fashion industry. The writer wanted the resume to have some creative design elements to complement the transition. Note the two Experience sections: Related Experience, which contains information of importance to the target industry, and

CORPORATE EXPERIENCE

Major Accounts Service Representative
telNET, Toronto, Ontario ▪ December '99–December '02

Personally selected by VP Sales and Marketing to provide elite-level account service for major corporate clients and Fortune 500 companies. Responsible for managing 12 major corporate accounts, resolving all client issues, ensuring account retention, and upselling on new service offerings. Client accounts include **Xerox, Coca-Cola, Dynamex, Loomis, Netricom, University of Toronto,** and **Durham Regional Police.**

Commercial Senior Accounts Representative
telNET, Toronto, Ontario ▪ July '97–December '99

Provided single point of contact in the resolution of billing, credit, and collection issues for a client portfolio of up to 3000 accounts (dealer, consumer, and commercial). Worked effectively with coordinating areas, including Client Care, Dealer Care, Credit, and Activation, to resolve common issues.

Process Coordinator
telNET, Toronto, Ontario ▪ March '96–June '97

Finalized financial month-end for 6 branches. Supervised client care representatives to ensure proper procedures and processes were followed, reconciled accounts to keep accurate financial records, and liaised with team leaders to ensure consistently high quality of client care.

COMPUTER SKILLS

- Proficient in all MS Office applications, including **Word, Excel, Outlook,** and **Explorer.** Particularly strong in developing and presenting **PowerPoint** presentations.
- Additional experience using Corel WordPerfect, AccPac, and specialty applications including Boss 1-2, BSCS, Clarity, AFP Viewer, DSS, and BOA.

EDUCATION

Broadcasting—Radio & Television, *Pinehurst College*   1992
Business Management, *Pinehurst University*   Ongoing

REFERENCES

Outstanding professional and personal references can be provided upon request.

Corporate Experience, which tells of the applicant's responsibilities and achievements as an Accounts Representative. White space makes the resume easy to comprehend at a glance.

Mark Quinn

Current Address:
123 Oak Street
Farmington, NY 99999

Cellular: (555) 555-5555
Email: mquinn22@yahoo.com

Permanent Address:
22 Main Street
Saratoga, NY 99999

Seeking an entry-level position in the capacity of
Political Analyst

A highly motivated individual with a strong work ethic and a passion for international politics. Tactful, diplomatic, and experienced in dealing with people from diverse backgrounds. Hold dual citizenship in the United States and England. Multilingual: fluent in English and Italian, functional in Swedish and Norwegian, and studying Spanish and French.

Summary of Abilities, Skills, and Attributes:
- ◆ Research ◆ Analysis ◆ Organize and interpret data ◆ Oral and written communication
- ◆ Problem solving ◆ Computer skills (MS Office, FrontPage; Internet; C++; HTML; Adobe Photoshop)
- ◆ Work well individually and in teams ◆ Excellent time-management abilities

Education

B.A., Political Science and Philosophy, New York University, NY—anticipated 2004
- **Multidisciplinary Political Science Major,** concentration in International and Global Affairs; minor in International Studies with a **3.3 GPA; Dean's List,** 2003.
- <u>Courses include</u> World Politics, Comparative Politics, Political Philosophy, Dynamics of International Conflict, Diplomacy in a Changing World, Democratization and Globalization, Global Democratic Revolution, Human Rights since 1945, International Economy—Global Issues.

College Papers: "The Balkans—Europe's Greatest Tragedy"; "How to Democratize Iraq—The Aftermath of Operation Iraqi Freedom"
Presentations: "What the Rest of the World Thinks of America"; "Europe and America"

Relevant Experience (while attending college)

INSTITUTE FOR WORLDWIDE RELATIONS, White Plains, NY   2000–2004
(A nonprofit organization with offices in London, New York, and Rome. Dedicated to increasing communication between cultures, promoting understanding, and facilitating dialogue on a political level.)

Conference Coordinator (Internship)
- Organized and coordinated two 50-person conferences on "European-American Relations in the 20th Century and Beyond" and "Young Leaders of Tomorrow":
  - o Worked closely with the directors on conference topics.
  - o Managed and planned all conference logistics.
  - o Corresponded accurately and clearly with participants and internal management.
  - o Solved problems and issues as they arose, ensuring a gratifying experience for all.

LITERACY, New York, NY   2001–2002
(A nonprofit organization focused on literacy in the New York City Metropolitan area.)

Intern
- Drafted and edited the charter application for the LITERACY New York Charter School, resulting in its approval by the New York State Board of Regents in March 2001.
- Researched city and state laws.
- Communicated orally and in writing with city and state officials, highlighted concerns between various agencies and the school, and problem-solved issues.
- Simplified, reorganized, and maintained computer network.

51

Joseph Imperato, Thiells, New York

This individual was working toward a four-year degree and was looking for his first position as a Political Analyst. He lacked experience but was multilingual, was well traveled, and had a good GPA.

Finance

Resumes at a Glance

RESUME NUMBER	LAST OR CURRENT OCCUPATION	GOAL	PAGE
52	Credit Union Teller	Not specified	117
53	Mortgage Division Loan Officer	Not specified	118
54	Business Development Officer	Commercial Loan Officer	119
55	Loan Officer	Loan Officer	120
56	Credit Reporting Analyst	Not specified	122
57	Personal Banker	Inside Sales Position	124
58	VP and Managing Partner	Business Management and Sales Professional	126
59	Managing Director	Financial Specialist	127
60	Finance Director/Financial Consultant	Not specified	128

Elizabeth J. Polawski

642 Deerfield Street Kalamazoo, Michigan 49002 269-555-0086

Profile
- ❖ Ten years of financial institution experience; additional experience in retail management.
- ❖ Reputation for building relationships with members and providing top-notch member service. Equally outstanding relationships with colleagues, supervisors and management.
- ❖ Exemplify the organization's commitment to quality through "knowledgeable and concerned professionals."
- ❖ Highly motivated to meet new challenges by capitalizing on experience and skills.

Highlights of Employment

- ❖ Exceeded personal sales goals for 18 consecutive months. Frequently receive recognition from management for cross-selling and referrals.
- ❖ Selected by management as one of two instructors to train teller staff in use of new Quality computerized system.

Employment History

Grand Valley Credit Union • Kalamazoo, Michigan 1994–Present

Teller (full-time)
- Process member transactions, ensuring thoroughness, accuracy and the protection of the organization's funds. Consistently balance cash drawer.
- Provide all aspects of customer service. Respond to and resolve questions and concerns.
- Introduce products and services to members; handle sales and make appropriate referrals.

Highlights:
- Act as resource person after training in and transition to new computerized system.
- Conduct on-the-job teller training for new employees following the classroom component. Monitor and support trainees during transactions and interaction with members; polish trainees' technical and communication skills. Evaluate trainees and report to management.
- Serve on Marketing committee; previously sat on Steering and Lunchbox committees.

The Deb Shop • Battle Creek, Michigan 1993–1994

Assistant Store Manager
- Participated in all aspects of daily operations:
  - Opening/closing   - Merchandising
  - Cash handling and bank deposits   - Employee supervision
- Assisted customers with merchandise selection and processed purchases. Provided personalized customer service.

Training & Education

- ❖ LEAD program through CUNA (currently participating)
- ❖ Sales Plus and Service Plus programs
- ❖ General course work through Grand Valley Community College

"The most important single ingredient in the formula of success is knowing how to get along with people."
—Theodore Roosevelt

52

Janet L. Beckstrom, Flint, Michigan

This candidate loved her job as a Credit Union Teller and wanted to position herself for promotion within the company. Acronyms are not defined because they are known within the industry.

Simon K. Pastor

21 George Drive
Syosset, New York 11791
516.555.5555
skp@optonline.net

Strong communication and interpersonal abilities, effective marketing and presentation skills; goal-oriented individual with a history of proven results.

Experience:

Direct Mortgage Corporation, Hicksville, New York
Mortgage Division Loan Officer, November 2003 through Present

- Manage loan process from prequalification through closing; research, create and distribute loan proposals for all clients, including but not limited to analyzing financial and risk assessments, satisfaction of loan requirements and sufficient payment schedule.
- Ensure that all loan documentation is submitted in a timely manner to guarantee efficient closings for all clients.
- Responsible for soliciting prospective clients via cold calling, networking with Realtors and implementing unique marketing programs/promotions.
- Develop and manage solid working relationships with Realtors, processors, underwriters and closers.
- Expert knowledge of principles of credit, income and appraisal guidelines.
- Order titles, appraisals, credit, payoff letters, insurance certificates and subordination agreements.

Colonial Corporation, Manhasset, New York
Mortgage Loan Consultant, August 2002 through November 2003

- Researched and developed loan proposals through a variety of third-party vendors for purchase or refinance of residential and commercial properties.
- Evaluated client's risk assessment; analyzed if prospective client met the lending institution requirements.
- Responsible for the solicitation of residential first and second mortgages through networking with Realtors, builders and developers.
- Cultivated and maintained exemplary relationships with third-party vendors, processors and underwriters.

GMZ Company, Flushing, New York
Operations Officer, March 1980 through July 2002

- Strategically enhanced customer service and company profitability through the effective management of all operational functions for a small chain of wholesale/retail footwear/sportswear establishments.
- Ordered and distributed merchandise for both wholesale and retail operations.
- Developed inventory control and quality assurance procedures and implemented shrinkage reduction strategies.
- Managed accounts receivable, accounts payable, payroll, banking and financial and tax reporting.
- Responsible for managing all phases of human resources, including interviewing potential candidates for hire, selecting employees for promotion or dismissal and implementing company health care plan.
- Successfully fostered solid working relationships with vendors, sales representatives and wholesale customers.

Computer Skills:

Microsoft Windows, Excel, PowerPoint, Access; Microsoft Works; Microsoft Money; Lotus 123; expert knowledge of Internet Explorer and Netscape Navigator browsers

Education:

Adelphi University, Garden City, New York
Course work completed in Sociology, 1980

53

Deanna Verbouwens, Hicksville, New York

This resume was the applicant's first. The writer wanted to highlight his experience in operating a business and his abilities in serving clients. Highlighted also are his communication skills.

Raynell Gardner

125 N.E. Woods Street • Boring, Oregon 88888

000-000-0000 *cell*   home **999-999-9999**

Commercial Loan Officer

Professional Profile

Top-producing, results-oriented **banking professional** with more than 20 years of experience in the banking industry. Strengths include business development, loan analysis, problem solving and top-quality customer service. Experienced in **Commercial Loans,** with a thorough understanding of the real estate business, construction loans, and business and consumer lending. Have expertise in procuring clients, analyzing needs, cross-selling, and a strong track record of "going the extra mile" to ensure client satisfaction and bank profitability. Possess outstanding communication skills. Personable, self-motivated, analytical, committed, an effective listener, and committed to a job well done.

Outstanding Achievements and Accomplishments

- Started with $0 and built portfolio to $3.5 million in loans—*largest portfolio of the Business Banking Officers.*
- Assisted in opening three branch offices.
- Top producer in referring to bank's strategic partners.
- Ranked in top three nationally in production—*1997.*
- Achieved above 130% of goal—*1997; 1996.*
- Retained 95% of book of business clients—*1996.*
- Received Chairman's Award for Outstanding Service.
- Top producer in Oregon—*1995; 1992.*

Career Progression

Umpqua Bank • Sandy, Oregon
Business Development Officer • *2002–present*

Centennial Bank • *purchased by Umpqua Bank,* Portland, Oregon
Business Banking Officer • *1998–2002*

Keybank • Portland Metropolitan area • Portland, Oregon
Small-Business Relationship Manager • *1992–1998*
Credit Analyst • *1989–1992*
Commercial Loan Assistant • *1983–1989*
Operations Assistant • *1981–1983*

Affiliations

Member • Soroptomist International • Sandy, Oregon
Chapter Secretary • LeTip International • Sandy, Oregon
Member of Mentor Committee • Gresham Area Chamber of Commerce • Sandy, Oregon

Certifications

Certified • Lending and Small Business
Licensed • Credit Life and Disability Insurance

Education

Small-Business Classes for certifications • Numerous training programs • Portland, Oregon
Accounting • Northwest College of Business • Portland, Oregon • *1972*

54

Rosie Bixel, Portland, Oregon

Two challenges were the age of this applicant and her being overqualified. The writer decided to play up the person's achievements. These appear within horizontal lines below the Profile.

Pamela Hernandez

7676 Royal Drive
Gainesville, GA 20144

Home Phone: (603) 744-6315
Cell Phone: (603) 318-6492
kygirls@aol.com

PROFILE

Loan Officer with more than 11 years of real estate and auto industry experience within increasingly responsible positions. Expertise in revenue generating, sales, employee training, recruiting, customer service, and relationship and team building. Recognized as top producer for consistently maintaining high monthly sales volumes and maximizing profits. Able to design and implement highly efficient business processes and programs and motivate teams of professionals toward achieving company goals. Results-oriented with keen eye for detail and perfect customer satisfaction ratings. Strong organizational skills with ability to manage multiple tasks and priorities simultaneously.

PROFESSIONAL BACKGROUND

First Horizon Home Loans, Centreville, VA   2001–Present
Loan Officer for home mortgage lending company with $450 million in annual sales.
- **Generate average sales volume of $1.5 million in loans per month.**
- Coordinate all details and phases of clients' loan process from application to closing.
- Maximize clients' credit rating by working with 3 credit bureaus.
- Boost sales by working with Real Estate Agents in selling property listings.
- Train Real Estate Agents on mortgage products and services.
- Seek ways to successfully move up homebuyers by exploring all financial options.
- Designed training course for new agents—specifically, Keller Williams Realty.
- Instituted highly successful mortgage application process.

Koons of Manassas, Manassas, VA   1999–2001
Finance Director for auto dealer with 3,000 new and used car sales per year.
- Oversaw average of 300 auto loans per month with 17 different lenders, including First Virginia Bank, GMAC, and First Union.
- **Doubled average profit per each car sold within 90 days after being hired.**
- Achieved most profitable GM dealer finance department on East Coast.
- Reduced sales costs by collaborating with accountants.
- Managed more than $4 million of contract dues per month.
- Supervised 4–6 Settlement Agents on a daily basis; hired, trained, and motivated agents on auto lending and selling finance products to customers.
- Assisted Sales Managers in selling cars and trained Car Salesmen.
- Planned and presented training programs and manuals for Auto Sales Staff and Settlement Agents and Sales Managers.

Continued...

55

John Femia, Altamont, New York

Read this resume from the end to the beginning, and you will recognize immediately the truth of the statement in the Profile that this candidate has had a career of increasingly responsible positions. In the Professional Background section, boldfacing calls attention to a notable

Pamela Hernandez Résumé / **Page 2**

Tyson's Ford, Tysons Corner, VA   1997–1999
Settlement Agent for auto dealer with 2,500 car sales per year.
- Ranked as top producer in sale of auto loans during entire time with dealer.
- **Handled nearly 50% of dealership's auto loans per year; processed and sold auto financing to 100 customers per month.**
- Controlled all finance deals and placed loans with lenders.
- Cut outstanding debts by working closely with accountants.
- Increased profits by finding best rates with various banks and leasing companies.
- Registered cars and processed titles with DMV and helped Sales Managers with sales.
- Liaised with Ford Motor Credit in developing a sales training process.
- Established more efficient sales process for customers by improving relationships with Managers.

Landmark Honda, Alexandria, VA   1993–1997
Settlement Agent for auto dealer with 3,000 car sales per year.
- **Top producer for American Honda for 2 consecutive years, receiving Top Gun Award 1995 and 1996 for highest profitability per car financed.**
- Sold greatest number of finance contracts for American Honda Finance throughout country in 1994 and 1995.

EDUCATION & TRAINING

NVAR, Fairfax, VA   2001
Certificate in Real Estate Sales

First Horizon University, Dallas, TX   2001
Certificate in Call Sales Reluctances

First Horizon University, Dallas, TX   2001
Certificate in Mortgage Lending, *Top Honors*

GM Training Center, Scottsdale, AZ   2000
Certificate in Maximizing Profit, *Best Auto Presentation Award*

Geneva, Arlington, VA   1999
Certificate in Showtime Sales and Lending

Honda Training Center, Arlington Heights, IL   1996
Certificate in Professional Selling

PROFESSIONAL AFFILIATIONS

Social Committee Chairperson, Keller Williams Realty

LANGUAGES

Working knowledge of Spanish

KEYWORDS: New Home Sales, Sales Representative, Sales Manager, Mortgage Loan Officer, Senior Loan Officer, Business Manager, Financial Analyst

achievement in each position held. Bold italic makes it easy to spot the positions held. Keywords at the end of the resume make it scannable for storing in a resume database for online searches.

Noreen Filbert

| 555 Drakewood Avenue | Brandon, Florida 33702 | (813) 555-7901 | nfilbert@yahoo.com |

More than 10 years of experience in banking and finance. Dependable and conscientious professional who is attentive to detail and produces quality work. Ambitious team player who enjoyed increasing responsibility levels during NationsBank/Huntington Bank career.

Attending college at night to get a B.A. degree with specialization in Management and Quality tracks. Previous entrepreneurial experience as 6-year owner and business manager of small business. Ready and eager to assume management training duties in Finance Department.

Skills and Accomplishments

Analytical and Detail-Oriented
- ☑ Conducted analytical procedures on financial data, spread financial data and tax returns, and calculated financial ratios to determine compliance.
- ☑ Researched media sources such as *Wall Street Journal* to gather external data on large corporate borrowers.

Cash Management
- ☑ Provided service and help for 50 Cash Management Program accounts pertaining to setup, wire transfers, and disbursement of funds to accounts.

Customer Service
- ☑ Resolved 10–15 customer problems per day due to changing corporate customer requirements and product limitations.

Trustworthy
- ☑ Created new position as Credit Associate to provide continuity and attention to detail in monitoring loans of less than $500,000.

Credit Policies
- ☑ Prepared Credit Review Committee meeting minutes and compiled essential reports for senior management.

Reports
- ☑ Significantly refined, improved, and regimented reports used by loan officers and senior management to determine when borrowers were out of compliance.

Accounting
- ☑ Completed Accounting I and Principles of Banking through American Institute of Banking (AIB).
- ☑ Mastered Financial Accounting for Managers, Management Accounting and Control (Cost Accounting), Financial Management, and Investments during B.A. program.

New Accounts
- ☑ Wrote procedures, communicated, and corresponded with new statewide accounts to set up customized account profiles and requirements.

Budget & Financial Statements
- ☑ Grew small business to profitable status and managed operations as Business Manager. Developed annual budget, administered payroll, administered banking, coordinated mailing, did purchasing, and developed advertising and public relations strategies.

Management
- ☑ Hired, trained, and managed 4 employees in addition to teaching 20 one-hour classes per week.
- ☑ Managed all aspects of annual and quarterly art shows: secured facility, sold advertising, contracted with artists, and created program.

56

Gail Frank, Tampa, Florida

This candidate worked her way up through banking with only an A.A. degree. She was told that to get into management training, she needed a B.A. degree. She is in the process of getting it; however, her job was eliminated. Wanting to get into a management training program

Noreen Filbert Page 2

Presentations	☑ Earned designation as Competent Toastmaster (CTM) after creating and delivering a number of successful oral presentations.
Office Management	☑ Coordinated physical move of entire banking department with minimal downtime: directed movers and utilities, developed floor plan and requirements, and notified employees about plans and progress.
Decision Making	☑ Thoroughly interpreted and made recommendations regarding financial position of borrowers.
Total Quality Management (TQM)	☑ Completed TQM training, including Foundations of TQM, Quality Implementation, Operations Management and Quality Enhancement, and Advanced Quality Management.
Leadership	☑ Voted "Educational Vice President" of Barnett Toastmasters due to strong organizational skills and trustworthiness.
Problem Solving	☑ Created system for loan officers to monitor financial loan covenants through design and implementation of standard compliance reports.
Computer Literate	☑ Competent in Microsoft Word and Excel 97, Lotus 1–2–3, Ami Pro, WinFast, WordPerfect. Familiar with Paradox and Word Pro.

Performance Review Excerpts

Noreen meets deadlines
Noreen is very meticulous
Noreen makes sound decisions
Noreen maintains excellent documentation
Noreen has easily met the targets set for her
Noreen's reports are readable and to the point
Noreen has been proactive in obtaining what is needed
Noreen is quickly able to serve as a resource to credit analysts
Noreen has very high standards regarding the accuracy of her work
Noreen does a good job of recognizing unclear requirements and obtaining clarification
Noreen demonstrated increased confidence in completing assignments that were not always "routine"

Professional Experience

HUNTINGTON BANK (formerly NationsBank)	**TAMPA, FLORIDA**	**1984–2003**
Credit Reporting Analyst, Credit Policy Administration		2002–2003
Credit Associate, Commercial Credit Department		1996–2002
Account Coordinator, Corporate Cash Management		1989–1996
Administrative Assistant to Senior Vice President and Branch Manager		1984–1989
MAJESTIC ART GALLERY	**BRANDON, FLORIDA**	**1980–1986**
Founder, Co-owner, and Business Manager		

Education

UNIVERSITY OF SOUTH FLORIDA	**TAMPA, FLORIDA**	**A.A.**
CONNECTICUT COLLEGE	**NEW LONDON, CONNECTICUT**	**2 YEARS**
SPRINGFIELD HIGH SCHOOL	**SPRINGFIELD, DELAWARE**	**HIGH SCHOOL**

immediately while working toward her B.A., she hoped that this resume would help her in her search. The writer showcased the person's experience and current B.A. work, plus excerpts from outstanding reviews.

Christian Sadler

1234 Any Drive ◆ Indian Trail, NC 28079 ◆ (704) 555–1212

Current Objective

Position in **Inside Sales** capitalizing on successful retail and financial product sales while leading to promotional opportunities.

Qualifications

- More than 5 years of successful banking and finance-related experience.
- Proficient in all areas related to customer service.
- Solid work ethic; proven ability to meet deadlines.
- Proven ability to manage staff and achieve positive results.

Home Management

Relocation
- Launched interstate relocation of entire family, coordinating moving services, trucks and packing schedules.

Budget and Purchasing
- Managed family finances, including budgeting, medical, dental, insurance packages, expenses and taxes.

Conflict Resolution
- Arbitrated personal and related business issues. Effective interpersonal skills.

Additional Professional Experience

Personal Banker (1997–1998)   My Bank   Orlando, FL
Customer Service Supervisor (1995–1997)

- Regularly managed 8 customer service employees in absence of immediate supervisor.
- Provided customer service in opening of new accounts as well as normal banking transactions.
- Lead teller responsible for preparing daily bank deposit and branch account summary.
- Posted daily rejects from the ACH credit/debit report.
- Experienced in providing the following services: checking, savings, money market and share loan accounts, CDs, IRAs, consumer loans, home equity loan closings and home equity lines of credit.

Retail Sales Associate (1994–1995)   Army and Air Force Exchange Services   Europe Operations

- Advised customers with product selections, processed customer sales and prepared nightly deposit slips.
- Proven ability to work accurately with large amounts of cash.

Bank Operations Processor (1992–1994)   Lender Bank Connecticut   Hartford, CT

- Researched, prepared and distributed requests for copies of documents for legal cases.
- Extracted and processed data from company's mainframe system for research purposes.
- Experienced in preparation of remittance and adjustment documents.

57

Nathan J. Adams, Indian Trail, North Carolina

This individual was a stay-at-home mom who needed to return to the workforce. The writer pulled out her home-management experience to show that she had developed skills while not being formally employed. Horizontal lines enclose the contact information. Partial lines

Christian Sadler
Page Two

Awards and Recognition _____

My Bank (1997–1998)

♦ Recipient of numerous cash awards for outstanding customer sales.

Valley High School (1988)

♦ Graduated with honors and received the Binkel Business College Award.
♦ Maintained the highest average in Business Administration.

Community Involvement _____

♦ Participant in the Juvenile Diabetes Foundation Walk (1995–1997)

Professional Development _____

1997
♦ Supervisory and Leadership Training
♦ Client Services and Sales Seminar
♦ Individual Retirement Accounts Training

Technical Ability _____

Fax ♦ Multiline Phone ♦ Data Processing ♦ Data Key Operations ♦ Microsoft Windows

Education _____

New Valley Vocational Technical Institute, Fairfield, CA
Studied Accounting and Marketing (1988)

---

extend from the end of each section heading to the right margin and so make more evident the overall design. Diamond bullets in almost all the sections tie together the resume's parts visually.

Sam T. Chapman

PO Box 1462, Winchester, VA 22602
540.555.0111 ♦ stc@hotmail.com

Business Management & Sales Professional
Client Relationship Specialist

❧ overview

Conceptual thinker with ability to define an overall vision and develop appropriate strategies and tactics to obtain end results.

Resourceful, decisive and persistent. Aggressive in financial dealings. Extremely self-confident; focused under pressure.

Dedicated to providing high-quality performance for a high-quality product, service or company.

❧ strengths

Background encompasses leasing and finance second-generation entrepreneurship; Marine Corps service and training; sales and leadership. Common thread of key skills:

- negotiation & problem solving
- verbal & written presentation
- organization
- autonomy
- adaptability
- financial & business acumen
- computer literacy

> ➤ Motivator
>> ➤ People Reader
>>> ➤ Risk Taker

❧ self-educated

"Anything worth knowing can not be taught in the classroom."

Oscar Wilde

❧ Skillfully employing the fine art of client-vendor relationships, which are firmly grounded in the principles of respect, open communication and trust.

Creator of customer loyalty. Executor of increased profits.

❧ professional experience

The Chapman & Rich Lending Company, Gaithersburg, MD
1998–present

- Vice President and Managing Partner of a financial lending firm, delivering customized financing solutions for individual and corporate clients, both domestic and international.
- Created an unconventional network of private lenders and business professionals to better service clients and ensure consistent referrals, transactions and closings.
- Manage financial transactions ranging from $10K to $5M; assess client needs, secure requested funds and negotiate/monitor payment terms.

ABC Financial Group, Baltimore, MD
1994–1998

- Consumer Finance Analysis and Lease Administration Manager for a financial firm negotiating automobile lease programs for credit-challenged individuals.
- Recruited by the Regional Business Development Manager to manage day-to-day operations, including staff management and training, marketing, customer service, portfolio and asset management and tactical business planning.
- Interfaced with the company comptroller, banks and credit lending institutions to ensure sufficient cash flow to support $1.5M in monthly operating costs.
- Collaborated with the company attorney in representing ABC Financial in legal proceedings.
- Made final determination on qualifying up to 300 applications per month, from a monthly applicant pool of 1500 to 2000 consumers.
- Managed a $20K monthly advertising budget; collaborated with radio and TV advertising personnel to design and execute an effective marketing campaign.
- Created and managed pay-plans and monthly bonuses for 10 independent brokers and 10 company sales personnel.
- Conceived and implemented a client monitoring system, which strengthened client relationships by proactively engaging them in self-monitoring of their lease status.

58

Norine Dagliano, Hagerstown, Maryland

This unique individual insisted on a unique design for his resume. The writer wanted the resume to be a window on the applicant's personality. Note the Education ("self-educated") section.

Thomas M. Worthington

123 Prince Road • Marlboro, NJ 07746 • 732.964.7790 (H) • tmw6762@aol.com

FINANCIAL SPECIALIST
Investments ~ Portfolio Management

Results-driven and well-organized *Investment Specialist* with extensive experience in stocks, bonds, securities, and other investment instruments. **Possess a talent for understanding market trends and emerging markets. A self-motivated professional with a proven record of financial success. Achieved significant positions through hard work, honesty, and a commitment to the workplace. Member of New York Stock Exchange.**

Excellent leadership, team-building, communication, and problem-solving skills. Provide superior customer service by cultivating strong relationships with clients.

Competencies

- Investment Management
- Portfolio Management
- Economic Forecasting
- Troubleshooting

- Financial Planning
- Financial Services
- Customer Relations and Retention
- Packaged Investment Products

Professional Experience

New York Stock Specialists, *New York, NY*   **(1986–2004)**
Managing Director—Specialist NYSE (2001–2004)
- Appointed as Managing Director when Morris Hart & Schultz merged with Merrill Lynch, forming the third-largest specialist firm on the New York Stock Exchange.
- Made fair and orderly markets in several securities at one time.
- Represented the firm in meetings with major clients, utilizing interpersonal communication skills, extensive business networking, and persuasive salesmanship.

Morris Hart & Schultz, *New York, NY*
Partner—Specialist NYSE (1995–2001)
- Promoted to Partner when Morris merged with Hart & Schultz.
- Earned increasing responsibilities as a partner maintaining close relationships with CEOs and CFOs of Fortune 500 firms such as Southern Company, Ingersoll-Rand, Navistar (International Harvester), and Puritan Funds.
- Trained and developed numerous employees to maximize their productivity in the services that they provide to traders.

Morris Partners, *New York, NY*
Associate—Specialist NYSE (1994–1995)
- Promoted to Associate when BET merged with Morris; received steady advancement, demonstrating achievement of company goals and a strong professional work ethic.
- Executed trade orders for clients specializing in 8 to 10 firms simultaneously.
- Assigned to desks with largest currency volume and consistently received the top bonus for performance. Knowledgeable regarding pricing and quick mathematical computations to trade a variety of equities earning the most profits for clients and the company.
- Developed excellent research skills and an intuitive sense regarding equities and the market. Identified and advised brokers of current trends reflecting buy and sell orders.

BET Partners, *New York, NY*
Trading Assistant NYSE (1986–1994)
- Promoted to First Assistant, having increased responsibilities, including the position of "Fireman," assisting traders when things got particularly hectic by providing a calm, detail-oriented manner to put out the fires.
- Recorded transactions, verified orders, and verified sales commissions.
- Researched questionable trades, analyzed trade data, and recorded all stock splits.

AL Colman, *New York, NY*   **(1985–1986)**
Trading Assistant NYSE
- Assisted the specialist, performing multiple tasks.
- Performed record keeping of trades and commissions.

United States Marine Corps   **(1981–1984)**

59

Beverly and Mitch Baskin, Marlboro, New Jersey

Follow the bold, and you will gain a quick overview of this well-designed resume with a page border and useful lines to separate the main sections. Note also the use of bold italic and regular italic.

MARGARET VENETTA
1500 South 22nd Place • Phoenix, AZ 85044
(480) 855-3710 • **mvenetta@cox.net**

PROFESSIONAL QUALIFICATIONS

- Proven history of achievements in **Loan Processing / Funding** for consumer and commercial credit organizations.
- Areas of expertise: **auto financing, mortgage loans, account management, market penetration, customer service, relationship development and office administration.**
- Ability to sort through broad range of financial options to find products best suited to customer=s needs.
- Organized, focused problem-solver who remains calm during stressful situations.
- Professional manner and appearance; able to easily build rapport with customers, peers and management.
- Computer skills: MS Windows, Word, Excel; Internet and intranet.

State of Arizona Insurance Sales License

CAREER HIGHLIGHTS

Office Management
- Performed all administrative functions, including A/P, A/R and bank deposits; organized bookkeeping records for accountant; purchased supplies and equipment; developed and implemented procedures. (Stanford)
- Conceived and installed showroom displays; interacted with walk-in customers. (Stanford)

Finance / Loan Administration
- Arranged consumer financing and performed credit analyses; administered and documented loans and leases; processed loans for 50–60 new and used cars per month. (Maxwell)
- Interfaced with loan officers of major banks and credit unions. (Maxwell)
- Completed commercial credit transactions and funded commercial loans against discounted notes. (Carnegie)
- Processed paperwork for home loans and interfaced with mortgage bankers. (A-Z Mortgage)
- Managed buy rates and reserves; promoted add-ons to generate maximum profit per transaction. (Maxwell)
- Tracked penetration into high-profit areas, reserves and total transactions on monthly basis, generating reports for corporate management. (Maxwell)

Sales / Customer Service
- Consistently achieved personal index of 97–98% for customer satisfaction. (Maxwell)
- Achieved Department CSI of 80%+ (1998, 1999), compared to company overall national average of 70–75%.
- Balanced profitability for company with customer needs, creating win-win situations and satisfied customers.
- Developed and implemented customer contact plans that significantly impacted sales. (Safety Plus)
- Assisted sales consultants in preparing individual marketing plans. (Maxwell)
- Used proven sales strategies to establish relationships with key accounts to expand territory. (Safety Plus)
- Interacted with vendors and sales representatives to promote sales. (Safety Plus)
- Built territory from 0 to 20 accounts in Nevada within one year, opening territory to allow addition of full-time sales representative for state. (Safety Plus)

PROFESSIONAL EXPERIENCE

Finance Director / Financial Consultant, MAXWELL CORPORATION, Tempe, AZ	1995 to Present
Office Manager / Sales Representative, SAFETY PLUS, Phoenix, AZ	1990 to 1995
Administrative Assistant—Funding Department, A-Z MORTGAGE, San Diego, CA	1986 to 1987
Office Manager, STANFORD & SONS, San Diego, CA	1980 to 1986

Prior to 1980:
Loan Administrator, CARNEGIE FINANCIAL CORPORATION, St. Paul, MN	7 years

EDUCATION / PROFESSIONAL DEVELOPMENT

- **University of Minnesota,** Minneapolis, Minnesota—Undergraduate studies
- **Training Courses**—Consultative Sales & Financial Consultative Sales Process
- **Anthony Robbins**—10-Hour Seminar

60

Wanda McLaughlin, Chandler, Arizona

This person had worked in jobs relating to mortgage and auto loans. She wanted to move into a banking or administrative position. The writer emphasized various skills for a flexible job search.

Firefighting

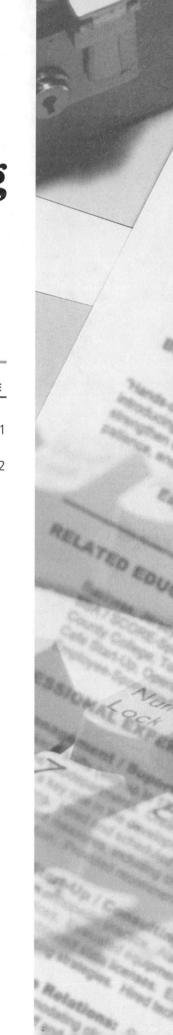

Resumes at a Glance

RESUME NUMBER	LAST OR CURRENT OCCUPATION	GOAL	PAGE
61	Captain of Operations	Division Chief, Special Operations	131
62	Fire Chief	Fire Chief	132

PHILLIP KNIGHT

71 Crater Avenue • Springfield, Oregon 99999 • (555) 555-5555

DIVISION CHIEF—SPECIAL OPERATIONS

Proactive leader and manager of personnel and programs, offering more than 14 years of experience as a firefighter. Extensive experience as a motivator and coordinator; able to focus the efforts of diverse groups to a common goal. Committed to providing innovative protection programs that reflect the values, diversity, aspirations, and priorities of the community they serve. Effective combination of interpersonal, analytical, and organizational qualifications with strengths in

- Coordination with Existing Organizations
- Public Speaking & Community Outreach
- Team Building, Training, & Management
- Program Development & Direction

- Administration & Reporting
- Federal & State Regulatory Compliance
- Strategic Planning & Critical Thinking
- Design of Policy & Procedures

PROFESSIONAL EXPERIENCE

SPRINGFIELD CITY FIRE DEPARTMENT; Springfield, OR   1989–Present
Captain—Operations Division
Currently supervise Engine 1B, Dive 1B, and coordinate shift manning as Captain of Operations. Scope of responsibility is broad and includes supervision, direction of fireground activities, tactical operation of emergency scenes, safety of firefighters, and the protection of life and property. Additionally responsible for ensuring continued compliance with all OSHA, NIOSH, and NFPA standards and regulations. Promoted on several occasions due to knowledge, skills, and high level of integrity and dedication.

- Developed extensive knowledge of all emergency response program plans, including Dive Rescue, Technical Rescue, Hazardous Materials, Airport Rescue Firefighting, and Special Events.
- Instrumental team member developing policies and procedures, including safety and minimum standards for Dive Rescue Company.
- Managed extensive firefighter training program for Recruit Academy and assisted in development of Firefighter II program currently being utilized, resulting in improved standards and operations.
- Proven ability to develop and maintain productive relationships and partnerships with a wide variety of organizations, officials, and individuals, including businesses and local citizens.
- Cooperatively worked with local government agencies such as EPA, DEQ, Springfield City Public Works, Springfield Parks and Recreation, and Springfield Police Department.
- Conducted public education classes on fire prevention, water rescue, CPR, and first aid training through gained knowledge of instructional methodologies.

PROFESSIONAL DEVELOPMENT & SPECIALTY TRAINING

Fire Officer I
Red Cross Lifeguard Instructor
American Heart Association BLS Instructor Trainer
Instructor Trainer National Fire Academy Leadership Series

Dive Rescue	**Technical Rescue**	**Hazardous Materials**	**Airport Rescue**
• Public-Safety Diver	• Rope Rescue Technician	• Awareness Level	• Operations Level
• Swift-Water Rescue	• Confined-Space Rescue	• Operations Level	
• Ice Diving	• Trench Rescue	• Technician Level	
• Ice Rescue		• Incident Command System	
• Current Diving			
• Deep Diving			

61

Denette Jones, Boise, Idaho

The opening section is a profile, a summary of qualifications, and areas of strengths without being titled as such. The bottom section lists areas of training grouped by rescue categories and materials.

MACK SEWARD

Award-winning, highly accomplished and seasoned Fire Chief with proven track record of leadership and team-building abilities within fire safety and rescue industry

SUMMARY OF QUALIFICATIONS

- ◆ More than 25 years of broad-based experience within fire safety design, hazardous-materials handling, rescue, medical emergency and security-services operations.
- ◆ Promoted quickly through series of increasingly responsible positions.
- ◆ Outstanding ability to improve team performance and create cohesive and strong working units.
- ◆ Known for exceptional leadership ability and for consistently performing at highest levels.
- ◆ Superior analytical, problem-solving and communication skills.
- ◆ Handpicked hardest assignments and executed each in a superior manner.
- ◆ Youngest professional in 10 years to hold Station Fire Chief position at Los Angeles Air Force Station.
- ◆ Willing to relocate anywhere in U.S.

CORE COMPETENCIES

- ▪ Fire Fighting, Fire Safety & Fire Rescue Procedures
- ▪ Fire Safety Design
- ▪ Aircraft Safety Considerations
- ▪ Hazardous-Materials Operations

- ▪ Leadership & Supervision
- ▪ Staff Development & Coordination
- ▪ OSHA Compliance
- ▪ Cost Reduction
- ▪ Project & Time Management

CAREER HIGHLIGHTS AND ACCOMPLISHMENTS

PROJECT MANAGEMENT

- ▪ Fully accountable for providing nonaggressive yet prominently displayed fire protection for President of United States and visiting Heads of State at Andrews Air Force Base, the nation's premier entry for highest-ranking dignitaries.
- ▪ Delivered significant savings of nearly $2.5 million in construction expenses by meeting safety requirements and utilizing materials and procedures with reduced costs.
- ▪ Led rescue and recovery operations at numerous air crash sites. Appointed as On Scene Commander at three major aircraft crashes. Conducted missions in methodical and meticulous manner, resulting in avoidance of all injuries and generation of insignificant damage to aircrafts.

1515 Clapton Dr., Hampton, Virginia 23663-1415 ◆ 703-555-1298

62

Rita Fisher, Columbus, Indiana

This resume is for a Fire Chief transitioning to civilian life after many years of service in the Air Force. All the positions of service are indicated in the Professional Background section beginning

Mack Seward **Page two**

(Project Management continues)

- Spearheaded three politically sensitive crash recovery operations on foreign grounds.
- Successfully strengthened fire security at Andrews Air Force Base, resulting in dramatic drop in number of yearly fires from 25 to 3.
- Pioneered development of airfield runway barrier operations standards, now widely used in United States and six other countries.
- Selected by upper management as having recognized industry proficiency to resolve problems with new P-23 Fire Fighting Vehicle.
- Initiated and spearheaded creation of current fire fighting standards for all wide-bodied Air Force airplanes.
- Demonstrated expertise regarding fire safety design by serving as final review authority at four fire safety design project installations.
- Developed hazardous-materials program from inception through successful operations within six months. Program was only one of 12 similar programs to pass series of comprehensive OSHA inspections with no write-ups.
- Coordinated with civil engineers to ensure building compliance with OSHA safety requirements.

SUPERVISION AND STAFF DEVELOPMENT

- Dramatically revitalized inadequately performing civil engineering unit within only 100 days and achieved "excellent" unit ratings from previous "barely acceptable."
- Effectively supervised several firefighter and hazardous-materials handling teams.
- Successfully led fire fighting unit to outperform more than 20 competitors and win distinction of "Best Large Fire Fighting Organization" in Europe.
- Generated highest possible rating for six fire fighting companies by transforming them from "satisfactory" to "outstanding" units.
- Created, developed and taught eight-months-long introductory class to numerous entry-level firefighters. Implemented new, highly successful and award-winning course on proper handling of burning toxic materials.
- Instrumental in attaining accreditation for Department of Defense from International Fire Safety Accreditation Council. First-ever accreditation review revealed 20 outstanding unit members without any discrepancies.

PROFESSIONAL BACKGROUND

132nd Civil Engineering Squadron, Burleson Air Force Base, Muleshoe, Texas   1992–Present
Fire Chief, Hazardous-Materials Program Manager, Fire Safety Design Review Authority
12th Air Force Headquarters, Isendorf Air Base, Isendorf, Germany   1988–1992
Fire Chief

1515 Clapton Dr., Hampton, Virginia 23663-1415 ♦ 703-555-1298

near the end of page 2. If these had been listed separately with responsibilities and achievements indicated under each position, the resume would have been lengthy with repetition. This is avoided by summarizing and listing key information in the first three sections: Summary of Qualifications, Core Competencies, and Career

Mack Seward   Page three

(Professional Background continues)

89th Civil Engineering Squadron, Andrews Air Force Base, Washington, DC
Fire Chief
45th Civil Engineering Squadron, Pusan Air Base, Korea   1987–1988
Deputy Fire Chief
916th Civil Engineering Squadron, Travis Air Force Base, Fairfield, California   1982–1987
Shift Supervisor
323rd Support Group, Los Angeles Air Force Station, Los Angeles, California   1978–1982
Station Fire Chief
USAF Fire Fighting School, Kessler Air Force Base, Mississippi   1975–1978
Instructor
555th Civil Engineering Squadron, Holloman Air Force Base,
Alamagordo, New Mexico   1972–1975
Firefighter
5th Civil Engineering Squadron, Travis Air Force Base, Fairfield, California   1968–1972
Firefighter

EDUCATION AND TRAINING

Incident Command System Training, National Fire Academy
Fire Protection Internships at Skilled, Advanced and Superintendent Levels
Fire Protection Management Applications
On-scene Commanders' Course
Advanced Fire Training Technology
Fire Investigation
Fire Prevention Technician Course
Ranger Propane Fire Safety School
Principles of Instructional Systems Development
Total Quality Management
Leadership for Mid-level Managers
Leadership for Selected Managers
USAF Fire Fighting School, Kessler Air Force Base, Mississippi
Graduate of Farley High School, Charlotteville, Virginia

AWARDS AND HONORS

Air Force Commendation Medal
Meritorious Service Medal
Air Force Achievement Medal
John P. Morely Memorial Award for Heroism in Lifesaving Operations
Airman's Medal for Courage

1515 Clapton Dr., Hampton, Virginia 23663-1415 ◆ 703-555-1298

Highlights and Accomplishments. Items in the third section are grouped according to Project Management and Supervision and Staff Development. The final two sections—Education and Training, plus Awards and Honors—bring the resume to an impressive close.

Health and Safety

Resumes at a Glance

RESUME NUMBER	LAST OR CURRENT OCCUPATION	GOAL	PAGE
63	Safety and Ergonomics Leader	Distribution/Warehousing Specialist	137
64	Health and Safety/Training Manager	Health and Safety Manager	138
65	Owner, Arbitration Company	Safety/OSHA Manager	140
66	Hazardous-Materials Technician/ Instructor	Occupational Health and Safety Professional	142

William S. Beyer

78 Holcomb Drive • Franklin Park, NJ 08823 • 732-378-1972 • wsbeyer7@aol.com

DISTRIBUTION / WAREHOUSING SPECIALIST

Top-performing and motivated manufacturing professional with 12 years' experience in distribution, warehousing, line production, supervision, team building, and equipment operation.

Successful track record of ensuring that the plant was in compliance with all local, state, and federal safety regulations. Self-disciplined administrator with the ability to troubleshoot and resolve problems in a timely manner. As **Safety Leader,** managed all monthly safety meetings and safety training programs for the 125 workers at the plant.

Experienced in supervising, mentoring, and training staff. Address process improvement issues to find better methods to get the job done with fewer injuries. Computer-proficient in Microsoft Word, email, and use of the Internet.

Areas of Expertise:

- OSHA Compliance
- Warehouse Operations
- Shipping/Receiving
- Good Manufacturing Practices (GMP)
- Real Time Control Inventory System (RTCIS)
- Ergonomics/Safety
- Problem Identification/Troubleshooting
- Licensed Fork Lift Driver

Professional Experience

Procter & Gamble—*Warren, New Jersey (1991 to 2003)*
Safety & Ergonomics Leader (1996 to 2003)
Fork Lift Technician/Materials Handler (1991 to 1996)

- Loyal, dedicated, efficient employee. Accepted an early retirement package from Procter & Gamble after a 12-year career.
- Knowledge of RTCIS inventory control system.
- Performed physical inventories using bar code scanners.
- Extensive knowledge of the processes and equipment in the food, beverage, bottling, and packaging industry. Calculated, weighed, and verified exact amount of ingredients per batch.
- Served as a forklift technician and driver on a computerized forklift.
- Thorough knowledge of procedures and techniques used for shipping and receiving and materials handling.
- Some of the many safety programs managed were
  - ♦ Job Safety Analysis (JSA)
  - ♦ Job Task Analysis (JTA)
  - ♦ Safety Inspections
  - ♦ Personal Protective Equipment (PPE)
  - ♦ Material Safety Data Sheets (MSDS)
  - ♦ Lock Out Tag Out (LOTO)
  - ♦ Ladders and Safety Climbing Devices
- Considered reliable and honest, with excellent follow-through. Ability to work alone and to build excellent rapport with employees, vendors, and customers.

Education

Orange High School, Orange, NJ
Bloomfield College, Bloomfield, NJ

Military

United States Army, Specialist 4th Class—Honorable Discharge, Vietnam Service Award

63

Beverly and Mitch Baskin, Marlboro, New Jersey

Boldfacing establishes down the page a path for seeing, in turn, key information and the main headings. A switch to a serif font in the final section adds a formal note. See Cover Letter 2.

FRANZ ROSENBERG

20 Manuel St.   Mobile: (816) 555 1212   Business: (816) 555 1884
Kansas City, Missouri 64111   Email: frosenberg@bigpool.com   Private: (816) 555 3211

Experienced workplace health and safety manager offering a verifiable record of achievement driving strong and sustainable gains in workplace culture. Combine exceptional technical, analytical and advanced health, safety and training qualifications with outstanding project-planning and project-management skills. Expertise includes demonstrated technical leadership in systems development, safety audits, team management, training programs and risk management.

KEY CREDENTIALS

- Occupational Health & Safety Legislation & Standards
- Project Planning & Management
- OHS & Environmental System Auditing
- Accident & Incident Investigation
- Risk Evaluation & Management

- Engineering Solution Development
- Ergonomic/Human Factor Assessments
- RULA, Strain Indices, AAMA & NOISH
- Safety System Development & Implementation

- Budget Management
- Strategic Planning
- Human Resources Management
- Quality Management & Improvement
- Training Program Development & Delivery

Information Technology: Microsoft Office Suite (Word, Excel, Access, PowerPoint, Outlook), Publisher, Windows 98/XP; WordPerfect; Internet; email

CAREER HIGHLIGHTS

- Effective change agent; evaluate, consult, design and implement workplace health and safety initiatives in commercial and volunteer sectors, adhering to legislative regulations and standards.
- Corrected risk management deficiencies; conducted safety audits and accident investigations; identified casual factors using Taproot, Mort, Event/Fault Tree, Failure Mode and Effect analyses.
- Profiled staff training needs; designed multimedia resources for effective presentations; delivered high-impact training programs and encouraged positive, proactive training culture.
- Exchanged ideas, challenges and encouragement as part of the management team; championed new strategies; maintained stringent budget controls for district expenditures.
- Planned, managed and conducted emergency, relief and rescue operations.
- Sampled sound, vibration and atmospheric contaminants; calculated air delivery and exchange rates.

CERTIFICATIONS & TRAINING

Graduate Diploma of Occupational Health & Safety
<u>University of Missouri</u>

- Workplace Rehabilitation Coordinator Certificate
- Statement of Attainment, Exercise Management
- Safety System Auditor
- Environmental Auditor
- TapRoot Accident Investigation

- Certificate II Incident Management System
- Qualified Road Accident Rescue, Rescue Boat, Land Search, Team Leader & Senior Instructor
- Certificate III/Licentiate in Workplace Health & Safety

- Workplace Health & Safety Officer (Stage 1&2)
- Certificate in Training & Development— Workplace Assessor
- Qualified Fitter & Turner

64

Gayle Howard, Chirnside Park, Melbourne, Victoria, Australia

This two-page resume contains much information because of a small font size, long lines of text, and compact three-column lists. Horizontal lines and centered headings make it easy to see at a

---

CAREER EXPERIENCE

CONSOLIDATED MINING   1/2001–Present

Health & Safety / Training Manager

Brief: To establish a portable and adaptable safety management system applicable to multiple projects.

Reviewed and improved safety management mechanisms, enforced compliance with contemporary legislative practices and spearheaded across-the-board organizational training systems. Presided over adherence to workplace health and safety training and revamped complete rehabilitation program design and delivery.

Core accountabilities include safety management, advice and legislative compliance; accident investigation and reporting; policy/procedure and management systems development/review; risk assessment; safety and compliance auditing; rehabilitation planning and management; strategic planning; training design, delivery and evaluation; training/safety record maintenance and analysis; external training/safety service procurement and human resources management.

Highlights:

- Reduced *"Lost Time Injury Frequency Rate"* from 45 to 0; reduced *"Disabling Severity Rate"* by 34.5% employing behavior modification principles at both manager and employee levels.

- Pioneered organizational shift to a "no blame" culture; reengineered accident investigation policy, spearheading an organization-wide investigation system (TapRoot).

- Introduced a more streamlined, user-friendly training and safety record system adopted throughout the organization that met stringent internal/external auditing requirements.

- Optimized early hazard identification and corrective action status tracking by developing a contemporary risk management system.

DEPARTMENT OF CRISIS SERVICES, Counter Disaster & Rescue Service   3/1998–1/2001

District Operations & Training Officer / Acting District Manager

GABSTONE BREWERIES   12/1997–3/1998

Service Department Supervisor

SELECTED PROJECTS & RESULTS

- Investigated ergonomic hazards and metabolic rate expenditure during night shift supermarket environment; considered extreme temperatures and workers' primary occupations.

- Examined potential effects of Sodium Azide from deployed vehicle restraining systems on panel beaters and tow truck drivers and potential hazards of inadequately storing faulty devices.

- Conducted extensive risk assessment report for cabinet manufacturing workshop, leading to company embracing comprehensive safety policy, including staff training, job descriptions, machine guarding and exhaust ventilation installations.

- Assessed operational competencies of small construction company from site preparation to handover. Company adopted and implemented all recommendations, including site-specific work plans, strict enforcement of safety on building sites and weekly inspections by external consultant.

- Investigated staff complaints of headache and nausea within an administrative building. Conducted detailed ventilation survey, concluding that contaminated air was returned to air-conditioning unit for recycling.

glance the sections of the resume and thereby its overall design. Careful use of white space between sections prevents this resume from appearing crowded. Note where italic is used effectively.

Joe Mitchum

555 Rose Drive
Delray Beach, Florida 33483

Fax (561) 555-8566   (561) 555-5095   JMSafety@comcast.net

More than 10 years of experience in the Safety/OSHA field as a manager and problem solver. Previous military career created special experience in management and training with additional accomplishments in OSHA, safety, risk management and logistics. Experienced fixed-wing/helicopter pilot.

Dependable and hardworking professional who solves tough problems and is attentive to detail. Multifaceted manager who analyzes needs, creates structure, develops systems, implements training and unifies staff. Strong mechanical ability.

Selected Management Accomplishments

OSHA
- Developed first-ever OSHA program in 3 different locations/companies and drastically improved safety compliance each time. Reduced hazards in areas of electrical, storage, fire detection, lighting, hazardous and flammable materials, medical equipment, first aid and airplane safety.
- Created first-ever safety inspection checklist for supervisors, resulting in ongoing detection of issues. Facility then established periodic inspections for prompt problem resolution.

Safety Manual Creation
- Selected to be on Safety Committee for independent aviation company that initially served the Rockefeller family and Chase Manhattan Bank. Created, researched and wrote 30-page safety supplement and inspection checklist for General Operating Manual.

Safety Program Development
- Developed system for 400–500-person organization to track injuries on the ground and begin measuring output and impact of injuries. After measuring, implemented safety program and drastically decreased auto, recreational and on-the-job injuries.

Management
- Appointed Airfield Manager in addition to Safety Director due to organizational and leadership abilities. Developed schedules for shift personnel and tower operations, maintained fuel and material inventories and assisted visiting air crews with accommodations.
- Managed workforces ranging from 30 to 350 people in variety of positions requiring training, standard setting and monitoring versus objectives.

Risk Analysis
- Initiated first risk analysis of the workplace, prioritized deficiencies for correction and instituted ongoing evaluation of deficiencies.

Logistics
- Organized and developed logistics for mock aviation accidents and mock invasions: contacted military police, fire departments and area hospitals; prepared reports; and secured airspace from the FAA. Coordinated all aspects of Present Reagan's base visit with Secret Service and Military Police to ensure smooth and safe exhibition.
- Selected as Air Mission Commander for nuclear warhead movement throughout Germany, Italy, Greece and Turkey. Also appointed member of Nuclear Inspection Team.

Instructional Design
- Developed objectives, program content and lesson plans for more than 25 different training courses.

Trainer
- Master Trainer for air safety. Tested instructor pilots on their ability to teach. Instructed them in methods and knowledge.
- Provided instruction on OSHA safety requirements to 20 participants.
- Created Training Board to track all required training courses and completion of courses. Developed and maintained weekly training schedule.

65

Gail Frank, Tampa, Florida

This candidate was an ex-military pilot and a private pilot who was laid off from his job of piloting small planes. He tinkered around with several different jobs and tried to find a new piloting job, but he was considered too old. He was trying to use safety/OSHA experience to land a job in

J. MITCHUM PAGE 2

Creativity
- Conceived and implemented innovative closed-circuit television system throughout company. Improved reach and accessibility of required training courses.

Mediation
- Started and currently run company representing homeowners in insurance arbitration. Inspect properties, create written report, present facts and evidence to arbitrator and insurance company, negotiate terms and approve settlement for client. 98% success in obtaining money for clients.

Quick Learner
- Completed intensive ground school training to become certified to fly Boeing 737 aircraft. Passed comprehensive 5-hour oral test, simulator checkride and flight test by FAA examiner.

Mechanical Ability
- Designed and remodeled bathrooms for area builder and construction company. Performed plumbing, electrical, carpentry and tile work in homes valued from $250K to $3M.

Bookkeeping
- Selected as political campaign Treasurer. Provide accounting to City Clerk for contributions and expenditures for City Council candidate. Approve all campaign checks and monies.
- Perform all bookkeeping, billing and tax filing for Johansen-Hale Associates, a consumer research company.

PR and Marketing
- Developed, wrote and produced training video that received attention from top officials.
- Secured extensive press coverage in radio and television for the high-priority Project Partnership in Europe. Arranged filming and briefings for press.

Inventory Management
- Tracked and maintained appropriate inventories for $10M worth of aviation parts and equipment.

PROFESSIONAL AND EDUCATIONAL BACKGROUND

ALTERNATIVE DISPUTE RESOLUTION — Delray Beach, Florida — 1998–Present
Owner of business that assists in arbitration, insurance appraisal and family mediation

CITY COUNCIL CAMPAIGN — Delray Beach, Florida — 1998–Present
Treasurer for Candidate

TROPIC ISLE CIVIC ASSOCIATION — Delray Beach, Florida — 1995–Present
Vice President, Board Member

PRIVATE CONTRACTOR — Delray Beach, Florida — 1997–1998
Designer for area builder and remodeler

CARNIVAL AIRLINES — Dania, Florida — 1995–1996
Student/Pilot

WAYFARER KETCH, INC. — White Plains, New York — 1988–1994
Corporate Pilot/Safety Manager

UNITED STATES ARMY
Airfield Safety Manager/Airfield Operations Manager/Pilot—Fort Campbell, Kentucky
Safety Manager/Airport Manager/Pilot—Germany and Italy
Pilot—second tour/Infantry—first tour/Maintenance Supervisor—Vietnam
Parts Supply Manager—Fort Riley, Kansas
Drill Sergeant Instructor—Fort Jackson, South Carolina

SPECIAL TRAINING AND EDUCATION

Aviation Officer Safety Course
OSHA Safety Course
Warrant Officer Senior and Advanced Course
Method of Instruction and Instructor Pilot Course
Saint Martins College—2 Years Liberal Arts

that field. Side headings in the Selected Management Accomplishments section make the long list of bulleted items easier to understand. Without those headings the long list would be overwhelming.

SAM SAFETY

1234 Toxic Drive • Anyton, Ontario L9T 5K9
ssafety@net.ca • 999.999.9999 • 999.999.9999

QUALIFICATIONS PROFILE

Highly accomplished **Occupational Health & Safety Professional** experienced in loss control, with 15 years of core career experience in R&D and operations in hazardous or high-risk areas.

➤ Very broad range of industrial experience, including chemical processing, machine tooling, fabrication, material handling, manufacturing, building controls, and laboratory settings.

➤ Practical experience in risk assessment, material and process hazards, emergency planning and response, hazmat, confined-space operations and rescue, firefighting, and incident investigation.

➤ In-depth knowledge of regulatory compliance requirements and legislation pertaining to transportation of dangerous goods, occupational health and safety, environmental protection, and fire code.

➤ Strong cross-functional management abilities for teams and projects. Able to apply theory in practical application.

➤ Currently pursuing Certificate in Occupational Health and Safety (OHS), with educational credentials in personal protective equipment, industrial hygiene practices, confined-space entry, toxicology, and monitoring of chemical/physical hazards.

➤ Professional background in chemical engineering technology and processes, with strong IT skills such as Windows, Word, Excel, PowerPoint, Access, Outlook, Explorer, MS Project, AutoCAD LT, Cameo, CCINFO, and Web-based reference sites.

PROFESSIONAL EXPERIENCE

ECHELON RESPONSE AND TRAINING, INC., Hamilton, ON   1999 to Present

Hazardous-Materials Technician / Instructor (Part-Time)

Start-up volunteer training firm employing 30, providing instruction to rural fire departments in basic spill response procedures.

Respond to environmental emergencies to stabilize situation, contain and remove hazardous waste, and perform site remediation. Prepare and present instruction in emergency services and hazmat emergency response skills to industrial technicians, including incident command responsibilities and roles, situational analysis, implementation of action plans, personal protective equipment, chemical and industrial process knowledge, and theory underlying NFPA 472 and other standards. Complete hazardous-waste manifests, work orders, and incident reports.

INCO TECHNICAL SERVICES LTD., Mississauga, ON   1987 to Present

Senior Research Technologist (2001 to Present)

Powder metallurgical industry.

Lead multidisciplinary team in providing technical development and stewardship of new value-added nickel powder products and manufacturing processes. Gather customer requirements to drive product development and support business planning and marketing efforts. Prepare and deliver management reports and customer presentations. Analyze root cause of process deviations and provide troubleshooting and technical support to plant commissioning and operations, working with department heads and peer project leaders in resource management. Review technical drawings, P&ID, PFD, fabrication, and assembly documentation. Design experiments, fabricate test equipment, and analyze results in support of

Continued...

66

Cathy Childs, Pompano Beach, Florida

Much important information justifies three full pages in this resume. Boldfacing and three-dimensional bullets call attention to the items in the Qualifications Profile. A pattern of company name (in small caps), position (in boldface), and explanation (in italic) appears in the first two

SAM SAFETY

laboratory operations, lending expertise in OHS and JHSC issues, compliance concerns, emergency response, first aid, and hazmat abatement and monitoring. Generate periodic reports.

- ◆ Played key role in design and commissioning of a $2 million process furnace in Wales.
- ◆ Greatly improved safety of handling of a lethal industrial gas by adapting existing technology to provide a means of risk assessment.
- ◆ Comanaged departmental respiratory protection program and facilitated formation of a chemical spill response team.
- ◆ Saved processing time and costs by developing a procedure to prevent agglomeration of nickel powder.
- ◆ As corporate expert on sintering process, launched and led a project team for new product/process development.
- ◆ Coauthored a paper (to be presented in October 2004), "Influence of Extra-Fine Ni Powder on P/M Steel Properties."

Research Technologist (1996 to 2001)

Worked in technical development of nickel foam sintering and other nickel processes for operations in Canada and Wales. Led second-generation process improvement initiatives for existing plants.

- ◆ Developed a fluid mechanics model to control reactor flow rates.
- ◆ Obtained patents for a process for removing polymer foam from nickel-coated substrate and for alloys containing insoluble phases along with manufacturing methods.
- ◆ Received Sheridan Science and Technology Park Technical Achievement Award for a new manufacturing process for nickel foam for batteries.

Technologist II (1992 to 1996)

Coordinated with production team in furnace commissioning. Interpreted and reported test results and modified production equipment to improve productivity. Trained operators in use of newly developed equipment.

- ◆ Performed electroplating of nickel, gold, and silver onto various novel substrates.
- ◆ Developed a new production coating process and refined a novel sintering process.

Technologist I (1989 to 1992)

Worked under supervision in fabrication and operation of experimental equipment, testing, data collection, and results analysis to improve output quality and productivity of production facilities. Acquired skills in fabrication, welding, and machining.

- ◆ Conducted initial research into a novel sintering process.
- ◆ Assisted in development of a metal powder treatment and a heat recovery system.

Building Technician (1987 to 1989)

Ensured reliable facilities functioning. Point of contact for trouble calls, installation, and maintenance of industrial and lab equipment. Performed minor repairs and fabrication in machine shop, including nonstructural welding. Maintained building emergency equipment inventory. Obtained readings from the building equipment and noted deviations. Participated in SCBA training.

- ◆ Promoted to R&D department.

Continued...

listings in the Professional Experience section. Thereafter, the company names are not given. Diamond bullets point to important responsibilities and notable achievements for the various positions held from 1987 to the present. The third page is devoted to the candidate's Educational

SAM SAFETY

EDUCATIONAL BACKGROUND

Mechanical Engineering Technician (1987)
GEORGE BROWN COLLEGE OF APPLIED ARTS AND TECHNOLOGY, Toronto, Ontario

Certificate in Occupational Health and Safety (Anticipated completion 9/04)
RYERSON UNIVERSITY, Toronto, Ontario
GPA: 3.53

SELECTED CERTIFICATIONS, SEMINARS, AND WORKSHOPS

Certificate, Hazardous Materials Technician (Echelon Response and Training, Inc.)
Certificate, Hazardous Materials Specialist (Transportation Technology Center, Inc.)
Medical First Responder, Level 1
Integrated Risk Assessment and Management for Continuous Improvement
Hazardous-Materials Specialist, Tank Car
Workplace Hazardous Materials Information System
Introduction to Interior and Exterior Firefighting
Transportation of Dangerous Goods
Standard First Aid
Environmental Compliance and Regulations for Managers and Supervisors
Powder Metallurgy Fundamentals
Hazard Training—Solvents, Flammables, and Combustibles
Hazard Training—Basic Machine Safety
Hazard Training—Lockout/Tagout
Hazard Training—Noise
Compressed Breathing Air and Systems—Canadian Standards Association (CSA) Z180.1
Respiratory Protection—CSA Z94.4
Confined-Space Entry and Rescue
Metro HazMat Conference
Hazardous Materials Technician—NFPA 472
Problem Analysis and Decision Making
Project Management
Material Science Fundamentals
Electricity I
Applied Chemistry
Introduction to Nondestructive Evaluation
Measuring Instruments
Metallurgy I&II
Practical Loss Control Leadership
Gas Fitter I&II
CPR Level C
World Powder Metallurgy Conference
Reg 347—Hazardous Waste

~ Excellent References Available Upon Request~

Background (including work on a certificate in progress) and Selected Certifications, Seminars, and Workshops. The impression given is that this individual is a lifelong learner. See Cover Letter 3.

Healthcare

Resumes at a Glance

RESUME NUMBER	LAST OR CURRENT OCCUPATION	GOAL	PAGE
67	Relocation Contractor	Medical Billing Specialist	147
68	Billing Specialist	Medical Assistant	148
69	Dental Assistant	Dental Assistant	149
70	Radiography Technician Assistant	Radiography Technician	150
71	Child Care Provider	Social Service/Healthcare Position	151
72	Owner/Personal Trainer	Youth/Athletic Director	152
73	Cosmetics Consultant	Physical Therapist Assistant	153
74	Co-owner/Cofounder, Health and Fitness Company	Fitness and Wellness Professional	154
75	Office Specialist	Medical Office Specialist	156
76	Chief Interventional Cardiac Technologist	Clinical Applications Specialist	158
77	School Nurse	Licensed Registered Nurse	160
78	Office Nurse, Psychiatric Services	Legal Nurse Consultant	162
79	Team Leader of Nurses	Not specified	164
80	Pharmacy Technician	Registered Nurse	165
81	Licensed Practical Nurse	Licensed Practical Nurse	166

KAREN CALLOWAY

402 East Main Street • Elmira NY 12995
607 111 0000 • kcalloway@myemail.com

▶ **Medical Billing Specialist** completing certificate program

▶ Will pursue credentials from American Health Information Management Association (CCS and CCS-P) and American Academy of Professional Coders (CPC and CPC-H)

▶ Dedicated self-starter who enjoys challenges, including learning and applying new skills

▶ Diverse career has included varied opportunities to work independently, in teams and as a manager, all of which have contributed to development of these key abilities:

- Detail focus
- Organization
- Coordination
- Research
- PC proficiency (Microsoft Windows/Office 2000, Internet, e-mail)

- Communication
- Customer service
- Maintaining confidentiality

EDUCATION

Medical Billing Specialist Certificate Program: Elmira TechEd Center, Elmira NY; completion anticipated July 2004. *A 19-week professional training program that includes*
- ICD-9 and CPT-4 Coding
- Basic and Advanced Medical Terminology
- Introduction to Insurance Plans/Forms
- Introduction to Medisoft

AAS, Optical Engineering Technology: Monroe Community College, Rochester, NY

HIGHLIGHTS OF EXPERIENCE

Contractor/Self-Employed   2000–2004
- Assisted in relocating individuals in their employment searches in the U.S. and Canada by researching and contacting appropriate potential employers through Internet, e-mail, telephone and direct mail
- Compiled reports of key data
- Honed computer and research skills in this remote-based position

Hospitality: Cuisine Italiano, Elmira, NY   1985–1999
- Held every position (front- and back-end) in this family-owned restaurant
- Applied exceptional customer service, organization and coordination skills

Business Manager/Owner: Petals Flower Shoppe, Elmira, NY   1990–1994
- Oversaw all facets of daily operations, including floral design, wedding coordination, staffing, purchasing and bookkeeping
- Expanded service and delivery area
- Added four wire services and managed this third-party ordering process
- Participated in wedding shows that resulted in a three-fold increase in wedding-related business
- Enhanced retail sales area of the shop with a wider gift line and selection of plants/flowers
- Substantially improved bottom-line revenue over previous ownership and sold business for profit

Optical Engineering Technician: Eastman Kodak Company, Rochester, NY   1981–1985
- Assisted engineers with quality assurance of confidential and cutting-edge photographic prototype development projects within the Consumer Products division
- Tested equipment in controlled and simulated "consumer use" environments
- Consistently received highest performance ratings and raises

Extensive community service/volunteer experience that has demanded and enhanced leadership, planning, coordinating and teaming abilities. Information available upon request.

67

Salome A. Farraro, Mount Morris, New York

This applicant had an outdated associate's degree and needed to update her skills through a Medical Billing Specialist program. A hospital hired her just after she got her certificate. See Cover Letter 4.

Jennifer Black

(555) 555-5555

email@address.com
1234 West Street
Hometown, NY 01234

MEDICAL ASSISTANT

Triage	Injections	Patient Scheduling
Medical Terminology	Phlebotomy	Chart Updating
Patient Intake	Vital Signs	ICD and CPT Coding
Dosage Calculations	Infection Control	Insurance Claims
Sterilization Procedures	Urinalysis	Accounts Payable / Receivable
Blood Smears and Blood Tests	Hematocrit	Collections
Lab Equipment Operation	EKG	Data Entry

EXPERIENCE

Patient Care
- Cared for in-home patients with complex, multisymptom illnesses for three years
- Eased patient discomfort by conducting accurate assessment and drawing techniques
- Fostered healthy environment for diabetic patient through meal preparation, medication dispensing, and glucose-level monitoring

Administrative
- Improved cash flow by recovering uncollectible accounts in excess of $1,000,000
- Increased accuracy of patient files by designing and implementing new patient update sheet
- Exceeded daily quotas and minimized overhead expenses with effective scheduling and management of part-time employees

Computer Skills
- Microsoft Windows, Word, Excel, and Works
- Corel WordPerfect
- Medical software including Medical Manager and Great Plains

EDUCATION

College of Medical Careers, San Diego, CA
Medical Assistant Certificate, 1996
Valedictorian

High School, Anytown, PA
Diploma—Science Emphasis, 1992

RELATED EMPLOYMENT HISTORY

Billing Specialist, Bookkeeper, Medical Assistant (various—Indiana and Somerset, PA)	1996–1997
Medical Assistant (Internal Medical Office—San Diego, CA)	1996
Long-term/Acute Care Provider (self-employed)	1992–1995

68

Tammy J. Smith, Olivet, Michigan

This person was a stay-at-home mom for several years. Her work experience was meager and dated. The writer played up the person's accomplishments, and she was hired on the spot at a job fair.

Carol A. Weiss
DENTAL ASSISTANT

62482 110th Avenue S., Federal Way, WA 99999   (000) 000-0000   email: cweiss@resume.com

PROFILE:

More than 15 years of Dental Assistant experience in meeting high infection-control standards, sterilizing and disinfecting instruments and equipment, preparing tray setup for dental procedures, and instructing patients on postoperative and general oral health care.

➢ **Supervised** two Dental Assistants.
➢ Trained in **product knowledge** (bonding, impression materials, and more).
➢ Experienced in working with all ages of people, from small children to senior citizens.
➢ **Managed office,** ensuring that it was organized, clean, fully stocked, and prepared daily.
➢ Worked in a **lab** within the same facility, making any shade changes or polishing of dentures, crowns, and bridge work.
➢ Caring, detailed-oriented, hard worker who has learned different state-of-the-art dentistry styles, **procedures, and techniques.** Always seeks ways to keep skills current.

SUMMARY OF QUALIFICATIONS:

▶ Root canal treatment
▶ Air particle machines
▶ Polishing of all fillings
▶ Soft and hard relines
▶ Rubber dam replacement

▶ Crown and bridge preparation and delivery
▶ Composite and amalgam fillings
▶ Denture and partial procedures
▶ Assisted with multiple extractions
▶ Took full-series radiographs and panolipse radiographs

OFFICE SKILLS:

▶ Windows, DOS, MS Office (Word, Excel, PowerPoint), word processing, spreadsheets, databases, Ex-Change+, Internet (Netscape, Explorer), email.
▶ Typewriter, word processor, copier, calculator, fax machine, printers, multiline phone systems
▶ Records management, medical terminology, healthcare plan knowledge, billing codes

PROFESSIONAL EXPERIENCE:

Dr. Ronald McPherson, DDS—Federal Way, WA Dental Assistant	2001–Current
Dr. D. Maynard Debus, DDS—Federal Way, WA Dental Assistant	1999–2001
Dr. Larry W. Howard, DDS—Federal Way, WA Dental Assistant	1999 (temp)
Dr. Abel D. Sanchez, DDS—Federal Way, WA Dental Assistant	1979–1989

69

Diana Ramirez, Seatac, Washington

Three-dimensional bullets and boldfacing point to key information in the Profile. Arrow bullets direct attention to the important content in the Summary of Qualifications and Office Skills sections.

MADISON GIBSON

555 West 120th Avenue, #000, Denver, CO 55555
Cellular (555) 555-5555, Home (555) 555-5555, lester@aol.com

Job Target Long-term association with a radiology facility that will benefit from academic preparation, radiology experience and a driving work ethic.

Skills

> Highly skilled in many modalities of radiology, including digital and regular fluoro, portables, c-arms, diagnostic, surgical, trauma, tomography and PACS. Eager to receive training on any additional modalities.
> Comprehensive knowledge of daylight and darkroom film processing.
> Capable in hospital environment, currently having completed 2,048 hours of clinical experience.
> Effectively manage multiple complex tasks simultaneously. Highly analytical, organized and detail-oriented.
> Consistently go the extra mile to ensure patient care and comfort.

Education

Associate, Radiography   August 2003
DPS Medical Institute, Denver, Colorado. GPA: 4.0.
Representative course work: Pathology, Radiography, Medical Ethics, Positioning, Physics, Anatomy, Patient Care and Medical Terminology. Hold CPR card.

Professional Experience

Radiography Technician Assistant   January 2003 to Present
Centura Health One, Aurora, CO—Accountable for taking radiographs, including operating portables, patient care, patient protection and positioning, operating x-ray machines and processing films in the darkroom. Conduct filing, answer phones, and schedule patients promptly. Commended by ER and clinical doctors, who went out of their way to call supervisor with appreciation for initiative and skill.

Radiography Technician Assistant   December 2001 to January 2003
Columbia Hospital, Thornton, CO—Performed all duties of radiology technician. Was hired before graduation based on superior performance in clinical work.

Item Processing Operator Level III   June 1999 to December 2001
Wells Fargo Bank, Denver, Colorado—Balanced customer transactions and large items, applied debits and credits accurately, audited transactions for customer and bank employee errors and met Federal Reserve deadlines. Consistently given raises, promotions and excellent reviews.

Bank Teller   September 1998 to June 1999
Wells Fargo Bank, Boulder, Colorado—Demonstrated efficiency, accuracy and speed when processing customer transactions. Assisted customers with inquiries about problems and banking products. Displayed ability to recognize forgery, counterfeit currency and kiting operations and observe security protocols. Recognized for speed, accuracy and dependability with promotions and raises.

Accomplishments

Received letter of recommendation from Dr. Anthony Stephen: "... skilled technologist... responsible, dedicated worker... great deal of energy... pleasant personality... utmost compassion for patients"

Worked 25 to 30 hours a week at bank, 32 hours per week on clinical requirement and 24 hours per week at Columbia Hospital while attending classes for Radiography degree and maintaining 4.0 GPA.

70

Michele Angello, Aurora, Colorado

This resume emphasizes academic preparation, clinical hours completed, and an impressive work ethic to make up for a lack of paid work experience. Testimonials are from a recommendation letter.

Lily A. Lucas

111 2nd Street
Racine, Wisconsin 00000
(333) 444-4444

PROFILE

- More than 5 years of experience in **social service** and **health care** positions requiring the ability to work with patients and customers of all ages and backgrounds.
- Reputation as a patient and sympathetic individual with a strong ability to troubleshoot emergency situations.
- Knowledge of computer software, including MS Word, WordPerfect and company database software.
- Proven telephone skills. Experience using multiline telephone.

EXPERIENCE

Childcare of Wisconsin   Milwaukee, Wisconsin
Child Care Provider   2001–2004

- Worked for residential program for teen mothers and their children.
- Monitored activities of mothers and children and recorded on daily charts.
- Advised mothers on parenting skills. Participated in planning for goals and career development.
- Provided court and field supervision.
- Oversaw clients in their daily living activities and housekeeping tasks.
- Administered medications and carried out medical treatments as instructed.

Kenosha Family Care   Kenosha, Wisconsin
Home Health Care Aide   1999–2001

- Assigned to clients who were elderly, disabled, or infirm.
- Visited clients in their homes and assisted them as needed with shopping, housecleaning and child care.
- Administered medications as instructed. Assisted clients with bathing and feeding as necessary.
- Acted as liaison with nurses, doctors and other medical staff assigned to patient.

Dil Computer Corporation   Milwaukee, Wisconsin
Production Clerk   1989–1999

- Updated and maintained production schedules on computer.
- Performed intermediate full systems backup for three computers and peripherals.
- Responsible for timely and accurate printing of documentation for United States military personnel.
- Coordinated activities with other offices.

TRAINING

College of Kane County   Milwaukee, Wisconsin
Completed college course work in customer service, basic computers and MS Word

71

Eva Locke, Waukegan, Illinois

The applicant was concerned about having held jobs in many different fields. The writer noticed that previous positions had the common quality of serving others. The resume highlights this theme.

ANTHONY DUBOIS

162 OXFORD AVENUE, RENO, NV 89501

775.555.9479

ADFIT@YAHOO.COM

Fitness Specialist

**A hands-on professional / goal-oriented strategist
whose confidence, perseverance and vision promote success**

GOAL: An opportunity to serve as a **Youth / Athletic Director**
employing my abilities to improve and motivate the physical fitness / rehabilitation of individuals

GENERAL QUALIFICATIONS

Recognize client's needs and set goals
Utilize initiative, achievement and independent judgment
Demonstrate record of high performance standards
Detailed attention to schedules, deadlines, budgets and quality results
Track record of creativity and innovation

PROFESSIONAL FITNESS EXPERTISE

20 years of progressive experience and responsibility with documented success in the areas of health / fitness

- ❖ Successfully develop, initiate and coordinate individual and group exercise programs
- ❖ Demonstrate correct and safe use of exercise equipment and routines
- ❖ Observe participants during exercise sessions for signs of physical stress; adjust pace
- ❖ Conduct group and independent aerobic, strength and flexibility sessions
- ❖ Supervise other instructors

MAJOR PROJECT: "TONY'S KIDS"

Developed franchised program implemented nationally in public / private schools

- ❖ Innovative fitness education program for improving overall health of at-risk children
- ❖ Encourage positive lifestyle choices to offset school violence and nutrition problems
- ❖ Detailed curriculum designed for infusion into school districts nationwide
- ❖ Utilize behavior style profiling and customized physical fitness equipment for children

SPECIALIZED TRAINING

Certifications: Strength & Conditioning / CPR / Athletic Trainer / American Red Cross
A.C.S.M. Exercise Specialist / Respiratory Technician

EXPERIENCE

DuBois & Associates, LLC	*Owner / Personal Trainer*	Barstow, NV
Reno Health & Rehabilitation	*Co-owner / Personal Trainer*	Reno, NV
Tower Fitness Industries	*Fitness Consultant / Wellness Center Program Director*	Las Vegas, NV
Reno Medical Center	*Respiratory Therapy Technician* (American Red Cross Certified)	Reno, NV

BODYBUILDING / WEIGHTLIFTING CHAMPIONSHIPS

1999	Western Power Lifting	*2nd Place*	1997	Beast of the Southeast Dead Lift	*2nd Place*
1998	Northeastern Power Lifting	*2nd Place*	1996	Nevada Strongest Man (lightweight)	*2nd Place*
1998	State Bodybuilding	*5th Place*	1995	Mid-Pacific Strongman (middleweight)	*1st Place*
1997	State Bodybuilding	*2nd Place*	1991	Northeastern Texas Bodybuilding	*3rd Place*

GYM DESIGN / LAYOUT	EQUIPPED / SET UP GYMS
Kansas City Royals	Washington Redskins
St. Joseph's Hospital	Ford Motor Company
J.T.O. Corporation	Phoenix Cardinals
McDonald Rehabilitation	Greenville Wellness Center
World Gyms	University of Missouri
Gold's Gyms	Texas State University
Federal Correctional Institute	Police and Fire Departments

72

Jane Roqueplot, Sharon, Pennsylvania

This resume uses blue ink for the contact information, the word Goal, and the section headings in small caps. The appearance is classy.

Darlene K. Jepson

1923 Church Road   Columbus, Michigan 48063   313-555-3098

Profile
- ❖ Physical Therapist Assistant **with more than 500 hours of clinical experience in sports medicine, outpatient, inpatient, and acute-care settings.**
- ❖ Recognized by supervising physical therapist as working and communicating effectively with other health care professionals, staff, and especially patients and their families.
- ❖ Proven ability to work with minimal supervision.
- ❖ Volunteered with the Michigan Special Olympic Games; provided one-on-one support and assistance to physically challenged children.

Education

Oakland Community College • Rochester, Michigan

Associate in Applied Science—Physical Therapist Assistant   May 2004

Clinical Skills

Treatment Modalities & Related Responsibilities

- Ultrasound
- Electric stimulation
- Cervical and lumbar traction
- Hot and cold packs
- Fluidotherapy

- Manual techniques including
  - Range of motion
  - Stretching
  - Soft tissue
- Patient transfers
- Patient charting

Patients & Diagnoses

- Traumatic brain injuries
- Cerebral vascular accidents
- Spinal cord injuries
- Gunshot and other wounds

- Total knee and hip replacements
- Amputees
- Burns
- ICU

Clinical Experience

- ❖ *Acute Care:* University of Michigan Medical Center—Ann Arbor, Michigan (240 hours)
- ❖ *Outpatient Rehabilitation/Sports Medicine:* Healthwise Rehabilitation Services— Ypsilanti, Michigan (240 hours)
- ❖ *Inpatient Rehabilitation:* Harper Hospital—Detroit, Michigan (80 hours)

Professional Affiliations

- ❖ Oakland Community College Physical Therapist Assistant Club—President
- ❖ American Physical Therapy Association—Member

Employment

Lord & Taylor • Troy, Michigan   1997–Present

Estee Lauder Consultant / Cosmetics Stock Handler / Shoe Department Clerk
- Earned Employee of the Month designation (2001)
- Named Most Valuable Team Player (2000)

*Additional experience as **Nanny** (seasonal 1994–2000)*

– References available on request –

73

Janet L. Beckstrom, Flint, Michigan

This individual had just completed her two-year program and had minimal experience (just clinicals through the college). The writer emphasized the person's skills and types of patients served.

CATHY PIPER CFC, PTS

46 Augusta Heights
Pinehurst, Ontario
A1A 1A1
(555) 444-7777

CERTIFIED FITNESS & WELLNESS PROFESSIONAL
Expert in sports, fitness, health, and wellness training and education

ENERGETIC, DRIVEN, AND PASSIONATE FITNESS PROFESSIONAL dedicated to promoting the benefits of health and wellness. Advanced communication and interpersonal skills, with a well-developed ability to motivate others to set and achieve realistic fitness and health goals. **Certified Personal Trainer and Fitness Consultant** experienced in working with athletes, teams, and individuals at all levels. **Women's "A" Ranked Squash Player.** Combine fitness expertise with a strong corporate background demonstrating outstanding customer service, leadership, and organizational skills.

RELATED EXPERIENCE & QUALIFICATIONS

WALKING WOMEN / THE ACTION FACTORY, Augusta, Ontario
Co-Owner / Co-Founder   (P/T) April 2001–Present
> Conceived and developed entire walking program, marketing plan, and promotional materials for start-up health and fitness company.
> Lead instructor and consultant responsible for acquiring client health history, assessing fitness levels and goals, and leading biweekly walks.

THE FITNESS FACILITY, Augusta, Ontario
Owner / Trainer & Fitness Consultant   (P/T) 2000–Present
> Founded and successfully operate a sole proprietorship offering specialized sports training programs for individuals, athletes, and teams.
> Personally consult with athletes to determine specific fitness levels and goals, and create customized programs designed to motivate clients to achieve success.

PINEHURST WOMEN'S FITNESS, Pinehurst, Ontario
Personal Trainer / Fitness Consultant   (P/T) 1999–2000
> Offered customized fitness testing and consulting for local women's fitness centre with more than 700 members.
> Tested individual clients to ascertain fitness level, assembled a realistic plan based on individual needs and goals, and conducted orientation on all gym equipment.

PROFESSIONAL TRAINING

Certified Fitness Consultant (CFC)—OASES   2000
Personal Trainer Specialist (PTS)—Can Fit Pro   1999
CPR, Heart & Stroke Foundation of Ontario   Current

74

Ross Macpherson, Whitby, Ontario, Canada

The applicant wanted to make a full-time transition to her passion for fitness and health. The writer placed all relevant information up front and created two experience sections: Related Experience & Qualifications and Professional/Corporate Experience. The graphic captures

PROFESSIONAL TRAINING, *continued*

Courses and seminars include

- Personal Training Psychology
- Heart Rate Training
- Core Training on the Ball
- Total Towel Training
- Motivating the Inactive Market
- Body Walk

- Personal Training Program Design
- Manual Resistance Training
- Healthy Eating on the Run
- Training for Prime Time
- Make It FITT for Kids
- Fat Loss

ATHLETIC ACHIEVEMENTS

Championship Squash:

- Canadian National Championships Masters—4th (2003)
- Bronze Medalist—World Masters Games (2000)
- Ontario Masters Squash Champion (1999)
- Ontario Women's "A" ranked

PROFESSIONAL / CORPORATE EXPERIENCE

DUPUY CANADA, Augusta, Ontario
Senior Customer Service Representative   1988–Present
Promoted to manage and service critical "performance coating" accounts with large automotive manufacturers and automotive suppliers throughout North America.

- Ensure that all customer orders are completed on time and to exacting specifications. Requires advanced customer service and organization skills and ability to accurately reconcile production schedules with forecasted customer requirements.
- Assemble and lead cross-functional teams from product support, technical, product scheduling, manufacturing, and planning to effectively manage multimillion-dollar accounts, meet tight deadlines, and solve customer problems.
- Consistently recognized and commended by clients and superiors for outstanding customer service, leadership, and organizational skills.
- Nominated for and awarded a variety of Employee Recognition Awards.

Previously promoted through a variety of increasingly responsible customer service and purchasing positions:

Customer Service Representative—Polyethylene Pipe Division, Pinehurst, Quebec
Purchasing Representative—Energy & Materials Division, Pleasantville, Quebec
Purchasing Control Clerk—Accounting and Finance Division, Pinehurst, Quebec
Control Clerk—Real Estate & General Services Division, Pinehurst, Quebec

attention instantly. Boldfacing pulls the reader's eyes to key information, including the various positions held, training certifications, and side headings that introduce additional education and athletic achievements.

SALLY K. JONES

1234 Oak Road
Portland, OR 55555
(000) 000-0000 Residence
sallyjones@yahoo.com

Medical Office Specialist

Professional Summary

Enthusiastic, dependable Medical Office Specialist with 6 years of experience in medical settings. Received superior ratings by employer for attendance, dependability, and availability to assist as needed. Recognized as an excellent communicator. Winner of customer service award. Demonstrated skill in training clients and patients. Fast learner. Computer literate.

Endorsements

"Demonstrates skill in fee-for-service collections with patients, which in part led to ending fiscal year 'in the black'…" Former Supervisor, Providence Hospital

"Outstanding customer service on phones." Former Supervisor, Binyon Optical

"We wish we had more employees that we could write a review like this for." Former Supervisor, Victorinox

Professional Experience

PROVIDENCE HOSPITAL, Portland, OR   2002–2004
Office Specialist

Managed office duties for contact lens clinic within one of Portland's largest employers, a 300-bed hospital with 8,500 employees. Answered phones, took messages, and scheduled appointments. Handled front desk reception and patient check-in. Trained patients in contact lens insertion / removal. Ordered and received contact lenses and solutions.

- Acknowledged by management for assistance in eliminating $100K deficit by requiring patients to pay before receiving products.
- Won Providence Award for patience in training customers in contact lens insertion / removal.

BINYON OPTICAL, Tigard, OR   1999–2002
Optometric Technician / Assistant Manager

Reported to optometric physician for single office within firm with nine locations and approximately 80 employees. Greeted and checked in patients, answered phones, scheduled appointments. Administered patient pretests, including autorefraction, noncontact tonometry, automatic neutralization of eyeglasses, Humphrey visual fields testing, and fundus photography. Taught patients how to insert / remove and care for their contact lenses.

- Promoted to assistant manager after only two years as optometric technician.
- Embraced additional duties, including ordering supplies, resolving patient customer service issues, and managing store operations.

75

Jennifer Rydell, Portland, Oregon

The challenge for this resume was to minimize multiple jobs and virtually no education after high school. The writer eliminated unnecessary jobs, using years only (instead of months and years), and left out the education section altogether, focusing on the applicant's wonderful performance

SALLY K. JONES   Page 2

Professional Experience, Continued

PALM HARBOR HOMES, Portland, OR   1998
Receptionist

Reported directly to owner of respected family-owned operation, the largest manufactured-home dealership in the Portland / Vancouver metro area. Greeted customers and answered phones. Took messages and directed them to appropriate individual. Photocopied and faxed documents. Assisted customers in filling out required forms. Answered customer questions.

▪ Acknowledged by supervisor as "delightful" to work with.

VICTORINOX / PORTLAND, Portland, OR   1995–1997
Stockroom Clerk / Quality Control

Hired to clerk stockroom for the original manufacturer of Swiss Army Knives, a company with 350 employees. Coordinated shipping and receiving. Weighed and prepared parts for shipment. Loaded and unloaded trucks. Provided production support. Issued supplies in lockdown environment. Inspected parts to blueprint specifications. Used calipers, micrometers, Rockwell hardness tester, and optical comparator.

▪ Handpicked to serve on communication and product development committees.
▪ Made several suggestions regarding existing drug testing policies that were implemented company-wide.
▪ Acknowledged by human resources manager for having "best communication skills in the company."
▪ Took on extra duties as quality control technician, helping to establish quality control department.
▪ Trained temporary staff to assist in implementing new quality control measures.

ANIMAL MEDICAL CLINIC, Portland, OR   1995
Veterinary Assistant / Technician

Assisted veterinarian in small-animal practice. Restrained animals during physical examinations. Prepared pets for surgery. Monitored and cared for hospitalized animals, administering medications and changing fluids. Sterilized instruments with autoclave. Prepared surgery packets. Greeted customers and answered phones. Checked pets in and out of office.

▪ Learned and excelled at job duties in a matter of weeks.

Computer Skills

MS Windows, MS Word, Novell GroupWise, SMS Health, Internet, and email

▪ ▪ ▪

reviews, customer service award, and current computer skills. Testimonials under Endorsements build confidence and interest in the applicant and more than offset the absence of an education section.

Mohammed Abi-Saleh

901 Oliver Street, Unit 17
South Paterson, NJ 00000

Phone: (000) 000-0000   Pager: (000) 000-0000   Cell: (000) 000-0000

Clinical Applications Specialist in Radiographic Invasive Cardiology

---

SUMMARY OF QUALIFICATIONS

Techniques: Right and left heart catheterization, angioplasty, rotoblator, pacemaker insertion, ICD implants, EP/ablation procedures, intra-aortic balloon pump insertion, peripheral and renal angiography, peripheral laser, and intracoronary laser.

Instruments: Intracoronary balloons, stents, diagnostic catheters, and interventional guide wires

- 7 years of experience with invasive cardiology in all its forms, with additional expertise in radiography procedures, including use of Picker 1200 CT Scan, injectable contrast, and digital cineless imaging (archiving).
- Prior background as a clinical instructor; sought out as a knowledge source by professional staff in general medical and cardiovascular matters.
- Entrusted by physicians and frequently requested to assist them in higher-risk procedures involving split-second decision making.
- Outgoing and motivated with high standards of performance and attention to detail in any assignment.
- Recognized for unique blend of intelligence, self-confidence, and sociable personality, enabling immediate rapport with people at all levels.
- Called upon as translator for Arabic-speaking patients in other units of the hospital.

PROFESSIONAL EXPERIENCE

ST. JOHN'S HOSPITAL AND MEDICAL CENTER, HACKENSACK, NJ   2000–Present
Chief Interventional Cardiac Technologist

- Hold leadership position in the cardiac catheterization lab of hospital, specializing in high-risk/invasive procedures such as peripheral and carotid work (1,000 cases/year).
- Train and act as preceptor in the electrophysiology process for 9 technologists and assign them according to their skill level for certain procedures.
- Prioritize cases as to medical necessity and ensure that rooms are available and properly equipped.
- Collaborate with administrative management in implementing departmental improvements and disciplinary requirements to meet patient care and caseload needs to retain reputation as a cardiac service of excellence.

MOUNTAINRIDGE HOSPITAL, RIDGEMONT, NJ   1996–2000
Interventional Cardiac Technologist

- Qualified for permanent position in high-volume cardiac catheterization lab (4,300 cases/year) after completing 2,400 hours of clinical instruction combined with prior radiography background and experience with trauma patients.
- Interacted effectively with medical team in all aspects of cardiac procedures.
- Helped ease patient anxieties by carefully explaining procedures.

PASCACK COUNTY COMMUNITY COLLEGE, PASCACK, NJ   1992–1996
Adjunct Instructor/Lab Assistant, Radiography Department

- Answered to Program Director and kept her updated on all program changes.
- Managed and maintained lab facilities and supplies, purchasing under grant and standard budget purchasing.
- Proctored didactic classroom instruction as well as clinical instruction.
- Evaluated students on lab competencies and charted their progress.
- Assisted with preparation of program to acquire JRCERT certification as one of the foremost programs in the state and region.

(Continued)

76

Melanie Noonan, West Paterson, New Jersey

This easy-to-read resume uses font enhancements to lead the reader through the resume. Boldfacing makes the person's name stand out in the contact information and highlights the section headings and the positions held. Bold italic calls attention to the position and field

ST. JOHN'S HOSPITAL AND MEDICAL CENTER, HACKENSACK, NJ   1984–1991
CAT Scan Technologist
- Performed all diagnostic CAT scan procedures, including invasive procedures (needle biopsy, aspirations, and tumor localizations).
- Disclosed potential problem areas to physicians.

Assistant Chief Technologist
- Worked closely with and assisted the chief technologist and held full responsibility for the Radiological Department in the chief's absence, which included supervising up to 24 full- and part-time personnel on 2 shifts.
- Oversaw patient care, ensured appropriate procedures, and served as troubleshooter in resolving any problem areas.
- Assisted with time analysis, upgrading of equipment, and scheduling of staff.
- Managed the darkroom (film processing and development) and ensured proper inventory levels of supplies. Negotiated with vendors to obtain best price and value-added features.

Senior Radiographer
- Answered to the chief technologist and assumed some staff and departmental duties during the chief's absence.
- Trained new staff in existing and new procedures.
- Worked effectively in a high-pressure, demanding environment, consistently earning excellent performance reviews.

EDUCATION/CERTIFICATION

PASCACK COUNTY COMMUNITY COLLEGE, PASCACK, NJ
- Associate of Applied Science in Radiography, 1984
- Registered Radiographer/Board Certified AART
- Basic Life Support (BLS) Certification

CONTINUING EDUCATION

- Use of GPI Inhibitors in Acute Coronary Syndrome
    St. John's Hospital and Medical Center, January 2002

- Cardiac Catheterization 2000: Diagnostic and Interventional Symposium for Cardiac Catheterization Laboratory Professionals
    HMP Communications, LLC, September 2001

- Siemens Coroskop Plus Clinical Applications
    Siemens Medical Systems, Inc., July 2000

- Intraoperative X-Ray Imaging
    OEC Medical Systems, Inc., February 2000

- Siemens ACOM Net PC Clinical Applications
    Siemens Medical Systems, Inc., July 1999

- Listening: Interpersonal Effectiveness
- Building Healthy Relationships
    Mountainridge Hospital, July 1998

- A Live Symposium of Complex Coronary Cases Focusing on Rotational Atherectomy
    The Mount Moriah Hospital School of Medicine, June 1998

- Multi-Link—Inservice, Mountainridge Hospital
    Guidant Corporation, October 1997

information in the box and to the subheadings under Summary of Qualifications. The workplace names and locations appear in small caps. Bullets throughout direct attention to the beginning of each new information item.

GRACE MADISON, R.N.

101 Oak Ridge Drive ▪ Victor NY 14564 ▪ 585-555-0001

- Licensed Registered Nurse with 5 years of practical experience gained in diverse medical arenas through employment and clinical training; solid generalist with excellent assessment and emergency-care skills
- Strong background in School Nursing and member of New York State Association of School Nurses; completed School Nurses Orientation Program and trained in Section 504
- Actively involved parent and community member with extensive history of volunteerism
- Personal strengths include patience, excellent organizational and communication skills, positive and collaborative team attitude, fast learner, practice with care and confidentiality, and life experience that offers stability, sense of responsibility and maturity

PROFESSIONAL CLINICAL EXPERIENCE

School Nurse: Webster Central School District, Webster, NY   *July 2001–present*
- One of two full-time nurses serving the district's staff and more than 800 students in grades 9–12
- Perform health assessments, treat emergencies, dispense medication and provide health counseling/patient education
- Perform routine health screenings (vision, hearing, scoliosis, lice) and ensure immunization compliance
- Maintain student health records
- Trained in WinSchool software
- Process accident and insurance documentation
- Manage the health office inventory; perform ordering
- Assist with physicals for sports participants and cafeteria staff
- Certified in defibrillator use; collaborated in school policy development; participated in placement of equipment throughout building; monitor equipment readiness and maintenance

Per Diem RN: MedPros of Rochester, Rochester, NY   *May 2001–present*
- Provide substitute nursing coverage in pediatric, OB/GYN, internist and family medicine practices

Substitute School Nurse: Victor Central School District, Victor, NY, & Rochester Public School District, Rochester, NY   *December 2000–July 2001*

Registered Nurse: Strong Memorial Hospital, Rochester, NY   *August 2000–May 2001*
- Provided direct care to mothers and infants, including medications and phlebotomy, in this busy 26-bed, low-risk birth center (labor, delivery, postpartum and nursery)
- Assisted doctors with deliveries
- Team member performing baby care during cesarean sections
- Assessed newborns and infants to age 2 months

Student Nursing Clinical Placements   *Fall 1998–Spring 2000*
- **Emergency Department:** Park Ridge Hospital, Rochester, NY
- **Pediatric Department:** Strong Memorial Hospital, Rochester, NY
- **Home Health Care:** Monroe County Visiting Nurse Service, Rochester, NY
- **Teaching Rotation:** Clara Barton School/School #2, Rochester, NY
- **Medical Rotation:** Park Ridge Hospital, Rochester, NY
- **Psychiatric Department:** Rochester General Hospital, Rochester, NY
- **Maternity Department:** Genesee Hospital, Rochester, NY
- **Surgical Rotation:** Genesee Hospital, Rochester, NY
- **Oncology Rotation:** Southview Commons Oncology, Rochester, NY
- **Long-term Care Rotation:** Jewish Home, Rochester, NY

Salome A. Farraro, Mount Morris, New York

This person completed her A.A.S. in nursing as an adult student. She applied for an R.N. position in her community's school to be closer to home and family. Five years of experience was a requirement. The writer included student nursing placements and focused on the applicant's

ADDITIONAL EMPLOYMENT

Pharmacy Clerk: Rite Aid, Victor, NY   *1998–2000*

Teacher Aide: Webster Nursery School, Victor, NY   *1995–1997*

Child Care: Private, Victor, NY   *1993–1995*

Additional background gained in bookkeeping and business management. Information is available upon request.

EDUCATION & CREDENTIALS

Associate in Applied Science, Nursing: Monroe Community College, Rochester, NY; May 2000
- GPA: 3.55

NCLEX-RN Exam; September 2000

Licensed Registered Nurse: State of New York; 2000

Fingerprint Clearance for Employment: New York State Education Department; September 2001

School Nurses Orientation Program; August 2002

CPR Certified: American Heart Association; through August 2004

PROFESSIONAL DEVELOPMENT

Understanding Section 504 in New York; March 2003

Child Obesity and Eating Disorders: What Schools Can Do; January 2003

School Automated External Defibrillator Training; August 2002

School Health Services Update 2002 Conference; May 2002

PROFESSIONAL AFFILIATIONS

New York State Association of School Nurses

Local School Nurse Zone

CURRENT VOLUNTEER INVOLVEMENT

High School Compact Committee: Schroeder Senior High School, Victor, NY

Member, past Treasurer and Vice President: Victor PTA

Youth Group Leader/past Faith Formation Teacher

commitment to the community and knowledge of it. The school hired her over several other candidates, some with far more experience. A gray background for each section heading is a nice touch. See Cover Letter 5.

CONFIDENTIAL

Lanina Crowne, RN, CLNC
legal nurse consultant

1111 New London Road
Montgomery, Alabama 36100
bnw002@soma.net ✆ 334.555.5555

WHAT I CAN OFFER DEWEY, CHEATAM & HOWE

❏ Gathering "bulletproof" support to assess the quality of medically based cases

❏ Building and maintaining a "stable" of expert witnesses

❏ Anticipating adversaries' theories

❏ Controlling costs and limiting liability

❏ Conducting fully documented discovery based on court-tested standards of nursing care

❏ Serving as an expert witness in nursing care

EXAMPLES OF PERFORMANCE

❏ Stepped in quickly to **correct a potentially actionable situation** involving a critically ill patient. With the family present, calmly corrected the situation and then fully documented every action. *Outcomes:* House counsel said he could have used my report without change because it was so complete and accurate.

❏ **Corrected a liability** that had been present for years. Redesigned how we documented suicide precautions for patients. *Outcomes:* Situation resolved in just two weeks. My new system also saved $5K in labor costs annually.

❏ Got control of expensive instruments with a **low-cost solution** that required no additional staff training. *Outcomes:* Treatments more efficient. Chronic misplacing of instruments stopped and never returned.

❏ Redesigned the security measures we relied on to track movements of psychiatric patients. *Outcomes:* **Reduced** our **liability** and **increased** the **safety** of our staff and patients in a hurry.

RECENT WORK HISTORY

❏ **Office Nurse,** Arista Psychiatric Services, Montgomery, Alabama   Jan 03 to Present
   APS is a statewide corporation offering services through four providers.

❏ **Staff Nurse** *with additional duties as* **Relief Charge Nurse,** Central Medical Center South, Montgomery, Alabama   Oct 00–Jan 03
   Served as direct supervisor of three registered nurses, a licensed practical nurse, and up to four mental health technicians.

❏ **Staff Nurse,** Central Medical Center East, Montgomery, Alabama   Nov 98–Nov 00
   Handled pre-admitting for surgical patients in wards with censuses of about 30.

❏ **Nurse,** Top Shelf Home Health, Montgomery, Alabama   Aug 98–Jan 99
   Provided at-home care for patients ranging from infant to adult with diabetic and wound care. Instructed patients and care providers in safe and accepted basic healthcare procedures.

CONFIDENTIAL   *More indicators Dewey, Cheatam & Howe can use…*

78

Don Orlando, Montgomery, Alabama

A common weakness of a resume Goal statement is that it expresses the hope that the company will do something for the applicant (such as "I'm looking for a place where I may improve my skills"). The first section of this resume clearly indicates how the candidate can benefit the

Lanina Crowne	**Legal Nurse Consultant**	334.555.5555

❑ **Charge Nurse** *promoted to* **Charge Nurse Supervisor,** Manor Nursing Home, Montgomery, Alabama — Aug 96–Aug 98
Supervised two licensed practical nurses and seven nursing assistants to care for 90 elderly patients.

❑ **Staff Nurse,** Quality Care, Montgomery, Alabama — Feb 90–May 96

❑ **Dental Health Technician** and **Hygienist,** Dracon Air Force Base, Louisiana — Oct 83–Sep 89
Supported eight dentists in a comprehensive practice that cared for thousands of patients annually.

RELEVANT PROFESSIONAL DEVELOPMENT

❑ **A.S., Nursing,** Central State University, Montgomery, Alabama — 93
Awarded Registered Nurse. Paid my own way to earn this degree while working seven days a week. Commuted 1,000 miles a week. One of 10, from a class of about 200, to be inducted into a national academic and service honorary society.

❑ **Certificate of Nursing,** Norton College, Montgomery, Alabama — 77
Awarded LPN.

❑ "Crisis Prevention Intervention for Psychiatric Patients," Horizon Corporation, one day — 02

PROFESSIONAL CERTIFICATIONS

❑ **Certified Legal Nurse Consultant** — 02
Certification awarded by the Medical Legal Consulting Institute, Inc.

❑ **Registered Nurse** — Expires 04
Registered to practice in the state of Alabama.

PROFESSIONAL AFFILIATIONS

❑ **Member, National Alliance of Certified Legal Nurse Consultants** — Since Oct 02

COMPUTER SKILLS

❑ Expert in medical support software; working knowledge of WordPerfect, Quicken, and Internet search protocols

LANGUAGE SKILLS

❑ Working knowledge of spoken Spanish and Italian.

prospective company. The Examples of Performance section presents significant achievements and their outcomes, which suggest additional benefits for a company. Study the italic comments as informative explanations.

MADELYN BUCKLEY

43 Parker Road
East Hartford, CT 00000
000.000.0000
00000@00000.000

PROFILE

Highly motivated professional with extensive teaching/training experience. Strong interpersonal skills. Able to explain theories, issues, and treatments clearly and completely. Promoted to Clinical Level III, which included training new nursing staff. Researched experimental jet ventilator from the idea all the way to government approval; this was a completely different concept in respiratory care. Trained nursing staff to use this new system. Passed CCRN and CORN examinations on first attempt.

EXPERIENCE HIGHLIGHTS

Team Leader of Nurses, Ophthalmology Department   1999–Present
Smith Hospital, West Hartford, Connecticut
- Supervised and trained nursing staff.
- Followed cases to ensure quality control.
- Ran tests on sterilizer, took cultures, and inspected all instruments to ensure sterility.
- Followed up on post-op infections to locate cause.
- Prepared budgets, purchased equipment, and oversaw all aspects of department administration.
- Certified—Registered Nurse Operation Room.

Clinical Level III Registered Nurse   1994–1999
Portland Hospital, Portland, Maine
- Charge Nurse in Medical Intensive Care.
- Supervised and trained nursing staff.
- Supervisor of Research Studies, including experimental jet ventilator (see Profile).
- Registered Nurse on Medical Floor.
- Certified—Registered Nurse, Critical Care.

EDUCATION

University of Portland, Portland, Maine
Associate of Science, Major: Nursing

E. C. Goodwin Vocational-Technical School, New Britain, CT
CT PCSW Pre-Apprenticeship Program

Capital Community Technical College, Hartford, CT
Computer courses in Word, PowerPoint, Excel, Internet

79

Ellen Mulqueen, Hartford, Connecticut

This person wanted a resume to return to college for a B.S.N. degree and to teach nursing. The writer therefore emphasized teaching/training in the Profile and Experience Highlights section.

SusanSpieker

215 Lincolnshire Lane
Findlay, OH 45840
419.420.1258
sspieker@msn.com

Seeking position as ...
★ REGISTERED NURSE ★

PROFILE

A **dedicated, compassionate** individual with the ability to maintain personal high-level-of-care standards by taking whatever steps necessary to ensure patient safety, comfort, and medical care. Recognized by supervisors and instructors for **team orientation, critical-thinking skills,** and a desire for continuous learning. **Problem-solving skills** gleaned by identifying solutions to challenging problems that arise when providing individualized care to those in need. Additional core competencies include

Charting by Exception—Meditech Software
Concise Written & Verbal Communications
Organizational / Time Management Skills
Pharmacologic Knowledge

Patient Relationship Management
Resourcefulness / Flexibility
Accurate Report Documentation
Patient Assessment / Analytical Judgment

EDUCATION

OWENS COMMUNITY COLLEGE, Findlay, OH
Associate in Applied Science Degree, May 2003
Major: Nursing Technology   GPA: 3.3

CLINICAL ROTATIONS

3/03–5/03	**OB,** Blanchard Valley Health Association, Findlay, OH
2/03–3/03	**Pediatrics,** Wood County Hospital, Bowling Green, OH
2/03–4/03	**Med/Surg and Peds**—Precepting
	Blanchard Valley Health Association, Findlay, OH
1/03–2/03	**Geriatric,** Winebrenner, Findlay, OH
11/02–12/02	**Psychosocial Dysfunction**—Inpatient Psychiatric Stress Unit
	Fulton County Hospital, Wauseon, OH
8/02–10/02	**Med/Surg, Oncology, PCU, ER, ICU**—Adult Health II
	Blanchard Valley Health Association, Findlay, OH
1/02–5/02	**Med/Surg, ER, OR**—Adult Health I
	Blanchard Valley Health Association, Findlay, OH
8/01–12/01	**Med/Surg and Bilio Floor**
	Wood County Hospital, Bowling Green, OH

> "As a clinical instructor for Susan in the acute medical–surgical setting, as well as long-term care of the elderly patient, I have found Susan to be very knowledgeable of disease process, medications, and treatments. She is well-prepared and organized and continues to build her confidence and experience with various nursing skills as well as nursing judgment."
>
> Erin Iglehart, RN, BSN
> Owens Community College
> Clinical Instructor

Responsibilities during the above rotations included

- Working cooperatively with patients, families, and other members of the healthcare team to provide individualized care.

- Providing a full range of patient care in the medical/oncology unit—monitoring vital signs and labs; working with ports, IV piggybacks, push meds, and heplocking; bathing; kinetic dosing; communicating patient status to nursing team; and delivering end-of-life care with empathy and compassion.

- Prioritizing patient care to deal with concerns and complex medical issues while making well-thought-out decisions and utilizing consultants and reference tools appropriately.

- Facilitating patient well-being by systematically assessing short- and long-term goals and by educating patients and their families about medical conditions and nursing procedures.

WORK EXPERIENCE

THE PHARM PHARMACY,	**Pharmacy Technician**	2000–PRESENT
SKIP TATE APPLIANCE,	**Secretary/Bookkeeper**	1999
SEARS & ROEBUCK,	**Sales Associate**	1998–2001
OLD MILL DAIRY,	**Cashier/Server**	1997–1998

Consistently worked part-time jobs to pay for college expenses.

80

Sharon Pierce-Williams, Findlay, Ohio

The applicant had only part-time jobs and clinical rotations. The writer included the testimonial and supplied much information. An HR director judged this "the best resume...in quite some while."

Katherine E. Masterson

321 Nickerson Point Avenue
South Kingstown, RI 12121
(401) 444-4444

OBJECTIVE:	A position as a Licensed Practical Nurse, utilizing 11 years of full-time, dedicated professional employment at the highest quality of nursing care.

- CAREER SUMMARY -

- Licensed Practical Nurse with 11 years of experience, including Cardiac Teaching and Pre-cardiac Catheterization
- Proven ability to meet the daily challenges of the nursing profession
- Work with the high standards and dedication expected of today's LPNs
- Received Highest LPN Service Award, two years

EDUCATION:	**Community College of Rhode Island,** Lincoln, RI

Diploma as a Licensed Practical Nurse, July 1994
GPA: 3.8/4.0
Graduated third in a class of 88

Community College of Rhode Island, Warwick, RI
Liberal Arts Courses (leading to Registered Nurse Degree)

EXPERIENCE:	**North County Memorial Hospital,** Cranston, RI

Licensed Practical Nurse, August 1998–Present
- Full-time staff member of the Coronary Care Unit
- Work in a team of three participants
- Maintain full awareness of monitored patients
- Care, assessment, charting, medicating, monitoring IV fluids/medications

North County Nursing and Subacute Unit, North Kingstown, RI
Licensed Practical Nurse, Primary Care, December 1994–1998
- Charge of nursing for 26 long-term and subacute residents
- Primary care nursing

LICENSES:	Current Practical Nursing license #LPN 07542
	CPR certification through November 2004
MEMBERSHIPS:	Wickford Glen Condominium Association, President
	Saint Paul's Parish Community Association
	Rhode Island LPN Consortium, Secretary
VOLUNTEER:	Annual Cancer Appeal Raffle ticket sales
	Kent County Hospital Annual Appeal Phonathons
	Toys for Tots Appeals

Excellent references will be furnished upon request

81

Edward Turilli, Newport, Rhode Island

A thin page border and a two-line horizontal line under the contact information are the two chief design elements. The centered Career Summary heading breaks up for variety the list of headings.

Hospitality

Resumes at a Glance

RESUME NUMBER	LAST OR CURRENT OCCUPATION	GOAL	PAGE
82	Cake Decorator	Cake Decorator	169
83	Waitress	Food Server	170
84	Banquet Captain	Computer Programming Position	171
85	Assistant Restaurant Manager	Restaurant Manager	172
86	Restaurant Supervisor	Not specified	173
87	Restaurant Operations District Manager	Food Service Manager	174
88	General Manager/Principal	Restaurant or Club Supervisor	175
89	Restaurant Manager	Manager	176
90	Executive Chef	Executive Chef	177
91	Restaurant Chef	Executive Chef	178
92	Executive Chef	Executive Chef/Operations Manager	180
93	Sous Chef and Food Production Manager	Sous Chef	182
94	Head Chef	Head Chef	184
95	Chef/Production Manager	Chef/Production Manager	186
96	Senior Associate Manager	Restaurant and Retail Manager	188
97	Director, Support Services	General Manager	190
98	Director of Sales, Resort Hotel	Senior Sales and Marketing Executive	192
99	COO/General Manager, Resort	Operations Manager	194
100	Corporate Executive Chef/ General Manager	Food Services Professional	196

TAMMY PARSONS
1422 HARTFORD ROAD · FOWLER, OHIO 44418 · (330) 555-0000

~ ~

CAKE DECORATOR

~ ~ Creative ~ ~

~ ~ Eye for detail ~ ~

~ ~ Flexible to changing priorities ~ ~

~ ~ Excellent organizational skills ~ ~

~ ~ Noteworthy interpersonal skills ~ ~

~ ~ Establish and maintain well-organized work area ~ ~

~ ~ Comply with all food safety and sanitation standards ~ ~

~ ~ Maintain high-quality standards and product integrity ~ ~

~ ~ Exceptional reading, writing and communication skills ~ ~

~ ~ Use production list to meet product needs throughout the day ~ ~

~ ~ Effectively merchandise all cake items according to plan-o-gram ~ ~

~ ~ Versatile, enthusiastic, hardworking individual; driven to meet or exceed expectations ~ ~

~ ~ Assist customers with bakery products or purchases using suggestive selling techniques ~ ~

~ ~ Work well as a team member with people of all professional levels and of various cultures ~ ~

~ ~ Computer systems knowledge includes Art Deco, Kopy Kake, Telxon, ACR and Label Machine ~ ~

~ ~ ~ ~ ~ ~ ~ ~ ~ ~ **PROFESSIONAL EMPLOYMENT** ~ ~ ~ ~ ~ ~ ~ ~ ~ ~

Shop-a-Lot, Hermitage, Pennsylvania
CAKE DECORATOR, 2002–Present

- Receive special orders from customers for cakes, pies, tortes, and cookies. Decorate cakes and pastries; duplicate customer-supplied drawings freehand or with Kopy Kake.
- Prepare a wide variety and assortment of fresh and appealing cake items. Assist bakery manager when ordering ingredients and decorator supplies. Rotate product to ensure optimum freshness.
- Introduced use of airbrush to cake business. Incorporated use of popular character images and recommended placing picture cakes in showcase. Saw immediate increase in cake business.

Farrell Bakery, Farrell, Pennsylvania
CAKE DECORATOR, 1996–1997

- Produced quality, appealing cakes to customer orders with consistent, on-time delivery.

Tastee Bakery, Hermitage, Pennsylvania
CAKE DECORATOR, 1989–1995

- Constructed beautiful cakes for special orders. Skilled in creating royal icing flowers. Reputation spread by word / taste of mouth, resulting in significant increase in volume of orders.

~ ~ ~ ~ ~ ~ ~ ~ ~ ~ **EDUCATION / TRAINING** ~ ~ ~ ~ ~ ~ ~ ~ ~ ~

Certificate, 1986, Advanced Cake Decorating, Trumbull County Joint Vocational School, Warren, Ohio
Graduate, 1984, Badger High School, Kinsman, Ohio

82

Jane Roqueplot, Sharon, Pennsylvania

This creative resume is for a creative applicant, and its design illustrates the applicant's occupation. Center justification and controlled line width create the cake's layers.

Valerie W. Butler

333 S.E. Riveredge Drive • Vancouver, Washington 33333

222-222-2222 *cell*   home 555-555-5555

Server

Professional Profile

Energetic and highly motivated **Food Server** with extensive experience in the food service industry. Expertise lies in working with the fine-dining restaurant, providing top-quality service, and maintaining a professional demeanor. Solid knowledge of the restaurant business, with strengths in excellent customer service and food and wine recommendations.

Get along well with management, coworkers, and customers. Well-developed communication skills. Known as a caring and intuitive "people person," with an upbeat and positive attitude. Highly flexible, honest, and punctual, with the ability to stay calm and focused in stressful situations. Committed to a job well done and a long-term career.

Outstanding Achievements & Recommendations

• Served notable VIP clientele, including clients associated with Murdock Charitable Trust.
• History of repeat and new customers requesting my service as their waitress.
• Known for creating an atmosphere of enjoyment and pleasure for the customer.

*"...Valerie was warm, friendly, kind, and very efficient.
We didn't feel rushed. She handled our requests, and
we appreciated her genuine 'May I please you' attitude...."*

Related Work History

Waitress • **Banquets** • Heathman Lodge • Vancouver, Washington • *2002–present*
Northwest seasonal cuisine.

Banquets • Dolce Skamania Lodge • Stevenson, Washington • *2001–2002*
Casual fine-dining restaurant.

Waitress • Hidden House • Vancouver, Washington • *1993–2001*
Exclusive fine-dining restaurant.

Waitress • Multnomah Falls Lodge Restaurant • Corbett, Oregon • *1992–1993*
Historic Columbia Gorge Falls restaurant serving authentic Northwestern cuisine.

Waitress • The Ahwahnee at Yosemite National Park • California • *1 year*
World-renowned, award-winning fine-dining restaurant—sister lodge to Timberline Lodge.

83

Rosie Bixel, Portland, Oregon

The applicant wanted to work for an upscale, fine-dining restaurant. The writer included a customer recommendation as a testimonial. Horizontal lines enclose each of the section headings.

Michael Kuchura

4 Pinehurst Avenue ▪ St. Augusta, Ontario A1A 1A1
(555) 555-5555 ▪ mkuchura@email.ca

Objective: Computer Programming

- Client/Server Applications
- Object-Oriented Programming
- Systems Analysis

- Networking
- Database Programming
- Staff & End User Training

Computer Programming graduate with proven technical abilities and a demonstrated track record of achieving in a team environment. Highly motivated, dependable, and driven to succeed. Consistently recognized for exceptional communication, interpersonal, and problem-solving skills.

Technical Skills

Operating Systems:	Windows (9x, NT, 2000 Pro, XP Pro, 2000 Server), Linux Mandrake 7.5
Languages:	Java, Oracle, SQL, Visual Basic 6.0, VBScript
Protocols:	HTTP, FTP, SMTP
Hardware:	Printers, hard drives, disc drives, and tower repair

Education

MCSA	2003
A+ Certification	2003
Computer Programming (Honours)—Welland College, St. Augusta, Ontario	2003

Work Experience

VANDERBELL INNS, St. Augusta, Ontario
Banquet Captain   2002–Present
First selected into new position responsible for ensuring the smooth execution of onsite and offsite banquet events. Supervised all banquet and kitchen staff, communicated directly with client, and finalized all client billing.
- Implemented a series of time-saving measures to improve service and ensure guest satisfaction.
- Recognized by General Manager, clients, and staff for commitment to excellence.

Maître D'   2001–2002
Hired to increase morale among staff in the dining room, coordinate staff scheduling, maintain budgeted hours for the week, and ensure guest satisfaction.
- Worked closely with staff to resolve outstanding issues and improve the work environment.

FAIRFIELD CHATEAU LAKE LORRIETE, Lake Lorriete, Alberta
Promoted through a series of increasingly responsible positions for one of Canada's most prestigious hotels. Handled the full range of service responsibilities for international clientele, with particular attention paid to courtesy and customer relations.
Fairview Fine Dining Server   1998–2000
Dining Room Supervisor   1996–1998
Dining Room Waiter   1992–1996

Personal Achievements

3rd-degree Black Belt in Karate
- Winner of 15 tournaments across Canada, including the Western Canadian Championships (2001).

84

Ross Macpherson, Whitby, Ontario, Canada

This applicant had solid hospitality experience but wanted to transition to IT. The writer used a graphic, a Technical Skills section, and relevant education to show his technology skills.

Rachel Marie Lindahl

227 N.E. 99th Street • Vancouver, WA 77777

555-555-5555 *cell*   home **555-555-5555**

Restaurant Management

Professional Profile

Driven, results-oriented, and energetic *professional* with 14 years of experience in *Restaurant Management,* offering an exceptional teamwork spirit and a positive attitude.

Experienced in managing within budget guidelines, maintaining an effective flow of inventory, and developing a strong team attitude among employees. Proven skills in setting and achieving goals, supplying above-average training skills, and adding to the bottom-dollar profit margin by improving service, reducing waste, and increasing efficiency.

Work well with all types of personalities; able to perform hiring and termination duties effectively and professionally. Conscientious, customer-service-oriented, and highly focused, with strong follow-through skills and effective time-management abilities. Loyal, possess strong common sense with a keen sense of humor, and committed to a job well done.

Expertise Includes

• Bookkeeping/Deposits	• HIV Awareness Training	• Quality Assurance
• Cash Handling	• Inventory Management	• Schedule Management
• Customer Service	• Operating within Budget	• Staff Training
• Event Planning	• POS Knowledge	• Supervisor
• Excellent Facilities Presentation	• Public Relations	• Team Player

History of Employment

Assistant Manager • Shari's Restaurant • Vancouver, Washington • *2001–current*

Chef / Manager • Van Mall Retirement • Vancouver, Washington • *1996–2001*
   250 residents—supplied full meal services.

Kitchen / Assistant Manager • Carrows Restaurant • Vancouver, Washington • *1989–1995*

85

Rosie Bixel, Portland, Oregon

The elaborate box around each main section heading is distinctive. The darker sides of the box create the illusion of a shadow. Without a box the Expertise Includes heading seems part of the Professional Profile.

LYNDA ROSEN

67533 NW Elm Street
Seattle, WA 88888
(555) 666-9999
2343856@lpst.com

QUALIFICATIONS

- Extensive experience in all aspects of restaurant operations, including supervising, food and dessert preparation, catering, inventory management, supplier relations, and service excellence.

- Skilled in training, motivating, and developing new staff members.

- A talent for identifying and developing new and creative business opportunities.

- Continually seeks ways to share knowledge and vitality.

- Thrives in a team-oriented environment that honors creativity and experience.

- Passionate about creating innovative food and dining experiences.

- Developed a comfortable management style based on integrity, excellence, and trust.

EDUCATION

WYOMING STATE UNIVERSITY
Undergraduate course work in business, art, and drama

EXPERIENCE

SEAFOOD GRILL & WINE BAR, Seattle, WA　　　　　**2000–present**
Front-of-the-House Supervisor for 125-seat seafood restaurant.
*Promoted rapidly from initial position of **Server** to **Daytime Maître d'** to **Floor Supervisor** and on to current position.*
- Manage, supervise, and set up floor.
- Ensure restaurant's high standards are being met.
- Provide training, labor management, and maintenance scheduling.
- Assist in budgeting and cost controls.

LA PRIMA TRATTORIA, Seattle, WA　　　　　**1998–2000**
Server and Pastry Chef for 75-seat Italian restaurant.
- Created and prepared in-house desserts, sauces, cookies, and special-order desserts.
- Trained new waitstaff, tracked dessert inventory, and gained experience on point-of-sale computer system.

HANES BAKERY, Renton, WA　　　　　**1997–1998**
Pastry Chef and Server for Cannon Beach bakery.
- Supervised sandwich counter and served when appropriate.
- Developed pastries, desserts, and special-order desserts.
- Improved staff scheduling and overall organization to maximize peak traffic flow.
- Introduced new lunch menu items to retain bakery vitality.
- Researched and developed wedding cake division that significantly increased overall revenue. Created marketing pieces, including product descriptions and price lists.

CAFÉ DE LA MER, Renton, WA　　　　　**1982–1997**
Assistant Manager and Co-Chef for 36-seat fine-dining restaurant (serving Northwest cuisine and wines) that became known as one of the most highly rated and exclusive restaurants on the West Coast.
- Provided business experience to new owners.
- Supervised and trained wait team and prep staff.
- Helped develop menus, prepare food, and create desserts.
- Introduced new signature items such as bouillabaisse, cassoulet, and scallop serviche.
- Planned and tracked inventory; ordered all food and wine.
- Prepared payroll and managed accounting.
- Managed restaurant in absence of the owners.

86

Rosie Bixel, Portland, Oregon

The writer wanted this resume to be creative for the creative Chef/Baker/Manager applicant. One vertical line crossing one horizontal line produced unequal quadrants suitable for the sections.

WILLIAM KENT

5555 North Orange Avenue • Los Angeles, CA 55555
(310) 555-5555 • wmkent@email.com

FOOD SERVICE MANAGEMENT—15 YEARS OF EXPERIENCE

RELATED SKILLS

- Multisite Operations Management
- Customer Service
- Menu Formulation
- Food & Labor Cost Control

- Purchasing & Inventory Management
- Warehouse Supervision
- Sanitation Control
- Facilities Management & Maintenance

QUALIFICATIONS

- ✓ Industry-wide reputation for superior leadership and team-building skills. Gain loyalty through ability to instill confidence and encourage growth in coworkers. Skilled in hiring, training and motivating team members.
- ✓ Track record of exceptional productivity and expense reduction. Effectively manage costs, consistently operating within or below budget.
- ✓ Work well independently and as a part of a team. Interface well with public and all levels of corporate and store management.
- ✓ Thorough in solving problems and taking preventative actions.
- ✓ Consistent award winner, including *Most Improved Sales, Most Improved Operating Profit, #1 in Sales Increases, #1 in Operating Profit Improvement.*

PROFESSIONAL EXPERIENCE

GOLD STAR RESTAURANT OPERATIONS   1992 to Present
Restaurant Operations District Manager (2000–Present)
Restaurant Manager, San Fernando Valley (1998–2000)
Previous Positions: Lead Cook, Assistant Restaurant Manager (1992–1997)
Achieved fast-track promotions through a series of increasingly responsible positions. Advanced based on consistent revenue production, earnings and customer satisfaction ratings.

- Coordinate corporate food service activities, policies and procedures for up to 40 diverse units encompassing cafeterias, grills, deli counters, fast food and snack bars. Territory extends throughout Los Angeles, Orange, Ventura and San Luis Obispo counties.
- Direct management team with up to 140 employees. Screen management applicants; hire, train, supervise, motivate and conduct performance evaluations.
- Consistently achieve revenues within top 5% company-wide with annual sales of $4 million.
- Secure vendors; negotiate contracts per corporate buying specifications and standards.
- Develop and implement creative promotional programs that have contributed to district-wide success.

JENNY'S RESTAURANT, Laguna Hills, CA   1990 to 1992
Lead Cook/Cook Trainer

EDUCATION

UNITED STATES NAVY
Mess Management, Class "A"
Honorable Discharge 1989

87

Vivian VanLier, Los Angeles, California

The Qualifications section highlights this candidate's strong record of food management skills and notable accomplishments. The list of Gold Star Restaurant positions shows his record of promotions.

L. STEPHEN WONDER

550 E. Ogden Avenue   000-983-8882
Naperville, Illinois 06063   lswonder@internetservice.com

CAREER FOCUS

Seeking a hospitality Supervisory or Management position in a new or established restaurant or night club. Diversified experience and abilities that are easily transferable.

SUMMARY OF QUALIFICATIONS

- Self-motivated, results-oriented Business and Operations Manager with a proven track record of establishing, operating and managing successful restaurant and beverage businesses.

- Background includes P&L management, sales, operations, security, facility maintenance, accounting, staffing, training, team leadership and development.

- Accomplished entrepreneur with excellent organizational, time-management and interpersonal skills; interact effectively with customers, associates and decision makers at all levels.

- Hands-on leadership style; meet goals, work well under pressure while providing high-level customer service to a demanding clientele.

EMPLOYMENT HISTORY & EXPERIENCE

IT'S THE BEST AROUND, Naperville, Illinois   1991–Present
Established restaurant/night club business providing entertainment, liquor and full menu.
General Manager / Principal
- Manage P&L, day-to-day operations and payroll
- Perform marketing, sales, advertising and customer service
- Hire, train, schedule and motivate bar and waitstaff, DJs and security personnel
- Determine capital equipment needs and purchase necessary fixtures and equipment
- Order food, beverages and supplies; maintain strong relationships with vendors
- Manage cash flow, prepare bank deposits and handle bookkeeping; authorize payments
- Maintain excellent working relationship with local community, police and citizens

BEN & JERRY'S HARD STUFF, Elgin, Illinois   1987–1991
Convenience store owner/operator
Manager
- Managed full-service liquor and convenience store; purchased beverages and inventory
- Maintained vendor relations; set up displays; managed cash flow
- Hired and supervised full- and part-time staff; controlled payroll and other costs

EDUCATION

University of Michigan, Ann Arbor, Michigan
Business and Psychology course work

88

Patricia Chapman, Naperville, Illinois

This entrepreneur Restaurant/Club Owner wanted to become an employee in the same industry. In the Summary and Experience sections, the writer presented items of greatest interest to an employer.

TODD RANDOLF

MANAGER
ENTREPRENEUR / MARKETER
INNOVATIVE PRODUCT DEVELOPMENT

BUSINESS EXPERTISE

- Problem Identification/Analysis
- Logistical Planning
- Product Specification
- Operations/Administration

- Process Optimization
- Troubleshooting/Problem Resolution
- Manufacturing Strategies/Techniques
- Patent Application Process

MARKETING EXPERTISE

- Lead Generation
- Account Development
- Customer Care

- Marketing Campaigns
- Publicity and Public Relations
- Sales Strategies/Incentives

PROFESSIONAL HISTORY

CANYON RESTAURANT, MORRISON, CO   1987–PRESENT

Todd has been the manager of Canyon since 1995 following a series of promotions in a career spanning 17 years. As manager, Todd manages the daily operations and monitors quality control and time management. He is responsible for guest relations, scheduling, staff management and development, point-of-sale administration, inventory control, and bookkeeping. Most notably, Todd has contributed in the following ways:

Employee Motivation and Retention: Closely managing a staff of up to 65 employees at peak times. Effectively motivating the staff through incentive programs and promoting a strong family atmosphere to achieve established sales objectives through performance improvement and increased customer satisfaction levels. Canyon enjoys a long-standing, loyal staff—many employees have been there for 17 years.

Tip/Gratuity Administration: Designed an innovative tip-tracking system to comply with IRS regulations. Employees receive their tips in their regular biweekly paychecks.

Reservation Matching: Implemented a successful reservation-matching system that eliminates overbooking, minimizes table wait times, and maximizes seating at Canyon.

FOUNDER AND PRESIDENT, FORMATIVE TECHNOLOGIES, MORRISON, CO   1998–PRESENT

Formative Technologies specializes in custom fabricated accessories for point-of-sale systems in the hospitality, grocery, and retail industries. The flagship product is a point-of-sale printer protective cover (patent pending) used to prevent damage caused by airborne particles, grease, spills, and foreign objects.

Faced with the ongoing problem of spills disabling the printers at Canyon Restaurant, Todd unsuccessfully searched for an off-the-shelf product to protect the printer. Further investigation revealed the problem was widespread in the hospitality industry, and a protective cover could serve the grocery market as well.

Todd enlisted the help of a product designer, and together they designed and specified a protective cover. After careful consideration, a manufacturer and thermal forming manufacturing process were selected. Production began. Word of the product spread, and orders for the protective cover were booked prior to launch.

A successful marketing campaign using advertising, trade press articles, and word of mouth won key accounts such as IBM, Micros, King Soopers, and P.F. Chang's. The printer cover has been so successful that the line will be extended to include other custom accessories for point-of-sale equipment and systems.

TGR TECHNOLOGIES INC., LITTLETON, CO   1999–PRESENT

TGR Technologies designs and fabricates self-contained housing units for ATMs. Todd is a hands-on technician, building and installing the housing units.

EDUCATION AND CERTIFICATIONS

Business Program, Arapahoe Community College, Englewood, CO
Computer Science and Business Programs, Red Rocks Community College, Lakewood, CO
CPR Certification
Dealing with Difficult Customers Certificate

1234 W. Cheyenne Drive • Morrison, CO 55555
555.555.1111 • truser@aol1.com

89

Roberta F. Gamza, Louisville, Colorado

This candidate—also an entrepreneur—was looking for a position with a start-up manufacturer or another entrepreneur. The writer used a narrative format to attract the right type of employer.

DONALD ARCHER

412 Old Castle Avenue • Sharon, Pennsylvania 16146 • 724-543-4671

"Compliments to the chef! This is the best prime rib I've ever eaten." — Ralph B
Monte Cello's, Sharon, PA

"Superb steak . . . cooked to perfection . . . excellent seasonings. My thanks to the chef." — Actress
Debbie Reynolds
Radisson Hotel, Sharon, PA

Knowledgeable in:
➢ Food Preparation
➢ Menu Creation
➢ Inventory
➢ Ordering Supplies and Food
➢ Event Planning
➢ Serving 1–2,500
➢ Nutrition
➢ Sanitation
➢ Security
➢ Policies & Procedures
➢ Personnel Management
➢ Staff Training
➢ Record Keeping
➢ Preparation of Reports

EDUCATION

Culinary Arts
International Culinary Academy—Pittsburgh, Pennsylvania

Winner Institute of Arts & Sciences—Transfer, Pennsylvania

Food Competitions and Food Shows

Liberal Arts
Criminal Justice/ Pre-Law Course Work Kent State University— Champion, Ohio

EXECUTIVE CHEF / PERSONAL CHEF / CATERING

- Select menu items with an eye toward quality, variety, availability of seasonal foods, popularity of past dishes and likely number of customers. Collaborate with owner(s) to plan menus to attract specific clientele.

- Estimate food consumption. Select and appropriately price menu items to cost-effectively use food and other supplies.

- Oversee food preparation and cooking, examining quality and portion sizes to ensure dishes are prepared and garnished correctly and in a timely manner.

- Proficient knowledge of computer programs, especially to create menus; analyze recipes to determine food, labor and overhead costs; and calculate prices for various dishes.

- Hardworking, self-motivated individual with proven record of responsibility. Equally effective working independently as well as in a team effort. Work well with a wide range of people at all levels; comfortable leading, collaborating or training.

- Able to view situations/issues in a positive way and propose solutions to streamline operations. Organized and detail-oriented. Identify and resolve challenges using available resources.

- Effective communicator. Monitor actions of employees to ensure health and safety standards are maintained. Represent an organization in a professional manner and appearance.

- Receptive to relocation.

EXPERIENCE

EXECUTIVE CHEF, Monte Cello's—*Sharon, Pennsylvania*
SOUS CHEF, Mr. D's Food Fair—*Brookfield, Ohio*
KITCHEN MANAGER, Sidetrack Inn—*Warren, Ohio*
STORE MANAGER, Pit Stop Pizza—*Cortland, Ohio*
GRILL AND SAUTÉ CHEF, Radisson Hotel—*Sharon, Pennsylvania*
PREP CHEF, Avalon Inn—*Howland, Ohio*
ASSISTANT MANAGER, Moovies, Inc.—*Cortland, Ohio*
PERSONAL SECURITY TECHNICIAN, Independent Contractor—*various locations*

MILITARY

Military Police, 1984–1987, Honorable Discharge
United States Marine Corp.

90

Jane Roqueplot, Sharon, Pennsylvania

As a printout from a color printer, this resume is two-color. The contact information, section headings, and round bullets are dark blue. The arrow-tip bullets are white over blue.

KRISTOPHER ROWLING

555 LAMIRADA DRIVE
HIGHLANDS RANCH, CO 00000 • KROWLING13@AOL.COM • (000) 000-0000
(000) 000-0000

ASPIRING EXECUTIVE CHEF WITH MORE THAN 19 YEARS OF CULINARY EXPERIENCE AND EXCELLENT MANAGEMENT SKILLS

SUMMARY OF QUALIFICATIONS

- 19 years of experience in culinary field. Expertise in classical cuisine.
- Strong management experience.
- Proven background in increasing covers and check averages.
- Considerable experience in ordering, inventory and costing, with improvements made that reduce waste and increase revenues.
- Consistently create innovative menus.

EDUCATION

CAT CERTIFIED THREE-YEAR APPRENTICESHIP PROGRAM, Los Angeles, CA
Century Plateau Hotel
Chef Michel Hofbrau, CMC
Certificates from CAT, Westin Hotels and State of California, 1995

California Certified Postsecondary Culinary Instructor, 1995

Nutrition Training—ACF approved, 1990

CULINARY ARTS CENTER, San Mateo, CA
Chef Robert Covey, CEC, CCE, ACC
Certificate, 1989

PROFESSIONAL EXPERIENCE

TONY'S ITALIAN RESTAURANT, Breckenridge, CO   02/02–present
Chef for Italian restaurant with 85 seats
Owner Mark Edison

- Supervise staff of 10, report directly to owner.
- Increased check average by almost $3.00 per person.
- Lowered labor costs by 15%.
- Accountable for all ordering, inventory and costing.
- Provided innovative menu development by standardizing recipes and establishing portion control.
- Instituted fundamental changes to reduce costs and waste, resulting in significant changes to bottom line.

BLUE RIVER GRILL, Jackson's Hole, WY   5/00–2/02 & 7/96–7/97
Sous Chef for American & Italian restaurant with 120 seats
Chef Drew Pike & Chef Kevin Medley

- Directed staff of 15, reported to chef.
- Initiated yield tests that changed New York steak cut, saving $2.40 per serving.
- Analyzed inventory and costing procedures, resulting in improved systems.
- Instrumental in opening of new restaurant, including menu development.
- Responsible for prep and line supervision and staff training.

91

Michele Angello, Aurora, Colorado

Education and the names of "chefs studied under" are important in the field of hospitality, even when a candidate like this one has had extensive experience as an Executive Chef. The writer therefore placed Education after the Summary of Qualifications and before Professional

KRISTOPHER ROWLING

PAGE 2

ASPEN RIDGE RESORT, Aspen, CO   3/99–5/00
Executive Sous Chef for Ski In/Ski Out Resort
Chef Mark Edison
- Oversaw crew of 25, reported to chef and Food & Beverage Director.
- Increased covers from average of 175 to 250 by improving staff training and designing more efficient menu.
- Supervised banquet preparation, in addition to restaurant and skier cafeteria.
- Introduced creative printed daily menus that featured daily specials.

COPPER COWBOY STEAKHOUSE, Jackson's Hole, WY   9/97–2/99
Sous Chef for Steakhouse with 75 seats
Chef Adrian Dunne
- Supervised crew of 6, reported to owner/chef.
- Created and produced daily specials.
- Accountable for ordering, prep and line during service.

Previous experience includes 11 years of increasingly responsible positions as Cook, Banquet Saucier/Apprentice, Chef de Partie and Sous Chef at such establishments as the Cheyenne Supper Club, the Century Plateau Hotel, Los Angeles International Culinary Institute, Los Angeles Country Club, Citrus and Hyden Grand Champions.

AWARDS & HONORS

General Foods Recipe Contest, Winner
CAT National Apprentice of the Year, Top Ten Finalist
Los Angeles Salon Culinaire, 1st Place Scholarship Award & Top Apprenticeship Honors

COMPUTER SKILLS

Microsoft Word, Works and Excel

REFERENCES AVAILABLE UPON REQUEST

Experience. Boldfacing makes it easy to spot the certifications and the restaurants served. Bullets in the Experience section point to responsibilities and achievements.

MAURICE K. DONOFRIO

66 ADAMS STREET, BROOKVILLE, NY 55555 ● 555-555-5555 ● CHEFMAURICE@MAIL.COM

EXECUTIVE CHEF
FOOD SERVICE OPERATIONS MANAGEMENT

Accomplished and extensive culinary and management career of twenty years. Directed high-volume restaurant and catering operations. Strong leadership and management qualifications combined with interpersonal and team-building skills. Significant contributor to cost reductions and profit growth through productivity, operational efficiencies, and quality improvements.

Expertise includes:

- Food & Beverage Cost Controls
- Procurement & Vendor Relations
- Inventory Management
- Efficiency Improvements
- Quality Assurance & Control

- Kitchen Staffing & Training
- Special-Events Management
- Renovations & Capital Projects
- County Health Code Compliance
- Nutritional, Dietary, Ethnic & Organic Cooking

PROFESSIONAL EXPERIENCE

EXECUTIVE CHEF   2000–Present
Carrie's, Woodbury, NY

Oversee all food operations of a 100-seat restaurant, on- and off-premises catering service, gourmet deli, and bakery.

- Plan menus and create innovative food selections. Oversee all details to ensure quality.
- Reduced food expenses 25–30% through effective price negotiations with vendors and improved inventory management and control. Consolidated procurement activities and reduced vendor accounts from 12 to 5. Secured more favorable delivery schedules and enhanced quality of provisions.
- Hire, train, schedule, and supervise a kitchen staff of 20. Provide dotted-line supervision to a waitstaff of 45.
- Optimize work flow by regularly evaluating individual and team productivity and modifying staff responsibilities as needed.
- Conduct performance evaluations, motivate staff, and provide opportunities for advancement.
- Increase staff retention by encouraging camaraderie and fostering a pleasant work environment.
- Assisted with a kitchen renovation and upgrade. Evaluated alternative plans and selected appliances and major kitchen items.
- Set standards for food and kitchen operations. Passed all county health code inspections.

EXECUTIVE CHEF   1990–2000
The Watermill, Nesconset, NY

Directed on- and off-premises catering events for this top Long Island catering establishment serving groups of up to 600.

- Planned and designed menus for breakfasts, brunches, luncheons, and dinners.
- Cut food costs approximately 25%.
- Enhanced food preparation efficiency by providing comprehensive staff training.

Continued...

92

MJ Feld, Huntington, New York

The challenge was to tell about each past job without being repetitive. Using a functional format (merely listing the workplaces in one part of the resume and summarizing elsewhere the candidate's common activities) was unsatisfactory because it was important to indicate

MAURICE K. DONOFRIO

EXECUTIVE CHEF, **The Watermill,** *Continued*

- Handled and coordinated procurement activities, cooking, and assembly of catered orders.
- Instituted food protection/sanitation program for all cooking and food preparation activities.
- Participated in philanthropic functions for Save Our Strength and other local charities.
- Assisted with a $300,000 construction project providing input for kitchen layout and equipment.
- Supervised 7–15 direct reports.

PRIOR CULINARY EXPERIENCE

SOUS CHEF   1987–1989
Muttontown Country Club, Muttontown, NY

Handled menu planning, cooking, station work, and ice carvings for this full-service golf and country club with several food service facilities on its grounds. Ran main kitchen in chef's absence.

EVENING A LA CARTE CHEF   1986–1987
Weisbord Inn, Southampton, NY

Created innovative nightly specials and directed menu planning and food preparation for this German restaurant. Cooked up to 300 meals nightly.

SOUS CHEF   1984–1986
The Bay Club, Huntington, NY

Gained extensive experience under the tutelage of a fine European-trained chef. Supervised a kitchen staff of 8–10.

EDUCATION / AWARDS

ASSOCIATE OF ARTS, CULINARY ARTS
Le Cordon Bleu Program Diploma
Atlantic Culinary Academy, Dover, NH

PROFESSIONAL AFFILIATIONS

American Culinary Federation (ACF)
International Chef Association Federation (ICAF)

ADDITIONAL

Several first and second place awards for cooking

pertinent information about each establishment (the number of seats, type of food served, and so on). The writer made certain that the information about each workplace was different—precisely to avoid repetition.

NATHAN PAGETTE

9 Lehigh Valley Road • Easton, PA 18100
610 999 5555 • pagette@myemail.com

Sous Chef with diverse experience spanning eighteen years in the culinary industry. Seeking opportunity to contribute to a successful upscale dining operation. Core competencies:

- Goal-oriented & dedicated
- Creative & energetic
- Relationship building & management
- Strong business operations skills

PROFESSIONAL EXPERIENCE

SOUS CHEF & FOOD PRODUCTION MANAGER *[five years]*

Jacobsburg Inn at Jacobsburg State Park — Nazareth, PA [2000–present]

Fine-dining establishment seating 150 and serving three meals daily spring through fall. Former estate of the Henry family, the Inn also contains 10 guest rooms. At 1300 acres, the park incorporates the Jacobsburg Historical District.

- Manage daily kitchen operations and staff of 20 (line chefs, pantry, and utility), including hiring, training, and discipline to ensure highest quality of product and presentation
- Participate in planning with Executive Chef and General Manager
- Jointly accountable for special catering events, including banquets, receptions, an annual 5K race, and picnics serving as many as 300 on-site and within the park
- Oversee limited room service to on-site guests
- Heavily involved in inventory and ordering
- Implement and maintain food cost control
- Open and close the Inn in the spring and fall, respectively

Achievements:

▶ Reduced food costs by 13%
▶ Developed menu items and specialties in response to patrons' requests and to effectively use inventory
▶ Identified and implemented measures that have noticeably improved sanitation
▶ Enhanced employee morale by modeling a positive attitude and resolving problems quickly

AMFAC, Yellowstone National Park Lodges — WY [1997–2000]

The largest concessionaire for national parks in the U.S. Assignments included three seasons at Yellowstone National Park (Wyoming) with six restaurants and lodges and winters at Everglades National Park (Florida) operating one lodge and restaurant located 70 miles within the park. Yellowstone is notable for the rich cultural and international diversity of both employees and guests.

- At Yellowstone, supervised the seasonal opening and closing of all facilities, which spanned from outdoor, campfire-type cooking to cafeteria operations and semi-fine dining, one serving 5,000 plates per day from the largest kitchen in the U.S.
- During tourist seasons at Yellowstone, assigned to a semi-fine dining operation (two different restaurants during tenure there)

93

Salome A. Farraro, Mount Morris, New York

This Sous Chef was working at a respected inn in a large state park. He wanted to relocate out of state and find an upscale dining operation within or outside a park environment. The writer showcased the applicant's achievements in managing food production and the range

AMFAC continued:
- In Everglades, oversaw a la carte services provided by the park's sole restaurant and lodge, which offered seating for 190 and three meals daily
- Planned, coordinated, and executed all kitchen operations, including staffing, inventory, cost control, and food preparation and presentation

Achievements:
- ▶ Consistently controlled food costs and achieved the company's lowest costs at Grant Village (Yellowstone)
- ▶ Built and led successful teams of diverse individuals who positively contributed to each restaurant's reputation

FIRST COOK *[eleven years]*

Fairlawn Country Club — Akron, OH [1994–1997]
Chili's — Cuyahoga Falls, OH [1994–1997]
Steak & Ale — Akron, OH [1991–1994]
Red Lobster — Akron, OH [1978–1983]

SALES REPRESENTATIVE & SERVICE MANAGER *[eight years]*

Pagette Construction Machine Company — Akron, OH [1983–1991]

This John Deere franchise was a family operation, started in 1941, and was purchased by the Deere Corporation in 1991. During tenure here, the company experienced rapid growth, expanding from one to three locations as one of Deere's top U.S. dealers.

- After learning the business in the Parts Department, promoted to Service Manager in 1985, supervising 12 mechanics
- Advanced to outside Sales role for all government accounts in a five-county territory
- Managed entire bid process, solicitations, and negotiations
- Built and maintained relationships with decision makers that resulted in per-item sales ranging from $40K to $100K

EDUCATION & PROFESSIONAL DEVELOPMENT

Course work toward Bachelor of Fine Arts, Business Administration: Ohio State University — Akron OH; two years

Certifications:
- Trainer & Safe Food Practices — Servsafe
- Food Safety & Sanitation — Dade County, Florida, & State of Wyoming

Extensive Management & Operations training throughout career

of restaurants he cooked for and managed. A large portion of a Sous Chef's job is to manage back-end operations. To reinforce his management abilities, the writer brought in earlier experience from a family business.

Jean Paul Rosseau, Chef

53 Goodfood Street
Seattle, WA 98122
206-888-1234 Cell
ccuisine1@yahoo.com

Objective: Head Chef for a high-volume corporate kitchen

Experience

HEAD CHEF ▪ **Murphy's,** Seattle, WA Opened December 2002–Present
Hired for ability to control food costs and construct a well-priced Northwest cuisine dinner menu for this neighborhood restaurant and nightclub. Rehired entire crew. Created first profitable month for restaurant 04/03.

HEAD CHEF ▪ **Tapatia** ▪ **La Place,** Seattle, WA   07/01–12/02
Spanish Tapa Neighborhood Café ▪ French Bistro
Rated "Top 10 Restaurant" —Seattle Dining Guide

Retained to develop tapa-based menu for Tapatia. Breakup between owners caused birth of La Place. Set up kitchen, hired a 4-person team, developed menu and handled all buying and planning, growing business from 80 to 120 entrees nightly in first six months. Trained Sous Chef from ground floor.

- Transitioned Spanish restaurant to a French bistro, receiving rave reviews.
- Delivered classic French dishes for a reasonable price (average entrée: $16).
- Grew loyal clientele on strength of "special sheet" offering upscale entrées at well-valued prices ($19–$25).
- Features included venison chops, steaks with Roquefort, halibut cheeks and rack of lamb. Served breakfast, lunch, brunch and dinner.

HEAD CHEF ▪ **L'Opera Cafe,** Seattle, WA   06/00–07/01
High-Volume French Bistro
Selected "100 Favorite Restaurants" —The Weekly, *2001*

Developed a well-trained kitchen staff that could surmount any theater rush. Served 100 covers in an hour, providing high-quality, fast-serve, full-course dinners to patrons of the neighboring Seattle Opera House prior to show time. Managed 2 salad chefs, a grill and a fryer chef. Handled all sauté and expediting tasks. Tapped by owner to create Spanish menu for new Tapatia venture.

- Reduced food costs from 30% to 25%.
- Adjusted scheduling, cutting staffing costs by 30%.
- Solved prior walkout problem 100%, serving all theatergoers promptly.
- Cut food and labor costs by 10% and increased sales by 20%. Went from 80 people nightly to 120 people nightly.

EXECUTIVE SOUS CHEF ▪ **The Marina Resort** ▪ **Mariner Restaurant** ▪ **Hyatt Resorts** ▪ **Hyatt Casa Marina & Resort,** Boca Raton, FL 09/99–06/00
Brunch Chef 09/99–12/99

Promoted to P.M. Chef in 3 months, overseeing a $.5M banquet kitchen, a full-service fine-dining restaurant and room service for a 150-room hotel. Completed formal hotel management training course. Handled full P&L for an $8M budget, hiring and supervision of a 15-person staff, menu planning, presentation and food quality assurance, purchasing and inventory and kitchen efficiency. Recreated historic 1950 upscale beach restaurant in location where four restaurants had previously failed. Established a solid local reputation in a tourist town as a quality place to eat. Did more with less, upgrading formula menu

★ Qualifications ★

20+ years of experience in country clubs, bistros, resorts and hotels, and high-volume fine dining. Full P&L for $8M budget. Proven trainer and leader. Record of creating profits for new/stagnant ventures.

Versatile and resourceful Chef, creating exciting, cost-effective menus, including Caribbean, Italian, Northwest, Spanish, Classic French and Fusion bistro fare.

★ Reviews ★

Murphy's
"Murphy's: great food at a great price" —Rave review, *The Weekly,* 2003

★ - ★ - ★ - ★ - ★

La Place
"Far from concept dining, La Place is ideal for any neighborhood. It serves espresso and morning pastries (not to mention satisfying pear tarts for dessert)....There is a French spin on eggs for brunch, quiche and a well-respected bouillabaisse for dinner—all without pretense or stuffiness. I hope more restauranteurs follow suit."
—The Weekly, 2001

★ - ★ - ★ - ★ - ★

The Mariner Restaurant
"Chef Jean Paul Rosseau has been around Boca Raton for years.... Rosseau's flare for turning ordinary dishes into tasty meals is unchanged.... Rosseau specializes in Conch-based entrees and Caribbean crab cakes."

—The *Boca Raton Citizen,* May 21, 2000

★ - ★ - ★ - ★ - ★

94

Alice Hanson, Seattle, Washington

A unique design, together with different levels of shading, sets this resume apart. Other original design elements are the staggered horizontal lines and the use of rows of five-pointed stars as dividers. The use of stars picks up on the five-star *Mobil Travel Guide* rating on page 2. Important

JEAN PAUL ROSSEAU, CHEF

EXPERIENCE (continued)

EXECUTIVE SOUS CHEF ▪ **The Marina Resort** ▪ **Mariner Restaurant** ▪ **Hyatt Resorts** ▪ **Hyatt Casa Marina & Resort** (continued)

to include fresh items, polenta, tuna and a 16 oz. steak for an average $16.95 entrée price. Grew local reputation for outstanding specials: Featured steak au poivre, rack of lamb and higher-end specials to attract a better clientele.

- Consistently delivered "four-star" presentations at a "two-star" restaurant.
- Received champagne toast by GM for achieving first $1M month and first profitable year for restaurant in ten years.
- Increased revenues per hotel guest: Average guest started "eating in" at the hotel restaurants at least three times a week.
- Decreased food costs 10% while increasing quality.
- Grew thriving banquet business based on local reputation.

CHEF / OWNER ▪ **Café Cuba Viva,** Boca Raton, FL   05/96–09/99
Ten-percent owner of a Caribbean café that introduced conch dishes to Boca Raton. Ran kitchen, including hiring, food costing, inventory and all aspects of kitchen efficiency. Served 200 diners, realizing $4,000–$5,000 nightly.

Mid-priced menu featured sautéed conch with fresh pineapple and ginger, conch piccata, steak-fried Martinique, calypso suite chicken, grilled pork tenderloin with cimicurri sauce, Barbados-style fried fish and a full range of appetizers. Bar featured authentic Cuban mojitos/Caribbean cocktails.

- Retained food and labor costs between 25–28% of overall revenues.
- Opened restaurant from ground floor, breaking even in a year.
- Promoted restaurant on local cable channel, quickly building clientele.

CHEF ▪ **Café Soleil,** Boca Raton, FL   10/93–05/96
Working chef handling all menu planning, personnel scheduling, food ordering and inventory. Introduced gallettes, creating $6,500 daily revenue and 350-order business with lines outside from 7 a.m.–3p.m. daily.

- Profitably introduced dinner menu to a "breakfast-lunch" tourist café.

CHEF ROUNDSMAN ▪ **La Belle Chateau,** Boca Raton, FL 09/92–09/93
★★★★★ Mobil Travel Guide. *Repeatedly listed as "Top Ten Restaurant."*
Pastry Chef 09/92–10/92

Classic French and Italian 150-seat fine-dining restaurant in a 1920 mansion, featuring a Grand Menu with 2 fixed seatings at 6 and 9:30 p.m.

- Formally trained to expedite a 10-person line. Maintained quality, handled large volumes yet always presented consistent quality.

NIGHT SOUS CHEF ▪ **Café Fleur,** Boca Raton, Florida 07/89–07/90
Nationally famous French restaurant

- Worked for chef trained by Paul Bocuse.
- Offered full chef position.

BANQUET CHEF ▪ **Alder Heights Golf Club,** Sarasota, Florida
Banquet Chef—Beach Grill ▪ High-end poolside banquets and events.

★ Reviews ★

Café Cuba Viva
"Rosseau fuses Indian, French and Spanish flavors to create an exciting café….Café Cuba features a nice mix of flavors and textures, perfectly fresh and attractively presented at a fair price. The appetizer list is simply delightful…." —*Boca Raton News,* 1997

★ - ★ - ★ - ★ - ★

La Belle Chateau
"The food is a throwback to the time when elegance was synonymous with French…. The kitchen emphasizes presentation….I came to La Belle Chateau fearful of pretentiousness….I leave having savored well-prepared foods with roots in the past. It is a pleasant relaxed event that comes at a high—but not unconscionable—price."

—Food review, *Florida Sentinel,* 1993

★ - ★ - ★ - ★ - ★

Education
Culinary Arts Degree
(French College 3 years)
Vannes, France

Apprenticeship: Le Meaban, Baden, France

Engagements in France
Charcuterie (Lyon)
First Cook, Garde Mgr.

Venezia Restaurant
Versaille, France
Chef de Partie Saucier

The Red Door Restaurant
Vannes, Brittany
First Cook, Saucier,
Garde Manager

---

to this resume is the use of italic. Note where it appears: in the contact information, in ratings comments in the Experience section, and in the review excerpts in the right columns of both pages.

PAUL M. BEATTY

23 Gates Road
Quincy, MA 55555
(555) 555-5555

CHEF/PRODUCTION MANAGER

Highly qualified and creative chef with more than 15 years of professional experience in managing, organizing, and executing the full spectrum of intensive catering in elite private boarding schools, college environments, and prestigious corporations. A successful and dedicated professional whose top concern is quality and client service while respecting budget mandates. Associate Degree in Culinary Arts.

- ▶ Managed catering teams in high-volume, fast-paced, multiunit facilities.
- ▶ Developed and executed record-breaking fund-raising and special-event dinners.
- ▶ Hired, trained, and supervised back-house operations and total food service staff.
- ▶ Traveled extensively to solve problems and troubleshoot in various locations.

PROFESSIONAL EXPERIENCE

NOVEAU INTERNATIONAL
An international food service management and public restaurant company with 600 institutional accounts generating revenues of $750 million.

Chef/Production Manager, Nichols Brown School, Nichols, MA	1999–2004
Regional Executive Chef, Plymouth Academy, Plymouth, MA	1996–1999
Regional Executive Chef, Massachusetts State College, Boston, MA	1992–1996

Chef/Production Management
- Oversaw an annual food budget of $800,000 with complete responsibility for all aspects of menu planning, preparation, presentation, special events, inventory, and purchasing.
- Managed all back-house operations and the coordination of buffet and banquet setups, maximizing kitchen productivity and staff performance while ensuring quality control and minimizing waste.
- Created and developed exciting new menus for special events, such as President's luncheons and banquets, Trustees' dinners, Chamber of Commerce breakfasts, and Alumni weekends.
- Increased client sales by marketing and promoting new accounts and making presentations of new, creative setup styles and menus to prospective clients.
- Supervised and implemented fund-raising events, organizing and coordinating multiple banquets and menus simultaneously, always meeting time requirements.

Personnel Management
- Managed food service production staff of 25 cooks and crew serving meals to 1200+ people daily.
- Trained and supervised new and existing culturally diverse staff to meet and exceed company standards of performance while conforming to strict procedures of safety, sanitation, and storage.
- Solved problems by troubleshooting existing accounts, traveling to facilities at various locations to assist in management and production.
- Initiated and promoted relationship building with all departments, collaborating and advising them in planning special events and menus.

95

Carol Nason, Groton, Massachusetts

The writer wanted to give this Chef/Production Manager "an aura of creativity," so she used at the top a food graphic that would appeal to vision and taste. Horizontal lines enclose the section

PAUL M. BEATTY – Page Two

SANTORINI FOOD SERVICE CORPORATION
A national food service management and public restaurant company generating revenues of $300M.

Chef, Prudential Travelers Insurance Company, Boston, MA	1990–1992
Chef/Supervisor, Rhodes Investment International, Boston, MA	1985–1990

- Supervised and implemented the setup and operation of cafeteria food line, serving more than 2,000 employees extensive luncheon menus within a two-hour time span.
- Scheduled, coordinated, and monitored staff assignments for back-house and dining room.
- Catered and organized special-event banquets and luncheons for executive staff and guests.
- Launched and developed a new menu for "Health Thyself" program, an awareness program for healthy eating that was highly praised and very successful.

EDUCATION

Associate Degree in Culinary Arts
Culinary Institute of New York, Lake Park, New York
Graduated 1985

PROFESSIONAL TRAINING

Cambridge Culinary Institute, Cambridge, MA
Food Show and Competition Buffet Presentations
Restaurant Desserts

National Hotel & Motel Association
Human Relations and Supervisory Development

National Institute for Food Service Administration
Applied Food Service Sanitation

headings and thus make them more noticeable. After an opening profile, triangular bullets point to key activities. In the Professional Experience section, bold italic statements describe each company, and bullets point to a mix of responsibilities and achievements. Training appears at the end.

Jay T. Mooney

520 Locust St., Apt. 2B, Columbus, OH 43215
Phone: (513) 294-2813 | jmooney@jitaweb.com

Restaurant & Retail Manager of a Multimillion-Dollar Operation
Personnel Management and Training / Multi-Shift / Facility Operations
History of Cutting Food Expenses, Labor Costs, and Shrinkage

Hospitality manager with an extensive background working within the food industry, including a retail operation. Track record of increased company revenues and customer satisfaction levels matched by a decrease in monthly overhead, food expenses, and labor costs. Handle all business logistics, from comparing daily revenues to sales quotas and workforce scheduling to securing customer satisfaction.

EDUCATION

A.A.S., Hotel and Restaurant Management, 1982
State University of New York (SUNY), Plattsburgh, NY

Certificate, Safety Practices for General Industry, 1993
OSHA Training Institute, New York Education Center

KEY ABILITIES

Personnel—Scheduling · Staffing · Work Flow Optimization · Employee Training & Supervision · Labor Relations · Turnover Reductions · Employee Evaluations

Operations—Restaurant Design & Layout · Floor Plan Optimization · Stock Levels · Vendor Relations · On-site Training · Waste Reduction

Financial—Goal Setting · Profit & Loss Statements · Weekly & Monthly Forecasting · Budgeting · Cash Management · Cost Avoidance · Operating Expenses · Payroll Analysis

Business Development—Staff Levels · Customer Satisfaction · Start-up / Grand Opening · Market Share Expansion · Safety Management

PROFESSIONAL EXPERIENCE

SENIOR ASSOCIATE MANAGER, 1998–2003
Rosewood Restaurant, Toledo and Columbus, OH
Oversaw a start-up location from the preliminary details to include staffing and scheduling for this restaurant and retail operation. Hired, trained, and scheduled up to 350 employees consisting of shift supervisors and support personnel (cleaning crew and stock personnel) manning $350,000 in yearly inventory. Tracked and compared all financial numbers, from retail to food sales. Concentrated employee training on providing 100% customer care to ensure a solid return client base. Checked/ordered stock and monitored levels closely to curtail employee theft and shrinkage issues.

- Promoted to senior status and transferred to the Columbus store for the grand opening and to manage the operation; opened one of the most successful operations in company's history with $323,000 in sales the first week, serving 28,000 people

- Assisted with new store location, from initial setup and budgeting to store stock levels, staffing requirements, and grand-opening event

- Selected to revisit and cut costs at the Toledo location; reduced food cost from 39.2% to 26.7% by implementing proper food preparation procedures and adequate food proportions while lowering labor cost by 5.8% and increasing staff levels by 48% after utilizing employment retention practices

- Trained employees on all aspects of the facilities operations: OSHA rules and regulations, Dept. of Health guidelines, HAACP, guest services, suggestive selling, safety and sanitation procedures, serve safe, workplace issues, and workman's compensation

96

Teena L. Rose, Huber Heights, Ohio

A thin horizontal line under each main section heading helps make apparent the resume's overall design. Boldfacing directs attention to the target occupation, the section headings, the degree and certification, the skill areas under Key Abilities, and the positions held. The key abilities are

Mooney, Jay T.

- Mentored other facility managers and supervisors on dealing with day-to-day concerns that plagued them and hindered revenues

- Added 6% to overall revenues by cutting labor, supplies, and food; reducing shrinkage; and conducting seminars that taught house staff about up-selling to guests, the benefit of knowing the products, and being conscious of politeness and common courtesies

- Worked with third-party contractors, including the negotiation of details surrounding contracts for landscaping, fresh produce, linen, equipment, and cleaning supplies

- Assisted with the creation and implementation of a "Best Practices" program that trained staff members on providing above-average guest services that also increased productivity; resulted in a sales record of $2,900 in sales per hour

- Reduced customer complaints by 68% at the Toledo store

- Utilized area media forums for grand openings and participated in a breakfast kick-off with community members and the mayor

CHEF, 1998
Juneau Cruise Ships, Juneau, AK
Six-month assignment aboard *Adventure Alaska* as a chef to prepare gourmet meals for 7- to 10-day cruises leaving the coast of Alaska. Addressed and attended to all aspects of kitchen management, from shopping list and meal preparation to staffing and management relations to ensure guests received high-end treatment. Prepared meals from scratch using top-quality and the freshest ingredients that "wowed" passengers.

- Promoted to chef (from assistant chef) within 2 weeks of joining the ship

DIRECTOR, FOOD AND BEVERAGE, 1991–1998
East Coast Parks and Resorts, Columbia, SC
Secured a number of promotions, from bar and pizza manager to a food and beverage management position and finally to a director position. Managed and supervised 80–190 employees at a food and beverage facility with up to $500,000 in monthly sales.

- Authored the Loss Control Program that focused on, informed, and trained on-site personnel in key OSHA safety standards

SOFTWARE

MS Word, MS Publisher, MS Excel, Lotus Notes, WordPerfect, SYSFLEX, Micros, Labor Pro, GS Order

presented as scannable keywords. In the Professional Experience section, both the paragraphs and the bulleted items under each workplace contain achievements as well as responsibilities.

Richard Johnson

2222 Indiana Avenue
Ocean Shores, WA 98343

(360) 888-1234
rjohnson3241@aol.com

GENERAL MANAGER
Hospitality – Class 3 Casinos – AAA Hotels – Fine Dining – New Venture Start-ups

Senior Hospitality Manager with more than 10 years of broad-based leadership history in gaming, luxury hotel management and fine-dining operations. *Strengths:* Finding efficiencies, motivating teams and creating on-time results.

Fast-track promotion record through all aspects of leading and operating large service-oriented businesses. Hands-on management style. Multitask easily. Strong supervisory, analytical, computer, and process-improvement skills.

Highly effective leader, guiding all business cycles: start-up, turnaround and stabilization. Proven ability to streamline systems, drive revenues, shrink staff turnover, build customer loyalty and restore profit centers. Expertise includes:

- **Design & Construction**
- **Policies, Staffing & Performance**
- **Food & Beverage**
- **Start-ups & Turnarounds**
- **Facilities & Security**
- **Regulatory Compliance**
- **IT & Communications Systems**
- **Marketing & Community Relations**
- **Vendor Management / Full P&L**

Professional Experience

HIGHLAND CASINO, Ocean Shores, WA   2000–present
Director, Support Services

Retained as part of a 5-person board and fast-track senior start-up team to plan, budget, design, license, contract, and open a $10 million class 3 casino in less than eight months.

Report to Chairman of the Board. Oversee all non-revenue functions (Housekeeping, Engineering, IT, Security, and Human Resources) for the largest casino in the state, operating 300 slot machines, 6 gaming tables, a full restaurant, a lounge with tabletop games and a bar with live entertainment 3 times a week.

Facilities, Security, IT & Construction Management: Selected vendors and negotiated contracts. Originated and monitored project budgets. Acted as sole point of contact for more than 50 vendors and contractors during construction phase, ensuring quality construction, promised price, and timely delivery of all construction services, communication systems (IT, security, telephones and cameras), hard lines, furniture and fixtures. Arranged construction and configuration for a 5,000-stall parking lot.

Regulatory Compliance: Quickly learned requirements posed by 3 casino regulators: National Indian Gaming Association (NIGA), Washington State Gambling Commission, and the Quilcene Tribe. Responded to 3 sets of requirements, writing policy and procedures manuals for each regulatory body. Addressed requests for further information, made revisions and successfully processed all licensing requirements in a tight 6-month period.

Staffing, Leadership & Human Resources: Manage 3 supervisors and 2 managers, overseeing a 46-person staff. Monitored the hiring for all personnel, pre-employment testing and establishment of all human resources procedures and policies. Trained all staff members in accordance with Casino Procedures Manual and Washington State Gambling Commission rules. Maintain positive relationships with the community and local law enforcement bodies.

- Handled buildout and securing of entitlements for $10 million casino, opening on time and under budget.

- Authored Standard Operating Procedures manual for casino, complying with 3 regulatory bodies.

- Commended by state as being the only casino in recent history to achieve regulatory review, compliance and licensing as scheduled and budgeted. Performed role as part of a tightly-knit 5-person management team.

97

Alice Hanson, Seattle, Washington

The contact information is presented in a balanced format, and the profile includes bold and bulleted areas of expertise. Boldfacing makes it easy to spot the positions held at the two workplaces.

Professional Employment (continued)

EXECUTIVE SUITES HOTEL, Seattle, WA   1992–2000

Privately held, AAA-rated, 3-star, 400-suite luxury hotel encompassing award-winning restaurant, high-energy nightclub, full-service banquet and catering facilities and 130 employees.

Assistant General Manager / Acting General Manager, 2000

Oversaw daily operations, including F&B Director and all internal financial reporting for the most profitable of 30 hotels held by Janus Capital Group in a 10-state region. Reported directly to the GM / Area Manager. Assumed decision-making and planning for facility, averaging 1 week out of every month, in GM's absence.

Accountable for revenues of $4 million, supervising performance of 10 department managers of the hotel's 12 departments, including Engineering, Housekeeping, Accounting, Front Office, Food and Beverage and Human Resources. Led by example. Built strong teams through improved recruiting and training. Complied with all local and federal laws. Managed security contracts and personnel.

Monitored and reviewed all department budget forecasts; P&L statements; STAR, promotions, marketing and sales projections; staffing plans; vendor contracts; and purchase log, inventory and expense reports. Identified and facilitated cost-saving measures with managers. Formulated short- and long-range marketing and budget plans for capital expenditures, construction / renovations and regular operations.

- Increased overall net revenues 6%, repeating 5-year record as top-producing hotel.
- Selected by Chief Operating Officer to serve on the elite Janus Capital Group Standing Committee, creating operations and food and beverage "best practice" policies for all 30 hotels.
- Reduced employee turnover 66%.
- Standardized and computerized purchase order tracking system, creating centralized managerial approval of all costs, accounting efficiencies and adherence to projected budgets.
- Incurred the fewest repair and maintenance costs company-wide.

Assistant General Manager / Food and Beverage Director, 1996–1999

Managed Food and Beverage Division, a vital profit center, producing 12% of the hotel's overall net revenues. Oversaw food service quality and profitability for 7 departments: kitchen, restaurant, lounge, banquet, comp breakfast, comp bar and suite service.

Oversaw quality and service of products within F&B outlets. Developed, marketed, rewrote and produced 8 weekly menus for restaurant, lounge and banquet service. Offered complimentary full cooked-to-order breakfast, Northwest casual fine dining, lunch and dinners in busy state-of-the-art kitchen facility.

Managed food, beverage and room items related to banquet service with banquet room that seated 350 diners, 500 theater-style, and provided 10,000 square feet of meeting space.

- Monitored food costs, producing lowest food cost budget in the company.
- Realized company's second-highest net beverage income figures for three years running.
- Increased sales 34% by upgrading menu. Won Executive Suites cuisine award for customer satisfaction.
- Contributed 60% of division's revenues by revitalizing banquet business.

Other Executive Suites positions: **Front Office Manager,** 1996; **Restaurant, Lounge and Banquet Manager,** 1993–1995; **Executive Chef,** 1993, and **Sous Chef,** 1992.

CERTIFICATIONS

Washington State Health Card Trainer   CPR Trained, July 2000   Sersafe Certified Trainer #000000000
Class 12, Class 13 Liquor Awareness Certification   Washington State Gambling Commission

EDUCATION AND TRAINING

Seattle Central Community College, Seattle, WA. Food Production Management Certificate and Hospitality Production Certificate. Programs accredited by American Culinary Federation. GPA 3.5

Activities at the casino are grouped according to underlined categories. Bulleted items throughout the Professional Experience section point to achievements, many of them quantified. The resume ends with sections on Certifications and Education and Training.

SAMUEL PECKHAM, CHME, CSP

60 Augusta Drive
Pinehurst, Ontario A1A 1A1

555.222.7777
speckham@email.com

SENIOR SALES & MARKETING EXECUTIVE
SPECIALIST IN DRIVING HOTEL & HOSPITALITY PROFITABILITY

*Business Development / Strategic Planning / Key Account Sales & Management
New-Market Development / Marketing Campaigns & Initiatives / Business Planning & Forecasting*

Dynamic sales and marketing career driving consistent revenue gains in the hotel and hospitality industry throughout Canadian and U.S. markets. Comprehensive understanding of hotel operations, sales, and profitability. Achieved strong revenue, market, and profit growth through expertise in business development, executive-level sales, and creative marketing initiatives. Extensive expertise supported by professional certification in the following:

➤ National & Executive Sales Management
➤ Hotel Management
➤ Food & Beverage Controls

➤ Hospitality Marketing
➤ Travel & Tourism
➤ Dining Room & Catering Management

★ **CERTIFIED HOSPITALITY MARKETING EXECUTIVE (CHME)** ★
★ **CERTIFIED SALES PROFESSIONAL (CSP)** ★

PROFESSIONAL EXPERIENCE

CENTENNIAL FALLS RESORT HOTEL, Niagara Falls, Ontario
(Exclusive 260-room "boutique-style" hotel and Centennial's flagship hotel in Niagara)

DIRECTOR OF SALES   May 2002–Present
Directed the strategic repositioning of the hotel following a $17 million renovation. Hired to optimize operations and rebuild the strategy to ignite growth across Domestic, Corporate, and International sales.
➤ Profiled the entire Sales Division to identify key areas for improvement and refocus areas of strength. Introduced dedicated Corporate and Domestic Sales Managers and augmented training division-wide.
➤ Developed a comprehensive AAA/CAA Travel Trade database and quickly launched a new promotion to more than 500 AAA/CAA offices across Canada and the Northeastern U.S.
➤ Redesigned all critical Corporate marketing tools and collateral materials and introduced simplified sales forms and operational contracts to focus more directly on F&B revenue protection and product upselling.
➤ Introduced a successful Preferred Rate Program with the Pinehurst Professional Sales Association (PPSA).

SELECT HOTELS INTERNATIONAL, Pleasantville, Maryland (Head Office)
(Largest international franchise hotel organization with over 5,000 locations and sales in excess of U.S. $1 billion)

NATIONAL SALES DIRECTOR—WORLDWIDE SALES   1999–2002
Selected to develop key association and consortia accounts throughout Canada and the Midwest/Western U.S. (American Express, Rosenbluth, World Travel, and Carlson Wagonlit). Scope of responsibility included all Canadian and U.S. regional sales and marketing initiatives, strategic sales and market planning, and the coordination of a team of Field Service Directors across North America.
➤ Exceeded annual revenue projection by $1 million within first 6 months.
➤ Primary accountability for $60 million CAA/AAA account, the largest single revenue-producing leisure account in the company.
➤ Developed highly successful joint marketing initiative between AAA Nebraska, AAA Colorado, and Alberta Motor Association (AMA) that increased gross room nights by 81%, increased gross revenue by 77%, and secured largest market share (14.83%) of any hotel company with AMA.
➤ AAA/AMA joint marketing initiative nominated for 3 distinguished MARQ Awards. AAA Nebraska initiative recently awarded top prize in competitive SYC&S category.
➤ Created CAA/AMA promotion that increased revenue from a 9.83% decline to a positive growth of 21.5%.
➤ Introduced two successful national marketing events designed to recognize high-performing CAA partners.
➤ Developed and produced all collateral marketing and training materials for Choice Hotels Canada.

98

Ross Macpherson, Whitby, Ontario, Canada

The writer aggressively highlighted keywords, professional certification, and expertise up front to help this Executive position himself as an expert in his field. The resume has features found in many executive resumes: relatively small print, giving the appearance of reduced leading

SELECT HOTELS CANADA, Augusta, Ontario (Head Office)
(Largest hotel franchise organization in Canada, operating 250 locations nationally under 8 leading brands.)

NATIONAL SALES MANAGER—TRAVEL INDUSTRY & CORPORATE   1997–1999

Hired to spearhead introduction and development of new corporate and consortia account portfolio, while revitalizing growth of leisure accounts nationally. Coordinated all strategic sales and marketing initiatives, market analysis, incentive management, budget planning, and management of largest-volume corporate account portfolio.

➢ Developed sales and marketing initiatives, promotions, and market education that assisted the licensee in increasing Revpar and developing yield management techniques.
➢ Personally secured 30 key corporate accounts from ground zero within 2 years.
➢ Grew major Quixstar/Amway corporate account by 2000% within 1 year.
➢ Generated exponential growth and dramatically improved product awareness within leisure market through aggressive sales and marketing strategies.

REGENCY VACATIONS, Augusta, Ontario
(Boutique travel business servicing high-end personal and corporate clients throughout Greater Niagara.)

PRINCIPAL / SALES & MARKETING DIRECTOR   1991–1997

Successfully built business from start-up into solid revenue generator with 2 years. Developed strategic direction, built infrastructure, and initiated all marketing, image development, sales, and public relations directives.

➢ Identified and capitalized on market trends through highly successful direct mail, presentations, and local promotional campaigns.
➢ Dramatically increased revenues by successfully targeting and penetrating lucrative corporate market.
➢ Grew sales from $0 to $1.5 million in less than 18 months and quickly established position as industry leader throughout Niagara.

ADDITIONAL EXPERIENCE

HOUSEWARE FINANCIAL CORP., Augusta, Ontario—**FINANCIAL ACCOUNT EXECUTIVE**   1996–1997
➢ Awarded "Top Sales" Ontario wide and ranked 3rd across Canada.
AUGUSTA COLLEGE, Augusta, Ontario—**AIRLINE TRAINING INSTRUCTOR**   1988–1995
WORLDWAYS LTD., Pinehurst, Ontario—**IN-FLIGHT SERVICE MANAGER**   1985–1991

INDUSTRY CERTIFICATION & EDUCATION

Certified Hospitality Marketing Executive (CHME) —Hospitality Sales & Marketing Association	2003
Executive Program in Sales Management—Sabbath School of Business, Yorktown University	2001
Skills for Sales Success—Pinehurst Professional Sales Association	2001
Certified Sales Professional (CSP)—Pinehurst Professional Sales Association	1999
National Professional Sales Manager Certification—Ontario Tourism Education Inc. (OTEI)	1998
Travel & Tourism—Augusta Business School	1983
Hotel Management: Food & Beverage Controls / Dining Room & Catering Management—Augusta College	1982

INDUSTRY AFFILIATIONS

Hospitality Sales & Marketing Association International (HSMAI)	2003
Canadian Hotel Marketing & Sales Executives (CHMSE)—Ontario Chapter	1998–Present
Pinehurst Professional Sales Association (PPSA)	1998–Present
Ontario Tourism Education Corp. (OTEC)—Hospitality Sales Manager Industry Evaluator	1998–Present

(less space between lines); wide lines of text; a variety of font enhancements (boldfacing, bold italic, regular italic, all caps, and small caps); horizontal lines that define main sections; and bullets pointing to many achievements.

JEFFREY W. RANDAL, JR.
555 Haleakala Street, Honolulu, Hawaii 00000
Residence: (808) 555-5555 • jwr.jr@hawaiinet.com

EXECUTIVE MANAGEMENT

More than 25 years of fine-dining restaurant, exclusive resort, and private club Operations Management experience. Guest-oriented business philosophy and focus. Assimilate to new environments quickly and thoroughly, consistently delivering top performance and providing strong leadership presence. Proven record of profitability.

• Restaurant & Club Operations	• Cost Controls Management
• Multiple-Site Operations	• Strategy Planning
• Staff Motivation & Development	• Presentations & Training
• Business Development	• Fine-Dining Ambiance
• Inventory & Purchasing	• Food & Service Quality

PROFESSIONAL HISTORY

CHIEF OPERATING OFFICER / GENERAL MANAGER   1998 to Present
THE PALMS CLUB—Honolulu, Hawaii

Oversee all operations for private beachfront club established in 1936. Currently 4,500 members, 160 employees, and annual club revenues of $11 million. Three food facilities on property with total sales of $4.2 million yearly. Active club functions every day of the year, including breakfast, lunch, dinner, private parties, and large club events.

- Reengineered expense control systems to run below budget and profitably for all 6 years at the helm.
- Increased revenues to meet operating and reserve budget without raising member fees and dues.
- Improved external and internal customer service in all aspects of operation.
- Enhanced quality, selection, and value of all food, beverages, and merchandise.
- Successfully implemented $3 million property upgrades.

DIVISION MANAGER   1994 to 1998
ABC RESTAURANT CORPORATION—Anaheim, California

Accountable for 6 restaurants in Los Angeles area for $30 million company operating dining establishments countrywide. Restaurants: *Outrigger,* Los Angeles; *Velvet Turtle,* Burbank; *Field of Dreams,* San Pedro; *The Beach,* Long Beach; *The Moon Room,* Monterey Park; *Proud Peacock,* Los Angeles International Airport.

- Steadily delivered gross profit of 10%, boosting sales during declining market.
- Reduced cost of controllables and improved manager performance.

99

Peter Hill, Honolulu, Hawaii

The challenge was to position this Hospitality Executive for a transition from Hawaii to the U.S. mainland. Hence, the profile asserts that the applicant could "assimilate to new environments quickly and thoroughly." In the Professional History section, each paragraph after the name of the

VICE PRESIDENT / GENERAL MANAGER　　　　　　　　　　　　1993 to 1994
THE VALLEY COUNTRY CLUB—Los Angeles, California

Recruited to inherit 66-year-old club after initially joining sister organization in Hawaii (The Hawaiian Club), taking over when operation began to lose members after a $14 million renovation. Extensive tennis, pool, dining room, and banquet facilities. Membership of 1,700.

- Increased annual revenues to more than $3 million, installing management controls and enhancing member amenities.
- Maintained staff level of 100+ by generating high level of team play and cohesiveness, despite front office pressure to reduce staff numbers.
- Simultaneously carried on general management responsibilities for 3,000-member Hawaiian Club.

DIRECTOR OF FOOD AND BEVERAGE　　　　　　　　　　　　1989 to 1993
THE COASTLINE RESORT—Newport Beach, California

Directed $4.5 million food and beverage operation for 350-room resort hotel. Worked closely with General Manager.

- Revamped food and beverage facilities during $23 million renovation.
- Developed new staffing guide, reducing labor costs by 32%.

VICE PRESIDENT OF FOOD AND BEVERAGE　　　　　　　　　1980 to 1989
NEWPORT BAY CLUBS—Balboa, California

Headed all food and beverage operations for the prestigious 33-year-old Sands Club. Annual sales of $4.5 million. Membership of 5,000.

ADDITIONAL EXPERIENCE

Vice President / General Manager—South Coast Fish Company
General Manager—Humpback Inn
District Manager—Specialty Enterprises / El Rancho
Airline Food and Beverage Consultant—Newport Bay Club and Southwest Airlines
Director of Restaurants and Entertainment—The Plaza Hotel
Director of Restaurants and Entertainment—Waikiki Hotel

PROFESSIONAL & COMMUNITY INVOLVEMENT

Founder of California Coast Chapter of Confre'rie de la Chaine des Rotisseurs
Advisory Board Member of Hawaii Pacific University Culinary School
Club Managers Association of America

club, restaurant, or resort indicates responsibilities, and the bulleted items are significant achievements. Boldfacing is used throughout the resume for the positions held by the candidate.

Michael J. Fisher, C.M.C.

56 Madison Avenue
Summit, New Jersey 07901
908-277-8796

Profile

Experienced Food Services Professional. Developed extensive management skills. Capable of speed and organization in a highly productive setting. Work cooperatively with a wide range of personalities. Successful executive chef and hotel/restaurant manager. Responsible for all aspects of culinary management catering to a discerning clientele. Ability to handle a multitude of details at once and meet deadlines under pressure.

Strengths and Abilities

- Profit and Loss
- Staffing and Supervision
- Forecasting

- Hotel/Restaurant Administration
- Training and Development
- Accounting and Controlling Functions

Experience

Hague Nieuw-York, New York, NY   1999–Present
Corporate Executive Chef/Promoted to General Manager

- Hague is a Dutch-style eatery that specializes in casual dining. The restaurant is part of Avanti Brands, owner of several well-known restaurant chains and the three top restaurants in London. Avanti Brands is partnered with Hague, PLC. Hired as corporate executive chef for North America. Developed key control systems and thorough inventory-control procedures.

- Responsible for the start-up of a 225-seat restaurant. Purchase all food and supplies. Manage a staff of 50 front-of-the-house, back-of-the-house, and marketing employees. Designed the facility and the kitchen, and coordinated all aspects of new construction with six professional trades during remodeling. Oversaw renovation of the entire property.

- Involved in yearly profit and loss and all financial reporting to Hague PLC, U.K., and Avanti Brands, Inc., USA. Accountable to the CEOs for accounting forecasting, projections, and cash flow. Develop all menus. Maintain a 27% cost of goods for beverages, wine and liquor, and food. The restaurant produces $4 million in yearly sales.

- Responsible for sales and marketing projections to attract target populations. Network with professional event planners to arrange major special-events functions. Involved in New York openings and premiers. Participate in large fashion shows for major designers and publishers. Oversee preparation of food for New York City food festivals.

- Travel internationally to the other locations to evaluate properties' performance. Worked in London and Dublin to facilitate a turnaround in failing restaurants. Studied Belgian cuisine in Brussels, Bruges, and Antwerp.

100

Beverly and Mitch Baskin, Marlboro, New Jersey

This resume is for an Executive Chef/General Manager. In the earlier part of his career, he was an Executive Chef, but in 1986 he assumed the dual roles of Executive Chef and Vice President of Operations. In 1990 his work shifted into management as Director of Operations of an upscale

Michael J. Fisher, C.M.C.

Achievements

- Established direct purchase from farm to restaurant from Maine and Nova Scotia.

- Presented First Friday Dinner at James Beard House.

- Worked with advertising people to market in-house beer seminars.

- Appeared on national syndicated television with Martha Stewart on NBC.

- Scheduled to appear on NBC's *Today* show to promote the restaurant and present a cooking demonstration.

- Made appearances on radio.

- Revised U.K. version of *Hague Cook Book* to include Signature Dishes Nieuw-York.

- Hague was reviewed in the *New York Times*.

Times Square Restaurant, Hoboken, NJ	1995–1999
Town Square Katering, Dover, NJ	1990–1999

Director of Operations

- Managed an upscale catering business and operated all phases of an American Cuisine theme restaurant. Obtained bookings for parties ranging from 10 to 4,000 people.

- Purchased all food and restaurant supplies. Responsible for marketing, purchasing, and directing 75+ kitchen staff, service staff, and maintenance employees.

- Combined Katering Operation still known as Town Square Katering with Times Square Restaurant (80 seats). Designed kitchen and restaurant layouts. Directed all kitchen, service, sales, and management.

- Taught Cooking School—Basic & Advanced & Pastry Courses M-W-F (weekly).

Pine Ridge Golf Course and Restaurant	1986–1989

Vice President of Operations
Executive Chef—American and International Cuisine

- Oversaw in excess of 10 department heads for both corporations. Responsible for profit and loss, including all accounting and controlling functions. Monitored capital expenditures of $350,000 with a gross of $4.5 million.

- Directed 152 employees and all administrative functions, including forecasting, budgeting, marketing, advertising, entertainment, and promotions.

- Directed a 1,000-seat banquet facility and a 165-seat a la carte restaurant. Responsible for operations of an 850-member golf club. Maintained excellent interpersonal relationships with members.

- Monitored standards of performance for all key control systems. Involved in developing a standard operations manual and employee manual.

catering business. His dual roles of Executive Chef and General Manager emerged again in 1999, and both were aspects of his career to the present. To gain a sense of his career path, you should read the resume from the end to the beginning. The Profile and Strengths and Abilities sections

Michael J. Fisher, C.M.C.   Page 3

Ordini's, Wellington, New Zealand   Prior to 1986
Executive Chef (Five-Star Rating) New Classical Cuisine
- Elevated the level of cuisine and service with a clientele including the Prime Minister, heads of state, and visiting dignitaries. Restaurant was booked 4 months in advance with a 50-seat cover.

Sheraton Corporation, *Executive Pastry Chef,* Kaanapali, Maui, Poipu Beach Kauai, Hawaii
Lahaina Yacht Club, *Executive Chef,* Lahaina, Maui, Hawaii
Summit Hotel, *Executive Chef,* Summit, New Jersey

Education

A.O.S. Culinary Institute of America, Hyde Park, NY

Awards

New Zealand Master Chef Certification
Certified Executive Chef
President, Les Amis d' Escoffier Society of New York, Inc.
Member, Société Culinaire Philanthropique De New York, Inc.

1988 NJRA Award-Winning Menus
   First Place   Best Banquet Menu
   Second Place Best a la Carte Menu

play up the person's management expertise. White space between the main sections and also between the bulleted items in the Experience section makes the layout pleasing. See Cover Letter 6.

Human Resources

Resumes at a Glance

RESUME NUMBER	LAST OR CURRENT OCCUPATION	GOAL	PAGE
101	Station Operations Supervisor	Human Resources Recruiter	201
102	Human Resources Generalist	Not specified	203

MICHELE M. CROWN

17188 Hunter Avenue, Apt. 301
Dallas, TX 77777
505.555.1212 ▪ mic1@aol.com

HUMAN RESOURCES RECRUITER

QUALIFICATIONS PROFILE

Talented professional with 16 years of proven performance recruiting, screening, and placing supervisory, customer service, and administrative candidates. Steadfastly exceed performance goals and customer service requirements. Capable communicator and high-energy motivator. Ably lead cross-functional teams.

Key Skills

✓ Recruitment & Hiring
✓ Training & Assessment

✓ Employee & Union Relations
✓ Negotiations & Collaboration

✓ Contract Interpretation
✓ Policies & Procedures

Key Talents

✓ People-Focused
✓ Confidence Builder

✓ Big-Picture Thinker
✓ Bottom-Line-Oriented

✓ Enthusiasm Creator
✓ Creative Problem Solver

RELATED SKILLS & ACHIEVEMENTS

Interviewing

- Led Supervisor Core Interviews as people services supervisor representative for 2 years, recruiting, screening, and placing candidates to fulfill corporate supervisory staffing profile.

- Personally coached 32 employees through Supervisor Core Interview process using role-playing and practice interviews.

- Conducted weekly interviews for customer service representatives and administrative assistants, recruiting, screening, and placing candidates.

Negotiation & Team Building

- Achieved 90% successful scheduling rate, interpreting and applying American flight attendant contract agreements for "win-win" results.

- Collaborated annually with union leaders to ensure effective ramp management and performance of 25 customer service employees.

- Ensured on-time flight departures for 329-flights-per-day operation by creating team environment among 7 critical departments.

Communication & Training

- Directed training team in developing new crew scheduler training program, including 6 new training modules with computer-based delivery system.

- Delivered formal 20-person classroom and on-the-job, new-hire, and in-service training for reservation sales and service representatives (RSSRs) labor force of 2000.

- Effectively disseminated timely operations and station performance information to 7 departments and 55 employees daily.

Program Management & Administration

- Managed all aspects of Airport and City Ticket Office operations over 2 years to achieve productivity and cost objectives, on-time performance, safety, security, FAA mandates, and all corporate core objectives.

- Managed promotional and customer support programs for 2 years, ensuring appropriate flight attendant staffing to maintain customer satisfaction and profitability.

101

Nick V. Marino, Bishop, Texas

This applicant received a severance package after 9/11 and wanted to transition to HR recruitment. The first page and a bit of the second page follow a functional format in detailing the person's skills and achievements. In the Qualifications Profile, check-mark bullets point to hard skills

RELATED SKILLS & ACHIEVEMENTS Continued...

Customer Service

- Selected and served successfully as customer support consultant for 2 years, providing assistance to RSSRs and customers.
- Earned solid problem-solver reputation, expeditiously resolving hundreds of customer complaints and sensitive situations to ensure customer satisfaction and on-time operations.

CAREER CHRONOLOGY

American Airlines, Nationwide Assignments, 1988–Present

Station Operations Supervisor, Dallas, TX   **1998–Present**
Direct all activities supporting 30 flights per day across 8 gates, 2 concourses, and 2 international and 4 domestic markets for a 329-flights-per-day operation. Manage 5 supervisors and 50 employees in 7 departments of cross-functional Station Operations Team. Report directly to station operations manager.

Airport Operations Supervisor, Los Angeles, CA   **1996–1998**
Directed all activities supporting an 11-flight-per-day operation across 4 gates and 2 domestic markets. Managed 55 employees in all functional areas of Airport Operations Team. Reported to Omaha city manager.

Onboard Service Crew Scheduling Coordinator, New York, NY   **1994–1996**
Managed all aspects of onboard service crew scheduling for 75% of airline, supporting entire international airport operations and hundreds of domestic airports. Reported to onboard service manager.

Sales and Services Representative Lead (Reservations), New York, NY   **1992–1994**
Oversaw 300–400 reservation agents as part of 25-person Customer Service Specialist Supervisory Team. Conducted new-hire and in-service training of sales and service representatives in 20-person classroom setting. Reported to manager of customer relations.

Lead Administrative Assistant (Revenue Accounting), New York, NY   **1988–1992**
Supervised 25 permanent and 15 contract employees for reconciliation of monthly ticket sales, performing data entry and providing various financial reports to management.

EDUCATION & RELEVANT TRAINING

Travel Degree, *Business and Communications*, McConnell Travel School, New York, NY

Business Management (various courses), International Correspondence School, New York, NY

Corporate Training
Customer Satisfaction Philosophy • United Commitment to Passenger Rights
Americans with Disabilities Act • Cultural Leadership • Team Leader Incumbent

COMPUTER SKILLS

Motorola Computer System ▪ Lotus 1-2-3 ▪ Microsoft Word, Excel, & PowerPoint ▪ Unimatic ▪ CMS

(key skills) and soft skills (key talents). The unbroken employment record with one airline is featured in the Career Chronology on page 2. The name in white on black makes the resume stand out even from across the room.

PHYLLIS MARTIN, PHR   (555) 555-5555
5555 Maxwell, Clearview, Texas 79000

■ QUALIFICATIONS SUMMARY ■

Results-driven human resources professional with progressive 20-year career including periodic managerial duties. Certification—Professional Human Resources. Particularly adept at training and development, safety program administration, new-hire orientations, benefits administration, and worker's compensation management. Fundraising and project management experience. Bachelor of Science degree in Occupational Education expected 2005. Other strengths include:

Open Communication	**Employee / Corporate Relations**	**Direct Problem Solving**
Leadership Development	**Negotiation / Mediation**	**Team Building**
Needs Assessment	**OSHA—Safety Awareness**	**Recruitment**
Presentations / Training	**Interviewing / Attentive Listening**	**Ethical Standards**

■ PROFESSIONAL EXPERIENCE ■

Human Resources Generalist, SUNLIT HIGH PLAINS, Panhandle, Texas   **1990–Present**

Integral team player of 5-member human resources staff overseeing personnel function for as many as 450 employees. Report to human resources manager. Recruit employees for current and future staffing requirements via local job fairs. Interview and evaluate qualified applicants; make hiring recommendations to supervisors. Deliver orientation presentations to 1–20 new hires. Establish business relationships with benefits companies and employment agencies. Calculate seasonal staffing needs.

Monitor earnings for exempt and nonexempt employees. Analyze and present statistical data via computer-generated spreadsheets and charts. Compile annual wage surveys and track turnover using HRIS technology.

Educate supervisors and employees on company benefits, policies, and procedures. Train 75% of interdepartmental positions to maximize departmental knowledge and skill. Conduct semiannual CPR classes to meet safety goals. Developed, designed, and directed entry-level MS Office computer classes.

Maintain comprehensive knowledge of Fair Labor Standards Act. Guide supervisors in disciplinary action procedures and review employee corrective action forms for compliance with company policy. Train and test supervisors to ensure EEO and ADA compliance. Abide by state and federal posting requirements. Promote safety awareness; investigate and administer worker's compensation claims; and maintain OSHA 200 Log. Govern Consolidated Omnibus Budget Reconciliation Act.

Key Achievements:
- *Earned Professional Human Resources certification.*
- *Regularly appointed to assume duties of HR manager in his absence.*
- *Instrumental in reducing accident frequency by 26% and costs by 76%.*
- *Raised $35,000 in donations as chair of 2000 Children's Miracle Network (CMN) Committee.*
- *Planned and organized annual Halloween event that raised $4,000 for CMN.*
- *Developed, organized, and implemented first Country for Kids Concert for CMN.*

Human Resources / Payroll Administrator, AGRESEARCH, Panhandle, Texas   **1984–1990**
Promoted to human resources / payroll administrator in 1989. Facilitated new-hire orientations and benefit classes; directed health, safety, and unemployment compensation programs; assisted senior leaders in developing federal and state employee compliance programs; and conducted interviews for general administration department.

Began as assistant controller, maintaining accounts payable / receivable and controlling vehicle registration.

102

Edith A. Rische, Lubbock, Texas

This HR Professional had extensive experience and responsibilities in her field. To avoid lengthy paragraphs, the writer broke the person's job description into categorized paragraphs. The resume is sprinkled with many keywords relevant to Human Resources. The writer added a

PHYLLIS MARTIN, PHR   Page 2

■ CERTIFICATION ■

- Professional in Human Resources, Human Resources Certification Institute, 2004

■ HR TRAINING AND DEVELOPMENT ■

- SHRM Diversity Development in the Workplace, 2004
- Perfect Fit, 2004
- Compliance Survivor with COBRA & HIPAA, 2004
- Make Your Presentation Skills Shine, 2003
- Instructional Techniques for New Instructors, 2003
- Creative Ways to Add Excitement to Your Training, 2001
- Communicating with Diplomacy and Tact, 2001
- Train the Trainer, ASTD, 2001
- Violence in the Workplace / Crisis Response Training, 2000
- Attentive Listening, 2000
- Listening and Speaking Effectively, 2000
- American Red Cross Instructor Candidate Training, 1999

■ PROFESSIONAL AFFILIATIONS ■

- National / Local Member, Society for Human Resource Management (SHRM), 2004
- 2002 United Way Loaned Executive
- Local Member, American Society for Training and Development (ASTD), 2000
  - Elected Treasurer, 2004

■ EDUCATION ■

HOPE BAPTIST UNIVERSITY, Centerville, Texas
Bachelor of Science in Occupational Education expected December 2005

green marble sidebar and squares as an attention-getting, yet professional, design element. The square bullets coordinate with the design. Key achievements have their own heading. See Cover Letter 7.

Information Systems/Information Technology

Resumes at a Glance

RESUME NUMBER	LAST OR CURRENT OCCUPATION	GOAL	PAGE
103	IT Support Analyst and Training Coordinator	Executive Assistant/ Administrative Assistant	207
104	Computer Professional	Computer Professional	208
105	Contract IT Support Specialist	Network Engineer	209
106	Computer Operator	Computer Operations Professional	210
107	Business Analyst	Technical Support Manager	211
108	Website Assistant Manager	Web Designer/Webmaster	213
109	Novellus Program Manager	Program Manager	214
110	Chief Information Security Officer	Not specified	217
111	Senior Application Developer	Application Architect/ Developer	219
112	Systems Engineer/Technical Consultant	Senior LAN Administrator/ Systems Engineer	221
113	Director of Informational Systems	Not specified	223
114	Application Development Supervisor	Information Technology Professional	225
115	IT Consultant/Senior Software Engineer	IT Web Contractor/Java Programmer	227
116	Senior Network Engineer	Senior Network Manager/ Engineer	229
117	Application Programmer	Applications Programmer— Visual Basic	231

Sherry Hill

25 Forest Street, Norwalk, Connecticut 00000
Phone / Fax: (203) 555-5555   Cell: (203) 555-5555
sherryhill@yahoo.com

Objective: EXECUTIVE ASSISTANT / ADMINISTRATIVE ASSISTANT

Excellent organizer and multitasker: day-to-day work is coordinated and flows smoothly; long-term projects are prioritized, updated, and on track; executives are kept organized, focused, and on schedule.

Highly proficient at compiling, revising, editing, and finalizing documents and presentations requiring quick, accurate production schedules that must adhere to inflexible deadlines. Strong interpersonal skills.

- Executive Administrative Assistant
- Editor / Proofreader
- Law Department Word Processor
- Graphics PowerPoint Presentation Specialist
- IT Support Analyst / Training Coordinator
- Website Designer, HTML

Expertise: MS Office 97 & 2000 (Word, PowerPoint, Excel), MS Word (PC, Mac), WordPerfect, Lotus 1-2-3, Harvard Graphics, & Freelance. **Proficient:** MS Outlook, MS Publisher, MS Access, Paradox, Q&A, & Quark. **Basic Proficiency:** Basic HTML & Mac version of Adobe Photoshop & Illustrator.

Experience

GREENWICH CONSULTING, Greenwich, Connecticut
Greenwich Consulting provides research-based consulting to leading commercial banks, investment banks, brokerage firms, bond dealers, and investment managers.

IT Support Analyst and Training Coordinator, IT Department   1998–2004
- Utilized Network Associates Support Magic Help Desk software module, redesigning default templates for specific company use.
- Coordinated and scheduled advanced software training for company members.

Graphics Presentation Specialist, Editorial Department   1997–1998
- Graphics presentation specialist utilizing Harvard Graphics and PowerPoint.

FREELANCE BUSINESSES, Stamford, Connecticut
Through various placement agencies, reported to vice presidential level and higher.

Executive Administrative Assistant, Graphics Presentation Specialist   1996–1997
- Law Department Word Processor reporting to Vice President and General Counsel.
- HRIS Reports Specialist for the Manager of Compensation and Employee Development.
- Engineering Editorial Assistant, Copy Editor and Copywriter, Proofreader, Junior Accountant, Accounts Receivable and Payroll Bookkeeper.

ENTREPRENEURIAL BUSINESSES, Stamford, Connecticut

AcoustiConcerts   1999–2001
- Promoted / presented concerts at Norwalk Concert Hall featuring well-known musicians.
- Managed bookings; hired sound engineers, labor crews; arranged catering, hospitality; coordinated advertising, ticket sales. Designed company website with links to area hotels and artists' websites.

Medical Transcription Service   1993–1996

Computer Software Tutoring Service   1991–1997
- Transitioned law firm's six administrative assistant WordPerfect users from DOS to Windows.

Licensed Realtor®   Prior to 1991

Education

Mathematics / Education   Hunter College
New York, New York

103

Diana Holdsworth, Rowayton, Connecticut

The applicant wanted an administrative position. The challenge was to display her many skills and her ability to coordinate people and things. She had many callbacks. After eight weeks she found a job.

Shultz Griggs
Computer Professional

1234 Valentine Street
Towers, WA 71234
Mobile Phone: (777) 777-7000
Fax: (777) 777-7001
email: Schultzie@email.com

Established reputation for expertise within the computer industry—more than 22 years of experience. Personable, conscientious, resourceful. Strong aptitude for learning. Willing to relocate.

EXPERTISE

- Set up, configure, enhance, upgrade, and support computers, computer systems, and peripherals—including server clusters and networks.
- Develop custom software for clients; resolve software compatibility issues.
- Develop programs that interface with computer-controlled test equipment.
- EXPERT in use, installation, configuration, troubleshooting, and problem-solving of the following:

Software

Operating systems: Windows NT 4.0, Windows XP, Windows 2000 Pro, Windows 95/98, and Windows 3.1; exposure to UNIX (various) and Linux

Protocols: TCP/IP, NetBIOS, and NetBEUI

Applications: MS Word 2002, MS Excel 2002, MS Access, MS Outlook, Photoshop, Macromedia Dreamweaver, MS Frontpage, Adobe Pagemaker, MS Visual C++ 6.0, MS Visual Basic 6.0, MS J++, and Borland JBuilder

Languages: C++, C, BASIC, HTML, Java, JavaScript, XML, and Assembly Language

Hardware

Desktop computers and small to midsize servers

HP servers, workstations, and RAID products; Adaptec SCSI and Fiber Channel Controllers; 3COM hubs, switches, and network cards; and SMC hubs and network cards

IDE, SCSI, and Fiber Channel hard disk drives and tape backup products from various manufacturers. Exposure to SAN and NAS storage devices.

EXPERIENCE

Computer Professional, Computer Service, Towers, WA   1991–present

Evaluated, tested, and recommended networking, storage, and server hardware to clients; provided problem resolution for MIS departments. Developed testing methods to ensure reliability and compatibility; performed testing of computer, storage, and networking products. Configured new computer, network, and storage hardware for clients. Installed and configured operating systems and drivers for workstations and servers. Configured server clusters, network software, RAID arrays, and other storage options. Aided clients with operating system and application upgrade rollouts. Undertook small to medium-size customer software development projects.

- *Major clients included* Texaco, Alcoa Aluminum, County Community College, City of Towers, and State University.

Lead Programmer, Rioters Insurance Group, Wooden, WA   1982–1991

Managed the development, installation, and support of software applications used by banks and automobile dealers. Provided technical support by phone for software. Installed and configured networking hardware and software on site. Resolved software problems on site.

- *Exemplary accomplishments:* Developed applications in C and BASIC to perform loan calculations and to print forms and contracts; developed algorithms to calculate various types of loans; developed basic email system for loan approval.

CERTIFICATIONS / EDUCATION

CompTIA A+ in progress; Network+ in progress; Microsoft MCSE in progress

State University, B.S. Program, Major in Technology and Mathematics
Community College, A.S. Program, Electronics and Technology

104

Janice Shepherd, Bellingham, Washington

Instead of a horizontal line above each section heading to divide the resume into three sections, the two horizontal lines have the effect of enclosing the Expertise section and calling attention to it.

JOHN WILLIAMS

382 White Elm Road • Unionville, NJ 07083
(222) 222-2222 • jwilliams@aol.com

Hands-on network engineer with strengths in diagnostic troubleshooting and customer satisfaction

SUMMARY OF QUALIFICATIONS

- More than 11 years in technical-support positions, including nearly one year as a network engineer.
- Skilled in configuring, networking, and troubleshooting computer systems in Windows NT & Novell environments.
- Outstanding diagnostic skills. Systematic and methodical in solving problems.
- Very strong work ethic with demonstrated commitment to providing outstanding customer service.
- Easy-going and accommodating personality. Known for going the extra mile to get the job done.

TECHNICAL SKILLS

Operating Systems: DOS, Windows NT 4.0, Windows XP
Software: Microsoft Office XP, NetWare, ProjectWise, Honeywell, proprietary refinery applications
Networking Protocols: TCP/IP, NetBEUI
Certifications: Microsoft Certified Professional

EXPERIENCE

<u>United Oil</u>, Port Murray, New Jersey   2002 to present
Contract IT Support Specialist
Provide on-site hardware and software support for 130 users throughout refinery. As part of two-person support team, build and network computer systems, install and configure software, and troubleshoot and repair all computer problems.
- Established reputation for prompt and effective response to service requests from customers, guaranteeing continued operation of workstations, servers, and refinery computer systems. Systematically troubleshoot problems to ensure quick and accurate resolution, collecting high customer satisfaction ratings.
- Effectively resolved problem with software used to allow remote downloads to networked computers, conducting research to identify possible causes and then pinpointing and addressing the source problem.
- Developed strong rapport with users, earning recognition as the "go-to" support person among users.
- Created Access database application to track inventory of computers and peripherals, monitor purchases and costs, and optimize allocation of computer resources.
- Effectively used ghost software to create and update machine images, improving speed and accuracy of custom computer configurations.

<u>ACS</u>, South Hills, New Jersey   1999 to 2002
Repair Technician
Provided on-site and in-house technical support for this distributor of automated warehouse equipment. Installed and repaired computer-based warehouse equipment and power supplies, effectively diagnosing problems.
- Worked closely with customer to determine and review scope and cost of repair projects.
- Consistently completed projects in accordance with established deadlines and customer expectations.

<u>PT Technologies</u>, South Hills, New Jersey   1997 to 1998
Repair Technician
Assembled, tested, and repaired telephone and peripheral equipment for this leading telecommunications firm.
- Worked with technicians and engineers to resolve complex technical problems. Trained new technicians.

<u>General Nissan</u>, Freeport, New York   1991 to 1996
Service Representative
Provided technical and customer support functions for this automobile dealership.
- Serving as liaison, interacted with customers to assess needs and recommend appropriate services.

EDUCATION & TRAINING

<u>Computer Institute</u>, Newark, New Jersey
Network Engineering Diploma, October 2000
- ✓ As part of team, networked classroom computers and effectively diagnosed problems introduced by instructor.
- ✓ Configured client workstations, servers, and peripherals.
- ✓ Gained hands-on experience in LAN/WAN configurations, hubs, routers, and networking protocols.

<u>Technical Institute</u>, Woodridge, New Jersey
Digital Electronic Technician Certificate

105

Carol A. Altomare, Three Bridges, New Jersey

This one-page resume offers much information through small type (10-point Perpetua) and narrower top and bottom margins. Note the use of bold, bold italic, italic, small caps, and underlining.

BRADLEY CUMMINGS

90 Parkway Road
Croton, NY 55555
555.555.9866
irwcu45@compuserv.com

Profile

Computer Operations Professional

- Skilled technical professional with 6 years of computer operations experience in mainframe systems, as well as leading and training staff.
- Desktop support includes installation and troubleshooting of PC hardware, operating systems and software applications.
- Recognized by management for dedication, strong service orientation and consistent record of quality performance.

Technical Skills

Hardware/operating systems: IBM 3083 and ES/9000; IBM 3880 disk drives; IBM 3203 printers; IBM-PC compatibles; Windows 97, 2000 and XP

Software: MVS, JES2, IDMS, CICS, PANVALET, TSO, DOS, MS Office (Word, Excel, PowerPoint and Access)

Programming languages: JCL, COBOL

Experience

HARTWELL INDUSTRIES, Croton, NY   1990 to present
Computer Operator (1998 to present)

Promoted to computer operator in Information Systems with oversight of 3 other operators on IBM ES/9000 mainframe system, using MVS, JES2, IDMS, CICS, PANVALET and TSO. Generate timely reports to all departments; perform daily and weekly system backups.

- Provide first-level technical support to internal users and monitor hardware to ensure effective operations.
- Selected to lead a continuous improvement team to enhance computer operations efficiency.
- Train and develop new operators in system procedures and processes.
- Support users on PC hardware, operating systems (Windows XP) and software (MS Office products) installation and troubleshooting.

Tape Librarian (1990 to 1998)

Performed all tape library functions to support daily computer operations in a timely manner.

- Monitored and filed tape media for midrange operations; scanned tapes for vaulting.
- Assisted with disaster recovery and media handling for backup/recovery operations.
- Maintained up-to-date documentation of tape and library operations.
- Supported customer requests for off-site storage or other needs.

Education

Certificate in Computer Technology/Programming, 1995
Dutchess Community College, Croton, NY

106

Louise Garver, Enfield, Connecticut

This person had only a certificate but wanted to apply for an internal position that would be a promotion. To offset his lack of education, the writer showcased his experience and technical skills.

(555) 555-5555
myname@email.com
123 West Grand Boulevard
Hometown, CA 01234-5678

Robert Brown

TECHNICAL SUPPORT MANAGER

Utilizing 15 years of proven success in customer service, supervision, and fiscal management to uphold company vision and deliver dependable operational support. A dedicated employee who accepts accelerated levels of responsibility and consistently delivers exceptional results.

SKILLS SUMMARY

- Administration: financial accountability, personnel supervision, policy making, executive presentation, achievement of performance metrics, results-oriented decision making, and efficient multitasking
- Computer operations: Microsoft Certified User Specialist—Word and Excel; Subject Matter Expert—Lotus Notes; proficient in Microsoft PowerPoint and Outlook, Vantive (Customer Relationship Management), WordPerfect, and IBM AS/400
- Customer service: situation analysis, problem resolution, and excellent customer satisfaction ratings

PROFESSIONAL EXPERIENCE

NATIONAL DATA SYSTEMS—San Francisco, CA   9/1997–Present
Business Analyst   1/2003–Present
NDS Midwest Regional Infrastructure
Business relations and statistics report specialist providing accurate information for successful contract negotiations. Consistently obtain quick results for customer service issues utilizing effective communication, targeted research, and action plan implementation.

Accomplishments
- Prevented loss of three major accounts by raising service levels to meet or exceed contractual obligation
- Earned company $6M contract through due diligence and contract negotiation activities
- Developed all service-level-agreement metrics and report capabilities for $16M account
- Established criteria and reporting procedures for tracking contract fulfillment requirements
- Provided seamless transition of service during takeover of national account

Operations Supervisor   1/2000–12/2002
BM Automotive Online Help Desk
Led team of 250 associates providing assistance to 120,000-customer base. Met all project management plan objectives on or ahead of schedule. Designed new hiring and training programs. Coordinated communication of policy changes and other areas of major impact with management and support staff. Supervised 2 teams, each having 20–25 direct reports.

Accomplishments
- Increased successful call handling 53% through creation of skill-based call routing standard (Super Queue) which has since been implemented nationwide by NDS call centers
- Reduced expenses 18% by completing detailed analysis and implementing corrective action, including successful petition to remove ineffective incentive program
- Presented new incentive program to appropriate management channels, reporting measurable productivity improvement within weeks of gaining implementation approval
- Enhanced productivity and staff confidence by obtaining onsite Microsoft Certification/Testing Center
- Improved team morale by developing and adhering to consistent personnel policies that met all legal and employee relations guidelines
- Invited to join Midwest Infrastructure Team as part of Operations Manager progression plan

107

Tammy J. Smith, Olivet, Michigan

The applicant's original, rough resume samples made him look like an entry-level employee, but he was "a great team leader with incredible success rates of achieving or exceeding goals." The writer overhauled and developed the resume, providing a profile, creating a Skills Summary,

PROFESSIONAL EXPERIENCE, *continued*

Team Leader, Operational Account Representative   12/1998–12/1999
BM Automotive Online Help Desk
Served as company representative in major contractual issues. Helped ensure service-level-agreement obligations were met. Invited to participate in global Digital Workflow Project as Subject Matter Expert; resulted in creation of standardized process manual—a project that had been in process 3 years as part of North American Operations' global responsibility. Final documents presented to and accepted by CEO.

Accomplishments
- Increased department productivity 37% by establishing team leader performance accountability
- Utilized management/leadership techniques to gain quick control of agents
- Developed policy and procedures for new Operational Account Representative position
- Managed 85,000-user Lotus Notes migration with no interruption in service

Geographic Specialist   9/1997–11/1998
RS Motor Works Customer Assistance Network
Handled RS Motor customer service inquiries, complaints, requests for financial assistance, negotiations, and arbitrations. Supervised 5 direct and up to 50 indirect reports.

Accomplishments
- Maintained one of highest customer satisfaction ratings for 2+ years while managing Western Region
- Resolved 97% of Better Business Bureau cases without arbitration or need for legal representation
- Exceeded expectations in all annual reviews, resulting in promotions from Divisional Help Desk Analyst to Corporate Help Desk Analyst to Subject Matter Expert to Team Leader in less than 3 years

PREVIOUS EMPLOYMENT HISTORY

FRIENDLY SKY AIR—Los Angeles, CA   4/1992–9/1997
Lead Flight Attendant   11/1994–9/1997
Flight Attendant   4/1992–10/1994
Exercised advanced time management skills and utilized extensive travel knowledge. Expert in emergency situation/negotiation procedures, safety, and CPR. Received U.S. Air Force Aerial Achievement Medal, Civilian Wartime Project Star Medal for Outstanding Achievement. Maintained FAA regulatory training requirements.

BILLIONAIRE BANK—Burbank, CA   6/1989–3/1992
Backup Head Teller/Floating Teller
Lowest error rate of branch tellers while balancing $150,000+ drawer daily. Consistently remained below $5 monthly variance. Responsible for dispersing $750K–$1.5M daily to and from main vault. Maintained excellent coworker and customer relationships.

SEMINARS / TRAINING

Foundations of Leadership—Instructor, 2 years
Diversity Training—Instructor, 2 years
Excellence in Customer Care I, II, III—Instructor, 1 year

Seven Habits of Highly Successful People
EOE, Behavioral Interviewing
Radiant Reading, Radiant Learning

PROFESSIONAL ORGANIZATIONS

Division Leader—United Way of San Francisco, 2001
Regional Manager—NDS Wellness Program, 2000
Member—Help Desk Institute, 2000–2003

and making two experience sections: Professional Experience and Previous Employment History. The Professional Experience section features bulleted accomplishments for each of the positions held.

WEB DESIGNER • WEBMASTER

internet & intranet solutions • creative • business-focused

Vibrant web design professional driving design innovations, implementations, and long-term strategies and projects for maximum business exposure. Distinctively creative—engaging a rich mix of conventional and contemporary ideas that seamlessly integrate with business image, market trends, demographics, and current business climates. Gregarious, expressive, and diligent; expert in inspiring others to build on ideas, refine concepts, and connect in a spirit of consensus and imagination. Acknowledged "firefighter"—able to steer projects through the inevitable minefields of issues, changing priorities, and disparate viewpoints for on-time and on-budget project completion. Reputed for visually appealing design, smart content, crisp layouts and navigation, and delivering improved efficacy, quality, and functionality.

professional strengths

- Client Relationship Management
- Stakeholder Management
- Graphic Design & Programming
- Research and Evaluation
- Cross-Browser Functionality Solutions
- Multimedia Web Interactivity
- Productivity Enhancements

- Project Coordination
- Issues Management/Strategic Planning
- Concept Development/Modeling
- Resource Allocations & Budgeting
- Client Briefs
- Supplier Negotiations
- Change Management

---

technology snapshot

HTML • JavaScript • DHTML • ASP • PHP • MySQL • Perl • VBA • Visual Basic • Delphi • Dreamweaver • Lotus Domino • Flash • Adobe Photoshop • PaintShop Pro • Adobe Premiere • Windows NT/XP/9x • Linux • Microsoft Office Pro • MS Project • MS Publisher • Lotus Notes • IE/Netscape • Streaming media • Xara & Asymetrix products • WISE • Install Shield • FrontPage • MS Visio • Linkbot Professional • Maximine • PC Anywhere

---

project showcase

Track record of accomplishment consulting for prominent companies, including UPS, Coles Myer Group, City of Rocklin, Collins Street Company, Direct View Consulting, Department of State Development, and more.

GLOBAL ONLINE TRADING & GLOBAL MARGIN LENDING
"MY WEALTH"
Website Assistant Manager

Projects: Multiple website projects ranging from $1K–$3.6M, including Global Online Trading, Global Margin Lending, My Wealth, and intranet.
Report to: Website Manager; Direct Reports: 2 (Content Administrator and Data Business Analyst)
Technologies: Lotus Domino, ASP

Leveraged the talents of the web design team to assess multifaceted user and system needs and institute strategic short- and long-term plans for developing an end solution. Expandable website environments were critical in meeting the organization's growing needs.

Produced the creative design and content for three websites. Documented site hierarchy, server structure, third-party relationships/processes, and work request procedures. Produced comprehensive briefings on recommended navigation flows and style guides for web content. Created all graphic optimization work and page mock-ups to reinforce the vision. Controlled all brainstorming sessions, tackled potential issues, and compiled solution reports for internal business analysts that provided a snapshot of project progress.

Special Contributions

- Transformed manual work request system plagued with inadequate instruction areas, slow processing, erroneous or missing data, and sign-off inadequacies into an automated electronic system based on Lotus Notes that cuts instances of complaints by 96% and reduced personal clarification visits to the requester by 80%.
- Elevated the usability and quality of websites, and arrested growing incidents of complaints regarding out-of-date content and errors, by developing a maintenance model that cemented biannual schedule dates exclusively for total website page reviews.
- Acknowledged "guru" appointed to investigate and resolve Internet-related software issues— from routine URL errors through complex browser configuration and plug-in anomalies.
- Selected to preside over proposed $3.6M website rebranding to mirror the Global image and transition to a new website platform. Collaborated with consultants on hardware/software needs and devised strategy for website redesign.

Anita Rosario

119 Gowan Drive, Rocklin, CA 91677 • Mobile: (916) 632 4545 • Website: http://anita.rosario.name • Email: anita@rosario.name

Page 1

108

Gayle Howard, Chirnside Park, Melbourne, Victoria, Australia

This applicant was an Administrator by day but wanted a job as a full-time Web Designer. She had formed her own freelance company for night and holiday work. The challenge was to play down her day work and showcase the minimal amount of design work she had performed for

Anita Rosario

119 Gowan Drive, Rocklin, CA 91677 • Mobile: (916) 632 4545 • Website: http://anita.rosario.name • Email: anita@rosario.name

project showcase
continued

PARKINSON'S SOCIETY
Webmaster

Project Scope: Live national convention broadcast across the Internet
Reported to: Multimedia and Information Services Manager
Technologies: Windows Media

With an "impossible deadline" of just 2 months from concept to delivery, presided over solution development and implementation for broadcasting the society's national convention across the Internet to a global audience.

Researched available technologies, interviewed and appointed specialist consultants, documented requirements, and collaborated on developing preseminar web pages for testing webcast signals and advertising prior to "go-live" date.

The project, delivered exactly to plan, was broadcast to a worldwide audience.

Special Contributions

- Seamlessly and successfully recorded and produced the seminar for live webcast.
- Devised multimedia PowerPoint slideshow that complemented the convention's theme. The seminar, live satellite connection, and slideshow seamlessly integrated to provide a premiere Internet broadcast.
- Offered real-time support for isolated users struggling to access the broadcast. Quickly identified individual browser plug-ins as the primary issue, providing instructions for download and installation.
- Seamlessly resolved one-time slideshow glitch by establishing alternative views on screen while re-establishing the lost connection.
- Collaborated with external companies to establish sponsorship technologies. Researched, pursued key decision-makers, presented case, and created/presented documents.
- Spearheaded e-commerce solution for donations, raffles, and merchandise. Recommended system that offered expandability, noninvasive implementation, and cost-effective pricing.
- Engaged children with the "Read-a-thon" website, designed to maximize children's enjoyment through interactivity, bright colors, and simple navigation.

career snapshot

THE WEB GURUS **Contractor/Consultant**	1999–Present
CITY OF ROCKLIN, Rocklin CA **Contract Administrator / Technical Administrator Coordinator**	1996–1998
MODEL SYSTEMS, Rocklin, CA **Computer Consultant**	1995–1996

education

Bachelor of Business (Accounting)
2 years successfully completed
Recipient, Faculty of Business Award (Computing)
Averaged Distinctions & High Distinctions in Computing & Accounting
University of California

Hundreds of hours devoted to ongoing professional development via formal short courses, workshops, information sessions, and meetings. Includes Dreamweaver MX, Photoshop, XML, Project Management, Time Management, Conflict Resolution, Introduction to Windows NT, Outlook and Office 97, Negotiation Skills, Software Testing, Workplace Communications, Designing User Documentation, Advanced Visual Basic, and more.

Page 2

her clients. The "technology snapshot" is a novel way to display her software expertise. Achievements are labeled "Special Contributions." The white-on-black contact information makes the resume stand out.

JEANNIE DANIELS

1639 Canyon Avenue • San Jose, CA 77777 • (555) 555-5555 • jdaniels@aol.com

A highly motivated, results-focused **Program Manager** with more than 8 years of information technology experience in the semiconductor industry. Encompasses strong leadership and successful team-building capabilities combined with excellent technical, communication, presentation, and customer-service skills. Resourceful problem solver with proven ability to bring quick resolution to challenging situations as well as building lasting relationships with vendors and customers.

Manufacturing Operations ◆ Continuous Process Improvement ◆ Global Partnerships
Strategic Planning ◆ Business Development ◆ Customer Relationship Management
Financial Analysis ◆ Team Building ◆ Product Development

ACHIEVEMENTS

- ◆ **Instrumental in becoming top service provider for Novellus Systems, Inc. in Asia (China, Taiwan, and Singapore).** Developed a service program in an effort to become the exclusive service provider for Novellus around the world. Hired resources, trained personnel, and implemented and managed program, ensuring customer and OEM satisfaction. Tracked equipment utilization and resource performance and established customer relationships.

- ◆ **Recognized as service provider with customer needs in mind.** Implemented new pricing structure based on client feedback from numerous meetings addressing past concerns about support and pricing. Established close customer relationships that increased revenues 90% and first-year revenues by more than $600,000.

- ◆ **Significantly improved practices and procedures throughout manufacturing area, increasing revenues from less than $100 million to more than $700 million annually.** Implemented ISO 9000, improving repair times and training processes, which reduced manufacturing cycle times and discrepancies while increasing mean time between failures, system availability, and on-time shipments.

PROFESSIONAL EXPERIENCE

AXIOM MECHANICAL, San Jose, CA
$35 million semiconductor services group with 480 employees throughout the United States, Asia, and Europe

NOVELLUS PROGRAM MANAGER   2000–Present

Manage operational and manufacturing personnel, continuous process and product improvement, and customer service program, creating overall operations efficiency. Play a key role in hiring, training, and scheduling, as well as implementing and supporting service plan.

- Negotiated use of Novellus training facility and equipment at no cost to company, resulting in comprehensive training and savings of $2,500 per student.
- Established database that allowed needed documentation to be retrieved for support field service efforts and training classes 24/7. Collaborated within organization to develop procedures that could be expanded on after contract agreement with Novellus.
- Increased service calls by 150% by developing strong customer relationships.
- Established accounts with key suppliers in U.S., Taiwan, and Singapore to provide nonproprietary parts, resulting in additional sales with 37% profit margin for material sold.
- Implemented new response time policy from 4- to 2-hour maximum, creating additional daily service and reduced average response time from 4 an hour to less than 1 an hour.

109

Denette Jones, Boise, Idaho

The resume gets off to a strong start with a profile and center-justified areas of expertise in bold-face and separated by diamond bullets. Big numbers justify a separate Achievements section. Each entry in the Professional Experience section has a company description in italic, a paragraph

JEANNIE DANIELS

JABIL, San Jose, CA
Fortune 500 company providing equipment leasing and financing services to venture capital-backed companies

TECHNICAL SERVICE MANAGER 1993–2000

Full authority over the remanufacturing, testing, and shipment of front-end fabrication equipment, including AMAT, Lam, and Novellus capital equipment. Ensured that refurbished equipment met OEM and customer specifications while targeting efforts toward quality equipment, reduced costs, on-time shipments, and improved manufacturing cycle times.

- Reduced manufacturing cycle times by 30%. Recruited technical writer to create procedures during manufacturing process, enabling staff to cross-train effectively and allowing trainees to work without constant supervision.
- Established material supply chain, improving employee morale and reducing manufacturing costs by more than 40%.
- Utilized original OEM to rebuild specific components to ensure quality and reduce costs over purchasing new, resulting in a warranty same as new and a 4-week lead time for rebuilds.
- Reduced crating times by 2 days, improving efficiency and on-time shipments. Coordinated partnership with shipping and crating vendor with prefabbed crates available for all company equipment.

NOVA CORPORATION, San Jose, CA
$1.3 billion supplier of sophisticated manufacturing systems employing more than 2,500 people in 26 locations worldwide

MANUFACTURING MANAGER 1987–1993

Responsible for all manufacturing activities and up to 104 personnel, ensuring quality and on-time delivery for more than 150 systems per quarter. Created operational budgets that consistently met or exceeded scheduled goals.

- Developed programs and employee incentives to promote quality, resulting in assembly discrepancies being reduced from 9 per module to less than 1, and final test discrepancies being reduced from 14 per system to less than 2 in 2 years.
- Achieved 100% on-time delivery 3 years in a row by reworking assembly procedures and training for better efficiency.
- Provided in-depth classroom training on ISO practices as well as Novellus workmanship standards that met production and shipment goals without increased discrepancies, which reduced cycle times by 40%.
- Reduced employee turnover rate to less than 5% a year. Encouraged employees to cross-train, increasing job challenge and employee morale.

EDUCATION / TRAINING

Completed numerous **professional training courses,** including Conflict Management, Managing to Stay Legal, Time Management, Problem Solving/Decision Making, Strategic Management, Project Management, ISO9001 Element Training, Concept I Operation and Maintenance, Capital Expenditure Linkage and Evaluation, Resource Management and Financial Performance, and Clean Room Training.

Proficient in several computer applications—Microsoft Word, Excel, Visio, Project, PowerPoint.

indicating key responsibilities, and bulleted items containing achievements. Each achievement is quantified in some way (with a dollar amount, a percentage, or some other figure). White space is used throughout.

BRUCE KATOSHI

2222 Pinehurst Crescent
Augusta, Ontario A1A 1A1

Phone: (555) 333-7777
Email: brucekat@email.com

PROFESSIONAL PROFILE
★ *Recipient of the highest corporate distinction for commitment to excellence* ★

Award-winning professional combining top-quality strategic, operational, and management expertise. Distinguished 24-year career providing high-level information security solutions designed to safeguard technology investments, services, facilities, and databases. Dynamic and results-oriented leader with outstanding communication, consulting, and team-building skills. Recipient of distinguished Wall of Winners Award for excellence.

Information Security & Disaster Recovery

- Expert in Information Security, Disaster Recovery, and Business Continuity
- 24 years of expertise planning and implementing enterprise-class security and recovery solutions to ensure integrity and protection of all critical corporate data and technology services
- Expert in mainframe and enterprise LAN/WAN technologies (Alpha, VAX, HP, Novell, and Unix)

Vendor Management & Contract Negotiations

- Outstanding contract procurement and negotiation skills—proven ability to secure comprehensive, top-quality, cost-effective vendor agreements
- Particularly skilled in managing long-term vendor relationships in a consistent and professional manner

Team Leadership & People Management

- Reputation for building and leading strong, high-performance teams
- Ability to create high team morale and to motivate teams to consistently meet and exceed corporate and departmental objectives
- Recognized for ability to create a positive and productive environment that effectively reduces staff turnover

PROFESSIONAL EXPERIENCE

TIRECO CORPORATION, Augusta, Ontario
Rapid advancement through senior technology and information security positions on the strength of advanced strategic planning, team leadership, process improvement, cost control, and vendor negotiation and relationship management capabilities.

CHIEF INFORMATION SECURITY OFFICER   1999–2004
Senior technology position charged with the strategic planning, maintenance, implementation, administration, and interpretation of all Information Security policies, standards, guidelines, and procedures across the organization to safeguard the corporation's vital technology services, facilities, and databases. Concurrently tasked with managing key technology projects and vendor negotiations.

- Revitalized the integrity of all security privileges and established comprehensive security and disaster recovery protocols that exceeded all audit security recommendations.
- Mandated disaster recovery procedures and offsite storage solutions for midrange and distributed systems (Alpha, VAX, HP, Novell, and Unix).
- Successfully renegotiated major outsource printing contract with Xerox Canada, securing more than $725,000 in savings for Canadian Tire over the term of the agreement, and further identifying a $100,000 cost avoidance opportunity for Xerox.
- Renegotiated critical Comdisco disaster-recovery contracts, resulting in cost savings of more than $700,000, improved client coverage, and the additional elimination of all 6% annual contract increases.
- Successfully managed implementation of a new fibre ring designed to reroute voice and data traffic in event of failure to the primary fibre option.

110

Ross Macpherson, Whitby, Ontario, Canada

This resume focuses on three areas that the candidate wanted to highlight and puts them up front in the Professional Profile, enclosed in horizontal lines. Even though he received his awards earlier in his career, they also are highlighted at the top of page 1 for greater impact. In the

MANAGER—
Disaster Recovery, Data Centre Security, Facilities Management, and Health & Safety   1997–1999

Challenged with safeguarding all enterprise technology services, security, and data in the event of a physical disaster. Included comprehensive planning and coordination of all network and mainframe recovery testing, physical security of computing facilities, environmental controls, and executive transportation to recovery site.

- Established infrastructure and procedures to ensure network connectivity to all business clients within 48 hours of disaster and relocation of corporate executive to recovery site in Andover, NJ, within 3 hours.
- Spearheaded implementation of SAE, effectively reducing erase time by 66% and resolving outstanding audit security issues.
- Successfully audited five corporate computing facilities to ensure integrity of environmental and employee safety controls, including fire alarm systems, air conditioning, environmental alerts, and use of UPS/diesel generators.
- Reduced mainframe and network recovery times by 25% and card authorization (Stratus) recovery by 50%.
- Re-evaluated and/or eliminated card access to secured areas and initiated weekly and monthly audits, reporting, and procedures to ensure security issues.

MANAGER—Program Delivery   1995–1997

Selected to build and manage key Project Management Team and coordinate multiple ongoing enterprise initiatives on time and within budget. Direct management of five Project Managers and resource pool of 40 technical specialists.

- Built and maintained an efficient and highly regarded professional unit through solid team leadership, process improvement, and priority management skills.
- Effectively controlled staffing costs through judicious training and redeployment within the resource pool.

MANAGER—Network Planning and Support Data & Voice   1993–1995

Coordinated all planning, support, and applicable outsourcing for enterprise telecommunications, voice (BPX), and WAN services across the corporation.

- Recommended technology improvements and outsourcing opportunities that allowed for significant cost savings while improving level of service.
- Effectively managed seamless crossover to outsourced voice services.
- Managed ongoing support of newly implemented Spacepac satellite communications system throughout all Associate stores and Express Auto Parts facilities.

MANAGER—Spacepac Satellite Information Systems   1992–1993

Concurrently seconded by Senior Technology Team to lead strategic planning and implementation of Spacepac satellite system across 400+ Associate Dealer network. Challenged to establish entire infrastructure and manage cycle through preinstallation, installation, training, and ongoing support.

- Doubled senior management mandate by signing all 400+ Corporate Associate Dealers in first year (met expectation of 200 signed orders within 6 months).
- Successfully managed all hardware and software installations without disruption to day-to-day operations.
- Established key service level agreements with corporate sponsors and associated vendors.

MANAGER—Computer Operations / Disaster Recovery   1990–1992

Coordinated all online computer services, computer planning, disaster recovery, and system development throughout the organization. Additionally accountable for all negotiation and relationship management with third-party vendors and technology partners. Managed 42-person team with 7 direct reports.

- Successfully instituted a number of industry and corporation firsts, including the first online automated cartridge system in Canada, the largest Amdahl single image processor in Ontario, and a new Data Centre Help Desk.
- Replaced and renegotiated more than 50% of current vendor relationships unable to meet business needs, resulting in significant cost savings and service improvements.
- Renegotiated all Micrographics contracts to reduce annual costs and turn around first profit of $500,000 for Operations department.

EDUCATION

Business Administration—Marketing, Augusta College, Augusta, Ontario

Professional Experience section, each entry exhibits the popular pattern of a paragraph with responsibilities that is followed by a list of bulleted achievements. The short Education section appears at the end.

MARTIN EBERLY

284 West Buffalo Court
Mapleton, MA 01122
(555) 333-8888
eberlym@company.com

QUALIFICATIONS SUMMARY

Forward-thinking application architect and developer with comprehensive range of information technology experience. Sophisticated command of advanced programming concepts and techniques.

- Passionate developer with an appetite for technology.
- Quick learner with interest in and ability to master new technologies and apply core programming concepts across technology boundaries.
- Avid reader with interests in service-oriented architecture and technologies, web services, code reusability, and Java and .NET compatibility.
- Self-motivated team member who enjoys sharing new ideas and mentoring other programmers.
- Multiple-award recipient recognized for personal contribution to high-profile projects.

SELECTED ACCOMPLISHMENTS

Enterprise Architecture and Application Development
.NET Object-to-Relational Framework—Architect
Reusable framework allowed seamless object persistence through relational database backend.
- Started personal project that ultimately was integrated into group's software development life cycle.
- Reduced development time by 30% for applications that used framework by eliminating need to write custom database mappings.
- Wrote sophisticated custom caching algorithms to improve database performance.
- Created database vendor-neutral strategy for maximum flexibility. Successfully implemented in projects using SQL Server and Oracle.

Publishing Tool—Architect and Developer
Administrative software used to make product and technical content available to corporate partners and customers.
- Formulated hierarchical user permissions to facilitate task delegation while ensuring data integrity.
- Designed administrative interface for users to upload and import content, to associate meta-data, and to manage content versions.
- Wrote visual dynamic page-building tool that allowed users to manipulate and format dynamic pages for website publication without any HTML knowledge.
- Relieved technical department of content management responsibility through distribution of maintenance tasks back to appropriate business departments.

MyGS Intranet—Architect and Developer
Corporate intranet website used by nearly 6,000 employees as centralized location for diverse department information.
- Designed portal software to integrate more than 30 websites into a single, personalizable view.
- Improved access to critical data and simplified overall user experience.

www.teacompany.com—Architect, Developer, and Consultant
E-commerce website and backend administrative software for specialty import company.
- Created custom-written website that grew nonexistent Internet sales to more than $1 million after one year of operation.
- Transitioned website into a robust, scalable application that supported increased business transactions and improved customer satisfaction.

111

Jessica Robinson, Westborough, Massachusetts

This applicant had extensive experience in his field but lacked a bachelor's degree, a qualification often listed as a requirement for the senior-level jobs he was considering. To eliminate any question of his competence, the writer highlighted some of the applicant's project successes and

<u>Technical Leadership</u>
Solutions Architecture Team—Member
Core supervisory group responsible for technology standards.
- Selected for participation through professional reputation and familiarity with wide range of technologies.
- Guided development teams, authored standards documents, and established IT procedures.

.NET Framework—"Ambassador"
Introduced .NET Framework to development group and initiated push for corporate acceptance of technology.
- Prepared and presented written and oral justification for numerous corporate approval committees.
- Realized adoption of .NET as company standard for nearly all new projects in functional organization.

"Brown Bag" Cross-Functional Training Program—Presenter
Independently researched, prepared, and presented seminars.
- Object-to-Relational Persistence: Examples in .NET
- Service-Oriented Architecture: A Decoupled World
- Web Services: Achieving Interoperability Between J2EE and .NET

Technology Newsletter—Editor and Contributor
Company-sponsored technical publication.
- Organized, published, and launched periodical to increase company-wide technical knowledge, to promote information sharing, and to enhance collaboration between developers.

Development Group—Application Developer
De facto team leader valued for technological competence and familiarity with programming techniques.
- Initiated collaborative meetings between members of five-person development team to discuss programming obstacles and brainstorm solutions.
- Reduced development timelines, improved quality of final product, and increased general team cooperation.

PROFESSIONAL EXPERIENCE

<u>Employment History</u>

Computer Corporation: Mapleton, MA—Senior Application Developer	2000 to Present
Tea Company: Mapleton, MA—Software Developer	1997 to 2000

<u>Education & Certification</u>

Boston University: Computer Science	2002 to Present
Sun Certified Java Developer	2002
Northeastern University: Java Certification	2001 to 2002

TECHNOLOGIES SUMMARY

<u>Development Languages</u>	C#, Java, C++, C, VB.NET, Perl, COBOL, Fortran, LISP, Ruby, Eiffel, SmallTalk
<u>Development Platforms</u>	J2EE, .NET, webMethods, ATG Dynamo, BEA WebLogic, IBW WebSphere, JBOSS, Oracle 9iAS, Orion, Autonomy, Documentum
<u>Web and XML Technology</u>	DTD, XML 1.0, XML Infoset, XML Schema, XPath, SOAP, WSDL, UDDI, WS-*, WS-I BP 1.0, Dime, SAAJ, XHTML, DOM, SAX, XSLT
<u>Databases and Database Software</u>	SQL, T-SQL, PL/SQL, SQL Server, Oracle, Sybase, mySQL
<u>Operating Systems</u>	Windows, Linux, Solaris

emphasized his true interest in computer technologies. Impressed with the applicant's qualifications, a reader might not even question whether the applicant was missing something by not having a degree.

JAMES L. TIERNEY

1450 Greenwood Drive • Chelmsford, MA 01824
Home: (222) 222-2222 • Mobile: (333) 333-3333 • E-Mail: jltiern3@attbi.com

SENIOR LAN ADMINISTRATOR / SYSTEMS ENGINEER

- **Certified Novell Engineer** with more than 15 years of experience in installing, upgrading, troubleshooting, configuring, and supporting network operating systems, hardware, software, servers, desktops, and a wide variety of computer peripherals.
- Highly proficient at establishing user accounts, implementing network security protocols, installing and supporting backup strategies, and planning/executing disaster recovery solutions.
- Excellent troubleshooting skills; tenaciously committed to the thorough resolution of technical issues.
- Exceptional ability to grasp and master new technologies quickly and easily.
- Strong communicator; able to interact effectively and positively with individuals of all technical abilities.

TECHNICAL SKILLS AND QUALIFICATIONS

- Novell NetWare 3.1x, 4.1x, 5.x
- TCP/IP, IPX
- IBM OS/2 2.x and 3.0
- BackupExec/Arcserve Administrator
- Lotus Notes

- Microsoft Windows NT 4.0, 2000, XP
- Microsoft Windows 95, 98, Me, XP
- Microsoft Office 4, XP
- Microsoft Exchange/Outlook/Express
- Microsoft Visio

PROFESSIONAL EXPERIENCE

Signet, Inc., Westford, MA   2000–2004
Start-up IT consulting firm offering high-end technology solutions to Fortune 1000 clients.
Systems Engineer/Technical Consultant

Provide NetWare operating systems support, file server installation, troubleshooting, and technical consultation to client companies with complex networking environments. Consult with clients to determine the optimal application of technology solutions to meet their current and future IT needs.
- Participated in the application of security policy standards to NetWare and NT servers at a leading New England financial institution to ensure their compliance for an upcoming FDIC audit.
- Planned, coordinated and implemented the relocation of 20 NT and NetWare servers to a new location over two weekends for a major New England Medical facility with zero loss in user productivity.
- Led the effort to upgrade 20 laptops from Compaq to Dell at a local New England medical center. Migrated user-specific data, mail, and software applications to the new laptops. Instructed users on VPN login, network access, and e-mail retrieval procedures.

Bryant Technologies, Concord, MA   1996–2000
National Professional Services firm providing Help Desk Support and Field Service Engineering to Fortune 1000 client companies.
Systems Engineer

Provided on-site technical support and network administration for clients, including installations, maintenance, upgrades, troubleshooting, and support for servers, fiber optics, printers, software applications, and workstations.
- Managed the upgrade of a NetWare 3.12 server to 4.11 for a global securities and lending firm. Administered and stabilized all other servers and developed and implemented a data backup solution.
- Installed 18 new servers and migrated all user-specific data to increase a client's network user storage space from 10 MB to 200 MB per user. Replaced 11 aging NetWare 4.11 servers, increasing total storage to 3.6 TB.
- Instrumental in the remediation of 12,000 desktops to ensure Y2K compliance for a New England financial institution. Provided technical support for hardware, DOS, Windows 3x and 95, and Y2K software.

112

Jeanne Knight, Melrose, Massachusetts

The strong opening profile, Technical Skills and Qualifications section, and Professional Experience section display this applicant's outstanding capabilities, offsetting his not having a four-year degree. In the Professional Experience section, each italic company description is useful to any

PROFESSIONAL EXPERIENCE (continued)

Larkus Corporation, Tyngsboro, MA   1992–1996
Consulting firm specializing in Novell Networks and computer support for small businesses.
Network Engineer (1993–1996)
Lead Technician (1992–1993)

Provided network systems administration for client Novell networks, including installations, troubleshooting, configuration, upgrades, support, and maintenance. Administered disaster recovery plans.

- Installed and configured NetWare 3.12 server supporting 40 users for a client divesting from its corporate headquarters. Migrated user and corporate data, created login scripts, and maintained desktops.
- Provided technical support and on-site preventive maintenance of computer hardware and peripherals for client companies.

Grenoble Information Services, Needham, MA   1992
National service provider of on-site computer repair service for PCs and peripherals supporting medium to large companies.

Field Engineer

Performed service calls and maintained spare-parts inventory for client companies. Performed lead engineering duties for two automotive manufacturer contracts supporting desktops and peripherals.

Centel Information Systems, Inc., Waltham, MA   1987–1992
National service provider of on-site computer repair service for PCs and peripherals supporting medium to large companies.
Branch Manager (1991–1992)
Lead Technician (1987–1991)

Performed service calls and diagnosed, troubleshot, and repaired computers and peripherals. Maintained spare-parts inventory. Dispatched technicians to service calls and tracked the status of those calls.

TECHNICAL CERTIFICATIONS

Certified Novell Engineer, CNE5
Certified Novell Engineer, IntranetWare
Certified Novell Administrator, CNA5
Certified Novell Administrator, IntranetWare

Microsoft Certified System Engineer, MCSE 2000
Microsoft Certified Professional, MCP (in progress)

EDUCATION

Associated Technical Institute, Woburn, MA—Certificate in Electronics and Computer Technology

reader who may not be familiar with the company. Boldfacing makes the positions held stand out. Bullets point to significant responsibilities and notable achievements. The Education section appears last.

BRUCE T. THOMAS

98 Ben Franklin Drive • Austin, TX 78734
Home: (555) 222–2222 • ThomasB@aol.com • Work: (555) 333–3333

QUALIFICATIONS PROFILE

Proactive, high-energy individual with more than 25 years of experience in law enforcement principles and practices, as well as state and federal laws relating to correctional and law enforcement agencies. Adept at building trust and developing effective relationships with county agencies and officials. Excellent organizational, time-management, and leadership skills, coupled with the ability to build and manage creative teams. Ability to think clearly and objectively, rapidly assessing the problem at hand while remaining calm in difficult situations.

☑ Penal Code	☑ IJS & RDMT
☑ Emergency Operations	☑ Public Speaking
☑ Community Awareness	☑ Technical Projects
☑ Educating & Mentoring	☑ Hostage Negotiations
☑ Multi-Agency Coordination	☑ Local Government Rules & Procedures

KEY ACHIEVEMENTS

- Pioneered the successful implementation of the RDMT project, an $11 million regional radio system and communications center involving 4 separate government entities. Liaised with Sheriff's office staff and county budget personnel for approval; developed specifications for vendors, and collaborated with attorneys over a 3-month period to write contract.
- Championed project management of IJS (Integrated Justice System) computer system, a $20 million project bringing together the Sheriff's office, Adult Probation, Constables, District Attorneys, County Attorneys, County and District courts, and elected County and District Clerks offices.
- Spearheaded writing of the Standard Operating Procedures (SOPs) for the SWAT unit, ensuring awareness by all parties (SWAT and uniformed patrol) of procedures for SWAT callout, arrival, deployment at scene, use of tactically trained medics, and handling of all victims and witnesses.
- Instrumental in leading more than 50 successful SWAT missions, ensuring the safety of all hostages, civilians, and team members.
- Played a pivotal role in Austin County agency's receiving parity pay with other local law enforcement agencies and retaining experienced staff; researched and created a detailed report to government officials, demonstrating that staff were relocating to other agencies due to pay issues.
- Wrote and submitted a successful grant request for the creation of a Warrant Research unit; unit still exists today.

PROFESSIONAL EXPERIENCE

AUSTIN COUNTY SHERIFF — Austin, TX   1987–Present
Director of Information Systems *(1999–Present)*
Report directly to Major of Austin County Sheriff's office overseeing all technical projects. Act as single point of contact for more than 20 government agencies, handling all data exchange and technology requests from staff. Execute all decisions on vendors used; develop specifications for vendors and recommendations for purchases; authority to handle all disciplinary matters up to, but not including, termination.

- Selected to research, develop, and write a successful budget request for a $5 million Training Facility; gathered outside support from numerous elected officials.
- Determined fiscal requirements and prepared budgetary recommendations for replacement PCs, staff promotions, and recruitment of new staff members.

113

Jennifer Rushton, Sydney, New South Wales, Australia

Printed on a color printer, this resume displays color (light blue) in the e-mail address in the contact information and light gray in the horizontal lines. A strong Qualifications Profile contains checked-box bullets next to areas of expertise. A Key Achievements section is put before a

Professional Experience Continued

- Independently coordinated complex "gap analysis" of the IJS, measuring differences between versions 6 and 7; saved thousands of dollars in maintenance fees and standardized growth ability with software. Collaborated with staff members in presenting results to Austin County agencies, resulting in successful conversion to version 7.
- Successfully rallied community support for the building of a radio antenna in the Austin School District; antenna is 1 of 17 towers in the new RDMT radio system, enabling full county coverage for all public safety agencies—Police, Sheriff, EMS, and Fire Department.

Lieutenant of Tactical Operations *(1994–1998)*

- Successfully led SWAT team to third place in SWAT Police Olympics; SWAT team achieved and maintained the highest level of physical fitness in the agency for 3 consecutive years.
- Planned and executed specialized training with other agencies for SWAT team; involved specialized training from the military in dignitary protection, hostage negotiations, drug lab raids, the use of helicopters in SWAT missions, raid planning, and bomb recognition.
- Independently gained authorization from Fiscal and Command staff to purchase the first "threat level 3 vests" and other costly essential equipment for the SWAT team.
- Collaborated with Sheriff's office and officials in opening a third "courthouse" in the Marks building due to growth; ensured Courthouse security and the safety of all court participants by determining security needs and establishing procedures, becoming the benchmark for Austin Courthouse security.

Lieutenant of Personnel & Training *(1990–1994)*

- Instrumental in managing grant providing Basic Peace Officer Training to students from a 10-county region, with 17 groups successfully graduating. Austin County held the State grant for Basic Peace Officer training and held the state record for 3 years, with a 100% pass rate.
- Played a key role in writing and implementing four annual promotion examinations for Corrections Sergeant, Corrections Lieutenant, Patrol Sergeant, and Patrol Lieutenant.

Sergeant of Special Operations *(1990)*

Sergeant of Patrol *(1987–1989)*

EDUCATION

University of Texas—Austin, TX
Criminal Justice (1994)

CERTIFICATIONS

Graduate of FBI National Academy, 2001
Professional License: Master Peace & Instructor License—TCLEOSE

PROFESSIONAL AFFILIATIONS

Member, Austin County Sheriff's Officers Association
Member, CLEAT

COMMUNITY ACTIVITIES

Original Founder/President—Employee's Association for the Sheriff's Office
Cadet Training Coach—University of Texas

REFERENCES AVAILABLE UPON REQUEST

Professional Experience section to ensure that these achievements will be seen. If you read the resume from the end to the beginning, you will better understand the applicant's growth in his career.

RONALD E. WHITTINGTON, CNE, MCP

1100 Residence Lane
Westings, IL 55555

Residence: (630) 555-0000
ronwhittington@cne.com

———— EXPERIENCED INFORMATION TECHNOLOGY PROFESSIONAL ————

Certified professional with almost 10 years of field experience. Expert in project management, design, development, migration, and implementation of enterprise networking technology. Diverse technical expertise derived from rapid learning and effective application of cutting-edge technology. Highly communicative team leader who motivates and mentors people at all levels of technical expertise. Facilitate problem-solving teams that accurately assess technical challenges and successfully transform ideas into appropriate, workable solutions.

———————————— PROFESSIONAL EXPERIENCE ————————————

ZOISE OFFICE SOLUTIONS, CHICAGO, IL   FEBRUARY 2000–PRESENT
APPLICATION DEVELOPMENT SUPERVISOR

In May 2002, received promotion from senior information systems engineer to application development supervisor. My team is responsible for Contracts and Pricing application development and backline support. Accountable for yearly performance evaluations, project management, total quality management, and priority resource scheduling. Meet with business analysts, managers, and directors to coordinate resources, forecast budgets, and meet deadlines.

Major project contributions:

- Automated Pricing Review for quarterly contract reviews: multi-CPU Intel platform with SQL database on EMC storage
- SOS Catalog: creation of a new pricing logic
- Timán-Zoise tier one joint venture: creation of a new DB/2 database and contract reporting structure
- Contract Access and Security: security profile and architecture enhancements in CICS environment
- Contract Purge Rearchitecture to reduce operating costs and make available valuable resources on AS/400
- Mainframe elimination by providing analysis information for proof of concept to reduce operating costs

SENIOR INFORMATION SYSTEMS ENGINEER

Top-level technical contributor responsible for highly available e-mail infrastructure and virus countermeasures. Provided technical consulting, evaluation, and reviews on complex projects. Qualifications in all facets of project life cycle development, from initial feasibility analysis and conceptual design through documentation, implementation, quality review, and enhancement. Provided long-range capacity planning of enterprise applications and operation systems, database management, and data networks. Effective communicator with associates and senior management. *Earned the Outstanding Achievement Award in October 2000 for demonstrating 110% total quality toward company goals.*

Defined project management methodology to optimize technology resources and applications:

- Implemented Sendmail MultiSwitch on Sun Solaris using EMC storage and Cisco Local Director.
- Replaced outbound fax acknowledgments with e-mail acknowledgments of orders placed by customers.
- Designed a stopgap solution for our customers to e-mail orders.
- Designed maintenance and support programs for the Enterprise Technology Assistance Center.
- Contributed to an enterprise management project to centralize monitoring of e-mail and antivirus software.
- Upgraded Norton AntiVirus to the corporate edition as project manager.
- Contributed to design of migration from GroupWise to Microsoft Exchange 2000.

■ ■ ■

114

Stephanie Whittington, Bolingbrook, Illinois

Printed on a color printer, this resume has elements in color (light blue): the applicant's name in the contact information and in the header at the top of page 2, the partial horizontal lines on each side of the main section headings, the small squares at the bottom of pages 1 and 2,

RONALD E. WHITTINGTON, CNE, MCP

(630) 555-0000   ronwhittington@cne.com

SENIOR TECHNOLOGY SPECIALIST—FRANKLIN HENDERSON LLC, GLEN BROOK, IL   APRIL 1998–DECEMBER 1999

In June 1999, received promotion from technology specialist to senior technology specialist. Was in charge of client relations. *Awarded the Client Partnership Award for 3rd and 4th quarters of fiscal year 1999.* Standardized on Microsoft Windows NT, Novell, Compaq, Cisco, and Computer Associates' ARCserver*IT,* Inoculate*IT,* and FAXserve products.

- Evaluated, tested, and implemented technologies and communications services.
- Developed database, procedures, and systems to support technology deployment.
- Delivered more than $95,000 in additional profit through value-added network consulting in less than one year.

INFORMATION TECHNOLOGY MANAGER—SPI MANAGEMENT ASSOCIATES, INC., NAPERBROOK, IL   JULY 1997–APRIL 1998

Planned and implemented the opening of a branch office. Used Nortel routers for WAN connectivity, 3Com workgroup hubs, and Cisco switches for LAN connectivity. Operated on Novell intraNetWare 4.11 network operating system. Multiple Compaq brand file servers, communications, and e-mail servers enabled task-specific operations.

- Managed help desk and software development personnel and tasks.
- Deployed, trained, and supported Novell GroupWise document management.
- Implemented Novell Application Launcher for central administration of applications.
- Planned Internet connectivity using ISDN dedicated service, IP-to-IPX gateway, and firewall technology.

COMPUTER SYSTEMS MANAGER—ON TOP OF LIFE, INC., DES MOINES, IA   DECEMBER 1995–JUNE 1997

This 24/7 multioffice traumatic brain injury rehabilitation center used NetWare 4.1 network operating system. Supported Marktech clinical and billing application, Kronos time tracking, and DaVince e-mail system. Established key business relationships with the CEO and various upper-level managers. Revitalized operations and led the corporation's launch into emerging technology designed specifically for health care organizations.

- Saved $1 million in travel by implementing video teleconferencing technology over fiber using PictureTel equipment.
- Updated network infrastructure to support switched Fast Ethernet using 3Com switches and workgroup hubs.

"Our organization has grown and benefited from [Ronald E. Whittington's] knowledge and expertise...his interpersonal skills are excellent...he is customer-oriented and responds quickly to any and all requests made of him." (President and CEO)

EDUCATION AND CERTIFICATIONS

BACHELOR OF SCIENCE IN TECHNICAL MANAGEMENT
DeVry University—anticipated completion December 2004

ASSOCIATE IN APPLIED SCIENCE
Joliet Junior College—graduated 1994

Microsoft Certified Professional   **Certified Novell Engineer**
Continuing Professional Education sponsored by Zoise, Sendmail, Omicron, and Martin Training Associates:
Accelerating Project Team Performance   Project Management Framework
Meeting Facilitation Skills   Your Role in Quality
Manager/Supervisor Training   Sendmail MultiSwitch
Negotiations and Conflict Resolution   Project Planning and Controls
                Directory Technology—Active Directory, NDS, Netscape, and LDAP

■ 2 ■

and the page number on page 2. Arial Narrow fonts in the resume make it possible to fit more information on a page. Note the testimonial at the end of the Professional Experience section.

R. K. Ashburn

156 Whittle Circle
Ashburn, GA 31714
rkashburn@AshburnIT.com
Home: (229) 555–2222
Work: (229) 555–3333

TECH PROFILE

IT WEB CONTRACTOR / JAVA PROGRAMMER
Web-focused Application Developer & Database Specialist

- **Strong technical lead and Web consultant** with nearly 10 years of experience in Java, Perl, JavaScript, Java Servlets, HTML, XML, C++, and Visual Basic programming.
- **Accomplished developer of Web-based systems** for e-commerce, monitoring and notification, problem tracking (PTS), multitiered architectures, distributed databases, business automation, and other client/server applications.
- **Versatile team leader and project manager** capable of managing the full application development life cycle for both corporate and government projects.
- **Knowledgeable database manager** skilled in MySQL, Microsoft SQL Server, and Paradox, as well as Windows Advanced Server/Active Directory/NT/CE/2000 and Linux Slackware/RedHat environments.
- **Reputation for self-taught, production-level skills** in more than 75 languages, protocols, application development packages, databases, APIs, IDEs, and operating systems.

AREAS OF EXPERTISE

- Web-based Multitiered Systems
- Java, C++, Perl, and Visual Basic
- Application Development Life Cycle
- Monitoring & Notification Systems
- E-Commerce Capability

- Active Directory Management
- XML / XSLT Programming
- Problem Tracking Systems / Help Desks
- Software Development Bids
- Team & Project Leadership

EXPERIENCE

ASHBURN IT CONSULTING (ASHBURN IT)—Ashburn, GA
Independent provider of Web, database, and related applications for regional businesses, large to small.
IT Consultant/Senior Software Engineer, 2001 to Present
Design, develop, test, and implement database, connectivity, and Web-based strategies.

WEB CONTRIBUTIONS

- **Delivered the full development life cycle of a Web-based multitiered PTS** (problem tracking system), including enhancements and streamlined base code. Used Java and MySQL on a Linux platform. (Georgia Postal)
- **Was tech lead for development of a multitiered XML-based Web site.** Used a MySQL database that was written using Java servlets. (Ashburn IT)
- **Bid/designed/tested/implemented a MANS alert system for the MIRS platform.** Sends alerts via e-mail, paging, and remote pop-up boxes for hardware carousel. Uses Visual Basic, XML, and MySQL. Developed for Northrop Grumman. (Georgia Postal)
- **Led redesign/implementation of the entire backend and database for a Web site** for accountants. Used a Perl backend and Microsoft SQL Server database. Currently maintain the production system to serve 100 affiliates with 1,000 end-user customers. (Ashburn IT)
  - o **Added e-commerce capability to the Web site.**
  - o **Automated the Web site's system administration and Active Directory tasks.** Integrated Microsoft Terminal Services and Active Directory components into the Web site using WSH, Visual C++, and Perl. Also automated the Active Directory tasks by creating WSH scripts in VBScript and Visual Basic.
  - o **Created a Windows-based client/server application and installation script** to transfer files via batch and process remote updates.
  - o **Currently developing a next-generation eXML-based Web site with a distributed multitiered architecture.** Involves components in Java, Perl, and C++.

115

Helen Oliff, Reston, Virginia

E-mail and Web addresses appear in light blue in this resume. A small font (11-point Garamond) allows quite a bit of information on each page. Not shown is a third page—a Technical Addendum—that indicates in detail the more than 75 Web languages and protocols,

R. K. Ashburn
Résumé — Page Two

EXPERIENCE

DATABASE & CONNECTIVITY CONTRIBUTIONS

- **Enforced uniform logging by the distributed components of an online system.** Created a centralized logging system, and integrated SOAP (simple object access protocol) into the applications written in Perl, Visual Basic, and Visual C++. Also created interface to display and filter logging data. (Ashburn IT)
- **Developed the systems and software to support creation, ingestion, and publication of survey metadata** for the Census Bureau. (AIS)
  - o In Java, created a rules-based system to ingest MIF files into a MySQL database.
  - o Developed a stand-alone Visual Basic interface to create MIF files.
  - o In Visual Basic, created a setup program to install the MIF ingestion application.
  - o Designed/implemented a spreadsheet to help create MIF files that used VBA.
  - o Created a Java wrapper to replicate MySQL data to different databases/providers/sites.
- **Helped bid a $900,000 contract to develop an MCD device for a vending machine** to enable credit card transaction processing and connectivity for remote maintenance. (GPS)
- **Helped design/develop a machine conversion device (MCD),** including ANSI C and microprocessor development, on a PBSM-624 vending machine. Designed/implemented the SSE messaging capability. Also ensured network connectivity and enhanced MCD functionality—as a key developer. Used Windows CE and eMbedded Visual C++. (GPS)

GEORGIA POSTAL SOLUTIONS, INC. (GPS)—Atlanta, GA (www.gapostal.com)
Global contractor of IT hardware, software, support, and training to postal services and corporations.
Software Engineer, 1998 to 2001
Provided technical development of mainly postal applications for contract clients.

- **Co-led the upgrade of a legacy IRT system from DOS to Windows** for the U.S. Postal Service. Developed Visual C++ device drivers and a Visual Basic GUI.
- **Customized Visual Basic applications for integration into a Remedy PTS,** including DLLs with the Remedy API in C++.
- **Created a change-of-address system for a self-service kiosk for the PMC/NT.**

ATLANTA INTEGRATION SYSTEMS (AIS)—Atlanta, GA (www.ais.net)
Regional contractor of IT, engineering, and logistics services for government and private industry.
Computer Programmer, 1995 to 1997
Participated in development teams/projects for major problem-tracking and database systems.

- **Helped the development team design a computer-based solution for a manual PTS** with 250 end-users. Used Remedy Help Desk.
- **Supported the development/maintenance of a Visual Basic app for economic data** from the Census Bureau. Included creating a WYSIWYG reporting interface from scratch.
- **Developed Java applets** and created/converted Visual Basic graphics into Java applets.

GEORGIA TECHNICAL COLLEGE (GTC)—Atlanta, GA (www.gatc.edu)
Educator of 15,000 students annually in architecture, engineering, science, technology, and liberal arts.
Computer Programmer, 1993 to 1994
Provided programming, GUI, and tech support services for the College's dining hall service.

- **Developed RMIS maintenance system from scratch for a dining service operation.** Replaced the existing system. Tracked equipment repair status using Paradox and Delphi.
- **Helped support a campus-wide information system for credit card processing** and tracking using Pascal and C.

application/development packages, programming interfaces, databases, and operating systems the person knows through self-teaching. He is working on becoming a Sun Certified Programmer (Java 2 platform).

ALAN MARSHALL

128 Sawdust Lane, Round Rock, TX 78664 • alanmar@yahoo.com

SENIOR NETWORK MANAGER / ENGINEER

13 Years of Verifiable Experience in Enterprise IT Project Management

Certified Internet Webmaster / CompTIA Network+ and Server+ Certified

Thrive in dynamic, changing, high-pressure environments

Consummate Senior Network Manager with proven performance in multiplatform enterprise system maintenance, management, and administration. Expert project manager in "best-in-class" design, redesign, and solutions development and implementation. Extensive experience in leading diverse project teams in multiple and complex projects. Detail-driven, results-focused professional with superior analytical, multitasking, and follow-up skills. Easily interact with all levels of management, staff, and customers. Known ability to translate complex information for universal understanding.

CORE COMPETENCIES

- Specification Analysis
- Test Schedule & Execution
- Project Management

- ISP/Systems Security
- Systems Implementation
- Network Development

- Diagnosis & Resolution
- Process Analysis/Design
- User Training & Support

COMPUTER SKILLS

Platforms:	Windows 3.x–XP, NT 3.01–2000, Linux 7.3–8.0, Novell 2.01-6.0, Cisco IOS 10.2–12.0
Networking:	LAN/WAN (wired/wireless), Ethernet, Fast Ethernet, Gigabit Ethernet, Token Ring, TCP/IP, IPX/SPX, NetBEUI, NetBIOS, NTP, SMTP, POP3, HTTP/S, FTP, NNTP, SNMP, VLAN, RIPv1, RIPv2, IGRP, EIGRP, BGP, PPP, SLIP, DDR
Applications:	Exchange, SMS, IIS, Website Pro, WebTrends, Backup Exec, Legatto, ARCserve, NTMail, Symantec & McAfee Anti-Virus, MRTG, IPTraf, WhatsUp Gold, Imail, Firewall-1, Citrix WinFrame & MetaFrame, MS Terminal Server, Sniffer Pro, Domino, HP-OpenView
Hardware:	Intel Desktop/Notebooks/Servers, Cisco Routers/Switches, Cisco PIX, 3Com/Bay Switches, SonicWALL Firewall Appliances, Orinoco AP1000, SmartBridge AP, SmartBridge Clients, Teletronics CPE, YDI EX-1 Wireless Bridge, MikroTik Routers, ImageStream Routers, Quantum DLT Drive, Miscellaneous Routers/Hubs/Switches

PROFESSIONAL EXPERIENCE

COMPUTER BUSINESS SERVICES OF TEXAS, Austin, TX   1997–Present
Senior Network Engineer
Direct Systems and Network department of 6 technicians in total oversight of enterprise network systems and infrastructure. Design, recommend, implement, and maintain equipment upgrades/modifications and network architectures. Ensure network security access over LAN/WAN, WiFi, telecommunications, and voice. Manage and collaborate with third-party vendors to complete requests for new service. Interview new hires, conduct staff performance evaluations, and provide training and guidance to junior staff.

- Saved $80,000 in annual telecom charges by designing Citrix solution using VPN and wireless technology.
- Recovered more than $35,000 in telecom overbilling.
- Oversaw acquisition of more than $3.5M in network servers and equipment.

CONTINUED...

116

Nick V. Marino, Bishop, Texas

A larger-than-average font (12-, 13-, and 14-point Arial) gets attention in the first part of a two-part profile (not titled) divided by a horizontal line. Elsewhere in the resume, a horizontal line appears under the contact information and each main heading. In the Computer Skills

ALAN MARSHALL
Page Two

PROFESSIONAL EXPERIENCE *CONTINUED...*

- Designed and developed wireless network infrastructure consisting of 10 access points and 9 wireless backhauls and covering more than 780 square miles.

- Installed fiber at no cost to company through proactive collaboration with telecom provider.

- Achieved near-zero downtime, directing conversion to DS3 from multiple frame circuits for DSL customers.

- Created 24/7 network monitoring system for all ISP structures.

TEXAS GENETICS CORP., Austin, TX   1995–1997
Network Administrator
Oversaw and managed all aspects of network systems, including workstations, user account information and rights, security and systems groups, MS Mail, and Exchange e-mail. Recommended, implemented, and maintained network architecture. Built and maintained external and internal web presence. Designed and supported server systems and supporting software. Ensured LAN/WAN security access, protecting against unauthorized access, modification, or destruction using Firewall-1 system.

- Migrated 6 network servers from NetWare to Windows NT on time and within budget, performing project after-hours to limit downtime.

- Migrated e-mail from MS Mail to Exchange for 3 locations and 500 clients without loss of accounts or e-mail.

- Designed and implemented sales-force automation Citrix solution to accomplish real-time access to inventory data over any dialup line.

- Significantly reduced backup time and file recovery for NT and Novell server environment by redesigning backup systems, schedules, and disaster-recovery plan.

- Built and implemented enterprise-wide Internet access using Firewall-1 solution for network security.

NIT COMPUTING, INC., Austin, TX   1991–1995
PC / Network Technician
Maintained, analyzed, diagnosed, upgraded, repaired, and documented computer systems, hardware, software, and peripherals. Supported and maintained user account information, including rights, security, and systems groups for assigned customers.

- Configured and installed more than 1,000 networked PCs in university student labs.

- Configured, installed, and maintained 57 network servers using Novell and Windows NT.

- Researched and implemented ISP department for company offering dedicated and dialup access.

EDUCATION & TRAINING

Associates Degree in Pre-Engineering & Math, Austin Community College, Austin, TX, 1995

Electrical Engineering Course Work, Texas State University, Austin, TX, 1998

CompTIA Network+, CompTIA, Austin, TX, 2000

CompTIA Server+, CompTIA, Austin, TX, 2000

CIW (Certified Internet Webmaster), ProSoft Training, Austin, TX, 2000

section, technical knowledge is conveniently grouped by categories (Platforms, Networking, Applications, and Hardware). In the Professional Experience section, bullets point to achievements.

JOHN STRONG

555 South Lynn Road
Pasadena, California 55555

(626) 555-5555
jstrong@email.com

APPLICATIONS PROGRAMMER—VISUAL BASIC

❑ Technical training plus more than 2 years of experience in program design, development, documentation, implementation and debugging.

❑ Able to understand and interpret needs of end user to design quality software. Consistent attention to detail with an ability to analyze and interpret the implications of decisions to minimize bugs and create user-friendly programs. Skilled in troubleshooting and problem solving.

❑ Quick learner who enjoys challenges and possesses a high level of energy and motivation. Dedicated to seeing projects through to completion.

❑ Experienced collaborating with clients and team members. Ability to convey technical information at all levels.

Computer Applications: Visual Basic... ADO... SQL... Crystal Reports... Windows... Word... Excel... Access... Outlook... FoxPro... Citrix... PC Anywhere... HTML (basic knowledge)... Internet

PROFESSIONAL EXPERIENCE

Application Programmer • 2001 to Present
APPLICATION LEADERS, INC., Pasadena, CA
Write programs in Visual Basic for company providing software solutions to manufacturing industry.
Representative Projects:
- Created, debugged and perfected entry screens for new release of company's main product.
- Produced reports providing critical information on gross profit, inventory transactions/projections, sales forecasts and purchase requirements.
- Wrote program to read EDI documents and generate sales-related reports.
- Collaborated on development of program that enables manufacturer to directly transfer orders to banks for approval using FTP.
- Developed customized programs to meet customer needs.

EDUCATION

PASADENA CITY COLLEGE, Pasadena, CA
Associate of Arts, Social Science May 2003
Honors: Deans List, Honors for Superior Achievement in Economics Award

COMPUTER LEARNING CENTER, Los Angeles, CA
Certificate in Client/Server Programming 2001
Relevant Course Work: Visual Basic, Integrating a Visual Basic Front-End with a SQL Server Back-End, Access, C, C++, Oracle, Client/Server Architecture
Honors: Awarded National Vocational Technical Honors Society Membership

UCLA EXTENSION, Los Angeles, CA, 2002
ActiveX Component Development with Visual Basic 6

117

Vivian VanLier, Los Angeles, California

This applicant completed a certification in client/server programming and wanted to become a Visual Basic Applications Programmer. Lines enclosing Computer Applications promote their readability.

Law/Law Enforcement

Resumes at a Glance

RESUME NUMBER	LAST OR CURRENT OCCUPATION	GOAL	PAGE
118	Merchandise Handler	Paralegal	235
119	Section Commander, Highway Patrol	Law Enforcement Officer/ Highway Patrolman	236
120	Lieutenant of Detectives	Not specified	238

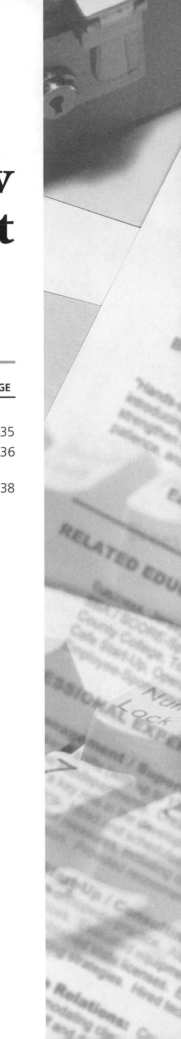

SELENA GAIL COOPERTON

2131 Aaronwood Drive, Gallatin, TN 00000

Home (555) 000-0000 – sgcooper@aol.com

PARALEGAL

Goal: To support attorneys and/or other professionals in a role where training, technical skills, and an understanding of legal concepts will be of value.

Summary of Attributes

- Resourceful and thorough in gathering information and conducting research. Follow through on assignments independently or as an interactive team player.
- Highly organized and detail-oriented; efficiently manage projects with close attention to deadlines and other time constraints.
- Computer experience includes Microsoft Word and WordPerfect in a Windows-based environment. Confident in learning and using new software applications.

Professional Training

PARALEGAL DIPLOMA—Nashville Career Center.. 2004

COURSE HIGHLIGHTS:	Legal Communications – Introduction to Law – Legal Terminology – Paralegalism and Ethics – Legal Documents – Computer and Manual Legal Research – Rules of Court and Procedures – General Legal Practice – Litigation and Business Law
LEADERSHIP:	Member of Student Advisory Board, serving as a liaison between students and staff members.

MCDONALD'S CORPORATION TRAINING CENTER, Brentwood, TN 1999–2000

COURSES:	Management Techniques – Communication Skills – Equipment Operations

Work Experience

THE GAP, Gallatin, TN 2003–Present
- **Merchandise Handler**—Move and transport inbound and outbound merchandise throughout the facility, up to 2,100 cartons per shift.
- Use customized inventory management software to track merchandise, measure inventory accuracy, and generate labels.
- Former team leader for coworkers. Provided direction regarding job assignments and equipment problems.

MCDONALD'S, Tullahoma, TN / Athens, AL 1996–2003
- **Store Manager**—Managed high-volume fast food operations with rapid customer turnover. Scope of responsibility included budget management, profit and loss, cost controls, cash management, purchasing, and inventory.
- Hired, trained, scheduled, supervised, and counseled 13 to 18 crew members.
- Honored as Manager of the Year (2001) and Employee of the Year (1997).
- Progressed through a series of increasingly responsible service and management positions; promoted to **Assistant Manager** in 1999 and Store Manager in 2001.

118

Carolyn S. Braden, Hendersonville, Tennessee

This person wanted to apply her recently acquired paralegal training to a position with a law firm or a company needing a paralegal. The writer focused on the person's education and relevant courses.

William T. Henry

16394 Clark Road   Charles City, IA 50616   henry@internet.com
641-555-8721

Qualifications Summary

- ❏ Veteran law enforcement officer/Iowa Highway Patrol lieutenant.
- ❏ Strong tactical background with expertise in narcotics and critical-incident response.
- ❏ One who leads by example and works to build a consensus among independent interests.
- ❏ Additional specific experience includes
  - Program implementation and administration
  - Building collaborative relationships with local, state and federal agencies
  - Grant writing
  - Officer training
  - Arms and ammunition

Selected Accomplishments

- ❏ Prepared and coordinated grant submissions generating $495,000 for narcotics investigations in Floyd and Butler counties.
- ❏ Earned designation as Expert Witness in Floyd and Johnson counties regarding clandestine methamphetamine labs.
- ❏ Sat on Office of Drug Control Policy (ODCP) committee charged with strategizing and developing policy on legal handling of methamphetamine labs in the state of Iowa.
- ❏ Received citations for Bravery and Professional Excellence.

Career History

IOWA HIGHWAY PATROL (IHP) • Statewide   1978–Present

Section Commander—Butler Area Narcotics Group & Rural Narcotics Unit (2003–Present)
- Manage two multijurisdictional drug enforcement teams (representing 14 agencies) in Floyd and Butler counties. Act as liaison with local agencies and ISP.
- Manage administrative functions, including employee supervision, fiscal management, vehicle fleet and facility maintenance.
- Develop and monitor $2.4 million budget with reporting responsibilities to local, state and federal officials.
- Coordinate and control forfeited property and funds totaling $196,000 per year. Ensure distribution to appropriate agencies.
- Monitor and participate in large-scale, multiple-agency narcotics investigations.
- Prepare grant submissions and oversee expenditures of funded grants.

Team Commander—Methamphetamine Investigation Team (2000–2003)
- Established, coordinated and supervised the state's first methamphetamine investigation team. Led team to become fully functioning within 6 months of appointment.
- Collaborated with local, state and federal law enforcement officials from multiple agencies to assist with policy development and provide training for clandestine lab response and investigation across the state. Also assisted with implementing area task forces.
- Acted as officer in charge on more than 140 investigations and subsequent raids of clandestine labs across the state. Collected evidence, dismantled equipment and coordinated clean-up activities in collaboration with the federal Drug Enforcement Agency and in adherence with OSHA requirements.

119

Janet L. Beckstrom, Flint, Michigan

The applicant had a career in the State Police/Highway Patrol. He was considering retirement to pursue a position with a little less stress, such as Police Chief of a small community. Read this person's Career History from the end of the resume to the first page to get a sense of his

William T. Henry   641-555-8721

Career History

IOWA HIGHWAY PATROL (IHP) • Statewide

Team Commander—Methamphetamine Investigation Team   *(continued)*

- Introduced equipment pool concept to methamphetamine investigation team to minimize need to purchase expensive OSHA-required equipment, thereby saving significant funds.
- Selected to make presentation to judges, law enforcement representatives and community leaders at Methamphetamine Strategy Summit hosted by the Iowa Department of Community Health Office of Drug Control Policy.
- Cowrote grant that received $50,000 to fund federal High-Intensity Drug Trafficking Area program.
- Coordinated the training of 100 local, county and state clandestine lab responders.

Assistant Team Commander—IHP Emergency Support Team (1997–2000)

- Helped supervise and develop team.
- Provided response planning and supervision at critical incidents across the state, including high-profile civil-disturbance events.
- Personally responded to several hundred critical incidents such as barricaded gunmen and hostage situations.
- Coordinated the team's training and equipment needs. Planned, coordinated and purchased equipment for a six-week (240-hour) basic training school.
- Implemented *less lethal use of force* training with the goal of reducing fatal-force incidents.

Shift Supervisor—Mason City IHP Post (1994–1997)

- Supervised post operations and 10 MSP troopers during shift.
- Served as Firearms Instructor. Researched and implemented "simmunitions" firearms training for post personnel.
- Conducted performance appraisals.
- Supervised property/evidence room.

Commanding Officer—Ordnance & Marksmanship Training Unit, IHP Training Academy (1993–1994)

- Oversaw firearms training for in-services and recruits.
- Implemented state-of-the-art decision shooting training and equipment.
- Researched and implemented ammunition changes for departmental rifle; participated in handgun selection.

Trooper—IHP Flint Post (1978–1993)

- Assigned to Floyd County to provide traffic enforcement and criminal investigation.

Training & Education

- ❏ Iowa Highway Patrol Training Academy (including credits from University of Northern Iowa)
- ❏ Iowa State University
- ❏ Selected training on relevant topics (comprehensive list available on request):
  - Leadership Development
  - Supervisor Development
  - Terrorism Responder
  - Hazardous-Materials Site Safety Officer
  - Technician-Level Hazardous-Materials Responder
  - Firearms Instructor
  - Less-Lethal Instructor
  - Chemical Munitions Instructor
  - Weapons Armorer (SigSauer, Remington, and H&K)

career path. Two levels of bullets are used in the Qualifications Summary. The Selected Accomplishments section put early helps ensure that special accomplishments will be seen and read.

John L. Sullivan

674 Loganberry Lane • Freehold, New Jersey 07728
732-467-1512 (Home) • 732-782-4576 (Cell) • 732-782-4579 (Fax) • JLSul@aol.com (Email)

Objective

I wish to utilize my leadership, management, and organizational experience to continue my career in the areas of <u>Operations</u>, <u>Inventory Management</u>, <u>Logistics</u>, and <u>Loss Prevention</u>.

Summary of Qualifications

Broad-based career with experience in the following:

- Supervisory/Management
- Surveillance
- Security and Safety
- Training and Development
- Inventory Control
- Interviewing/Interrogations
- Project Management
- Loss Prevention

Profile

A highly professional individual with diverse experience in law enforcement.....known as a results-oriented professional.....supervised major investigations leading to final solutions including apprehension or restitution.

Obtained state-of-the-art education in criminal justice techniques and technology.....developed excellent communications and data-collection abilities to assist in investigations.

Excellent interpersonal skills utilized to disseminate information to individuals at all levels.

Professional Experience

Bergen County Sheriff's Office, Jersey City, NJ   **1970–Present**

Lieutenant of Detectives	**1991–Present**
Sergeant	**1985–1991**
Officer	**1970–1985**

- Supervise a staff of 25 police officers, including patrolmen, detectives and plainclothes officers. Prepare work schedules, assign duties, and develop and revise departmental procedures.
- Train new personnel, setting goals and objectives and evaluating performance; administer budgets; handle employee relations, labor relations and grievances; write policies and procedures; conduct in-house investigations/oversee disciplinary actions and coordinate public/community relations activities.
- Assist with and monitor arrests; review major reports and collaborate with officers regarding investigative procedures.
- Utilize aggressive investigative work for successful apprehension of suspects; confirm that proper legal procedures are followed for possible judicial presentations.
- Obtain suspect information, apply for search warrants or subpoenas and, when necessary, travel nationwide to apprehend fugitives.
- While on loan to the Prosecutor's Office, performed homicide investigations. Surveillance and investigative process included identifying and locating suspects and proper handling of evidence.
- Knowledge of laws, legal codes, court procedures, precedents, government regulations, executive orders, agency rules and the democratic political process.

120

Beverly and Mitch Baskin, Marlboro, New Jersey

This resume begins with an Objective statement, a resume opener that was common a decade ago but is seen less in contemporary resumes. One reason for the Objective statement's decline in popularity is that, in the hands of an amateur, a poorly worded or too narrowly focused

John L. Sullivan

Pennsylvania Railroad, Newark, NJ　　　　　　　　　　　**1960–1970**

Electrician

- Served a 4-year apprenticeship from entry level to completion as a first-class electrician.
- Maintained and repaired or replaced wiring, equipment and fixtures at Pennsylvania Station in Newark.
- Inspected systems and electrical parts to detect hazards, defects and need for adjustments or repair. Maintenance was approximately 80% of the job.
- Installed electrical wiring, equipment, apparatus and fixtures using hand tools and power tools. Performed new installations approximately 20% of the time.

Awards

Executive Member of New Jersey Police Honor Legion

Member of New York City Police Honor Legion

Twelve commendations for exceptional performance, bravery and superior investigative work

Affiliations

Past President, Policeman's Benevolent Association Local 109

Trustee, Fraternal Order of Police Lodge 127

Military

United States Air Force
Master Sergeant

Active Duty	1956–1960
Reserves	1954–1956, 1960–1965

Education

Jersey City Junior College, Jersey City, NJ—attended for criminal justice courses

New York University, New York, NY—attended for criminal justice courses

Objective statement can lead to an early screening out of the applicant. The Objective in this resume exhibits breadth in declared areas of interest. Another notable feature in this resume is the third page, which lists continuing professional seminars in ascending chronological order

Continuing Professional Seminars

FBI Combat Firearms	1970
Jersey City Police Dept. Combat Shotgun	1971
Jujitsu for Police	1971
Hudson County Prosecutor's Office—Firearms	1972
45 Thompson SMG	1972
9 MM Uzi	1972
M1 Carbine	1972
Electronic Surveillance—Wiretap	1973
Jersey City Police Academy	1973
Photo Surveillance School	1974
Jersey City Police Department Narcotics	1974
Homicide Investigation	1975
Hostage Confrontation Seminar	1976
Criminal Investigation New Jersey State Police	1976
Defensive Driving	1977
Introduction to 2C	1978
Investigation Refresher Jersey City Police Dept.	1982
New Jersey State Police Breathalyzer School	1984
Emergency Medical Technician	1984
Civil Liability	1986
Methods of Instruction	1986
Breathalyzer Refresher	1986
Managing a Detective Unit	1988

from 1970 to 1988. The applicant participated in these continuing-education events while he was first an Officer and then a Sergeant with the Bergen County Sheriff's Office in Jersey City, New Jersey.

Maintenance

Resumes at a Glance

RESUME NUMBER	LAST OR CURRENT OCCUPATION	GOAL	PAGE
121	Apartment Housekeeper	Housekeeper	243
122	Pool Maintenance Technician	Not specified	244
123	Maintenance Leader	Maintenance Specialist	246
124	Airframe and Power Plant Mechanic	Aircraft Maintenance Supervisor	248
125	Lead Aircraft Maintenance Technician	Airframe and Power Plant Mechanic	250
126	Lead Ground Maintenance Technician	Ground Support Equipment Technician	252

KATHRYN TAMBURRO

76 Columbia Street   (555) 555-5555
Frankfort, NY 00000   kart@aol.com

EXPERIENCED HOUSEKEEPING PROFESSIONAL

Offering an excellent customer service philosophy, a professional attitude and proven skills in project coordination

---

PROFILE   Hardworking and self-directed individual with vast experience in providing comprehensive housekeeping services for a multibuilding apartment complex. Qualifications include strong organization skills, a good eye for detail and a bottom-line focus. Effective time manager with great people skills and a reputation for high-service standards. Able to function in a multidimensional role and can perform under pressure.

HOUSEKEEPING SKILLS & EXPERIENCE
- Identifying Deficiencies / Damage Assessment
- Investment Protection / Quality Control
- Carpet & Surface Care Techniques & Systems
- Move-Ins / Move-Outs & Inspection Reports

AREAS OF SUPERVISORY EXPERIENCE
- Work Order Management & Scheduling
- Inspection Procedure Improvement
- Owner Relations / Personnel Training
- Contractor Selection & Scheduling

HIGHLIGHTS
→ Highly skilled at organizing time, resources and workload to maximize daily productivity

→ Able to meet client expectations and overall objectives despite sudden setbacks and changing priorities

→ Experienced in responding to demanding situations and tactfully resolving difficult issues

→ Maintain a high degree of awareness of property owner/tenant sensitivities

→ Skilled at communicating with work crews and able to facilitate cooperation among all groups

EMPLOYMENT EXPERIENCE

1990 to Present **Housekeeping Department**   *Guy Prindle Apartments—Frankfort, NY*

Provide housekeeping services for this 835-unit garden-style apartment complex. Accountable for maintaining all common areas, 31 in-house laundry rooms, main office and the gym. Inspect vacant units to assess overall condition and identify any deficiencies. Prepare inspection reports, formulate damage estimates and schedule work. Coordinate contractor crews (paint, maintenance, carpet) and direct daily efforts to maintain cost and schedule guidelines necessary for apartment turnovers.

Accepted increased responsibilities (3/03) to include some supervisory functions. Oversee work order management and contractor coordination, which includes distributing maintenance calls among seven Maintenance Techs and two Porters. Coordinate maintenance requests and daily tasks to comply with owner's expectations. Credited with resolving a three-month work order backlog despite a staff shortage.

1998 to Present **Owner**   *Kat's Cleaning Service—Frankfort, NY*

Built business from start-up to a consistent client base acquired through referrals only. Provide weekly and biweekly cleaning services for single-family homes, apartments and townhomes. Achieved high levels of customer satisfaction based on honesty, reliability and thorough work.

ADDITIONAL INFORMATION

QUALITIES   Detail-oriented / Persistent / Patient / Good Judgement / High Energy / Friendly Personality
OTHER   Cleaning Product Knowledge / Appliance Life Expectancy / Carpet Wear Issues / Quality Factors
CIVIL SERVICE Completed the General Custodian Civil Service Test (5/02)

121

Kristin M. Coleman, Poughkeepsie, New York

A pair of horizontal lines acts as a banner that attests to the person's excellence and professionalism. Small type (10-point Times New Roman) makes it possible to fit much information on one page.

Jared Davis

320 Fayette Road   Beaumont, Texas 77683   H: (409) 227-3854   C: (409) 929-4512

PROFESSIONAL PROFILE

Multifaceted construction, operations and customer service background includes experience in supervision, plant equipment operations, construction, safety, maintenance, project management, customer service and product sales.

Summary of Skills

Supervision	Organization	Inventory Control
Equipment Maintenance	Scheduling	Problem Solving
Chemical Treatment	Customer Relationships	Sales / Customer Service
Mechanical Troubleshooting	Bid Estimates	Residential Trades

PROFESSIONAL EXPERIENCE

POOL MAINTENANCE TECHNICIAN / CHEMICAL ANALYST   April 2001 to Present
BEAUMONT POOL SERVICES—Beaumont, Texas—Beaumont Pool Services specializes in the construction / installation, maintenance, structural / equipment repair and product sales of residential and commercial pools and spas.

- Manage 24 residential accounts on a biweekly basis.
- Provide customer service and sales for pool / spa chemicals and supplies.
- Coordinate and follow up on equipment repair.
- Retain customer accounts by providing excellent customer service.
- Recognized in a letter of commendation from a "difficult" customer, resulting in "saving" the account..

SALES ASSOCIATE   Aug. 1997 to April 2001
LACK'S—Beaumont, Texas—Lack's is Texas' largest supplier of quality home furnishings, bedding, electronics and appliances, with more than 60 years of dependable family-owned service from 39 home furnishing centers.

- Recognized in the following achievements:
  - *TOP 10% SALES CLUB,* Sealy Posterpedic Mattress, national level
  - Number one sales team, corporate level
  - Highest number of sales generated in a specific period, local level
- Accomplished a 50% ratio of repeat and referred customer database.
- Achieved high closing ratio by gauging customer response and adjusting presentations to resolve customer concerns. Proven success in overcoming resistance to close sales.
- Established a successful sales record in a strictly commission-based environment.
- Enhanced customer satisfaction through continuous implementation of communication and problem-solving techniques.
- Generated $380,000 worth of merchandise sales in the first 12 months.
- Initiated customer financing and maintained database for follow-up.

SALES REPRESENTATIVE   May 1996 to August 1997
COLOR TILE, INC.— Beaumont, Texas—Color Tile was founded in 1953 and is the most recognized name today in the flooring industry with stores nationwide. Color Tile partnered with CarpetsPlus in 2002 to create a national chain of premier floor covering design centers. Color Tile closed the Beaumont store in August 1997.

- Achieved *PRESIDENT'S CLUB* status within 2 months of employment.
- Enhanced production in the areas of negotiating sales, closing sales and customer satisfaction.

122

MeLisa Rogers, Victoria, Texas

The applicant had a multifaceted background in construction, inside retail sales, and part-time domestic work, and he wanted to present it all together in an attractive package. The writer summarized all the applicant's skills early in the resume and then—in the Professional Experience

Jared Davis

Résumé page two

OWNER / MANAGER / SUPERVISOR   May 1994 to December 1996
FRONTIER CONSTRUCTION—Jackson, Mississippi—Frontier Construction consisted of a four–man framing crew specializing in residential home construction in the Northern Mississippi area.

- **Project Management:** Managed up to four concurrent new-construction projects ranging in value from $50,000 to $250,000. Increased business by 20% through positive client relationships and a positive reputation. Secured bid estimates, purchased supplies, hired and trained personnel.
- **Bid Management:** Reviewed and selected bids and proposals, with a proven history of bringing projects in on time and at budget. Developed construction schedules for all phases of work and delegated duties to site lead personnel. Secured various trade crews for 75% of the projects.
- **Safety Management:** Achieved a zero accident rate for crew as a result of follow-through and the implementation of all safety regulations at every project site in a variety of environmental conditions.

CREW SUPERVISOR   October 1990 to May 1994
KRUEGER FRAMING—Jackson, Mississippi—Krueger Framing consisted of two four–man framing crews specializing in residential home construction in the Northern Mississippi area.

- Supervised a four-man crew in residential framing jobs.
- Processed contract bid and negotiation under direction of owner.
- Fielded customer complaints and renovations.
- Assisted in project management of a new venture awarded in a commercial assignment.

OPERATOR / LEAD MAN   February 1988 to October 1990
JENSON FOODS—Biloxi, Mississippi—Jenson Foods was the third-largest poultry operation in the U.S. with corporate offices in Birmingham, Alabama. The Biloxi facility processed approximately 173,000 birds in two production shifts. Tyson Foods acquired Jenson Foods in 1997.

- **Whole-bird Line Lead Man:** Operated bagging /stapling equipment, rerouted non-A-grade birds to packing lines, stacked and moved product to 28-degree room and managed rework process. Assisted supervisor in setting up department for the shift, assigning/motivating department personnel, training new employees and communicating with USDA Grader.
- **Weldatron:** Stacked multiple product lines, managed rework process, moved product to 28-degree room, and trained new employees.

ADDITIONAL TRAINING AND EXPERIENCE

- Currently facilitate employment workshops for a vendor trainer for the State of Texas for the Orange County Development Board. These workshops consist of job search techniques, interviewing skills, career assessments and positive work habits training.
- Achieved Bronze and Silver Award for Sealy Bedding training.
- Completed multiple courses in product knowledge for appliances, technology, fabric types, furniture lines/styles, bedding and floor coverings.
- Completed multiple courses in sales and customer service training.
- Proficient in data entry software programs.
- Knowledge of food processing equipment operations and maintenance.

section—detailed each business, listing under each any corresponding achievements. Notice the use of horizontal lines, the box, and underlining in this resume. Notice, too, the second level of bullets.

Robert Render

147 Englishtown Road ~ Old Bridge Township, NJ 08857
(732) 555-5555 (H) ~ E-mail: render538@aol.com

MAINTENANCE SPECIALIST

Top-performing and motivated maintenance professional with 20 years of experience in manufacturing, distribution, warehousing, line production, maintenance, and equipment operation. Strengths include excellent communication with all levels of personnel. Known as a results-oriented professional with attention to detail.

Self-disciplined leader with the ability to troubleshoot and resolve problems in a timely manner. Enjoy performing multiple tasks/projects while keeping an eye on bottom-line profits for the company.

Experienced in supervising, mentoring, and training staff. Address process improvement issues and find better methods to complete the job with fewer injuries.

Areas of Expertise:

- Project Management
- Equipment Maintenance
- Budget Management
- Preventive Maintenance
- Hydraulic Maintenance

- Low-Pressure Boiler License
- Electrical Maintenance
- Troubleshooting
- Maintenance Supervision
- Licensed Forklift Driver

Experience

PROCTER & GAMBLE, Dayton, NJ   1996–2004

Maintenance Leader

- Perform preventive maintenance and repair of equipment and facility grounds for this food and beverage manufacturing operation with seven manufacturing lines.
- Responsible for machine ownership during product changes, including maintenance and process adjustments.
- Recommend process machinery improvement projects.
- Familiar with conveyors, bottle cleaners, labelers, packers, palletizers, and filling machines.
- Perform work as an electrician, millwright, plumber, and forklift mechanic.
- Thorough knowledge of mechanical, electrical, hydraulic, and plumbing systems for process equipment, as well as for building and grounds.

PHILIPS WAREHOUSE, Bridgewater, NJ   1991–1995

Facility Maintenance Supervisor

- Managed five people at this public warehouse, which stored everything from hazardous chemicals to pencils.
- Responsible for eight different facilities, ordering supplies and scheduling manpower and boiler operations.
- Saved the company $5,000 by upgrading the electrical panels using in-house labor.
- Thorough knowledge of procedures and techniques used for shipping, receiving, and materials handling.

Continued

123

Beverly and Mitch Baskin, Marlboro, New Jersey

A two-line page border ties together visually the two pages of this resume. One thick line appears below the contact information, and two thinner lines enclose the Areas of Expertise. The result is that these areas are easily spotted on the first page. In the Experience section,

Robert Render

Page 2

LARRY'S ELECTRICAL SERVICE, Helmetta, NJ   1987–1991

Electrical Technician

- Installed electrical wiring, equipment, apparatus, and fixtures for both residential and commercial customers.
- Inspected systems and electrical parts to detect hazards, defects, and need for adjustments or repair.
- Tested electrical systems and continuity of circuits in electrical wiring, equipment, and fixtures using testing devices such as ohmmeters and voltmeters.
- Diagnosed malfunctioning systems, apparatus, and components using test equipment.

LOUIS FAMILY FOODS, Lansdale, MD   1986–1987

Facility Maintenance

- Responsible for daily maintenance of the facility and grounds, as well as the process equipment for the manufacture of food.
- Skills necessary to perform the job were the functions of a welder, pipe fitter, rigger, and millwright.

AMERICAN STRUCTURAL STEEL, Manville, NJ   1984–1986

Welder / Blueprint Coordinator

- Daily duties included layout of parts, interpreting locations from the blueprints; welding; and fabrication of steel structures.

Special Training/Licenses

EAST BRUNSWICK VOCATIONAL TECHNICAL SCHOOL, East Brunswick, NJ
Electrical Career Path

Black Seal Low-Pressure Boiler License, State of New Jersey

Forklift License

CPR and First Aid Training, Procter & Gamble, Dayton, NJ

bullets point to a mix of responsibilities and achievements. Boldfacing helps the reader spot key information, such as headings, company names, job positions, and dates. See Cover Letter 8.

Ready to relocate to the Clovis area

Charles Henry Kraft

2102 Sledgeway Street
Anchorage, Alaska 99517

✆ 907.555.5555 (Cell)
apmaster@whiz.att.net

WHAT I CAN OFFER TOPLINE AIRLINES AS YOUR NEWEST AIRCRAFT MAINTENANCE SUPERVISOR

❑ Credibility at every level, from management to line mechanic ❑ Skill to find, interpret, and act on trends to build productivity and limit liability ❑ Focus that removes every distraction from the workplace ❑ Skill to find, reward, and retain the best in aircraft maintainers ❑ Knowledge to separate symptoms from problems

LICENSURE AND CERTIFICATIONS

❑ Airframe & Powerplant License Number 44409976

RECENT WORK HISTORY WITH EXAMPLES OF PROBLEMS SOLVED

❑ **A & P Mechanic** *promoted from 10 eligibles (all with years more experience) to* **Alternate Lead Mechanic.** *Promoted from 3 eligibles in just 90 days to* **Lead Mechanic** *and* **RII Inspector,** Alaska Wings, Anchorage, Alaska   Dec 90–Present
Alaska Wings operates nine all-cargo aircraft, primarily in state. Annual sales approach $45M.

Supervise six A & P professionals.

Serve as the **only maintenance decision maker** on my shift. Regularly guide pilots in assessing write-ups that occur hundreds of miles from our home base. *Results:* Consistently **strike the right balance** between **maximizing time in the air** and operating in **complete safety.**

Made myself the key person in bringing on a new model aircraft critical to a major expansion. Oversaw the cargo conversion. Plowed through half a room full of boxes of records to **ensure compliance** and convert MX records to our standard. *Results:* **Easily trained our people on a type they had never seen before.**

Zeroed in on a **tiny indicator of a potentially large problem:** a newly painted-over screw. Quickly realized my finding pointed to a missed critical inspection of flight control surfaces. Got the right checks done fast. *Results:* We placed our **new airplane online with complete confidence.**

Removed a major frustration for our mechanics: reference materials that were too far from our work area. Created a mobile library. *Results:* **Saved nearly $4K** in lost labor hours alone. New arrangement made it easier for me to **help new people** find just the references they needed.

124

Don Orlando, Montgomery, Alabama

This individual wanted to leave Alaska for the warmer climates of the lower 48. The writer wanted to set the applicant apart by showing "the unusually harsh conditions under which he succeeded." A company wants to know what a prospective employee can offer the

CONFIDENTIAL

Charles Henry Kraft   **Aircraft Maintenance Supervisor**   907.555.5555

Used my "systems view" to fix a critical write-up that had not only stumped our maintainers, but also threatened a late departure. *Results:* Not only fixed the problem in 30 minutes, but **made certain everybody in the shop could do the same thing.**

Make training a part of everyday operations. My regular follow-ups help us **find and reward the best.** *Results:* **Directors** of Maintenance and Quality Control **accept my recommendations** for task assignments without change.

❏ **A & P Mechanic** *with later additional duties as* **RII Inspector.** Northern Lights Air, Kenai, Alaska   Dec 87–Dec 90
Northern Lights Air operated eight aircraft to carry passengers and mail as a commuter service.

Supervised three A & P mechanics.

PROFESSIONAL DEVELOPMENT

❏ "Line Maintenance for the PW100 Series Engine," SECA, one week, 03
My employer chose me as one of 6 (from a group of 18) to attend this training funded by my company.

❏ "Updating Hot Section Inspection of the Pratt & Whitney PT6 Engine," Pratt & Whitney, one day, 02.

❏ "Maintaining the EMB 120 Aircraft Propeller," Hamilton-Sunstrand, two days, 02.
One of 5 selected from a group of 18 eligibles.

❏ "EMB 120 Aircraft Line Maintenance," Skywest, one week, 99. *Paid for by my employer.*

❏ "Hot Section Inspection of the Pratt & Whitney PT6 Engine," Dallas Aeromotive, one day, 99.

❏ "Maintenance Procedures for the Beechcraft 1900 Airliner Series," Flight Safety International, two weeks, 87. *I paid for this program myself.*

COMPUTER SKILLS

❏ Proficieint in **proprietary aircraft maintenance software suite**

❏ Working knowledge of Word and Outlook

PROFESSIONAL AFFILIATIONS

❏ Member, Professional Aviation Maintenance Association, since 99

company. The resume begins with this issue and meets it head on. A company also wants results, not a lot of talk. The Recent Work History section presents, one after another, results of problems solved. See Cover Letter 9.

THOMAS A. NABORS

476 Murray Lane • Goodlettsville, TN 00000 • Home (555) 000-0000

AIRCRAFT MAINTENANCE & TECHNOLOGY

FAA-LICENSED A&P MECHANIC with more than 18 years of experience in the maintenance, repair, troubleshooting, and inspection of civilian and military aircraft. Familiar with all Federal Aviation Regulations (FARs). Qualified by experience, education, and training to assume new leadership and supervisory challenges. Expertise includes the following:

<u>Civilian Aircraft:</u>	Saab 340 (A, B, B+ models) – Saab 2000 – British Aerospace Bae-146 100/200 and JS 3100/3200 – Canadair CRJ – Embraer 120/135/145 – ATR-42/72 – DeHavilland Dash-8 – Shorts 360
<u>Military Aircraft:</u>	B-52 (G, H models) – C-130
<u>Airframe Structures:</u>	Sheet Metal – Composite – Painting
<u>Systems:</u>	Electrical Hydraulic – Landing Gear – Instrument – Flight Controls – Pneumatic – Heating/Pressurization – Fuel – Oxygen – Fire Extinguishing
<u>Powerplant:</u>	Turbine Engine – Fuel-Metering Systems – Ignition Systems – Propeller and Governing Systems

PROFESSIONAL EXPERIENCE

READYSTEP AIRTECH (a full-service, FAA Class 4 certified repair station) – Nashville, TN 1997–Present

Lead Aircraft Maintenance Technician (2001–Present)
- Promoted to manage and schedule work assignments of four Technicians and supervise training and performance. Make certain that Technicians use correct technical data.
- Ensure that planes are inspected according to schedule and are ready by delivery date. Order parts for various aircraft models.
- Follow FARs and airlines' procedures on standard maintenance and custom-requested items.

Aircraft Inspector (2000–2001)
- Evaluated the quality of maintenance and repair work performed by Technicians. Inspected and followed up on completed work and advised supervisor of any problem areas.

Aircraft Maintenance Technician (1997–2000)
- Performed maintenance, troubleshooting, and repair of aircraft systems.

U.S. AIR FORCE – Stationed at various AFBs throughout the country 1986–1997

Advanced through a series of increasingly responsible assignments based on knowledge of aircraft maintenance and repair, technical abilities, and overall performance. Received numerous medals for meritorious service and outstanding achievement throughout military career, including Commendation Medal, Achievement Medal, Outstanding Unit Award, and National Defense Service Medal. Served four years in support of Operation Desert Shield/Desert Storm. Held Secret Security Clearance.

Aircraft Maintenance Supervisor / Crew Chief – Ellsworth AFB, SD (1992–1997)
- Achieved impeccable quality assurance and safety records and was cited for superior after-flight inspections.

Continued . . .

125

Carolyn S. Braden, Hendersonville, Tennessee

The aviation industry has been hit hard with downsizing and cutbacks. This candidate felt that his position was in jeopardy. He wanted to step up to a senior supervisory or management role. The writer designed the resume so that it reflected the applicant's experience, education, and

THOMAS A. NABORS   Page 2

PROFESSIONAL EXPERIENCE (continued)

Aircraft Maintenance Supervisor — Wurtsmith AFB, MI (1991–1992)
- Selected for special maintenance position servicing B-52 aircraft for first-strike "real-world" missions in the Persian Gulf during Desert Storm. Inspected and troubleshot all types of problems under time-critical schedules. Twelve planes launched and 17 recovered in 48 hours; 24 ready aircraft launched in only five days.

Aircraft Maintenance Assistant Crew Chief — Fairchild AFB, WA (1987–1991)
- Trained and mentored mechanics servicing B-52H airplanes.
- Member of a team that achieved unprecedented aircraft sortie rates and systems reliability; received consistent 100% pass rates on safety practice evaluations.

Aircraft Maintenance Team Technician — Fairchild AFB, WA (1986–1987)
- Completed on-the-job training program ahead of peers with a final "closed book" test score of 90% in all areas (significantly above unit average).

EDUCATION & PROFESSIONAL DEVELOPMENT

FAA AIRFRAME & POWERPLANT LICENSE, 1994
License #000000000

AIRCRAFT MAINTENANCE TECHNOLOGY
Community College of the Air Force — Maxwell AFB, AL
Successfully completed 110 hours toward A.A.S. degree.

Supervisory Training:
Management & Human Resources Development / Total Quality Concepts, 1993
Introduction to Supervision & Training Management Courses, 1989

Technical Training:
Fam Classes in Saab 340 and ATR 72
Canadair CRJ Training
Weight and Balance & Hazardous Materials Handling Training, 1994
B-52H Engine Operations Certification Training
Aircraft Maintenance (B-52G/H) Crew Chief & Follow-On Training Courses
Aircraft Maintenance Career Development Course (with Honors), 1987
Aircraft Maintenance Technical Training School (160 hours), 1987

Computer Skills:
Sperry Remote Computer Terminal for Maintenance Data Collection
Microsoft Office (Word), Windows 3.1/95/98/Me/2000/XP
Internet navigation and research, e-mail, faxing, scanning

ADDITIONAL INFORMATION

Member of Tennessee Air National Guard (1998–Present)
Maintain and repair C-130H aircraft.

Willing to travel worldwide. Hold current U.S. passport.

---

training, plus his knowledge and skills acquired in private industry and the military. The Aircraft Maintenance & Technology section thus provides technical information as an indication of the person's expertise.

Lewis Smith

4702 NW 1659 SE, Seattle, WA 99999
Home: (555) 555–5555 ◆ Mobile: (777) 777–7777

Experienced Ground Support Equipment Technician with more than 17 years of experience in the airline ground maintenance industry. Extensive hands-on expertise in performing and supervising minor and major maintenance for airline ground equipment. Key strengths include:

- Maintenance Operations
- Vendor Relationship Management
- Hazardous Materials Awareness
- Project Management
- Program Coordination
- Fabrication
- Staff Training & Leadership
- Inventory Control
- Team Building

Outstanding troubleshooting ability and a proven track record of high levels of quality assurance, cost savings, productivity, and overall equipment readiness. A skilled training instructor with expertise in parts management and interpretation of system schematics. Committed to quality workmanship and ethical conduct.

Professional Experience

ALASKA AIRLINES, Seattle, WA 1987–Present
Progressed to Senior-level Technician in Seattle. Rated #2 GSE shop in the Northwest for Alaska Air Group in 2002 and 2003.

Lead Ground Maintenance Technician

- Oversee and coordinate service operations for more than 300 pieces of ground equipment for up to 20 city stations throughout Washington, Idaho, California, and Canada.
- Substantial mechanical and electrical systems training and experience aid in immediate repair of breakdowns, avoiding air flight delays.
- Trained more than 25 agents on correct operation of ground equipment, resulting in proper safety and injury-prevention practices.
- Awarded the Top Performer bonus for first-class commitment and service in 2001 and 2002.
- Instrumental in development of ongoing out-station repair and maintenance program.
- Provide courtesy technical support to other airlines, establishing solid relationships with station managers and agents.
- Recognized mechanical resource person. Interpret nontechnical descriptions, aiding in troubleshooting and correcting problems over the phone to outstations.
- Compose maintenance flow sheets and parts ordering sheets; maintain detailed documentation records on all equipment and parts.
- Fabricate various ground equipment, including bag carts, tow bars, LAV carts, deicers, truck flat beds, and bulk tanks with heat systems.
- Basic hands-on computer knowledge, including Windows and the Internet.
- Rapid advancement through series of progressively responsible positions in recognition of leadership capabilities, performance, and technical expertise. Other positions included On-Call Ground Maintenance (1994–1996), Ground Service Agent (1988–1994), Aircraft Groomer (1987–1988).

Continuing Education

Lektro Maintenance and Troubleshooting—model AP8850SDA-AL-100
Aero Specialties—Hobart models 600 & Jet-Ex4D
Maintenance and Troubleshooting—Hobart models GPU-600, Jet-Ex4D, & 90CU24P5
Charging Systems & Starting Circuits
Automotive Painting
Delta Weld 451-641
GPU Training, Welding, & Basic Hydraulics

126

Denette Jones, Boise, Idaho

The horizontal lines enclose and thereby call attention to the applicant's key strengths that are relevant to aircraft maintenance. Under Professional Experience, bulleted items include achievements.

Management

Resumes at a Glance

RESUME NUMBER	LAST OR CURRENT OCCUPATION	GOAL	PAGE
127	Office Manager	Office Manager	255
128	Office Manager	Not specified	256
129	Medical Assistant and Accounting Manager	Apartment Managers	257
130	Manager, Service Department	Project Manager	258
131	Budget Manager	Insurance Professional	259
132	President, Supermarkets	Retail Executive	260
133	General Manager	Retail Manager	261
134	Junior Logistician	Office Manager	262
135	Project Manager	Business Manager	264
136	Senior VP/CRM Business Process Integration Manager	Senior Manager	266
137	Hazardous Waste Manager	Executive Manager	268
138	Warehouse Manager	Operations Manager	270
139	Manager, Purchasing and Materials	Administrative/Business Manager	272
140	Director of Resource Planning	National Workforce Manager	274
141	Senior Account Manager	Visual Merchandising Manager	276
142	Store Manager	Customer Service/Operations Manager	278
143	Manager, CD Superstore	Retail Store Manager	280
144	Store Manager	Manager/Consultant/Trainer	282
145	Store Director	Retail Store Operations Director	284
146	Lead Consultant Supervisor	Regional/District Retail Manager	286
147	Store Manager	Retail Manager	288

CINDY WALSTROM

111 Beech Street
Fort Norris, PA 99999

(555) 555-5555
cwalstrom@dotresume.com

CAREER SUMMARY

Award-winning office manager with solid experience in bookkeeping and finance, supervision, customer service, and computer troubleshooting.

PROFESSIONAL EXPERIENCE

Fifteen years of office and related management experience with Shop Fresh at Darby and other locations in the western Philadelphia suburbs. Promoted rapidly through increasing levels of responsibility: Bakery Manager (1988–1990), Front-End Night Manager (1990–1992), Front-End Manager (1992–1994), Backup Office Coordinator (1994–1997), and Office Coordinator (1998–present).

SELECTED ACCOMPLISHMENTS

- Received excellent performance evaluations from nine managers at four locations.
- Won five five-star recognition awards for outstanding customer service.
- Achieved 100 percent success rate selecting and training more than 20 employees for more-responsible customer service and office duties. All performed well in new assignments.
- Ranked first in loss prevention among similar departments in district covering 20 locations.
- Resolved budgeting and scheduling problems resulting from erroneous wage reports by developing a procedure that accurately calculates daily wages.

BOOKKEEPING / FINANCE

Manage all financial aspects of store with annual sales exceeding $20 million.

- Balance cash and other sales receipts daily.
- Compute weekly and yearly sales, analyze trends, and prepare forecasts.
- Calculate weekly payroll for 100 employees on different pay schedules.
- Develop weekly labor cost analysis and compare against budget.
- Process accounts payable.

MANAGEMENT

Oversee 50 supervisory, clerical, and support personnel—20 as direct reports—and advise backup managers at six other locations.

- Assist director in hiring, firing, rewarding, and disciplining employees.
- Schedule employees to provide sufficient coverage while remaining within budget.
- Train employees in job responsibilities, system changes, and new policies and procedures.
- Ensure that customers receive courteous, efficient service.
- Maintain confidential employee records.

COMPUTER SKILLS

Hardware: Proven ability to troubleshoot and repair computers, printers, and scanners. Provide first-level support in store. Upgrade, rebuild, and build PCs from scratch in spare time.
Applications: Proficient in Microsoft Word and Excel. Use Excel daily to record sales and generate trends for forecasts. Also utilize specialized sales balance and payroll software.
Operating Systems: Working knowledge of Microsoft Windows 98, NT, Me, and XP.

EDUCATION, SEMINARS

Seminars: Americans with Disabilities Act, EEO Policy, Handling Employee and Customer Accidents, Point-of-Sale Balance Software, Visual Labor-Management (VLM) Scheduling and Payroll Software.

Richmond Area High School, Oak Glenn, PA. Honor roll student.

127

Jan Holliday, Harleysville, Pennsylvania

This individual wanted to move from retail to a corporate environment. The writer therefore emphasized accomplishments and transferable skills that would be valued by any employer.

ELAINE MIRAMONT
78 Norwalk Street
New York, NY 00000
(555) 555-5555

QUALIFICATIONS SUMMARY

Offering 19 years of **MEDICAL OFFICE** experience. Excellent planning, organizational and administrative skills combine with strong performance in staffing, productivity improvement and patient service/satisfaction. Demonstrate high level of professionalism and compassion with patients. Equally comfortable with front or back office. Qualifications include the following:

- Medical Assistant Skills
- Patient Appointments / Surgical Scheduling
- Medical Office Terminology & Transcription
- Purchasing & Inventory Management

- ICD-9 Codes
- Physician & Provider Relations
- Staff Training & Development
- Files & Records Management

PROFESSIONAL EXPERIENCE

Executrix, Edward Jones Trust, Dublin, CA (2001 to present)

Wilson Group, New York, NY (1988 to 2001)
Office Manager

Managed administrative activities at a surgical practice with 6 surgeons and several support personnel. Maintained well-organized, efficient office operations. Oversaw human resources, office systems, purchasing, finance/accounting, patient relations, record keeping and regulatory affairs. Clinical functions encompassed assisting physicians with minor surgical procedures, patient exams, disposal of hazardous materials, patient flow and preparation of tissue samples and cultures.

Contributions

- Conducted phone triage, booked surgeries and surgical assistants, obtained pre-authorization from insurance companies and scheduled patient pre-op appointments.
- Directed human resources functions of interviewing, hiring and training in office procedures and sterile techniques.
- Managed physicians' monthly production reports that involved tracking number of referrals, referrals source, and accounts receivable.
- Spearheaded new office opening, including layout of business area, reception room, 3 exam rooms, 2 physicians' offices, lab and kitchen and installation of phone service; established office procedures.
- Enrolled physicians with 15 insurance companies.

Richard Murray, M.D., New York, NY (1980 to 1986)
Office Assistant & Receptionist

Assigned to 3 dentists in a practice with 5 dentists, 2 hygienists, 2 insurance secretaries and 5 dental assistants. Fielded a high volume of telephone calls in a fast-paced, demanding environment.

Contributions

- Spearheaded the initial computerization to fully automate record keeping, appointments, insurance, billing and patient database functions; assisted in entering patient data for more than 2000 patients.
- Managed Capitation Program that encompassed managing appointments and enrollment verification of patients serviced with accounts receivable.
- Recommended and implemented new filing system that increased efficiency and accessibility.

EDUCATION

A.S., Medical Assisting, Valmore Community College, New York, NY

128

Louise Garver, Enfield, Connecticut

This person had to take a leave from her career to serve as a Trust Administrator in another state. She was now ready to resume her career. The resume focuses on her strengths and accomplishments.

Pamela Heshe ◆ Katherine Heshe

1234 SE 23rd Avenue   Rhododendron, Oregon 55555   555-555-5555

Apartment Managers

Professional Profile

✓ Highly motivated, dynamic and energetic, with more than 30 combined years of experience successfully working with diverse personalities.

✓ Experienced management and maintenance of various houses and plexes.

✓ Possess strong organizational skills and effective paper-processing techniques.

✓ Expert bookkeeping abilities.

✓ Skills include minor repairs, simple plumbing, light electrical, painting, pool maintenance, landscaping, strong maintenance and clean-up experience.

✓ Effective in prequalifying new lease applicants and collecting rents in a timely fashion.

✓ Personable, loyal, honest, committed and creative. Able to maintain property impeccably and get along well with tenants and management.

✓ Able to be bonded if necessary.

✓ Computer-literate.

◆

Pamela Heshe	**Katherine Heshe**
Employment History	**Employment History**
Medical Assistant · Portland, Oregon · *1990–2004*	**Accounting Manager/Administrative Assistant** · National Metal Distributors, Inc. · *2000–2001* Vancouver, Washington
· OHSU Sellwood/Moreland Clinic · *1999–2004*	**Bookkeeper** · *1998–2000* · Aerospace & Corrosion International Vancouver, Washington
· Medical Temporary · *1990, 1991, 1995, 1997, 1999*	**Letter Carrier** · *1976–1997* · United States Postal Service Portland, Oregon
· Mount Tabor Medical Group · *1996–1997*	
· Dr. Samuel Miller · *1991–1995*	
Education	**Military**
Medical Emphasis · *1988* · Clackamas Community College · Oregon City, Oregon	**United States Air Force** · *1971–1975* · Disbursement Accountant
Graduate · Portland Community College · Portland, Oregon	**Education**
Graduate · Oregon X-Ray Institute · Portland, Oregon	**Elliott Bookkeeping School** · *1998* **Portland Community College** Accounting · *1976*

129

Rosie Bixel, Portland, Oregon

This is a rare resume because it is for two people: members of an apartment management team. The writer combined their skills in one Profile but presented their individual backgrounds separately.

Roger Grant

2345 N.E. 302nd Lane • Portland, Oregon 33333

555-555-5555 *cell* rg32812@easystreet.org *home* 555-555-5555

Project Manager

Professional Profile

Hardworking, disciplined, and energetic *Project Manager* with extensive experience in all aspects of the electrical industry. Proven strengths in effective Project Management with a history of finishing projects ahead of schedule and under budget while increasing company profits. Possess great "people" skills and a well-developed sense of humor. Strong business networking skills with a commitment to professionalism and a job well done while thoroughly enjoying a challenge.

Outstanding Accomplishments

- Advanced from Purchasing Agent to Management in four years, increasing sales from $8 thousand to $4 million per year.
- Tripled business in two years while managing Dynaelectric Service Department.
- Produced largest profits in twenty years while at Siriani.

Selected Projects

Lloyd Center Mall—Security camera installation
Most sophisticated system on the West Coast—Finished **ahead of schedule** and **under budget**
City of Portland—Portland Building electrical retrofit
Class A high-rises and various other projects for City of Portland and Multnomah County
Port of Portland—Portland International Airport
Duty-free Stores • Hudson News • Satellite Installations • Tenant Installs
Tyco—various projects—Honored as outstanding Project Manager
Oregon Health Sciences University—Primate facility
Nike—various projects

Related Employment History

Manager • Service Department • Dynaelectric, *a division of Emcor* • Portland, Oregon • *1998–present*
Emcor is the largest specialty contractor in the world.

Start-up Assistant • Team Electric • Portland, Oregon • *1998*
Assisted in development of service division. Extensive estimating and project management.

Service Manager • Siriani Electric • Portland, Oregon • *1994–1998*
Developed service department to $500,000–$700,000 with an approximate gross profit of 35%.
Dispatched, scheduled, estimated and billed using "Estimation" and "Contest" computer programs.

Purchasing Agent • Grasle Electric • Portland, Oregon • *1989–1994*
Functioned as Interim Service Manager and purchased all items as necessary for service department.

Deliveries / Customer Service • Pepco Electric • Portland, Oregon • *1983–1989*
Drove route truck, pulled orders and supplied customer service.

Training

Graduate • NECA *(National Electrical Contractors Association)*
Project Management *and* **Estimating Classes** • NECA

130

Rosie Bixel, Portland, Oregon

The writer sought to display this Electrician's major projects and outstanding accomplishments with well-known corporations. The Professional Profile makes clear his status as a Project Manager.

LAKEISHA JOHNSON

100 Laurel Lane
Brooklyn, NY 00000
000.000.0000
zzz@zzzzzzz.zzz

INSURANCE PROFESSIONAL

Extensive experience in increasingly responsible positions encompassing pension-plan administration and record keeping, customer service, employee supervision, strategic financial planning, budgeting and expense management, and general ledger maintenance.

- ◆ **Saved department more than $500,000** by identifying and resolving chargeback discrepancies.
- ◆ Managed development of 100-page Small Group Department's Key Operating Measures Package.
- ◆ Revised new business-reporting procedures, resulting in twenty-fold increase in frequency reports produced in support of management decision making.
- ◆ Communicated section of department's business plan as part of formal presentation to Small Group Department.

SKILLS

PeopleSoft	Access
Lotus	Excel
Word	Harvard Graphics
DisplayWrite 4	XYZ Expense Processor System
XYZ General Accounting System	Corporate Budget and Reforecast System
Voice Chargeback Reporting System	XYZ Hardware, Software Purchasing System

RELATED EXPERIENCE

XYZ Healthcare, New York, NY   *1992–2004*

Budget Manager, 1999–2004

- ◆ Managed and implemented annual expense budget for 1,000-employee department, generating $1 billion in revenue.
- ◆ Identified and recommended opportunities for managing risk and achieving budget, profit objectives.
- ◆ Reviewed and approved all department purchases and expenses.
- ◆ Prepared and presented comprehensive array of financial and statistical reports for key department decision makers.
- ◆ Cocreated Key Operating Measures Package for Senior Management.

Senior Pension Accountant / Supervisor, 1992–1999

- ◆ Supervised team of six analysts, providing record-keeping services for clients with defined-contribution pension and profit-sharing plans.
- ◆ Hired and trained new staff.
- ◆ Serviced clients' unique reporting requirements.
- ◆ Evaluated and recommended improvements to system work flows and processes.
- ◆ Orchestrated successful conversion of client files to new administration system.

EDUCATION

Kings County Community College, Brooklyn, NY
A.S., Business

131

Ellen Mulqueen, Hartford, Connecticut

This candidate had only an associate's degree. The writer wanted to emphasize the applicant's skills, illustrate her achievements, and show how far she had come without a bachelor's degree.

JEFF GOLDMAN

Performance-driven executive with a wealth of operations and management experience whose accomplishments reflect outstanding leadership skills and a long-term focus on maximizing efficiency and productivity

SUMMARY OF QUALIFICATIONS

Goal-oriented executive with extensive experience in retail operations and administrative management. Demonstrated expertise in orchestrating performance turnarounds. Long-standing track record of success in identifying and exploiting key improvement opportunities to drive sales and increase profits. Open, honest, and respected manager who leads by example and is effective at motivating team to achieve outstanding results. Demonstrated commitment to efficiency and productivity that carries through entire organization. Driven leader with passion for excellence.

PROFESSIONAL EXPERIENCE

GREAT AMERICA SUPERMARKETS, Mountainview, Pennsylvania   1985 to present
President, Southern Region (6/02 to present)
Currently oversee network of stores in southern region, directing 4500 staff members through team of direct reports. Worked way up through organization, holding a series of management positions of increasing responsibility.

Performance Excellence

- Recognized for ability to effect change and improve profitability. Brought in to turn around performance of troubled Southern Region.
- Led New England team that earned ranking as top-performing group in the company.
- Effectively orchestrated new-store openings in Pennsylvania. Oversaw opening of seven stores in seven months, each of which exceeded all performance goals.
- Established long-standing record of productivity excellence, leading teams ranked best nationwide. Consistently maintain shrink at levels that are among the lowest in the industry.
- Implemented seasonal programs throughout 900 stores, achieving 25% growth in two years.

Operations Improvement

- Analyze and organize all areas of operations, instituting plans, policies, and controls to support business goals.
- Developed planning technology and operating guidelines for unit, district, divisional, and chain-wide operations that took into account the unique challenges and requirements of individual locations.
- Coordinated with merchandising management to implement strategies to exploit unique local opportunities.
- Integrated technology and education to dramatically elevate productivity, cultivating an environment for the successful implementation of new processes and procedures that substantially improved operations.
- Instituted shrinkage control measures that consistently reduced losses through the establishment and communication of team goals, enhanced staff training, and improved monitoring.
- Introduced proactive customer service culture, elevating service levels, enhancing company profile, and contributing to profit growth and competitive advantage.

Administrative Management

- Prepared and administered annual operating and expense budgets of up to $3 billion, applying skill in financial forecasting and analysis.
- Observed and evaluated consumer and market data to discover emerging trends, determine competitive position within the industry, and identify future opportunities.
- Developed and implemented performance management initiatives that used incentive programs to communicate performance expectations and motivate staff to attain them.
- Planned, organized, and directed comprehensive staff and management training programs. Successfully trained 65 new corporate managers and 12 new store managers within twelve-month period.
- Organized and administered employee recruitment and retention programs, including efforts successful in consistently reducing turnover.

8 WILSON AVENUE ▪ MIDDLEBORO, PA 22222 ▪ (333) 333-3333

132

Carol A. Altomare, Three Bridges, New Jersey

This Supermarket Executive had no degree but had worked his way up through the organization. He wanted to keep things simple and direct. He liked grouping his accomplishments under headings.

Jason J. Gill

9803 Clinton Avenue ▪ Houston, TX 77068 ▪ name@yahoo.com
home: 000-000-0000 ▪ mobile: 000-000-0000

Career Target: Retail Management

Results-driven, customer-centered manager with 3 years of experience in store-management positions. Verifiable talent for maintaining profitable retail operations, with success in capitalizing on growth opportunities, implementing promotional/marketing strategies, and upholding fiscal efficiency. Articulate communicator and effective trainer skilled in achieving employee buy-in on organizational goals. Respected, trusted manager who upholds the highest ethical and professional standards. Core skill areas include

- Customer Management
- Inventory Control/Shrinkage
- Customer Service/Loyalty
- Staff Training & Mentoring

- Financial Management
- Loss Prevention/Security
- In-Store Promotions
- Performance Management

- Buyer Behavior/Awareness
- Visual Merchandise Displays
- Specialty Retail Operations
- Profit-and-Loss Management

Relevant Experience

Retail Outlet—Houston, TX

GENERAL MANAGER, 2002–2004 / **ASSISTANT MANAGER,** 2000–2002 / **ASSOCIATE,** 1999–2000

Earned promotion to GM position based on performance in Assistant Manager role, directing sales and customer service activities for team of 15 employees in fast-paced mall location. Scope of management accountability included financial management, staff training and evaluation, inventory management and loss prevention, marketing and promotions, and general management functions. *Selected Accomplishments:*

- **Performance Improvement**—Demonstrated ability to produce results and drive year-to-year increases in core revenue and profit categories, illustrated by the following:

	Inventory Shrinkage	Store Revenues*	Pre-Order Sales
2001 Totals	2.1%	$667,000	30
2002 Totals	0.4%	$691,000	310
Increase	1.7%	10.3%	1033%

Generated sales increase despite downturn market and against totals of –21.3% company-wide average, –26.5% in region, and –28.35% in district.

- **Business Development**—Led store to earn distinction as only mall store ranked in top 50 for 2 months. Store achieved exemplary company rankings following my promotion, including #1 overall in district, #1 in Texas (3 months), #1 in region (2 months), and #21 in company for 10/02 among 410 stores.

- **Profit Enhancement**—Maintained profitability by reducing operating costs 39%, performing inventory procedures that earned location excellent audit ratings, and identifying employee theft incidents.

- **Marketing & Promotions**—Secured approval from Marketing Manager for in-store promotions and sponsorships for local musical groups. Managed successful "appreciation day" programs.

- **Performance Recognition**—Groomed assistant manager to take over general manager position; requested promotion to District Manager position prior to company's Chapter 11 filing.

- **Customer & Employee Relations**—Built and sustained excellent relationships with customers, leading to frequent repeat business. Demonstrated fair, respectful treatment of team members.

PRIOR EMPLOYMENT:
LABORER—Enterprises, Santa Fe, NM (1998–1999)
FILE CLERK—Collections, Santa Fe, NM (1997–1998)
DELIVERY DRIVER—Office Equipment, Santa Fe, NM (1996–1997)

Education & Technical Skills

UNIVERSITY OF HOUSTON, Houston, TX / 106 Hours, Emphasis in Business Management & Graphic Design

Technical Summary: Microsoft Word, Excel, Access, FrontPage; Adobe Illustrator, Photoshop, Streamline, Acrobat; CorelDRAW, QuarkXPress; proprietary applications used in retail environments

133

Daniel J. Dorotik, Jr., Lubbock, Texas

Accomplishments don't need to be a list of bulleted items. The writer of this resume liked the use of a table and an italic note to illustrate revenue and profit increases. Gray shading simulates color.

TOMI SPRINGFIELD

1000 Page Blvd., Springfield, MA 01151 ▪ Tspringfield@aol.com ▪ Home: 413-788-2008

OFFICE MANAGER ▪ LOGISTICS ▪ SALES SUPPORT

*Objective: To provide office or project management, logistics, and/or sales support
for a high-tech, security, or financial services firm.*

CAREER PROFILE & SKILLS

Versatile people person and problem solver with 20 years of experience in field support, office management, logistics, and project management. Organized facilitator with excellent follow-through. Analytical self-starter able to think on her feet.

▪ Office Management	▪ Customer Service	▪ Special Events
▪ Logistics & Coordination	▪ Credit Management	▪ Meeting Planning
▪ Operational Support	▪ Proposals & Job Costing	▪ Marketing Support
▪ Project Tracking/Reporting	▪ Purchasing & Procedures	▪ Field Sales Support
▪ Training & Supervision	▪ Budget Management	▪ Account Management

Cited for *"diligence, competence, a positive attitude, and being a team player on a consistent basis"* by MA-Logistics President while providing logistics for a Homeland Security contract.

Cited as a *"competent and recognized contributor in a stressful environment with minimal supervision"* by Broadband Cable's President while supporting SASR—the federalization of high-risk airports.

OFFICE & PROJECT MANAGEMENT HIGHLIGHTS

▪ **Comanaged a team of 25 account clerks in a commercial credit/loan environment** as Credit Manager for Cambridge Credit Corporation. Included team scheduling, performance reviews, and credit training. Also reviewed, analyzed, and investigated credit applications and contracts.

▪ **Managed a 5-person customer service department that handled 1500 transactions per week** for Cambridge Credit Corp. Included hiring, training, and evaluating employee performance; managing budgets, payroll, and scheduling; and developing customer service manuals and procedures.

▪ **Tracked/reported the status of multimillion-dollar fiber optic network construction** for Broadband Cable Corporation. Used MS Project 2000.

▪ **Developed tracking/reporting procedures for hundreds of millions of dollars of equipment purchases** for Broadband Cable fiber optics business.

▪ **Managed entire office for an exhibits design and fabrication firm** in the President's absence. Included accounts payables/receivables, collections, proposals and job costing, invoicing, travel, and meeting plans for NE Trade Show Products. Helped administer two other companies in shared office space.

LOGISTICS & SALES SUPPORT HIGHLIGHTS

▪ **Helped manage logistics to federalize 429 airports in 180 days** for SASR (the Strategic Airport Security Rollout). Provided customer service and operational support for 1700 mobile/permanent airport screeners. Used AIM Help Desk Software to analyze, track, and report problems for MA-Logistics.

▪ **Provided customer service, inventory management, and high-volume sales to 200 retail accounts** quarterly for Kraft Foods. Assisted special promotions, set up new stores, and sold marketing programs.

▪ **Won two All Star Awards for 1st Place in regional sales/support** from Kraft Foods.

▪ **Provided field support for merchandising, marketing, sales, and service** for Helene Curtis.

▪ **Planned and managed special events and Board of Directors meetings** for Broadband Cable Corporation. Backed up the senior administrator who supported the Vice President of Sales.

134

Helen Oliff, Reston, Virginia

The writer demonstrated this candidate's "strength through versatility" and diminished her job hopping by using the variety and short length of multiple jobs to show progressive skills and responsibilities. Look for the comment in italic after each position indicated in the Chronological

TOMI SPRINGFIELD
Page Two

CHRONOLOGICAL EMPLOYMENT HISTORY

Junior Logistician, Task Force Homeland Security, 2002 to Present
MA-LOGISTICS, INC.—Springfield, MA
Provides solutions for supply-chain logistics challenges and project management to public/private businesses.

Project Administrator, Network Planning, 2000 to 2002
Office Manager, Network Services, 2000 to 2002
BROADBAND CABLE CORPORATION—Medford, MA
A start-up that provides bundled cable, Internet, and telephone services for broadband customer networks.

Office Manager, President's Office, 1999 to 2000
NEW ENGLAND TRADE SHOW PRODUCTS—Portland, MA
Provides millwork, casework, graphics, and fabrication for exhibit/museum displays and trade show marketing.

Office Support Specialist, 1995 to 1998
MASSACHUSETTS DESIGN ASSOCIATES—Portland, MA
Provides architectural design for both commercial and residential structures and spaces.

Sales Representative/Sales Support
SHISEIDO COSMETICS AMERICA, LTD.—Cambridge, MA Office, 1993 to 1995 (job share)
SMOKELESS TOBACCO COMPANY—Cambridge, MA, 1993 to 1995 (job share)
Major distributors of retail and consumer products and services distributed worldwide.

Sales Representative/Sales Support
KRAFT FOODS, CONFECTIONERS DIVISION—Dorchester, MA, 1990 to 1993
Major distributor of retail and food products and services to consumers worldwide.

Customer Service & Credit Manager, 1986 to 1989
Marketing & Collections Representative, 1984 to 1986
CAMBRIDGE CREDIT CORPORATION—Cambridge, MA
Provides credit services and credit management to hardware and other retail stores.

PROFESSIONAL TRAINING

Marketing & Sales Training—Kraft Foods
Customer Services & Selling Symposium—Cambridge Credit Corp.
Motivation & Productivity—Cambridge Credit Corp.

Computer Skills: MS Office 2000/97 (Word, Excel, and PowerPoint), MS Project 2000, PageMaker, AIM help desk software, e-mail, Web browsers, and Windows 2000/98

E-mail: Tspringfield@aol.com • Home: 413-788-2008

Employment History. The three expertise areas of office management, logistics, and sales support, indicated at the top of page 1, are illustrated by highlights in two sections at the bottom of the page.

CONFIDENTIAL

Carol Trona

400 Conch Drive, Pacifica, California 94044
ctrona1111@aol.com ✆650.555.5555 (Home) — 650.555.6666 (Cell)

What I can offer **TopLine** as your newest **Business Manager**

❏ Bringing in projects on time and on budget ❏ Knowing the difference between symptoms and problems ❏ Maximizing profits by getting the right resources to the people at the right time ❏ Serving customers so well they become our unpaid "sales force" ❏ Limiting liability ❏ Controlling costs ❏ Building and maintaining excellent, motivated teams ❏ Freeing senior management for things only they can do

Recent work history with examples of problems solved

❏ *Hired away to become* **Office Manager,** *and then given additional responsibilities as* **Project Coordinator,** *and later promoted with additional responsibilities to* **Project Manager,** Carter Winslow, General Contractor, Punta Gordita, California

Sep 99–Present

This custom builder of high-end homes in the Bay Area has annual sales of more than $1.5M.

As **Office Manager,** have **near-total P&L responsibility** for this small office. As **Project Coordinator** and **Project Manager,** control all the resources—people, time, equipment, money, cooperation, and facilities—for every major project we have.

Turned around an operation that ran on handshakes—and increasing lawsuits—for six years. Built a complete system for documenting business from scratch. *Payoffs:* **Costly disputes replaced by amicable relationships** with customers and vendors. Owner freed for things only he could do.

Put management in complete control of critical resources. Helped employees draw the straight line from their responsibilities to our corporate success. *Payoffs:* Disputes over scarce resources disappeared. More than **doubled the number of projects** we worked on simultaneously. **Sales rose more than 100 percent.**

❏ *Hired away to be* **Office Manager** *with later additional responsibilities as* **Event Planner** and Event Planning **Sales Professional,** Crux & Associates, Pinetop City, California

Sep 97–Aug 99

Crux & Associates is a complete event-planning solutions provider serving major corporate clients in the Bay Area. Annual sales topped $2M.

Won over what later became a major account. Got them to buy into the "perfect" vision of the product we could provide—then realize we were best suited to deliver the goods. *Payoffs:* Customer so pleased that **we became their "sole service provider."**

135

Don Orlando, Montgomery, Alabama

This applicant had been taken for granted too long by her current company. Her job search was an opportunity for her to "spread her wings" and proceed to the next level. The "What I can offer..." section summarizes the individual's most significant abilities, which are documented in

Carol Trona   **Business Manager**   650.555.5555 (Home) — 650.555.6666 (Cell)

Stepped in smoothly to work with demanding musicians as we planned a major event 2,500 miles away. By listening carefully, found just what they wanted. *Payoffs:* **Used differential costing** to meet their needs yet **get their services at considerable savings.**

Pulled together—**single-handedly**—every detail of what would normally be a week-long project for four people. Did it all over a three-day weekend. Tracked down suppliers even though their businesses were closed. Convinced vendors I could provide promotional value in exchange for **moderate pricing.** *Payoffs:* **Customer was thrilled** with the event we planned for 500 people at such short notice.

❑ **Office Manager,** Triangle Company, Inc., San Francisco, California

Nov 92–Sep 97

This public financial advisory firm helped customers across the state prepare to float school bond issues. Sales: $5M.

Transformed a challenge into new revenue. Persuaded owner to create a subsidiary to handle the mountain of publications we produced each quarter. *Payoffs:* **Netted $100K** in new revenue in the first year alone—**from an investment of $20K.**

Volunteered to rescue a "small" account others said couldn't be serviced when workload threatened to overcome our staff. Made the time to master our customers' needs. *Payoffs:* Of five major efforts running at the same time, mine was **the only successful venture**—even though I had no experience in this field.

Language skills

❑ Read, write, and think in fluent German

Computer skills

❑ Expert in Word

❑ Proficient in Excel, QuickBooks, FileMaker Pro (database software)

❑ Working knowledge of Outlook and Internet search protocols

the "Recent work history…" section. In that section, look for shadowed square bullets as pointers to companies where the candidate distinguished herself by performing tasks beyond expectation.

KEELE A. PERKINS

KAPerks@yahoo.com

BUSINESS PROCESS DEVELOPMENT/REENGINEERING PROFESSIONAL
- ➤ *Program / Project Leadership*
- ➤ *Change Management / Continuous Improvement*
- ➤ *Customer Relationship Management (CRM)*
- ➤ *Team Building / Mentoring*

Profile

Proactive, hands-on **senior manager** and **operational specialist** savvy in quickly identifying actual and potential business problems, **formulating strategic plans, developing requirements** and **implementing solutions** in challenging and diverse environments. Proven innovative and experienced professional with rich background in strategic design, **cross-functional business process reengineering, process management, project management** and **implementation.** Keen ability to uncover and execute **revenue enhancement** and **cost-control initiatives.**

Experience

CITIZENS BANK & TRUST—Flint, Michigan; 1997–current
$13 billion financial services provider serving U.S. mid-Atlantic and Midwest regions and selected national and international markets

Senior Vice President, CRM Business Process Integration Manager
Manage enterprise work teams to develop, design and translate CRM requirements into new business processes, customer delivery integration, systems selection and functional specifications for Siebel application.

Built CRM strategic plan and defined 5-year road map, redesigned and formalized disciplined organizational approach to project management, implemented campaign management for call center and operationalized new sales management practices for enterprise.

Select accomplishment:
- Developed enterprise business case and won approval for largest capital investment in company history

Senior Vice President, Customer Process Reengineering Manager
Led enterprise initiative, reporting to President/CEO, to enhance customer experience, improve employee efficiency and increase revenue. Designed and implemented companywide customer servicing application and simplified loan documentation and processing.

Select achievements:
- Generated more than $15 million in incremental revenue through management consulting and multiple business process changes
- Reengineered Customer Contact Center sales, servicing and fulfillment areas, which resulted in a reduction of 10 FTEs, increased booked loan ratio 55% and improved customer servicing turnaround by 7 days

Vice President, Consumer Loan Change Manager
Managed and oversaw all activities within Technology Support, Continuous Improvement, Training, and Communications groups.

Select accomplishments:
- Partnered with Marketing department to change product structure, resulting in consumer loan growth of nearly $500 million in one year
- Improved Secured Loan turnaround from 60 to 5 days, simultaneously reducing FTEs 12%
- Led successful Iaams Bank Direct and Indirect Loan merger; completed 37 systems upgrades or conversions, overhauled process flows, and hired and trained 79 new employees in 60-day period

248-969-9933 residence
248-601-5202 work

4983 Menominee Lane
Clarkston, Michigan 48348

136

Jennifer N. Ayres, Clarkston, Michigan

Putting most of the contact information at the bottom of the first page lets you place more important material—the areas of expertise and the Profile—at the top of the page, where this prime information will surely be read. In the Experience section, italic subheadings (for

U.S. BANK—Washington, D.C.; 1980–1997
A world leading financial services company with 4,400 domestic offices and 30 international offices, serving individuals, small businesses and commercial, corporate and institutional concerns

Vice President, Regional Administrative Manager
Managed daily operations performance of 52 banking centers and developed and managed $30 million operating budget. Responsible for capital planning, budgeting, expense management, staffing allocation and scheduling. Assessed and developed regional ranking plan of personnel resources for two regions, including staff assignment master plan for more than 700 employees; troubleshot human resources, security and operational problems; and provided technical support and training. Represented Consumer Bank division on numerous special-project work groups to evaluate, develop and implement initiatives for mid-Atlantic region.

Select accomplishments:
- Achieved 7% expense reduction directives three months into operating year
- Successfully implemented staffing project, reducing FTEs and operating expenses by 29%

Banking Officer, Regional Sales & Service Manager
Developed regional sales, service quality and financial plans for consumers and small businesses. Directed sales activities and managed regional floating pool, staffing optimization programs, daily operations, training and sales for 19 banking centers. Established regional incentive programs to complement bank-wide promotional activities and piloted innovate product knowledge and sales training programs.

Select accomplishments:
- Created strategic and tactical product plan for business development; exceeded regional sales goals by 25%
- Planned and executed regional product promotions, achieving two consecutive 1st-place finishes for Home Equity Loan sales

Additional Experience:

NBD BANK—More than 10 years of progressive experience from entry-level branch position through various higher-level branch sales and regional administrative assignments.

Education

UNIVERSITY OF MICHIGAN, FLINT; SCHOOL OF PROJECT MANAGEMENT
Managing Projects in Organizations, Project Leadership, Management & Communications

AMERICAN INSTITUTE OF BANKING
Financial Services Course Work

OMEGA
Commercial Lending, Consumer Lending, Understanding Business Cash Flow

Professional Affiliations

UNITED WAY—Wings Program

WOMEN ENTREPRENEURS OF FLINT

KEELE A. PERKINS
KAPerks@yahoo.com

248-969-9933 residence
248-601-5202 work

example, *Select accomplishments* and *Select achievements*) ensure that the bulleted achievements are seen and also make it possible to glance through the section and spot just these statements.

James Howard

7777 Tracer Downs ♦ Perry, GA 00000 ♦ (H) 000-000-0000 ♦ (C) 000-000-0000

Operations Management ♦ Personnel Management ♦ Materials Management
Inventory & Logistics ♦ Purchasing & Procurement

Goal-oriented management professional with more than 20 years of progressive and stable experience in executive-level management positions. Offer background and qualifications in personnel and human resources administration, facilities management, operations administration, budgeting, materials, team leadership, security management, problem resolution, professional development, training and education analysis, public and motivational speaking, customer relations, research and investigation, international travel, and report and forecast development. Understand intricacies of regulations governing personnel issues. Ensure that subordinates remain in continual compliance with all health, safety, and security directives and specifications, including those of OSHA and the EEOC.

CAREER ACCOMPLISHMENTS

☑ Managed facilities maintenance team responsible for the upkeep of 490,000 square feet of commercial building space.
☑ Managed all aspects of logistics, transportation, and delivery support functions for assigned U.S. Marine Corps units.
☑ Spearheaded and implemented cost control measure resulting in $40,000 in annual savings for assigned unit.
☑ Chosen from 2,000 qualified candidates to serve as liaison aboard the USS Tripoli in support of logistics operations between Marine Corps and Navy personnel.

PROFESSIONAL EXPERIENCE
OPERATIONS MANAGEMENT

- Planned, directed, and coordinated human resources management activities, maximizing the strategic use of human resources and maintaining facilities maintenance department.
- Provided supervision for the equipment and supply manager, the maintenance supply manager, and all personnel responsible for the performance and management of equipment maintenance.
- Analyzed maintenance management and personnel functional areas, proficiently utilizing equipment and materiel.
- Assigned to the completed functions required by the maintenance information systems coordination office to ensure the proper functioning of the field maintenance subsystem of the Marine Corps Integrated Maintenance Management System.
- Interacted with management to formulate and implement administrative, operations, and customer relations policies.
- Analyzed expenditures and other financial reports to develop plans, policies, and budgets for increasing profits.

PERSONNEL MANAGEMENT

- Supervised and monitored the work activities of subordinates and staff.
- Developed employment policies, processes, and practices, and recommended changes to executive management personnel.
- Met with team leaders and supervisors to resolve grievances.
- Conducted new-employee orientation to foster positive attitude toward company objectives.
- Wrote directives advising department managers of organizational policy in personnel matters.
- Maintained records and compiled statistical data to identify and determine causes of personnel problems.
- Analyzed statistical data and reports to identify and determine causes of personnel problems and develop recommendations for improvement of organizational personnel policies and practices.
- Planned, directed, and coordinated the training activities of all personnel under personal authority.
- Analyzed training needs to develop new programs or to modify and improve existing programs.

TRANSPORTATION & LOGISTICS

- Reviewed transportation schedules, personnel assignments, and routes to ensure compliance with standards for personnel elections, safety, and contract terms.
- Orchestrated activities relating to dispatching, routing, and tracking of transportation vehicles, aircraft, and railroad cars.
- Monitored the process of investigation and response to complaints relating to operations department.
- Directed team responsible for tariff classifications, billing preparation, mode of transportation, and destination of shipment.
- Inspected and supervised the maintenance of equipment, vehicles, and facilities and enforced all applicable regulations.

MATERIALS MANAGEMENT, PURCHASING, & PROCUREMENT

- Oversaw procurement process, including research and testing of equipment and vendor contacts and approval of requisitions.
- Negotiated and authorized contracts with equipment and materials suppliers.
- Formulated, implemented, and interpreted policies and procedures.
- Developed plans to meet expanded needs, such as increasing capacity of facilities or modifying equipment.

137

Lea J. Clark, Macon, Georgia

The first page of this resume has design elements found in many executive resumes: narrow margins, wide lines, and small type (here, 10-point Times New Roman). Areas of expertise (in boldface and separated by diamond bullets), a profile, and Career Accomplishments

James Howard
Page Two

MATERIALS MANAGEMENT, PURCHASING, & PROCUREMENT (Continued)

- Authorized repair, movement, installation, and construction of equipment, supplies, and facilities.
- Analyzed data, trends, reports, consumption, and test results to determine adequacy of facilities and system performance.
- Investigated and evaluated new developments in materials, tools, and equipment.
- Forecast consumption of utilities to meet demand or to determine construction, equipment, or maintenance requirements.
- Developed, prepared, and distributed reports, directives, records, work orders, specifications for work methods, and other documents.

EMPLOYMENT HISTORY

Hazardous-Waste Manager, Environmental Outsourcing	2003–present
Inventory Support Supervisor, U.S. Air Force Logistics Center	2001–2003
Operations and Project Management, Facilities Management Corp.	1999–2001

MILITARY SERVICE

Transportation/Facilities/Communications/Operations Management, U.S. Marine Corps	1978–1999

EDUCATION
Graduate, Austin High School, Chicago, IL

TRAINING
Chapman College, Twentynine Palms, CA
Public Speaking, Communications, English, Math

U.S. Marine Corps, Various Locations
Advanced Staff NCO Administrative Academy, Personnel Administration, Marine Corps Leadership, Advanced Staff NCO
Non-Resident Program, Ground Safety Managers Training, Logistics and Embarkation Specialist Course,
Substance Abuse Information Program, Maintenance Management Course

Additional Employment-Related Course Work
Total Quality Management, Equal Opportunity Representative, Public Speaking,
Written Correspondence, Assertiveness Training, Safety, First Aid

COMMUNITY SERVICE AND AFFILIATIONS
Local Coordinator, Habitat for Humanity, Cobb County, GA
Volunteer Driver, Meals on Wheels, Marietta, GA
Volunteer Team Member, Boy and Girl Scouts of America, various international locations
Little League Basketball Coach, Gwinnett County

HONORS & AWARDS
United States Armed Forces
Meritorious Service Medal ♦ Navy Achievement Medal ♦ National Defense Service Medal
Armed Forces Expeditionary Medal ♦ 3 Letters of Commendation ♦ 8 Letters of Appreciation

Cobb County Division of Habitat for Humanity—Letter of Appreciation

are all placed just below the contact information to be the first information seen. The Professional Experience section lists items by categories rather than by workplaces. See Cover Letter 10.

Charles Gladstone

555 Franklin Drive
Ramsey, NJ 55555

(555) 555-5555 (Cell)
(555) 555-5555 (Home)
myname@mysite.net

OPERATIONS MANAGEMENT

PROFILE: Multifaceted, proactive operations manager with more than 11 years of experience in managing all aspects of warehousing and inventory control. Skilled at designing and implementing new systems and procedures to increase efficiency and decrease costs. Combine outstanding management skills with strong qualifications in distribution, budgeting, and human resources. Excellent computer skills.

- Inventory Processes & Controls	- Purchasing	- Production/Assembly Planning
- Quality Control	- Contract Negotiations	- Compensation Incentives
- Expense Control	- Traffic Control	- Testing & Sampling

PROFESSIONAL EXPERIENCE

<u>DICKINSON, INC.</u>   Paterson, NJ
Warehouse Manager   7/97–4/04
International distributor of hand-tooled instruments. Reported to Operations Manager. Promoted to this position because of knowledge of warehouse operations. Managed staff of three, including Shipping Manager, Receiving Manager, and Production Assembly Manager, and workforce of 22. Managed all facets of warehouse operations. Responsible for maintaining inventory and reducing costs. Scheduled deliveries of inbound receipts to all 3 departments. Planned daily workloads for each department. Developed and scheduled weekly production/assembly plan. Produced weekly stockout report covering more than 2,500 items.

- Improved inventory accuracy from 92% to 99.5% on $2 million inventory.
- Reduced operating expenses by $100,000 annually by reducing staff 30% and combining positions.
- Improved space utilization by introducing blanket order/release system for corrugated purchases that resulted in lower on-hand inventory, less wasted space, and improved tracking of expenses.
- Received overall rating of "Outstanding" on last 2 performance reviews.

Challenge: Ensure that all sales orders received by 2:30 p.m. were picked, packed, and shipped the same day. Initially, 50% of orders (on volume of 300 orders per day) were not being shipped the same day.
Action: Revised inventory locations, designed more efficient pick/pack flow, implemented incentive program, increased training, and designed and installed powered conveyor system.
Results: All sales orders received by 2:30 p.m. are now shipped the same day.

Challenge: Reduce shipping costs by 25%.
Action: Identified and introduced new equipment (strapping machine) and identified and implemented better void fill system (sealed plastic bag filled with air).
Results: Reduced labor and material costs by $34,000 annually (30% less than prior year).

Challenge: Develop better reports regarding daily business workloads for top management.
Action: Designed (with MIS) and implemented information tracking system that kept track of current workload on daily/hourly basis.
Results: Provided in-depth reports that allowed management to respond to changing patterns quickly. Also provided means for evaluating pick/pack personnel.

Assistant Operations Manager/Special Projects Coordinator   7/95–7/97
Reported to Operations Manager. Oversaw activities of 25. Responsible for monitoring and maintaining company-wide inventory levels. Monitored backorder levels. Negotiated rates and contracts with small package and common carrier freight companies. Formulated plans for reducing costs and increasing efficiencies.

138

Igor Shpudejko, Mahwah, New Jersey

This individual did not go to college but has done very well for himself with an A.A.S. degree in Electronics. Because the applicant is a "doer," the writer wanted to focus on his many accomplishments and to use the CAR (challenge, action, results) format to present achievements. This

Charles Gladstone

- Saved more than $10,000 in annual costs by replacing old shipping manifest system with new system provided free of charge by United Parcel Service.

Challenge: Identify causes of $700,000 in backorders and reduce them.
Action: Discovered flaw in releasing backorder documents to warehouse. Designed backorder report (with MIS) that reported backorders by sales territory and released product as needed.
Results: Reduced backorders to $250,000 in 2 months.

Challenge: Conduct study to determine whether California public warehouse was cost-effective.
Action: Studied cost per item for storage and handling and shipping. Analyzed work flow in Paterson warehouse to determine possibility of absorbing extra volume.
Results: Shut down facility after it was determined that $25,000 could be saved annually without sacrificing customer satisfaction. Extra freight charges to customers were reduced.

Challenge: Obtain compensation from vendors for defective returns.
Action: Designed report (with MIS) that identified and tracked vendor defective returns over 18-month reporting period. Data showed items returned because of manufacturing defects. Presented data to vendors for defective return compensation. Initiated monthly defective return report.
Results: Recovered more than $56,000 in initial discovery and more than $40,000 on annual basis.

ONSITE GRAPHICS, INC.   Fairlawn, NJ
Plant Manager   8/92–7/95
A wholly owned subsidiary of Nu-Kote International, a leading remanufacturer and supplier of premium-quality laser printer cartridges. Directed all aspects of the East Coast pick/pack distribution and recovery center through staff of 15. Managed 15,000-square-foot facility and 2,000 SKUs. Shipped $1.5 million of merchandise monthly. Ensured that 97% of orders shipped same day. Maintained entire computer system.

- Increased distribution from 20% of total company distribution to 50% without increase in staff.
- Saved more than $50,000 annually by negotiating better international and domestic freight rates.
- Developed workable inventory and raw materials min/max levels, which decreased warehousing freight costs by 20%.
- Designed and implemented new pick/pack operation using conveyor and pallet rack systems that reduced picking time.
- Cross-trained all personnel on one other position, which improved productivity and staff morale.
- Improved operational efficiency by moving invoicing into shipping department and all receiving department data entry into receiving department.

PC SYSTEMS   Norwich, CT
Field Service Manager   8/89–8/92
Regional company specializing in service and maintenance of PC-based computer systems. Directed staff of 6 field technicians responsible for troubleshooting and resolving routine and complex service calls. Handled large volume of inbound technical questions. Maintained extensive parts inventory.

Field Technician   8/87–8/89
Responsible for handling both on- and off-site repairs of computers and peripherals.
- First technical person hired in this branch. Played key role in launching business.

COMPUTER SKILLS
- **Software:** MS/PC DOS, WordPerfect, Lotus 1-2-3, Symphony, Q&A, ProComm, Carbon Copy, Sidekick, and Smartcomm
- **Hardware:** IBM PCs and clones, HP, Epson, Okidata, and Citoh printers

EDUCATION
- **AAS in Electronics,** DeVry Technical Institute, Woodbridge, NJ, 1987

format appears in the Professional Experience section at the end of the information about the first two jobs mentioned. An italic explanation of each workplace is helpful information.

DARLENE DAVIS

123 Main Street ▪ Philadelphia, PA 19000
215-555-5555

ADMINISTRATIVE / BUSINESS MANAGER

Start-Up, Turnaround, and High-Growth Organizations

PROFILE

MANAGEMENT PROFESSIONAL with more than 10 years of experience in increasingly accountable positions requiring a high level of business operations knowledge. Recognized for consistent success in developing systems, processes, and methodologies to reorganize/revitalize purchasing operations, increase revenues, and enhance profit performance.

Demonstrated accomplishments with strategic planning, organizational development, key account management, and general management expertise. Cross-functional background in corporate communications, vendor negotiations, resource allocation, and project management. Proficient with MS Office 2000 (including advanced training in Word and Excel), Solomon System, Fourth Shift ERP/MRP, and Crystal Reports.

CORE COMPETENCIES

PURCHASING MANAGEMENT & BUSINESS ADMINISTRATION

Key player in the launching of a fast-paced, worldwide, interactive television Internet company from start-up to a public company by successfully managing major production purchases and building purchasing/materials department.

- Reduced freight costs by 15% by renegotiating rates with carriers, taking advantage of free shipping, marking up/invoicing all freight for customer shipments, and reducing volume of overnight shipments. Significantly decreased costs on mature products by sourcing alternate vendors, renegotiating existing prices, and obtaining preferred payment terms with key vendors.

- Successful in liquidating inventory as cash problems developed and sales dropped. Negotiated the return of $270,000 in excess inventory to vendors, sold specific items to cable industry vendors, and sold nonindustry items generating $800,000 in cash.

PROJECT PLANNING & MANAGEMENT

Skilled at leading cross-functional teams in the planning and execution of special projects. Able to critically evaluate project requirements and coordinate delivery of appropriate resources to meet operating demands.

- Instrumental in administering procedures and processes to streamline flow between sales, material planning, manufacturing, and materials from start to finish (inventory to time of shipment). Execution of new processes resulted in inventory accuracy moving to less than 1% (from 9% variance).

- Researched ERP/MRP software packages ranging from $300,000 to $1 million and justified product selection and cost savings to executive team. Oversaw project implementation teams, ensuring sales, IT, engineering, materials, finance, and manufacturing departments met project objectives and deadlines.

139

Darlene Dassy, Harleysville, Pennsylvania

This individual was laid off because of a company bankruptcy. She had extensive corporate experience but was afraid that her lack of a four-year degree would prevent her from getting a challenging job. The writer emphasized the applicant's most important qualifications on the

CORE COMPETENCIES (continued)

PERSONNEL MANAGEMENT & LEADERSHIP
Excellent qualifications in providing flexible leadership in a fast-paced work environment. Demonstrated proactive leadership practices and directed staff to be reactive when projects were altered to meet corporate deadlines.

- Consistently met and exceeded department objectives. Oversaw administrative efforts to bring various products into organization with unrealistic deadlines, which resulted in the deployment of product into field, allowing it to "go public" before originally scheduled timeframe.

- Built work teams that continually exceeded goals for productivity. Instrumental as a team leader who promoted employee ideas/input and implemented newly suggested procedures to help department run more smoothly and effectively.

CUSTOMER SERVICE & CLIENT RELATIONS
Served as the direct liaison to maintain cooperative relationships and resolve operating problems for sales administration and order fulfillment departments.

- Effectively handled customer reconciliations, ultimately restoring tenuous customer relations on many critical overseas shipments.

- Troubleshot various issues within the organization and was considered the "go-to person" among staff for solving problems within different areas of the company.

EDUCATION AND CERTIFICATIONS

Pursuing <u>Bachelor of Business Administration</u> at **Anytown College USA**

Attended **The American Institute of Paralegal Studies** for Paralegal Program

Continuing Professional Education & Seminars sponsored by the Management Development Institute of the MidAtlantic Employers' Association (1999–2000):

- Supervisory Skills Certificate
- Coaching and Team Building
- Human Resources Overview
- Basics of Supervision
- Leadership Skills for Today's Workplace
- Time Management Systems
- Successful Communication
- Managing People

CAREER EXPERIENCE

<u>Manager—Purchasing and Materials</u>	**WorldWide Communications**	1997–2004
<u>Purchasing & Inventory Control Manager</u>	**Corporate Data, Inc.**	1995–1997
<u>National Account Contract Specialist</u>	**Corporate Data, Inc.**	1991–1995

first page and placed her education and career experience at the end. The writer also beefed up the Education section with certifications and management seminars.

MARIA D. SCHERING

832 Sandy Lane   Corpus Christi, Texas 78132   361-275-4739

National Workforce Manager—Call Center Industry
offers eight years of global experience in workforce planning and management

Technology Background
TCS versions 4.0, 5.0, and 6.0; IEX; Lucent (CMS) ACD Administration; CentreVu Supervisor; Administration for Expert Agent System (EAS); WinQSB; Crystal Reports

Value-Added Competencies
Generate $50K in additional annual revenue as an external workforce management consultant to Fortune 100 and 500 companies. Own a reputation as a polished, organized, enthusiastic professional with excellent communication skills and a high level of expertise in the workforce management arena.

Professional Achievements

- *Increased efficiency in and span of control* over eight remote call center operations as a result of establishing an effective Global Support Center for the Workforce Management sector located in Phoenix, AZ. Functioned in the capacity of project manager from ground zero implementation of this operation.
- *Empowered 1200 agents* in personal performance management through the implementation of the Performix Reporting Integration System. Served in capacity of project manager and corporate liaison for multiple site implementations.
- *Generated an additional $50K in revenue for 2002* in role of external consultant to Dell Home Sales, La Quinta Reservations, and Humana Service Centers. This assignment required a dynamic relationship with the client. *Solutions were created in software implementation, best practices in workforce management, forecasting, staffing, and process reengineering.*

Professional Profile

CORESTAFF
February 2003 to present
Corporate office, Boise, Idaho

Director of Resource Planning Group—On Site—Corpus Christi, Texas. Manage a staff of 30 support personnel: Staffing and Scheduling, Traffic Desk Coordinators, Telecommunications, Reporting, and Time and Attendance.
- Lead Resource Team in planning, recommending, implementing, and tracking of hiring plans and productivity for 1,000 agents networked in a "virtual" call center consisting of three multisites.
- Provide analysis and consultative support to cross-functional partners and other lines of business.
- Implemented an escalation procedure within call center for recovery and escalation notification.

CRICHTON TECHNOLOGIES—GLOBAL NETWORK SOLUTIONS
1994–February 2003
Corporate office, Cincinnati, Ohio

National Workforce Manager—Remote Office—Corpus Christi, Texas   **2000 to February 2003**
- Managed a staff of 11 workforce support personnel in both domestic and international customer service centers.
- Created and generated forecasting models for existing and newly acquired operations.
- Identified and implemented programs to improve service, performance, and productivity.

140

MeLisa Rogers, Victoria, Texas

The candidate had a strong background in workforce management with promotions, but her resume did not display the level of management she had attained and her knowledge of technology. The writer remedied this situation by making certain that this new resume

2

Site Resource Manager—Call Center, GNS—Corpus Christi, Texas   **1994 to 2000**

- Administered TCS and workforce management for a multiskilled, 24/7, 250-seat center.
- Incorporated Real Time Adherence, Vacation Planner, and Meeting Planner modules.
- Presided over the hiring strategies, which supported the client volume forecast on a daily and annual basis.
- Managed and trained a team of administrators designated to manage call center operations and a real-time traffic center.
- Established procedures to deliver budget-conscious solutions while meeting the forecast expectations of the client and senior management.

DAMSON GENERAL FOODS
1992 to 1994
Corpus Christi, Texas

Territory Sales Manager—Successfully expanded the Corpus Christi market for this purveyor to hotels, restaurants, hospitals, and institutions.

- Through aggressive sales and marketing, doubled monthly revenues, expanded customer base, increased market penetration, and established a track record of strong customer service.
- Selected as the Gross Profit Leader for the Texas Region.

Prior Professional Experience

Restaurant Manager	RED LOBSTER—Houston, Texas	4/91 to 11/91
Catering Manager	BARNACLE CATERING, INC.—Houston, Texas	9/89 to 11/90
Kitchen Manager	SPAGHETTI WAREHOUSE—Houston, Texas	8/86 to 11/88
Assistant Manager	HOLIDAY INN—Beaumont, Texas	9/84 to 7/86

Professional Training and Certifications

Crystal Reports—40 hours of classroom training—2002
Benchmark Portal—Certified Specialist 2002
Lucent Custom Reports—2000
IEX Database, Process, Real-Time Adherence, and Skill Training—Certified
TCS versions 4.0 and 5.0—Certified
TCS and IEX Users Forum—1999, 2000, 2001
ICCM Forecast and Scheduling Seminar—1999
Microsoft Office Suite—Excel, Word, Outlook, PowerPoint, Access, Project
Visio

Education

Texas A&M University, College Station, Texas—Finance—1982 to 1986

Military Experience

Active-Duty USAF—Honorable Discharge—1976 to 1980—Medical Administration
Assignments:
> *Inactive Reserves—Lackland AFB—1980 to 1984*
> Clerk Office of Professional Education
> Highest rank attained: Sergeant—Active Duty
> Staff Sergeant—Inactive Reserves
> *Lackland AFB—1978 to 1980*
> Inspector General Specialist, Medical IG Office
> *Elmendorf AFB—1976 to 1978*
> CHAMPUS Clerk, Budget Office AAC (Alaskan Air Command)

M A R I A   D .   S C H E R I N G

8 3 2   S A N D Y   L A N E   C O R P U S   C H R I S T I ,   T E X A S   7 8 1 3 2   3 6 1 - 2 7 5 - 4 7 3 9

communicated early the applicant's position, her level of technology, and her global experience. With this resume she got the new position she was seeking, and her salary increased by approximately $30,000!

MARY ANNE SMITH

7777 West Main Street, Anytown, ST 55555
masmith@aol.com • (555) 555-5555

PROFESSIONAL PROFILE

Visual Merchandising Manager with a broad base of retail experience, including strategic concept planning for national corporations, fiscal responsibility for multimillion-dollar budgets, product development and importation and major account development to drive sales and profits. Innovative visionary with fresh ideas, a keen sense of style and fashion, trend intuition and creative design techniques. Motivational presenter and articulate public speaker who trains store management and educates corporate executives to deliver consistency of merchandising concepts throughout large retail networks. Self-sufficient and resourceful problem solver with meticulous organizational, planning, problem identification and decision-making skills.

AREAS OF EXPERTISE

National Retail Corporations	Marketing Communications	Project Management
Brand Strategy/Imaging	Executive Presentations	Training Programs
Retail Merchandising	Channel Management	Vendor Negotiations
Visual Presentation Standards	Strategic Partnerships	Team Building

SAMPLE OF CAREER ACHIEVEMENTS

➢ Directed a major collateral rollout for a nationally known merchandise brand that far surpassed corporate expectation and created consumer-recognized brand identity throughout the United States.
➢ Developed merchandising standards to maintain visual consistency throughout large retail network that optimized fashion apparel assortments, maximized sales revenue, promoted product/category awareness and improved in-store traffic patterns.
➢ Devised guidelines for implementing visual merchandise concepts, including training videos and written marketing communications.
➢ Prepared and delivered compelling, persuasive presentations to win senior executive approval of and support for new concepts, corporate direction and program rollouts.
➢ Primary visionary for new and innovative visual merchandising concepts for specialty departments of two Fortune 500 retailers throughout the United States.
➢ Redesigned and implemented a new specialty department for a major retailer at an upscale mall in San Juan, Puerto Rico, that targeted the Hispanic consumer and featured a tropical theme.
➢ Managed multimillion-dollar budgets and directed field visual merchandising teams in the development of presentation concepts and installation of 500 specialty departments in new and remodeled stores.
➢ Initiated and designed the *Innovative Concept I* and *Innovative Concept II* merchandising concepts.
➢ Created original branding concepts for private-label merchandise product lines.

PROFESSIONAL EXPERIENCE

ABC COMPANY, Anytown, ST   1998–present
Senior Account Manager
Develop new business and deliver exemplary service to existing accounts to increase market penetration, annual revenue and profit margins.
• Develop respected customer relationships through comprehensive industry knowledge, keen understanding of visual merchandising, superior customer service and meticulous attention to detail.
• Grew account base by 54% through targeted research, trade show participation, persistent prospecting and highly successful sales techniques.
• Formulate cohesive, sales-driven marketing plans and presentations based on client profiles and a thorough understanding of customer needs and what motivates consumer purchases.
• Manage the entire sales process from prototype design to in-store installation using exceptional communication and project management skills to deliver best results on time and within budget.

XYZ COMPANY, Anytown, ST   1997–1998
Manager, Merchandise Presentation—Corporate
Directed the development of visual presentation strategies for all apparel divisions nationwide. Managed a multimillion-dollar budget and coached a team of 12 direct reports. Reported directly to the Division Vice President.
• Developed merchandising standards to maintain visual consistency throughout 236 stores by defining space, adjacency, zone and fixture orientation to optimize fashion assortments, maximize sales, promote product/category awareness and improve traffic patterns.
• Corroborated with senior management, division merchandise managers, buyers and trend office personnel to create new merchandise assortments to quickly respond to changing trends and consumer buying preferences.
• Initiated and implemented product placement and visual presentation plans for all categories of merchandise to promote special sales and highlight targeted merchandise.
• Mentored creative merchandising team in designing and installing visual components, including in-store signage, trend graphics, POS collateral and POP fixture concepts.
• Provided visual merchandising direction and training for all 138 remodeled stores nationwide.

141

Rosemary Fish Justen, Schaumburg, Illinois

This applicant had a long career in retail with increasing levels of responsibility; however, without a four-year degree, she worried about progressing further in the industry. After an extensive interview and fact-gathering session, the writer presented the applicant's qualifications in a

MARY ANNE SMITH_____

LMN AND COMPANY, Anytown, ST   1994–1997
Category Creative Manager—Corporate   (1996–1997)
Responsible for strategic development of visual merchandising initiatives for entire specialty category in 573 full-line stores with $695 million annual revenue throughout the United States.
- Primary visionary for creating new and innovative visual merchandising concepts.
- Corroborated with Senior Vice Presidents to develop a visual support plan for respective businesses consistent with sales and profit objectives, marketing goals and customer perception.
- Designed fixtures, collateral elements and graphic programs. Delivered persuasive presentations of conceptual prototypes to win approval and support of the President and Senior Executives.
- As point of contact for architectural firm of record, engaged design firms, production vendors, outside consultants and contractors to meet clearly stated build-out objectives on time and within budget.
- Drove transition of projects to successful completion through articulate written and verbal communication, anticipation of obstacles and timely resolution of problems.

National Visual Presentation Manager—Corporate   (1994–1996)
Developed and directed visual presentation and merchandising concepts for specialty departments nationwide. Fiscally responsible for multimillion-dollar operating budgets, maintaining bottom-line control without sacrificing high quality of visual presentation programs and materials. Coached a team of three direct reports. Dotted-line management and training responsibility for a field implementation team who installed more than 500 specialty departments in new and remodeled stores.
- Directed all design, development and implementation of fixture programs, POP marketing materials, signage and visual collateral to create a compelling environment for the customer.
- Coordinated all elements of project initiatives with planning, fixture purchasing, construction, marketing and outside sources to maintain phasing schedules and control project expenditures.
- Initiated all merchandising standards and traveled nationally to educate region and district management to ensure consistency and seamless execution.

ANY COMPANY, INC., Anytown, ST   1990–1994
Vice President
Directed sales, product development and marketing functions for import of private-label packaging and gift items with annual sales of $162 million. Developed key packaging items for major accounts and national retail clients.
- Managed overseas sourcing and the design of decorative containers and gift items for promotional marketing programs, traveling to Hong Kong, China and the Philippines.
- Designed and delivered persuasive sales presentations to major gift accounts and specialty markets.
- Created original branding concepts for private-label merchandise product lines.

BEST CORPORATION, Anytown, ST   1984–1990
Specialty Visual Manager—Corporate   (1987–1990)
Responsible for creative design, strategic planning, vendor relations and visual program implementation to contribute to the profitability of all specialty promotions for major merchandise brands.
- Initiated gift-with-purchase and purchase-with-purchase merchandise promotion, developed visual and merchandising concepts, directed in-store implementation and monitored financial results.
- Coordinated all aspects of celebrity appearances and special events in store's most heavily promoted department. Personally presented category seminars to audiences of up to 400 key managers.

Assistant Director—Visual Presentations/Merchandising / Assistant Fashion Director / Staff Visual Positions—
Flagship Store—Best Corporation, Anytown, ST   (1984–1987)

*EDUCATION AND AFFILIATIONS*_____

     ***Industry Standard* Magazine** • *Editorial Board*   **2000–2002**
     Recognized School of Art, Anytown, ST • **Associate in Arts Degree**   **1987**

     <u>Computer Skills</u>: ACT • Goldmine • MS Office Suite • Adobe Photoshop, PageMaker and Illustrator

Professional Profile that emphasizes her innate abilities. The writer also included industry keywords in the Areas of Expertise section and highlighted her industry successes in the Sample of Career Achievements section.

TREVOR HUTCH

555 5th Street NE, Byron, Minnesota 55555
(555) 555-5555 ■ Email: thutch@network.net

Management ■ Customer Service ■ Operations

High-energy, goal- and results-oriented manager with fifteen years of experience in a customer service environment and a track record of performance and sales turnarounds. Leadership style includes team motivational techniques, training and staff development, mentoring and coaching, and individual accountability. High school Spanish courses and direct experience interacting with Hispanic, Asian, Somali, Arabic and other cultures and customs.

AREAS OF EXPERIENCE

- ➤ Execution of corporate directives … Policy planning and implementation … Retail operations
- ➤ Budget management and implementation … Finances
- ➤ Loss prevention … Inventory management … Shipping and receiving
- ➤ Customer service and community relations
- ➤ Sales, marketing, merchandising and promotions
- ➤ Employee retention … Salary determination … EEO adherence … Recruitment, interviewing and hiring of management personnel … Scheduling and work flow … Staff motivation

MANAGEMENT EXPERIENCE

◆ **LEIFSON STORES, Minnesota, 1993 to 2004**

STORE MANAGER, 1998 to 2004, Ralston MN: Provided oversight of store, pharmacy and optical center with sales volume of $23 million, 150 regular staff, 12 hourly supervisors and management team of 10.

STORE MANAGER, 1996 to 1998, Bresden MN: Led store, pharmacy and optical center consisting of 85 employees, 7 managers and 6 hourly supervisors.

ASSISTANT STORE MANAGER, 1993 to 1996, Ralston MN: Accountable for success of apparel, front end, hard lines and backroom operations.

Results and Achievements

TURNAROUNDS: Proven track record of turning around poorly performing stores in profits and execution of customer service, resulting in promotion from small- to large-volume store. Sent to store failing to meet profits and sales goals (Bresden), achieving 5% sales and 15% profit increases (exceeding goals) and transforming store from 138th in customer service corporate-wide to 8th in 1 year (earning large bonus).

HEAVY COMPETITION: Achieved success during highly competitive and rapidly expanding community retail growth involving new superstores, department stores and home-improvement megastores. Exceeded corporate goal of 15% annual sales decrease, losing only 5% of previous sales during the first year of store-to-store competition. Kept employee retention at 100% in both markets, receiving 2001 corporate award and garnering status of #1 in region and #10 nationwide. Recognized as #8 in "average store sales" company-wide.

OPERATIONS and PROGRAMS: Assisted in developing updated in-store marketing program involving merchandising presentations, displays and logistics that was adapted for use by other company stores. Decreased inventory loss last 3 years through loss prevention program that was acknowledged corporate-wide for shrink reduction.

EXECUTIVE DEVELOPMENT: Mentored numerous employees to management-level promotions and was assigned to train managers in other stores.

142

Beverley Drake, Rochester, Minnesota

The individual wanted to get away from retail management and move to some other type of management. Three areas of expertise appear in a heading above the profile. The Areas of Experience section elaborates on the person's abilities. In the Management Experience

TREVOR HUTCH, Page 2

MANAGEMENT EXPERIENCE, continued

◆ **DIVERSE PRODUCTS, Dixon, Minnesota, 1989 to 1993**

MANAGER: Oversaw 54-employee, 6-manager team and coordinated $4.5 million sales base. Trained new managers.

<u>Results and Achievements</u>

TURNAROUNDS: Transitioned previously unprofitable store from losing money to break-even stage within 2 years of being hired, turning a profit by the 3rd year.

OPERATIONS and TRAINING: Assigned to assist store managers in other locations to get back on track and improve operations.

◆ **SUPERIOR LTD., Minnesota, 1986 to 1989**

MANAGER, 1988 to 1989, Rochester MN
MANAGER, 1987 to 1988, Rochester MN
ASSISTANT MANAGER, 1986 to 1987, Faribault MN

ONGOING EDUCATION and PROFESSIONAL DEVELOPMENT

GRADUATE of Corporate Leadership Program, with courses covering Diversity, Leadership, Motivation, Problem Solving and Troubleshooting, Employee Disciplinary Action, Interviewing, Hiring and Peer Leadership

OTHER TRAINING: Change Management … Team Motivation and Planning … Positive Thinking … Using Employee Strengths … OSHA Communication and Compliance … MSDS Sheets … Hazardous Materials … Bloodborne Pathogens … Workplace Safety

TECHNOLOGY

PC in Windows XP environment … MS Word, Excel and Outlook … Norton AntiVirus … Email … Internet and intranet … Customized Merchandising Control and Inventory Programs … Computer Programming

COMMUNITY INTERACTON

Guest Speaker, Ralston Community and Technical College—Retail Management Program

Coach, Ralston Youth Soccer Association

Classroom Volunteer, Chimron Elementary School

Member, Neighborhood Watch Program

Member, Chimron Sportsmen's Club

Member, Church Council

section, Results and Achievements are grouped according to the categories at the beginning of the paragraphs. A diamond bullet directs your attention to each new workplace.

STEPHEN P. SMITH

555 5th Ave.	smith@email.net	(Home) 555-555-5555
Shoretown, NJ 11111		(Cell) 555-555-5555

SUMMARY

Retail Store Manager with extensive experience in a variety of industries, including music, food, entertainment, and hospitality. Effective interpersonal and communication skills are used to develop and maintain customer relationships. Known for product knowledge and superior customer service. Strong organizational and prioritizing skills are used to successfully manage large, diverse inventories. Highly respected and valued by peers and employees for positive and practical management style, integrity, hard work, and business expertise.

PROFESSIONAL EXPERIENCE

CD Superstore, Northfield, NJ   Nov. 1997–Present
Manager

Manage the financial and physical operations of an independent, high-volume retail store selling compact discs and related items. Supervise staff and personally provide sales and service to customers. Maintain accurate inventory and order and receive products and supplies. Select and install software and perform computer maintenance.

- Led staff in attaining 125% sales growth in four years.
- Guide employees in achieving company standards by controlling problems, identifying trends, solving personnel issues, and rewarding accomplishments.
- Increase repeat customers by offering superior service, demonstrating product knowledge, and personally addressing questions and concerns.
- Maintain accurate records for more than $1 million worth of inventory through compiling detailed sales and purchase reports, reconciling cash registers, and delivering bank deposits.

Boardwalk Casino Hotel, Atlantic City, NJ   Sept. 1993–Nov. 1997
Administration Services / Reservations Clerk

Performed administrative duties for record retention department, including processing requests, researching confidential records, distributing interoffice correspondence, and compiling information for various departments within high-profile casino and hotel. As reservations clerk, interacted effectively with patrons to coordinate and confirm reservations.

- Avoided fines and penalties by adhering to all Casino Control Commission regulations.
- Consistently processed requests quickly and accurately in a fast-paced environment using strong organizational and prioritizing skills.
- Met or exceeded company and departmental guidelines for responding to calls and coordinating reservations while demonstrating quality customer service.

143

Karen S. Carli, King of Prussia, Pennsylvania

This candidate's two-year degree was unrelated to management. The writer wanted to create a resume that focused on the individual's management skills rather than on the particular type of store he managed. The writer therefore composed an effective Summary, which

STEPHEN P. SMITH, 555-555-5555   Page 2

Spirit Airlines, Egg Harbor Township, NJ   Feb. 1995–Oct. 1996
Flight Representative, Line Service

Performed a variety of activities in person and over the phone to provide customer service and support to the airline and its passengers, including gate services and reservations.

- Effectively maintained radio communications with flight crews directly after takeoff and before landing to relay pertinent information regarding aircraft and airport status, ensuring proper procedures, security, and passenger safety.
- Requested and performed additional duties on the flight line in order to facilitate the daily operations of the airline.

World Casino Hotel, Atlantic City, NJ   April 1993–Sept. 1993
Diamond Club Ambassador

Promoted casino's Diamond Club program to patrons and photographed jackpot winners.

- Consistently exceeded daily goals for enlisting new members by effectively presenting membership benefits to patrons.

Bruno's Finer Foods, Atlanta, GA   Jan. 1990–Feb. 1993
Assistant Front End Manager (1992–1993)

Supported the financial and physical operations of a high-volume, full-service grocery store, supervising up to 10 cashiers per shift and maintaining the cash offices.

- Ensured accurate transactions and financial records while leading employees to exceed company standards for customer service.

Maintenance Activity Clerk (1991–1992)

Received large volumes of products, maintained inventory, and ensured accurate pricing for every store item using an electronic inventory system.

Cashier (1990–1991)

Completed customer transactions promptly and accurately. Promoted to Maintenance Activity Clerk in recognition of product knowledge and professional initiative.

EDUCATION

The Art Institute of Atlanta, Atlanta, GA   March 1990
Associate Degree, Music Entertainment Management

PROFESSIONAL DEVELOPMENT

Cash Office Management   *Successful Customer Relationships*

lists core skills, and focused on accomplishments in the Professional Experience section rather than on the industry in which he was working. For each workplace, bullets point to the accomplishments.

GARY KILBURN

1743 Dickinson Place
Amarillo, Texas 79109

806-555-9211
gkilburn@aol.com

MANAGER/CONSULTANT/TRAINER

Customer Service • Human Resources • Financial Management • Operations • Sales
Merchandising • Inventory Management • Payroll • Purchasing • Loss Prevention

➢ Solid P&L management, training, strategic planning, budgeting, financial reporting, and leadership qualifications. Lead companies to substantial revenue gains by establishing sales goals, initiating cost containment processes, providing hands-on training, and motivating personnel. Well-informed in current best practices.

➢ Self-motivated, results-driven manager; understand overall industry position and appropriate competitive strategies in market development. Readily visualize target and identify steps required to attain goal. Creative and effective at capturing cost reductions through performance training, employee retention, and strict inventory controls.

➢ Skilled in staff training, development, and performance management to meet/exceed operational and financial goals through performance/quality improvements and adherence to established procedures. Team player; establish standards for self and others, embrace visions, and see the "big picture."

➢ Computer-literate; proficiency includes MS Excel, MS Word, PeopleSoft, LRT scanner, and Internet research and communication.

RETAIL STORE MANAGER

Howe's Home Improvement Warehouse   *1996–2004*
Profitably managed 114,000–118,000 sq. ft. home improvement stores with 150–220 employees and annual sales volume of $25 million–$45 million with a product inventory of $6 million (45,000 SKUs). Oversaw $600K weekly inventory purchasing to procure merchandise mix specific to location's demographic needs. Tracked inventory and implemented systems to reduce inventory shrink.

STORE MANAGER, #372, Houston, Texas *(2001–2004)*
STORE MANAGER, #80, San Antonio, Texas *(1999–2001)*
CO-MANAGER, #372, Houston, Texas *(1998–1999)*
OPERATIONS MANAGER, #173, Austin, Texas *(1996–1998)*

• Achieved $45 million in annual sales and $6.7 million in net-before-taxes. Managed operating budget up to $7 million at approximately 15.5% to sales. Consistently improved sales performance and produced bottom-line profits in each facility by ensuring superior customer service, efficient staff scheduling, and appropriate product merchandising while maintaining facility's appearance.

• Spearheaded numerous cost-saving initiatives:
   ➢ Employee Turnover/Retention—Achieved best rate out of 60 stores in region.
   ➢ Inventory Shrink—Reduced inventory shrink from $500K at 2% to sales to $220K at .97% to sales by introducing new programs and executing existing procedures. Maintained this standard in all facilities.
   ➢ Labor Scheduling—Implemented effective automated labor scheduling, reducing man-hours while improving productivity. Introduced night stocking of merchandise, decreasing labor to process freight by 25%.
   ➢ Supply Management Program—Resulted in 35% savings in supply expense.
   ➢ Delivery Income/Expense—Turned around significant loss in delivery to break-even status by accurately calculating load, time, and distance.
   ➢ Bad Checks/Cash Over-Short—Introduced in-store campaign with expectations and rewards, reducing losses by as much as $10K annually.

144

Jane Roqueplot, Sharon, Pennsylvania

A color printer prints this resume in black and brick red. The brick red is evident in all the contact information, the information between the top two horizontal lines, the arrow-tip and round bullets, and the section headings. For each corporation, work positions are clustered to avoid

Howe's Home Improvement Warehouse, continued

- Implemented operational and management changes to dramatically boost profits in every facility under my management. For example, in store #372, increased profits 48% ($2 million). Oversaw several expansion projects as well as numerous major remerchandising efforts in excess of $500K each.

- Hired best possible staff; facilitated appropriate training and emphasized customer service. Drove customer service standard in each store.

- Boosted customer satisfaction through numerous initiatives:
  - ➢ Through proper scheduling, eliminated major front-end operations problem (long lines at cash registers) as well as sales floor department coverage issues.
  - ➢ Created program to verify customer received product in undamaged condition.
  - ➢ Improved communication and accountability by adding missing element to corporate Manager On Duty Program, providing direct access to manager.

Century Supermarkets   *1987–1996*
Managed 12,000–62,000 sq. ft. grocery stores with 25–300 employees and annual sales volume of $6 million–$35 million with a product inventory of 60,000 SKUs.

STORE MANAGER, #904, Wichita Falls, Texas *(1995–1996)*
STORE MANAGER, #897, Vernon, Texas *(1990–1995)*
STORE MANAGER, #901, Wichita Falls, Texas *(1987–1990)*

- Achieved highest volume of $35 million in sales and $2 million in profits out of 50 stores in chain.

- Succeeded in challenge to keep store productive while overseeing 12-month, $7 million construction project adjacent to facility being replaced. New facility recorded profit in first financial reporting period—a first in company history.

- Spearheaded use of computerized staffing program, which optimized efficient use of employee time during peak and off-peak store hours.

SEMINARS/TRAINING/WORKSHOPS

Recent training topics:
- Conflict Management Training
- Harassment Training
- Diversity Training
- Essentials of Communicating with Diplomacy and Professionalism

- Excelling as a Manager or Supervisor
- Substance Abuse in the Workplace
- Dale Carnegie, Effective Public Speaking

PERSONAL HIGHLIGHTS

Descriptive terms of personal strengths in the workplace based on professional Personality Profiling

Objective ~ Realistic ~ Looks for Logical Solutions ~ Competitive ~ Excellent Troubleshooter
Goal-oriented ~ Ambitious ~ Innovative ~ Responsible ~ Accurate

EDUCATION

Business Management, Texas Tech University, Lubbock, Texas

repetition in describing common duties. Attention is directed instead to achievements, cost-saving initiatives, and other initiatives for each cluster.

Tom S. Richards

1297 Silver Creek Road, Fort Worth, Texas 78413
(H) 817-897-1153 (W) 817-828-2236 (C) 682-442-6258 e-mail: tsr5125@yahoo.com

---

RETAIL STORE OPERATIONS DIRECTOR
Regional Director of Diversity

*Proven career history as a **market-driven store director** with an outstanding background in **managing multimillion-dollar retail operations**. Recognized for **increasing sales volumes, consistently beating expense goals** and successfully leading the region's 5,000 partners in corporate diversity initiatives.*

CORE STRENGTHS

Visionary Leadership / Innovation Management
Production and Efficiency Optimization
Customer Service and Retention Management
Organization / Team Leadership
Sales & Shrink-Inventory Control
Profit & Loss Management
Strategic Planning
Facility Maintenance

Strategic-Alliance / Partner Development
Regional Initiatives / Location Management
Human Resources Management
Financial Forecasting
Staff Supervision & Management
Stringent Cost Control Measures
Safety / Sanitation / Premises Liability
Training & Development

SELECTED PROFESSIONAL ACHIEVEMENTS

- Significantly increased community volunteerism and partnerships resulting in increased sales volume.
- Increased sales per man-hour 13% with no impact to service levels.
- Slashed store losses 50% by implementing systems and controls in premises liability.
- Reduced employee turnover 50% by transitioning to a fair and equitable management style, penetrating the store's leadership team from the top down.

PROFESSIONAL EXPERIENCE

H·E·B **STORE DIRECTOR**   **May 2001–Present**

H.E. BUTT GROCERY COMPANY, Fort Worth, Texas
H.E.B. is a $10 billion company with 300 stores operating throughout Texas, Mexico and Louisiana with corporate offices in San Antonio, Texas.

Manage retail operations, inventory control, premises liability, safety/sanitation, overall facility maintenance, human resources, and revenue / cost control with full P & L responsibility in a 24/7 operation consisting of 10 departments and 250+ partners. Support and implement regional objectives, including the execution of targeted advertising efforts.

- Yield a net profit of 7–9% of total sales while managing an annual sales volume of $3–6 million per year with a bottom-line profit of $300,000 to $400,000 per quarter.
- Achieved a first-time-ever expense record of 17.99%, and consistently maintain an average of 18.33%, comparable to a corporate goal of 18.50% and store history of 19.20%. This was accomplished through an effort to refocus attention on expenses and educate store partners in the identification of opportunities to reduce waste such as electricity.
- Reduced inventory from 22 to 16 days as a result of incorporating tighter management practices combined with the successful implementation of SRS—Store Replenishment System.
- Increased achievement of strategic operating goals though the implementation of a partner-centered leadership philosophy.
- Quadrupled participation in community volunteerism activities such as Junior Achievement as a result of assembling diversity programs and building community relationships.

MeLisa Rogers, Victoria, Texas

This candidate did not have a college degree but did have director-level responsibility in his current position. He wanted to relocate to a major metropolitan area in another part of the country but had only an outdated, amateurish resume. The writer constructed from scratch this

Tom S. Richards   page 2

Regional Director of Diversity   **January 2002–Present**
In conjunction with Store Director responsibilities

- Spearheaded the corporate diversity program on the regional level for 29 stores and 5000 partners. Led the region's management team in "getting excited" about diversity. Installed a 12-member council and 29 diversity champions (one representative per each location) to promote diversity throughout the region. As a result, HEB has gained a reputation as an active volunteer leader in each of its respective communities in the South Texas Region.

 STORE DIRECTOR   **1999–2001**

ALBERTSON'S INCORPORATED, Seattle, Washington
Albertson's is an NYSE $38 billion retail grocery company consisting of 2,300 stores operating in 31 states with the corporate office located in Boise, Idaho. Albertson's merged with Lucky Stores, a division of American Stores, Inc., in 1999.

Store located in heart of Seattle with 80–100 partners.

- Saved $920,000 in annual premises liability expense—$20,000 to $250,000 per quarter—through the execution of community-based initiatives that led to increased community support and operational awareness.
- Founder of Diversity Group Leadership Committee, which assisted the regional marketing team in implementing diversified community advertising campaigns that were previously nonexistent.
- Transitioned a store with a history of incurring losses of up to $300,000 per quarter to profitability within one year of promotion to store director.

ASSISTANT STORE DIRECTOR   **1995–1999**
AMERICAN STORES, INC. (LUCKY STORES DIVISION), Portland, Oregon

- Promoted every six months within four years to Assistant Store Director.
- Created and spearheaded a marketing initiative to enhance the store's snack program, "Snacks Across Your Tracks." This resulted in .4–.6 base points in profitability and margins.

ENTRY-LEVEL MANAGER / CASHIER / COURTESY CLERK   1988–1995

AWARDS AND RECOGNITIONS

2002 – Leadership for Diversity – HEB
2002 – Retail Grocery Industry – Diversity Edge – TAMU Sorority – Fort Worth – Plaque

EDUCATION AND PROFESSIONAL TRAINING

UNIVERSITY OF TEXAS "ON-LINE"—Course of Study: Business Administration, 1996–1998
WASHINGTON STATE UNIVERSITY, Seattle, Washington—Liberal Arts, 1987–1989

Diversity   Career Advancement Program
Behavior-Based Feedback   Store Management Training
Store Operating Statement Analysis

CERTIFICATIONS

Forklift Operation   Food Preparation and Safety State Certification
Anti-Money Laundering   AST—Alcohol Sellers Training

resume, which describes the candidate's extensive background, so that he could be competitive in achieving a position he was seeking in a preferred demographic area. The logos are in bright colors.

EDWARD W. JONES

| 256 Snowcrest Ave. | | Home Phone (555) 555–5555 |
| Anytown, CA 95555 | edjones@isp.com | Cell Phone (555) 444–4444 |

REGIONAL / DISTRICT RETAIL MANAGER

Strategic Business Planning / Team Leadership & Training / Revenue & Profit Growth
Customer Service / Multisite Operating Management / Investor Relations

SUMMARY OF QUALIFICATIONS

- ✓ More than twenty-five years of progressively responsible experience, with seven years in multistore supervisory positions.
- ✓ Highly successful in team building, merchandising, planning, organizing, and monitoring to achieve goals.
- ✓ Successful track record of increasing sales, driving profits, and meeting company goals. Ability to drive sales under adverse circumstances.
- ✓ Great communication skills, with proven ability to motivate, train, and lead employees to provide high level of professional standards and accomplishments.
- ✓ Unquestionable integrity and total commitment to providing outstanding customer service and creating value for shareholders.
- ✓ Earned Home Center's top award and recognition as "Store of the Year 1995" for best overall performance in sales and profitability.
- ✓ Awarded Home Improvement's top award and recognition as "Store Manager of the Year 1979" for Home Improvement's Southwest Region of 30 stores.

"I had the opportunity to watch Ed Jones do a great job of taking complete operational control of the entire chain. With his small staff he was able to completely manage the operational process of the chain, replacing a senior vice president, three regional vice presidents, and eight district managers....In the latter stages of this process, the events of 9/11/01 had an impact on the sale, and Ed was able to make the strategic adjustments needed to salvage an acceptable outcome." —George Hamilton, Senior Vice President of Merchandising of Home Improvement Stores

PROFESSIONAL EXPERIENCE

NATIONAL MERCHANT RESOURCES, Redding, Illinois—1999 to Present
<u>LEAD CONSULTANT SUPERVISOR</u>
Set direction and provide leadership to Regional and Store Consultants for achievement of maximum sales and profit goals while controlling expenses during liquidation sales of merchandise inventory and assets of retail clients across nation.

- Supervised staff of 12 Regional Consultants, 50 Store Consultants, and 3 Finance Personnel while closing up to 100 stores and 2 distribution centers during 16-week sale.

- Developed and ensured effective sales promotions, merchandise directions, personnel functions, operation systems, and accounting requirements, resulting in maximum sales, high staff motivation, productivity, and cost-effectiveness.

- Successfully increased profitability as much as 20% over budget through cost-effective operations.

- Saved $1.3 million in operating expenses on a budget of $25 million by controlling payroll, effectively utilizing advertising/marketing events, and reducing store-operating expenses.

146

Carla Barrett, Redding, California

The applicant's original resume did not list his achievements so that they stood out. They were hidden in the job description after each company listed. The original resume also had very little formatting. The writer reformatted the resume to give it a professional look and placed at

EDWARD W. JONES ▪ Page 2

THOMPSON BROTHERS RETAIL PARTNERS, Boston, Massachusetts—1995 to 1999
<u>REGIONAL SUPERVISOR</u>
Performed consulting and related services at locations designated by the company throughout the United States.

  - Promoted to Regional Supervisor in May 1997 to supervise Store Consultants in top-performing regions during liquidation of Johnson's/Home Quarters Company.

FRANKS HOME CENTER, INC., Tacoma, Washington—1987 to 1989 / 1992 to 1995
<u>AREA MANAGER/STORE MANAGER</u>
Recruited to improve sales, customer service, and profitability for the Tri-Cities market (1987 to 1989). Supervised staff of 2 assistant managers, 10 department managers, and 60 associates with an annual operating budget of $6 million in new store in the Northern California market (1992 to 1995).

  - Established special-order business, contractor sales, and second-highest cabinet sales in company, resulting in sales increases of more than 22% above previous year.

  - Increased store profits from $760,000 to $840,000 in 1993, resulting in largest percentage increase in 48-store chain for that year.

NORTHERN HARDWARE STORE, San Jose, California—1989 to 1992
<u>STORE MANAGER</u>
Hired as Assistant Manager after relocating back to California. Promoted to Store Manager to open new store in Sonora, California. Supervised staff of 3 assistant and 12 department managers.

  - Hired and trained 80 new associates while setting up fixtures and merchandise for new store.

  - Developed and implemented new check stand program to increase impulse sales of everyday items needed by store customers.

ALPINE LUMBER, INC., Stockton, California—1985 to 1987
<u>GENERAL MANAGER</u>
Accountable for total operations and sales. Maintained margins of a 9-acre lumberyard, including a 22,000-square-foot retail store and a customizing door shop.

  - Increased sales from $3.5 million in 1986 to $5.5 million in 1989, which consisted of a customer base of approximately 85% contractor and 15% retail.

HOME IMPROVEMENT CORPORATION, Placerville, California—1974 to 1985
<u>DISTRICT MANAGER TRAINEE/STORE MANAGER</u>
Assisted District Manager in district activities while managing highest-volume store in the district.

  - Totally remodeled a 56,000-square-foot store. Assisted in opening of five new stores. Supervised three additional stores without Store Managers in Irving, Texas.

PROFESSIONAL TRAINING

Management Corporation, Paradise, California: Managing for Motivation – Managing by Objective for Results – Creative Problem Solving – Essentials for Management – Causes of and Solutions to Shrinkage – Customer Service, Number One Priority

the end of the Summary of Qualifications a glowing testimonial about the person's outstanding achievements. This was embedded in a letter the applicant possessed and made available to the writer.

STEPHANIE LEIGH BIXBY

555 Farmington Lane ◆ Anytown, ST 00000
555-555-5555 ◆ mysearch@mynet.com

ACTION-ORIENTED MANAGEMENT PROFESSIONAL OFFERING EXPERIENCE IN RETAIL OPERATIONS, MERCHANDISING, CUSTOMER SERVICE AND HUMAN RESOURCES

PROFILE

Team Builder with proven record of motivating staff to achieve peak performance. Able to develop credibility and confidence with the public. Solid organizational and multitasking skills. Troubleshooter with demonstrated ability to identify problems and implement solutions. Excellent interpersonal and communication skills. Bilingual–English and Spanish. Computer literacy includes **Word, Excel, PowerPoint** *and* **Internet applications.**

EMPLOYMENT HISTORY

ALMOST FAMOUS	Watertown, CT	11/95 to Present

Store Manager

Orchestrate all facets of daily operations for upscale retail apparel and accessories store with annual sales of $3 million.

- ❑ Oversee activities and efforts of 23 full-time sales associates. Train staff in providing superior customer service.
- ❑ Coordinate work and vacation schedules. Arrange coverage for absences.
- ❑ Manage recruiting efforts, including screening resumes, interviewing and hiring personnel. Refer for termination. Conduct exit interviews.
- ❑ Evaluate staff and deliver constructive performance appraisals. Compensate employees based on corporate guidelines and policies.
- ❑ Maintain, monitor and troubleshoot computer sales and inventory programs. E-mail weekly reports to District Manager.
- ❑ Coordinate creative merchandising efforts by adapting corporate-provided materials to customer demographics.
- ❑ Address and resolve problems with vendors and suppliers.
- ❑ *Spearheaded efforts to resolve and correct overstock problems, resulting in $2,000 monthly additional sales along with improving efficiency.*
- ❑ *Reduced employee theft 100% by developing and instituting team sign-out policy. Received $500 bonus and commendation from company President. Policy now implemented in all stores nationwide.*

BOX OFFICE VIDEO	West Hartford, CT	7/90 to 11/95

Customer Service Manager

Oversaw operations for independently owned video rental store with average weekly revenues of $15,000.

- ❑ Supervised 12 Service Representatives in establishing memberships, processing rentals, arranging merchandise and dealing with customer service issues.
- ❑ Handled recruiting functions, including reviewing applications, conducting on-site interviews, hiring and performance reviews. Counseled, disciplined and terminated staff in appropriate instances.
- ❑ Maintained, monitored and updated sales and inventory records on customized software program.
- ❑ *Reduced employee turnover and enhanced morale by instituting store-sponsored health insurance plan along with monthly bonus program.*
- ❑ *Increased sales by more than 45% by instituting Favorite Customer Reward Plan.*

EDUCATION

NAUGATUCK VALLEY COMMUNITY COLLEGE, Waterbury, CT
Associate's Degree in **Management**

147

Ross Primack, Torrington, Connecticut

This person had been in retail operations/management, but she wanted to keep her options open. The writer indicated her other areas of experience so that she could pursue other opportunities.

Manufacturing

Resumes at a Glance

RESUME NUMBER	LAST OR CURRENT OCCUPATION	GOAL	PAGE
148	Assembler Installer	Assembler Installer/Toolmaker	291
149	Team Coordinator and Leader/ Production and Line Technician	Supervisor, Team Coordinator, Trainer	292
150	Quality Inspector/Supervisor	Not specified	293
151	Manufacturing Process Engineering Technician	Manufacturing Technician	294
152	VP and General Manager	Manufacturing Operations Executive	296
153	Production Manager	Manufacturing Manager	298
154	Machine Operator	Not specified	300

Michael K. Wilson
4621 McMurphy Avenue, Summer, WA 99999
(000) 000-0000

Summary of Qualifications

More than 12 years of experience in all phases of Assembler Installer and Toolmaker work in a manufacturing environment. Construct, maintain and repair tooling fabricated from all types of materials. Skill requirements involve jigs, fixtures, templates, plaster and plastic tools, wooden tools and press plate dies. Install parts and assemblies in Join and Installation (J&I), System and Installations (S&I), Wing Body Join, Final Body Join and Final Assembly shops for fuselage, wing buildup and joining and other major subassemblies.

Notables

◆ Past security clearances: U.S. Army—Top-Secret Clearance, The Boeing Company—Secret Clearance
◆ Able to work with others as part of a team, which includes giving and receiving feedback and helping others complete tasks. Possess interpersonal, listening and participation skills.

PROFESSIONAL EXPERIENCE

Toolmaker
◆ Read and interpret engineering, machine and tooling drawings. Capable of visualizing a three-dimensional shape from a two-dimensional view, converting left-hand to right-hand views and understanding symbols, flag notes, general notes and geometric dimensioning and tolerancing.
◆ Coordinate system to identify multiple axis (e.g., X, Y and Z) and airplane dimensional references (e.g., buttock, water and station lines).
◆ Operate various types of jacks to lift heavy machinery and mechanical lifts of various types (e.g., scissor lifts, elevated work platforms).
◆ Set up and operate conventional optics such as alignment scopes, levels, transits, optical scales, optical squares and laser alignment kits.

Assembler Installer
◆ Operate computing equipment to access job information (e.g., drawings, specifications and other online information systems).
◆ Use various jigs and fixtures to orient parts into predefined positions for part fabrication and assembly.
◆ Use various types of precision measuring tools.
◆ Drill, ream and countersink straight and close tolerance holes.

WORK HISTORY

Assembler Installer, The Boeing Company, Renton, WA   1992–2004
Small-Arms Repair Specialist, U.S. Army, Camp Kasey, Korea   9 years, honorable discharge

EDUCATION/TRAINING

◆ Associate of Technology Degree, <u>Machinist</u>—1 year complete: Bates Technical College, Tacoma, WA
◆ Certification, <u>Tool Fabrication</u>: Lake Washington Vocational College, Kirkland, WA
◆ Course, Tig and Mig Welding: Central Texas College–Satellite Course, U.S. Army–Korea
◆ <u>Crane Operations</u>: Rigging/Ground Control, Overhead Material Handling, Safety for overhead and shop operations
◆ <u>Safety</u>: First Aid and CPR Certified, Hazardous Communication, Emergency Preparedness, Fire Safety, Earthquake Preparedness, Chemical Safety and Health Awareness, Hazardous-Waste Management, Confined-Space Awareness, OSHA Hand Radio, Hearing Protection, Storm Pollution Prevention, Machine Tool Safety, Eye Protection, Reducing Air Pollution
◆ <u>Specialized Training</u>: Electrical Bonding Certification Type I, II, IV, V and VI; Face Surface Seal; Sealing Essentials; Coupling; Tubing Installation

148

Diana Ramirez, Seatac, Washington

A special horizontal line appears after the contact information. The Notables section includes information about secret clearances. Experience is listed according to occupation categories.

Jennifer D. Perrozi

116 Simpson Road • Jamesburg, NJ 08831 • 732.521.3929 (H) • 609.510.4823 (C)

MANUFACTURING ~ PRODUCTION ~ MANAGEMENT ~ CUSTOMER SERVICE
Supervisor/Team Coordinator/Trainer

Top-performing and motivated manufacturing professional with 28 years of experience in line production, supervision, team building, and machine and equipment operation.

Successful track record of maximizing resources to increase production capacity with the ability to troubleshoot and resolve problems in a timely manner. Computer-proficient. Assigned numerous projects with oversight of staff training, mentoring, diversity training, and production improvement. Aided in the design of new processes for production; excellent mediator.

Modeled customer service attitude and strong ethics within the work environment. As **team leader,** developed daily production schedule and served as a liaison between plant employees and management.

Experienced in supervising and training staff, addressing process-improvement issues, **production scheduling,** and adherence to quality standards. Mastered and implemented Good Manufacturing Practices (GMP).

Areas of Expertise:

- Manufacturing Operations
- Management & Supervision
- Production Scheduling
- Process Improvements
- Statistical Analysis
- Training/Mentoring/Team Building
- Communications/Presentations

- Good Manufacturing Practices (GMP)
- Quality Assurance/Inspection
- Problem Identification/Troubleshooting
- Customer Relationship Management
- Calibration & Instrumentation
- Lean Manufacturing
- Business & Strategic Planning

Professional Experience

General Foods—*Dayton, New Jersey (1976 to Present)*
Team Coordinator & Leader/Production & Line Technician

Challenged to supervise and coordinate 15 staff members working in manufacturing line production. Cross-trained and assisted in all business aspects by writing production schedules, attending production strategy meetings, and calculating production statistics. Functioned as Line Technician, Equipment Operator, and Quality Inspector. Known for excellent communication skills. Ability to resolve conflicts and motivate staff.

- Recognized by management for excellent product knowledge, supervisory skills, and plant machinery and equipment operation.
- Liaison between technicians and executive staff.
- Promoted to Team Coordinator for exemplary work and appointed as Diversity Trainer.
- Chosen to conduct training and development operations for various plants as Site Coordinator. Training workshops include diversity, process management, production, quality control, and project management training programs.
- Completed and facilitated Zenger-Miller training and team building operations with company departments.

Education and Training

Zenger-Miller, High Performance Workshop (HPO), and Team Development Workshop

149

Beverly and Mitch Baskin, Marlboro, New Jersey

This applicant had worked at the same company since 1976. Four areas of activity are indicated at the top of the resume. In the profile a paragraph is devoted to each of these areas in some way.

LEONARD COLLETTA

926 Augusta Blvd.
Pinehurst, Ontario A1A 1A1
Phone: (555) 888-3333

Assembly / Factory Production / Light Industrial
Quality Control / Team Supervisor

- Extremely **hardworking** and **dedicated,** with the ability to work in **physically demanding and high-pressure environments**
- Ability to **read blueprints** and complete **precision work** to exacting technical specifications
- Excellent **problem-solving skills**—able to quickly determine and repair source of problem
- **Highly reliable, self-motivated,** and **focused** on achieving tasks to highest standards
- Demonstrated ability to **meet and exceed production** quotas while maintaining standards for **accuracy and safety**
- Comfortable and proficient working in a **team** or **team-leader** capacity
- Solid **communication and interpersonal skills** interacting with coworkers and suppliers, with additional experience in customer service and sales

Experience

Quality Inspector / Supervisor
AVENUE METALS, Augusta, Ontario   1999–Present
- Supervise staff and monitor quality in the production of precision sheet metal components for the electronics industry.
- Produce and insert hardware components based on blueprints and specific technical requirements. Includes setup and use of punch press, kick press, and pemserter machines.

Installer
DESIGN WAVE, Pinehurst, Ontario   1998–1999
- Working from floor plans, installed entire offices for government departments around the GTA. Included all cubicle assembly and furniture installation.

Sales / Service Advisor
COLLETTA CORVETTE, Augusta, Ontario   1991–1998
- Sold new and used Corvettes to walk-in clients. Managed the store during night shifts.
- Served as Service Advisor and assisted in car detailing as needed.
- Appraised and bought used cars, handled customer service, and supervised service staff.

Education

Precision Sheet Metal Fabrication
AUGUSTA COLLEGE SKILLS TRAINING CENTRE, Augusta, Ontario   1998–2000

O.S.S.G.D.
MAJOR OAKS SECONDARY SCHOOL, Augusta, Ontario   1992

References available upon request

150

Ross Macpherson, Whitby, Ontario, Canada

A bold one-page presentation and graphic turn an otherwise blue-collar resume into an eye-catcher that had the applicant's phone ringing off the hook. Note the use of boldfacing.

Millie C. Router

222 Laminated Rd., Circuit Board, NY 00000
Residence: (555) 555-5555

OBJECTIVE

Manufacturing Technician

OVERVIEW OF QUALIFICATIONS

✓ **More than 20 years of experience** in technical manufacturing positions.

✓ **Promoted twice during a 5-year period** to current position supporting Manufacturing Engineers in the evaluation and testing of new products and materials.

✓ **Recognized for practical solutions** that have drastically **cut costs** and **saved** manufacturing **time** in the use of drill bits and materials and in the making of laminated circuit boards.

✓ **Positive, hardworking team player** who works well within company guidelines. Always willing to share information. Able to work effectively both as a contributing member of a team and independently. Organized and focused to function well under strict deadlines.

✓ **Dedicated to quality.** Not afraid to say something went wrong. Committed to doing the job right, developing the most efficient processes, and producing the best possible product.

✓ **New York State Certified** CNC Vertical Mill Set-Up Operator. Qualified Journey Person.

WORK EXPERIENCE

PRECISION MICROWAVE, INC., Circuit Board, NY   *1991 to Present*
ISO 9000–compliant manufacturer with $95 million in sales to the world's leading OEMs in the wireless-infrastructure, satellite, defense electronics, and select other sectors using complex microwave technology.

Manufacturing Process Engineering Technician *(2003–Present)*
CNC Router Manufacturing Technician *(1998–2003)*
Production Operator and Inspector *(1991–1998)*

✓ **Promoted** twice within 5 years.

Manufacturing Process Engineering Technician
- Assist engineers in evaluating and testing new products and materials.
- Determine ways to save money and time by improving processes and extending limits.
- Organize, compile, and evaluate data on new and existing processes. Create spreadsheets from data and submit results to Engineers. Follow the procedure all the way through.
- Communicate problems to management. Inform management how even more money can be saved through simple and practical changes.

Highlights of Accomplishments
- Saved time and money by cutting 2–4 hours off the time to manufacture boards by finding a way to eliminate the dry run.
  Challenge: 300 hits per drill is the standard when drilling via holes into circuit boards. Get more hits per drill, you save time and money on the use of drill bits.
  Action: In assignment with current vendor, tested and challenged the process to see if more hits could be made per bit.
  Result: Goal was 500 hits per bit. Accomplished the goal.

151

Bruce Baxter, Liverpool, New York

The applicant was moving out of state to create a new life for herself. Her excellent background and experience called for two resume pages. The writer set up her qualifications in a series of headlines to announce to her target company what she could do for them. The writer

MILLIE C. ROUTER   (PAGE TWO)

WORK EXPERIENCE (continued)

<u>PRECISION MICROWAVE, INC.</u>, Circuit Board, NY (continued)
CNC Router Manufacturing Technician

- Evaluated procedures to save costs while processing new product.
- Ran experiments and ensured that high-cost projects were run properly while working closely with Process and Project Engineers and CNC Programmers.
- Kept monthly and weekly utilization and efficiency charts. Ordered supplies, prioritized jobs, and assisted the Supervisor in administrative duties.
- Trained new employees.
- Assisted with inspections and safety procedures.

Production Operator and Inspector

- Set up and operated machines—CNC, NC, CMM measuring, lamination presses, and drill presses.
- Coordinated and worked all phases of lamination.
- Executed duties as Mechanical Inspector for the Machine Shop. Assisted with inspections of the Chemical Process Areas and with incoming inspections.

<u>CASTING-DIE MOLDING CORPORATION</u>, Lathes, NY   *1984 to 1991*
Develops and manufactures thermoset components for the automotive industry.

Technical Products Set-Up Operator
Mold Room Inspector

- Machined phenolic brake pistons on lathes.
- Set up machines according to blueprint specifications and measurements of phenolic products.
- Inspected Mold Room processes and conducted SPC data verification.

EDUCATION

Lake Community College, Wordsworth, NY (completed *December 1999*)
Associate in Applied Science Degree in Machine Trades

Keats Senior High School, Coleridge, NY
Business Degree with a BOCES Certificate—2-year program in Data Processing

TRAINING AND CERTIFICATIONS

✓ **Certificate of Completion for Apprenticeship Training,** New York State Department of Labor, *May 2000.* Qualified CNC Vertical Mill Set-Up Operator. Qualified Journey Person.

✓ **Certificate of Completion in IPC-A-600 Training and Certification Program,** IPC Association Connecting Electronics Industries. Course completed *June 2003.* Certification expiration *June 2005.*

✓ **CE 301 Introduction to MS Excel,** *Train the Trainer,* Burns College, Ayrshire, NY, *November 2001.* Also proficient in MS PowerPoint and Word.

✓ **Dale Carnegie Course in Effective Speaking and Human Relations,** Dale Carnegie & Associates, Inc. Awarded 4.9 Continuing Education Units, *April 1994.*

✓ **Advanced Validator Computer Technology,** Brown and Sharp.

✓ **Blueprint Reading,** Technicomp SPC Basic Series.

✓ In-house training through Precision Microwave, Inc.—Geometric Tolerancing, Dimensioning, Blueprint Reading.

also included her New York licenses and certifications because of their high standards for certain industries. The target company in Florida called her immediately and wanted to interview her when she got to Florida.

ROBERT W. PETERS

1078 Monet Lane
Edisto Bay, Nova Scotia 99999
Home: (777) 555-6767
Cell: (904) 555-7272

- Operations Turnaround
- Product Line Transitioning
- EDI Stock Replenishment
- KANBAN & CFM
- Capital Improvements
- JIT & Cell Manufacturing
- TQM & MRP

Results-driven **Manufacturing Operations Executive** with 14 years of management experience. Strong general-management skills in strategic business and market planning, quality and performance improvement, customer-relationship management, contract negotiations, capital improvements/renovations, cost reduction and revenue gains and multisite manufacturing operations.

Delivered strong revenue and profit gains at an international facility
while reversing a $9.4 million loss in 8 months.

CUSTOMER-FOCUSED ▪ COST-CONSCIOUS ▪ SOLUTION-ORIENTED

PROFESSIONAL EXPERIENCE

ABBA MANUFACTURING CORPORATION (ABBA)—Sydney, Australia   1990–Present
Formerly Piccadilly Design Co., the company was acquired in 1997 by ABBA, a $500 million, global, NYSE-traded (ABBA) manufacturer of printed circuit boards.
Vice President and General Manager—Caribou, Nova Scotia/Chinchilla, Mexico (2000–Present)
Senior operating executive with full P&L responsibility for a 120,000 sq. ft., 600-employee manufacturing facility with revenues of $120 million annually. Plant operates within a high- and medium-volume, complex, box-built, system-integrated production environment. Promoted to Vice President, August 2000.

Hold full accountability for all strategic and business planning, production control and master scheduling, manufacturing engineering, materials management, purchasing, inventory control, QA/QC, finance, marketing and human resources. Lead a 7-person management staff.

- Challenged in January 2002 by corporate COO and President to plan and direct the turnaround and return to profitability of a manufacturing center in Chinchilla, Mexico, while simultaneously managing the Caribou facility. Achieved all turnaround objectives, returning the Chinchilla operation to profitability within 8 months. Contributed strong and sustainable operating gains:
  - Reduced labor costs by 15% at this then-1,200-employee facility.
  - Improved product quality by 61%.
  - Increased on-time customer delivery from 65% to 85% in 90 days.
  - Reversed $9.4 million revenue loss, generating $4.1 million in operating revenues.

- Oversaw transition of $120 million contract from Caribou to full-scale production in Mexico. Transferred 2 major accounts from Caribou over 15 months. In Mexico, transitioned several new accounts from 3 sites and new assemblies from 4 long-term customers.

- Spearheaded introduction of a series of continuous flow manufacturing (CFM) initiatives for the Caribou facility that strengthened productivity, product quality and customer satisfaction. Reduced work-in-process (WIP) from 10 days to 5 days.

- Delivered significant improvements in quality, production time and cycle time for a major customer through implementation of KANBAN scheduling. Restored credibility and resolved long-standing quality and delivery issues. Achieved and sustained 100% on-time delivery for this high-volume line.

- Pioneered introduction of process changes, such as microBGA, cell manufacturing and EDI.

152

Doug Morrison, Charlotte, North Carolina

With an A.A.S. degree in Electronic Engineering from a community college, this individual had risen through the ranks the old-fashioned way—sweat equity. He started as a Test Engineering Technician at one company, became a Manufacturing Manager at another

Robert W. Peters, page 2

- Implemented time analysis studies and SMED procedures that reduced production setup time by 83%.

- Directed $750,000, 20,000 sq. ft. renovation, including multiple conference, training and break rooms. Monitored costs for leasehold improvements.

- Negotiated contracts and letters of understanding (LOUs) with major computer and server vendors, covering materials, pricing, payment terms and related liability, warranty and disclaimer issues.

- Delivered operating cost reductions totaling $480,000 over 9 months to accelerate profit gains. Led team toward brainstorming creative solutions.

- Created and managed a focus team for scrap-reduction program. Reduced scrap from 1% to .3%.

- Played key role in winning 3 major contracts in 2½ years. Worked closely with sales, production and customer in consummating agreement. Built sales from $6 million to $22 million for one account.

Operations Manager—Caribou, Nova Scotia (1990–2000)

Managed production controls, including materials allocation, scheduling, shop floor tracking and inventory control. Supervised 3-person production planning team.

- Reduced production cycle time from 10 days to 6 days.

- Decreased indirect costs by 30%.

- Established process controls that improved and maintained test yields above 97.2% in-circuit and 98.5% functional.

GREEN BAY ELECTRONICS—Green Bay, Wisconsin   1989–1990
Manager of Manufacturing and Testing

Led 18-person team (6 supervisors, 12 technicians) for this electronics facility with 130 production employees responsible for auto-insertion, SMT, wave-soldering, burn-in and testing operations.

RONSICO, INC.—Hoboken, New Jersey   1980–1989
Quality Assurance Engineer (1987–1989)

Identified and resolved negative trends in production.

- Reduced quality defects within electromechanical assembly from 1.2 per unit to .23 per unit.
- Implemented wave-soldering techniques that improved soldering and decreased solder defects.

Manufacturing Supervisor (1985–1987)
Quality Control Technician (1982–1985)
Test Engineering Technician (1980–1982)

EDUCATION

A.A.S., Electronic Engineering, Manhassett Technical Community College, Long Island, New York, 1980
Professional Development—(APICS Courses, 1998–1999): Basics of Supply Chain Management; Inventory Control Management; Master Scheduling

company, and then secured a position of Vice President and General Manager at a third company. The writer framed the contact information in a box at the top left and placed the keyword section to the right.

SHINGO T. KAIZEN

5555 East Town Road ▪ Pennsylvania, Indiana 00000 ▪ myemail@myaddress.com ▪ (555) 555-5555

MANAGEMENT PROFESSIONAL

Specialist in Production Efficiency / Quality Assurance / Project Management

Results-driven manufacturing professional with more than 10 years of management experience seeks career advancement within dynamic, high-growth organization that welcomes **fresh ideas, initiative, dedication, and experience** and demands excellence in consistently **meeting business objectives.** Exceptional ability to work under high pressure, offering **expertise in troubleshooting, problem solving,** and **management of multishift production operation.** Possess **outstanding interpersonal skills** complemented by **solid management acumen** and proven **ability to make sound, time-critical decisions**.

AREAS OF EXPERTISE

▪ Strategic Planning	▪ Production Scheduling	▪ Project Management
▪ Budgeting	▪ Inventory/Material Control	▪ HR Affairs
▪ Assembly	▪ Performance Improvement	▪ Team Building
▪ Training & Leadership	▪ Crisis Management	▪ Presentations

MANAGEMENT PROFICIENCY

PROVEN METHODOLOGY
- Drive business growth through aggressive initiatives that result in increased revenue growth
- Balance production initiatives with leadership via conceptual thinking and strategic planning
- Identify, establish, and manage strategic relationships to leverage significant long-term business opportunities
- Ensure customer service and satisfaction is afforded highest attention and priority
- Successfully build and maintain key corporate relationships

DEMONSTRATED RESULTS
- Skillfully **reduced labor costs** by 30%
- Participated in **work-flow redesign to increase production efficiencies** and reduce cycle time
- Successfully and dynamically consolidated valve designs to **reduce supply base** with an annual **savings of more than $1.5M**
- Implemented **one-person final assembly line,** reducing the need for three operators online and **realizing an annual savings of $1.2M**
- Participated in **transition of production facility** from Town, New York, to This Facility, Ohio, skillfully **absorbing new business without affecting customer** or current plant operations

CAREER PATH

PRODUCTION FACILITY—This Facility, Ohio   **1991–Present**
Fast-track promotion through a series of increasingly responsible manufacturing leadership positions

PRODUCTION MANAGER   **1998–Present**
Challenge: Coordinate production priorities with team leaders while ensuring cost efficiencies
Responsibility: Foster continuous improvement through Toyota Production System Methodology
Selected Accomplishments:
- Substantially increased production outputs
- Drove a series of successful productivity, quality, and operating improvement programs
- Facilitate team meetings, Quality Operation System (QOS) meetings, and problem-solving teams
- Motivate production employees to achieve team goals

153

Tammy K. Shoup, Decatur, Indiana

This applicant had a great deal of experience in manufacturing and management but never completed the business degree that many organizations require. To overcome this obstacle, the writer highlighted the applicant's methodology and then showed the results achieved. The

S H I N G O   T .   K A I Z E N

CAREER PATH CONTINUED

SCHEDULER   **1996–1998**
Challenge: Prioritize production schedules based on capacity requirements planning (CRP) and communicate with Sales, Manufacturing, and suppliers
Responsibility: Meet customer demand for shorter lead times
Selected Accomplishments:
- Introduced Lean Manufacturing Principles such as one-piece flow cells, Kanban, and Heijunka Scheduling to New Haven Plant
- Reduced work-in-process by 60%

PROCESS TECHNICIAN   **1994–1996**
Challenge: Analyze work flow and develop processes to standardize work
Responsibility: Streamline processes and procedures for increased efficiencies
Selected Accomplishments:
- Assisted with development and launching of new products

TEAM LEADER   **1991–1994**
Challenge: Communicate work directives to employees and provide leadership necessary to accomplish goals
Responsibility: Ensure productivity of work cell
Selected Accomplishments:
- Ensured quality of parts built

MY BUSINESS—Anytown, Ohio   **1988–1991**
Entrepreneurial venture with full-charge responsibility for all aspects of business and growth initiatives

GENERAL MANAGER
Challenge: Build profitable business from ground up
Responsibility: All aspects of operations management
Selected Accomplishments:
- Increased customer base by 500% over 4-year period

THE QUICKSTOP SHOP—Corner Lot, Ohio   **1985–1988**
Recruited to plan and implement strategies that would increase market share

GENERAL MANAGER
Challenge: Motivate employees, maintain low turnover rate, and increase store profitability
Responsibility: All store HR functions and operations management for four locations
Selected Accomplishments:
- Improved profitability for each location

TECHNOLOGY

- MS PowerPoint
- MS Word
- MS Excel

EDUCATION & PROFESSIONAL DEVELOPMENT

Ongoing professional development through seminars and classes in

- Excellence in Manufacturing I & II
- Strategic Financial Decision Making
- Facilitation & Coaching
- Shingo Prize Cell Redesign
- Workplace Organization
- Physical Inventory Control

BS in Business Management in Progress
Business School University

individual received an offer the first time out with this resume. Boldfacing of important information in the profile, the Demonstrated Results section, and the Career Path section help sell the candidate.

Relocating to Yourtown, IN

Gene Kelley, Jr.

Phone: (555) 555-5555

Quality-Focused — Quantity-Driven

Hard worker, contributes more than asked, reports to work prior to start of shift,
promotes teamwork, accurate, fast learner, excellent attitude.

Recent Work Experience

**LINE LEADER, MACHINE OPERATOR, QUALITY CONTROL, TRAINER, LICENSED FORKLIFT
DRIVER, HIGH-SPEED INK-JET OPERATOR**
CPP—Springfield, IL   1998–2001 and 2004
Commercial printing, packaging, distribution, and fulfillment service

Machine operator (drill press, trimmer, drop-bagger, ink-jet printer, glue/folder, mechanical
taper, GBC bindery machines); completed setup of new jobs; performed routine machine
maintenance (belt and blade changes, oiling, teardown, miscellaneous part replacement).

- Reduced turnaround time of recurring glue/folder job by 50% (from two days to one)
- Met or exceeded parts-per-minute quota
- Completed 95% of projects on time
- Received no customer complaints on work produced
- Trusted with special projects requiring confidentiality and highest level of responsibility

STEEL PRESS OPERATOR
Automation, Inc.—Springfield, IL   2003
Car-parts manufacturer primarily supplying Ford cross members, gas tank covers, and bumpers

- Gained knowledge and experience on every line
- Met production rate 100% of time
- Progressed quickly to operate six different presses
- Performed QC duties (not a responsibility given to all employees)

LINE ASSEMBLY ASSOCIATE
AutoTech—Springfield, IL   2002–2003
Leading supplier of automotive technology, systems, and components for major automakers

- Self-taught paperwork procedures to become backup for Assistant Team Leader
- Proficient in six stations of HVAC line
- Performed visual safety checks for quality control

Education

Graduate, JFK Memorial High School
Springfield, IL

154

Tammy J. Smith, Olivet, Michigan

This person had gaps in his work history and had worked at many companies in his town.
The writer emphasized the applicant's work ethic to make him stand out and be what employers
really look for.

Purchasing

Resumes at a Glance

RESUME NUMBER	LAST OR CURRENT OCCUPATION	GOAL	PAGE
155	Assistant Buyer/Sales Analyst	Assistant Buyer	303
156	Manager, Import Purchasing	Purchasing/Merchandising Management Professional	304
157	Purchasing Manager	Senior Buyer	306

Mary J. Sanders

111 East End Avenue • Elmhurst, New York 55555 • (555) 888-0000 • shop2drop@retailworld.net

Assistant Buyer

Skilled in areas of

- Wholesale / Retail Buying
- Product Merchandising
- Information Systems Training

- Product Distribution and Tracking
- Sales Analysis & Reporting
- Regional Marketing Campaigns

- Inventory Replenishment
- Vendor Relations
- Order Management

Computer Skills: Windows 2000; MS Word/Excel; Management Information Systems

Professional Experience

Merchandise Buying / Coordination

- Report directly to LAC's Director of Sales, providing support in areas of commodities buying and merchandising activities that reach annual sales volumes of $3 million for the division.
- Collaborate with multiple buyers to facilitate the marketing efforts of new products and the development of promotional calendars, product launches, and employee incentive programs.
- Maintain open lines of communication between manufacturers, sales teams, vendors, and warehousing personnel to expedite product orders, distribution, and problem resolutions.
- Reported directly to the Senior Buyer of Steinway Bedding in charge of day-to-day retail merchandise buying and merchandising activities impacting bedding sales across 37 Northeast locations.
- Successfully trained more than 45 Steinway employees on a complex LAN database management system.

Sales Tracking, Analysis, & Reporting

- Perform LAC's weekly sales analysis activities on regional/local transactions, achieving a recovery of $1,800,000 from 1998 to 2004 resulting from identification and resolution of accounting discrepancies.
- Develop sales books reflecting product lines, monthly promotions, discontinued items, order forms, and transparencies used by sales teams and personnel throughout 26 store locations.
- Formulate price breakdowns and track sales levels to determine product volume adjustments, replenishments, and allocations with a demonstrated proficiency in internal networking systems.
- Researched, compiled, and recorded Steinway's historical data to develop innovative sales strategies through close examination of inventory and product availability, pricing, and store promotions.

Work History

Assistant Buyer / Sales Analyst   7/97–present
LONDON-AMERICAN COMMODITIES, LTD. (LAC), Valley Stream, New York

Assistant Buyer / Merchandise Coordinator   4/93–7/97
STEINWAY BEDDING, Woodbury, New York

Education

Associate's Degree in Science, Business Management, 1993
STATE UNIVERSITY *of* NEW YORK *at* COBLESKILL

155

Ann Baehr, Brentwood, New York

Because the applicant had held two positions in 11 years, the writer split the Professional Experience section into two categories for impact and clarity. Note the easy-to-read keywords at the top.

ELIZABETH GREEN

5555 Oak Tree Lane • Northridge, CA 55555
(818) 555-5555 • egreen@email.com

PURCHASING • MERCHANDISING MANAGEMENT

Results-oriented Purchasing / Merchandising Management Professional with demonstrated success in streamlining operations and reducing costs of multimillion-dollar purchasing units. Proven ability to develop long-term partnerships with key suppliers. Highly responsive to organization objectives and customer needs.

—Core Competencies—

Project Management • Systems Development & Implementation • Product Development
Team Building & Leadership • Vendor Selection & Negotiations • Purchasing of Imported Goods
International Transportation • Letters of Credit • International Wire Transfers • Foreign Trade Documentation
U.S. Customs Regulations • Customer Relations • Communications • Hiring, Training & Supervision

PROFESSIONAL EXPERIENCE

WEST COAST ENTERTAINMENT COMPANY, Burbank, California • 1990 to Present
Achieved fast-track promotions from initial hire as Purchasing Assistant through positions of increasing responsibility, challenge and complexity.

Manager, Import Purchasing (1999 to Present)
Full accountability for day-to-day operations of $200 million unit, including managing staff of six. Report to Vice President/Global Controller. Oversee broad range of functions, including production sourcing, material planning, shipping and receiving, vendor contract negotiations and purchasing of resale and promotional inventory for seven divisions.

Specific Areas of Accountability
- Oversee issuance of all import purchase orders for merchandise supplied by foreign agents and factories.
- Consult with various business units on establishing and/or maintaining successful import programs. Provide expertise on complete import process, including supplier selection, product development, quality control, export documentation requirements, payment options, international transportation and U.S. Customs and other government agency clearances.
- Communicate corporate importation guidelines and requirements to all foreign suppliers, ensuring compliance with all applicable international and U.S. laws.
- Approve all international Letters of Credit to support $160 million annual import purchasing volume. Coordinate daily activity with outside banking partners, ensuring timely transmission of critical data.
- Partner with internal sourcing, merchandise and logistics departments to leverage combined purchasing and shipment volumes, gaining significant efficiencies and cost savings.
- Review and approve all open account (non–letter of credit or wire transfer) payment transactions.

Representative Accomplishments
- Developed and executed automated download of purchase order transactions to letter of credit system, improving on-time issuance from 20% to 75% in less than two years.
- Streamlined operations by consolidating merchandise supplier base from 1200 to 850 in twelve months.
- Implemented adoption of buying agent agreement representing approximately 50% of current international vendors and manufacturers.

Continued...

156

Vivian VanLier, Los Angeles, California

This individual had strong competencies and accomplishments as a purchasing manager, including expertise in import purchasing. She also had held several positions of increasing responsibility over a ten-year period. The writer, however, described only the past two positions

ELIZABETH GREEN
PAGE TWO

WEST COAST ENTERTAINMENT, *continued…*

Assistant Manager, Import Purchasing (1994 to 1999)
Introduced new programs for internal/external clients, including product launches and special promotions. Primary interface between customer and internal operations. Provided recommendations and organized conversion to a new integrated software program for import purchase order generation.

Representative Accomplishments
- Instituted new infrastructure to support distribution to foreign drop-ship destinations required for third-party promotional needs.
- Created new client checklists with a standardized format that provided consistent flow of information throughout the import transaction, reducing time and costs associated with error resolution and rework.
- Participated in contract and settlement negotiations with European suppliers to develop, purchase and install theme park equipment in excess of $100 million.

Prior Positions at West Coast: Promoted through four positions from Purchasing Assistant to Buyer.

EDUCATION

CALIFORNIA STATE UNIVERSITY, Northridge, CA
Major: Communications

PROFESSIONAL DEVELOPMENT

Letter of Credit Rules and Regulations—Los Angeles Bank, CA (Annually 1999 to Present)
Laws of Letters of Credit Workshops—Bank of America, Los Angeles, CA (1994, 1997)
United States Customs Broker Examination Course—Foreign Trade Association, El Segundo, CA (1996)
International Trade Regulations—Women in World Trade Association, Irvine, CA (1995)

PROFESSIONAL AFFILIATIONS

Foreign Trade Association
Women in World Trade

COMPUTER SKILLS

Windows, Microsoft Office (Word, Excel, Outlook, PowerPoint)

—Available for Travel and/or Relocation—

because the earlier positions were a progression of nonmanagement responsibilities. Nevertheless, a broad range of responsibilities and representative accomplishments are indicated in the resume. See Cover Letter 11.

Nora T. Collins

56 MacArthur Road • Somerset, NJ 08873 • 732.958.4791 • noracol7@prodigy.net

SENIOR BUYER
Procurement ~ Materials Management ~ Sourcing ~ Inventory

Performance-driven, dynamic professional with demonstrated abilities in procurement, outsourcing, and negotiating for manufacturing or wholesale distribution environments.

An independent self-starter with a solid history of utilizing out-of-the-box approaches, adapting to new business environments, and negotiating win-win agreements.

Competencies

- Purchasing/Buying
- Stock Control/Leveling
- Customer Relations
- Organizational/Project Management
- Material Distribution/Supply Chain
- Inventory Control/Management
- Resource/Materials Management
- Contract Negotiations/Vendor Relations

Professional Experience

American Bouquet Company, Inc. *(1984–Present)*
Purchasing Manager

Performed all buying functions for the New Jersey, Florida, and South America manufacturing facilities. Promoted numerous times over a 20-year career with the company.

Continually acknowledged for dramatically improving the firm's profitability with each assignment.

Handle disposition of defective merchandise and determine inventory levels in the warehouse while analyzing new order trends and then conducting precise inventories.

With a solid knowledge of hard-goods pricing, designed and created several new products and product lines that were significant revenue earners for the company.

Coordinated vendor operations with factory and shipping schedules and developed "Just in Time" procedures.

Improved quality and consistency of incoming merchandise by taking a tough stance with vendors.

Final authority for approving all vendor invoices for payment.

- Reduced a $1 million inventory by 50% with improved delivery scheduling.
- Reduced costs and price levels by selecting innovative vendors and changing the inventory system to augment production.
- Pioneered a company import program to purchase hard goods, reducing manufacturing costs substantially.

157

Beverly and Mitch Baskin, Marlboro, New Jersey

A pair of horizontal lines draws attention to the applicant's competencies. Bullets at the bottom of the page point to achievements. Extra-large type makes the applicant's name and position stand out.

Real Estate

Resumes at a Glance

RESUME NUMBER	LAST OR CURRENT OCCUPATION	GOAL	PAGE
158	Community Sales Manager	Community Sales Manager	309
159	Real Estate Development Consultant	Real Estate Development Consultant	310
160	Property Manager/Realtor	Real Estate Industry Professional	312

DENISE WEYLAND

6666 Ralston Commons
Sunnyvale, CA 94080

dweyland2000@aol.com

408-555-0000 (home)
408-555-0001 (cell)

COMMUNITY SALES MANAGER

Versatile, goal-oriented new-home sales manager with a track record of producing successful results in challenging market conditions. Proven ability to establish rapport and trust with diverse individuals, including home buyers, lenders, construction staff and warranty staff. Strong negotiating and closing skills.

REAL ESTATE SALES EXPERIENCE

Elegance Homes   2000–Present
Community Sales Manager, Atlantia Creek, Foster City, CA (2001–Present)

♦ Despite a difficult economy, lack of model homes and a less-than-desirable location, sold and closed 26 of 27 homes in the $600,000–$700,000 range between May 2001 and May 2002. Generated approximately $18 million in gross revenue.

♦ Interacted with both an in-house lender and outside lenders to overcome numerous obstacles and complete the closings.

♦ Joined the community as the fourth sales manager in approximately two months.

Sales Associate, Sunrise Shores, Santa Clara, CA (2000–2001)

♦ Performed selling and closing for a top-producing Community Sales Manager during a period when the home-buying situation changed from long waiting lists to a challenging sales market.

♦ Played a key role in assisting the manager to close approximately 50 of 84 homes in the $600,000–$800,000 range.

♦ Recommended by the manager for promotion to Sales Manager at Atlantia Creek.

Home Resale Experience:

Richardson Mortgage, Palo Alto, CA   1998–2000
Sales Representative

Porter-Martinson, Woodside, CA   1997–1998
Sales Representative

Previous Experience:

Employed in the South Bay and Sacramento-area real estate industry in a non-sales capacity, including office management and agent assistance, 1985–1997.

LICENSE

California Real Estate License obtained in 1997

PROFESSIONAL AFFILIATIONS

Member: Home Builders Association of Northern California
Former member: National Association of Realtors®, California Association of Realtors
and Woodside Association of Realtors

158

Georgia Adamson, Campbell, California

This person wanted a new job in a highly competitive field—new-home sales. The writer saw that the person could produce exceptional results in a difficult business climate. This becomes the lead idea.

JOSEPH K. THORNSTEIN

400 Rindge Avenue Worcester, MA 55555	thornstein42@earthlink.net	Office: (555) 555-5555 Mobile: (555) 555-5555

REAL ESTATE DEVELOPMENT CONSULTANT

Strong record of completing more than 35 development projects, from the development review, licensing, and permitting process through to final approvals. Recruited to manage the most high-profile, controversial, and environmentally sensitive projects.

- Exceptional ability to build agreement with town boards and community groups and to guide projects through complex regulatory and litigation processes on time and on budget.

- Broad and deep expertise in the industry. Able to quickly develop a feel for the community and assess whether a project is likely to be a "go," saving time and money and improving the company's bottom line.

- Excellent reputation within the New England real estate development industry. Extensive network of positive relationships with town officers, planning boards, and state and federal agencies.

- Politically and interpersonally savvy with expert conflict-management, communication, and presentation skills. Adept at breaking down barriers and turning opposing stakeholders into allies.

Development Projects

- Skilled Nursing & Alzheimer's Facilities	- Single-Family Homes
- Medical Office Buildings	- Condominiums & Apartment Complexes
- Corporate Office Centers	- Assisted Living Facilities
- Industrial Facilities	- Multiuse Facilities

Real Estate Development Skill Set

- Development review, permitting, & licensing	- Hire & manage development consultants
- Liaison with federal, state, & local agencies	- Make presentations to town planning boards &
- Negotiate option / purchase agreements	community groups
- Perform due diligence	- Conduct real-estate & construction-loan closings
- Develop & administer budgets	- Siting & land acquisition

PROFESSIONAL EXPERIENCE

WORCESTER PROPERTIES, Worcester, MA   2001–Present
Real Estate Development Consultant

Representative Project

- **Southbridge Corporate Center,** Southbridge, MA
  A $110 million project to develop an 82-acre stone quarry into a high-end corporate office building.

  Full development review, licensing, and permitting accountability from day one to final approvals.

  Challenge: Lay the groundwork for developing a controversial project in a strongly anti-development town. Solve zoning and jurisdictional problems concerning wastewater treatment. Work against a December 2001 deadline to avoid the company's having to negotiate a costly new land option.

  Actions: Successfully drove the project through a land court, an appeals court, and the State Supreme Court. Hired corporate consultants who could communicate well with town planning boards and community groups. Represented the project at 120 public hearings and neighborhood-group meetings. Negotiated with selectmen. Built relationships with local board members. Cleared a major roadblock— resulting from a decision by a neighboring town not to accept other towns' waste—by developing a plan for a $1.2 million on-site treatment plant. Completed entire MEPA, DEP, MHD, and ACOE processes.

  Results: Won all final permits and approvals for the development of "the most-litigated land parcel in the Commonwealth of Massachusetts going back 45 years."

159

Jean Cummings, Concord, Massachusetts

The individual did not have a bachelor's degree but did have exceptional gifts that made him effective in his field. The writer sought to make clear what those special skills were and to give examples of how he achieved results in the face of community opposition and other

JOSEPH K. THORNSTEIN

BERTRAND COMPANIES, Worcester, MA 1992–2001
Second-largest nursing home developer in the U.S.
Development Officer for Massachusetts

Accountable for project development from inception to final approvals. Projects included nursing home facilities, medical office buildings, high-end single-family homes, and corporate office centers. Performed due diligence; hired and managed development team of architects, engineers, and other specialists; and made presentations.

Representative Project

- **Southbridge Nursing Home,** Southbridge, MA

  Challenge: Site is a $15 million facility in a suburban town. Overcome strong neighborhood and community opposition by developing negotiated solutions. Determine optimal use for the 40% of the existing structure not required by the architectural plans.

  Actions: Hired the development team. Researched possible sites. Met with town officials and planning boards. Established a "good neighbor" relationship by allowing $1-a-time use of the auditorium. Made a strategic decision to install a CORF (comprehensive outpatient rehabilitation facility) and medical offices in the 32,000 sq. ft. of space not required by the nursing home. Neutralized strong opposition from the planning board and neighbors by negotiating creative solutions such as lowering the height of light poles, moving the parking lot, and building buffers.

  Results: Achieved buy-in from all necessary groups and gained project approval within a tight nine-month time frame and within the development process budget.

SANDERSON ASSOCIATES, INC., Manchester, NH 1986–1992
Vice President

Charged with developing the NH and MA markets for the company's real estate acquisition / development business. Staffed a 10-person acquisition department. Managed the development review process.

- Instrumental in growing sales from $2 million to $115 million in four years.
- Established new divisions in NJ, CT, ME, FL, and DC/VA.

Representative Project

- **Residential / Multifamily Condominium Housing,** Salem, NH

  Challenge: Overcome strong community opposition to the proposed 204-unit housing development. Address concerns about the tax increases and quality-of-life impacts resulting from a large influx of new residents using the roads and requiring costly town services (schools, police, fire).

  Actions: Actively listened to citizen concerns and then performed in-depth research on actual impacts. Hired a finance specialist to determine costs and benefits. Made a convincing case in a public presentation that the project would result in a financial net gain.

  Results: Successfully achieved all approvals within nine months.

EDUCATION

MOUNT MONADNOCK COMMUNITY COLLEGE, Princeton, MA
A.A. Degree in Mathematics

roadblocks to successful development. His special skills are indicated in the extended profile. His successes in spite of opposition are shown in the Challenge...Actions...Results portions.

MARTIN E. COLEMAN

227 Hillcrest Drive   Home (555) 000-0000
Mt. Juliet, Tennessee 00000   Cellular (555) 000-0000

REAL ESTATE INDUSTRY PROFESSIONAL

Property Management – Lease Negotiations – Tenant Relations

Experienced **PROPERTY MANAGER** and **LICENSED REALTOR** with 16 years of experience in residential and commercial property management and land sales. Oversee the performance of income-producing properties, lease negotiations, tenant relations, and property maintenance. Effective networking and communication abilities. Highly regarded for professionalism and integrity in all transactions. Computer experience includes Multiple Listing Service (MLS), credit-report software, Internet navigation and research, and email. Member, Real Estate Investors of Nashville.

PROFESSIONAL EXPERIENCE

DUNWOODY & COMPANY—Nashville, Tennessee
Property Manager / Realtor—1988 to Present

Oversee and manage 140 residential units, including single-family and multifamily homes, as well as an 18,000-square-foot office building. List and sell vacant land and lots throughout the metro Nashville area. Report to Owner / Investor.

- Show available space to prospective tenants, negotiate lease terms, and oversee collections and delinquent accounts. Coordinate eviction proceedings and make court appearances.
- Direct a maintenance staff of three in the repair, cleaning, and upkeep of rental properties.
- Review and approve office plans for build-outs and renovations.

WYATT & GREENE, INC.—Nashville, Tennessee
Purchasing & Inventory Manager—1971 to 1988

Scheduled and purchased all materials for this wholesale jobber of upholstery fabrics, vinyl, and supplies. Maintained inventory levels for 6,000 items. Promoted from warehouse position.

- Placed orders with manufacturers' representatives. Kept in daily contact with supplier mills and manufacturers regarding orders and shipment dates.
- Managed and negotiated terms with insurance representatives for health insurance plans and workers' compensation coverage. Filed employee claims and monitored claim status.

PROFESSIONAL DEVELOPMENT

CONTINUAL LEARNING INSTITUTE—Nashville, Tennessee

Earned **Realtor** designation and license in 1989.

Completed numerous continuing education courses, including
Real Estate Office Management, Property Management, and Real Estate Law.

160

Carolyn Braden, Hendersonville, Tennessee

This person had only two jobs his entire career. For the past 16 years he had worked for a real estate development company. The owner was retiring, and the applicant wanted to stay in real estate.

Recruiting

Resumes at a Glance

RESUME NUMBER	LAST OR CURRENT OCCUPATION	GOAL	PAGE
161	Recruiting Consultant	Recruiting Manager/Consultant	315
162	Recruiter/Trainer	Banking/Finance Position	317

Steven Brooks

1111 Lawrenceville Road ◆ Haven, CT 00000 ◆ 000–000–0000 ◆ user@adelphia.net

SUMMARY

An energetic, motivated and highly effective Recruiting Manager and Consultant with more than 20 years of experience in building teams of Sales, IT and Staffing professionals. Achieve astonishing success in developing and maintaining cohesive sales units, designed to fulfill organizational staffing needs. Employ extensive experience in areas of departmental operations, budget administration, lead generation and contract negotiation to directly affect financial growth and bottom-line profitability. Possess excellent command of written and verbal communication, as well as public speaking, sales presentation, staff development and resource allocation skills.

CAREER ACCOMPLISHMENTS

➢ Redesigned and transformed Sales and Recruiting processes for 3 geographic locations, resulting in up to 60% increase in full-time hires.
➢ Created diversified, motivated and innovative sourcing team responsible for filling 100 open positions nationwide.
➢ Integrated standardized applicant tracking, Internet posting procedures, timeline reporting and costing processes, increasing staff proficiency through detailed metrics.
➢ Directly contributed to hiring of more than 500 professionals on behalf of SAP America in 1998, positioning company to grow revenues from $1 billion to $2 billion in 1-year timeframe.
➢ Negotiated and closed contracts with Fortune 100 organizations, growing revenues for assigned branch by $3 million.

QUALIFICATION HIGHLIGHTS

- Multitasking professional with background in business development, recruiting management, personnel training and resource allocation.
- Interact and effectively communicate with executive and management personnel with decision-making authority to successfully generate client base and increase profit margins.
- Build and foster progressive, continuous business relationships, directly affecting overall bottom-line profitability.
- Utilize extensive, diversified lead-generation processes such as networking, cold-call prospecting and sales presentations to grow recruiting success and increase client base.
- Successfully interact with top-line professionals to negotiate and close employment contracts and establish qualified, motivated, cooperative and successful Sales, IT and Recruiting teams.
- Spearhead, create and implement departmental processes to increase efficiency and decrease expenditures.
- Plan and prepare for industry-specific job fair attendance.

PROFESSIONAL EXPERIENCE

IT Recruiters   2000–2004
Recruiting Consultant

- Successfully redesigned all Sales and Recruiting structures and processes for 3 national regions of $200 million IT consulting firm.
- Spearheaded and monitored restructuring of Internet and "brick and mortar" Recruiting Centers in Philadelphia, Chicago and Washington, DC.
- Created and conducted effective recruiting and sales presentations and designed employment packages to attract and retain top-quality professionals.
- Developed and integrated processes to streamline applicant tracking, Internet posting, timeline and metrics report generation to ensure recruiting and sales team met and exceeded personal, departmental and organizational goals.
- Implemented innovative interviewing and hiring processes to maintain compliance with new Affirmative Action Plan.
- Researched and contracted personnel development training, resulting in all recruiting staff being AIRS-certified, as well as improving interpersonal skills and increasing contract closures and continuous compliance with organizational/governmental regulations.

Continued…

161

Lea J. Clark, Macon, Georgia

This resume has a couple of design elements that avoid an impression of sameness: section headings that are bold, underlined, all caps, and without a blank line below them; and a staggered indentation pattern for three sets of bulleted statements under the section headings.

Steven Brooks **Page Two**

Technology Resources, Inc. 1999–2000
Operations Manager
- Instrumental in the establishment and growth of IT consulting firm.
- Prospected and grew accounts, leading to strong, foundational client base.
- Developed, conducted, researched and contracted personnel development training, ensuring that all team members remained knowledgeable in cutting-edge industry advancements.

Staffing America, Inc. 1996–1999
Recruiting Consultant
- Maintained responsibility for the recruitment and staffing of all departments in division, including product development, instructional design and data center.
- Improved and integrated company-wide recruiting processes, resulting in the hiring of more than 500 professionals in 1998 alone.
- Managed and administered $2 million advertising budget in support of marketing plan designed to enable timely fulfillment of open requisitions.

US Technologies 1995–1996
Manager of Recruiting
- Spearheaded and implemented nationwide recruiting strategy for start-up IT project organization.
- Researched, evaluated and integrated online applicant tracking system.
- Recruited, interviewed and hired applicants with n-Tier, OO application infrastructure and architecture qualifications.
- Administered recruiting budget of $500,000.
- Interacted with market researchers and print media to develop and implement strategic recruiting campaigns.

ACME Limited, Inc. 1992–1995
Recruiting Manager
- Managed and monitored activities related to recruiting and staffing, as well as new account development.
- Created and integrated new and innovative recruiting processes, leading to contract acceptance with globally recognized firms.
- Identified, evaluated and negotiated contracts with professional development and training companies to increase productivity, efficiency and knowledge of administrative management and technical contract employees.
- Developed and trained recruiters at 12 nationwide geographic locations.

Tech Search, Ltd. 1982–1992
Founder/Operations Manager
- Built and grew successful organization from ground floor, negotiating and retaining accounts with high-end organizations such as Franklin Mint, Lotus Corp., and PECO Energy.

COMPUTER SKILLS
Microsoft Office

In the Professional Experience section, bold italic makes it easy to spot the various positions held for the different companies. Bullets point to a mix of duties and achievements. See Cover Letter 12.

TED CARMICHAEL

1652 Toad Hill Road ▪ Newfoundland, PA 00000
(555) 555-5555 ▪ tedcarmichael10@mydomain.com

OBJECTIVE

BANKING/FINANCE position requiring hard work, sound business ethics, professionalism and innovation.

PROFESSIONAL SKILLS/KNOWLEDGE

- Leadership
- Documentation
- Quality
- Methods and Procedures

- Project Management
- Supervisory Skills
- Interpersonal Skills
- Customer Service

TECHNICAL SKILLS

Strong working knowledge of Microsoft Word and Microsoft Excel

PROFESSIONAL EXPERIENCE

THE INVESTMENT GROUP, Stroudsburg, PA
Recruiter/Trainer, 2004–Present

Initiate recruiting efforts for new telemarketers and stockbroker trainees. Arrange training sessions for entry-level staff specific to successful telemarketing, customer service and general telephone techniques.

ILC MANAGEMENT GROUP, East Stroudsburg, PA
Account Executive, 2001–2004

Complete management, development and service of diversified, nationwide client base. Designed customized short- and long-term financial plans based on clients' objectives by customizing questions and providing appropriate programs and services designed to meet financial goals.

- Increased understanding of asset allocation, risk management and risk tolerance of the client as they apply to the client's long-term goals and needs
- Built relationships with high-net-worth individual accounts
- Developed structured prospecting techniques, including cold calling, mailings, computer tracking, follow up, rapport building, persistence and closings
- Established niche marketing techniques
- Established standards for customer service, including sales, advisement and problem resolving

WJP PARTNERS, Warren, NJ
Investment Advisor, 1998–2001

Made contact with prospective customers, presenting corporate capabilities and offerings. Opened new accounts, advised clients on available financial options, educated clients on market trends and customized financial solutions designed to achieve short- and long-term

162

Patricia Traina-Duckers, Edison, New Jersey

Partial horizontal lines on each side of centered section headings are a distinctive design element in this resume. In the Professional Experience section, bold capital letters make the company names stand out. Italic for the job positions makes it easy to spot them if you look for italic only.

TED CARMICHAEL
Page 2

customer goals. Assisted with completion of complex paperwork. Trained new customer service representatives and brokers on ways to attract new customers. Expanded dealings to global market. Advised customers on buying/selling and performed detailed market analysis.

- Obtained required Series 7 and 63 licenses on first attempts
- Opened ten new accounts within two-week period
- Managed portfolios of high-net-worth individuals and corporate accounts

EZ CREDIT, Allentown, PA
Data Entry Operator, 1995–1998

Entered and modified orders for high-volume call center; resolved customer disputes and trained new employees.

- Handled more than 200 calls per shift, recognized as the highest of Quarter 1, '98
- Created online templates to expedite call resolution and increase personal productivity 50%

EDUCATION

Diploma, William Penn High School, Radnor, PA—1995

Dates are just after the job position so that you can associate the two items quickly. The paragraph below each job position indicates responsibilities, and bullets point to accomplishments. Education is last.

Sales and Marketing

Resumes at a Glance

RESUME NUMBER	LAST OR CURRENT OCCUPATION	GOAL	PAGE
163	Sales Associate	Sales Supervisor	321
164	On-Site Sales Manager	Not specified	322
165	Senior Sales Representative	Sales Professional	323
166	Sales Manager	Operations and Sales Management Professional	324
167	Sales Director	Sales Director	325
168	Parts Counter Sales Position	Management Professional	326
169	Sales and Marketing Representative	Sales and Management Professional	328
170	General Manager	Retail Sales Manager	330
171	Partner/General Manager	Not specified	332
172	General Manager	General Manager/Director of Sales	334
173	Account Executive	Sales and Promotions Professional	336
174	Consulting Sales Executive	Senior Sales Executive	338
175	Director, New Business	General Manager/Senior Sales Manager	340
176	Senior Account Executive	Not specified	342
177	Business Solutions Consultant	Sales Professional	344
178	Yacht Broker	Senior Product Development/ Operations Management Executive	346
179	Regional Vice President	Senior Retail Executive	348
180	Regional Vice President	Senior Account Manager/ Technology Consultant	350
181	Business Partner	Not specified	352

Tammy Wilson

| P.O. Box 8215 | Richmond, Texas | H: 832-449-5182 |

OBJECTIVE

SALES SUPERVISOR
To lead, coach, and teach a team of sales associates in the winning techniques of achieving sales that result in the increased commission and revenue for the associate, corporation, and client.

SUMMARY OF MARKETING SKILLS

Sales	Customer Service	Product Promotions
Personnel Training	Vendor Contract	Inventory Control
Cash Accountability	Displays	Order Processing
Computer Processing	Data Entry	Problem Solving

SALES and CUSTOMER SERVICE EXPERIENCE

Long Distance Service
- Achieve 85% of sales goals on a regular basis.
- Demonstrate winning sales techniques to client's corporate personnel.
- Negotiate and close sales for long distance services and miscellaneous packages for a leading telecommunications firm.
- Proven success in overcoming resistance to achieve sales.

Cellular Sales
- Generated sales of $.5 million annually in communication products and services.
- Managed an in-house inventory of a minimum of $75,000.
- Utilized manufacturer's literature in sales presentations.
- Trained sales staff on current and changing technology.
- Dealt with vendors while selecting products.
- Achieved high closing ratio by gauging customer response and adjusting presentations to resolve customer concerns.
- Initiated customer financing and maintained database for follow-up.
- Managed customer satisfaction by addressing customer complaints and solving problems.

Furniture Sales
- Generated annual sales of $216,000.
- Monitored sales in market trends of interior design to maximize sales and customer satisfaction.
- Achieved a 50% ratio of repeat and referred customer database.

Customer Service
- Maintained customer satisfaction and sales in a fast-paced, multitasked environment.
- Achieved daily sales of $2,000.

EMPLOYMENT HISTORY

Sales Associate, Precision Telecom, October 2001–present
Sales Representative, Fort Bend Communications, June 1999–December 2000
Sales Consultant, Zarowsky Furniture, January 1998–June 1999
Customer Service Representative, various organizations, May 1994–January 1998

EDUCATION and TRAINING

General Office Operations: fax, ten-key calculator, copy machines, Microsoft Office suite
Houston Baptist University, Houston, Texas, 1998–2001

163

MeLisa Rogers, Victoria, Texas

This person did not have supervisory experience in sales but wanted to be promoted to a supervisory position to double her salary. The writer focused on achievements. The person got the promotion.

Gloria James
5555 Princeton Lane
Hometown, IL 00000
555-555-5555 home
555-222-2222 cellular
gj5555@aol.com

Summary of Accomplishments

Consistent top sales producer for new-home developments in the Chicago area.
Responsible for more than $150 million in closings since 1993.

Professional Experience

Jansen Homes, Hometown, IL
1999 to Present
On-Site Sales Manager. Recruited by the founder of Jansen Homes to manage the sales of various home-development projects, with price points ranging from moderate to upscale. Prepare marketing plans, set up model homes, hire staff and manage sales results.

- Played a key role in the company's growth from 80 to 400 average closings per year.
- Earned "Diamond" or "Gold" level sales awards each year.

Supreme Homes, Westerville, IL
1993 to 1999
On-Site Sales Manager. Originally hired as a Model Homes Hostess. Promoted to Sales Associate and then Sales Manager within the first two years with the organization. Prepared marketing plans, set up model homes, hired staff and managed sales results.

- Earned "Manager of the Month" designation nine times in five years.
- Earned "National Salesperson of the Year" award from the National Association of Home Builders, 1997.
- Earned "Diamond" level sales award for 1998; "Gold" for 1997, 1996 and 1995; and "President" for 1994 and 1993.

Gained early career experience as a Retail Staff Assistant for Global Oil, helping to manage company-owned stations, and as an Associate for Mega Real Estate Relocation Corporation.

Education

Continuing education through industry conferences and seminars.
Real Estate License, Illinois, 1994

State College, Stateville, IL
Completed two years of general and business courses.

164

Christine L. Dennison, Lincolnshire, Illinois

This applicant kept current with her knowledge of the industry by attending seminars and conferences. The writer emphasized the applicant's energy, initiative, and sales accomplishments.

AMBER PATRICK

amberpatrick@email.com

5555 Central Avenue, #1   Residence (818) 555-5555
North Hollywood, California 55555   Mobile (818) 555-5554

SALES PROFESSIONAL

Expertise in Client Development / Sales Management / Sales Training

- Motivated sales professional with seven years of experience; includes three years of outside sales as well as experience in sales management and training. Experienced in working with organizations of all sizes, including national and high-revenue accounts.

- Natural communicator and team leader with strong motivational and interpersonal relations skills. Easily establish and maintain strong working relationships with clients and coworkers at all levels. Outstanding networking abilities.

—Strengths—

Account Development & Retention • Client Relations • Sales Training • Coaching
Time & Task Management • Negotiations • Strategic Alliances & Business Partnerships
Cold Calling, Prospecting & Closing • Event Planning & Coordination

---

PROFESSIONAL EXPERIENCE

SOCAL CREDIT ASSOCIATION, Burbank, CA • 2000 to Present
Senior Sales Representative
Cold call, prospect and forge relationships with business owners to generate new clients for leading credit card processing company. Conduct presentations, analyze profitability of credit card volume and respond to questions. Actively network at chambers of commerce and community organizations to increase company visibility and develop new business.
- Generated highest revenues in state, first quarter 2003.
- Achieved #1 in district production two consecutive years: 2000, 2001.
- Named "rookie of the year," 2000.
- Selected to represent company at job fairs to recruit new hires.

GOLDEN STATE DEPARTMENT STORE, Glendale, CA • 1997 to 2000
Department Manager, Junior Sportswear
Advanced from Sales Associate within six months to manage apparel department catering to trend-oriented, high-end clientele. Trained new hires, scheduled and supervised staff of six, oversaw merchandising and displays, assisted customers with selections and processed purchases.
- Surpassed 1999 sales targets by 12%—the highest in region.
- Recommended merchandising enhancements that maximized product visibility.
- Monitored client preferences and communicated with buyers.

EDUCATION

CENTRAL HIGH SCHOOL, Burbank, CA
Graduated in 1997

PROFESSIONAL AFFILIATIONS / COMMUNITY ACTIVITIES

Burbank Chamber of Commerce, Member—Ambassador Committee, Education Committee
Red Cross Blood Bank, Volunteer

165

Vivian VanLier, Los Angeles, California

This individual did not have a college degree and hadn't completed college-level course work, but she proved herself in the workforce. The writer built on the person's track record of accomplishments.

GEORGE E. DOWNING

7777 Salem Drive ■ Tyler, TX 75701 ■ (903) 888-5555 ■ gdowning@mail.com

OPERATIONS & SALES MANAGEMENT PROFESSIONAL
Consistent winner of Medallion Manager and Customer Satisfaction awards

QUALIFICATIONS & COMPETENCIES
**New Start-Ups ~ Business Revitalization & Optimization ~ Sales Revenue Acceleration
Change Management ~ Strategic Planning & Execution ~ Team Development & Empowerment**

Operations Management: Verifiable ability to astutely manage all facets of automotive business, including operations, sales, marketing, media advertising, P&L, legal, merchandise procurement, inventory control, service/repair, personnel recruitment/development/supervision, and problem/conflict resolution. Recognized for ensuring maximum revenue growth and profit margins, minimal expenditures, and continuity in operations while escalating customer satisfaction and Quality Commitment Performance (QCP) ratings. Consistently honored with **Medallion Manager awards.**

Sales Management: Proven track record of increasing volume and sales revenues through comprehensive team development, innovative incentive programs and sales strategy implementation, and unsurpassed customer service. Capture new business through media advertising (commercials and newspaper advertising) and customer referrals. Received many **Customer Satisfaction awards.**

Personnel Management: Recruit and build synergetic teams committed to common goal attainment. Implement hands-on, open-door management approach and fair, but firm, discipline principles to gain respect, trust, and cooperation from team members.

Finance & Insurance: Full P&L, banking, credit audit/approval, and add-on sales and insurance plan accountability.

CAREER CHRONICLE

BROWN'S AUTO SALES—Tyler, TX (2004–Present)
Sales Manager
- Joined forces with owner to launch new automobile business engaged in selling used vehicles. Manage all sales, banking, financing, and inventory procurement efforts.

WHITE'S TYLER FORD—Tyler, TX (1995–2004)
Operations Manager (1997–2004)
General Sales Manager (1995–1997)
- Orchestrated operations and sales efforts for dealership employing an average of 19 salespeople and selling 250–300 units monthly. **Increased total departmental revenues 233%, accelerated Customer Satisfaction Index, and received Medallion Manager award five consecutive years,** until sale of dealership in 2003.

COVINGTON PIKE CHRYSLER-PLYMOUTH—Memphis, TN (1993–1995)
General Manager
- Collaborated with owner in establishing new dealership from ground level. Assumed full accountability for dealership, **spearheading growth to realize profitability in first month and increasing sales revenue and profitability annually.** Presented with several **Customer Satisfaction awards.**

PRESTON II CHRYSLER-DODGE—Dallas, TX (1990–1993)
Sales Manager
- Hired, trained, and directed sales team of 15. Purchased and controlled large inventory of new vehicles. Instrumental in guiding dealership to recognition as **#1 volume dealership in district.**

HENRY BUTTS OLDSMOBILE—Dallas, TX (1985–1990)
Lead F&I Manager
- Managed financing and credit audits for prestigious dealership with sales of 450–500 new units per month.

166

Ann Klint, Tyler, Texas

A bold page border and boldfacing for the person's name, profile, section headings, competencies, areas of expertise, awards, job positions, and significant achievements establish this resume's tone.

Marty Clayton

Sales Director
Fractional Aircraft Sales

"I have been amazed at, surprised by, and appreciative of the number of hours you work and your accessibility....We reviewed many options for partial jet ownership, but you helped us decide that Flying Options was the absolute right choice." Tom M., Senior V.P., Morgan Stanley, Retired	"Marty has been a joy to work with at the company and has done a great job in terms of accommodating my needs with the utmost professionalism and integrity.... I look forward to working with him again." Jerry P., Capital Management, Founder

Strengths

- Leading and building high-performance teams, driving market share and revenue growth.
- Applying innovative marketing strategies to increase client acquisition, retention, and penetration.
- Building a solid client pipeline through referrals and focused efforts to create awareness and preference.
- Identifying customer issues to achieve customer satisfaction levels that enable further sales.
- Ability to adapt to changing business requirements, market conditions, and emerging technologies.

Expertise

- Strategic Planning	- Strategic Alliances	- Leadership
- Needs Assessment	- Customer Acquisition/Retention	- Business Development
- High-Impact Presentations	- Marketing Strategies	- Budget Management
- Persuasive Communications	- Building Relationships	- Time Management
- Closing Skills	- Strategic Planning/Implementation	- Territory Management

Professional Experience

Flying Options, Denver, CO   **August 1999–Present**

Sales Director, Rocky Mountain Sales Territory   April 2000–Present

Navigator (Sales Lead Coordinator and Inside Sales Rep)   August 1999–April 2000

- ✓ Managed the toughest U.S. territory (Rocky Mountain) and achieved the second-highest closing rate (61% compared to company average of 23%) of 11 sales directors.
- ✓ Achieved the highest demo-to-sales conversion rate (64% compared to average of 37%) in the company.
- ✓ Turned the Rocky Mountain Territory (RMT) into a significant contributor to the bottom line.
  RMT received only 2.6% of the qualified leads and contributed
     4.5% of the Total Earned Revenue
     6.5% of the Total Hours Sold
- ✓ Doubled the Rocky Mountain region's sales revenue within 12 months of taking over the territory.
- ✓ Promoted to Sales Director within 6 months of joining the company as Navigator and Inside Sales Rep.
- ✓ Assistant to Vice President of Sales and Marketing while working at corporate headquarters.

Marty Clayton Excavating, Inc., Tampa, FL   **1984–1999**

Founder and Chief Operating Officer

Owned and operated business for 15 years. Built business from the ground up. Recruited, managed, and developed staff. Managed the daily operations, planned and implemented marketing and sales activities, and supervised all accounting tasks and tax filings. Sold business in 1999.

- ✓ Achieved profit within 12 months. Doubled annual gross revenue in both the first and second years.

Education

Attended University of Miami, Miami, FL 1980–1983

123 Ristal Place • Castle Rock, CO 00000 • 555.555.5555 • marclay@hotmail.net

167

Roberta F. Gamza, Louisville, Colorado

This person had the company's worst sales territory. Instead of comparing him with peers, the writer compared his closing and conversion ratios, which show him maximizing his territory results.

Jamie Anderson, Jr.

1672 North Riding Drive · Spring Oak, AL 99999
(555) 555–5555 · janderson@att.net

Profile

Management professional with 14 years of experience in the Class-8 Vehicle Parts industry, including general management, human resources, and general sales. Background includes the establishment of programs to increase sales, improve productivity, reduce costs, and enhance customer relations. Decisive and direct, yet flexible in responding to the constantly changing demands of staff members, customers, and operations throughout the company. Key strengths include the following:

- Customer-Driven Management
- Marketing & Sales
- Leadership & Team Building
- Human Resources
- Recruitment & Training

- Efficiency Improvement
- Strategic Planning
- Organizational Development
- Policies & Procedures
- Labor Relations

Use excellent communication skills to maintain positive relations with customers; provide outstanding customer service and follow-through. Bring dedication and commitment to the highest level of service within the industry.

"Jamie looks for economical alternatives when purchasing for stock…he does a good job looking out for improving our branch. He has proven he can be trusted and charged with important duties and responds positively to working with other managers and employees. He is a good addition to management."

—Ken Brooks, Baker Transport Equipment

Professional Experience

GREENWOOD SALES & SERVICE, Spring Oak, AL 1999–Present
Parts Counter Sales

- Instrumental in establishing solid customer base, including dealer-level customers, for new company through expansive network of contacts. Set up more than 150 new customers, building customer base to more than 300 within region.

- Consistently surpass set sales goals by servicing up to 50 customers daily through e-mail, telephone, and outside parts sales communications.

- Handle stock, customer special orders, and repair shop orders with 500 various vendors nationwide, providing technical information regarding equipment, order parts, returns, and special orders.

- Design monthly sales flyers, brochures, and line cards featuring all heavy equipment products sold.

- Established shipping and receiving procedures, which streamlined operations and increased efficiency.

Continued…

168

Denette Jones, Boise, Idaho

Horizontal lines enclose the Profile, which ensures that it will be seen. The Profile not only contains a quick sketch of the applicant but also includes a two-column list of bulleted key strengths.

Jamie Anderson, Jr. Page 2

Professional Experience Continued

BAKER TRANSPORT EQUIPMENT, Spring Oak, AL   1989–1999
Outside Parts Sales *(1998–1999)*
Office Manager *(1996–1998)*
Assistant Parts Manager / Purchasing Agent *(1989–1996)*

- Defined and streamlined human resources systems; coordinated all HR functions, including recruiting, employee evaluation, and yearly sexual harassment awareness courses.

- Instrumental in branch gross sales increasing from $2.5 million to $4.8 million annually.

- Supervised and trained office personnel; total branch accountability during Branch Manager's absence.

- Integrated branch planning in compliance with corporate mission statement; assisted in defining branch mission and vision.

- Served as secretary for company. Directly involved during collective bargaining contract negotiations and employee contractual agreements.

- Negotiated with vendors to arrange optimal pricing and service for all departments.

- Researched and determined best shipping methods to distribute parts to customers and vendors, utilizing UPS, USPS, Federal Express, Air Freight, and Common Carrier.

Professional Development

Participated in several courses and workshops to ensure skills were up-to-date and professional education was ongoing. Courses included

· The Art of Hiring Smart	· Taking Physical Inventories & Cycle Counts
· Sales Territory Management	· ADP Payroll Systems
· Refining Interview Techniques	· Employment Law Update
· Understanding Unemployment	· Forklift Training & Safety
· Basic Air Brake Systems	· Confined-Space Safety
· Notary Public Training	· Basic First Aid & CPR

Technical Skills

Microsoft Office · Word · Excel · Publisher · PowerPoint · Photoshop · MS–DOS

The testimonial below the Profile helps dispel any reservations a reader may have about the applicant's worth. In the Professional Experience section, bullets point to accomplishments for each employer. Grouping positions under the second employer prevents unnecessary repetition.

Catherine Elizabeth Browning

SALES & MANAGEMENT PROFESSIONAL

Driving Growth, Revenues, & Market Share to Unprecedented Levels
Through Relationship Building, Enthusiastic Presentations, Ingenuity, & Perseverance

AREAS OF EXPERTISE

Consultative Sales & Marketing	*Business & Budget Management*
Long-Term Relationship Cultivation	*Revenue & Market Share Escalation*
Dynamic Presentations/Public Speaking	*New-Product Introduction & Marketing*
Fund-Raising Organization & Coordination	*Synergetic Team Development/Leadership*

SALES CHRONICLE

Sales & Marketing Representative, SPECIALTY MEDICAL, INC. — Tyler, TX (2001–Present)

Call on physicians, nurses, home health providers, and hospital discharge planners within 100-mile radius of Tyler to market, demonstrate, and provide in-service training on medical devices/equipment. Promote handicap mobility equipment to auto dealers in Northeast Texas. Market/advertise Specialty Medical through publications and advertising methodologies. Represent Specialty Medical at healthcare organizations/charities. Cultivate positive, long-term business relationships throughout community.

Significant Accomplishments
> ➤ **Acquired new accounts generating $139,000 monthly from new-patient referrals**.
> ➤ **Highly successful in reestablishing lost accounts** (ongoing effort).

Independent Sales Consultant, HEALTH RESEARCH CENTER, INC. — Tyler, TX (1998–2001)

Established/penetrated target territory to develop and expand client base. Scheduled appointments with hospital CFOs, administrators, and ER physicians and directors. Delivered presentations to promote Compliance Precision Reimbursement (CPR), which facilitates and improves accuracy of physician charting in emergency room settings.

In-serviced/educated physicians and administrative staffs on product knowledge and usage. Purchased/installed hardware/software in each facility. Diligently followed up to resolve issues and ensure satisfaction. Shrewdly managed self-employed business.

Significant Accomplishments
> ➤ **Acquired 17 new accounts while promoting new product** within first six months.
> ➤ Generated average of $63,000 monthly in highly competitive market.

Account Executive, TCA MEDIA SERVICES — Tyler, TX (1996–1998)

Marketed commercial advertising for 24 cable networks to key accounts in Tyler territory. Extensively researched marketplace and masterminded strategic marketing plan to optimize success. Prepared detailed reports (sales, expense) and established goals weekly. Executed all billing, collecting, and posting functions for own accounts.

Significant Accomplishments
> ➤ **Secured key accounts,** including Murphy Furniture; White's Tyler Ford; Elder Plymouth, Dodge, Jeep. Generated annual revenue of **$1.5 million.**
> ➤ **Recaptured lost accounts** by building rapport and providing personalized, congenial service.

District Sales Representative, AMERICAN TOBACCO COMPANY — Chester, VA (1992–1996)

Promoted/sold ATCO products and displays to distributors within large territory. Preplanned and organized route to maximize daily visits. Reported sales via PenRight computer software and completed daily call summaries. Prepared daily/weekly sales reports, coupon reports, and personal expense reports.

33000 Lovers Lane ➢< Tyler, TX 75700
Residence: (903) 999-5555 ➢< CatherineBrowning@internet.net ➢< Cellular: (903) 555-8888

169

Ann Klint, Tyler, Texas

This striking resume has a number of design features that make it stand out: the 3-D page border, the other vertical and horizontal lines, the applicant's name in large type and rotated counterclockwise 90 degrees, the contact information at the bottom of pages 1 and 2,

Catherine Elizabeth Browning

SALES CHRONICLE (Continued)

AMERICAN TOBACCO COMPANY (Continued)

Significant Accomplishments

➢ **Consistently exceeded all sales goals.** Recognized for **outselling leading district sales representative.**

➢ Honored with two **"Tough Nut" awards** in 1993 for **attaining highest volume of new contract commitments in chain accounts** and for **clinching display contract in chain account unattainable by other representatives during preceding six years.**

➢ Presented with **"Commitment to Excellence" award** in recognition of **exceeding national sales goals.**

➢ Received numerous **"Achievement Through Performance" awards** for recommending strategies to improve company operations and revenues.

Sales Manager, J. RIGGINGS — Tyler, TX (1991–1992)

Developed, scheduled, and directed team of 2 assistant managers, 6 full-time sales associates, and 15 additional seasonal sales personnel in upscale, high-volume men's clothing store. Astutely controlled labor costs and shrinkage.

Significant Accomplishments

➢ **Spearheaded store to #1 in the region in sales and shrinkage control for six consecutive months,** outperforming high-volume Dallas stores.

➢ Recognized as **"Number One Manager in the Region"** for eight consecutive months. Achieved honor first time in only second month as manager.

COMMUNITY LEADERSHIP & PERSONAL DISTINCTIONS

Member, TOASTMASTERS CLUB
Completed **Toastmasters Program** ⊱ **Won "Impromptu Speaking" Award**

Chairperson, MARCH OF DIMES
(Organized, coordinated activities of 15 volunteers and participated in 5K Walk-a-Thon)

Volunteer / Committee Chair — East Texas Chapter, AMERICAN HEART ASSOCIATION
(Facilitated and participated in myriad fund-raisers, such as Heart Ball, 5K Run, golf tournaments)

Chair (various committees), TYLER JAYCEES

Volunteer / Golf Tournament Committee Chair, AZLEWAY BOYS' RANCH
(Organized and executed fund-raising golf tournaments)

Care Group Volunteer, ROSE HEIGHTS
(Initiated and launched 5K Fun Run, fund-raisers, and golf tournaments to help disadvantaged)

Certified Personal Trainer

Soccer Coach (5 years) ⊱ **Soccer Captain,** Co-Ed Adult Team (3 years)

Top 10 in Nation Finalist — EAS Fitness Contest (1997)

Mrs. Texas Semifinalist (1997)

⊱⟨⟩⟨⟩⊰

33000 Lovers Lane ⊱ **Tyler, TX 75700**
Residence: (903) 999-5555 ⊱ CatherineBrowning@internet.net ⊱ Cellular: (903) 555-8888

the Areas of Expertise items left-aligned and right-aligned, the arrow-tip bullets in the contact information and at the end of the second page, and the handling of Significant Accomplishments.

KAREN COPELAND

12 Augusta Street
Pinehurst, Ontario A1A 1A1
(555) 555-5555

RETAIL MANAGEMENT
SPECIALIZING IN FOOD SERVICES & CONSUMER GOODS

☑ Strategic Planning   ☑ Merchandising & Promotions
☑ Staff Leadership & Development   ☑ Inventory Management
☑ Customer Service   ☑ Budgeting & Cost Control

Retail Sales Manager with more than 12 years of experience in all phases of retail operations. Consistently successful in achieving P&L, sales, productivity, budget, inventory, and shrinkage goals. Skilled in marketing, merchandising, management, accounting, budgeting, staffing, and overall profitability. Motivating and results-oriented leader who balances commitment to revenue growth with outstanding interpersonal and people-management skills. Persuasive sales and customer-service skills.

KEY STRENGTHS

➤ **Staff Management**
- Extensive people management and human resources experience with full-time, part-time, and seasonal staff. Includes hiring/firing, training, performance management, policy enforcement, and salary/promotion decisions.
- Known for approachable management style and ability to motivate employees to meet performance goals.

➤ **Merchandising & Business Growth**
- Extremely creative approach to promotional events and customer incentives that attract new business, build visibility, encourage repeat business, and increase sales.
- Skilled in creating eye-catching merchandising solutions to boost sales and increase impulse purchasing.

➤ **Finances & Cost Control**
- Strong financial planning, budgeting, and profit-and-loss management skills.
- Able to maintain and optimize profitability through effective scheduling, inventory maintenance, and shrinkage control.

WORK EXPERIENCE

ST. AUGUSTINE SPRING WATER TO WINE, Pinehurst, Ontario

GENERAL MANAGER   1998–Present

Hired and quickly promoted to manage all day-to-day operations for local distributor of high-quality springwater and U-Brew wines. Selected to manage new retail facility on the strength of retail expertise and track record of increasing sales revenues.

- Opened and currently manage all day-to-day operations for U-Brew retail franchise in Oshawa. Developed marketing plan, implemented processes and procedures, handled all administration and staffing, and grew loyal customer base to more than 1500.
- Selected to coordinate transition from St. Augustine's water distribution business to retail franchise operations following purchase by Crystal Springs in 1999. Responsible for all staff release, rehiring, and administration associated with the dissolution of the company.
- Assumed full responsibility for all marketing, sales, distribution, and business development for new biodegradable soap product line in 1995. Quickly expanded territory stretching from Pickering to Cobourg.

Achievements...

170

Ross Macpherson, Whitby, Ontario, Canada

This applicant had made a career change into retail management just a few years ago. The writer wanted to focus heavily on retail management as the target on page 1. He provided a strong profile, featuring the applicant as a Retail Sales Manager, and he made Key Strengths

KAREN COPELAND   (555) 555-5555   Page 2

ST. AUGUSTINE'S SPRING WATER TO WINE, *continued*

Key Achievements:

➢ Successfully increased annual revenues for U-Brew wine franchise by 8–10% annually.

➢ Conceived successful Fall & Winter wine campaigns that consistently increase sales by 300–400%.

➢ Enhanced company image through effective customer and employee relations.

➢ Spearheaded successes in annual trade shows, including Canada Blooms and The Cottage Show. Coordinated, set up, and managed booths for all events.

➢ Conceived and coordinated highly successful co-marketing partnership with CAA Travel, highlighted by a BBQ event and drawing for a free trip to Paris, France.

➢ Key contributor to St. Augustine's recognition by Pinehurst Chamber of Commerce for business and operational excellence (placed second for all businesses throughout Pinehurst within that category).

ABC FINANCIAL, Pinehurst, Ontario

INDEPENDENT INSURANCE BROKER   1990–1998

Marketed and sold a full range of home and business insurance products, including life, health, casualty, and property insurance. Prospected new clients through targeted cold calling and direct-mail campaigns.

• Consistently maintained a high-standard performance and sales record through exceptional service and follow-through, strong product knowledge, and outstanding communications, sales, closing, and customer service skills.

VIDEO WORLD, Augusta, Ontario

OWNER / OPERATOR   1981–1990

Grew single video store into small seasonal chain with locations in Pinehurst, Kirkland, and Cobot Cove. Managed all retail operations, hired and trained staff, and personally oversaw all marketing, merchandising, purchasing, and business development. Sold business in 1990.

• First within market to offer VIP membership cards with prepaid values. Successfully captured return client base and significantly increased revenues.

• Recognized and capitalized on untapped opportunity within seasonal cottage market.

Previous experience includes successes in insurance sales and sales management.

PERSONAL INTERESTS & ACTIVITIES

• Actively purchase and renovate single and multiunit residential properties
• Enjoy fitness, swimming, and the performing arts

REFERENCES

• Provided upon request

the first main section. The applicant's strengths are grouped according to three categories presented as subheadings. In the Work Experience section, a Key Achievements subheading directs the reader to accomplishments.

Susan Lee

Top performer
ready for a new challenge

PROFESSIONAL PROFILE

Positive attitude, committed to excellence, present a strong **Sales / Marketing / Management** background in the book industry and in private store ownership.

Track record of continuous growth and customer satisfaction in highly competitive and mature markets. Consistently beat market trends.

Participative management style, with proven talent for generating enthusiasm, motivating, achieving, and maintaining high team morale. Instill confidence and ensure highest level of productivity.

Relentless learner; value adaptability, innovation, and flexibility. Highly intuitive with a keen instinct for and genuine enjoyment of people.

#1 Funology Way
Circus City, WA 99999
(777) 777-7777

"I believe that the way you treat people, whether

employees or customers, is vital in creating

a successful business."

CAREER SUMMARY

Partner/General Manager, TEXTBOOK PALACE, Circus City, WA, 1996–present
Created and put into operation single family-owned retail store serving university and college students, teachers and homeschoolers, and the general public. Sell course books, general books, office supplies, computer products, university insignia clothing, and gifts. Annual sales approximately $3 million. Employees: 6–10 full-time and 15–25 part-time, depending on the season, with less than 10% employee turnover. Total P&L responsibility for the entire store and operation.

- Statistically valid marketing research conducted by Cole-Geyer Marketing concluded "Textbook Palace has an incredible report card. In service, pricing, selection, and atmosphere, Textbook Palace excels."

- Secured 33–40% share of overall market and 50% in course books—exceeding national average of 20–25% market share—in less than 3 years from date of opening.

- Achieved levels of 56% gross sales in used textbooks—exceeding national average of 14%.

- Marketing research revealed 90% of the students surveyed said Textbook Palace was preferred overall to the campus store.

- Since store opening in 1996, sales in every quarter exceeded previous years' same-quarter sales without exception.

- Stun competition annually with new programs, services, and products.

- Negotiated smooth transfer of company ownership with no disruption of service to customers or public image.

171

Janice Shepherd, Bellingham, Washington

This resume begins with an unconventional, free-form, two-column layout, with the applicant's name at the right and right-aligned, and a Professional Profile on the left and left-aligned. The contact information is farther down and right-aligned in the right column. Farther down still

Susan Lee

CAREER SUMMARY CONTINUED

COLORADO BOOK COMPANY, INC., Boulder, CO, 1976–1996
The nation's largest used textbook wholesaler, providing innovative products and services that help bookstore managers run efficient and profitable operations.

Director, Canadian Division / Coordinator, Canadian Accounts, 1991–1996
Accepted challenge to expand Canadian market for Colorado Book Company. Trained and managed sales representatives. Trained and supervised company buyers. Wrote manuals and procedures for employees. Monitored monetary markets and strategically moved funds to take advantage of fluctuations. Arranged brokerage and shipping for international sales and purchases. Reviewed expenses and reports of Account Sales Representatives and provided basic bookkeeping functions consistent with management goals. Negotiated contracts with universities and college bookstores for purchasing and selling textbooks.

- Succeeded in establishing strong market presence in Canada.

- Reduced shipping costs by up to 50% by implementing system of national brokers and shippers and consolidating shipping points into larger shipments.

- Established Canadian national bank account to fund purchases, which reduced financing costs due to more-favorable exchange rates, less time lost setting up individual arrangements, and reduced travel and labor costs associated with such arrangements.

Account Representative, 1980–1991
Built relationships and created sales opportunities with new, existing, and prospective customers. Maintained accurate contact records and conscientiously followed up with clients and prospects. Represented company at trade shows and conferences.

- Consistently met or exceeded weekly, monthly, and annual sales goals.

- Collaborated with company accounting offices and software programming department to create a program that allowed prices to be adjusted instantly and made conversions from U.S. to Canadian values. Saved 5–10% on purchase prices while maintaining a favorable status for "fair market" with customers.

Buyer, 1976–1980
Purchased inventory for wholesale resale. Managed travel, funds, and shipping of books purchased. Entertained clients and represented company. Kept accurate records. Coordinated with banks and schools for cash transfers.

"...skills at selling are very good...certainly has a good work ethic...a woman of her word.... One of Susan's strong traits is her ability to get along with people." MWO, President/CEO, Colorado Book Co., Inc.

"...a person of high integrity, and she throws her whole being into whatever she undertakes....you'll recognize patience, sincerity, organization, and communication skills...." MOL, Commodity Broker

"...superior ability to train her employees in human resources, consumer behavior, and customer satisfaction...her motivation and willingness to work motivate her employees to work harder and more efficiently....a person with such motivation, dedication, and leadership skills is hard to come by, and Susan is one of those rare people." CK, Middle School Instructor

"...an intelligent person...good management skills...works well with people...a person of honesty and integrity. As an employer and business operator, she is well respected by her employees and customers alike." JOS, Attorney

is a quotation, double-spaced and right-aligned. The Career Summary is a page long, reporting on four positions at two employers. The resume ends with a strong set of four testimonials.

TIMOTHY DAWSON

469 Clover Pathway
Newmarket, Ontario
L3X 9T9

555–555–5555
Cell 555–555–6666
Email myname@mysite.com

GENERAL MANAGER • DIRECTOR OF SALES • SALES MANAGEMENT PROFESSIONAL

EXECUTIVE PROFILE

Solutions-driven, innovative, and results-oriented, offering the benefit of 18 years of success in leading teams that serve highly competitive and volatile markets. **Track record of strong and sustainable revenue gains based on talent for growing client base, developing productive sales and marketing programs, and maximizing behind-the-scenes administrative operations.** Excellent networking, presentation, and negotiation skills. A dynamic and persuasive communicator, able to cultivate and maintain long-lasting business ties with staff, management, and clients from all organizational levels and cultural backgrounds. Earlier professional experience includes more than 5 years of managing a catering firm; more than tripled business in 2 years. Speak conversational Italian. Computer knowledge includes MS Office (Word, Excel, PowerPoint) and Internet research.

Sales Management Expertise

Public Speaking • Account Development & Retention • Brand Management • Buyer Awareness
Sales Closing Techniques • Consultative Sales • Field Sales Management • Incentive Planning
Dealer Relationship Management • Customer Satisfaction Index Creation • Marketing Materials Creation
New-Business Development • Territory Penetration & Optimization • Trade Show Representation
Profitable Sales Strategy Conception • Trend & Competitive Analysis

General & Operations Management Expertise

Budgeting & Forecasting • Cost Avoidance & Reduction • Job Description Creation & Monitoring
Tactical Planning & Execution • Operational Troubleshooting • P&L Management
Policy & Procedure Formation • Staff & Dealer Training, Coaching, & Counseling
Team Building & Organizational Leadership • Transition Management

Manufacturing Management Expertise

Automated & Cell Manufacturing • Distribution Management • Ergonomic Efficiency
Inventory Planning & Control • JIT Processes & On-Time Delivery • Logistics Management
Master Scheduling • Materials Planning • Project Management • Safety Training

CAREER HIGHLIGHTS

General Manager—North America, Storage Products Division (report directly to the V.P. of Sales)
  Cadbury Industrial, Toronto   2000–present
(Global leaders in metal manufacturing with 100,000 sq. ft. of factory space and annual revenues in excess of $20 million)
Recruited, based on Storage Products Division's aggressive expansion, with a mandate to build product awareness. Accountable for daily divisional operations that include on-time product delivery, product manufacture, high-expectation customer service, and quote and tender generation. Extensively interact with external distribution network in envisioning additional uses for a myriad of products. Create all presentations for dealers, sales representatives, and end-users. Supervise 3 Customer Service employees.
  Selected Achievements:
- Grew sales from $1.8 million to $2.3 million in a 6-month span.
- Nearly doubled client base for sales reps and dealers through tireless marketing and product awareness promotion.
- Led a 3-person team in the dramatic overhaul of back-office administrative functions. **Results:** Boosted quote turnaround time, streamlined commission pay-out procedure, and accelerated distribution network in an effort to enhance Company awareness and better promote services offered.
- Created numerous selling strategies, customized for 10 independent sales agencies. **Result:** Captured an additional 20% to 25% in yearly revenues.
- Expanded the concept and promotion of volume selling. **Result:** Generated—and continue to maintain—a heightened interest in product encompassing new and established markets.
- Customized client satisfaction index programs according to individual agency. **Result:** Obtained effective tracking results, which revealed agency strengths and areas for improvement.

172

Marian Bernard, Aurora, Ontario, Canada

The applicant, a top-flight executive, wanted to bid good-bye to the manufacturing industry. With each new company, he had earned promotions. He felt that his original resume did not do him justice. This new resume cites a wealth of achievements. For these, look at the

TIMOTHY DAWSON • 555-555-5555 • Cell 555-555-6666   **Page Two**

<u>**CAREER HIGHLIGHTS (continued)**</u>

National Sales Manager (reported directly to the V.P. of Sales)
 Vita-Flow Industries, Ltd., Oshawa   1999–2000
(National automotive outfitters catering to trucks and vans)
Recruited to oversee daily sales and operations of the Sales Fleet Dept. and Commercial Sales Staff.
   Selected Achievements:
- Single-handedly captured 5 key accounts through extensive network relationship-building. **Result:** Dramatically grew sales levels from zero to $1.5 million in only 5 months.
- Designed and implemented a sales and marketing program geared toward service fleet. **Result:** Successfully elevated client base.
- Overhauled in-house collections and trimmed receivables to less than 30 days.
- Introduced new VIP card program designed to increase repeat customer usage.
- Elevated awareness of Aftermarket Product Division to promote added value to customers. **Result:** Grew revenues by 9% within 1 year.
- Pioneered Company's first Customer Satisfaction Index to determine overall Company performance.

National Sales Manager (reported directly to the V.P. of Sales & Marketing)
 Quick-Fix Window Glass, Toronto   1995–1999
(A highly respected Canadian retailer and wholesaler with more than 175 locations in all 10 provinces and 3 territories)
Originally recruited as Account Executive and promoted in record time based on unprecedented and self-generated revenue growth. Assisted Sales and Service Depts. with calling on their client base.
   Selected Achievements:
- Extended current network with a mandate of expanding business activity. **Result:** Won most improved territory for 2 years based on commitment to exceed business targets and grew national revenues from $1.1 million to $3.9 million in less than 3 years.
- Elevated awareness of Aftermarket Product Division to promote added value to customers. **Result:** Realized noticeable increase in sales within 12 to 15 months.
- Introduced new VIP card program designed to increase repeat-customer usage.
- Pioneered Company's first Customer Satisfaction Index to determine overall Company performance.
- Overhauled in-house collections and trimmed receivables to less than 30 days.
- Appointed Chairman of Safety Committee for the National Association of Fleet Admin. in Ontario.
- Earned recognition in the following areas:
  - Won 3 sales competitions for most product sold within a 4-month period.
  - Won most increased number of clients in 3 months / 1 year.
  - Won most organized territory.

General Manager
 Blue Lion Auto Parts Sales, Toronto   1986–1995
(A local mobile franchiser serving mechanics, gas stations, and the general public)
   Achievement:
- Improved territory ranking from 29th to 3rd in Ontario through aggressive marketing and sales programs

<u>**EDUCATION AND PROFESSIONAL DEVELOPMENT**</u>

Completed a variety of company-sponsored courses:
- Modern Manufacturing Management
- Delegation Management
- Project Management
- Accounting for Non-Financial Managers
- Fred Pryor Sales & People Management
- "Sell Like the Pros"
- "The 7 Habits Coach" (originated by Stephen Covey)
- Nonverbal Communication Training

Business Administration Certificate, Chincousy College

Selected Achievements subheadings in the Career Highlights section. Many of the achievements include a Result (or Results) statement. Areas of expertise are grouped according to three categories and are center justified.

Barbara Bonnell

222 Hickory Avenue
Augusta, Ontario A1A 1A1
(555) 555-5555
bb@email.com

SALES & PROMOTIONS PROFESSIONAL

- ➢ Sales & Business Development
- ➢ Sales Closing / Negotiations
- ➢ Promotions / Marketing
- ➢ Communication

- ➢ Key Account Management
- ➢ Sales Presentations / Demonstrations
- ➢ Brand Management
- ➢ Total Client Satisfaction

Energetic, personable, and results-driven professional with solid track record of increasing revenues through superior sales and relationship-building expertise. Outstanding interpersonal skills—personable and professional with the ability to build rapport and close sales at all levels of management and executives. Creative marketing and promotional mind-set—able to conceive, source, develop, and sell marketing/promotional solutions that consistently generate revenue gains. Highly efficient, organized, and self-motivated. Proficient in MS PowerPoint, Excel, and Word; Internet research; and contact management/database applications.

RECENT ACHIEVEMENTS

- ➢ **Doubled annual sales revenues to $2.6 million in less than 4 years** for marketing/promotions firm
- ➢ **Revitalized lagging accounts** for leading manufacturing supplier, growing portfolio to more than 60 accounts and injecting an **additional $1 million** into company revenues
- ➢ **Ignited 40% sales increase** for leading construction supplier

PROFESSIONAL EXPERIENCE

ABC PROMOTIONS, Augusta, Ontario
Corporate promotions firm specializing in print, POS, and gift pack campaigns for major corporate clients across Canada.

ACCOUNT EXECUTIVE   1997–1998; 2000–Present

Quickly promoted to senior sales and account management position responsible for managing and developing key corporate accounts. Scope of responsibility includes all sales, relationship management, campaign consulting, end-to-end production, and delivery. Major clients include **Morantz Group of Canada, Corbett Distilleries, Maxximum Canada, Raymond Kitchens,** and **Appleby Jamaica Rum.**

- Developed lucrative relationships with client Brand Managers, recommending successful promotional campaigns, supporting product launches, and dramatically increasing annual account revenues.
- Routinely coordinated with external agencies, design teams, and print houses to complete production, meet delivery requirements, and ensure total client satisfaction.
- Personally sourced promotional items worldwide and/or developed items from scratch to meet exact design and cost specifications.
- Successfully developed accounts through strong interpersonal skills, dedication to client, and consistent commitment to excellence.

  - ➢ **Doubled key account sales from $1.3 million to $2.6 million in less than four years.**
  - ➢ **Grew Maxximum account from smallest to largest client in less than two years.**
  - ➢ **Designed, pitched, and sold a variety of seasonal promotions, resulting in 98–100% sell-through (Canada Club and Appleby Jamaica Rum gift packs)**

173

Ross Macpherson, Whitby, Ontario, Canada

In this resume, achievements and big-name clients are highlighted with boldfacing to show this candidate's performance. She left her company for two years and then returned. Dates for the current position show this gap in employment. Areas of expertise are put at the top

Barbara Bonnell

(555) 555-5555
bb@email.com
Page 2

CENTURY ALLOYS & RESEARCH CO., Pinehurst, Ontario
Canadian arm of a leading international producer of high-grade welding rod for the manufacturing and industrial production industries.

SALES REPRESENTATIVE—OUTDOOR SALES   1998–2000

Hired to revitalize sales and manage existing accounts throughout Augusta-Pinehurst territory. Required extensive knowledge of more than 30 key products, including all technical specifications and related applications.

- Successfully rebuilt existing relationships, conducted onsite product demos and sales presentations, and further introduced and sold new clients.

  ➢ **Grew portfolio to more than 60 accounts, generating more than $1 million in sales within 10 months.**

  ➢ **Successfully rebuilt key 6-figure account with General Motors.**

SOUTHERN BUILDING, INC., West Pinellas, Florida
$20 million manufacturer and supplier of roof trusses and floor joists throughout the southern United States.

SALES REPRESENTATIVE—OUTDOOR SALES   1995–1997

Sold volume and custom-built trusses and joists to major builders and contractors throughout Florida. Additionally, consulted on technical specifications and repair issues and provided drafts of truss layouts.

  ➢ **Increased sales by 40% by effectively rebuilding key accounts, generating an additional $800,000 in annual revenues.**

PERRY & ASSOCIATES INSURANCE, Augusta, Ontario
Midsized home, auto, and farm insurance broker with 5 offices throughout Ontario.

INSURANCE BROKER   1993–1995

Promoted to assume one of only five broker positions. Responsible for all cold calling, walk-in sales, account maintenance, and customer service.

- Effectively sold and serviced more than 200 accounts. Secured sales, executed policy renewals and endorsements, and collected client premiums.

PROFESSIONAL DEVELOPMENT / TRAINING

Managing the Relationship—FRED PRINCE SEMINARS   2001
Managing Your Time—FRED PRINCE SEMINARS   2001

VOLUNTEER & COMMUNITY INVOLVEMENT

MEMBER / VOLUNTEER—LIONESS CLUB OF AUGUSTA   1999–Present
- Volunteer participant in a variety of community fund-raising and charitable events.

before a profile paragraph. The Recent Achievements section is a strong addition because of the "big numbers" it contains. A horizontal line under each main section heading makes it easy to see the overall design.

CHARLES FUNG

9 Greenway Crescent
Augusta, Ontario A1A 1A1

cfung@email.com

Phone: (555) 555-5555
Cellular: (222) 222-2222

SENIOR SALES EXECUTIVE
Specializing in High-Tech Business Development & Key Account Management

★ <u>RECIPIENT OF MORE THAN 16 AWARDS FOR EXTRAORDINARY SALES PERFORMANCE</u> ★

TOP-PRODUCING SALES EXECUTIVE with 25 years of professional experience in managing key accounts and generating outstanding revenue gains in the IT industry. Combine outstanding customer-needs assessment and solutions-selling skills with advanced negotiation and relationship-management capabilities. High-level understanding of complex systems management, networks, databases, mainframe and distributor products, and software. Outstanding leadership, communication, and presentation skills. Fluent English and French.

SALES ACHIEVEMENTS

➤ **5 "PRESIDENT'S CIRCLE" AWARDS, granted to top 10% for extraordinary sales achievement**
➤ **11 "100% CLUB" AWARDS for sales results above quota**
➤ *Recent sales results:*

YEAR	% A	YEAR	% A
2004	**143% YTD**	1999	**153%**
2002	**228%**	1997	**183%**
2001	**128%**	1996	**182%**

PROFESSIONAL EXPERIENCE

XYZ CORPORATION   **1980–Present**
Exemplary career in the sales and marketing of IT solutions across a wide variety of hardware and software lines. Rapid advancement through increasingly responsible sales account, executive, and leadership positions on the strength of solid relationship-building skills and consistent ability to exceed revenue targets.

CONSULTING SALES EXECUTIVE—Tripoli Systems, Inc., Augusta, Ontario (1997–Present)
Tripoli Systems, Inc., is a wholly owned XYZ subsidiary marketing integrated IT Systems Management software solutions.

Charged with the sale and account management of multimillion-dollar enterprise IT solutions to key corporate accounts across financial, insurance, and telecommunications industries. Promoted through Sales Executive (1997) and Senior Sales Executive (1998) positions. Scope of responsibility includes account ownership, business development, strategic sales planning, team leadership (10 direct reports), consultation on client business casing, and negotiations.

- Successfully built entire client base from scratch by establishing solid relationships with client executive team, selling expertise, and delivering powerful multimedia presentations on Tripoli's integrated solutions.
- Established key business relationships with XYZ Business Partners and XYZ Global Services to deliver complimentary services and technology components.

  ➤ **Within first year, single-handedly sold key corporate accounts and effectively realized 148% of sales targets.**

  ➤ **Continued to overachieve all targets in subsequent years—228% (2002), 143% YTD (2004).**

174

Ross Macpherson, Whitby, Ontario, Canada

This resume uses an eye-catching chart to highlight exceptional sales results. Awards and achievements also are highlighted to position the individual as a top candidate. Lines enclosing the profile make the information there highly visible. In the Professional Experience section, a statement

CHARLES FUNG   Page 2

SOFTWARE ACCOUNT MANAGER, Augusta, Ontario (1996–1997)

Managed all sales, sales strategy, and account management of enterprise database and applications development software products (DB2, Java). Responsible for negotiating complex software solutions and supporting services to major players in the financial services industry. Focused on the development of solid client relationships and assistance with business case development to correctly identify specific client architecture, resource, and service requirements. Assembled and led a team of 6 Technical Specialists.

➢ **Achieved sales results of 182% (1996) and 183% (1997).**

PROGRAM MANAGER, NORTH AMERICA—Augusta Software Lab (1995)

Specifically recruited to manage internal sales and marketing of new database and AS/400 software applications throughout U.S. and Canadian markets. Developed and delivered highly effective sales presentations promoting software capabilities and illustrating sales potential.

➢ **Introduced creative incentive program, resulting in a significant sales increase across market.**

BUSINESS DEVELOPMENT MANAGER, Pinehurst, Ontario (1987–1994)

Promoted to run Pinehurst XYZ branch, focusing on the management and development of all mainframe and associated software sales to key government ministry accounts. Unique client group required patience; persistence; high degrees of creativity; and solid relationship-building, negotiation, and business casing skills. Success hinged on ability to recognize and market to unique government requirements, anticipate and work within strict budget restrictions, and negotiate creative leasing/financing options. Full management and leadership responsibilities for team of 10 System Engineers and 6 Sales Representatives.

➢ **Consistently exceeded sales targets, averaging 128% over six years.**

ACCOUNT MANAGER, Centennial, British Columbia (1980–1987)

Recruited to take over mainframe sales and manage multimillion-dollar financial and commercial accounts. Responsible for all front-end sales, relationship building, and account management.

➢ **Consistently exceeded targets, averaging 148% over six years.**

PROFESSIONAL DEVELOPMENT

- IBM Management Program—Levels I & II
- CRM Practices
- Solutions Selling Process
- Signature Selling Methodology
- Negotiation & Soft Selling
- Selling E-Business
- Messaging and Collaboration Sales—Lotus
- IT Systems Management Principles

PERSONAL ACHIEVEMENTS / ACTIVITIES

➢ Private Pilot's License—more than 5000 flying hours
➢ Skydiving—more than 350 jumps
➢ Additional interests include rock climbing (indoor and outdoor), equitation, mountain biking, and boating.

in italic describes the company. Arrow-tip bullets point to significant achievements for each of the positions held at this same company since 1980. At the end we learn that he is a pilot and sky-diver.

CHRIS ANDERSON

698 Cranberry Street
Salt Lake City, UT 84117

Email: canderson@hotmail.com

Mobile: (801) 555-5555
Residence: (801) 277-5511

GENERAL MANAGER • SENIOR SALES MANAGER • BRANCH MANAGER
Profit & Loss Accountability

Consensus-driven senior executive, expert in delivering realistic, repeatable outcomes; driving spirited profit performances in declining markets; and sourcing the right solution for the right time. Considered an "enabler of success" with a clear resolve for quality, revenue growth, and cost containment, underpinned with integrity and big-picture vision. Proven track record of propelling startups to market prominence and restoring prosperity to ailing companies—applying a mix of innovation, fiscal accountability, and rational decision-making to the process of management.

Professional strengths:

- General Management
- Sales & Marketing Management
- Market Expansion Initiatives
- Profit Turnarounds
- Budget Management
- Staff Recruitment & Training
- Succession Planning & Motivation

- Strategic Planning
- Business Forecasting
- Vendor Relationship Building
- Process Reengineering
- Change Management
- Sales & Contract Negotiations
- Lead Generation/Prospecting
- Executive Presentations

- Distribution Channel Development
- VIP Client Management
- Cost Containment
- New Startups
- Technology Sales
- Business Operations

BENCHMARKS & MILESTONES

- Launched new IT startup in partnership, establishing a dealership network **delivering $3 million per annum in revenues by year three.** By year four, product **attained "Top 3" marketplace status.** (Pointer Research Corporation)

- Pioneered the first distribution network across three states for a software startup company targeting the accounting industry with the *DDA* product. From humble beginnings, the software enjoyed enormous market brand awareness, becoming the **leading product in its market segment by year three,** installed at more than 10,000 sites and boasting 100 dealerships nationwide. (Pointer Research Corporation)

- Spearheaded introduction of call center designed to arrest declining customer service rates and boost field consultants' productivity. **In three months, customer satisfaction rates rose by 242%,** and consultants' write-off time **was cut by 400%.** (Bill Dollar)

EMPLOYMENT CHRONOLOGY

ECLIPSE IT, Salt Lake City, UT

4/2000–11/2004

Reseller and installation provider of information systems to $5M–$50M SME market. $14 million turnover.

Director, New Business

Products: Account distribution costing software and reporting tools.

Transformed cold leads generated through telemarketing into firm prospects, entering into protracted sales cycles frequently spanning 12 months of negotiations and implementation works. Drove new business strategies across Utah, winning rare audiences with CFOs and project committees.

- Reversed a long-held history of heavy discounting negatively impacting profit margins; focused instead on winning the sale by emphasizing value-added services and quality.

- Despite a steeply declining IT market, secured multiple appointments and drove fledgling sales negotiations; interpreted business needs and provided cost-effective solutions. Active contributor to the business, achieving the "Microsoft Business Solutions Inner Circle" for 2002.

175

Gayle Howard, Chirnside Park, Melbourne, Victoria, Australia

A lack of education has not been a handicap for this Senior Business Development Executive who was seeking the next step on his career path to general management. Note in this resume the use of italic, boldfacing, font sizes, page borders, lines of different lengths, parentheses,

---

EMPLOYMENT CHRONOLOGY (continued)

BILL DOLLAR, Salt Lake City, UT   1/1998–4/2000
Software producer of information systems for the SME market.
Director, New Business
Reported to IT Partner; Direct Reports: 5; Operational Budget: $3 million.
Products: Account distribution costing software.

A short-term sales role transitioned to full divisional management upon request to arrest the swift decline of staff morale and eliminate increasingly unproductive work practices. **Restored operations to a tight, cost-effective operation** and spearheaded a series of infrastructure improvements designed to increase customer satisfaction, win new business, and increase market share.

Daily accountabilities included strategic sales planning and execution, contract negotiations/renewals, call center management, and consulting to business clients to devise a range of technology solutions and conduct full process reviews. **Consistently met all sales volume and profit targets.**

- Reengineered the entire sales cycle to maximize profits and eliminate the company-held belief in the value of price discounting. The cultural shift from "cheaper price wins the sale" to a renewed focus on value and quality was a new strategy that paid solid dividends, with the company achieving "President's Club" status—**one of only two U.S. companies to reach this benchmark.**

- Key contributor in elite three-person team **winning gross product sales of $1.3 million and service sales of $1.3 million**—including nabbing a "personal best" sale of $700K.

- Identified and attributed significant drops in customer satisfaction rates to slow service responses, which in turn affected the productivity of field staff restricted from sales activities by routine "customer service" matters. Spearheaded new call center initiative that **in just 3 months elevated customer service rates from 14% to 48%** and **cut field consultants' non-selling times from 25% to 5%.**

POINTER RESEARCH CORPORATION, Salt Lake City, UT   1/1990–12/1997
Startup software company distributing accounting software through a national dealership network.
Sales & Marketing Director
Reported to Board of Directors; Operational Budget: $3 million
Direct Reports: 6 (Managers: State, Sales, Marketing, Support, and Operations)

Formed startup enterprise with two partners to facilitate the distribution of the (then) newly developed Pointer Accounting software through a national dealership. From a market novice in 1990, the aggressive establishment of a dealership network combined with intense brand-awareness campaigns propelled the software to become **one of the top 3 products in the marketplace** by the company's fourth year, with more than 100 dealerships nationally, and to become **profitable in the first 12 months.**

- Influential contributor in all phases of the software's development from concept to reality to a marketplace leader, **generating $3 million in revenues by year 3.** By 1997, 22 product modules were successfully on the market, and the product was installed at more than 6000 sites.

- **Introduced revenue-generating** "enhancement fee" billed directly to end users requesting product customization. Revenues burgeoned **to cover fixed costs,** ensuring product's profitability.

TRAINING

Hundreds of hours of training throughout career via formal short-courses, workshops, conferences, information sessions, and on-the-job training. Topics included

Strategic Selling, Negotiation Skills, Project Management, Structured System Design, COBOL Programming, Advanced Crystal Reports Design, and Conflict Resolution.

Chris Anderson   Page 2   Confidential

quotation marks, and use of a page number. Blank lines ensure white space even though the resume is full of information. Center justification of the main headings makes the overall design easy to see.

DIANA RETT

25512 Drayton Way ● Santa Clarita, California 91350   661-333-5775

SALES/MARKETING/BUSINESS DEVELOPMENT/KEY ACCOUNT MANAGEMENT

Dynamic 16-year sales and management career marketing products, technologies, and artists within high-growth, emerging, mature, and competitive business markets. **Top-Producing Sales Professional** with strong presentation, negotiation, and sales-closing skills. Deliver outstanding customer service. Excellent analytical and organizational skills; meticulous, professional, articulate. Qualified for client interaction at all levels. Success in the training and development of other sales professionals. Delivered consistent revenue growth through expertise in

◆ Sales Planning and Strategy	◆ New-Product Introduction
◆ Sales Forecasting and Measurement	◆ Key Account Relationship Management
◆ Sales Training and Development	◆ Multichannel Development and Management
◆ Team Building and Leadership	◆ Consultative Solutions Selling
◆ Dealing with Difficult People	

Proficient in Microsoft Word, Excel; versatile with WordPerfect.

PROFESSIONAL EXPERIENCE

> Integrity is crucial to customer care, and customer care makes *the* difference.

NTT/VERIO ● Los Angeles, CA   2001–Present
Senior Account Executive

Research and identify sales leads and opportunities as well as customer requirements that necessitate customized and complex solutions from NTT/VERIO's eBusiness services; effective handling of entire sales cycle followed by comprehensive account management. Provide leading role in new-business negotiations requiring in-depth knowledge of product strategy and NTT/VERIO's sales objectives. Accounts average $10,000 a month.

WORLDCOM ● Los Angeles, CA   2000–2001
Major Account Executive

Prospected corporations in Southern California to develop partnerships by providing telecommunica- tion solutions for Internet access, ATM, Frame Relay, managed web hosting services, colocation services, videoconferencing, and global applications as well as facility-based services. Researched and tailored proposals to clients' needs. Grew, maintained, and serviced all accounts. Networked with vendors and attended networking sessions and seminars.

SPRINT CORPORATION ● Universal City, CA   1999–2000
Business Account Manager

Analyzed, presented, and sold all aspects of telecommunications (long-distance services, voice, and data) to small and midsize businesses. Maintained and serviced all existing accounts. Continuously developed territory. Successfully utilized telemarketing techniques in setting appointments to increase market share.

Pinnacle Award for 1999 (outstanding sales achievement)

176

Myriam-Rose Kohn, Valencia, California

This applicant has a multifaceted life, being a Business Manager for an entertainment company while pursuing a professional career in sales and working on a bachelor's degree. You can gain a better sense of this individual's career path if you start at the end of the Professional Experience

DIANA RETT

CONNECTION III ENTERTAINMENT, INC. ● Los Angeles, CA   1995–Present
Business Manager   (concurrently)
    Challenged to launch an entrepreneurial venture, combining expertise in sales, marketing, and general business management. Full responsibility for Ross Bagley's career. Manage legal, financial, and administrative affairs; develop organizational infrastructure (legal, accounting); establish goals; design staffing patterns; and create sales functions. Keep all articles of incorporation current, file taxes, and set up trust account.

    Interface with acting/voice coaches, producers, studio moguls, and attorneys. Involved in theatrical contract negotiations.

SPRINT CORPORATION ● Gardena, CA   1991–1995
Account Manager Outside Sales (1993–1995)
Account Manager Inside Sales (1991–1993)
    In **Outside Sales,** analyzed market segments, developed marketing plans, and designed territory coverage. Key areas of management included sales/marketing, staff recruitment and supervision, employee training, scheduling, customer relations, and daily administrative affairs. Prospected tremendously to acquire new business. Developed, tailored, and wrote proposals to address clients' needs. Followed through on each account.

    Clients included mostly senior management in charge of telecommunications. Became valuable team asset.

    Accomplishment: Increased sales in territory by **25%** within first **6 months.**

    In **Inside Sales,** received several quarterly awards for **consistently exceeding revenue goals.** Requested by senior management to develop *The Revenuers* program for other employees to reach quota.

THOMAS SERVICES ● Los Angeles, CA   1988–1991
Account Manager
    Interfaced with middle to senior management and service coordinators to build strategic relationships, as well as to gain competitive advantage and market positioning for this temporary agency. Acquired thorough knowledge of government contracts (The Gas Company being one of many such clients), OSHA, and HAZMAT.

    Interviewed and placed temporaries. Handled disability and workman's compensation claims.

EDUCATION

Working toward **Bachelor of Science, Health Administration;** Minor: Psychology; California State University, Northridge, CA

Generation D Certification, WorldCom, January 2001

Computer courses in Lotus 1-2-3, Microsoft Excel
Technical Sales Training through Sprint Technical Support
Day-Planner Course
Courses in OSHA and HAZMAT regulations
Numerous sales seminars
Real estate training

section and read to the beginning. Note the design touch of the philosophical statement in a shaded box. Boldfacing highlights an award and notable achievements.

P J L PATRICIA J. LALLY

1515 Pinehurst Court • Augusta, Ontario A1A 1A1
Bus: (555) 555-5555 • Home: (222) 222-2222 • Cellular: (777) 777-7777

SENIOR SALES / MANAGEMENT / TRAINING
16 Years of Outstanding Sales Performance & Team Leadership
★ **WINNER OF MORE THAN 30 PRESTIGIOUS AWARDS FOR SALES ACHIEVEMENT** ★

HIGHLY RESPECTED SALES PROFESSIONAL skilled in high-level sales, account management, and team leadership. **Dynamic, aggressive, competitive, and driven to be the best.** Proven ability to pull together sales teams around a common goal and motivate to exceed expectations. Expertise includes

- ➢ **Key Account Management**
- ➢ **Sales Training & Development**
- ➢ **Team Building & Leadership**
- ➢ **Territory Management & Development**
- ➢ **Goal Setting & Achievement**
- ➢ **Labor Negotiations**

SALES AWARDS & ACCOMPLISHMENTS

- ➢ **Ranked #1 Sales Consultant 12 out of 16 years (out of 50 Sales Consultants)**
- ➢ **Achieved highest level within President's Gold Circle out of 300 Sales Consultants across company:**

  $3 Million Net Sales—fourth and highest plateau (2002)
  (highest level ever achieved by Sales Consultant)
  $2.5 Million Net Sales—third plateau (1999)
  $2 Million Net Sales—second plateau (1997)
  $1 Million Net Sales—first plateau (1993)

- ➢ **Winner of company Customer Service Award for 7 of the last 10 years:** 2003, 2002, 2000, 1999, 1997, 1996, & 1995
- ➢ **Earned 14 Canvass Awards for most advertising sold per geographic area**

SALES LEADERSHIP

- ➢ Successfully **led sales teams to exceed highest targets** within company.
- ➢ Consulted as **Sales Subject Matter Expert** for creation of seven in-house training courses on Professional Selling Skills.
- ➢ Chosen to participate in a variety of **Executive Focus Groups** developing and introducing new corporate products, incentives, business strategies, marketing, and training courses.
- ➢ Specifically requested to deliver **motivational sales presentations** for departments throughout company designed to ignite staff and model sales skills and excellence.
- ➢ Demonstrated **excellent communication and negotiation skills with all levels of management and executives,** including two collective agreement contracts as Chief Steward for OGEU, the only union representing $100,000+ Sales Consultants in Canada.

177

Ross Macpherson, Whitby, Ontario, Canada

This applicant was making a shift upward into sales management. A strong profile with keywords and a Sales Awards & Accomplishments section worked well to position this client as an expert in sales performance and leadership. The white-on-black graphic containing the individual's initials

P J L PATRICIA J. LALLY
Bus: (555) 5555-5555 • Home: (222) 222-2222 • Cellular: (777) 777-7777   Page 2

PROFESSIONAL EXPERIENCE

YP ACTIMEDIA, INC. (Formerly TeleSales), Augusta, Ontario   1988–Present
$600+ million corporation specializing in database and directory publishing and e-commerce business solutions. Currently operating in nine countries across four continents worldwide.

BUSINESS SOLUTIONS CONSULTANT *(1997–Present)*
Sell print directory advertising, Internet, and e-commerce business solutions to highest-value client group throughout greater Augusta area. Maintain accounts, increase account revenues, and provide advanced consultative and strategic advice on most effective combinations of advertising media.

- Manage and increase exclusive high-value client base consisting of more than 200 accounts generating $1.7 million in existing revenue.
- Maintain highest level of customer service in high-stress environment, coordinating with client executive and meeting all publishing and artwork deadlines.

  ➢ **Currently maintaining a 91% renewal rate on a $1.7 million customer base.**
  ➢ **Currently generating a 14% net gain, exceeding department average of 9%.**

DIRECTORY ADVERTISING CONSULTANT *(1988–1992; 1994–1997)*
Directory advertising sales to medium to large corporate accounts throughout GTA and bonus canvass areas (London, Sarnia, Windsor, Thunder Bay, Kitchener)

- Managed and increased high-value accounts generating minimum $1,000–$20,000/month.
- Provided strategic advice on advertising methodology, design, and overall program.

  ➢ **Recognized 16 times as #1 Top Sales Performer.**
  ➢ **Generated more than $3 million in net sales, achieving highest level within prestigious President's Gold Club.**

BUSINESS MANAGER *(1993)*
Selected to lead teams of 10–14 Sales Reps to improve previous performance and meet highest sales targets within company.

- Applied years of sales expertise to coach, consult with, and mentor team on advanced sales techniques, encouraging individual goal setting, creativity, and calculated risk taking.
- Provided team and individual development through advanced sales and account management training.

  ➢ **Successfully led team to exceed 14% net gain target on $14 million client base.**
  ➢ **Consistently exceeded sales targets and modeled best team practice within company.**

TRAINING / PROFESSIONAL DEVELOPMENT

➢ **Xerox Training Courses I & II**

➢ **Richard Horne Selling Course**—4-day

➢ Numerous courses and workshops on topics including **Consultative Selling, Handling Objectives, Closing Techniques, Teamwork Development, Coaching, and Counseling**

catches attention immediately. The graphic is echoed in smaller form at the top of page 2. Note how boldfacing also captures attention. Follow the bold through the resume to the key information.

Thomas A. Anderson

2929 Bowling Lane · Malibu, CA 90263
HP: 310-287-2321 · CP: 310-405-3691 · tander@msn.com

SENIOR PRODUCT DEVELOPMENT/OPERATIONS MANAGEMENT EXECUTIVE
Driving Growth & Profits in Retail Environments

Two Decades of Highly Successful Business/Industry Leadership
Proven Ability to Capitalize on Emerging Markets

Extensive Production Experience from Costing to Shipping
Start-ups / Market & New-Business Development / P&L Responsibility

Visionary, results-driven professional with demonstrated performance in strategic planning, long- and short-term goal setting, forecasting, budgeting, and cost control. Equally effective in needs evaluation, identification, implementation, and outcome assessment. Talent for creating motivating environment and interorganizational collaboration.

Core Competencies

- Business Plan Development
- Strategic Planning & Logistics
- Contract Management & Negotiations
- Performance Monitoring/Evaluation
- Quality Control Management

- Budget/Expense Control & Analysis
- Start-up Capital & Financial Reporting
- Sales, Marketing, & Business Expansion
- High-Level Presentation & Training
- Marketing & PR Initiatives

SELECTED EXAMPLES OF QUALIFICATIONS IN ACTION

- Founded and established Los Angeles design studio as $21M annual major force in textile and apparel markets, developing nationally acclaimed and editorially praised products.

- Led Pickford Mills to become foremost national textile manufacturer.

- Developed JIT inventory system for Pickford, raising on-time deliveries 87%.

- Invented unified merchandising model empowering textile companies to sell to coordinated sportswear companies.

- Collaborated with major chemical and fiber companies on market direction, product development, and advertising.

- Conceived and manufactured products for national brands.

- Created and ran highly successful national merchandising and marketing initiatives.

- Hundreds of retail ads and more than 100 editorial credits.

178

Nick V. Marino, Bishop, Texas

Center justification of the information in the early part of this resume makes a nice contrast with the two-column arrangement of the Core Competencies section and the full-page spread of the Professional Experience section. Centered main headings throughout tie the two

Thomas A. Anderson
Page Two

PROFESSIONAL EXPERIENCE

STAR ISLAND YACHT CLUB, Malibu, CA 2002–Present
YACHT BROKER
Sell 31-foot to 125-foot yachts regionally, ranging from $250,000 to $8.9M.

DESIGN STUDIO LTD, Los Angeles, CA 1996–2001
PRESIDENT
Product development consulting firm specializing in production/design packages for national start-ups.
Oversaw design, product development, sourcing, purchasing, manufacturing, and QC for major names in apparel industry. Full profit-and-loss responsibility.

- Accomplished $6M sales and 95% sell-through for first-year product launch on one-week turn.
- Product advertised by all major retailers.

FAR STYLES, LTD., Los Angeles, CA 1992–1996
VP SALES and PRODUCT DEVELOPMENT
Start-up with $9M in volume serving retail and wholesale markets with wide range of product development and production services using strong national sales force.
Acquired financing, hired sales force, stood up production, directed all product development, and oversaw all major accounts. Full profit-and-loss responsibility.

- Achieved $8.2M annual sales on modest start-up capital.
- Established quick turn on dollars with low inventory levels.

TAA, INC., Los Angeles, CA 1987–1992
PRESIDENT
Manufacturer with $3.5M in volume selling to national discount chains and department stores.
Directed design, finance, and sales operations. Hired and oversaw staff of 17 in sales, production, shipping, administration, and bookkeeping.

IN-MOTION, New York, NY 1983–1987
PRESIDENT
Start-up with $18M in volume selling to national and regional "budget" and "off-price" chains.
Acquired financing, and established and directed design/product development, sourcing purchasing, production, and QC.

- Turned $100,000 start-up capital 55 times and inventory 18 times first year for $5.5M in volume.

EDUCATION
Hunter College, New York, NY
Long Island University, Brooklyn, NY

pages together visually. Larger square bullets point to important qualifications at the bottom of the first page. Square bullets on the second page call attention to significant achievements. Education is last.

John J. Withers

Senior Retail Executive

Operations ▪ Marketing ▪ Merchandizing ▪ Sales

Increasing Revenue ▪ Enhancing Profitability ▪ Maximizing Productivity
Capturing Market Share

Top-performing executive with impeccable ethics, integrity, and a keen desire to succeed. Respected for consistently delivering results and

- Reversing underperforming operations and transforming them into top operations.
- Attracting, hiring, challenging, and effectively utilizing talent; building cohesive organizations; facilitating ownership/pride; and motivating team members through shared vision.
- Driving market share and revenue growth.
- Reducing costs and expenses and managing budget.
- Defining and enhancing the customer experience.

Expertise

▪ Strategic Planning	▪ P&L	▪ Organizational Restructuring
▪ Revenue Growth	▪ Operational Execution	▪ Relationship/Team Building
▪ Margin Improvement	▪ Budgeting/Forecasting	▪ Training/Mentoring
▪ Expense Reduction	▪ Marketing/Merchandizing	▪ Employee Development/Recognition

Professional Experience at Lowe's Home Improvement Warehouse 1988–2004

Regional Vice President 2002–2004

Directed retail sales for the Eastern Region of the Northwest Division (CO, WY, UT, ID, and NV) producing $2.5B of annual revenue. Accountable for P&L, strategic market planning, business development, sales, forecasting, marketing/merchandizing activities, pricing, shrink/safety control, training, and personnel. Managed nine district managers and two remote division support partners as direct reports; supported by a regional team of 10,000 associates. Worked from Denver, CO.

Key 2003 and 2004 Results

- Achieved 12% increase in retail sales and 32% increase in profit over previous year.
- Exceeded sales-per-square-foot goals by $28.
- Recaptured $25M in annual profit through stringent shrink control—reduced shrink by 47% in 18 months.
- Achieved 86% customer service satisfaction rating, 8 points higher than company average.
- Increased operating profit in low-volume stores $1.2M over plan.
- Achieved the third-lowest operational expense in company and sixth-highest safety rating.
- Grew store count by 36% while reducing employee attrition by 37% in 18 months.
- Attained:
    #1 company-wide new-store performance ranking. Realized $1.4M over operating profit plan.
    #1 company-wide ranking for professional tool rentals, achieving 38% profit margins.
    #1 company-wide ranking for on-time training of associates (101% Curriculum Score).
- Finished 2003:
    $3.1M under Workman's Compensation and General Liability Plan.
    $0.10 under effective wage plan, reducing labor costs by $1.5M/year.

123 South Circle ▪ Highlands Ranch, CO 00000 ▪ 123.456.7890 ▪ jjw@warmail.net

179

Roberta F. Gamza, Louisville, Colorado

This applicant was an accomplished, top-performing executive who spent many years with one company and now was seeking employment with a new company. The writer stressed the individual's most recent accomplishments and impact on the bottom line in order to

John J. Withers

Page 2

Vice President Operations, Contractor Business 2000–2002

Assumed leadership for Lowe's Pro Initiative, a start-up program to increase revenues by capturing a greater share of annual spending from existing contractor base. Challenged to reduce the much-higher-than-anticipated program costs and to accelerate roll-out speed.

- Identified/resolved bottlenecks and unnecessary costs in the program. Reduced expenses by 40% and accelerated roll-out speed by 200% (30 stores in 2000; 335 stores in 2001; 512 stores in 2002).
- Developed additional services necessary to enable further sales, including contractor sales associates who were able to capture more products per sale than general sales associates.
- Pro Initiative stores realized $1.2–$2M more in incremental sales revenue and 10% higher profit margins than non-Pro stores.
- Restructured stores' G&A, resulting in $22M savings.
- Created "Walk the Talk" and "The Pro Show" live video training programs delivered via the Lowe's internal network. Personally scripted and anchored "The Pro Show."
- Developed labor model for the Lowe's Supply concept store and corporate staffing model for low-volume stores.

District Manager, San Francisco, CA 1998–2000

Promoted from store manager and challenged to turn around and return to profitability the worst-performing district in the division (highest shrink rate, worst safety and attrition record). First district manager to work from San Francisco location.

- Developed and executed strategic plan that reversed the district's overall performance, resulting in market growth of 167%, from 3 stores to 8 stores.
- Achieved 109% of sales plan and 159% of profit plan in 1999.
- Significantly reduced Workers Compensation and General Liability costs by finishing 33% under plan.
- Achieved the largest shrink reduction in the Western Division. Climbed from #21 of 21 to #2 in two years.
- Became the first test market for online business operations. Established staging areas, order fulfillment procedures, shipping stations, and UPS interface processes to facilitate e-commerce initiative.

Store Manager, San Jose, CA 1995–1998

Managed all phases of daily operations of this Bay-area store while maximizing store sales and profitability.

- Achieved 107% over sales plan and 140% of profit plan.
- Awarded Store Manager of the Year, 1997 (#1 of 160 store managers).

Education and Professional Development

Babson Executive Education, Retail Seminar, August 2003
Selected for the elite Lowe's Executive Learning Program, April 2003
Lowe's Regional Vice President Training, July 2002 (2-week intensive program)
Lowe's CEO Dinner Series Events (quarterly dinners/discussions with CEOs from outside companies)
John Chambers, Cisco, August 2001
Ram Charam, Charan Associates, Inc., April 2001
David Glass, Walmart, January 2001

Mission College, Cerritos, CA 1987 (56 units in pre-med studies)

123 South Circle ▪ Highlands Ranch, CO 00000 ▪ 123.456.7890 ▪ jjw@warmail.net

demonstrate his value. The Key 2003 and 2004 Results section contains an impressive list of achievements. Bulleted items on the second page are a continuation of extraordinary accomplishments.

ROBERT A. JOHNSON, MSS

1805 NW 23rd Street
Tamarac, Florida 33321
954-555-1411 • rjohnson@go.com

SALES • MANAGEMENT • TRAINING
Senior Account Manager • Total Quality Management • Technology Consultant

➤ **Account Management**—Excellence in penetrating key accounts and increasing revenues through solution selling. Quickly establish rapport with individuals at all professional levels and from diverse cultures. Clearly focus product/services; identify target customers; capitalize on market trends; work to maximize client satisfaction together with revenue and profit expectations.

➤ **Team Building**—Decisive team leader with extensive experience in recruiting and hiring salespeople and managers. Create an environment that is positive and motivating and fosters a competitive spirit that fuels cooperation and teamwork while maximizing personnel's skills.

➤ **Training/Communication**—Promotion of corporate training initiatives in the classroom/field to motivate and develop first-rate sales team/managers. Review materials/manuals and update as needed.

➤ **Quality**—Superior aptitude in developing high-level relationships that maximize company profits and revenues along with customer and employee retention using Total Quality Management and Technology Resources.

➤ **Professional**—High-energy achiever; use outstanding organization, communication, and correspondence skills to build solid relationships. Generate top-quality results by demonstrating superior product knowledge and integrity. Equally skilled at budgeting and financial management.

➤ **Motivating**—Dedicated, ambitious, goal-oriented self-starter. Strong "closer" with emphasis on strategic solutions selling to major account markets, including established firms and small start-ups. Persuasive negotiator. Consistently achieve/surpass established sales goals. Lead by example.

➤ **Skills**—Technology savvy. Proficient in numerous computer applications. Microsoft Sales Specialist.

TRAINING / CERTIFICATIONS

e-Learning Summit; e-Lectrify to Learn, 2001	Total Quality Management
Certified Microsoft Sales Specialist (MSS), 1998	Mission of Excellence, Rollins University, 1996
Finding the Technology Buyer, 1998	Quality I and II
Quality at Work	A Guide to the Tools and Processes

AWARDS / ACHIEVEMENTS

Gold Club Member, 2000	Rolex Elimination Derby #1 Sales Manager, 1988
Million Dollar Round Table, 1999, 2000	National Sales Manager of the Year, 1986, 1987
Winner, Spring Madness Sprint Challenge, 1997	Manager of the Month, 1981
General Manager of the Quarter (Q1, Q2), 1994	Salesperson of the Month (3 months), 1980
Sales Manager of the Quarter, Q3, 1993	President's Club (recurrent member)

PROFESSIONAL EXPERIENCE

Quality Tech Services, Inc., Baltimore, Maryland   *2002–Present*
REGIONAL VICE PRESIDENT
- Manage college partners in Florida and develop enterprise relationships with corporate clients. Collaborated with college partner in securing $3M grant.
- Closed $500K in business during first 90 days.
- Won bid to implement Microsoft MCSE program at Magnet High School for 11th and 12th grade students. Coordinated training plan and trained test administrator. Students achieved an unprecedented 77% pass rate after one semester.

180

Jane Roqueplot, Sharon, Pennsylvania

The upper-left and upper-right graphics on the first page are in color. The one on the right has multiple colors and different levels of shading. In addition, the person's name, the contact information, the centered headings, and both kinds of bullets are dark blue. The profile's content

ROBERT A. JOHNSON, 954-555-1411, *Page 2*

PROFESSIONAL EXPERIENCE, *continued*

Production Point International, Orlando, Florida   *1997–2002*
SENIOR ACCOUNT MANAGER / ENTERPRISE CONSULTANT
- Deliver Technology Learning Solutions and Workforce Performance Improvement Strategies for software, network OS, and business skills development to targeted customer base.
- Profitably direct account management programs for key customers in South Florida. Built account base from ground floor to more than $1M in revenue within 2 years. Increased customer satisfaction ratings with implementation of account management and retention strategies.
- Consistently maintain highest GM and lowest discount percentage in region.
- Gold Club Member 2000; consistently in top 10% in National Sales Ranking.

Professional Business Systems, Pompano Beach, Florida   *1996–1997*
MAJOR ACCOUNT MANAGER
- Sold digital imaging and reproduction software and hardware. Generated $500K in new gross revenue within first 12 months with $112K gross profit.

Barton Protective Services, Atlanta, Georgia   *1992–1996*
GENERAL MANAGER, Tampa, Florida (1995–1996)
GENERAL SALES MANAGER, Lanham, Maryland (1993–1995)
SALES MANAGER, Springfield, Virginia (1992–1993)
- Within one year turned around Tampa branch from 60% of sales and profit plan to 100% of sales and profit plan in Q1 1996.
- Managed first office to exceed $100K/month in sales in first year, March 1994.
- Achieved 117% Profit Plan, 1994. Recognized as #1 in company; President's Club 1994.
- Managed and motivated team members to achieve National Sales Champion, 1992, 1993, and #2 Rookie, 1993.

Production Resource Group, Greenwich, Connecticut   *1989–1992*
CONSULTANT / REGIONAL SALES MANAGER
- Oversaw sales and distribution of consumer products; provided management, marketing, and sales consulting in U.S. and internationally.
- Generated $500K in wholesale first-year sales for Environmental Products Division. Developed more than 350 new distributors through December 1990. Produced $150K annual revenue in Telecom Division in first six months.

ADT Security Systems, Greenwich, Connecticut   *1982–1989*
BRANCH MANAGER
- Built sales force, increased major accounts, spearheaded customer growth, and developed sales branches as profit centers in Westchester County, NY, and Fairfield County, CT. Grew office from 9 employees and less than $500K in annual sales to more than 60 employees and $2.5M in sales.
- Hired and trained salespeople who achieved National Sales Status in several divisions: Residential (1986, 1987, 1988), Commercial (1988), and Rookie (1985, 1987).

Copy Systems, Inc., Glastonbury, Connecticut   *1980–1982*
SALES MANAGER / SALESPERSON
- Increased territory production by 30% within one year. Ranked 2nd of 14 managers in average sales per man (1981) and 3rd of 14 managers in total sales ($1.1M).

EDUCATION

1977–1980, NORTHEASTERN UNIVERSITY, Boston, Massachusetts
Business Administration
Major: Marketing • *Minor:* New-Venture Management

is grouped according to categories in boldface. In the Professional Experience section, round bullets point to notable achievements.

— NANCY WILLIAMS —
455 Knots Lane
Kettering, Ohio 00000
(555) 555-5555

— PROFILE —

Capable and self-motivated professional with a strong desire to apply skills in sales, client relations and communications • Ability to coordinate people and activities • Special talent for relating easily to others and inspiring confidence • Equally effective in self-managed projects and as a team member • Creative, enthusiastic and positive • Computer-literate

— STRENGTHS —

Problem Solving ... Organizational Skills ... Communications
Interpersonal Effectiveness ... Bilingual ... Client Relations

— SUMMARY of SKILLS —

Sales / Business Development

- Developed and sold residential properties ranging from $50,000 to $350,000.
- Utilized cold calling, direct mail, promotions, open houses and advertising to develop new clients.
- Researched, prepared and presented market analyses to prospective clients based on current market data.
- Established partnership in a start-up wholesale craft supply business.

Customer Relations & Service

- Utilized strong client relations and problem-solving skills to ensure optimum service.
- Prepared contracts and managed all aspects of real estate transactions/negotiations through closing.

Communications / Languages

- Proficient in both English and German.
- Extensive knowledge of European cultures from experience in living and traveling abroad.
- Provided freelance translation services from German to English.

Community Service

- Served as volunteer assisting with programs provided at battered women's shelter in Bergen County.
- Contributed as volunteer during children's enrollment at Merritt Memorial School Library.

— EXPERIENCE —

Crafts Company • Kettering, Ohio • 1992 to Present
Business Partner/Full-Time Parent

Barnes Real Estate • Kettering, Ohio • 1991 to 1992
Real Estate Associate

Bordeaux Restaurant • Kettering, Ohio • 1986 to 1990
Hostess

— EDUCATION —

A.A. in **Liberal Arts,** Ohio Community College, Akron, Ohio

---

181

Louise Garver, Enfield, Connecticut

This person had combined a crafts business with full-time parenting. She wanted to return to the workforce full time in sales or customer service. Featuring related skills helped her win an offer.

Technology

Resumes at a Glance

RESUME NUMBER	LAST OR CURRENT OCCUPATION	GOAL	PAGE
182	Welder	Machinist/Welder/Fitter	355
183	Steamfitter	Steamfitter	356
184	Overhead Crane Mechanic	Licensed Elevator Mechanic	357
185	Air Conditioner Repairer	HVAC Technician/Mechanic	358
186	Quality Control Inspector/ Electronic Assembler/Machinist	Not specified	359
187	Prewire Technician	Service Technician	360
188	Machinist	Machinist	361
189	Contractor	Heavy Equipment Diesel Fitter	362
190	President, Telecommunications	Training Professional	364
191	Senior Technician	Not specified	366

LEONARD BAKER
10 Blackbird Lane • Bridgetown, Pennsylvania 16466

(555) 645-3219   lbaker@hotmail.com

MACHINIST • WELDER • FITTER

◆ Proficient and skilled in technical specialty. Recognized for dedicated work ethic and productivity. Capable of doing work that requires concentration, high degree of patience and attention to detail. Mechanically inclined. Able to work independently.

◆ Thrive in a team- and deadline-oriented environment. Exceptional organizational skills; capable of prioritizing, scheduling and managing heavy work flow.

◆ Proficiency in technical skills/machine operations/equipment processes:

✓ MIG	✓ Fluxcore	✓ Computer Numeric Control
✓ TIG	✓ Submerged Arc	✓ Gantry Crane
✓ Stick	✓ Inner Shield	✓ Tolerancing
✓ Pulse	✓ Drill Press	✓ Forklift Operator
✓ Aluminum	✓ Technical Math	✓ Machine Print Reading
✓ Blueprint Reading	✓ Applied Math	✓ Lathes and Milling Machines

PROFESSIONAL EXPERIENCE

CLASS A WELDER, Forker Industries, *Bridgetown, Pennsylvania*   *1988–Present*
- Fit and weld boxcars with Fluxcore and submerged arc welding. Examine welds to ensure they meet specifications.
- Instrumental on shift that slashed project hours from 11 (by another shift) to 8 hours while maintaining quality of workmanship.

WELDER ASSEMBLER, Sun Engineering, *Walton, Texas*   *1987–1988*
- Used spray arc welding equipment. Assembled dock levelers and functioned as a saw operator, forklift driver, truck driver and member of installation crew.

WELDER FITTER, Perfection Metal Products, *Hazen, Texas*   *1986–1987*
- Fitted and welded frames for the electronic industry using MIG and TIG welding. Recognized for outstanding workmanship by lead man.

LABORER, City of Wilding, *Wilding, Texas*   *1985–1986*
- Received commendation from mayor for exemplary service to the citizens of Wilding by working more than 96 hours during a winter storm to repair water main leaks.

CERTIFICATIONS

◆ Arc Welding	◆ Gas Metal Arc Welding, Advanced	◆ Plumbing and Pipefitting Fundamentals
◆ 1/8" LH	◆ AWS SMAW 3/8" Butt Weld	◆ Flat and Vertical, Inside Corner Filler
◆ 7018 AWS Structural	◆ Flat, 3/8" Dia. Plug Weld	◆ 75-Fillet Vertical and Overhead Positions
◆ Vertical Outside Corner	◆ Vertical, T-Butt Weld Vertical	◆ 86 GMAW, Spray Arc Single V Groove with Backing 1G-Flat
◆ AWS D1	◆ GMAW AWS D7.7	
◆ Code D1.1		

EDUCATION

A.S., Machine Technology, anticipated November 2004
Dean's Certificates; *3.94 GPA to date;* ***Perfect Attendance;*** *Class President*
Capitol School of Trades, *Weathersfield, Pennsylvania*

182

Jane Roqueplot, Sharon, Pennsylvania

The overall design of this one-page, four-section resume is easily grasped at a glance. Boldfacing and three kinds of bullets ensure that the reader sees all of the most important information.

Fred G. Jamisen
9999 Abernethy Road • Oregon City, Oregon 99999
555-555-5555

Steamfitter

Professional Profile
Highly skilled, conscientious, and precise **Steamfitter** with more than 6 years of experience and more than 10,000 hours of training in all aspects of steam fitting. Familiar with all required codes, appropriate use of equipment, steam-fitting techniques, safety standards, and proper procedures to prevent injuries. Proficient in reviewing plans, blueprints, and specifications for steam-fitting projects with proven ability to provide expert recommendations. Well-developed troubleshooting skills with accurate and precise repairs. Experienced EMT willing to volunteer EMT services on the job. Excellent communication skills, personable, trustworthy, adaptable, and committed to a long-term career.

Expertise and Training:
- Air Conditioning and Refrigeration Systems and Equipment
- Boilers
- Commercial and Industrial
- Conduit Flex, Duct, and Controls
- Electrical and Electronic Contracting
- HVAC, Air Conditioning, and Refrigeration
- Instrumentation
- Outdoor Installations
- Overhead and Underground
- Process Systems and Equipment
- Steam and Heating Systems and Equipment
- Troubleshooting and Maintenance
- Welding Processes, Including Orbital Welder and Arc 207
- Wire Pulling, Wiring Devices, Removal and Finish

Licenses
Pressure Vessel and Boiler License Class V • *State of Oregon*
United Association of Steamfitters • *Local 290*

Employment History
Steamfitter • United Association of Steamfitters • Portland, Oregon • *6 years*
Assigned to various companies and projects as needed.

Paper Machine Operator • Crown Zellerbach Corp. • West Linn, Oregon • *11 years*
Previously owned by James River and Simpson Paper Company.
EMT *(Emergency Medical Technician)* • Served as volunteer EMT for the paper mill.

Sales Representative • Pepsi Bottling Company • Portland, Oregon • *8 years*
Beverage sales.

Military
U.S. Army • **Specialist E-4—Nuclear Missile Technician** • *Honorable Discharge* • *1976*

Education
Associate of Applied Arts • **Humanities**
Carroll College • Helena, Montana, *and* Clackamas Community College • Oregon City, Oregon

183

Rosie Bixel, Portland, Oregon

This applicant's position was highly specialized. His resume was designed for an international job opening. Bold italic side headings indicate the resume's main sections.

RAYMOND FINNEGAN

887 Ballinger Road
Springfield, IL 00000
(555) 555-0789 • rayfin@aol.com

QUALIFICATIONS

Licensed Elevator Mechanic with specialized skills in hydraulics, motor controls, wiring controls, rigging, electrical print reading, solid-state computers and print boards.

➤ Experienced in troubleshooting, repair, installation and testing of electromechanical systems, including pumps, drives and reducers.

➤ Contributor in self-directed, high-performance team environment with proven ability to complete multiple projects in a timely, efficient manner.

➤ Skilled in welding (steel, aluminum and industrial equipment), pipe fitting, millwrighting and machining. Strong mathematical, organizational and time-management skills.

CURRENT EMPLOYMENT

BAYSTATE ELECTRO-MECHANICS, Springfield, IL
Overhead Crane Mechanic (1998 to present)

• Perform on-site service calls on overhead cranes for customers in the chemical, power and paper industries.
• Diverse responsibilities include repairing, troubleshooting, removing, installing and testing electromechanical equipment to ensure safe operations.
• Repair and install chemical processes and related equipment such as pumps, drives and reducers.

ELEVATOR SERVICE EXPERIENCE

VANGUARD ELEVATORS, Springfield, IL
Elevator Mechanic (1990 to 1998)

• Performed all aspects of elevator installations, from setting up and aligning brackets, rails and car, to setting up motors on tractions and wiring the elevators.
• Serviced contracts for elevator equipment at major area companies: American Technologies, Payne & Company, Montgomery Corp., Dover Enterprises and others.

INTERNATIONAL UNION OF OPERATING ENGINEERS, West Springfield, IL
Hoisting Engineer (1986 to 1990)

• Operated and maintained heavy equipment, including backhoes, cranes, bulldozers and rollers.

Additional Experience: Service Manager, MARLAND PROPERTIES, Chicopee, MA
Supervised staff of 9 in all aspects of property maintenance for 300 residential units. Ensured that repairs were completed in a timely, cost-effective manner while maintaining quality standards. Prepared and maintained up-to-date documentation on all repairs performed *(1984-1986)*.

EDUCATION

Electronics courses
Illinois Technical Community College, Westfield, IL

International Union of Elevator Constructors' School, Springfield, IL
Completed training in Elevator Mechanics, Electronics, Hydraulics, Motor Controls, Electrical Theory

184

Louise Garver, Enfield, Connecticut

This applicant wanted to return to his preceding occupation as an Elevator Mechanic. To emphasize his prior experience in relation to his goal, the writer created the heading Elevator Service Experience.

John Simpkins
P.O. Box 000, Franconia, PA 99999
(555) 555-5555 ▪ simpkins@dotresume.com

Objective	**HVAC Technician / Mechanic**

Profile	**CFC / EPA Universal Certificate** (Type I, Type II, and Type III) **Strong Mechanical Skills:** Installation, setup, maintenance, repair **Quick Learner:** Excellent grades, easily grasp mechanical concepts and application **Responsible Employee:** Trustworthy, able to work with little supervision

Education	**Marcom Tech,** Bell Meade, PA, EPA Universal Certificate, 2004
	Maintained 94 average on exams while attending school full-time and working full-time.
	
	    Courses: Heating / Air Conditioning Theory, Commercial Air Conditioning, Heating
	    Air Conditioning Labs: Charging, Leak-Checking, and Superheat-Checking a System; Creating Electrical Diagrams; Testing Electrical Circuits; Troubleshooting / Repairing Split Systems; Piping a System; Assembling / Installing / Wiring a System
	    Heating Labs: Wire-Heating an Electrical Circuit; Wiring an Electrical Furnace; Wiring Controls, Components, and Safety Devices on a Gas Furnace; Using Test Instruments to Determine Gas Furnace Efficiency
	
	Northeast Area High School, Bell Meade, PA, 2000

Experience	**Air Conditioner Repair** Troubleshot and repaired window air conditioning units. Overhauled an abandoned air conditioner to perfect working order. (Independent Projects) **Machine Setup & Operations** Set up machinery to draw wire through furnace and onto spools. Checked spools and rewired any that failed inspection. Learned job in a few days—typically takes several months. (Aberwelton Alloys) Operated 200-, 400-, and 600-ton metal-stamping presses and set up dies and parts according to blueprints. Inspected machines for safety based on OSHA standards. Performed first-piece inspection and adjusted machinery when necessary. Maintained conveyor belts, air lines, fuses, and other machine components. (Mila Technology) **Management** Promoted to setup supervisor after learning to operate and set up metal-stamping presses in only four months. Earned eight raises in four years. Supervised six operators, training on machine operations and evaluating performance. Prepared paperwork to ensure on-time shipment of orders. Served as back-up foreman—wrote production reports and closed and secured building at end of shift. (Mila Technology) **Work History** Aberwelton Alloys (wire manufacturer), Morrisville, PA, 2003–2004 *Setup Mechanic* Mila Technology (metal-parts manufacturer), Penlyn, PA, 2000–2003 *Setup Supervisor, 2001–2003* *Machine Operator, 2000–2001*

Skills	**Tools:** brazers, drill presses, electric drills, grinders, measurement gauges, metal snips, pliers, pipe cutters and benders, sawsalls, socket sets, wrenches **Special Equipment:** calipers, CMMs (Coordinate Measuring Machines), comparators, micrometers, plasma cutters, pressure gauges, protractors, set squares, voltmeters **Material-Moving Equipment:** diesel trucks, forklifts, overhead cranes **Other:** blueprint reading, computers (Windows XP, Internet), shop math / algebra

185

Jan Holliday, Harleysville, Pennsylvania

Dual-weighted lines are the conspicuous design feature, appearing thicker above the section headings. The thickening is the result of placing a short, heavy line below a thin, full line.

Denise Sylvestor
467 Appleton Street
Dayton, OH 00000
(555) 555-5555

Summary

More than 13 years of experience in electronic assembly, quality-control inspection, shipping and receiving and production. Experience in leading and training other employees to perform productively.

Proficient in sub and final assembly, testing and inspection of electronic components, including printed circuit boards, wiring and other products.

Skilled in operating a variety of hand tools and machinery; able to assemble and handle simple to complex operations.

A team-oriented, dedicated, punctual employee recognized for the ability to learn quickly and produce quality work.

Computer skills include Microsoft Word for Windows.

Experience

Electronic Assembly/Machining

- Assemble and build printed circuit boards and automotive parts (exhaust and intake for Chrysler cars) from blueprints/schematics, using soldering iron, gauges and various other hand tools.
- Operate exhaust machine and make any necessary minor repairs/adjustments to Bradley Allen computer to maintain top production levels and minimize downtime.

Quality Control Inspection/Shipping & Receiving

- Inspect more than 340 boxes of electronic parts each day to ensure compliance with company standards, using chemicals and electric equipment.
- Record incoming and outgoing shipments as well as prepare items for shipment; verify information against bills of lading, invoices, orders and other records.

Team Leadership

- Selected by management in recognition of dependability and excellent performance as lead person on Cybex production line, overseeing team of 16 assemblers.
- Provide ongoing guidance, training and leadership to assembly team, maintaining top levels of productivity.

Employment History

Full-Time Caregiver, Dayton, OH (2002 to present)

AUTOMOTIVE CORPORATION, Dayton, OH (1994 to 2002)
Quality Control Inspector
Electronic Assembler
Machinist

WIRE COMPANY, Dayton, OH (1990 to 1994)
Automotive/Electronic Assembler

NEW VISIONS, Dayton, OH (1989 to 1990)
Electronic Assembler

Education

A.S. in Electronics Technology
Dayton Community College, Dayton, OH

186

Louise Garver, Enfield, Connecticut

This person's mother became ill, and the applicant served as a full-time caregiver. After her mother died, the applicant wanted to return to work. This skills-based resume helped her land a job.

James Karberg
11100 S.W. Cork Avenue • Trenchville, Georgia 99999
555–666–7777

Service Technician

Professional Profile

Energetic, self-motivated, and resourceful *Technician* offering a solid background in installations, service, and technical support of all security systems, as well as voice and data systems. Able to read blueprints, provide inconspicuous wiring, and supply efficient and accurate installations. Experienced working with Alarmnet cellular backup systems.

Possess outstanding "people skills," with strong customer-service abilities and strengths in working well with all types of personalities. Excellent troubleshooting and problem-solving skills. Learn quickly, work well independently and effectively as a team member. Career-oriented, honest, loyal, and committed to a job well done.

Projects Include
Prewire new construction, including retirement, condominium and apartment projects.
State of Georgia—Networked all buildings.
First Interstate Tower
One Financial Building
Nordstrom's

Related Employment History
Prewire Technician • *2002–2004*
Century Cable Services • Trenchville, Georgia

Installation Manager • Service • *1998–2002*
Great Western Security Systems • Los Angeles, California
(Satellite office—Trenchville, Georgia)
Supplied technical support, installation and service for security systems.
Maintained full operation of satellite office in Georgia.

Technician • *1984–1987; 1991–1997*
Various temporary jobs.

Technician • *1987–1990*
Christenson Electric • Lancaster, Georgia
Provided voice and data installations.

Installer • *1982–1984*
TCI Cablevision of Georgia, Inc.
Installed broadband cable TV.

Community Service
Volunteer • Trenchville Food Bank • Trenchville, Georgia • *11 years*

Education
Machine Technology • Trenchville Community College, Trenchville, Georgia • *1989*
Electrical Codes • Landcaster Community College • Trenchville, Georgia • *1989*

187

Rosie Bixel, Portland, Oregon

The writer displayed projects and chronological information in a different format (centered) with a page border for emphasis. Centered section headings complement the center-justified information.

JOHN ROCKFORD

1234 Trident Road	555-555-1234 Home
Akron, OH 12345	555-555-1234 Cell

KEY QUALIFICATIONS

- Twenty-six years of applied Machinist experience
- Ten years of experience as an HBM Operator
- Recognized for significant increases in work productivity
- Skilled in machining, mechanical and welding trades
- Excellent problem-solving and communication skills
- Ability to take initiative and ownership of work outcomes

WORK EXPERIENCE

The Steam Program, 2001 to Present
Completed more than 1000 hours in super-heated steam area and high- and low-pressure steam drum internals.

Walker Machining, Akron, OH
Machinist, Mechanic and Welder, October 1998 to October 2004
Repaired essential parts and components of machines utilized during the process of crushing coal.

Equipment Technologies, Akron, OH
September 1978 to May 1998

- Performed multiple roles in the manufacturing division of an equipment technologies company.
- Progressed from Helper to the highest position of HBM Operator.
- Experienced as Grinder, Milling Machine Operator, Drill Press Operator, Engine Lathe Operator, NDT Inspector, Visual Inspector, Master Fitter and Layout Specialist.
- Received two individual recognition awards for engineering novel parts that improved the performance and functionality of machine components.
- Worked collaboratively with a Participative Task Team that was awarded a recognition plaque for productivity increases in both quality and quantity of work outputs.

EDUCATION

Diploma from Akron High School, Akron, OH
Vocational course work in machining, heat treatment and electrical principles, 1976–1978

State College of Technology, Akron, OH
Fulfilled requirements of a six-month program in Computer Numerical Control (CNC), 1990

Akron Career Center, Akron, OH
Completed a 40-hour course in Welding, 2002

ADDITIONAL ACTIVITIES

- Member of Akron Fitness Center. Active in several physical fitness programs, including kickboxing, martial arts, yoga and aerobics.
- Owner and Operator of Faster Road Racing, a supplier of drag racing and motorcycle supplies.

188

Tara G. Papp, Mogadore, Ohio

This retired Machinist was applying for a position in Iraq. He wanted his years of experience and physical activities highlighted. The writer included an Additional Activities section to show his fitness.

PAUL THOMAS

3 Etwell Court
Fairborn, OH 45324

Email: thomas_paul@bigpool.com

Telephone: (937) 855-3358
Fax: (937) 855-3351

PRODUCT SUPPORT FITTER • FIELD SERVICE FITTER • WORKSHOP FITTER

Equipment:

Blasthole drills D45K, D55K, D75K, D90K

Caterpillar off-highway trucks to 789B

All auxiliary plant

Dozers to D11 Series III

Loaders to 992G

Graders to 16G

Liebherr R994A, R994 200 series, R994B 200 series, R996

Komatsu—all equipment including excavators to PC1800

Hitachi excavators to EX2500 Super

Dragline Marion 8050

Licenses:

Licensed to drive forklifts, earthmovers, mobile equipment, passenger vehicles, and trucks.

Training:

- Workplace Health & Safety
- Safe Operating Procedures
- Coal Surface
- Generic Induction
- Codes of Conduct

Heavy equipment diesel fitter with expert technical troubleshooting and leadership capabilities. Acknowledged for capacity to juggle multiple projects and priorities simultaneously; restore order from chaos; and consistently reinforce the importance of quality, deadlines, and safety across multidisciplined teams. Competent technical lead, team member, or solo performer.

Vast experience working in inhospitable and remote terrains has sharpened talents in "making do"—fashioning tools and components using available resources for minimal downtime. Specialist experience in production blasthole drill rigs, air conditioning, electrics, hydraulics and pneumatics, engine, power train, final drive, hydraulic pumps, and full hydraulic tune-ups.

Professional strengths:

- Service Scheduling
- Hydraulic Faults: Diagnosis and Repair
- Preventive Maintenance Planning
- Component Records Management
- Parts & Component Procurement
- Time Management
- Workload Allocation & Direction
- Client Relationship Management
- Critical Problem Solving
- Staff Education & Awareness
- Workplace Health & Safety
- Safe Operating Procedures

Trade Qualifications

Qualified Heavy Equipment Diesel Mechanic

ISO 9002 (Hydraulics & Pneumatics)
Parker Jackson College (1995)

Certificate of Motor Mechanics
Ohio Community College (1988)

Project Highlights

- **Overcame stock availability issues** on 24-hour operation by analyzing regularly needed parts, stringently monitoring stock levels, and modifying equipment for longer equipment life.

- **Consistently passed exacting standards** enforced by independent product representatives inspecting maintenance works for compliance to product warranties.

- Completed drill rig rebuilds in 8 days, **saving 2 days from plant department's estimates.**

- Skirted major breakdown incidences by conducting a regime of regular inspections and identifying fault defects prior to negative impact. Careful recordkeeping of faults in drill rigs **drove plant availability from 40% to 90% in six months.**

- Delivered accountability to workshop operations by implementing 24-hour inspections.

189

Gayle Howard, Chirnside Park, Melbourne, Victoria, Australia

It takes some time to see all the information on this two-page resume. The Equipment, Trade Qualifications, and Project Highlights sections are different but particularly relevant to this individual's situation. In studying this resume, note the use of page borders, boxes, columns,

PAUL THOMAS

Employment Experiences

Computer Technologies:

- Microsoft Word
- PowerPoint
- Outlook
- Internet
- Email
- Windows 2000
- Caterpillar ET: engine power train software
- Caterpillar SIS (spare parts and electronic workshop manuals)
- PlantPac (component records management)

References

Ian Vincent
Support Supervisor / Consultant
Johnson Peck
Tel: (937) 555-6789
Ian.V@johnpeck.com

Peter Barrons
Workshop Foreman
RTG Pty Ltd
Bus: (937) 555-4433
pbarrons@rtg.com

George Barton
Product Support Manager
Mines Australia P/L
Tel: +61 3 9776 8112
gbarton@optus.com.au

ATC DIESEL SERVICE & REPAIRS P/L   1991–Present
Contractor
Projects: Major mining site projects.

Building a reputation as an accomplished diesel fitter with specialist talents in multimillion-dollar heavy earthmoving equipment. Successfully won long-term contracts to repair, rebuild, troubleshoot, and maintain project-critical equipment at several major mining sites in remote locations.

As an expert in fault-finding, diagnostic works, and full hydraulic tune-ups, recommendations to schedule equipment for repair or remove for immediate service are observed rigorously by management, with project costing relying heavily on sustained levels of productivity.

- **RTG Pty Ltd:** Leading contractors servicing 60% of mining contracts across the largest area of coal infrastructure in Australia, conducting full mining operations for major companies such as RAG Australia BHP Billiton, MIM, and Camel Resources on multimillion-dollar projects.

With heavy emphasis on minimum equipment/machinery downtime and quick turnarounds, regular service checks to identify potential defects and assess risks are vital to sustaining production levels and circumventing costly lost equipment time and parts. With much of the repair/maintenance and troubleshooting tasks both unsupervised and solo assignments, performances are measured on the quick identification of problems, resolution, and turnaround of equipment to commission.

Frequently achieved minimum downtime targets of 7 days each quarter.

- **EXEL Hydraulics, Mobile Hose Doctor and Contract Diesel Fitter.** Mount Isa, Queensland, Australia. Top 3 Australian company specializing in hydraulic and pneumatic service and repairs to plant and equipment in transportation and mining industries. On 24-hour call for machinery modifications and setups, shut-down maintenance, and component overhauls for Mount Isa Mines, Universal Transport Operations, Atlas Copco, Tamrock, and Selwyn Mines underground and surface. On-call 24/7 diesel fitting onsite and remote work.

Workshop Manager & Contract Diesel Fitter. Supervised 5 staff (administrative, trades assistant, and customer service). Multifaceted role managing $1.1 million budget, overseeing daily workshop operations, customer and supplier liaison, scheduling servicing projects, and juggling "hands-on" technical diesel fitting projects. Trained workers in assembly line technique, time management, and order dispatch. Achieved 12-hour turnarounds from receipt to dispatch.

CARTERS EARTHMOVING, Fairborn, OH   1988–1991
Serviced and maintained plant and machinery in remote sites across the United States.
Contract Diesel Fitter
Repaired and restored mobile plant equipment and earthmoving machinery and equipment in remote locations. Designed, refurbished, and overhauled parts and components where immediate "fixes" and difficult terrain for transportation inhibited parts procurement and deliveries.

FRED SIVYER HOLDEN, Fairborn, OH   1984–1988
Apprentice Motor Mechanic

boldfacing, italic, short lines, very small type (for e-mail addresses), and reduced leading (less space between lines). Observe how some white space is achieved through some center justification.

ROBERTA MAGNOTTI

Telecom Training Solutions

1234 Pinehurst Road
Augusta, Ontario A1A 1A1

Office: 444.555.8888
Home: 555.444.3333

TRAINING PROFESSIONAL

Expert in Technical, Sales, and Product Training

Dynamic training professional skilled in providing top-quality training and learning programs to individual and corporate audiences throughout Canada and the United States. Outstanding reputation and success built on ability to design and deliver enriching and engaging learning programs focused on specific development needs and client objectives. Skilled in a wide variety of learning methodologies, including classroom, online, distance learning, and CBT. Motivating and enthusiastic facilitator.

➢ Learning Needs Assessment	➢ Curriculum Design & Development
➢ Program Facilitation	➢ Consulting
➢ Train-the-Trainer	➢ Assessment Strategies

Fully Certified in Adult Learning and Distance Education

"Best instructor ever!"
Account Executive
Bell Telecom

"Fantastic! The instructor explained everything in a way that could be understood by everyone."
—Sales Representative
SaskTel

"Amazing instructor…kept the course alive and interesting. Was able to teach to entire class at their level of understanding."
—Service Director
Bell Nexxium

"This is by far the best course I've been on…[Instructor's] knowledge level is amazing. Speaks to you so you understand."
—Sales Associate
Bell Nexxium, Vancouver

"..excellent presentation and style."
—Account Consultant
SaskTel

"The instructor is really terrific! She made the course easy to understand."
—Business Office Rep
Bell Telecom

TRAINING & FACILITATION EXPERTISE

➢ Personally trained more than 3000 employees for industry leaders throughout Canada and the United States.

➢ Solid reputation for outstanding program design and facilitation skills.

➢ Polished, professional, and personable training style. Innovative and flexible approach ensures success with both beginner and advanced audiences.

➢ Extremely self-motivated and customer-focused. Dedicated to providing first-rate service and guaranteeing client success.

➢ Polished consulting and learning needs assessment skills. Able to identify key learning need, design solution, and meet objectives.

➢ Advanced troubleshooting, analysis, and problem-solving skills. Able to accurately identify problems and implement effective solutions.

TRAINING EXPERIENCE

TELECOM TRAINING SOLUTIONS, *Augusta, Ontario*

PRESIDENT 2001–Present

Founded successful telecommunications training company offering more than 30 cutting-edge training courses and development programs to 35 leading Telcos throughout North America. Provide all learning consulting, design and develop curricula, and facilitate all programs.

• Train corporate telecom audiences throughout North America in data and voice technologies, product positioning and pricing, data sales training, and technology overviews.

• Consistently receive highest rating of participant and client feedback. Majority of business acquired through word of mouth and client recommendations.

continued…

190

Ross Macpherson, Whitby, Ontario, Canada

This unique format allows this Training Professional to show off some of the comments from her workshops. Furthermore, the two Experience sections, Training Experience and Additional

BELL TELECOM, *Augusta, Ontario*   1993–1999
TRAINING TEAM LEADER / DESIGNER—Bell Institute for Professional Development
Managed and led Bell's in-house training facility for Ontario & Quebec. Required to revise all outdated programs, introduce new learning technologies, and facilitate all courses. Managed team of 4 designers and training support staff.

- Revamped entire Bell curriculum, transferred all supporting materials to updated technologies, and revised 12 comprehensive in-house programs. Content covered Network Concepts, Data Network Protocols, New Emerging Technologies, ATM Concepts, DMS Family of Switches, and Frame Relay.
- Consistently received outstanding participant feedback for course design, content, and facilitation style.
- Liaised with product managers to ensure all product updates incorporated into state-of-the-art training modules.

ADDITIONAL TELECOM EXPERIENCE

BELL TELECOM, *Augusta, Ontario*   1988–2001
Rapid promotion through a series of increasingly responsible positions based on solid industry expertise, strong leadership and team development skills, and consistent ability to generate results.

DIRECTOR—Advanced Solutions (1999–2001)

- Led strategic development and growth of new corporate division mandated to protect Bell interests in the face of open telecom competition.

ACCOUNT EXECUTIVE—Bell Executive Service (1989–1993)

- Full key account management responsibilities for **$180 million CIBT account**. Sold full-scale data and voice systems in response to detailed needs analyses. Consulted on comprehensive technology solutions, designed and monitored blueprints, negotiated pricing, and managed account relationships with key lines of business.

NETWORK CONTROLLER (1988–1989)

- Contributed to the coordination and implementation of Canada's first Voice/Data Trans-Canada Megastream T1 Network.

PROFESSIONAL DEVELOPMENT

Distance Learning Certificate—Ohio State University   1997
Effective Planning—TICA Learning   1995
Project Management—TICA Learning   1995
Instructor Training—Lange Learning   1993
Seven Steps of Highly Effective People—Steven Covey   1990

Computer Communications—Electronic Engineering

- Senegal College of Applied Arts & Technology

Corporate clients:

Bell Nexxium

SaskTel

Bell Telecom

AT&T (TigerTel)

Qwest

Alaint

Northern Telephone

NWTel

USwest

IntrisHP

Newbell Networks

Dell Canada

Telecom Experience, allow her to clearly show both her training experience and her professional experience in her target industry. If you read the workshop comments, you can see how testimonials strengthen a resume, particularly if it—unlike this resume—has some conspicuous weaknesses.

ROBERT C. KELLY

1862 Glen Oaks Drive • Sacramento, CA 77777 • (555) 555-5555 • bobckelly@myexcel.com

PROFILE

More than 15 years of experience in troubleshooting and repairing electrical and electronic systems and equipment, including robotic, pneumatic, mechanical, control circuit, power supply, hydraulic, and vacuum systems. Adept at providing technical equipment support and developing new processes through ongoing maintenance, defect resolution, and enhancement solutions. Combine excellent technical, analytical, and engineering qualifications with outstanding customer-service skills. Expertise includes

- Customer Service, Support, & Communication
- Training & Team Leadership
- Blueprints & Schematics
- Problem Identification & Resolution
- Inspection & Maintenance

- Technical Documentation
- Project Scheduling & Management
- Systems Design & Installation
- Quality Control & Assurance
- Interpersonal Communications

PROFESSIONAL EXPERIENCE

EXTREME TECHNOLOGIES—Sacramento, CA   1989–2004
Senior Technician—Engineering Equipment Support

Conducted and scheduled investigative tests, repairs, and overhauls of robotic and automated manufacturing and processing equipment to ensure proper operation. Documented inspections, maintenance, repair work, and failures in maintenance logs and statistical process control charts. Trained employees on operational procedures with emphasis on quality, productivity, and overall equipment readiness.

- Designed and fabricated several equipment modifications, including a parts handler to prevent breaking of tie bars in encapsulated parts, which resulted in saving $40,000 per breakdown.
- Created and installed low-level alarm system for slurry barrels, preventing $80,000 in damage to machine and product by sounding an audible alarm when slurry was low.
- Developed and implemented wafer guide for the Westech 372 Planarizer. Ensured nonbreaking feed of wafers, saving up to $6,000 in materials cost.
- Reduced lot count time to seconds by designing electronic handheld lead frame counter.
- Selected to participate in Mirra Polisher installations and training located in Singapore. Created a team approach to problem solving and technical support.

ADDITIONAL EXPERTISE

Assembly Encapsulation

· Nickolet X-Ray Machine
· Lawton Encapsulation Press L.A. Rose Preheater
· AIS Automated Handler
· Blaser 5000 Laser
· Boschman & Fico Automold
· MTI Media Deflash
· Dia Ichi Seiko

Chemical Mechanical Planarization (CMP)

· Nel Taper & De-taper Ontrak Scrubbers (Series 0, 1, 2)
· Strasbaugh 6DS
· Applied Materials Mirra & Ebara Planarizers
· Ipec 676
· Westech 372
· Shibayama Back Grinder
· ADE Ultra Gauge 9500 NOVA Scan 210
· 420 Prometrix UV-1050

EDUCATION

Associate's Degree (1989), Electronics Engineering Technology, ITT Technical Institute—Sacramento, CA

191

Denette Jones, Boise, Idaho

The horizontal lines before and after the Profile make it the first area of attention. Bulleted areas of expertise are listed after the descriptive Profile paragraph. The Additional Expertise section is a plus.

Transportation

Resumes at a Glance

RESUME NUMBER	LAST OR CURRENT OCCUPATION	GOAL	PAGE
192	Maintenance/Driver	Sales Position, Food Industry	369
193	Truck Driver	Truck Driver	370
194	Area Fleet Supervisor	Not specified	371
195	Pilot	Pilot	372

Timothy Turner

520 E. Ogden Avenue
Naperville, Illinois 06000
000-983-8882

PROFESSIONAL PROFILE

Focus: Sales Position / Food Industry

Creative, resourceful, peak-performing individual offering strong management, business development, sales and customer-service skills, as well as a variety of hands-on skills such as carpentry, electrical and mechanical. Thorough understanding of transportation, distribution and logistics required to meet tight schedules and operation efficiencies. Excellent interpersonal and client-relations skills. Ability to establish and maintain active relationships with people at all levels. Motivational management style. Recognized for professionalism, knowledge, sound judgment and commitment to exceeding customer expectations. Good work ethic, combined with strong organizational and communications skills, ensures ability to make an immediate and positive contribution.

KEY COMPETENCIES

- P&L Management
- Purchasing / Inventory Control
- Business Strategies
- Organization and Multitasking

- Training and Mentoring
- Building Strong, Lasting Relationships Between Customers and Suppliers
- Persuasive Communicator

- Collections
- Problem Analysis and Resolution
- Contract Negotiations

SELECTED ACCOMPLISHMENTS

Transportation
- Highly competent driver handling a variety of routes
- Responsible for maintaining clean, safe vehicle
- Successful at maintaining on-time delivery schedules
- Provided excellent customer service to all customers
- Trained staff and mentored new drivers

Sales Account Management
- Owned and managed distribution/delivery business
- Facilitated all inventory control measures and maintained working levels
- Provided supervision and leadership for up to 15 drivers
- Scheduled routes
- Motivated and trained staff

EMPLOYERS

TWIANNE INDUSTRIES, Naperville, IL (2000–Present)
Maintenance

DIAMOND–WILLIAMS CO., Elgin, IL (1995–1999)
Driver

CAESAR ALLEN TRUCKING, Chicago, IL (1995)
Driver

CONSOLIDATED, INC., Naperville, IL (1994–1995)
Driver/Salesman

A-1 BOTTLED WATER, Aurora, IL (1970–1994)
Branch District Manager (1972–1994)
Relief Training Specialist (1972)
Driver (1970–1972)

ACCREDITATIONS AND LICENSES

- Awarded Employee of the Month at Twianne Industries after 4 months on the job
- Won numerous sales promotions for Route Sales and Sales Management
- Nationwide representative for Driver of the Year while employed at A-1 Bottled Water
- Passed National Safety Council defensive driving course 12/13/86

192

Patricia Chapman, Naperville, Illinois

Centered headings enable you to see all the headings quickly and therefore size up the resume's overall design at a glance. Boldfacing helps you spot the person's occupations under Employers.

Jason A. Zimmerman

2513 West Vista Lane   Miami, FL 33166   (cell) 786.522.9875   (home) 305.779.0036

> *Professional truck driver offers a winning combination to an organization that values stability, dependability, and timely deliveries*

- ❖ *3 Million Miles*
- ❖ *Multiple Safety Awards*
- ❖ *32 Years of Experience*

Single and Team Driver of the following rigs:

Vans	Step Deck	Reefers
Doubles	Flat Deck	Tankers

SAFETY AWARDS

SCHROEDER NATIONAL
6-Year Driver Safety Award
GREENWAY/LOADSTAR
5-Year Driver Safety Award
EAST POINT TRANSIT
800,000-Mile Driver Safety Award
SOUTHEAST EXPRESS
7-Year Driver Safety Award
PULMAN GROUP
2-Year Driver Safety Award

PROFESSIONAL EXPERIENCE

Nov 1996–Present
SCHROEDER NATIONAL
Richmond, Virginia

- Drive vans transporting general freight throughout the United States.
- Supervise the dock management of product: loading, unloading, and accounting.

Oct 1991–Oct 1996
GREENWAY/LOADSTAR
Buffalo, New York

- Drove single and double vans, flatbeds, and step decks transporting general freight throughout the United States.
- Supervised the dock management of product: loading, unloading, accounting, securing freight, and customer interaction.

Jan 1991–Oct 1991
GLOBAL MARINE
Charleston, South Carolina

- Drove specialized boat trailers transporting high-value yachts.
- Supervised the crane work and tie-down of the yachts.
- Coordinated delivery times with the customer.

1970–1991
**GLENDALE SHIPPING / REINOLD TRUCKING CO. / EAST POINT TRANSIT
INTERSTATE TRUCKING CO. / SOUTHEAST EXPRESS / COASTAL TRANSPORT
PULMAN GROUP**

193

MeLisa Rogers, Victoria, Texas

The original resume was a hodgepodge of company listings. The writer transformed it into a precise background document that emphasizes the person's tenure in the industry and his safety record.

John Mullin
66 Fox Drive
Farmingville, New York 11735
516.555.5555

Qualifications:

Effective management and communication skills; ability to identify, define and provide solutions in a timely manner; ability to multitask. 18 years of experience in automotive diagnosis and repair.

Experience:

DHK Airways, Long Island City, New York
August 1997 to Present

Area Fleet Supervisor
- Operate and manage vehicles in 11 service centers and airport operations at Newark Airport.
- Manage a fleet of 325 vehicles and 30 pieces of ground support equipment.
- Supervise staff of 11 ground mechanics; activities include but not limited to managing PM services and daily assignments, scheduling vacation and personal time, and interviewing potential candidates for hire.
- Develop and implement monthly department budgets.
- Created training procedures for all new hires; responsible for training and supervising all new hires.
- Effectively communicate with suppliers and vendors.
- Repair foreign and domestic cars and light- and medium-duty trucks; maintain ground support equipment, including specializing in electronic fuel injection and carburetor and engine rebuilding.

Awards and Promotions
- Promoted to M3 Mechanic, November 1998
- Promoted to Lead Mechanic, November 1999
- Mechanic of the Year, December 1999
- Promoted to Area Fleet Supervisor, September 2000

Mulligan Service Center, Seaford, New York
October 1986 through August 1997

Mechanic
- Repaired foreign and domestic cars, specializing in electronic fuel injection and carburetor and engine rebuilding.
- Defined problems and presented solutions to clients in an effective and personal manner.

Certifications:
- Class BCDL Certification
- DHL Dimension of Leadership
- DHL New Supervisor Training
- NYC Certificate in Fundamental Engine Electronic Training (1992)
- ASE Refrigerant Service Recycling Certificate (1991)
- ASE Certified Master Technician (1990)
- NYS Inspection License
- FAA Drug and Alcohol Training
- Competency-Based Selection

Education:
- Wyoming Technical Institute, Certificate of Completion in Automotive Technology
- Nassau County Technical Institute Center, Automotive Mechanics Program, 1986 through 1988

194

Deanna Verbouwens, Hicksville, New York

Large, bold print makes the contact information readable from across a small room. Boldfacing and underlining highlight the section headings and the subheadings in the Experience section.

JEFFREY COLLINS

Permanent Address:
1234 Red Baron Lane
Tempe, AZ 82345
(123) 456-7890

Present Address:
1 Maple Street
Speedway, IN 46789
(999) 555-1212

CAREER OBJECTIVE
Flight Crew Position

CERTIFICATES

ATP
Instrument
Multi-Engine
FAA Class I Medical

Flight Instructor—Single-/Multi-Engine
Flight Instructor—Instrument Airplane
Ground Instructor—Advanced/Instrument
FCC Radio Telephone Permit

FLIGHT TIME

5500	Total Time	4300	Multi-Engine
3400	Pilot in Command	3500	Turboprop
2100	Second in Command	400	Actual Instrument
1000	Instructor Pilot	100	Simulated Instrument
4400	Cross-Country	1100	EMB-110
1900	Night	300	PA31-T1040
4000	FAR 135	2000	SF-340

EDUCATION

Germantown High School, Germantown, Indiana; Graduated May 1982

PREVIOUS EMPLOYERS

May 1999 to Present	Express Airlines I, Inc.	First Officer, SF-340
April 1993 to April 1999	Flight Line, Inc.	Captain, EMB-110
May 1991 to January 1993	Northwestern State University	Flight Instructor
September 1989 to March 1991	Jack Adams Company	Ferry/Demo Pilot
August 1988 to August 1989	Memphis Aero Charter/AMR	First Officer, BE-300
October 1986 to July 1988	Metro Flying School	Flight Instructor

OPERATIONAL EXPERIENCE

My pilot experience has progressed from both flight and ground instructor for Private, Commercial, Instrument, Multi-Engine, and CFI candidates; to Captain and Check Airman for Flight Line, Inc., a part 135 Scheduled Cargo/Air Taxi Operator; to First Officer for Express Airlines I, Inc./Northwest Airlink, a scheduled Regional Airline.

My Pilot-in-Command experience includes flight operations in all types of adverse weather and airfields, ranging from major international aerodomes with high-density traffic to small, isolated airports with limited navigational aids.

195

Julie C. Thomas, West Monroe, Louisiana

The writer prepared this resume for a commercial airline pilot who had 18 years of aviation experience, including work as a flight instructor. The person was seeking a major airline position.

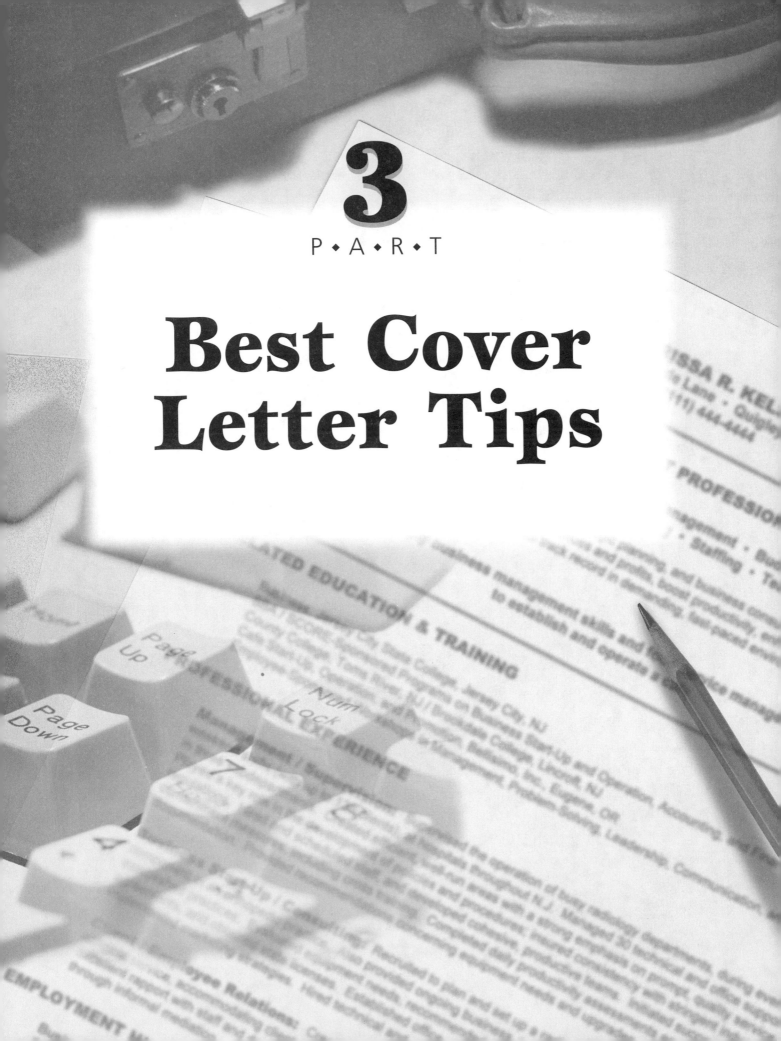

Best Cover Letter Tips

3

P·A·R·T

Best Cover Letter Tips at a Glance

Best Cover Letter Writing Tips 375

Myths About Cover Letters. 375

Tips for Polishing Cover Letters 376

- Using Good Strategies for Letters 376
- Using Pronouns Correctly. 377
- Using Verb Forms Correctly 378
- Using Punctuation Correctly. 379
- Using Words Correctly 383

Exhibit of Cover Letters 385

Best Cover Letter Writing Tips

In an active job search, your cover letter and resume should complement one another. Both are tailored to a particular reader you have contacted or to a specific job target. To help you create the best cover letters for your resumes, this part of the book mentions and debunks some common myths about cover letters and presents tips for polishing the letters you write.

Myths About Cover Letters

1. **Resumes and cover letters are two separate documents that have little relation to each other.** The resume and cover letter work together in presenting you effectively to a prospective employer. The cover letter should mention the resume and call attention to some important aspect of it.

2. **The main purpose of the cover letter is to establish a friendly rapport with the reader.** Resumes show that you *can* do the work required. The main purpose of cover letters is to express that you *want* to do the work required. But it doesn't hurt to display enthusiasm in your resumes and refer to your abilities in your cover letters.

3. **You can use the same cover letter for each reader of your resume.** Modify your cover letter for each reader so that it sounds fresh rather than canned. Chances are that in an active job search, you have already talked with the person who will interview you. Your cover letter should reflect that conversation and build on it.

4. **In a cover letter, you should mention any negative things about your education, work experience, life experience, or health to prepare the reader before an interview.** This is not the purpose of the cover letter. You might bring up these topics in the first or second interview, but only after the interviewer has shown interest in you or offered you a job. Even then, if you feel that you must mention something negative about your past, present it in a positive way, perhaps by saying how that experience has strengthened your will to work hard at any new job.

5. **It is more important to remove errors from a resume than from a cover letter because the resume is more important than the cover letter.** Both your resume and your cover letter should be free of errors. The cover letter is usually the first document a prospective employer sees. The first impression is often the most important one. If your cover letter has an embarrassing error in it, chances are good that the reader may not bother to read your resume or may read it with less interest.

6. **To make certain that your cover letter has no errors, all you need to do is proofread it or ask a friend to do so.** Trying to proofread your own cover letter is risky, even if you are good at grammar and writing. Once a

document is printed, it has an aura about it that may make it seem better written than it is. For this reason, you are likely to miss typos or other kinds of errors.

Relying on someone else is risky, too. If your friend is not good at grammar and writing, that person may not see any mistakes either. Try to find a proofreader, an editor, an English teacher, a professional writer, or an experienced secretary who can point out any errors you may have missed.

7. **After someone has proofread your letter, you can make a few changes to it and not have someone look at it again.** More errors creep into a document this way than you would think possible. The reason is that such changes are often done hastily, and haste can waste an error-free document. If you make *any* change to a document, ask someone to proofread it a final time just to make sure that you didn't introduce an error during the last stage of revision. If you can't find someone to help you, the next section gives you advice on how to eliminate common mistakes in cover letters.

Tips for Polishing Cover Letters

You might spend several days working on your resume, getting it just right and free of errors. But if you send it with a cover letter that is written quickly and contains even one conspicuous error, all your good efforts may be wasted. That error could be just the kind of mistake the reader is looking for to screen you out.

You can prevent this kind of tragedy by polishing your cover letter so that it is free of errors. The following tips can help you avoid or eliminate common errors in cover letters. If you become aware of these kinds of errors and know how to fix them, you can be more confident about the cover letters you send with your resumes.

Note that you can apply some of the following tips to your resume, especially the tips on grammar, punctuation, and word usage.

Using Good Strategies for Letters

1. **Use the postal abbreviation for the state in your mailing address.** See resume writing Tip 1 in Part 1.

2. **Make certain that the letter is addressed to a specific person and that you use this person's name in the salutation.** Avoid using such general salutations as Dear Sir or Madam, To Whom It May Concern, Dear Administrator, Dear Prospective Employer, and Dear Committee. In an active job search, you should do everything possible to send your cover letter and resume to a particular individual, preferably someone you've already talked with in person or by phone, and with whom you have arranged an interview. If you have not been able to make a personal contact, at least do everything possible to find out the name of the person who will read your letter and resume. Then address the letter to that person.

3. **Adjust the margins for a short letter.** If your cover letter is 300 words or longer, use left, right, top, and bottom margins of 1 inch. If the letter is shorter, you should increase the margins' width. How much to increase them is a matter of personal taste. One way to take care of the width of the top and bottom margins is to center a shorter letter vertically on the page. A maximum width

for a short cover letter of 100 words or fewer might be 2-inch left and right margins. As the number of words increases by 50 words, you might decrease the width of the left and right margins by two-tenths of an inch.

4.   **If you write your letter with word-processing or desktop-publishing software, use left justification to ensure that the lines of text are readable and have fixed spacing between words.** The letter will have a "ragged right" look along the right margin, but the words will be evenly spaced horizontally. Don't use full justification (having each line end even with the right margin) in an attempt to give your letter a printed look. Unless you do other typesetting procedures, such as kerning and hyphenating words at the end of some lines, full justification can make your letter look worse by giving it some extra-wide and extra-narrow spaces between words.

Using Pronouns Correctly

5.   **Use *I* and *My* sparingly.** When most of the sentences in a cover letter begin with *I* or *My*, you might appear self-absorbed, self-centered, or egotistical. If the reader is turned off by this kind of impression (even if it is a false one), you could be screened out without ever having an interview. Of course, you need to use these first-person pronouns sometimes because most of the information you put in your cover letter is personal. But try to avoid using *I* and *My* at the beginnings of sentences and paragraphs.

6.   **Refer to a business, company, corporation, or organization as "it" rather than "they."** Members of the Board may be referred to as "they," but a company is a singular subject that requires a singular verb. Note this example:

New Products, Inc., was established in 1980. It grossed more than $1 million in sales during its first year.

7.   **If you start a sentence with *This*, be sure that what *This* refers to is clear.** If the reference is not clear, insert a word or phrase to clarify what *This* means. Compare the following:

You should receive my revised application for the new position by fax on Friday. *This* should be acceptable to you.

You should receive my revised application for the new position by fax on Friday. *This method of sending the application* should be acceptable to you.

A reader of the first sentence wouldn't know what *This* refers to. Friday? By fax on Friday? The revised application for the new position? The insertion after *This* in the second sentence, however, tells the reader that *This* refers to the use of faxing.

8.   **Use *as follows* after a singular subject.** Literally, *as follows* means *as it follows,* so the phrase is illogical after a plural subject. Compare the following:

Incorrect:	My plans for the day of the interview are as follows:
Fixed:	My plans for the day of the interview are these:
Correct:	My plan for the day of the interview is as follows:
Better:	Here is my plan for the day of the interview:

The last version avoids a hidden reference problem—the possible association of the silent "it" with *interview.* Whenever you want to use *as follows,* check to see whether the subject that precedes *as follows* is plural. If it is, don't use this phrase.

Using Verb Forms Correctly

9. **Make certain that subjects and verbs agree in number.** Plural subjects require plural forms of verbs. Singular subjects require singular verb forms. Most writers know these things, but problems arise when subject-verb agreement gets tricky. Compare the following:

Incorrect:	My education and experience has prepared me....
Correct:	My education and experience have prepared me....

Incorrect:	Making plans plus scheduling conferences were....
Correct:	Making plans plus scheduling conferences was....

   In the first set, *education* and *experience* are two separate things (you can have one without the other) and therefore require a plural verb. A hasty writer might lump them together and use a singular verb. When you reread what you have written, look out for this kind of improper agreement between a plural subject and a singular verb.

   In the second set, *making plans* is the subject. It is singular, so the verb must be singular. The misleading part of this sentence is the phrase *plus scheduling conferences.* It may seem to make the subject plural, but it doesn't. In English, phrases that begin with such words as *plus, together with, in addition to, along with,* and *as well as* usually don't make a singular subject plural.

10. **Whenever possible, use active forms of verbs rather than passive forms.** Compare the following:

Passive:	My report will be sent by my assistant tomorrow.
Active:	My assistant will send my report tomorrow.

Passive:	Your interest is appreciated.
Active:	I appreciate your interest.

Passive:	Your letter was received yesterday.
Active:	I received your letter yesterday.

    Sentences with passive verbs are usually longer and clumsier than sentences with active verbs. Passive sentences often leave out the crucial information of who is performing the verb's action. Spot passive verbs by looking for some form of the verb *to be* (such as *be, will be, have been, is, was,* and *were*) used with another verb.

    In solving the passive-language problem, you might create another problem, such as using the pronouns *I* and *My* too frequently (see Tip 5 in this list). The task then becomes one of finding some other way to start a sentence while keeping your language active.

11. **Be sure that present and past participles are grammatically parallel in a list.** See Tip 50 in Part 1. What is true about parallel forms in resumes is true

also in cover letters. Present participles are action words that end in *-ing,* such as *creating, testing,* and *implementing.* Past participles are action words that usually end in *-ed,* such as *created, tested,* and *implemented.* These types of words are called *verbals* because they are derived from verbs but are not strong enough to function as verbs in a sentence. When you use a string of verbals, control them by keeping them parallel.

12. **Use split infinitives only when *not* splitting them is misleading or awkward.** An *infinitive* is a verb preceded by the preposition *to,* as in *to create, to test,* and *to implement.* You split an infinitive when you insert an adverb between the preposition and the verb, as in *to quickly create, to repeatedly test,* and *to slowly implement.* About 50 years ago, split infinitives were considered grammatical errors, but opinion about them has changed. Many grammar handbooks now recommend that you split your infinitives to avoid awkward or misleading sentences. Compare the following:

    Split infinitive: I plan to periodically send updated reports on my progress in school.

    Misleading: I plan periodically to send updated reports on my progress in school.

    Misleading: I plan to send periodically updated reports on my progress in school.

    The first example is clear enough, but the second and third examples may be misleading. If you are uncomfortable with split infinitives, one solution is to move *periodically* further into the sentence: "I plan to send updated reports periodically on my progress in school."

    Most handbooks that allow split infinitives also recommend that they not be split by more than one word, as in "to quickly and easily write." A gold medal for splitting an infinitive should go to Lowell Schmalz, an Archie Bunker prototype in "The Man Who Knew Coolidge" by Sinclair Lewis. Schmalz, who thought that Coolidge was one of America's greatest presidents, split an infinitive this way: "to instantly and without the least loss of time or effort find...."[1]

Using Punctuation Correctly

13. **Punctuate a compound sentence with a comma.** A compound sentence is one that contains two main clauses joined by one of seven conjunctions (*and, but, or, nor, for, yet,* and *so*). (A clause is a group of words containing a subject and a verb.) In English, a comma is customarily put before the conjunction if the sentence isn't unusually short. Here is an example of a compound sentence punctuated correctly:

    I plan to arrive at O'Hare at 9:35 a.m. on Thursday, and my trip by cab to your office should take no longer than 40 minutes.

    The comma is important because it signals that a new grammatical subject (*trip,* the subject of the second main clause) is about to be expressed. If you use

---

[1] Sinclair Lewis, "The Man Who Knew Coolidge," *The Man Who Knew Coolidge* (New York: Books for Libraries Press, 1956), p. 29.

this kind of comma consistently, the reader will rely on your punctuation and be on the lookout for the next subject in a compound sentence.

14.   **Be certain not to put a comma between compound verbs.** When a sentence has two verbs joined by the conjunction *and*, these verbs are called *compound verbs*. Usually, they should not be separated by a comma before the conjunction. Note the following examples:

> I *started* the letter last night *and finished* it this morning.

> I *am sending* my resume separately *and would like* you to keep the information confidential.

Both examples are simple sentences containing compound verbs. Therefore, no comma appears before *and*. In either case, a comma would send a wrong signal that a new subject in another main clause is coming, but no such subject exists.

15.   **Use (or don't use) the serial comma consistently.** How should you punctuate a series of three or more items in a sentence? If, for example, you say in your cover letter that you increased sales by 100 percent, opened two new territories, and trained four new salespeople, the comma before *and* is called the *serial comma*. It is commonly omitted in newspapers, magazine articles, advertisements, and business documents. However, it is often used for precision in technical documents or for stylistic reasons in academic text, particularly in the Humanities.

16.   **Avoid using *as well as* for *and* in a series.** Compare the following:

> Incorrect: Your company is impressive because it has offices in Canada, Mexico, as well as the United States.
>
> Correct: Your company is impressive because it has offices in Canada and Mexico, as well as in the United States.

Usually, what is considered exceptional precedes the phrase *as well as,* and what is considered customary follows it. Note this example:

Your company is impressive because its managerial openings are filled by women as well as men.

17.   **Put a comma after the year in a grouping of month, day, and year.** Similarly, put a comma after the state when it appears after the city. Compare the following pairs of examples:

> Incorrect: On January, 28, 2004 I was promoted to senior analyst.
> Correct: On January, 28, 2004, I was promoted to senior analyst.

> Incorrect: I worked in Springfield, Illinois before moving to Dallas.
> Correct: I worked in Springfield, Illinois, before moving to Dallas.

18.   **Put a comma after an opening dependent clause. An opening dependent clause often begins with a word such as "When," "If," "Because," or "Although" and cannot stand by itself as a separate sentence.** Compare the following:

> Incorrect: If you have any questions you may contact me by phone or e-mail.

Correct:	If you have any questions, you may contact me by phone or e-mail.

Actually, many writers of fiction and nonfiction don't use this kind of comma. The comma is useful, though, because it signals where the main clause begins. If you glance at the example with the comma, you can tell where the main clause is without even reading the opening clause. For a step up in clarity and readability, use this comma. It can give the reader a feel for a sentence even before he or she begins reading the words.

19. **Use semicolons when they are needed.** Semicolons are used to separate two main clauses when the second clause starts with a *conjunctive adverb* such as *however*, *moreover*, or *therefore.* Compare the following:

Incorrect:	Your position in sales looks interesting, however, I would like more information about it.
Correct:	Your position in sales looks interesting; however, I would like more information about it.

The first example is incorrect because the comma before *however* is a *comma splice,* which is a comma that joins two sentences. It's like putting a comma instead of a period at the end of the first sentence and then starting the second sentence. A comma may be a small punctuation mark, but a comma splice is a huge grammatical mistake. What are your chances of getting hired if your cover letter tells your reader that you don't recognize where a sentence ends, especially if a requirement for the job is good communication skills? Yes, you could be screened out because of one little comma!

20. **Avoid putting a colon after a verb or preposition to introduce information.** The reason is that the colon interrupts a continuing clause. Compare the following:

Incorrect:	My interests in your company are: its reputation, the review of salary after six months, and your personal desire to hire handicapped persons.
Correct:	My interests in your company are these: its reputation, the review of salary after six months, and your personal desire to hire handicapped persons.

Sometimes it is better to avoid the colon.

Better:	My interests in your company are its reputation, the review of salary after six months, and your personal desire to hire handicapped persons.

Although some people may say that it is OK to put a colon after a verb such as *include* if the list of information is long, it is better to be consistent and avoid colons after verbs altogether.

Incorrect:	My areas of expertise include: life insurance, health insurance, disability insurance, tax-deferred annuities, and retirement plans.
Correct:	My expertise includes these areas: life insurance, health insurance, disability insurance, tax-deferred annuities, and retirement plans.

Better:	My areas of expertise include life insurance, health insurance, disability insurance, tax-deferred annuities, and retirement plans.
Incorrect:	In my interview with you, I would like to: learn how your company was started, get your reaction to my updated portfolio, and discuss your department's plans to move to a new building.
Correct:	In my interview with you, I would like to discuss these issues: how your company was started, what you think of my updated portfolio, and when your department may move to a new building.
Better:	In my interview with you, I would like to discuss how your company was started, what you think of my updated portfolio, and when your department may move to a new building.

21. **Understand the use of colons.** People often associate colons with semicolons because their names sound alike, but colons and semicolons have nothing to do with each other. Colons are the opposite of dashes. Dashes look backward, whereas colons usually look forward to information about to be delivered.

Dash:	William joined the company—last week, I believe.
Colon:	Three items are on the agenda: a staff party, extended vacation time, and salary increases.

One common use of the colon does look backward, however. Here are two examples:

My experience with computers is limited: I have had only one course in programming, and I don't own a computer.

I must make a decision by Monday: that is the deadline for renewing the lease on my apartment.

In each example, what follows the colon explains what was said before the colon. Using a colon this way in a cover letter can impress a knowledgeable reader who is looking for evidence of writing skills.

22. **Use slashes correctly.** Information about slashes is sometimes hard to find because *slash* often is listed in grammar books under a different name, such as *virgule* or *solidus*. If you are unfamiliar with these terms, your hunt for advice on slashes may lead to nothing.

At least know that one important meaning of a slash is *or*. For this reason, you often see a slash in an expression such as ON/OFF. This usage means that a condition or state, such as that of electricity activated by a switch, is either ON *or* OFF but never ON *and* OFF at the same time. This condition may be one in which a change means going from the current state to the opposite (or alternate) state. If the current state is ON and there is a change, the next state is OFF, and vice versa. With this understanding, you can recognize the logic behind the following examples:

Incorrect:	ON-OFF switch (on and off at the same time!)
Correct:	ON/OFF switch (on or off at any time)
Correct:	his-her clothes (unisex clothes, worn by both sexes)
Correct:	his/her clothes (each sex had different clothes)

Note: Both his-her and his/her are clumsy. Try to find a way to avoid them. One way is to rephrase the sentence so that you use *their* or *your:*

> Campers should make their beds before breakfast.

> Please make your beds before breakfast.

Another way is to rephrase the sentence without possessive pronouns:

> Everyone should get dressed before going to breakfast.

---

23. **Think twice about using *and/or*.** This stilted expression is commonly misunderstood to mean *two* alternatives, but it literally means *three*. Consider the following example:

    If you don't hear from me by Friday, please call and/or e-mail me on Monday.

    What is the person at the other end to do? The sentence really states three alternatives: just call, just e-mail, or call *and* e-mail on Monday. For better clarity, use the connectives *and* or *or* whenever possible.

24. **Use punctuation correctly with quotation marks.** A common misconception is that commas and periods should be placed outside closing quotation marks, but the opposite is true. Compare the following:

Incorrect:	Your company certainly has the "leading edge", which means that its razor blades are the best on the market.
Correct:	Your company certainly has the "leading edge," which means that its razor blades are the best on the market.
Incorrect:	In the engineering department, my classmates referred to me as "the girl guru". I was the youngest expert in programming languages on campus.
Correct:	In the engineering department, my classmates referred to me as "the girl guru." I was the youngest expert in programming languages on campus.

    Note this exception: Unlike commas and periods, colons and semicolons go *outside* double quotation marks.

Using Words Correctly

25. **Avoid using lofty language in your cover letter.** A real turn-off in a cover letter is the use of elevated diction (high-sounding words and phrases) as an attempt to seem important. Note the following examples, along with their straight-talk translations:

Elevated:	My background has afforded me experience in…
Better:	In my previous jobs, I…
Elevated:	Prior to that term of employment…
Better:	Before I worked at…

Elevated:	I am someone with a results-driven profit orientation.
Better:	I want to make your company more profitable.
Elevated:	I hope to utilize my qualifications…
Better:	I want to use my skills…

In letter writing, the shortest distance between the writer and the reader is the most direct idea.

26. **Check your sentences for excessive use of compounds joined by *and*.** A cheap way to make your letters longer is to join words with *and* and to do this repeatedly. Note the following wordy sentence:

> Because of my background and preparation for work and advancement with your company and new enterprise, I have a concern and commitment to implement and put into effect my skills and abilities for new solutions and achievements above and beyond your dreams and expectations. [44 words]

Just one inflated sentence like that would drive a reader to say, "No way!" The writer of the inflated sentence has said only this:

> Because of my background and skills, I want to contribute to your new venture. [14 words]

If, during rereading, you eliminate the wordiness caused by this common writing weakness, an employer is more likely to read your letter completely.

27. **Avoid using abstract nouns excessively.** Look again at the inflated sentence in the preceding tip, but this time with the abstract nouns in italic:

> Because of my *background* and *preparation* for *work* and *advancement* with your *company* and new *enterprise*, I have a *concern* and *commitment* to implement and put into *effect* my *skills* and *abilities* for new *solutions* and *achievements* above and beyond your *dreams* and *expectations*.

Try picturing in your mind any of the words in italic. You can't because they are *abstract nouns*, which means that they are ideas and not images of things you can see, taste, hear, smell, or touch. One certain way to turn off the reader is to load your cover letter with abstract nouns. The following sentence, containing some images, has a better chance of capturing the reader's attention:

> Having created seven multimedia tutorials with my video camera and Gateway Pentium computer, I now want to create some breakthrough adult-learning packages so that your company, New Century Instructional Technologies, Inc., will exceed $50,000,000 in contracts by 2005.

Compare this sentence with the one loaded with abstract nouns. The one with images is obviously the better attention-grabber.

28. **Avoid wordy expressions in your cover letters.** Note the following examples in the first column and their shorter alternatives in the second column:

at the location of	at
for the reason that	because
in a short time	soon

in a timely manner	on time
in spite of everything to the contrary	nevertheless
in the event of	if
in the proximity of	near
now and then	occasionally
on a daily basis	daily
on a regular basis	regularly
on account of	because
one day from now	tomorrow
would you be so kind as to	please

Trim the fat wherever you can, and your reader will appreciate the leanness of your cover letter.

29. **At the end of your cover letter, don't make a statement that the reader can use to reject you.** For example, suppose that you close your letter with this statement:

> If you wish to discuss this matter further, please call me at (555) 555-5555.

This statement gives the reader a chance to think, "No, I don't wish to." Here is another example:

> If you know of the right opportunity for me, please call me at (555) 555-5555.

The reader may think, "I don't know of any such opportunity. How would I know what's right for you?" Avoid questions that prompt yes-or-no answers, such as, "Do you want to discuss this matter further?" If you ask this kind of question, you give the reader a chance to say no. Instead, make a closing statement that indicates your optimism about receiving a positive response from the reader. Such a statement might begin with one of the following clauses:

> I am confident that....

> I look forward to....

In this way, you invite the reader to say yes to further consideration.

Exhibit of Cover Letters

The following Exhibit contains sample cover letters that were prepared by professional resume writers to accompany resumes submitted for this book. In most cases, the names, addresses, and facts have been changed to ensure the confidentiality of the original senders and recipients. For each letter, however, the essential substance of the original remains intact. Because each cover letter was written for a resume displayed in the Gallery, the resume number is indicated first, along with the name of the resume writer.

LISA A. WELLER

(555) 555-5555

7030 Birmingham Road   **mynameis@aol.com**   Grand Rapids, MI 49000-9476

July 25, 2004

Premier Accounting
1234 York Street
Grand Rapids, MI 49000

I am interested in the position of Bookkeeper for Premier Accounting. My experience includes more than ten years in processing accounts receivable, accounts payable, payroll, and general-ledger entries; preparing tax payments; auditing; and generating financial reports.

The focus of my accounting experience lies with small businesses that have specialized in marketing, consulting, real estate, service manufacturing, and construction. I have an innate attention to detail and zero tolerance for errors. In addition, most of my positions have placed me in situations that require multitasking and prioritizing—again, areas in which I thrive.

My educational credentials exceed those of an Associate's Degree and include an Accounting Certificate (with a GPA of 4.0); the computerized portion was taught using Peachtree software. I also have an impressive amount of software and computer experience. My home office is equipped with a wireless network, DSL Internet connection, and Windows XP operating system. For the last 18 months I have maintained accounting records for a small business that uses QuickBooks, currently version 2003. In addition, I have just downloaded the trial version of MYOB Plus 12.0 and look forward to exploring it in detail.

I hope that this summary of my experience has encouraged you to consider me as a candidate for a PA Bookkeeper. Please contact me at your convenience so that we can determine whether we are, in fact, a good match. In addition to my email address and home phone, you may contact me on my cell phone at (444) 444-4444.

Looking forward to hearing from you,

Lisa A. Weller

For Resume 5. *Tammy J. Smith, Olivet, Michigan*

Horizontal lines enclosing the contact information make it easily seen. The letter expresses, in turn, the candidate's interest in the announced position, her focus, her credentials, and a probe for an interview.

William S. Beyer

78 Holcomb Drive • Franklin Park, NJ 08823 • 732-378-1972 • wsbeyer7@aol.com

DISTRIBUTION / WAREHOUSING SPECIALIST

Re: Distribution Position

Dear Sir or Madam:

Enclosed is my resume for your review. I am confident that my long-term chemical/food experience with various types of manufacturing positions would serve as an asset to an opening in your company.

I have 12 years of experience in working at Procter & Gamble as a Warehouse Specialist, Safety Leader, and Fork Lift driver. I have taken an early retirement package and would like to continue my manufacturing career with another company.

I am considered a quick learner with high concentration skills. As a Safety Leader, I have had the responsibility of making sure all plant personnel were properly trained and in compliance with OSHA guidelines. In addition, I feel that my interpersonal skills, honesty, and rapport with fellow employees will benefit the company.

Other skills that I have gained though my employment are ergonomics and shipping and receiving, as well as inventory control. I have always been known for my accuracy and hard-working attitude.

Thank you for your consideration. I look forward to speaking with you personally so that we may discuss my qualifications in greater detail.

Sincerely yours,

William S. Beyer

Enclosure

2

For Resume 63. *Beverly and Mitch Baskin, Marlboro, New Jersey*

The page border and bold, large type in the contact information complement the applicant's claim of being a confident, take-charge kind of employee. Short paragraphs make the reading tempo fast.

SAM SAFETY

1234 Toxic Drive • Anytown, Ontario L9T 5K9
ssafety@net.ca • 999.999.9999 • 999.999.9999

August 1, 2004

Name, Title
Company Name
Address
City, State, ZIP

Dear Hiring Executive:

Having worked for 15 years in chemical engineering for the power metallurgy industry before beginning course work for my forthcoming Certificate in Occupational Health and Safety, I have both the theoretical knowledge and practical hands-on experience in loss prevention and control in industrial settings to qualify for a challenging position as an **Occupational Health & Safety Professional** in your organization.

Offering outstanding team and project-management skills and a strong background in operations in hazardous chemicals environments and training of technical emergency response crews, I am ever flexible and accepting of increased responsibilities. My work has enabled me to develop expertise in a broad range of industrial applications, including chemical processing, machine tooling, fabrication, hazardous materials handling, manufacturing, building controls, and laboratory setup and experimentation. In addition to my full-time job as a research technologist, I have devoted my spare time to serving as an instructor for rural volunteer fire departments in techniques for environmental emergency response. The highlights of my work include the following:

- ◆ Lessening handling risks for a dangerous industrial gas by configuring available technology to provide a means for evaluating levels of concentration.
- ◆ Comanaging a respiratory protection program for a chemical research department, and facilitating the formation of a chemical-spill response team.
- ◆ Leading project teams to develop new products and processes, including environmental health and safety procedures.

I would appreciate the opportunity to discuss how I may be of service to your company. In the interim, I appreciate the time you have spent reviewing this letter and the accompanying resume.

Sincerely,

Sam Safety

Enclosure

3

For Resume 66. *Cathy Childs, Pompano Beach, Florida*
Boldfacing makes the target position stand out in the first paragraph. Diamond bullets call attention to achievements as work highlights after the second, main paragraph, which "sells" the candidate.

KAREN CALLOWAY

402 East Main Street • Elmira NY 12995
607 111 0000 • kcalloway@myemail.com

December 10, 2004

Recipient Name
Title
Company
Address
City State Zip

Dear _____:

Currently completing professional training as a **Medical Billing Specialist**, I am contacting you/your organization regarding positions in Billing and/or Coding.

Through this specialized program, I have gained a knowledge base in

- ▶ ICD-9 and CPT-4 Coding
- ▶ Basic and Advanced Medical Terminology
- ▶ Insurance Plans and Forms
- ▶ Medisoft

Additionally, I plan to pursue CCS and CCS-P credentials from the American Health Information Management Association and CPC-H and CPC credentials from the American Academy of Professional Coders.

Earlier positions in engineering/manufacturing, retail and employment industries have allowed me to develop exceptional skills in detail orientation, organization, research and customer service. Maintaining confidentiality while communicating effectively and coordinating diverse activities to meet a goal is easily achieved. I possess strong PC skills and am comfortable learning new applications.

I am confident that my abilities, dedication and enthusiasm will allow me to contribute successfully to your operations as a Medical Billing Specialist. It would be a pleasure to discuss potential openings with you; I will contact you shortly to confirm receipt of my enclosed résumé. Should you wish to speak with me sooner, I can be reached at 607 111 0000.

Thank you for your time and consideration.

Sincerely,

Karen Calloway

Enclosure

For Resume 67. *Salome A. Farraro, Mount Morris, New York*

The letter makes clear the applicant's target position, recently acquired knowledge, plans for additional learning, experience and skills, and interest in contributing to the prospective company.

GRACE MADISON, R.N.
101 Oak Ridge Drive ▪ Victor NY 14564 ▪ 585-555-0001

May 19, 2004

Dr. Samuel Walters
Superintendent of Schools
Victor Central School District
10 East Street
Victor NY 14564

Dear Dr. Walters:

As a Licensed Registered Nurse with five years of related experience, including public school nursing, I have great interest in your opening for a School Nurse.

For the past three school years, I have been employed at Webster Central School, providing routine and emergency health services to its staff and school population of more than 800 students. In addition, I gained experience in school nursing as a substitute with your district as well as the Rochester Public School District. In these roles, I have been able to apply and hone my generalist skills, most notably in assessment, emergency care, and health counseling. Notable accomplishments in my current position include the following:

- Completion of School Nurses Orientation Program
- Training in Section 504 regulations
- Automated External Defibrillator Training and Certification as well as involvement in school policy development for defibrillator use and placement selection (I also manage the equipment maintenance program)
- Management of student attendance using a custom software application

As a lifelong resident of Victor and a parent of school-aged children, I have been actively involved in the community and the school for more than a decade. I believe this gives me a unique perspective and understanding—of the environment in which I would work, of the individuals receiving care and their families, and of the impact to our community.

A collaborative professional, I am both dedicated and visionary. I will use my clinical and personal skills in partnership with the administration to support the school's mandate to provide and maintain a healthy and safe environment for its students and employees.

It is my hope that we can meet to discuss your School Nurse opening and my background in greater detail. I will follow up this letter and résumé with a call to your office, but I invite you to contact me anytime at 555-0001.

Thank you for your consideration and time.

Sincerely,

Grace Madison

Enclosure

5

For Resume 77. *Salome A. Farraro, Mount Morris, New York*

The first paragraph expresses the candidate's interest in the position, and the next three paragraphs show how she is the best match for the position. The last paragraph calls for an interview.

Michael J. Fisher, C.M.C.

56 Madison Avenue
Summit, New Jersey 07901
(908) 277-8796

Dear Sir/Madam:

Enclosed is my resume for your review. I am confident that my extensive experience as an executive chef and hotel/restaurant manager would serve as an asset to a position in your organization. My career began 23 years ago as an apprentice training under several internationally known chefs. Since that time I have been involved extensively in the area of food services management and marketing.

I am currently General Manager and Corporate Executive Chef of Hague Nieuw-York. In 1999 I was hired to start up this 225-seat restaurant. The casual dining establishment is part of Avanti Brands, Inc., USA. I am responsible for all financial reporting and instituted key control systems to meet the standards of the parent company. Additional achievements include gaining excellent media publicity, creative menu development, and directing on- and off-site catering for many New York City premiers. I was asked to coordinate all aspects of our new construction and to assist in the design aspects of the kitchen.

As Director of Operations for Town Square Katering and Times Square Restaurant in Hoboken, New Jersey, I expanded the business to accommodate parties ranging from 10 to 4,000 people and grossed more than $1.5 million in sales.

Working as Vice President of Operations and Executive Chef for Pine Ridge Country Club, I oversaw all profit-and-loss functions for a 165-seat a la carte restaurant and a 1,000-seat banquet facility. The club had an 18-hole Championship Golf Course that I managed, with an active membership of 1,000 members.

I gained extensive international experience working as Executive Chef for Ordini's, a five-star restaurant in New Zealand, where I prepared food for the Prime Minister, various heads of state, and visiting dignitaries. I obtained my New Zealand Master Chef's Certification. In addition, I served as an Executive Pastry Chef and Chef for a Hawaiian hotel owned and operated by the Sheraton Corporation.

Thank you for your consideration. I look forward to speaking with you personally regarding my qualifications and how I can contribute positively as a member of your management staff.

Sincerely yours,

Michael J. Fisher, C.M.C.

Enclosure

6

For Resume 100. *Beverly and Mitch Baskin, Marlboro, New Jersey*

The opening paragraph gives an overall picture of the candidate's career. The next four paragraphs express, in turn, the major positions, responsibilities, and achievements of his notable career.

PHYLLIS MARTIN, PHR

(555) 555-5555

5555 Maxwell, Clearview, Texas 79000

July 12, 2004

Sid Critefelder
Vice President of Human Resources
NATURAL GAS COMPANY
P.O. Box 5555
Panhandle, Texas 79408

RE: HUMAN RESOURCES GENERALIST

Dear Mr. Critefelder:

Your recent HR generalist vacancy has prompted me to send you my résumé for review. As you will discover, I offer the depth of experience necessary to successfully administer safety, benefits, and compensation programs; recruit, train, develop, and retain staff; build community relations; assess and fulfill staffing needs, and evaluate/revise policies and procedures. **My 14 years of collective HR experience** also indicates a comprehensive knowledge of state and federal personnel regulations. Additionally, my history reflects a loyal, stable employee who thrives on increasing responsibility and progressive learning. It would be an honor to contribute to a corporate culture, such as yours, that values people and appreciates differences.

The following attributes and well-developed skills are additional reasons to take a close look at my credentials:

HUMAN RESOURCES ADMINISTRATION
- Integrity, loyalty, and diligence earn respect and reflect distinction.
- Ownership of responsibility and accountability demonstrate leadership and character.
- Time-management and organization skills help streamline tasks and cultivate efficiency.
- Investigation and discernment foster effective problem resolution.
- Analysis and interpretation skills assist in understanding guidelines, policies, and procedures.

COMMUNICATION / INTERPERSONAL SKILLS
- Direct communication and appropriate interpersonal style enhance understanding.
- Enthusiastic presentation stimulates interest in and retention of material.
- Attentive listening enhances interviewing, counseling, and mediating.
- Professional/personal security reflect a genuine person who easily integrates into teams.
- Ability to build rapport strengthens community ties and maintains valuable resources.
- Persuasiveness sells ideas and promotes acceptance of change.

PERSONAL CHARACTERISTICS
- Friendly, personable, helpful attitude contributes to an accommodating environment.
- Attention to details and focus on excellence inspire others to excel.
- Capacity to easily learn and retain procedural information suggests decreased training time.
- Willingness to embrace challenging, changing situations indicates flexibility and adaptation.
- A sense of humor and positive outlook help ease stress in the workplace.

Experience, confidence, and drive will enable me to make significant contributions to your HR goals. Since a personal interview would benefit us both, I will contact you within the week to schedule an appointment at your convenience. In the meantime, thank you for your consideration.

Sincerely,

Phyllis Martin, PHR

Enclosure: Résumé

For Resume 102. *Edith A. Rische, Lubbock, Texas*

Boldfacing in the first paragraph makes the applicant's experience stand out. Each bulleted item is a sentence indicating the person's value or potential benefit to the prospective company.

Robert Render

147 Englishtown Road ~ Old Bridge Township, NJ 08857
(732) 555-5555 (H) ~ E-mail: render538@aol.com

MAINTENANCE SPECIALIST

Dear Sir/Madam:

As a professional **Maintenance Specialist**, I understand that success depends on several factors. These include attention to detail during manufacturing, continual upkeep of machinery, supervision of maintenance programs, and monitoring outside contractors. My extensive work experience has allowed me to ensure product quality during production, timely completion of projects, and adherence to corporate safety requirements.

Throughout my career I have been promoted and have acquired increasing responsibilities within every position. In my latest position as a Maintenance Leader for Procter & Gamble, I had the reputation for excellent machinery knowledge.

Procter & Gamble is downsizing the plant in Dayton, New Jersey, and I have accepted a voluntary separation package from the company. I would like to continue my career with a different company offering me new challenges.

Thank you for your consideration. I possess excellent hands-on knowledge as well as supervisory expertise. I look forward to meeting with you personally so that we may discuss how I can make a positive contribution to your team.

Very truly yours,

Robert Render

Enclosure

8

For Resume 123. *Beverly and Mitch Baskin, Marlboro, New Jersey*

The first paragraph summarizes the candidate's success as a worker. The second and third paragraphs indicate his last position, his reason for leaving it, and his desire for a new position.

CONFIDENTIAL   *Ready to relocate to the Clovis area*

Charles Henry Kraft
2102 Sledgeway Street – Anchorage, Alaska 99517
☎ 907.555.5555 (Cell) – apmaster@whiz.att.net

November 26, 2004

Mr. Joe North
Director of Maintenance
TopLine Airlines, Inc.
500 Northridge Parkway
Suite 400
Clovis, New Mexico 87000

Dear Mr. North:

I want to make it easy for you to add me to your team as your newest aircraft maintenance supervisor.

As a first step, I thought you deserved to see more than the usual tired lists of jobs held and training completed. In their place you'll find a half dozen examples of maintenance teams motivated, productivity boosted, liability reduced—in short, problems solved. And, while a résumé format tailored to your needs is good at documenting results, it cannot tell you *how* I contribute to our leadership's peace of mind.

Therefore, as you read, I hope the following ideas stand out:

- ❏ I am only as good as the last job I signed off—conditions in the remote parts of Alaska leave even less room for maintenance errors.

- ❏ I am only as good as my last quarter's MX statistics. If I don't spot and correct trends, we'll lose time and money.

- ❏ I am only as good as the teams I attract, recruit, train, and retain. Our labor market is among the tightest in the nation.

I'm employed now, and my company likes my work. However, I want to relocate to be closer to my family. That's why I am testing the waters with this confidential application.

When it comes to something as important as finding TopLine Airlines's next aircraft maintenance supervisor, words on paper are no substitute for people speaking with people. So let me suggest a next step. I'd like to get on your calendar in a few days so we can explore how I might serve your special maintenance needs.

Sincerely,

Charles Henry Kraft

Encl.: Résumé

CONFIDENTIAL

9

For Resume 124. *Don Orlando, Montgomery, Alabama*

The writer of this letter is a master at avoiding the typical, the expected, and the dull. As you examine this letter, note the many ways it avoids being a conventional, ordinary cover letter.

James Howard
7777 Tracer Downs ♦ Perry, GA 00000 ♦ (H) 000–000–0000 ♦ (C) 000–000–0000

(Date)

Mr. (Ms.) _____
(Company)
(Address 1)
(Address 2)

Dear Mr. _____:

(Insert 2-line paragraph about how you heard of the position and why you are applying for it. For example: "If the information in the *Times Courier* is still accurate, I am currently seeking to fill the position of Customer Service Manager. This letter is to introduce myself as a candidate for just such a position.")

I am an experienced and highly qualified management professional. My areas of expertise lie in operations management, facilities management, transportation and embarkation, inventory and logistics, purchasing and procurement, personnel and human resources, materials management, public and motivational speaking, written and oral communications, information gathering, data analysis, team coordination and budget administration. I accepted my current position with the Air Logistics Center at Robins AFB, GA, in an attempt to gain meaningful employment within the infrastructure of civil service. Because opportunities for advancement from this position are quite limited, I am seeking a position within the community at large where my wealth of knowledge and expertise can be fully utilized to the benefit of both my employer and myself.

The enclosed résumé briefly outlines my experience and accomplishments. If it appears that my qualifications meet your current needs, I would be happy to discuss my background in a meeting with you. Please feel free to contact me at the above telephone number.

Sincerely,

James Howard

Enclosure

10

For Resume 137. *Lea J. Clark, Macon, Georgia*

The letter begins with a "stage direction" for you to follow at the beginning if you adapt this letter to your own situation and job search. You would then tailor the next paragraph to your experience.

ELIZABETH GREEN

5555 Oak Tree Lane • Northridge, CA 55555
(818) 555-5555 • egreen@email.com

[Date]

[Name]
[Address]
[City, State Zip]

Dear [Salutation]:

If you are seeking a motivated and detail-oriented Purchasing Professional with a proven ability to streamline operations, motivate teams and achieve significant cost savings in a multimillion-dollar environment, my enclosed résumé should be of interest to you.

Common themes that have run throughout my professional career have included outstanding team-building and leadership strengths, as well as my ability to see the "big picture"—integrating the purchasing function into corporate goals. Representative of my past accomplishments are the following:

- Directed $200 million purchasing unit for West Coast Entertainment Company
- Hired, trained and motivated top-performing team members
- Consistently identified and developed talent in others
- Employed technology to streamline procedures, including automating the downloading of purchasing orders to the Letter of Credit system, improving on-time issuance from 20% to 75% within two years
- Consolidated supplier base from 1,200 to 650 within one year
- Sourced and developed excellent working relationships with outside and internal vendors
- Participated in key negotiations

I am currently seeking a new professional challenge where I can make a positive contribution to future goals and success. I possess a high level of energy and motivation, learn quickly, adapt well to new environments and enjoy challenges. I look forward to a personal meeting at which time we can discuss your needs and my qualifications in detail. Please don't hesitate to call me at the above number to set up a meeting. Thank you in advance for your time and consideration.

Sincerely,

Elizabeth Green

Enclosure

For Resume 156. *Vivian VanLier, Los Angeles, California*

This letter draws attention to the applicant's scope of responsibilities and strengths. Bullets point to achievements, enabling the reader to see at a glance what the applicant brings to the table.

Steven Brooks

1111 Lawrenceville Road ◆ Haven, CT 00000 ◆ 000–000–0000 ◆ user@adelphia.net

(Date)

(contact name)
(company name)
(street address)
(city, state, zip code)

Dear Hiring Professional (or insert contact name):

As a goal-oriented, progressive individual with more than 20 years of combined experience in positions that allowed for the development of diverse skills and proactive management in the areas of Recruiting and Information Technology, I feel my skills and qualifications are ideal to fill the position of (insert job title) in your (insert department), as listed with (insert source) on (insert date).

My background has positioned me to accept employment where I can make use of a wide range of skill sets within a small to midsized organization. The ideal position will allow me to provide a wealth of experience to employ a combination of strategic marketing, budget administration, and technological and sourcing skills to grow revenues and increase bottom-line profitability.

I have enclosed a copy of my résumé for your review. Please feel free to contact me, at your convenience, if you have any questions or would like to schedule an interview. I look forward to discussing the mutual benefit of our association.

Thank you for your time and consideration.

Sincerely,

Steven Brooks

12

For Resume 161. *Lea J. Clark, Macon, Georgia*

You can easily adapt this letter to your own job search by noting the information called for within parentheses and changing the language to match your worker traits, experience, skills, and goals.

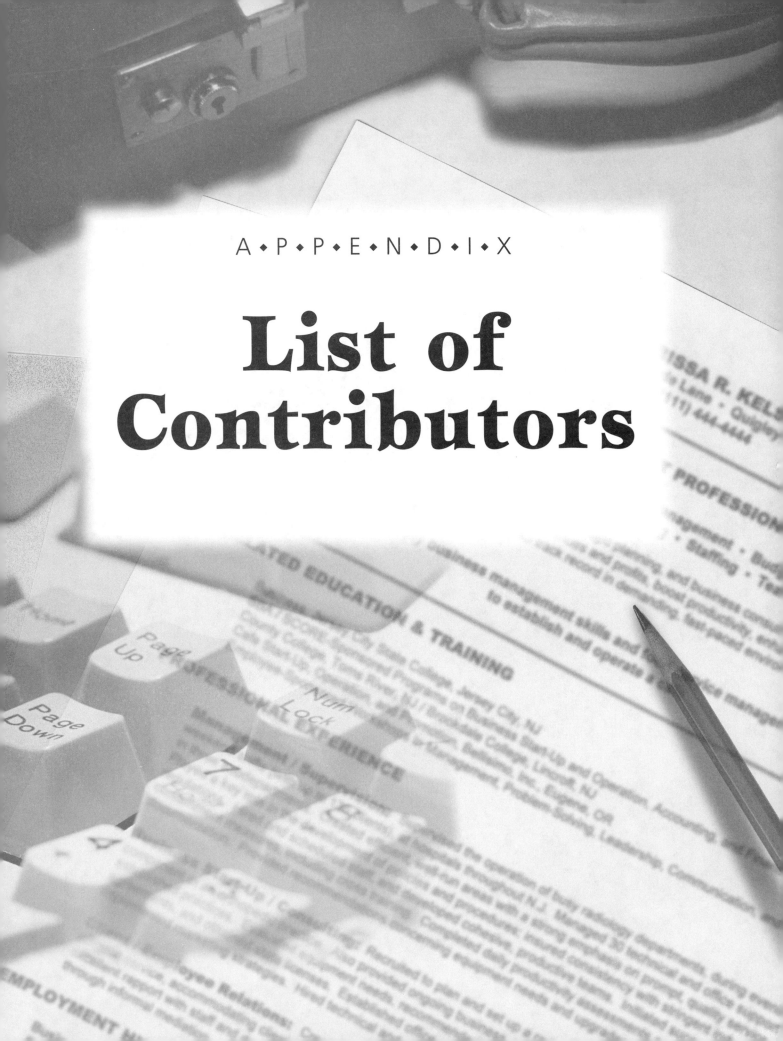

A·P·P·E·N·D·I·X

List of Contributors

List of Contributors

The following professional resume writers contributed the resumes and cover letters in this book. All the contributors are professional resume writers. To include in this appendix the names of these writers and information about their businesses is to acknowledge with appreciation their voluntary submissions and the insights expressed in the e-mails that accompanied their submissions. Resume and cover letter numbers after a writer's contact information are the *numbers of the writer's resumes and cover letters* included in the Gallery, not page numbers.

Australia

New South Wales

Sydney

Jennifer Rushton
Keraijen
Level 14, 309 Kent St.
Sydney NSW 2000
Phone: 61 2 9994 8050
E-mail: info@keraijen.com.au
Web site: www.keraijen.com.au
Member: CMI, PRWRA, AORCP
Certification: CRW
Resume: 113

Victoria

Hallum

Annemarie Cross
Advanced Employment Concepts/AEC
    Office Services
P.O. Box 91
Hallam, Victoria, 3803
Phone: 61 3 9708 6930
Fax: 61 3 9796 4479
E-mail: success@aresumewriter.net
Web site: www.aresumewriter.net
Member: CMI, PARW/CC, PRWRA
Certifications: CEIP, CPRW, CRW, CCM,
    CECC
Resume: 9

Melbourne

Gayle Howard
Top Margin Résumés Online
P.O. Box 74
Chirnside Park, Melbourne, Victoria 3116
Phone: 61 3 9726 6694
Fax: 61 3 9726 5316
E-mail: getinterviews@topmargin.com
Web site: www.topmargin.com
Member: CMI, PARW/CC, PRWRA, ASA
Certifications: CPRW, CCM, CERW
Resumes: 64, 108, 175, 189

Canada

Ontario

Aurora

Marian Bernard
Principal
The Regency Group (d.b.a. Regency
    Secretarial)
6 Morning Crescent
Aurora, Ontario
Canada L4G 2E3
Phone: (905) 841-7120
Fax: (905) 841-1391
E-mail: marian@neptune.on.ca
Member: CMI, PARW/CC
Certifications: CPS, CPRW, JCTC, CEIP
Resume: 172

Whitby

Ross Macpherson
Career Quest
131 Kirby Crescent
Whitby, Ontario
Canada L1N 7C7
Phone: (905) 438-8548
Toll-free: (877) 426-8548
Fax: (905) 438-4096
E-mail: ross@yourcareerquest.com
Web site: www.yourcareerquest.com
Member: CMI, PARW/CC, ACP
    International
Certifications: MA, CPRW, CJST, CEIP, JCTC
Resumes: 42, 50, 74, 84, 98, 110, 150, 170, 173,
    174, 177, 190

United States

Alabama

Montgomery

Don Orlando
The McLean Group
640 South McDonough St.
Montgomery, AL 36104
Phone: (334) 264-2020
Fax: (334) 264-9227
E-mail: yourcareercoach@aol.com
Member: CMI, PARW/CC, Phoenix Career Group
Certifications: CPRW, JCTC, CCM, CCMC
Resumes: 45, 78, 124, 135
Cover letter: 9

Arizona

Chandler

Wanda McLaughlin
Execuwrite
314 N. Los Feliz Dr.
Chandler, AZ 85226
Phone: (480) 732-7966 or (866) 732-7966
E-mail: wanda@execuwrite.com
Web site: www.execuwrite.com
Member: PARW/CC, CMI, NRWA
Certifications: CPRW, CEIP
Resume: 60

Tucson

Kay Bourne
CareerConnections
5210 E. Pima St., Suite 130
Tucson, AZ 85712

Phone: (520) 323-2964
Fax: (520) 795-3575
E-mail: CCmentor@aol.com
Web site: www.bestfitresumes.com
Member: CMI, PARW/CC
Certifications: CPRW, JCTC, CEIP
Resume: 21

California

Campbell

Georgia Adamson
Adept Business Services/A
    Successful Career
180 W. Rincon Ave.
Campbell, CA 95008
Phone: (408) 866-6859
Fax: (408) 866-8915
E-mail: success@ablueribbonresume.com
Web site: www.ABlueRibbonResume.com
Member: CMI, NRWA, PARW/CC
Certifications: CCMC, CCM, CEIP, CPRW, JCTC
Resume: 158

Los Angeles

Vivian VanLier
Advantage Resume & Career Services
6701 Murietta Ave.
Valley Glen, CA 91405
Phone: (818) 994-6655
Fax: (818) 994-6620
E-mail: vvanlier@aol.com
Web site: www.CuttingEdgeResumes.com
Member: CMI, NRWA, PARW/CC
Certifications: CPRW, JCTC, CEIP, CCMC
Resumes: 7, 16, 87, 117, 156, 165
Cover letter: 11

Redding

Carla Barrett
Career Designs
6855 Irving Road
Redding, CA 96001
Phone: (530) 241-8570
Fax: (530) 248-3351
E-mail: carla@careerdesigns.com
Web site: www.careerdesigns.com
Member: CMI, NRWA
Certifications: CCM, Certified Career Coach
Resumes: 33, 146

Torrance

Gail Taylor
A Hire Power Résumé
21213-B Hawthorne Blvd., #5224
Torrance, CA 90503
Phone: (310) 793-4122
Fax: (310) 793-7481
E-mail: hirepwr@yahoo.com
Web site: www.call4hirepower.com
Member: CMI, NRWA, PARW/CC
Certifications: CEIP, CPRW
Resume: 38

Valencia

Myriam-Rose Kohn
JEDA Enterprises
27201 Tourney Road, Suite 201M
Valencia, CA 91355-1857
Phone: (661) 253-0801
Toll-free: (800) 600-JEDA
Fax: (661) 253-0744
E-mail: myriam-rose@jedaenterprises.com
Web site: www.jedaenterprises.com
Member: CMI, NRWA, PARW/CC
Certifications: CPRW, CEIP, IJCTC, CCM, CCMC
Resumes: 19, 176

Colorado

Aurora

Michele Angello
Corbel Communications
19866 E. Dickenson Place
Aurora, CO 80013
Phone: (303) 537-3592
Fax: (303) 537-3542
E-mail: corbelcomm1@aol.com
Web site: www.corbelonline.com
Member: PARW/CC
Certification: CPRW
Resumes: 70, 91

Louisville

Roberta F. Gamza
Career Ink
211 Springs Drive
Louisville, CO 80027
Phone: (303) 955-3065
Toll-free: (877) 581-6063
Fax: (303) 955-3065
E-mail: roberta@careerink.com
Web site: www.careerink.com

Member: CMI, NRWA, PARW/CC, PRWRA
Certifications: CEIP, CTC, CJST
Resumes: 89, 167, 179

Connecticut

Enfield

Louise Garver
Career Directions, LLC
115 Elm St., Suite 203
Enfield, CT 06082
Phone: (860) 623-9476
Toll-free: (888) 222-3731
Fax: (860) 623-9473
E-mail: careerpro@cox.net
Web site: www.resumeimpact.com
Member: CMI, NRWA, PARW/CC, ACA, NCDA,
    ACPI, CPADN
Certifications: MA, JCTC, CMP, CPRW, MCDP,
    CEIP
Resumes: 2, 106, 128, 181, 184, 186

Hartford

Ellen Mulqueen, MA
Vocational Counselor, Department of Rehabilitation
    Services, The Institute of Living
200 Retreat Ave.
Hartford, CT 06106
Phone: (860) 545-7202
Fax: (860) 545-7140
E-mail: emulque@harthosp.org
Web site: www.instituteofliving.org/Programs/
    rehab.htm
Member: CMI, NRWA, PARW/CC, PRWRA
Certifications: CRW, CECC
Resumes: 35, 40, 41, 79, 131

Rowayton

Diana Holdsworth
Action Communications Résumé Services
P.O. Box 234
Rowayton, CT 06853
Phone: (203) 831-0070
Fax: (203) 831-0070
E-mail: hold@optonline.net
Member: CMI, PARW/CC, PRWRA
Certification: CPRW
Resume: 103

Torrington

Ross Primack
Connecticut Labor Department/Torrington CT
  Works
486 Winsted Road
Torrington, CT 06790
Phone: (203) 879-3242
Fax: (203) 879-3242
E-mail: rossprimackcprw@hotmail.com
Member: CMI
Certifications: CPRW, CEIP, GCDF
Resume: 147

Florida

Pompano Beach

Cathy Childs
133 N. Pompano Beach Blvd., #310
Pompano Beach, FL 33062-5720
Phone: (954) 946-3953
E-mail: hitchy-koo@juno.com
Member: PARW/CC
Certification: CPRW
Resume: 66
Cover letter: 3

Tampa

Gail Frank
Frankly Speaking: Resumes That Work!
10409 Greendale Drive
Tampa, FL 33626
Phone: (813) 926-1353
Fax: (813) 926-1092
E-mail: gailfrank@post.harvard.edu
Web site: www.callfranklyspeaking.com
Member: PARW/CC, NRWA, PRWRA, CMI,
  SHRM, ASTD
Certifications: NCRW, CPRW, JCTC, CEIP, MA
Resumes: 31, 56, 65

Georgia

Macon

Lea J. Clark
Lea Clark & Associates
4521 Dorset Drive
Macon, GA 31206
Phone: (478) 781-4107
Fax: (478) 781-6960
E-mail: lclark352001@cox.net
Web site: www.gacareercenter.com

Member: PRWRA (Region 4 Rep), Who's Who in
  Executives and Professionals
Certifications: CRW, BIT
Resumes: 137, 161
Cover letters: 10, 12

Hawaii

Honolulu

Peter Hill
Distinctive Resumes
1226 Alexander St.
Honolulu, HI 96826
Phone: (808) 306-3920
E-mail: distinctiveresumes@yahoo.com
Web site: www.peterhill.biz
Member: CMI, NRWA, PARW/CC
Certification: CPRW
Resume: 99

Idaho

Boise

Denette D. Jones
Jones Career Specialties
4702 Gage St.
Boise, ID 83706
Phone: (208) 331-0561
Fax: (208) 361-0122
E-mail: dj@jonescareerspecialties.com
Web site: www.jonescareerspecialties.com
Member: CMI, NRWA, PRWRA
Resumes: 18, 61, 109, 126, 168, 191

Illinois

Bolingbrook

Stephanie Whittington
Prairie Professional, LLC
1136 Jennifer Lane
Bolingbrook, IL 60440
Phone: (630) 605-4251
Fax: (630) 226-0555
E-mail: swhittington@prairieprof.com
Web site: www.prairieprof.com
Member: NRWA
Resume: 114

Glen Carbon

Heather Eagar
Professional Approach
Glen Carbon, IL 62034
Phone: (618) 288-0742
E-mail: heather@professionalapproach.com
Web site: www.professionalapproach.com
Member: PARW/CC, CMI
Certification: CPRW
Resume: 14

Lincolnshire

Christine L. Dennison
Dennison Career Services
Lincolnshire, IL 60069
Phone: (847) 405-9775
Fax: (847) 405-9775
E-mail: chris@thejobsearchcoach.com
Web site: www.thejobsearchcoach.com
Member: PARW/CC, Greater Lincolnshire
    Chamber of Commerce, BBB of
    Chicago/Northern Illinois
Certification: CPC
Resume: 164

Naperville

Patricia Chapman
CareerPro-Naperville, Inc.
520 E. Ogden Ave., Suite 3
Naperville, IL 60563
Phone: (630) 983-8882
Toll-free: (866) 661-2269
Fax: (630) 983-9021
E-mail: pat@career2day.com
Web site: www.career2day.com
Member: CMI, PRWRA, NAFE
Certification: CRW
Resumes: 26, 88, 192

Schaumburg

Rosemary Fish Justen
Creative Communication Services, Inc.
1025 Southbridge Lane
Schaumburg, IL 60194-2265
Phone: (847) 490-8686
E-mail: rosemary@CCSResumes.com
Web site: www.CCSResumes.com
Member: PARW/CC
Certification: CPRW
Resume: 141

Waukegan

Eva Locke
Lake County Workforce Development
415 Washington St., Suite 104
Waukegan, IL 60085
Phone: (847) 249-2200, ext. 110
Fax: (847) 249-2214
E-mail: elocke@co.lake.il.us
Web site: www.co.lake.il.us/workforce
Member: PRWRA
Resume: 71

Indiana

Columbus

Rita Fisher
Career Change Résumés
2826 Hawcreek Blvd.
Columbus, IN 47203
Phone: (812) 375-6190
Toll-free: (866) 645-6350
Fax: (928) 569-5114
E-mail: resumes@reliable-net.net
Web site: www.careerchangeresumes.com
Certification: CPRW
Resume: 62

Decatur

Tammy K. Shoup
Breakthrough Resume Writing Service
Decatur, IN 46733
Phone: (260) 223-1821
E-mail: AWordpro@aol.com
Web site: www.breakthroughresumes.com
Member: PARW/CC
Certification: CPRW
Resume: 153

Louisiana

West Monroe

Julie C. Thomas
Julie's Typing & Notary Service
1134 West Olive
West Monroe, LA 71292
Phone: (318) 322-2199
Fax: (318) 322-2199
E-mail: jcthomas@bellsouth.net
Member: NRWA
Resume: 195

Maryland

Hagerstown

Norine Dagliano
ekm Inspirations
616 Highland Way
Hagerstown, MD 21740
Phone: (301) 766-2032
Fax: (301) 745-5700
E-mail: ndagliano@yahoo.com
Web site: www.ekminspirations.com
Member: CMI, PARW/CC
Certification: CPRW
Resume: 58

Massachusetts

Concord

Jean Cummings
A Resume For Today
123 Minot Road
Concord, MA 01742
Phone: (978) 371-9266
Toll-free: (800) 324-1699
Fax: (978) 964-0529
E-mail: jc@aResumeForToday.com
Web site: www.aResumeForToday.com
Member: CMI, PARW/CC
Certifications: M.A.T., CPRW, CEIP
Resume: 159

Groton

Carol Nason
Career Advantage
95 Flavell Road
Groton, MA 01450-1536
Phone: (978) 448-3319
Fax: (978) 448-8948
E-mail: nason1046@aol.com
Web site: acareeradvantageresume.com
Member: CMI, PARW/CC, NRWA
Certifications: MA, CPRW
Resume: 95

Melrose

Jeanne Knight
Career and Job Search Coach
P.O. Box 828
Melrose, MA 02176
Phone: (617) 968-7747
E-mail: jeanne@careerdesigns.biz

Web site: www.careerdesigns.biz
Member: CMI, NRWA
Certification: JCTC
Resume: 112

Needham

Wendy Gelberg
Advantage Resumes
21 Hawthorn Ave.
Needham, MA 02492
Phone: (781) 444-0778
Fax: (781) 444-2778
E-mail: WGelberg@aol.com
Member: NRWA, CMI, Career Planning and Adult
   Development Network
Certifications: M.Ed., CPRW, IJCTC
Resume: 3

Westborough

Jessica Robinson
RA Résumé
P.O. Box 513
Westborough, MA 01581
Phone: (508) 284-9950
Fax: (508) 870-0911
E-mail: jessica@raresume.com
Web site: www.raresume.com
Member: PARW/CC
Certification: CPRW
Resume: 111

Michigan

Clarkston

Jennifer N. Ayres
Executive Director
Nell Resources
P.O. Box 2
Clarkston, MI 48348
Phone: (248) 969-9933
E-mail: jennifer@nellresources.com
Web site: www.nellresources.com
Member: CMI, PRWRA
Certification: CRW
Resume: 136

Flint

Janet L. Beckstrom
Word Crafter
1717 Montclair Ave.
Flint, MI 48503-2074
Toll-free: (800) 351-9818
Fax: (810) 232-9257
E-mail: wordcrafter@voyager.net
Member: CMI, PARW/CC
Certification: CPRW
Resumes: 52, 73, 119

Olivet

Tammy J. Smith
Professional Image Design, LLC
7030 Marshall Road
Olivet, MI 49076
Phone: (269) 209-3539 or (877) 588-7459
Fax: (877) 588-7459
E-mail: ProResumeWriter@aol.com
Member: NRWA
Resumes: 5, 68, 107, 154
Cover letter: 1

Portage

Richard T. Porter
CareerWise Communications, LLC
332 Magellan Court
Portage, MI 49002-7000
Phone: (269) 321-0183
Fax: (269) 321-0191
Toll-free fax: (888) 565-7109
E-mail: careerwise_resumes@yahoo.com
Member: CMI, PARW/CC
Resume: 44

Minnesota

Rochester

Beverley Drake
CareerVision Resume & Job Search Systems
1816 Baihly Hills Drive SW
Rochester, MN 55902
Phone: (507) 252-9825
E-mail: bdcprw@aol.com
Member: CMI, PARW/CC
Certifications: CEIP, IJCTC, CPRW
Resume: 142

Missouri

Kansas City

Evelyn E. Maddox, SPHR
Employment Services, Inc.
1625 NE Clubhouse Drive, #201
Kansas City, MO 64116
Phone/Fax: (816) 421-5166
Cell: (913) 634-3976
E-mail: eemaddox@aol.com
Member: CMI, SHRM
Certification: SPHR
Resume: 34

New Jersey

Edison

Patricia Traina-Duckers
The Résumé Writer
P.O. Box 595
Edison, NJ 08818-0595
Phone: (732) 239-8533
Fax: (732) 906-5636
E-mail: sales@theresumewriter.com
Web site: www.theresumewriter.com
Member: CMI, PRWRA
Certifications: CPRW, CRW, FRWC
Resume: 162

Flemington

Carol A. Altomare
World Class Résumés
P.O. Box 483
Three Bridges, NJ 08887-0483
Phone: (908) 237-1883
Toll-free: (877) 771-6170
Fax: (908) 237-2069
E-mail: caa@worldclassresumes.com
Web site: www.worldclassresumes.com
Member: PARW/CC
Certification: CPRW
Resumes: 15, 105, 132

Iselin

See Marlboro.

Mahwah

Igor Shpudejko
Career Focus
23 Parsons Court
Mahwah, NJ 07430
Phone: (201) 825-2865
Fax: (201) 825-7711
E-mail: Ishpudejko@aol.com
Web sites: www.careerinfocus.com and
      www.anexecutiveresumewriter.com
Member: CMI, PARW/CC
Certifications: CPRW, JCTC, MBA, BSIE
Resume: 138

Marlboro

Beverly and Mitch Baskin
Baskin Business & Career Services
6 Alberta Dr.
Marlboro, NJ 07746
Other offices: 120 Wood Ave. South, Iselin, NJ
      08830; Forrestal Village, Princeton, NJ 08540
Toll-free phone: (800) 300-4079
Fax: (732) 972-8846
E-mail: bbcs@att.net
Web site: www.baskincareer.com
Member: NRWA, NCDA, NECA, MACCA,
      AMHCA
Certifications: Ed.S, MA, MMS, LPC, NCCC,
      CPRW, MCC, PE, NAJST
Resumes: 8, 59, 63, 100, 120, 123, 149, 157
Cover letters: 2, 6, 8

Princeton

See Marlboro.

West Paterson

Melanie Noonan
Peripheral Pro, LLC
560 Lackawanna Ave.
West Paterson, NJ 07424
Phone: (973) 785-3011
Fax: (973) 256-6285
E-mail: PeriPro1@aol.com
Member: NRWA, PARW/CC
Certification: CPS
Resumes: 20, 25, 47, 76

Phone: (518) 872-1305
Fax: (518) 872-1305
E-mail: customresume1@aol.com
Web site: www.customresumewriting.com
Member: PARW/CC
Certification: CPRW
Resumes: 13, 55

Brentwood

Ann Baehr
Best Resumes
122 Sheridan St.
Brentwood, NY 11717
Phone: (631) 435-1879
Fax: (631) 977-2821
E-mail: resumesbest@earthlink.net
Web site: www.ebestresumes.com
Member: CMI, NRWA, PARW/CC
Certification: CPRW
Resume: 155

Hicksville

Deanna Verbouwens
Ace in the Hole Resume Writing and Career Services
14 Mitchell Court
Hicksville, NY 11801
Phone: (516) 942-5986
E-mail: verbouwens@yahoo.com
      and info@aceinthehole.net
Member: PARW/CC
Resumes: 53, 194

Huntington

M J Feld, MS
Careers by Choice, Inc.
205 East Main St., Suite 2-4
Huntington, NY 11743
Phone: (631) 673-5432
Fax: (631) 673-5824
E-mail: mj@careersbychoice.com
Web site: www.careersbychoice.com
Member: PARW/CC
Certifications: MS, CPRW
Resumes: 17, 28, 39, 92

New York

Altamont

John Femia
Custom Résumé & Writing Service
1690 Township Road
Altamont, NY 12009

Liverpool

Bruce Baxter
Baxter Communications
4186 Gemini Path
Liverpool, NY 13090
Phone: (315) 652-7703
Fax: (315) 652-7758
E-mail: baxtercom@juno.com
Web site: baxtercom.com
Member: PARW/CC
Certification: CPRW
Resumes: 12, 151

Mount Morris

Salome A. Farraro
Careers TOO
3123 Moyer Road
Mount Morris, NY 14510
Phone: (585) 658-2480
Toll-free: (877) 436-9378
Fax: (585) 658-2480
E-mail: sfarraro@careers-too.com
Web site: www.careers-too.com
Member: PARW/CC
Certification: CPRW
Resumes: 67, 77, 93
Cover letters: 4, 5

Poughkeepsie

Kristin M. Coleman
Career Services
44 Hillcrest Drive
Poughkeepsie, NY 12603
Phone: (845) 452-8274
Fax: (845) 452-7789
E-mail: kristincoleman44@yahoo.com
Member: CMI
Resumes: 49, 121

Smithtown

Linda Matias
CareerStrides
37 East Hill Drive
Smithtown, NY 11787
Fax: (631) 382-2425
E-mail: linda@careerstrides.com
Web site: www.careerstrides.com
Member: CMI, NRWA, PARW/CC
Certifications: CEIP, JCTC
Resume: 30

Thiells

Joseph Imperato
XSolutions Résumé Service
P.O. Box 76
Thiells, NY 10984

Phone: (845) 362-9675
Fax: (845) 818-3676
E-mail: resumes@xsresumes.com
Web site: www.xsresumes.com
Member: NRWA
Resumes: 6, 51

North Carolina

Charlotte

Doug Morrison
Career Power
2915 Providence Road, Suite 250-B
Charlotte, NC 28211
Phone: (704) 365-0773
Fax: (704) 365-3411
E-mail: dmpwresume@aol.com
Web site: www.CareerPowerResume.com
Member: CMI, PARW/CC, PRWRA
Certification: CPRW
Resume: 152

Indian Trail

Nathan J. Adams
First Impressions Résumé & Career Management
    Center
P.O. Box 1653
Indian Trail, NC 28079
Phone: (704) 882-2839
Fax: (775) 244-1310
E-mail: rezumay4u@aol.com
Web site: www.firstimpressionscount.com
Member: PARW/CC, CMI
Certification: CPRW
Resume: 57

Ohio

Athens

Melissa L. Kasler
Résumé Impressions
540 W. Union St., Suite D
Athens, OH 45701
Phone: (740) 592-3993
Toll-free: (800) 516-0334
Fax: (740) 592-1352
E-mail: resume@frognet.net
Web site: www.resumeimpressions.com
Member: CMI, PARW/CC
Certification: CPRW
Resumes: 23, 48

Findlay

Sharon Pierce-Williams, M.Ed.
The Résumé.Doc
609 Lincolnshire Lane
Findlay, OH 45840
Phone: (419) 422-0228
Fax: (419) 425-1185
E-mail: Sharon@TheResumeDoc.com
Web site: www.TheResumeDoc.com
Member: CMI, PARW/CC, PRWRA, Findlay-
    Hancock County Chamber of Commerce
Certifications: M.Ed., CPRW
Resume: 80

Huber Heights

Teena L. Rose
Résumé to Referral
7211 Taylorsville Road, Office 208
Huber Heights, OH 45424
Phone: (937) 236-1360
Fax: (937) 236-1351
E-mail: admin@resumetoreferral.com
Web site: www.resumebycprw.com
Member: PARW/CC, CMI
Certifications: CPRW, CEIP, CCM
Resume: 96

Mogadore

Tara G. Papp, M.S.
Accomplished Résumés
1196 Waterloo Road
Mogadore, OH 44260
Phone: (330) 628-0073
Fax: (330) 628-0073
E-mail: TGPapp@aol.com
Web site: www.accomplishedresumes.com
Member: NRWA, PARW/CC, SHRM, SIOP
Certification: CPRW
Resume: 188

Oregon

Portland

Rosie Bixel
A Personal ScribeRésumé Writing & Design
    (a division of BHH Group)
4800 SW Macadam Ave., Suite 105
Portland, OR 97239
Phone: (503) 254-8262
Fax: (503) 255-3012
E-mail: aps@bhhgroup.com
Web site: www.bhhgroup.com/resume/asp

Member: NRWA
Resumes: 22, 29, 54, 83, 85, 86,
    129, 130, 183, 187

Jennifer Rydell
Simplify Your Life Career Services
6327-C SW Capitol Hwy PMB 243
Portland, OR 97239-1937
Phone: (503) 977-1955
Fax: (503) 245-4212
E-mail: jennifer@simplifyyourliferesumes.com
Web site: www.simplifyyourliferesumes.com
Member: CMI, NRWA, PARW/CC
Certifications: CPRW, NCRW, CCM
Resume: 75

Pennsylvania

Harleysville

Darlene Dassy
Dynamic Résumé Solutions
602 Monroe Drive
Harleysville, PA 19438
Phone: (215) 368-2316
Fax: (215) 368-2316 (call before faxing)
E-mail: darlene@attractiveresumes.com
Web site: www.attractiveresumes.com
Member: CMI, NRWA, PRWRA
Certifications: BBA, CRW
Resume: 139

Jan Holliday
Arbridge Communications
Harleysville, PA 19438
Phone: (215) 513-7420
Toll-free: (866) 513-7420
E-mail: info@arbridge.com
Web site: www.arbridge.com
Member: NRWA, CMI, IWA
Certifications: MA, NCRW, Certified Webmaster
Resumes: 4, 127, 185

King of Prussia

Karen S. Carli
Carli Career Consulting
P.O. Box 62003
King of Prussia, PA 19406
Phone: (610) 337-8891
Fax: (610) 337-1013
E-mail: kscarli@comcast.net
Member: NRWA
Certifications: MS, LPC, CRC, CCM
Resume: 143

Media

Karen L. Conway
Premier Resumes
1008 N. Providence Road
Media, PA 19063
Phone: (610) 566-8422
Toll-free: (866) 241-5300
Fax: (610) 566-3047
E-mail: premresume@aol.com
Web site: www.ResumesInADay.com
Member: PARW/CC
Certifications: CPRW, CEIP
Resume: 24

Sharon

Jane Roqueplot
JaneCo's Sensible Solutions
194 N. Oakland Ave.
Sharon, PA 16146
Phone: (724) 342-0100
Toll-free: (888) 526-3267
Fax: (724) 346-5263
E-mail: jane@janecos.com
Web site: www.janecos.com
Member: CMI, NRWA, PRWRA, PARW/CC, AJST,
    NCDA
Certifications: CPBA, CWDP, CECC
Resumes: 11, 72, 82, 90, 144, 180, 182

Rhode Island

North Kingstown

Edward Turilli
Director, Career Development Center
Salve Regina University
100 Ochre Point Ave.
Newport, RI 02840
Anthem Resume & Career Services (ARCS)
918 Lafayette Road
North Kingstown, RI 02852
Phone: (401) 268-3020
Fax: (401) 341-2994
E-mail: turillie@salve.edu
Web site: www.salve.edu/office_careerdev
Member: CMI, PARW/CC, NCDA, NACE, EACE,
    RICC
Certification: MA
Resumes: 1, 32, 81

Tennessee

Hendersonville

Carolyn S. Braden
Braden Résumé Solutions
108 La Plaza Drive
Hendersonville, TN 37075
Phone: (615) 822-3317
Fax: (615) 826-9611
E-mail: bradenresume@comcast.net
Member: CMI, PARW/CC
Certification: CPRW
Resumes: 118, 125, 160

Texas

Bishop

Nick V. Marino
Outcome Résumés & Career Federal Résumé Service
710 Aurora Drive
Bishop, TX 78343
Phone: (361) 584-3121
Toll-free: (866) 899-6509
Fax: (270) 837-3852
E-mail: CareerResumPro@stx.rr.com and
    CertFedResWriter@stx.rr.com
Web sites: www.OutcomeResumes.com and
    www.FederalResumeService.com
Member: CMI, PARW/CC, AJST, CPADN
Certifications: CPRW, CRW, CEIP, CFCM,
    CFRW/C, CFJSP
Resumes: 101, 116, 178

Lubbock

Daniel J. Dorotik, Jr.
100PercentResumes
9803 Clinton Ave.
Lubbock, TX 79424
Phone: (806) 783-9900
Fax: (214) 722-1510
E-mail: dan@100percentresumes.com
Web site: www.100percentresumes.com
Member: NRWA, PARW/CC
Certification: NCRW
Resume: 133

Edith A. Rische
Write Away Resume
5908 73rd St.
Lubbock, TX 79424-1920
Phone: (806) 798-0881
Fax: (806) 798-3213
E-mail: erische@door.net
Web site: www.writeawayresume.com
Member: NRWA
Certifications: NCRW, JCTC
Resume: 102
Cover letter: 7

Tyler

Ann Klint
Ann's Professional Résumé Service
2130 Kennebunk Lane
Tyler, TX 75703-0301
Phone: (903) 509-8333
Fax: (734) 448-1962
E-mail: Resumes-Ann@tyler.net
Web site: www.geocitles.com/ann_klint/
    ann_klint2.html
Resumes: 46, 166, 169

Victoria

MeLisa Rogers
Ultimate Career
270 Live Oak Lane
Victoria, TX 77905
Toll-free phone: (866) 573-7863
Fax: (361) 574-8830
E-mail: success@ultimatecareer.biz
Web site: www.ultimatecareer.biz
Member: PARW/CC, SHRM, ASTD
Certifications: M.S. HRD, CPRW
Resumes: 27, 36, 37, 122, 140, 145, 163, 193

Virginia

Reston

Helen Oliff
Principal Turning Point
2307 Freetown Court, #12C
Reston, VA 20191
Phone: (703) 716-0077
Fax: (703) 995-0706
E-mail: helen@turningpointnow.com
Web site: www.turningpointnow.com
Member: CMI, PARW/CC
Certifications: CFRWC, CPRW, ECI
Resumes: 115, 134

Washington

Bellingham

Janice M. Shepherd
Write On Career Keys
Bellingham, WA 98226-4260
Phone: (360) 738-7958
Fax: (360) 738-1189
E-mail: Janice@writeoncareerkeys.com
Web site: www.writeoncareerkeys.com
Member: CMI, PARW/CC
Certifications: CPRW, JCTC, CEIP
Resumes: 104, 171

Seatac

Diana Ramirez, RC
Ramirez Consulting Services
Seatac, WA 98198
Phone: (206) 870-7366
Mobile: (253) 332-5521
E-mail: ramirezconsulting@yahoo.com
Web site: www.ramirezconsulting.us
Member: NRWA, NCDA, NAWW
Certifications: NCDA; Registered Counselor,
    Project Management, Human Resources
    Management
Resumes: 10, 43, 69, 148

Seattle

Alice Hanson
Aim Resumes
P.O. Box 75054
Seattle, WA 98175-0054
Phone: (206) 527-3100
Fax: (206) 527-3101
E-mail: alice@aimresumes.com
Web site: www.aimresumes.com
Member: CMI, NRWA, PARW/CC, PSCDA,
    NWRA
Certification: CPRW
Resumes: 94, 97

Professional Organizations

If you would like more recommendations of resume writers and career coaches in your area, see the following information.

Career Masters Institute

119 Old Stable Road
Lynchburg, VA 24503
Phone: (800) 881-9972
Fax: (434) 386-3200
E-mail: wendyenelow@cminstitute.com
Web site: www.cminstitute.com

www.CertifiedCareerCoaches.com
www.CertifiedResumeWriters.com
National Résumé Writers Association

P.O. Box 184
Nesconset, NY 11767
Toll-free phone: (888) NRWA-444
E-mail: AdminManager@nrwaweb.com
Web site: www.nrwaweb.com

Professional Association of Résumé Writers and Career Coaches

1388 Brightwaters Blvd., NE
St. Petersburg, FL 33704
Toll-free phone: (800) 822-7279
Fax: (727) 894-1277
E-mail: PARWCCHQ@aol.com
Web site: www.parw.com

Professional Résumé Writing and Research Association

1106 Coolidge Blvd.
Lafayette, LA 70503
Toll-free phone: (800) 225-8688
E-mail: laurie@prwra.com
Web site: www.prwra.com

For information on the certification programs for Certified Federal Job Search Trainer (CFJST) or Certified Federal Resume Writer & Coach (CFRWC), see the following information.

Ten Steps to a Federal Job™
The Resume Place, Inc.
89 Mellor Ave.
Baltimore, MD 21228
Phone: (410) 744-4324
Fax: (410) 744-0112
E-mail: kathryn@resume-place.com
Web sites: www.resumeplace.com and
    www.tensteps.com

Occupation Index

Job goals do not appear in this index. Only the applicants' current and last positions are included.

Note: Numbers are resume numbers in the Gallery, *not* page numbers.

A

Account Executive, 173
    Senior, 35, 176
Account Manager, Senior, 141
Accounting Clerk/Technology
    Specialist, 1
Accounting Manager, 129
Accounts Payable Clerk, 3
Administrative Assistant, 13,
    14, 15
    Executive, 18, 19
Air Conditioner Repairer, 185
Aircraft Maintenance
    Technician, Lead, 125
Airframe & Power Plant
    Mechanic, 124
Analyst
    Business, 107
    Credit Reporting, 56
    Sales, 155
    Support, IT, 103
Apartment Housekeeper, 121
Application Developer, Senior,
    111
Application Development
    Supervisor, 114
Application Programmer, 117
Arbitration Company, Owner,
    65
Area Fleet Supervisor, 194
Assembler Installer, 148
Assistant
    Administrative, 13, 14, 15
    Dental, 69
    Executive, 16, 17, 20, 21
    Instructor's, 44
    Medical, 129
    Radiography Technician, 70

Assistant Buyer, 155
Assistant Manager, Website,
    108
Assistant Restaurant Manager,
    85
Assistant Stylist Coordinator,
    50
Associate Manager, Senior, 96
Aviation Flight Line Hostess,
    46

B

Banker, Personal, 57
Banquet Captain, 84
Basketball Coach, 48
Billing Clerk, 2
Billing Specialist, 68
Bookkeeper
    Full Charge, 7
    Senior, 6
Budget Manager, 131
Business Analyst, 107
Business Development Officer,
    54
Business Partner, 181
Business Solutions Consultant,
    177
Buyer, Assistant, 155

C

CAD Designer, Senior, 42
Cake Decorator, 82
Captain of Operations, Fire
    Department, 61
Cardiac Technologist,
    Interventional, Chief, 76
CD Superstore, Manager, 143
Chef
    Executive, 90, 92
        Corporate, 100

    Head, 94
    Restaurant, 91
    Sous, 93
Chef/Production Manager, 95
Chief, Fire, 62
Chief Information Security
    Officer, 110
Chief Interventional Cardiac
    Technologist, 76
Child Care Provider, 71
Clerk
    Accounting, 1
    Accounts Payable, 3
    Office/Billing, 2
Coach, Basketball, 48
Community Sales Manager, 158
Computer Operator, 106
Computer Professional, 104
Conference Coordinator
    (Intern), 51
Construction Manager, 28
Consultant
    Business Solutions, 177
    Cosmetics, 73
    Financial, 60
    IT, 115
    Leisure Travel, 22
    Real Estate Development,
        159
    Recruiting, 161
    Technical, 112
Consultant Supervisor, Lead,
    146
Consulting Sales Executive, 174
Contract IT Support Specialist,
    105
Contractor, 189
    Relocation, 67
COO/General Manager, Resort,
    99

Coordinator
    Conference (Intern), 51
    Customer Services, 33
    Database Marketing, 25
    Program, National, 49
    Stylist, Assistant, 50
    Team, 149
    Training, IT, 103
Co-owner/Cofounder, Health &
    Fitness Company, 74
Corporate Executive
    Chef/General Manager, 100
Cosmetics Consultant, 73
Credit Portfolio Specialist/
    Executive Assistant,
    21
Credit Reporting Analyst, 56
Credit Union Teller, 52
CRM Business Process
    Integration Manager, 136
Customer Relations, Director,
    38
Customer Service
    Representative, 30, 31
    Supervisor, 32, 36
    Trainer, 34
Customer Services Coordinator,
    33

D

Database Marketing
    Coordinator, 25
Dental Assistant, 69
Design and Drafting, Manager,
    45
Designer
    CAD, Senior, 43
    Graphic, 39
Detectives, Lieutenant, 120
Development Consultant, Real
    Estate, 159
Director
    Customer Relations, 38
    Finance, 60
    Information Systems, 113
    Managing, 59
    New Business, 175
    Resource Planning, 140
    Sales, 167
        Resort Hotel, 98
    Store, 145
    Support Services, 87
Director of Customer Relations,
    38
Director of Information
    Systems, 113

Director of Resource Planning,
    140
Director of Sales, Resort Hotel,
    98
District Manager, Restaurant
    Operations, 87
Driver, Truck, 193

E

Editor, Senior, 23
Electronic Assembler, 186
Engineer
    Network, Senior, 116
    Software, Senior, 115
    Systems, 112
Engineering Technician,
    Manufacturing Process, 151
Excavating Company,
    Owner/Operator, 29
Executive
    Account, 173
        Senior, 35, 176
    Sales, Consulting, 174
Executive Administrative
    Assistant, 18, 19
Executive Assistant, 16, 17, 20,
    21
Executive Chef, 90, 92
    Corporate, 100

F

Finance Director/Financial
    Consultant, 60
Financial Consultant, 60
Fire Chief, 62
Fire Department, Captain of
    Operations, 61
Flight Line Hostess, Aviation,
    46
Food Production Manager, 93
Foreman, General, 27
Full Charge Bookkeeper, 7

G

General Foreman, 27
General Manager, 100, 133,
    152, 170, 171, 172
    Resort, 99
General Manager/Principal,
    Restaurant and Nightclub,
    88
Generalist, Human Resources,
    102
Graphic Designer, 39
Ground Maintenance
    Technician, Lead, 126

H

Hazardous-Materials
    Technician/Instructor, 66
Hazardous Waste Manager, 137
Head Chef, 94
Health & Fitness Company,
    Co-owner/Cofounder, 74
Health & Safety/Training
    Manager, 64
Highway Patrol, Section
    Commander, 119
Housekeeper, Apartment, 121
Human Resources Generalist,
    102

I

Import Purchasing, Manager,
    156
Information Security Officer,
    Chief, 110
Information Systems, Director,
    113
Inspector
    Quality, 150
    Quality Control, 186
Installer, Assembler, 148
Instructor's Assistant/
    Laboratory Technician, 44
Intern
    Conference Coordinator, 51
    Media Services, 24
Interventional Cardiac
    Technologist, Chief, 76
Inventory/Receiving/Laborer,
    26
Investments, Recruiter/Trainer,
    162
IT Consultant/Senior Software
    Engineer, 115
IT Support Analyst/Training
    Coordinator, 103
IT Support Specialist, Contract,
    105

J-L

Junior Logistician, 134

Laboratory Technician, 44
Laborer, 26
Lead Aircraft Maintenance
    Technician, 125
Lead Consultant Supervisor,
    146
Lead Ground Maintenance
    Technician, 126

Leisure Travel Consultant, 22
Licensed Practical Nurse, 81
Lieutenant of Detectives, 120
Loan Officer, 55
    Mortgage Division, 53
Logistician, Junior, 134

M

Mac Operator (Graphic
    Design), 42
Machine Operator, 154
Machinist, 186, 188
Maintenance/Driver, 192
Maintenance Leader, 123
Maintenance Technician
    Aircraft, Lead, 125
    Ground, Lead, 126
        Pool, 122
Manager
    Account, Senior, 141
    Accounting, 129
    Assistant, Website, 108
    Associate, Senior, 96
    Budget, 131
    CD Superstore, 143
    Construction, 28
    CRM Business Process
        Integration, 136
    Design and Drafting, 45
    District, Restaurant
        Operations, 87
    Food Production, 93
    General, 100, 133, 152,
        170, 171, 172
        Resort, 99
        Restaurant and
            Nightclub, 88
    Hazardous Waste, 137
    Health & Safety/Training,
        64
    Import Purchasing, 156
    Office, 4, 5, 20, 127, 128
    Production, 95, 153
    Program, Novellus, 109
    Project, 135
    Property, 160
    Purchasing, 157
    Purchasing & Materials,
        139
    Restaurant, Assistant, 85
    Sales, 166
        Community, 158
        On-Site, 164
    Service Department, 130
    Site, Senior, 37
    Store, 142, 144, 147
    Warehouse, 138

Managing Director, 59
Managing Partner, 58
Manufacturing Process
    Engineering Technician,
    151
Marketing Coordinator,
    Database, 25
Mechanic
    Airframe & Power Plant,
        124
    Overhead Crane, 184
Media Services Intern, 24
Medical Assistant, 129
Merchandise Handler, 118
Mortgage Division Loan
    Officer, 53

N

National Program Coordinator,
    49
Network Engineer, Senior, 116
New Business, Director, 175
Novellus Program Manager, 109
Nurse
    Office, Psychiatric Services,
        78
    Practical, Licensed, 81
    School, 77
Nurses, Team Leader, 79

O

Office/Billing Clerk, 2
Office Manager, 4, 5, 127, 128
Office Manager/Executive
    Assistant, 20
Office Nurse, Psychiatric
    Services, 78
Office Specialist (Medical), 75
On-Site Sales Manager, 164
Operator
    Computer, 106
    Mac (Graphic Design), 42
    Machine, 154
Overhead Crane Mechanic, 184
Owner, Arbitration Company,
    65
Owner/Operator, Excavating
    Company, 29
Owner/Personal Trainer, 72

P

Partner
    Business, 181
    Managing, 58
Partner/General Manager, 171
Parts Counter Sales Position,
    168

Personal Banker, 57
Personal Trainer, 72
Pharmacy Technician, 80
Pilot, 195
Pool Maintenance Technician,
    122
Practical Nurse, Licensed, 81
Preschool Teacher, 47
President
    Supermarkets, 132
    Telecommunications, 190
Prewire Technician, 187
Production & Line Technician,
    149
Production Manager, 95, 153
Program Coordinator, National,
    49
Program Manager, Novellus,
    109
Programmer, Application, 117
Project Manager, 135
Property Manager/Realtor, 160
Psychiatric Services, Office
    Nurse, 78
Purchasing & Materials,
    Manager, 139
Purchasing Manager, 157

Q-R

Quality Inspector/Supervisor,
    150

Radiography Technician
    Assistant, 70
Real Estate Development
    Consultant, 159
Realtor, 160
Receptionist, 8, 9
Recruiter/Trainer, Investments,
    162
Recruiting Consultant, 161
Regional Vice President, 179,
    180
Relocation Contractor, 67
Repairer, Air Conditioner, 185
Resort, COO/General Manager,
    99
Resort Hotel, Director of Sales,
    98
Resource Planning, Director,
    140
Restaurant and Nightclub,
    General Manager/
    Principal, 88
Restaurant Chef, 91
Restaurant Manager, 89
    Assistant, 85

Restaurant Operations District Manager, 87
Restaurant Supervisor, 86

S

Safety and Ergonomics Leader, 63
Sales & Marketing Representative, 169
Sales Analyst, 155
Sales Associate, 163
Sales Director, 167
　Resort Hotel, 98
Sales Executive, Consulting, 174
Sales Manager, 166
　Community, 158
　On-Site, 164
Sales Position, Parts Counter, 168
Sales Representative, Senior, 165
School Nurse, 77
Secretary, 10, 11, 12
Section Commander, Highway Patrol, 119
Senior Account Executive, 35, 176
Senior Account Manager, 141
Senior Application Developer, 111
Senior Associate Manager, 96
Senior Bookkeeper, 6
Senior CAD Designer, 43
Senior Editor, 23
Senior Network Engineer, 116
Senior Sales Representative, 165
Senior Site Manager, 37
Senior Software Engineer, 115
Senior Technician, 191
Senior VP/CRM Business Process Integration Manager, 136

Server, 83
Service Department, Manager, 130
Site Manager, Senior, 37
Software Engineer, Senior, 115
Sous Chef and Food Production Manager, 93
Specialist
　Billing, 68
　Credit Portfolio, 21
　IT Support, Contract, 105
　Office (Medical), 75
　Technology, 1
Station Operations Supervisor, 101
Steamfitter, 183
Store Director, 145
Store Manager, 142, 144, 147
Stylist Coordinator, Assistant, 50
Supermarkets, President, 132
Supervisor, 150
　Application Development, 114
　Area Fleet, 194
　Consultant, Lead, 146
　Customer Service, 32, 36
　Restaurant, 86
　Station Operations, 101
Support Analyst, IT, 103
Support Services, Director, 97
Support Specialist, IT, Contract, 105
Systems Engineer/Technical Consultant, 112

T

Teacher, Preschool, 47
Team Coordinator & Leader/Production & Line Technician, 149
Team Leader of Nurses, 79
Technician
　Aircraft Maintenance, Lead, 125

Engineering, Manufacturing Process, 151
Ground, Lead, 126
Hazardous-Materials, 66
Laboratory, 44
Pharmacy, 80
Pool Maintenance, 122
Prewire, 187
Production & Line, 149
Radiography, Assistant, 70
Senior, 191
Technologist, Interventional Cardiac, Chief, 76
Technology Specialist, 1
Telecommunications, President, 190
Teller, Credit Union, 52
Trainer
　Customer Service, 34
Training Coordinator, IT, 103
Travel Consultant, Leisure, 22
Truck Driver, 193

U-V

Vice President, 40, 41
　Regional, 179, 180
　Senior, 136
Vice President and General Manager, 152
Vice President and Managing Partner, 58

W

Waitress, 83
Warehouse Manager, 138
Website Assistant Manager, 108
Welder, 182

X-Z

Yacht Broker, 178

Features Index

The following sections are common and therefore are not included in this Features Index: Work Experience, Work History, Professional Experience, Related Experience, Other Experience, Employment, Education (by itself), Student Teaching, Additional Information, and References. Variations of these sections, however, are included if they are distinctive in some way or have combined headings. As you look for features that interest you, be sure to browse through *all* the resumes. Some important information, such as Accomplishments, might not be listed if it is presented as a subsection of another section.

Note: Numbers are resume numbers in the Gallery, *not* page numbers.

A

Abilities, 96, 100
Academic Achievements, 46
Accomplishments, 21, 35, 54, 56, 62, 65, 70, 111, 119, 130, 137, 161, 164, 177, 192
Accreditations and Licenses, 192
Achievements, 3, 36, 46, 54, 74, 83, 84, 101, 109, 113, 140, 141, 145, 173, 174, 180
Activities, 18, 113, 165, 170, 174, 188
Administrative Management, 20
Affiliations, 22, 45, 54, 55, 73, 77, 78, 92, 98, 102, 113, 120, 124, 136, 137, 141, 156, 158, 165
Areas of Experience, 142
Areas of Expertise, 44, 63, 115, 123, 141, 149, 153, 169
Athletic Achievements, 74
Attributes, 118
Awards, 39, 100, 120, 177, 193
Awards and Achievements, 180
Awards and Honors, 24, 46, 62, 91, 137
Awards and Recognition, 57, 145

B

Benchmarks and Milestones, 175
Bodybuilding/Weightlifting, 72
Business Expertise, 89
Business Proficiencies, 20

C

Career Accomplishments, 62, 137, 161
Career Focus, 88
Career Highlights, 20, 60, 62, 64
Career Objective, 195
Career Profile and Skills, 134
Career Summary, 127
Career Target, 133
Certificates, 195
Certifications, 22, 54, 78, 97, 102, 113, 145, 182, 194
Certifications and Education, 21, 76, 89, 104, 114, 139
Certifications and Licenses, 27, 123, 151, 180
Certifications and Training, 64
Clinical Skills, 73
Coaching, 48
Committees and Memberships, 37
Community Activities, 18, 113, 175
Community Interaction, 142
Community Involvement, 23, 57, 77, 81, 99, 173
Community Leadership and Personal Distinctions, 169
Community Outreach, 44
Community Service, 24, 29, 187
Community Service and Affiliations, 137
Competencies, 59, 62, 116, 139, 157, 178, 192
Computer Skills, 3, 5, 13, 14, 15, 21, 28, 35, 39, 45, 50, 53, 75, 78, 91, 96, 101, 116, 124, 127, 135, 138, 156, 161

Continuing Education, 11, 20, 76, 126
Continuing Professional Development, 38
Coordination, Project, 20
Core Competencies, 62, 116, 139, 178
Core Strengths, 27, 145
Credentials, 64, 77
Culinary Experience, 92
Current Objective, 57
Current Volunteer Involvement, 77

D

Development, Professional, 6, 21, 34, 38, 49, 57, 77, 124, 142, 143, 156, 160, 168, 173, 174, 190
Development Projects, 159

E

Education and Affiliations, 141
Education and Awards, 92
Education and Certifications, 21, 76, 89, 104, 114, 139
Education and Credentials, 77
Education and Professional Certifications, 36
Education and Professional Development, 9, 18, 33, 52, 93, 119, 125, 142, 153, 172, 177, 179
Education and Professional Training, 145
Education and Relevant Training, 101
Education and Seminars, 127
Education and Technical Skills, 133

Education and Training, 32, 55, 62, 65, 82, 97, 105, 109, 116, 148, 149, 163
Education, Continuing, 11, 20, 76, 126
Education, Honors, and Academic Achievements, 46
Employment Highlights, 52
Endorsements, 75
Examples of Performance, 78
Executive Profile, 172
Experience Highlights, 67, 74, 79, 142
Expertise, 44, 63, 104, 115, 123, 141, 149, 153, 167, 169, 179, 191
Extracurricular Involvement, 23

F

Fitness Expertise, 72
Flight Time, 195
Focus, 44

G

General Qualifications, 72
Goal, 24, 72, 118
Graphics, 11, 35, 37, 40, 42, 44, 46, 48, 50, 72, 74, 80, 82, 90, 95, 101, 102, 108, 129, 133, 145, 150, 174, 177, 180

H

Highlights, 4, 8, 121, 144
Highlights of Employment, 52
Highlights of Experience, 67
Home Management, 57
Honors and Awards, 24, 46, 62, 91, 137
Human Resources Training and Development, 102

I

Industry Affiliations, 98
Industry Certification and Education, 98
Interests, 170

J-K

Job Target, 70

Key Abilities, 96
Key Achievements, 113

Key Competencies, 192
Key Credentials, 64
Key Qualifications, 188
Key Strengths, 170

L

Language Skills, 55, 78, 135
Leadership, Sales, 177
Licenses, 22, 81, 123, 158, 183, 192
Licenses and Certifications, 27, 29, 123, 124, 151, 180
Logistics and Sales Support, 134

M

Major Projects, 33, 72
Management, 65, 153
  Administrative, 20
  Home, 57
  Office and Project, 134
Marketing Expertise and Skills, 89, 163
Memberships, 37, 81
Milestones, 175
Military Service, 29, 32, 63, 90, 120, 129, 137, 140, 183

N-O

Notables, 148

Objective, 1, 2, 12, 13, 48, 57, 81, 84, 94, 103, 120, 151, 162, 163, 185
Office and Project Management, 134
Office Skills, 69
Ongoing Education and Professional Development, 142
Outstanding Accomplishments, 130
Outstanding Achievements and Accomplishments, 54
Outstanding Achievements and Recommendations, 83
Overview, 58
Overview of Qualifications, 151

P

Performance Examples, 78
Performance Review Excerpts, 56
Personal Achievements, 84

Personal Achievements and Activities, 174
Personal Highlights, 144
Personal Interests and Activities, 170
Problems Solved, 45, 124, 135
Professional Achievements, 36, 140
Professional Affiliations, 45, 55, 73, 77, 78, 92, 102, 113, 124, 136, 156, 158
Professional Affiliations and Community Activities, 165
Professional and Community Involvement, 99
Professional Associations and Organizations, 18, 107
Professional Certifications, 78
Professional Development, 21, 34, 38, 49, 57, 77, 78, 124, 143, 156, 160, 168, 174, 190
Professional Development and Training, 6, 173
Professional Profile, 21, 22, 29, 54, 83, 85, 110, 122, 129, 130, 140, 141, 171, 183, 187, 192
Professional Qualifications, 20, 60
Professional Skills and Knowledge, 162
Professional Summary, 75
Professional Training, 36, 74, 95, 134, 146
Professional Training and Certifications, 140
Profile, 6, 10, 25, 26, 34, 38, 42, 43, 44, 52, 55, 69, 71, 73, 79, 80, 100, 106, 120, 121, 136, 138, 139, 147, 168, 181, 185, 191
Project Coordination, 20
Project Management, 134
Projects, 33, 46, 64, 72, 108, 130, 187, 189

Q

Qualifications, 24, 47, 57, 74, 86, 94, 151, 161, 184, 188, 194
Qualifications and Competencies, 166
Qualifications Profile, 9, 66, 87, 101, 113

Qualifications Summary, 2, 13, 15, 23, 28, 38, 48, 49, 62, 69, 76, 88, 91, 102, 105, 111, 119, 120, 128, 132, 146, 148

R

Real Estate Development Skills, 159
Recent Achievements, 173
Recent Work History with Examples of Problems Solved, 45, 124, 135
Recommendations, 83
Related Experience and Qualifications, 74
Related Skills, 26, 87
Related Skills and Achievements, 101
Relevant Experience and Selected Projects, 46
Relevant Professional Development, 78
Relevant Qualifications, 24
Reviews, 94

S

Safety Awards, 193
Sales Achievements, 174
Sales Awards and Accomplishments, 177
Sales Leadership, 177
Sales Support, 134
Sample of Career Achievements, 141
Selected Accomplishments, 21, 111, 119, 192
Selected Achievements, 3

Selected Certifications, Seminars, and Workshops, 66
Selected Examples of Qualifications in Action, 178
Selected Highlights, 49
Selected Management Accomplishments, 65
Selected Professional Achievements, 145
Seminars, Training, Workshops, 144, 107
Skills, 12, 20, 56, 70, 107, 122, 131, 181, 185
Software, 5, 39, 96
Special Skills, 49
Special Training and Education, 65
Special Training and Licenses, 123
Specialized Training, 72
Specialized Training and Certifications, 27
Strengths, 27, 58, 145, 165, 167, 170, 181
Strengths and Abilities, 100
Summary, 1, 3, 12, 32, 143, 161, 186
Summary of Accomplishments, 164
Summary of Attributes, 118
Summary of Marketing Skills, 163
Summary of Qualifications, 2, 13, 15, 23, 28, 38, 48, 49, 62, 69, 76, 88, 91, 102, 105, 111, 119, 120, 128, 132, 146, 148

Summary of Skills, 122, 181
Support, Sales, 134

T

Technical Ability, 57
Technical Certifications, 112
Technical Proficiencies, 18
Technical Profile, 115
Technical Skills, 33, 84, 105, 106, 112, 162, 168
Technology, 9, 108, 111, 142, 153
testimonial(s), 18, 23, 47, 75, 80, 90, 146, 167, 168, 171, 190
Trade Qualifications, 189
Training, 43, 71, 72, 130, 137, 175
Training and Facilitation Expertise, 190
Training, Certifications, and Licenses, 27, 123, 151, 180
Training, Education, and Professional Development, 52, 119, 177

U-V

Volunteer and Community Involvement, 77, 81, 173

W-Z

What I Can Offer, 45, 78, 124, 135

More Good Books from JIST: Resumes and Cover Letters

Gallery of Best Cover Letters

A Collection of Quality Cover Letters by Professional Resume Writers

Second Edition

416 pp., 8.5 x 11
Price: $18.95
ISBN: 1-56370-990-2
Order Code: LP-J9902

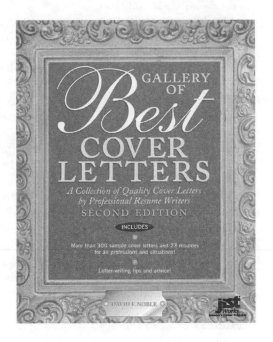

- More than 300 letter-perfect cover letter examples selected from thousands submitted by professional writers.

- Cover letter writing and strategy tips.

- Bonus resume samples and tips!

Same-Day Resume

Write an Effective Resume in an Hour

192 pp., 6 x 9
Price: $8.95
ISBN: 1-59357-005-8
Order Code: LP-J0058

- A quick and easy way to put together an effective resume in a hurry! This compact guide gives readers the essential tools to apply for jobs on the fly!

- Includes sample resumes with tips and critiques.

- Help with other job search correspondence: cover letters, follow-up letters, thank-you letters, and more.

To order, call 1-800-648-JIST, fax 1-800-JIST-FAX, or visit www.jist.com.

More Good Books from JIST:
Job Search

Seven Steps to Getting a Job Fast

160 pp., 6 x 9
Price: $8.95
ISBN: 1-56370-888-4
Order Code: LP-J8884

1. Identify your key skills and develop a powerful skills language.

2. Define your ideal job.

3. Use methods that can cut your job search time in half.

4. Write a superior resume.

5. Organize your time to get two interviews a day.

6. Dramatically improve your interview skills.

7. Follow up on all leads.

The Very Quick Job Search

Get a Better Job in Half the Time!

Third Edition

544 pp., 7.5 x 9.25
Price: $17.95
ISBN: 1-59357-007-4
Order Code: LP-J0074

- Bestseller—more than 215,000 copies in print!

- All the tools you'll need for conducting a fast job search: resumes, cover letters, interviewing, networking, job trends, and much more!

- Used widely in college and high school career courses.

To order, call 1-800-648-JIST, fax 1-800-JIST-FAX, or visit www.jist.com.

More Good Books from JIST:
Career Choice

America's Top 101 Jobs for People Without a Four-Year Degree

Detailed Information on Good Jobs in Major Fields and Industries

Seventh Edition

368 pp., 8.5 x 11
Price: $15.95
ISBN: 1-59357-072-4
Order code: LP-J0724

- Covers nature of the work; working conditions; job outlook through 2012; education needed; earnings; related occupations; and additional information sources, including Web sites.

- Practical and effective job search information to identify your skills, make career decisions, write resumes, prepare for interviews, and learn the most effective job search methods.

- Features resume examples written by professional resume writers.

300 Best Jobs Without a Four-Year Degree

464 pp., 7.5 x 9.25
Price: $16.95
ISBN: 1-56370-861-2
Order Code: LP-J8612

- Includes more than 50 "best jobs" lists, including best pay, fastest growth, and most openings.

- Information-packed job descriptions from a wide range of fields and industries, based on the U.S. Department of Labor's Occupational Information Network (O*NET) database.

- Should be part of any library, placement office, admissions, or media center career collection.

To order, call 1-800-648-JIST, fax 1-800-JIST-FAX, or visit www.jist.com.